His Masterly
Pen

His Masterly Pen

A BIOGRAPHY OF

JEFFERSON

THE WRITER

Pen

Fred Kaplan

HARPER

An Imprint of HarperCollins*Publishers*

HarperCollins books may be purchased for educational, business, or sales promotional use. For information, please email the Special Markets Department at SPsales@harper collins.com.

FIRST EDITION

Library of Congress Cataloging-in-Publication Data has been applied for.

ISBN 978-0-06-244003-7

22 23 24 25 26   LSC   10 9 8 7 6 5 4 3 2 1

In Memoriam:
Rhoda Ackerson Weyr, 1937–2021

MR. JEFFERSON HAD THE REPUTATION OF A MASTERLY PEN; HE HAD BEEN CHOSEN A DELEGATE IN VIRGINIA, IN CONSEQUENCE OF A VERY HANDSOME PUBLIC PAPER WHICH HE HAD WRITTEN FOR THE HOUSE OF BURGESSES, WHICH HAD GIVEN HIM THE CHARACTER OF A FINE WRITER.

—John Adams, *Autobiography*

"THE SHINING TRACES OF HIS PEN."

—James Madison, *Letters*

GETTING ITS HISTORY WRONG IS PART OF BEING A NATION.

—Ernest Renan

CONTENTS

Thomas Jefferson is the most controversial Founding Father for our times, above all due to his relationship with slavery. He inherited slaves, bought and sold slaves, and, after the death of his wife, had six children by Sally Hemings, a slave woman who was a half sister to his wife. It is that part of his life that we condemn today. It is useful to keep in mind, however, that Jefferson was also hated by many of his contemporaries as a Jacobin revolutionary, a populist demagogue, an agnostic or atheist, a slaveholder who believed in liberty in principle but not in practice, who preached against big government and centralized power but did not hesitate to use it in the interest of his policies, and a man whose vision of America's future minimized banking, industry, and urbanization. All of which is to say, Jefferson has always been a controversial figure, and our attitudes toward him will be divided for as long as we study and reflect on our history. Indeed, his legacy—especially his Declaration of Independence, which says that "all men are created equal"—is so central to the American experience and the reality of the United States today that Jefferson is the Founding Father who cannot be ignored. I hope my readers will find in this book an increased understanding of Jefferson as a whole, his strengths and weaknesses, and particularly the degree to which his brilliance as a writer is a key to his personality and public service and to the fact that his words still have meaning and resonance.

This book anchors the narrative in Jefferson's growth and development as a writer: the relationship between his literary gifts, his personal life, and his public service. They are an inseparable triad. In this narrative, Jefferson is often holding a pen. It is a dynamic element in his life and career from his earliest letters to *A Summary View of the Rights of British America*, the Declaration of Independence, and *Notes on the State of Virginia*, to his religious and scientific writings, his inaugural addresses, his correspondence with Washington, Madison, and Adams, his relationships with his wife, daughters, grandchildren, and slaves, his letters to male and female friends, and his brief, self-concealing autobiography. The narrative is biographical but selective. It proceeds chronologically by highlighting key moments when Jefferson had pen in hand. It is a pen used both to show and to hide. This master writer is a master of the shifting line between revealing and concealing from others and himself the complications, inconsistencies, and contradictions between his principles and his policies, between his optimistic view of human nature and the realities of his personal situation and the world he lived in.

Jefferson was constantly defining himself by literary acts, from his first letters to his self-created description for his tombstone. Only occasionally did he write explicitly about himself—his feelings, experiences, and relationships—and almost always in letters, which are among his most powerful and revealing writings. To approach Jefferson through his writings helps us to get into his mind and feelings. It contributes to our understanding of his strengths and limitations. It fosters an appreciation of his role as a propagandist of the Revolution, of the way he both made and recorded crucial aspects of the history of the first years of our republic. This approach shows how Jefferson wrote in different voices to different people and groups. It highlights his ability to change tone and language, as in his addresses to

Indian nations, adjusting his appeal to the needs of his audience, and it also allows a focus on Jefferson as a revisionist historian attempting to mold the historical record in favor of himself and his policies. To focus on what and how he wrote helps us understand his personal and political tensions and reveals the complexity and fullness of his personality. Moreover, it allows us to read and appreciate prose of the highest literary and intellectual quality. It bookmarks Jefferson with Lincoln as a master of the English language. Jefferson was a superb writer, with a genius particularly suited to his needs as a Virginia legislator, wartime propagandist, governor, congressional delegate, secretary of state, vice-president, president, and the premier intellectual, cultural, and moral voice of the republic he helped create and then lived in for fifty years.

Jefferson gave eloquent articulation to the founding ideas of the United States. Many are still the bellwether values of American society. He channeled the widespread sentiment and language of rebellion into a declaration whose first paragraph became a worldwide affirmation of personal liberty and republican government. As a leader in the Virginia legislature, his pathbreaking proposals on issues from religious liberty to inheritance reform resonated with a set of values that the country was to embrace over time. And in his few years in the Confederation Congress, his writing talent, his gift for logical organization, concision, and precision, his assiduous work ethic, and his diplomatic tactfulness made him a prominent force in moving disparate interests toward a more unified expression of national priorities. He and his colleagues recognized the need for the confederated states to have a national Congress responsible for interstate commerce and foreign affairs, though how to do this and how far to go required a consensus difficult to achieve. As the second United States minister to France, Jefferson's work ethic, social amiability, writing skills, and aristocratic bearing made him the right person for the assignment. When, in 1789, he returned to America to become its first secretary of state, he had already contributed to the making of the new nation what most others would have considered a full career. As secretary of state and president, he advocated his version of republican values, emphasizing frugality, decentralization, agriculture, westward expansion, and an extension of the franchise.

Jefferson, though, was a public man who preferred his private home to the civic square. He could not, in March 1809, get out of Washington fast enough. Much of his desire for privacy was personal, but he also had intimations of an American future of which he did not approve. He disapproved of the federal court system, especially the Supreme Court as the unelected determiner of the Constitution's meaning; of the influential role of banks, paper currency, and stock markets in the emerging commercial nation; and of the power of money to influence legislation. He also believed that over time the American people were always right. Jefferson embodies the paradox of an elitist who preached populist rule on the assumption that the people would always elect people like him. In his last decade, with the election of Andrew Jackson, whom he detested, he discovered to his horror that his assumption was wrong.

Jefferson died a disillusioned man, touched with an edge of bitterness, so distraught was he by the way in which the country was defining itself. The populace did not always elect the best people. By 1826 the country had rejected his vision of a pastoral republic and was well on its way to embracing financial and industrial activism. In that regard also, he was considerably out of step with history. Even in his own day, Americans cared very much about many things Jefferson thought they should care less about, especially money and material objects—and they had few of Jefferson's scruples about how to get them. He would have been appalled at twenty-first-century America.

CHAPTER ONE

My Watch Had Lost Its Speech

1743–1765

On a cold, sunstruck January day in 1961, at the inauguration of the youngest American president ever, the poet Robert Frost, his white hair touched by the wind, his puckish elderly face lined with years and griefs, had a message for America. It reached from the present to the past, from one end of the continent to the other. His raspy New England voice was rich with the tones and substance of American history. His gift to John F. Kennedy and to the huge audience he addressed was a poem called "The Gift Outright." It is a good poem with which to begin this biography of Thomas Jefferson:

> The land was ours before we were the land's.
> She was our land more than a hundred years
> Before we were her people. She was ours
> In Massachusetts, in Virginia,
> But we were England's, still colonials,
> Possessing what we still were unpossessed by,
> Possessed by what we now no more possessed.
> Something we were withholding made us weak
> Until we found out that it was ourselves

We were withholding from our land of living,
And forthwith found salvation in surrender.
Such as we were we gave ourselves outright
(The deed of gift was many deeds of war)
To the land vaguely realizing westward,
But still unstoried, artless, unenhanced,
Such as she was, such as she would become.

For Jefferson and his contemporaries, the land was everything.
And they wanted more of it, more fully than they had it in 1743, the
year in which Jefferson was born. They were to get it more fully in
the next decades. It was, though, never to be fully enough possessed,
as Frost noted, until many wars, treaties, and extensions later. It was
to extend from the Atlantic to the Pacific, from the Bering Sea to the
Rio Grande. It should have contained, many Americans believed, especially in Jefferson's day, Canada and Cuba. They were near misses.
All this, as it was gained, was both a conquest and a bequest. Most
Americans believed that some force or power, from God to guns, had
given the land to them. It began with Massachusetts and Virginia, the
two places where the possession started in depth and in earnest. And
the commitment to be possessed by the possessions gradually became
paramount. America began to define itself, its people and values, in
terms of the land they occupied, from small farms to plantations,
from "sea to shining sea." And then in big cities of the sort that Jefferson not only disapproved of but thought already were (and would
become even more so) black holes of moral degeneration. Eventually,
one became the possession of the land one possessed. It was the key to
moral values and national character.

That was especially so for Virginians. It was from the land itself
and from what one built on it that Americans like Jefferson drew their
self-identity and sustenance. Americans were more than house proud.
They were land hungry. From the start, Jefferson called Virginia his

"country." The union came afterward. Important as it was, for many, especially Southerners, it was a construct, a convenience, until in 1861 it wasn't convenient anymore. The nation that Jefferson helped create was based on the belief in the right of land possession—to have it for oneself, with as few restrictions or constraints as possible. It was a legal as well as a moral matter. To grow one's crop and be master of it was the essence of personal and communal pride. Jefferson was the archetype of the house-proud American. Moreover, land ownership by white men included the right to extend ownership and wealth westward, to possess more land to be possessed by. Real estate was the highest form of material wealth.

Land wealth was also psychological, spiritual, and self-affirming. It provided self-worth, moral stature, and civic power. Without land ownership or its equivalent, one did not have the right to vote. The more one had, the better, and one needed private ownership of guns to defend it from enemies, internal and external. In Virginia, the elites, like Jefferson, who owned large plantations, also needed slaves to keep their cash flow positive and their self-worth affirmed. From the start, they needed a nonwhite labor force. Tobacco was a labor-demanding, soil-destroying staple. The crop made it hard to possess the land, and it exacted a heavy price from those who were possessed by it. But it had international market value. Fragile and unreliable as it was, it was the wealth Virginia provided. Even those who had little or no land still approved of that distinctive form of wealth. Slaves were part of the land. They were possessions, inseparable from the soil and buildings. Jefferson built Monticello as an act of possession. Eventually, it possessed him. He owned slaves as a necessary component of the wealth his land created. His slaves, as extensions of the land, also possessed him.

Robert Frost visualized the act of creating America, from Jefferson to John F. Kennedy and beyond, as an act of language, as a storytelling enterprise, a narrative that over time became increasingly rich and complex. To have a story, a myth, a narrative about what one had was to have it emphatically, to possess it entirely. Language helps make reality; it makes, guides, improves, and projects forward a people and a nation. And the story can and usually does exist on multiple levels, from the simple to the sophisticated, from the borrowed to the stolen, from the honest to the dishonest. It's written in the textbooks and monuments, the scholarship and politics, the facts and fictions. At first, in seventeenth- and eighteenth-century America, as the land went from colony to independent nation, it was "still unstoried, artless, unenhanced." The poet implies that the narrative Jefferson's predecessors and his own generation constructed was simple and unsophisticated. They were "artless" storytellers, in Frost's words, history describers and myth creators.

Actually, colonial Americans, especially in Virginia and Massachusetts, were from the start sophisticated tellers of stories about themselves, their origins, their settlements, and their relationship to those who lived there before them, to the people, Red and Black, whom they subjugated or owned. Their stories were also about their connection to the mother country, Great Britain, from which most had come, stressing whom they owed their allegiance to and from whom they got the right to possess the land they had settled. Usually they knew exactly what they were doing and why. Fact and fiction, reality and desire, action and thought, aspiration and imagination, history, natural science, and theology, the access through language to narrative patterns and claims were part of the American experience from the start. The earliest settlers of Virginia and Massachusetts began the making of American identity. Jefferson was one of its most gifted and influential storytellers.

In 1757, at the age of fourteen, Jefferson inherited a large share of the property his father had amassed, "the lands," he later wrote, "on which I was born and live." Peter Jefferson was the largest property owner in Albemarle County in west-central Virginia. A surveyor, cartographer, planter, and slave-owner, he had married upward. A native Virginian, he came from a moderately well-to-do but not wealthy family. His wife, Jane Randolph, made him and their ten children, two of whom were sons, kin to one of the most influential families in the colony. Peter and Jane Randolph Jefferson's children belonged to the privileged elite. Peter had an eye for wealth, power, and adventures, for settlement and expansion, and even for books, which his eldest son inherited. In his will, he made customary provision for his wife, his daughters, and his sons. It was an unusually equitable will for its time.

Beyond specific bequests to each child, at his death at the age of forty-nine, Peter Jefferson bequeathed "unto [his eldest] son Thomas all the residue of my Estate whether real or Personal of what kind soever," the plantations and slaves to be held in trust for him until he came of age. The eldest son benefited from the custom, though not the letter of *primogeniture*, one of numbers of laws to keep estates intact. It was a feature of *entail*, requiring future generations to keep or pass on their property according to restrictions created by previous owners. It was meant to keep estates intact, to keep wealth and power concentrated. None of Thomas's sisters inherited land. They inherited domestic slaves, a small amount of money, and their educations at the expense of the estate. Peter Jefferson's wife got life tenancy of the family home, Shadwell, about three miles from the small village of Charlottesville. The will provided that each son should inherit either one of two large properties, one on the Fluvanna River, about 2,300 acres, the other on the Rivanna River. The Rivanna land, including Shadwell, was on the southern part of the lower ridge of the South Mountains, which ran north to south for about eighty miles, about thirty miles east of the Blue Ridge. Its highest point was almost 1,500 feet above sea level. As the first son to come of age, Thomas chose the land on the Rivanna, about five thousand acres.

Peter Jefferson had risen through energy, personality, skill, marriage, kinship connections, land speculation, and a favorable legal and political structure to a line of "demarcation" which most Virginians were below. It was a line that his eldest son respected in some ways and challenged in others. "To state the differences between the classes of society, and the lines of demarcation which separated them would be difficult," Jefferson wrote to William Wirt in 1815. "The law . . . admitted none, except as to the twelve counsellors," rich and supposedly wise men who, with the royal governor, governed the colony. "In a country insulated from the European world" and "its sister colonies with whom there was scarcely any intercourse . . . certain families had risen to splendor by wealth and the preservation of it from generation to generation under the law of entails; some had produced a series of men of talents; families in general had remained stationary on the grounds of their forefathers, for there was no emigration to the Westward" beyond the Blue Ridge Mountains.

"In such a state of things, scarcely admitting any change of station, society would settle itself down into several strata, separated by no marked lines, but shading off imperceptibly, from top to bottom, nothing disturbing the order of their repose." There were no titles, as in the mother country, but "there were . . . Aristocrats, half breeds, pretenders." A large part of the population was landless or had only enough to sustain themselves and their families. There also existed "a solid independent yeomanry, looking askance at those above" but essentially docile. Life, for them, was largely hardscrabble. "And last, and lowest" were the "Overseers, the most abject, degraded and unprincipled race. . . ." The overseers managed the daily life of the slave laborers who did the manual work on the thousand and more–acre tobacco farms on which the governing class resided. The on-site work of the Jeffersons and Randolphs was to oversee the overseers. They were a privileged class, possessors of and possessed by their property in all its material forms.

———

Rain dripped through the roof of a plantation called Fairfield into the room in which nineteen-year-old Thomas Jefferson was sleeping. It was Christmas Day 1762. He was two years away from coming into his inheritance. He awoke to find his pocket watch, which he had placed by his bedside, floating in water. His "poor watch," he jokingly complained to his closest friend, John Page, "had lost her speech." It had also lost a representation, probably a silhouette, of a young lady he was passionate about. His wallet, stored for the night a foot from his head, had also been attacked. It had been eaten through by rats. Owned by the husband of Jefferson's newly married sister Mary, Fairfield was a convenient stopover on the way from Williamsburg to Shadwell, the house in which Jefferson had been born on April 13, 1743. The 108-mile distance between William and Mary College and home usually took three days by horseback, longer in bad weather. The main houses of plantations like Fairfield and Shadwell were not grand. Large families were crowded into small spaces. Rats and rain frequently shared occupancy. In warm weather, there would be many more insects in the house than people. Outside were hundreds and often thousands of acres of tobacco farmland.

Christmas Day was not a religious day in Church of England Virginia. It was a day of social celebration. The first thing on the young man's mind that morning was his need to communicate with his good friend. One of the first things in his hand, other than the "poor watch" that he rescued, was his pen. He had a story to tell and a state of mind to write about. The rain and rats didn't spoil his humorous, satirical, and self-revealing mood. Very little he wrote after his school days reveals a notable sense of humor or an inclination toward self-satire. There's no record of his telling jokes or responding to other people's. But on Christmas Day 1762, he had his moment as a humorist, a self-mocking memoirist, the kind of writer he never was to become. Still, the story creator, the exaggerator, the tall-tale teller, the writer who could use language effectively to define himself to himself and others was there from the start. "This very day, to others the day of greatest mirth and jollity," he wrote to Page, "sees me overwhelmed with more and greater misfortunes than have befallen a descendant of Adam for these thousand years past I am sure."

John Page was the heir to Rosewell, a spectacular house and plantation overlooking the York River. He was almost exactly Jefferson's age. His classmate at William and Mary College, Page was to be a lifelong friend. He was to have a successful minor political career. Page's family had been in Virginia since the middle of the previous century, his great-great-grandfather having migrated from the London area. When the Jefferson family had arrived and from where is unknown. The descendants of the grandfather of Peter Jefferson assumed that the family came from Wales at about the turn of the seventeenth into the eighteenth century. Like most of the first settlement families, the Pages had established themselves on a river with access to the ocean; they married well, expanded their property, and became one of the colony's leading families. Peter Jefferson went to what was then considered the frontier, later to be named Albemarle County, its "3d or 4th settler," just short of the Blue Ridge. The Pages already had their fortune. Peter Jefferson went to Albemarle and beyond to make his. In 1762 the Pages were at the top of the social and political "lines of demarcation" that the elderly Thomas Jefferson described to William Wirt. The Jeffersons had risen to it through Peter Jefferson's marriage to Jane Randolph.

Jefferson's lamentation about the loss of the image in his watch was spontaneous self-expression. Job's "misfortunes," he humorously acknowledged, "were somewhat greater than mine, for although we may be pretty nearly on a level in other respects, yet I thank my God I have the advantage of brother Job in this, that Satan has not as yet put forth his hand to load me with bodily afflictions." At least he was young and healthy. He was also indulging his pen in playful self-mockery. "You must know, dear Page, that I am now in a house surrounded with enemies, who take counsel together against my soul and when I lay me down to rest they say among themselves Come let us destroy him."

These enemies were a host of aggressive rats in a parodic and comic misfortune, with a semiserious complication. The rats had, he wrote, animating them into playful agency, conspired against him as agents of the devil. "I am sure if there is such a thing as a devil in this world, he must have been here last night and have had some hand in contriving what happened to me. Do you think the cursed rats (at his instigation I suppose) did not eat up my pocketbook which was in my pocket within a foot of my head? And not contented . . . they carried away my . . . silk garters and half a dozen new minuets," sheet music he needed for his violin practice and pleasure. "But of this I should not have accused the devil (because you know rats will be rats, and hunger without the addition of his instigations might have urged them to do this) if something worse and from a different quarter had not happened."

To blame the devil was not a religious construction. Jefferson was never to believe in supernatural creatures except for a first cause. That was his view from early on. "When I went to bed I laid my watch in the usual place, and going to take her up after I arose this morning I found her, in the same place it's true but! . . . all afloat in water . . . and as silent and still as the rats that had eat my pocket-book." As a storyteller he could have it both ways: it could not have been accidental, though the denial was an affirmation that it was accidental. He had been unlucky. He also had been careless. It was good fun to make the Devil take the blame. "There were a thousand other spots where it might have chanced to leak as well as at this one which was perpendicularly over my watch. But I'll tell you: It's my opinion that the Devil came and bored the hole over it on purpose. Well as I was saying, my poor watch had lost her speech: I should not have cared much for this, but something worse attended it: the subtle particles of the water with which the case was filled had by their penetration so overcome the cohesion of the particles of the paper of which my dear picture and watch paper were composed that in attempting to take them out to dry them Good God! . . . my cursed fingers gave them such a rent as I fear I never shall get over. This, cried I, was the last stroke Satan had in reserve for me: he knew I cared not for anything else he could do to me. . . ."

It was, he mock angrily concluded, his fingers that were "cursed." But the clumsy fingers whose touch had completed the shredding of the image firmly held the pen that created this expressively imaginative letter. Among his gifts as a writer, he had at times, for eighteenth-century prose, a colloquial and conversational voice.

In Jefferson's Virginia, courtship between members of the same class was highly ritualized. He was marginally too young to marry; the lady in the silhouette was of marriageable age. The woman whom nineteen-year-old Jefferson had fallen in love with was sixteen-year-old Rebecca Burwell. He had attempted to engage with her in Williamsburg, with no significant success. Shy and almost speechless, his first attachment of the heart was strong but recessive. She was the recipient of and the projection of the dialectic between his desires and his shyness. With Rebecca, his body talked awkwardly and mostly in flight. Expressive and bold on paper, in her presence he tended to be irresolute, tongue-tied. Apparently, sex and courtship both enticed and confused him. Whatever his physical intensity, he gave it no expression for the record. Rebecca seems not to have taken him seriously enough to advance their relationship beyond Williamsburg dances and social gatherings. Much of the relationship was in Jefferson's head. It was also in his letters to friends. The image that had been enclosed in his watch had been, he wrote to Page, "defaced." But "there is so lively an image of her imprinted in my mind that I shall think of her too often I fear for my peace of mind, and too often I am sure to get through Old Cooke [Edward Coke's *Institutes of the Lawes of England*] this winter: for God knows I have not seen him since I packed him up in my trunk in Williamsburg."

———

Less than three years before, in March 1760, Jefferson had arrived at William and Mary College in Williamsburg. He was sixteen years old. He had been an active if not avid student almost since he had first learned to read. At nineteen, he had a knowledge of Latin, Greek, classical literature, Shakespeare, Milton, English poetry, and British and European history; he was keen on arithmetic and what he and his contemporaries called natural science—phenomena that later generations began to differentiate into specialties like botany, chemistry, physics, anthropology, and climate studies. He was to be an enlightened amateur student of these subjects all his life. He had also developed a passion for lists and record keeping, an obsessive insistence on recording the details of his activities, with numbers and fractions. He kept a daily record of the weather, partly because he owned farms but mostly because he had a passion for facts and records, as if somehow they clarified and enhanced his life. At nineteen, he still had a long way to go to be learned, which eventually he did become, though with gaps, lapses, and qualifications. Overall, his education was to be self-education, the autodidacticism of a compulsive reader and collector of books.

Eager for his son to have the education he had not had, Peter Jefferson had sent his eldest son to a basic starter school at the age of five; then at nine to a Latin school, where he learned the rudiments of the ancient languages and considerable French; then, in 1758, to the more sophisticated school of Reverend Richard Maury, whose exemplary level of scholarship, pedagogy, and character made him a lifelong model. In the spring of 1760, three years after his father's death, Thomas himself made the decision to become a student at William and Mary. It meant leaving his mother and siblings for much of the year. Not yet of age, he needed the formal permission of one of his father's executors. The request is the earliest extant example of his putting words on paper. He began with a reference to Shadwell as "the mountain." It was about 360 feet above sea level. Close to it was another of Peter Jefferson's properties, which Thomas was also to inherit. Its highest point, from which Shadwell and Charlottesville were visible, was about 850 feet above sea level. That small mountain was to become Jefferson's lifelong home, where his children were to be born and where he was to die.

"I was at Colo. Peter Randolph's," a relative on his mother's side, "about a Fortnight ago," he wrote to his father's executor John Harvie, "and my Schooling falling into Discourse, he said he thought it would be to my Advantage to go to the College, and was desirous I should go, as indeed I am myself for several Reasons," including that his "absence will in a great Measure put a Stop to so much Company, and by that Means lessen the Expences of the Estate House-Keeping." At Shadwell, visitors were constant. Family and friends stayed with family and friends. That was the custom and the practicality. Costly and time consuming, it was to be the mature Jefferson's pleasure and expense at Monticello. "And on the other Hand," he continued, "by going to the College I shall get a more universal Acquaintance, which may hereafter be serviceable to me; and I suppose I can pursue my Studies in the Greek and Latin as well there as here, and likewise learn something of the Mathematics. I shall be glad of your opinion." It was a no-brainer for everyone involved. In March, he began attending classes. He was, by family connections, a known and valued quantity. His Randolph great-grandfather had been a founding trustee of the college. His Randolph grandfather had been a student. One of his Randolph cousins had been William and Mary's third president. His father's business partner and fellow mapmaker had been its professor of mathematics.

Jefferson was to write to his grandson in 1808 that "when I recollect that at 14 years of age the whole care and direction of myself was thrown on myself entirely, without a relation or friend qualified to advise or guide me, and recollect the various sorts of bad company with which I associated from time to time, I am astonished I did not turn off with some of them, and become as worthless to society as they were." Who the bad company was, whether it was at home or in Williamsburg, he never clarified. The comment seems a recollective reconstruction of how deserted the young boy felt at the death of his father. Actually, his childhood had been inseparable from the Randolph connection. Jane Randolph's brother William had been one of Peter Jefferson's closest friends. Peter Jefferson had agreed that if his friend should predecease him with children not yet of age he would take responsibility for William Randolph's family. The agreement had been written into William's will. When, in 1746, Randolph died prematurely, Peter Jefferson fulfilled his promise. It was a kinship and friendship promise so powerful that he moved his family, including two-year-old Thomas, to the great estate of Tuckahoe, the Randolph plantation on the James River, to take over its management and the care of Randolph's family. Thomas's earliest memory was of being carried on horseback, cradled on a pillow in the arms of a slave, from Shadwell to Tuckahoe. The two families remained merged for six years, the siblings and cousins attending a one-room plantation schoolhouse. Jefferson's oldest daughter was to marry a Randolph, and all his grandchildren except one were to have the Randolph name. The obligations, responsibilities, and advantages of tribal kinship among the Virginia elite were immense.

On the morning of Christmas Day, 1762, Rebecca Burwell's disintegrated image between his fingers was his subject. He was not turning out to be a successful suitor. "Whatever misfortunes may attend the picture or lover," he wrote to Page, "my hearty prayers shall be that all the health and happiness which heaven can send may be the portion of the original, and that so much goodness may ever meet with what may be most agreeable in this world, as I am sure it must in the next." If he could not have her, he would bless her anyway. But he feared that he would "think of her too often" for his "peace of mind." Still, he could and would rise above that. "What! are there so few inquietudes tacked to this momentary life of ours that we must need be loading ourselves with a thousand more? . . . And as for admiration I am sure the man who powders most, parfumes most, embroiders most, and talks most nonsense, is most admired. Though to be candid, there are some who have too much good sense to esteem such monkeylike animals as these, in whose formation, as the saying is, the taylors and barbers go halves with God almighty." It was to become a lifelong motif. The best condition human beings could attain emphasized pleasure, not pain; hope, not despair; the future, not the past. And whining is not allowed. As always, he was immersed in the details of social engagement. "I would fain ask the favor of Miss Becca Burwell to give me another watch paper, of her own cutting . . . however I am afraid she would think this presumption. . . . If you think you can excuse me to her for this I should be glad if you would ask her. . . . My mind has been so taken up with thinking of my acquaintances that till this moment I almost imagined myself in Williamsburg talking to you in our old unreserved way, and never observed till I turned over this leaf to what an immoderate size I had swelled my letter." The letter is as much an expression of affection for Page as it is an expression of love for Rebecca Burwell.

Jefferson's passion found comic relief in dramatizing the limitations of its subject and object, a satirically exaggerated complaint for comic effect, a touch of self-mockery to accentuate how seriously he thinks himself worth taking, and the deflection of pain by a comic lament for his misfortune in love. The lovestruck nineteen-year-old revealed that he had the potential to become the kind of writer he never would or wanted to be—a writer of sensibility, of narrative and feeling, of imaginative self-expression. That talent occasionally surfaces later, but rarely. With an extraordinary gift for literary prose, Jefferson apparently never fantasized about being "literary"—about writing poetry or engaging with any of the other traditional literary genres. He had no desire to be another Shakespeare or Milton or Pope. He never wrote a line of poetry. The question is not so much: Why not? The question is: What did he want to be? One of the things he most wanted to be was educated and learned. His father had shown the way, modestly but forcefully. From his father, he inherited a small library, though large by Virginia standards and for a man who had received no formal education. He had also inherited the means and the desire to become an educated and productive Virginia gentleman. His plantations, run by overseers whom he would oversee, often from a distance, would produce crops. What would he himself do and produce? His thought in 1762 was that a career in the law would provide a satisfactory foundation for his mind and his citizenship.

Arriving at Shadwell three days after Christmas 1762, he brought his books with him, intending to spend the winter applying himself to legal reading. "All things here appear to me to trudge on in one and the same round: we rise in the morning that we may eat breakfast, dinner and supper and go to bed again that we may get up the next morning and do the same: so that you never saw two peas more alike than our yesterday and to-day." He was still, though, obsessing about Rebecca. Would he have been better off staying in Williamsburg? he wrote to Page. "What do you think of my affair, or what would you advise me to do? Had I better stay here and do nothing, or go down and do less? . . . Inclination tells me to go, receive my sentence, and be no longer in suspense: but, reason says if you go and your attempt proves unsuccesful you will be ten times more wretched than ever." His intention had been to propose marriage. Proposing nothing seemed the better alternative. Marriage, he imagined, would provide love, sex, and stability. "Why cannot you and I be married too, Page, when and to whom we would chuse? Do you think it would cause any such mighty disorders among the planets? Or do you imagine it would be attended with such very bad consequences in this bit of a world, this clod of dirt, which I insist is the vilest of the whole system? Nobody knows how much I wish to be with you."

Though despondent, his words still had a hint of playful exaggeration. "I verily believe Page that I shall die soon, and yet I can give no other reason for it but that I am tired with living. At this moment when I am writing I am scarcely sensible that I exist," though the spirited writing belies the claim. He would build a boat (clearly an imagined one) to which he would give the name Rebecca. When finished, "I intend to hoist sail and away. I shall visit particularly England Holland France Spain Italy (where I would buy me a good fiddle) and Egypt and return through the British provinces to the northward home. This, to be sure, would take us two or three years and if we should not both be cured of love in that time I think the devil would be in it." If he could not have Rebecca, he would have Europe and other adventures.

What he had in hand were his law books. He burrowed into them in the winter, spring, and summer of 1762–1763. He did other reading as well. Rural isolation and family companionship gave time and freedom to pursue his studies. And he had opportunities for long walks, including to the highest point on the property, and for his favorite form of exercise, horseback riding. An assiduous student and encyclopedic reader, he believed regular exercise essential to bodily and mental health.

His mind and heart, though, were still on Rebecca, with a late adolescent obsessiveness. He was incapable of not writing at length to Page about his dedication to her. He still seemed convinced, in the summer of 1763, that he was an eligible suitor. And that Page could serve as an intermediary. If she "will not accept of my service it shall never be offered to another," he wrote—both a youthful absurdity and an anticipation of his vow to the woman he did marry that, after her death, he would never remarry.

He prayed "most sincerely" that Rebecca would accept his proposal "but . . . she never gave me reason to hope. With regard to my not proceeding in form I do not know how she may like it: I am afraid not much: that her guardians would not if they should know of it is very certain. But I should think that if they were consulted after my return, it would be sufficient. . . . This is a subject worth your talking over with her; and I wish you would and would transmit me your whole confab at length. I should be scared to death at making her so unreasonable a proposal as that of waiting until I returned from Britain, unless she could be first prepared for it." His proposal would be for an engagement that would allow him to travel to Europe for two or three years, perhaps more, and marry afterward. "I am afraid it will make my chance of succeeding considerably worse. But the event at last must be this, that if she consents, I shall be happy; if she does not, I must endeavor to be as much so as possible."

There was, he knew, a lesson in all these hopes, desires, and fantasies. It was embodied in the philosophy of the Greek Stoics and their followers. Their guide for a satisfactory life particularly appealed to Jefferson. He put to Page what was to be his lifelong attitude toward fortune and misfortune. "Perfect happiness I believe was never intended by the deity to be the lot of any one of his creatures in this world." This deity, though, "has very much put in our power the nearness of our approaches to it." This is what I "steadfastly believe. The most fortunate of us all in our journey through life frequently meet with calamities and misfortunes which may greatly afflict us."

Deprived of his father at fourteen, aware of the fragility of life, he had determined at an early age that he needed to create bulwarks against pain and ways of finding compensations for loss. Stoic strength of mind seemed to him essential. We need, he wrote to Page, "to fortify our minds against the attacks of these calamities and misfortunes." It "should be one of the principal studies and endeavors of our lives. The only method of doing this is to assume a perfect resignation to the divine will, to consider that whatever does happen, must happen, and that by our uneasiness we cannot prevent the blow before it does fall, but we may add to its force after it has fallen." Post-event pain management was essential. He had it in mind to minimize the pain of today by not allowing it to undermine the equilibrium of tomorrow. "These considerations and others such as these may enable us in some measure to surmount the difficulties thrown in our way, to bear up with a tolerable degree of patience under this burthen of life, and to proceed with a pious and unshaken resignation." It was his recipe for moving through life with as little emotional, let alone aggressive and confrontational, stress as possible.

When he returned to Williamsburg in October 1763, he again pursued his desire to be engaged to Burwell, as if not yet ready to treat rejection with Stoic acceptance. He was still hopeful, unrealistically. In preparation for a social event at which he knew she would be present, he rehearsed and memorized what he wanted to say. No doubt he expressed himself more effectively in his account to Page of what had happened than he had been in expressing himself directly to her. "In the most melancholy fit that ever any poor soul was, I sit down to write to you. Last night, as merry as agreeable company and dancing with Belinda [Rebecca] in the Apollo could make me, I never could have thought the succeeding sun would have seen me so wretched as I now am! I was prepared to say a great deal: I had dressed up in my own mind, such thoughts as occurred to me, in as moving language as I knew how, and expected to have performed in a tolerably creditable manner. But, good God! When I had an opportunity of venting them, a few broken sentences, uttered in great disorder, and interrupted with pauses of uncommon length, were the too visible marks of my strange confusion."

He tried again in early January. This time the words came. "I then opened my mind more freely and more fully. I mentioned the necessity of my going to England, and the delays which would consequently be occasioned by that. I said in what manner I should conduct myself till then and explained my reasons, which appeared to give that satisfaction I could have wished." He misapprehended Rebecca's response.

Two months later, when Rebecca's engagement was announced, the news gave him "a violent headache," which lasted for two days, probably a tension headache of the sort he was to have periodically throughout his life. Williamsburg was now "Devilsburg." When, the next year, he was unexpectedly "dubbed a bridesman" at a friend's wedding he treated it both as a joke and an affliction. He wrote to Page, who was on a courting visit near Yorktown, where the newly married Rebecca was also a guest, "How does your pulse beat? . . . What a high figure I should have cut had I gone! When I heard who visited you there I thought I had met with the narrowest escape in the world. I wonder how I should have behaved? I am sure I should have been at a great loss." He wrote to another friend, that "St. Paul only says that it is better to be married than to burn. Now I presume that if that apostle had known that providence would at an after day be so kind to any particular set of people as to furnish them with other means of extinguishing their fire than those of matrimony, he would have earnestly recommended them to their practice." His words suggest that he was not an innocent in such matters.

Jefferson had arrived in Williamsburg to go to college. The capital of colonial Virginia provided a community entertainingly different from rural Shadwell and tiny Charlottesville. It had a population of about 750 white people and 750 slaves, probably doubling when the legislature and the courts were in session. With a tavern life, street spectacles, social events, well-dressed dignitaries, a flirtation and marriage market, and of course young ladies, it offered sights and experiences unavailable in rural Virginia. Inevitably, the ladies occupied the attention of many of the all-male students attending the college. Jefferson frequently immersed himself in his studies. But he already knew how to express himself in writing about the ups and downs of believing he was in love, about male and female hormones colliding with and sometimes merging with the fortunes of the children of the best families of Virginia.

In addition to his affair of the heart, Jefferson had a passion for extended hours of reading, by daylight and candlelight. The education William and Mary provided was mostly education by books. That suited him well. There were classes also, but they emphasized guidance, an impetus to Jefferson's lifelong preoccupation with reading lists for himself and others. He never tired of lists about everything and anything, though especially books. Later, he was to spend extraordinary amounts of time writing out encyclopedic reading lists, containing titles for a lifetime of reading, classified by areas and subjects, for eager young men who asked for guidance. Never a teacher in any formal sense, he had a teaching inclination. He also developed and began to perfect his lifelong technique of making concise abstracts of everything he read. When "I began a regular course of study," he noted late in life, "I determined to abridge in a common place book, everything of value which I read. At first I could shorten it very little: but after a while I was able to put a page of a book into 2 or 3 sentences, without omitting any portion of the substance." It was "an aid to memory." It will also "learn you the most valuable art of condensing your thoughts and expressing them in the fewest words possible. No stile of writing is so delightful as that which is all pith, which never omits a necessary word, nor uses an unnecessary one."

Reading and writing were, for Jefferson, inseparable. A good reader had to know how to put his reading into his own words. His own words became an embodiment of a literary style in which reading and writing were inseparably connected. His primer to young writers gave highest value to substantive concision, the art of not one word too much and not one too little. He was learning, partly from his teachers, partly from his own feel for effective techniques, to be a sharp student of any subject he studied, to connect reading and studying skills with good writing, and to set a standard for his own writing style. This standard was practiced and expressed by many eighteenth-century writers, most of them in young Jefferson's collection of books. It was famously epitomized in the poet Alexander Pope's advocacy of the delicate balance between communal wisdom and originality in his *Essay on Criticism*: Good writing is "What oft was thought, but ne'er so well express'd." It was to be the intellectual and stylistic hallmark of Jefferson's most famous contribution to English prose.

In fits and starts, he remained a student for four years, from 1760 to 1764. For the first two, he was an undergraduate; the other two, a law student. The latter activity had no formal connection to the college. These were four of the most formative years of his life. His fumbling attempts to reach an arrangement with Rebecca had no long-term consequences. His letters to Page and others about this affair of the heart are a prelude to the more intense, mature, self-exploratory letters he was to write later in life.

At Williamsburg, concentrating on his studies, he successfully earned, consistent with the requirements of the curriculum, his undergraduate degree. For the next two years, he did a legal apprenticeship, which led to his short-lived and disappointing life as a lawyer. His undergraduate courses came under the direction of the college's school of moral philosophy, comparable to a modern degree in the humanities or the liberal arts, widely defined to include the social sciences, sciences, and mathematics. The curriculum was strategically focused to represent the educational and moral values of the eighteenth-century British American Anglican world. The school of moral philosophy included almost all subjects and knowledge that the world valued. It was assumed that a good student could master all or most of it, or at least get a good head start into a life of learning. Jefferson gave it his best, as he was to do all his life.

Jefferson had two teaching models. They became enduring guides to his most important value: moral conduct. His main undergraduate teacher, William Small, had come with an MA from Aberdeen, Scotland, two years before Jefferson enrolled, the only teacher on the small faculty with an Enlightenment mind-set. Ten years older than his student, his specialties were the sciences and mathematics. He was also trained in the moral-philosophy curriculum. He was a teacher with "an enlarged and liberal mind," Jefferson was later to reminisce. The first William and Mary professor to give "regular lectures in Ethics, Rhetoric," and literature, he became Jefferson's mentor. He also became a friend. "Most happily for me, [he] became soon attached to me and made me his daily companion when not engaged in the school; and from his conversation I got my first views of the expansion of science and of the system of things in which we are placed." To seventeen-year-old Jefferson, Small was an irresistible magnet. "It was my great good fortune, and what probably fixed the destinies of my life that Dr. Wm. Small" brought with him European learning, an analytical and questioning mind, the Scottish philosophical Enlightenment, and the experimental approach to the physical sciences.

At William and Mary, Jefferson stood out from what were mostly intellectual mediocrities. He had an open mind and an avid interest in what Small taught. He also had a quiet charm; he was a good listener; he came from an established family; he already wrote well; he could be assumed to be a young man of integrity; and he studied with an impressive intensity. In 1764, Small returned to Great Britain to purchase books and equipment for the college. He did not return. Jefferson apparently missed him considerably.

Small introduced Jefferson to George Wythe (pronounced "with"), later to become the first professor of law at William and Mary. Seventeen years older than Jefferson, Wythe also became his "faithful and beloved Mentor." From a Quaker family, whose values of dress and manner he perpetuated, he had inherited the profits but not the values of the tobacco plantation that over three generations had produced his family's wealth. Wythe was strongly antislavery. In Jefferson's later estimate, he was "the best Latin and Greek scholar in the state." Stocky and short, he was "kindly-looking, with a very round head, the first traces of a double chin, and striking blue eyes, inquiring yet soft and cheerful." He was to become "my most affectionate friend through life. . . . He was my antient master, my earliest and best friend; and to him I am indebted for first impressions which have had the most salutary influence on the course of my life."

In the days to come, Wythe and Jefferson were to be colleagues in the law, in revolution, in legislation, and in the politics of the new republic. When Jefferson became Wythe's law student, an intimacy and mutual trust began that was to last until Wythe's death in 1806. It included a political and legislative collaboration in which Wythe distinguished himself as a member of the Virginia legislature and as a signer of the Declaration of Independence. The most important lessons that Small and Wythe taught Jefferson were embodied in their moral presence. They had their most sustained effect on him in the values that they expressed and by which they lived. "Under temptations and difficulties, I would ask myself" what would William Small and George Wythe "do in this situation? what course in it will ensure me their approbation?"

Jefferson found a third mentor whose moral standards would also guide his decision-making process, his cousin Peyton Randolph. Twenty-two years older than Jefferson, Randolph had by 1762 risen to high office in Williamsburg. Like Wythe and Jefferson, he also was to embrace the new American world that was shortly to develop.

Busy in the daily activities of government, Randolph does not seem to have been someone the young student saw as frequently as he did Small and Wythe. But he was a moral model whose approval Jefferson invoked all his life. "I am certain that this mode of deciding on my conduct tended more to its correctness than any reasoning powers I possessed. Knowing the even and dignified line" that Small, Wythe, and Randolph "pursued, I could never doubt for a moment which of two courses would be in character for them."

If he had relied, he later told his grandson, on his own reasoning processes, "with the jaundiced eye of youth, I should often have erred. From the circumstances of my position I was often thrown into the society of horse racers, cardplayers, foxhunters, scientific and professional men, and of dignified men; and many a time have I asked myself, in the enthusiastic moment of the death of a fox, the victory of a favorite horse, the issue of a question eloquently argued at the bar or in the great council of the nation, well, which of these kinds of reputation should I prefer? that of a horse jockey? a foxhunter? an orator? or the honest advocate of my country's rights?" That Jefferson, at the age of twenty, was in any danger of becoming best known as a horse jockey or a foxhunter or even an influential orator like Patrick Henry, given his weak skills as a public speaker, hovers between an exaggeration and an absurdity. It was, though, an exaggeration of the sort that Jefferson often allowed himself in the service of the point he wanted to make. That all he wanted to be was "an honest advocate of my country's rights" was retrospective. In 1762, his nationality was British, his country a prosperous colony of Great Britain. His own ambitions had nothing to do with his "country's rights" or a public career.

At its start, the relationship between Wythe and Jefferson was as much pedagogic as fraternal: how best to train Jefferson to become a lawyer. There was a standard pattern to follow. Probably sometime in late 1762, Wythe set out a reading list for Jefferson, beginning with Coke, the volume that Jefferson had had with him during his Christmas visit to Fairfield. It was the beginning of an apprenticeship that included attendance in April and October at the four-week sessions of the General Court in Williamsburg and occasional attendance at the sessions of the House of Burgesses, alternating with intensive reading at home at Shadwell. There were no law schools. A course of guided study typically lasted from as little as six months to as much as two years, sometimes longer, culminating in an examination somewhere between perfunctory and semiserious. Some apprentice lawyers had a talent for assiduous study. Others felt more attracted to learning by watching, listening, copying, and clerking. Jefferson did both.

A frequent traveler on horseback between the capital and Albemarle, he aimed to qualify to practice before the General Court. There were two court systems, the county courts, spread around the colony, and the General Court in Williamsburg. The latter was where the most important litigation was tried. It was where distinctive cases originated and contested cases from the county courts were appealed. The judges of the Court, appointed by royal authority, were the governor of the colony and his Council. Those qualified to practice before the Court were also a small body of about eight or ten elite lawyers. Their legal stature was inseparable from the mainstream of the governance of the colony. Self-perpetuating, they determined who was to be allowed to practice before the Court. As an institution, the Court was, like the Council, a family affair of the Virginia elite, familiars of the governor, the Council, and the House of Burgesses, the lower house of the state's legislative body. Wythe was one of its distinguished members. Most Court lawyers were connected to wealthy planter families, an especially pertinent fact if you were related to a Randolph or if your family stature had brought you into contact with members of the Virginia oligarchy: Peyton Randolph, Robert Burwell, William Byrd, Robert Carter, Philip Lee, William Nelson,

George Mason, John Blair, and Robert Carter Nicholas, among others, all members of the Court fraternity. They were to welcome Jefferson into the club.

Some of the General Court lawyers were also licensed barristers, having attended the Inns of Court in London, which qualified them to practice in the General Court *and* in the county courts. Those, like Jefferson, who were not London-trained barristers, practiced in the county courts before applying to practice in the General Court. Many who qualified to practice in the county courts practiced only there. It was likely to be where the most money could be made. It required, though, frequent travel. Exclusive practice in the General Court brought more prestige but less money. But practice before the Court kept one close to and sometimes at the center of legal and political power. It also had social advantages. And it also dealt with more intellectually stimulating cases. Supported by George Wythe and relatives like John Randolph, his brother Peyton, and John Robinson, the speaker of the House, Jefferson was early on identified as a candidate for admission to the General Court.

At first it seemed a promising career. Most likely he passed the qualifying exam to practice in the county courts in the autumn of 1765. A year later, he was admitted to the General Court by oral examination by three Court members, one of whom might have been Wythe. Jefferson never practiced in the county courts. He didn't need the money; the travel may have been unappealing; the roads were terrible; the inns nonexistent or almost uninhabitable for a gentleman; and, anyway, his limited passion for the practice of law flourished mostly on the intellectual level. Reading, digesting, epitomizing, and observing suited him more than oral advocacy.

Two contentious realities dominated the daily life of Williamsburg lawyers: disputes about land and disputes about money. The land disputes revolved around claims in a colony slowly evolving westward from a wilderness into a rural civilization: who had gotten there first, who had registered ownership first, who had thereafter fulfilled the legal requirements for ownership and who had not, and what devices were available to protect land claims and thwart competitors seeking land for settlement or for speculation. It was about taking possession of the land and being possessed by it, about expanding and defining Virginia, about the competition for the property that was the highest form of wealth and privilege. And inseparable from property considerations was debt. Within a year of starting practice, Jefferson had numbers of debt cases that came on appeal to the General Court. Fees were set by the legislature and the Court. Since fees were low, to make a profit he needed, as did his colleagues, many cases in various stages of process and progress, wending their way through the legal system. He kept detailed files. He made notes and kept lists. He got paid most of the time, but not always. Few cases, though, raised issues beyond the bone-dry litigation and paperwork that were the bread and butter of the legal profession. Still, he took the law seriously. As a body of knowledge, it seemed to him essential.

In a few cases he had the opportunity to hone his legal mind on theoretical matters. A divorce case came before the General Court that involved a claim of nonconsummation and adultery. There was no precedent in Virginia for divorce on any grounds. Both parties had claims against the other that informal separation, the usual resolution, could not resolve. The situation was both scandalous and novel. It riveted the attention of Williamsburg. Most everyone knew the principals, an elderly leading citizen of Williamsburg and a young lady of social standing. The only possible forum for resolution was the General Assembly, on the assumption that Virginia should follow the British model, in which divorce could be granted by a special act of the legislature. Apparently, after years of public and bitter maneuvering, in early 1772 Dr. James Blair, the male principal in the case, retained Jefferson to draw up a private bill to submit to the legislature. Jefferson began to research everything that he could discover about divorce, from the ancient world to the present. It was a writing as well as a research challenge.

The case provided an opportunity to hone important skills, the two sides of an argument on an issue that had widespread resonance: marriage, incompatibility, separation, divorce. He treated the subject, as he had been retained to do, as if he were preparing a detailed outline for an argument before a legislative body that was also a judicial forum. He headed it "Blair v. Blair. On a bill of Divorce to be proposed to the General Assembly," with arguments pro and con. It has some of the flavor of one of Jefferson's favorite modes of analysis: a dialogue or at least a dialectic between two different ways of apprehending an issue or a reality, as if he were thinking with his pen, though in this case without a conclusion. The sweep is wide and deep, including the argument that divorce "restores to women their natural right of equality." His sources ranged from the Bible to contemporary analysis, a testimony to the young Jefferson's reading and research skills. It has some of the range of the highest-level judicial decisions without, however, a conclusion; a cross between a legislative bill and a judicial analysis, an intense in-depth exercise in presenting the evidence for and against. The arguments Jefferson cites in favor seem surprisingly compelling, given that he shared his culture's conservative views. He himself was to marry happily. He was, after his wife's death, to fall in love with a married woman. The possibility that she might divorce her husband was never a consideration. And he was in his intimate family to experience the painful reality of his eldest daughter's unhappy marriage. Jefferson the lawyer presented both sides of the issue in what was more a brilliant exercise than anything else. The case became moot when James Blair died in late 1772.

Jefferson was now a young man with a public presence. He had begun to have a noticeable voice. What did he actually sound like when he appeared in court, when he chatted with friends, when he was with his mother and siblings? He spoke in the cadences and inflections that a native of Albemarle County would speak in today. The land that possessed him gave his voice regional distinctiveness. He was unmistakably a Virginian in speech—soft, low, and effectively precise in most circumstances, with the rhythms of the region he had lived in during his formative years. A good listener, his tone usually amiable and companionable, he was reserved in private conversation, though less so with intimate friends, and formal with professional peers and visitors. He was capable of cold formality, his most severe form of disapproval expressed by vocal tone. It's likely that he mostly spoke much as he wrote in letters: careful word choice, balanced sentences in the eighteenth-century style, intensity derived from precision rather than expletive, the personal in a restrained dance with the factual and the objective. As a young lawyer, he had to speak as persuasively as he could before the General Court, but there's no indication that he ever spoke impressively, let alone memorably.

He had a noticeable physical presence, mostly because he was a little over six foot two in an age in which the average height was considerably less. He was almost always the tallest man in the room. He was also thin, lanky, trim in an athletic way, his main exercise walking and horseback riding. Abstemious in his eating, health was always a consideration. He ate well, enjoying the best of Southern and then French cooking, though his passion, eventually, was for vegetables, fruits, and wine. If left to himself, he probably could not boil an egg, though he would have soon learned how. With soft gray eyes, his face longer than round, there was a proportionate compatibility between his stature and his look. Light complexioned, given to freckles, his hair was sandy with a suffusion of red, usually worn long enough in the back to be tied into a short trail in the contemporary style. He had no special feeling for distinctive dress. In public, he wore the white silk socks, the garters, the half pants and waistcoats in subdued colors typical of the gentlemen of his class and profession. In private, he dressed for country life. In his rooms in Williamsburg, he was casually informal. Habit and custom were his instinctive standard. He wore slippers on occasions when others would have worn fancy shoes. He slouched, though apparently he did it mostly when sitting, extending his legs to decrease the appearance of height from his waist up. It became habitual, a physical expression of his desire to put people at ease. His look expressed his temperament and social philosophy.

By birth, community, conditioning, and philosophy, he was an intensely social being. He wanted always to be part of a community, from family, neighbors, and friends to the larger worldwide consanguinity, wherever it was to be found, though he was later to find it especially in France. It was an affirmation of his belief that human beings are social animals. They need other people. It meant at its core an identifiable location, a community made coherent by its attachment to the land of a particular place. For him that was still Shadwell. Beyond Virginia, it was extended to the South, his distinctive region. Later, he was as much, if not more, a localist than a nationalist.

Jefferson was committed to the widespread claim among eighteenth-century philosophers that people had a natural affinity for and flourished best within social communities. His reading at college and as a law student encouraged this view. William Small, George Wythe, and Peyton Randolph embodied it. These social communities required, Jefferson believed from early on, "good humor as one of the preservatives" of its "peace and tranquility." The concept of "good humor," as he wrote in 1808, had nothing to do with humor in the modern sense. It embodied the politeness that his temperament embraced, the conventional politeness that a Virginia gentleman valued, and the commitment always to act with "good humor" no matter whom one was in conversation with. It meant the avoidance of confrontational disagreement, tolerance when in disagreement, the practice of polite accommodation in every instance and activity. Good humor's "effect is so well imitated and aided artificially by politeness," he believed, "that this also becomes an acquisition of first-rate value. In truth, politeness is artificial good humor . . . [a] substitute nearly equivalent to the real virtue. It is the practice of sacrificing to those whom we meet in society all the little conveniences and preferences which will gratify them, and deprive us of nothing, worth a moment's consideration; it is the giving a pleasing and flattering turn to our expressions which will conciliate others, and make them pleased with us as well as themselves." Its practice provided a model; it taught those who were remiss its value. "When this is in return for a rude thing said by another, it brings him to his senses, it mortifies and corrects him in the most salutary way"—a teaching moment.

It was also, for Jefferson, a guiding value in the public sphere. "In stating prudential rules for our government . . . I must not omit the important one of never entering into dispute or argument with another," at least face-to-face and never on a personal level. "I never yet saw an instance of one of two disputants convincing the other by argument. I have seen many of them getting warm, becoming rude, and shooting one another. . . . When I hear another express an opinion, which is not mine, I say to myself, he has a right to his opinion, as I to mine; why should I question it. His error does me no injury . . . if a fact be misstated, it is probable he is gratified by a belief of it, and I have no right to deprive him of the gratification. If he wants information he will ask it, and then I will give it in measured terms; but if he still believes his own story, and shews a desire to dispute the fact with me, I hear him and say nothing. It is his affair not mine, if he prefers error."

There are, he readily granted, "ill-tempered and rude men in society who have taken up a passion for politics. . . ." His advice to his grandson: Keep away from them "as you would from the infected subjects of yellow fever or pestilence. Consider yourself, when with them, as among the patients of bedlam needing medical more than moral counsel. Be a listener only, keep within yourself, and endeavor to establish with yourself the habit of silence especially in politics. In the fevered state of our country, no good can ever result from any attempt to set one of these fiery zealots to rights either in fact or principle. They are determined as to the facts they will believe and the opinions on which they will act. Get by them therefore as you would by an angry bull: it is not for a man of sense to dispute the road with such an animal." It was an acute observation. But neither his own career nor the future of American politics would allow its implementation.

For Jefferson, a confrontation avoided was a difficult or tense disagreement made less dangerous. As a lawyer, he accepted that it was better to settle a disagreement than to litigate it. "Good humor" was his synonym for self-control in the face of provocation; it was also a synonym for putting one's best face forward, to keeping its expression in place, for not allowing disagreement, let alone anger, to be expressed by gesture, body language, or facial expression. It was, as Jefferson explained to his grandson, a kind of high-level, persistent, and strategic politeness in the interest of self-control and harmony. Good humor, as in Pope's *Rape of the Lock*, a poem that Jefferson knew well, had nothing to do with being humorous. It had to do with a way of fine-tuning the mind and the emotions to elicit social harmony in interactions with people, from the personal to the public.

Jefferson, though, did not always follow his own advice. In many instances he conspired, tacitly or openly, with surrogates whose assignment was to be confrontational with those he came to see as enemies. And while "good humor" was his personal ideal, as a standard it would sometimes be breached by his own emotions: he was capable of resentment, anger, even hatred. His disagreements, his antagonisms, became explicit with some issues and some people. With George Washington, he was to try hard to stay in good humor, and partly succeed. He soon lost the good humor of his relationship with Patrick Henry and then Aaron Burr. He never had it with Alexander Hamilton and John Marshall. And by 1765 and certainly between 1765 and

1772, he turned against Great Britain with a passion, an acidity, and a prejudice that he seems never to have felt or expressed previously. Eventually, there was hardly a touch of good humor in it. Many of his countrymen did the same, but for most of the Americans who became haters of everything English, it was a passion consistent with their self-interest and principles. It was that for Jefferson also, but good humor in regard to Great Britain was by the early 1770s also in the process of disappearing from his private feelings and his political life.

By the early 1770s, Jefferson was ending his legal career. The skills he had honed as a lawyer were to be an excellent preparation for the role he was soon to play in the Anglo-American world of public dispute and resolution. He had by personality, training, and philosophy a stratagem for getting along with people. He could develop both sides of an argument with logic, evidence, and writerly precision. His extensive notes for a proposal for a legislative divorce in *Blair v. Blair* was an instance of how thoroughly and forcefully he could marshal evidence, and, if the goal was advocacy, to state a case. It was a talent he was soon to have the opportunity to exercise in the historical drama that was already in the making. At the same time that he was having his brief career as a lawyer, events in Virginia and Massachusetts were directing his mind and heart to a public role for which he was well prepared by his studies and his legal training. He had become, for a young man, impressively learned in history and the law. He had sharp skills as a writer. He had the potential to be forensically dramatic in prose. And he was developing a passionate commitment to possessing more fully the land he owned and the country he lived in.

CHAPTER TWO

Building Houses

1765–1773

In early February 1770 Thomas Jefferson's family home burned to the ground. He had been born there. His father had died in that house. His mother and siblings lived there. After her life tenancy, Shadwell was to be his, though he had begun to implement plans for a residence of his own, an assertion of his coming-of-age. Almost the entire record of his and his family's life was turned into ashes. There's no record of what time of day the fire occurred or how it started. There seems reason to doubt that Jefferson was there when it happened. He and his mother may have been visiting a neighbor. But absent or present, he soon had the ashes in hand. The fire destroyed most of his law books. One survived because it had been lent out and not returned. He had prepared notes for the cases he was scheduled to argue in the next session of the General Court. None survived. He had lost all the personal letters he had ever received. Among them may have been letters from his mother. Any letters of his to her would have been there.

Shadwell's entire "contents were consumed," he wrote three weeks later, except for "two or three beds." He was terse and cool about what had to have been a painful, dislocating experience: the loss of the site of many of his childhood memories and possessions. The destruction of the physical building perhaps less so. It was not grand or beautiful. He was already moving on. What he regretted most was the loss of his books, "for a lawyer without books would be like a workman without tools. . . . These are gone, and 'like the baseless fabric of a vision,'" the young Shakespeare reader remarked, "'Leave not a trace behind.' The records . . . which furnished me with states of the several cases, having shared the same fate, I have no foundation whereon to set out anew." Jefferson's earliest words on paper were ashes and dust. Friends tried to console him. "You bear your misfortune so becomingly," George Wythe wrote to him, "that, as I am convinced you will surmount the difficulties it has plunged you into, so I foresee you will hereafter reap advantages from it several ways."

The fire that destroyed Shadwell was a marker of change in Jefferson's life, the accidental exclamation point to the purposeful. It expanded an already expanding coming-of-age, an ongoing redefinition of how he envisioned himself in relation to the land he lived in and the land from which his ancestors had come. As a man, he wanted the pleasures and the fulfillment of marriage. As a lawyer, he wanted something both less and more. As a colonial citizen of the British Empire, he was entering into an uneasy clarification, the resolution of which was unclear. As a writer, he was also starting anew. He was soon to become the prose expositor of his generation's redefinition of itself. In the next six years, he and his contemporaries would overwrite and rewrite the founding documents of the world into which they had been born, transforming history and texts to serve new purposes. It was not what he and they started out to do. It was something that happened, gradually, then swiftly. It was a revolutionary version of starting anew.

Between 1765 and 1773, Jefferson was trying the law as a profession. It provided an intellectual discipline and a grounding in governing realities. It helped him think and write with precision and clarity; it intensified his potential as a writer about public matters by adding substance to skill. It gave him a familiarity with legal language and legal structure, a training in the logic and rhetoric of stating a case and making an argument. He was never to lose the skill of writing contracts and briefs. He was always to have himself at hand as a lawyer when he wanted one. Practicing law, though, seemed to him intellectually thin and repetitive. It did not excite or gratify. And there was little to no profit in it. Fees were so low that, as he was ending his practice, he signed with his General Court colleagues a statement printed in the *Virginia Gazette* that "we find it can no longer be continued on the same Terms. The Fees allowed by Law, if regularly paid, would barely compensate our incessant Labors, reimburse our Expenses, and the Losses incurred by Neglect of our private Affairs; yet even these Rewards, confessedly moderate, are withheld from us, in a great Proportion, by the unworthy Part of our Clients." It was unsatisfying not to be paid, regardless of whether or not he needed the money. He profited from the law mainly in his training and preparation of cases. In his notes and notebooks, summarizing and copying out quotations, he practiced the certainty, if he had ever had any doubt, that one of the most powerful forces of his life expressed itself when he had his pen in hand. He liked writing better than talking. And he was better at it. It seemed almost instinctive to write about what in his reading struck him as intellectually interesting.

In May 1769, the Virginia House of Burgesses asked its newly elected twenty-six-year-old member from Albemarle County to write a resolution of thanks to the recently appointed royal governor, Norborne Berkeley, Baron Botetourt. The young legislator thanked the governor for "his very affectionate speech at the Opening of this session." It was "the first assembly" the governor had addressed. Jefferson's words of thanks were the first that were entirely his own to become part of the public record. They were not, as has been remarked, "purely ceremonial." At the opening of each spring session, the response to the governor, though polite in formal diction, alluded to the main issues of the day, emphasizing the expectation that the House and governor would work together to resolve the colony's internal problems and remove or manage any tensions between the colony and the mother country. There were significant tensions. Since the end in 1763 of the French and Indian War (the Seven Years' War), differences about governance had become consequential. They were about the relationship between governance and taxes.

In 1765, the American colonies had a serious difference of view with their London superiors about money. That became inseparable from the question of who was to decide how much and through what mechanisms the American colonies were to contribute to the British treasury. From the earliest permanent settlements in North America, the British settlers who controlled the colonies' wealth and power took it as a given that each colony's assembly determined internal policy, including taxation. The British Parliament was not motivated to test that claim until March 1765. Great Britain had been triumphant in the recent war. It now ruled the seas and more of the earth's land than any other country. To pay for the war, fought to protect and expand the empire, Britain had pioneered in deficit financing. It now needed increased revenue to pay interest and pay down principal. To most residents of the British Isles, including its heavily taxed ordinary citizens, it seemed only fair that the colonies ought to pay their share. The war had been fought to keep Britain the dominant world power, especially in international commerce. It had been fought to keep the colonies Protestant and British. It had been fought to protect American settlers from Catholic France and its Indian allies, and especially to expand the reach of English commercial power.

At the start of his law practice, Jefferson had an up-front view of how strongly his fellow Virginians disagreed with the British attempt to tax them. In Williamsburg, in 1765, he was an attentive observer of the explosively hostile reaction to Parliament's command that the colonies, through a tax on every use of paper, from playing cards to legal documents, help pay Great Britain's debts. To Parliament and the king, it seemed a no-brainer. Five years older than Jefferson, George III had started his long reign in 1760. In legislating a tax on anything for which paper needed to be used, Parliament and the king believed it was taxing what it had every legal right to tax. After all, the American colonists were citizens of the United Kingdom, living in what was an extension of Great Britain, subjects of George III. The Stamp Act's requirement that a modestly priced stamp be purchased and affixed to all paper products seemed a reasonable way to raise money. In March 1765, Parliament legislated that the Stamp Act take effect in November.

From Georgia to Massachusetts, it was denounced as an assault on the colonists' belief that its own assemblies determined the kind and extent of internal taxation, a conviction based on custom, not on explicit statute. The favorite tax of all Americans was no tax at all. If there was to be internal taxation, the colonists believed it should be legislated locally. And it should not have to be paid in specie (silver or gold coins), which most colonists rarely had. Transactions in Virginia were often by barter, tobacco the major medium of exchange. Letters of credit were also a type of currency. And, for most Virginians, the enforcement of law was local, county by county. Common law, not statutory law, determined civil liberties and legal procedures. The British constitution was not a written document. It consisted of precedent, custom, judicial decisions, and Parliamentary acts. Every governmental agency and most prominent officials in Great Britain believed it had the right to require that the American colonies pay their fair share of the cost of what they benefited from. British public opinion was divided or unclear about what the imperial constitution decreed and what was the best way to raise revenue from the colonies. But the American response shocked the British establishment.

At the end of May 1765, twenty-two-year-old Thomas Jefferson, having just begun his legal practice, stood at the door of the Virginia House of Burgesses listening to passionate debates about the new tax. The House passed four resolutions addressed to Parliament, unanimously declaring that the Stamp Act was unfair and exploitative. It should not and would not be honored. Americans should refuse, whatever the inconvenience, including the inability of the legal system to operate, to purchase the stamps that the act required. The tax should be revoked. The House resolved that each colony should send representatives to an anti–stamp tax meeting in New York. Later in the year, nine of the thirteen colonies did participate, the first time they were to act as a collective body, though without representation from Virginia. To prevent the election of delegates, Governor Fauquier refused to call the House into session. For some time, Jefferson had been sharing musical entertainments and sophisticated conversations with his Williamsburg mentors, including the personally amiable Governor Fauquier. Neither the actions of the House nor those of the governor had a personal resonance.

In Virginia, as in the other colonies, views differed about how opposition should be expressed. In concert with some other House members, newly elected Patrick Henry, seven years older than Jefferson, urged assertive and confrontational resolutions. It was the first time Jefferson heard Patrick Henry speak. The non-orator was impressed by the supreme orator, whose debut showcased his talent for spontaneous eloquence. Most legislators looked for a balance between honey and vinegar. There was enough vinegar in the final resolutions to emphasize that the legislature demanded retraction. In the streets, reaction ranged from intimidation to violence against the tax agents. Some were tarred and feathered. Stacks of stamps were burned. There was both a legislative and a popular voice. The former used words; the latter, violence.

The language of Virginia's anti–Stamp Act resolutions implied that it and other colonies could be provoked into stronger acts of defiance. Very few Virginians, though, entertained the possibility of independence, let alone expressed that view publicly. For most elite Americans, the Stamp Act represented a disagreement about boundaries between local and London-based authority. In March 1766, one year after its passage, a nervous Parliament repealed the act. It was a tactical retreat, a temporary concession.

And whose real estate was America anyway? It was, most Americans believed, the land of those white colonists from Great Britain who had the means to possess it, obtained by grant, purchase, or conquest. It belonged to them as far as the eye could see, as legs could go, and the imagination extend. In 1763, by royal proclamation, Great Britain had declared that the colonists could not own, settle, buy, or sell land west of the Appalachians. Native Americans would have exclusive right to that land. Parliament had decided that conflict between white settlers and Native Americans was unacceptably costly. They should be kept geographically separate. The colonists reacted with outrage and anger. Many Virginians believed they had long-standing claims to Western land. Colonists were already farming west of the Appalachians. The fact that the land was occupied by Indian tribes who had claims of ownership was inadmissible to settlers and speculators eager for land and money. Some colonists assumed that Western land would be their reward for service in the French and Indian War. They had shed blood on behalf of the empire. Many believed it was their God-given right to obtain land by settling on it. Or adding by one mechanism or another to what they already owned, as if the land were a divine gift from a Protestant God to a Protestant people. Virginians believed that their 1609 royal charter extended the colony's sovereignty almost infinitely westward. The 1763 proclamation was robbing them of Western land they felt rightfully theirs.

After 1765, Parliament considered other ways than the Stamp Act to skin the same cat. The postwar recession that had reduced economic activity in the colonies pinched the British treasury. Revenue needed to be raised. Between 1766 and 1769, Parliament enacted import taxes or tariffs, called the Townshend Acts after the chancellor of the Exchequer, on selected items imported to the colonies. To most Americans, these were "Intolerable Acts." Massachusetts reacted first. Boston merchants evaded the taxes by widespread smuggling, a long-standing lucrative industry anyway. In response, the British navy attempted to enforce the law. Boston merchants then began a movement to boycott British goods. All this seemed to the royal governor treasonous: the perpetrators should be arrested and transported to London for trial. London sent British soldiers to Boston to impose martial law. Which city and colony would be next? A new sense of crisis vibrated along the Atlantic seaboard. Elite American voices began debating seriously how much autonomy the colonies were entitled to by royal edict, Parliamentary law, and long-standing custom. The debate focused on the historical record.

For Jefferson, as a lawyer, historian, and emerging legislative leader, engagement was irresistible. Like many Americans, he found historical grounds to stress significant local autonomy. In Massachusetts, James Otis, a comparatively singular voice, openly challenged Parliamentary sovereignty. Parliament interpreted the historical record differently. But neither side, in the main, believed there to be reason or desire for the colonies to become independent, separately or as a nation. Differences of policy and principle, it was hoped, could be reconciled.

Many American colonists, including Jefferson, believed that as British Americans, the British constitution exempted them from the authority of Parliament in regard to internal taxes. The colonists, particularly in Virginia, were produce rich but cash poor. British monetary regulations drained what little gold and silver they had. At the same time, Parliament forbade the colonies to print paper money. When outstanding bills to British merchants were called in, payment was required in sterling. The requirement that American colonists trade only with Great Britain, to the great advantage of British merchants, seemed corruptly oppressive. Britain, in effect, collected import taxes on British goods sold to the colonists and export taxes on American goods shipped abroad. It had begun to seem to Jefferson and his contemporaries that the governing powers of Great Britain viewed the colonies as tributary streams to be governed and taxed for the benefit of the British treasury.

Having been given the honor of writing the welcoming address to the new governor, Jefferson spoke optimistically for himself and his fellow legislators: "If in the Course of our Deliberations, any Matters shall arise, which may in any way affect the Interests of Great-Britain, these shall ever be discussed on this ruling Principle, that her interests, and ours, are inseparably the same." Jefferson was, in March 1769, a loyal citizen of the British Empire. Most colonists wanted a better deal, not independence. If Parliament and the king would recognize, at a minimum, that the constitution supported the claim that local colonial assemblies determined internal taxation, the otherwise seamless biological, linguistic, and cultural consonance between the two sides of the Atlantic could continue to cohere harmoniously.

Two members of the House of Burgesses, in response to the Townshend Acts, took the lead in calling for a resolution of remonstrance. Both were wealthy planters from Fairfax County in northeastern Virginia. George Washington, eleven years older than Jefferson, was a surveyor, then a soldier by profession. Ambitious for distinction, he had felt unappreciated by his British superiors, his military career balked. A land entrepreneur and businessman, he had married well. Over time, he became wealthy rather than well-to-do, a planter eager to increase his landholdings, to support western expansion, to grow his capital, and to encourage commerce.

Eighteen years older than Jefferson, George Mason was heir to a plantation close to Mount Vernon. Both Washington and Mason had been delegates to the House of Burgesses since 1758. Mason had a facile pen, a quick intelligence, and a libertarian mind. Both resented that land west of the Alleghenies had been closed to American ownership. In 1765, Mason, printing a satiric attack on British paternalism, had put himself on public record in opposition to the Stamp Act. By 1769, he and Washington strongly resented what they felt to be economic oppression. Both felt insulted to their existential British core by what seemed to them Parliamentary tyranny. They were being treated as second-class citizens, inferior to those born and based in England. They agreed with their Bostonian co-protesters: the best nonviolent weapon available to the colonists was to pinch the British economic shoe by refusing to purchase British imports. Not everyone in the House of Burgesses was on the same page about tone and substance. Still, the majority agreed that a colony-wide pledge to boycott products imported from Great Britain, though difficult to enforce, was the best counter to the new import duties on paint, glass, lead, paper, and tea. Their debts were growing. Their pocketbooks were being hurt. So too their pride. They felt deprived of the constitutional protection guaranteed to all British citizens.

The same people and forces that had smoothed Jefferson's path into the law and legislature now chose him, a kinsman, a gentleman, and a fellow plantation owner, for prominence. They also had to have had a sense, even if not immediate corroboration, of his competence as a writer, his attentiveness to detail, and his noncombative personality. Appointed to the committee to write a remonstrance, he made his first appearance in a role he was to excel in. His peers had reason to believe that he could be counted on to be amiably assertive, to seek the middle ground, to push ahead but not precipitously. Whatever his personal views, he would be attentive to others; he would not make inflammatory speeches; he would be an excellent committeeman by instinct and training, a leader who would not lead too far and too fast; and his most aggressive weapon would be his pen.

Jefferson later wrote that "Mr Pendleton asked me to draw the resolutions, which I did. They were accepted by the house, and Pendleton, Nicholas, myself, and some others were appointed a Committee to prepare the Address. The Committee desired me to do it; but when presented . . . Mr Nicholas chiefly objected . . . and was desired by the committee to draw one more at large which he did . . . and it was accepted." Jefferson's draft was not strong enough. "Being a young man . . . it made on me an impression proportioned to the sensibility of that time of life." He resented the editorial oversight just as, seventeen years later, he was to object to the changes Congress imposed on his draft of the Declaration of Independence.

Jefferson and his colleagues believed that the British economy would suffer considerably if Americans practiced nonimportation. They also assumed that the call for nonimportation would be widely implemented. They were wrong on both counts. The language of the remonstrance was not explicitly rebellious. It existed to make a point and apply pressure.

> Being deeply affected with the Grievances and Distresses, with which his Majesty's *American* Subjects are oppressed . . . which threaten the Ruin of ourselves and our Posterity, by reducing us from a free and happy People to a wretched and miserable State of Slavery; and having taken into our most serious Consideration the present State of the Trade of this Colony, and of the *American* Commerce in general, observe with Anxiety, that the Debt due to *Great-Britain* for Goods imported from thence is very great, and that the Means of paying this Debt, in the present Situation of Affairs, are likely to become more and more precarious. . . . The late unconstitutional Act, imposing Duties on Tea, Paper, Glass . . . is injurious to Property, and destructive to Liberty. . . . Therefore,

in Justice to ourselves and our Posterity, as well as to the Trad-ers of *Great-Britain* concerned in the *American* Commerce, we, the Subscribers, have voluntarily and unanimously entered into the following Resolutions. . . . First . . . that the Subscribers . . . will promote and encourage Industry and Frugality, and discourage all Manner of Luxury and Extravagance. Secondly, . . . they will not . . . import, or cause to be imported, any Manner of Goods, Merchan-dize, or Manufactures, which are, or shall hereafter be taxed by Act of Parliament, for the Purpose of raising a Revenue in *America*. . . . Thirdly, . . . the Subscribers will not hereafter, directly or indirectly, import or cause to be imported from *Great-Britain*, or any Part of *Europe* . . . any of the Goods herein after enumerated. . . . Lastly . . . these Resolves shall be binding on all and each of the Subscribers . . . upon his Word and Honour, agree that he will strictly and firmly adhere to and abide by every Article in this Agreement.

The language of the resolutions presents the economic argument as an effort at logical persuasion. That any members of the House of Burgesses who signed the nonimportation resolutions believed that it would move Parliament to renounce its claim of sovereignty and su-premacy is questionable. And what would these colonists do if Great Britain were to reject the appeal, other than continue to urge, without the power to enforce, nonimportation? The remonstrance also relies on the language of victimization, an irrational comparison of Parlia-mentary supremacy and indirect taxation with slavery. That emo-tionally charged trope would become more widespread and intense in the next decade. It was a slightly credible argument that the taxes imposed on the colonies undermined the American economy, though each of the colonies differed in its vulnerability to particular taxes. Apparently, none of the signers of the resolutions detected any irony in the slavery metaphor. Jefferson and his contemporaries used the word in this context as if it had nothing to do with those who tilled their fields. It stood for non-self-governance in regard to internal taxes. To be an actual slave was probably, for Jefferson, unimaginable. It took a very human and contextual act of mental dissonance for the signers of the resolutions to hold human slaves while at the same time arguing that if they accepted Parliamentary supremacy they themselves would also be slaves.

There were other important concerns for Jefferson besides his political activities. By the start of the 1770s, he was well along to phasing out his legal career. Having come of age in 1764, he had met the excitement of the anti–Stamp Act fervor as a legally mature and well-to-do member of the Virginia elite. He was a Jefferson; he was also a Randolph. He was the owner of a large estate, about five thousand acres spread among a few plantations, and about two hundred slaves. He could be exclusively a farmer, a vocation he increasingly valued, though farming always was ownership of land that others worked for him. He seldom got his hands dirty, except with occasional light pruning. He was the master, the proprietor, and the ultimate supervisor.

Later he recognized that he had been a poor farmer, not in wealth, though that turned out also to be the case, but in managing his estates—poor in discipline, conception, and implementation. On a day-to-day basis, he gave orders. Others implemented them. And tilling the soil was always a risky business. Nature did not cooperate often enough. Plantation farmers faced problems of scale, weather, and pests; the labor force had to be controlled and cared for; crops had to be transported to rivers, then seaports, and from seaports to Northern cities or distant Europe. Markets were uncertain and variable. The owners of or squatters on smaller parcels of land faced most of the same obstacles. Jefferson romanticized the latter as the yeoman class. He himself did not belong to it. He always, though, elided the distinction between large scale, slave-based farming and the small farms of the vast majority of Americans, who worked with few or no slaves and got their hands dirty.

In mid-May 1766, Jefferson traveled northward for the first time, to Annapolis, then Philadelphia and New York City. He wanted to get vaccinated against smallpox, along with yellow fever one of the two deadliest diseases Americans faced. He may also have been restless. And curious. It was his first visit to any part of the world other than Virginia. The bare mechanics of travel had its dangers. He traveled alone in a two-wheeled open carriage pulled by a single horse. He was lucky to do twenty miles a day. Roads were minimal, often muddy and obstructed. River crossings were challenging. He almost didn't make it to Maryland. In the first few days, his horse ran away with him twice. His neck was almost broken, he wrote to John Page. Crossing a tributary of the York, he misjudged its depth. "I passed through water so deep as to run over the cushion as I sat on it, and to add to the danger, at that instant one wheel mounted a rock which I am confident was as high as the axle, and rendered it necessary for me to exercise all my skill in the doctrine of gravity, in order to prevent the center of gravity from being left unsupported." For a moment it seemed as if "myself, chair and all" would be tossed "into the water. . . . I confess that on this occasion I was seized with a violent hydrophobia."

He passed near what decades later would be the capital of a country that did not yet exist. It was a bucolic wilderness. Jefferson made no mention in his letters of his first sight of the Potomac. At Annapolis, he went to observe the Maryland Assembly in action. "I was surprised on approaching it to hear as great a noise and hubbub as you will usually observe at a public meeting of the planters in Virginia," he wrote to John Page. It seemed a chaotic assembly of unruly lawmakers, hardly distinguishable from a mob, gathered in a particularly ugly building. He had no need to emphasize the comparative sophistication of their Williamsburg world. Annapolis itself he thought "extremely beautiful," its bustling and commodious port impressive. Virginia had nothing like it. Nor had it anything like Philadelphia or New York, the first sizable cities he ever visited. Virginia made almost nothing but tobacco. People in Philadelphia and New York had busy commercial and artisanal lives.

And Philadelphia, with about forty thousand people, had the colonies' best medical professionals. Eager to be protected against smallpox, he made use of a letter of introduction and had himself infected with the variola virus. He then traveled to New York, the second largest city in the colonies, about which he had nothing to say. He made it back to Williamsburg by late July, "after a long, but agreeable trip along the continent as far as New York." If he had any complaint, it was the "want of a companion, whose equal curiosity might have kept one in countenance in rambling over the different places which lie on the road." It was mostly a solitary trip, and he was a sociable man who liked company and companionship.

In 1768 he initiated having slaves build a home for himself on the 867-foot rise a mile from Shadwell. He called it his little mountain, Monticello. It was not a replacement for Shadwell. The fire didn't occur until two years later. The idea may have been conceived at the time of his father's death. Perhaps, without his father, Shadwell was less his home of choice than it had been. His mother and siblings were there, but he either wanted out or he wanted something more, a house of his own on the summit of the hill that had been in sight since he first had eyes to notice. By February 1769, the mountaintop had been cleared and leveled. He was planning, he wrote to John Page, "to remove to another habitation which I am about to erect."

In his head he was already gone from the home of his birth. His much-loved sisters would still be close, his mother also. This project was not a rejection of his family but a personal aspiration and affirmation. Twenty-five years of age, he desired marriage and physical love, and a family of his own. He had lost Rebecca Burwell, whom he had never had except in his imagination. There were alternatives. Marriage was indirectly and sometimes directly on his mind, always seriously, even if his language and tone were playful. Page, who had married in 1765, was already a father. Jefferson wanted that happiness for himself. Having his own home would advance that possibility. Even if his marital life would be some years off, the decision to build a house was a coming-of-age affirmation of who he was and whom he wanted to be.

As his slaves began leveling the mountaintop, Jefferson had little idea of what a challenge it would be to build there. Building at that height would take a great deal of labor and time. It would be expensive. And how to get water for human consumption and for a kitchen garden, let alone flower beds and orchards, to that height? Would he have wells dug? How deep would he have to go to get water? At times of drought, wouldn't the wells fail? He could augment his wells with rainwater collected in cisterns, but how large and strong would those cisterns have to be in order to contain enough water for a large house? What about when it hardly rained? Also, a house at that height required a well-constructed road to carry the weight of heavy carts loaded with supplies and building materials. It would have to be winding; the angle of ascent should not place too heavy a strain on oxen and donkeys. All this would have to be done by manual labor and animal strength.

In addition, flattening a mountaintop would disturb if not damage the ecosystem that kept the soil in place, though that does not seem to have occurred to him. The soil was shallow. Beneath it was hard red clay. It did not readily absorb water. Over time, the quick, heavy rainfalls typical of the area would wash much of the soil down the slopes. In dry times, it would disintegrate into dust. Erosion was inevitable. It would have made more sense to build on a level plot in a location that sloped gently down to sea level, close to a navigable river. Apparently, what outweighed all other considerations was the view, almost limitless westward toward the eastern slope of the Blue Ridge Mountains. Its beauty, its privacy, and the sense of being above lower levels appealed to Jefferson. To build there was an assertion of possession of some of the things he most valued. The decision was also an assertion of his own distinctiveness. It had its base in class, and it was also very personal.

Experts with special skills had to be employed and paid. And when Jefferson's slaves cleared and leveled the area and made bricks for the building, they were not working at profit-producing tasks like tending tobacco fields. They could be assumed to be cost-free labor, though every plantation owner was aware that slave labor involved profit-and-loss bookkeeping. From the start, Jefferson was good at and preoccupied with lists of almost everything that could be represented numerically, including the cost of maintaining slaves. He enjoyed the sense of control that lists provided, but the appearance of control was not the reality. Jefferson could be demanding but was never brutal. Still, he had no doubt about the relationship between himself and his slaves: they were property.

He had some tolerance for slave misbehavior; after all, free persons also misbehaved. But when, in 1769, "a Mulatto slave called Sandy, about 35 years of age," ran away, he paid for an advertisement in the *Virginia Gazette*. With his writing skills, he contributed to that widely published genre a nicely expressed descriptive sketch. Sandy's "stature," he wrote, "is rather low, inclining to corpulence, and his complexion light; he is a shoemaker by trade, in which he uses his left hand principally, can do coarse carpenters work, and is something of a horse jockey; he is greatly addicted to drink, and when drunk is insolent and disorderly, in his conversation he swears much, and his behaviour is artful and knavish. He took with him a white horse, much scarred with traces, of which it is expected he will endeavour to dispose; he also carried his shoemakers tools. . . . Whoever conveys the said slave to me in Albemarle, shall have 40 [shillings] reward, if taken up within the county, 41 if elsewhere within the colony, and 101 if in any other colony, from Thomas Jefferson." The sketch is vivid. And he wanted his property back.

Did twenty-five-year-old Jefferson have any idea, in 1768, how much Monticello would cost, what a price he would pay over his lifetime for its construction, expansion, and furnishing? His taste and education compelled him to spend lavishly for the Palladian architectural distinction that he aimed for, a European design alien to the American experience. At the start, the major expense was site preparation. A year later, with second thoughts, he confided that if the fire at Shadwell "by which I am burned out of a home, had come before I had advanced so far in preparing another, I do not know but I might have cherished some treasonable thoughts of leaving . . . my native hills." And where was he getting the cash in 1768 for the initial construction, even discounting the use of slave labor? His legal practice brought in little. His inheritance provided a variable and undependable cash flow. Like many plantation farmers, he had and needed very little cash. He resorted mainly to debt, barter, and the self-sufficiency of vegetable garden and slaughterhouse.

The one-room small brick building built in 1768 was to be one of several superimposed and enlarged over a forty-year period. Jefferson's eventual "suite" of three rooms—library, cabinet (study), and chamber (bedroom), with a greenhouse separated by glass compartments and doors, and characteristic pseudo-Palladian details, like the colonnades, the columns, and the dome—was not in place until decades later, starting in 1809, when he was sixty-eight. There were improvements after 1809, in his retirement years, but there was also deterioration. He could have had no idea in 1768 that the project would take about forty years to be completed, that the cost would be almost ruinous, and that, in the end, he would leave to his heirs a house mainly characterized by discomfort and decay. The reconstructed Monticello that visitors see today is not the house that Jefferson lived in. It is an idyllic version, made possible by the Monticello Foundation and by modern technology. Its weedless and well-watered garden is what most modern gardeners dream of. Even with slave labor, Jefferson's actual garden had lots of weeds, always.

In late November 1770, Jefferson moved into what was now his own one-room home. Late in life, he wrote that "I have often thought that if heaven had given me the choice of my position and calling, it should have been on a rich spot of earth, well-watered, and near a good market for the productions of the garden." The good fortune of his birth indeed had given him his choice of both. Monticello was not heaven's decision. He had been born wealthy. He was soon to obtain more wealth by marriage. He could have chosen to be entirely a farmer or entirely a politician, or neither. He could have created his home almost anyplace on the land he had inherited. Or he could have sold and bought land. He need not have built his house on the top of a mountain where the runoff from rainstorms would wash away the thin topsoil, where a water supply would always be uncertain, which was at an impractical distance from a market, and where the cost of hauling materials for leveling, building, and maintenance would be huge. The Monticello of Jefferson's lifetime was a slow, costly, and improvident creation.

The nonimportation resolutions encouraged self-sufficiency. For Jefferson, certain kinds of possessions were a birthright and an addiction. For example, in 1774 he badly wanted fourteen pairs of glazed window sashes for Monticello. They could only be obtained from England. He ordered them, their cost to be added to his bill, which would be paid for by a tobacco crop not yet harvested. He knew it was likely that Congress, the newly created national legislature, was about to put in place a nonimportation embargo. He thought the sashes might be delivered before the embargo legislation was passed, but the dates worked against him. When he wrote to cancel the order, it was too late. In December, in an overly argued, lengthy letter to the Virginia Committee of Correspondence, he explained what had happened. His explanation misdated in his favor the sequence of events. "I thought it better previously to lay before your committee . . . a full state of the matter by which it might be seen under what expectations I had failed to give an earlier countermand." He would, he wrote, be perfectly content to have the goods confiscated on arrival. There was, though, a subtext. He so much wanted the sashes that he seems to have deceived himself into believing that the dates were actually in his favor. Of course, he wrote, he would leave it to others to determine whether he would get them or not. "To your committee therefore if landed within their county I submit the disposal of them, which shall be obeyed as soon as made known to their and your most humble servant." There is an evident tension between his patriotism and his flawed argument. It seems likely that he hoped his explanation would allow the committee to be enough convinced of his patriotic fidelity to allow him to have what the facts did not support.

Between 1768 and 1770, law took up some of Jefferson's time. He continued to be a constant reader, soon re-creating and adding to his lost library. He read widely in history, science, poetry, fiction, and drama. The latter two he especially valued for how effectively they taught moral lessons. The greatness of great literature resided, he believed, in its use of imagination and emotion to convey moral lessons vividly and memorably. It taught wisdom and moral conduct better than did dry historical narratives or philosophical disquisitions.

His months in Williamsburg twice a year were sociable, though not satisfying. John Page was at Rosewell, happily married, by 1770 the father of two children and the center of a community of young people. Jefferson envied Page's situation. He missed his friend's lively hospitality, including the women who shared it. "Indeed I should be much happier were I nearer." He reflected often "with pleasure on the philosophical evenings I passed . . . in my last [visit]s there. I was always fond of philosophy even in its dryer forms, but from a ruby [lip] it comes with charms irresistible. Such a feast of sentiment must exhilarate and lengthen life at least as much as the feast of the sensualist shortens it. In a word I prize it so highly that if you will at any time collect the same" attractive company "I shall certainly repair to my place as a member of it." He was, though, mostly alone in his "very small house," on an isolated mountaintop, "with a table, half a dozen chairs, and one or two servants." By comparison with Rosewell, Shadwell had been a social and cultural desert. So too was Charlottesville. The small house in progress, in which he had started to live, was even more isolated. "My friends sometimes take a temperate dinner with me and then retire to look for beds elsewhere."

Always eager to be the optimist, he played with the notion that even in his solitude he could be "the happiest man in the universe." It required "the art of extracting comfort from things the most trivial. Every incident in life," he wrote to Page, referring to himself in the third person, as if he could transform what was the personal into the objective and universal, "he so takes as to render it a source of pleasure." He would be an embodiment of benevolence, by which he meant goodwill toward mankind, while at the same time utterly neglecting "the costly apparatus of life," by which he meant the painful experiences of the human condition. He could go on and on like this, he wrote, but "I am determined not to enter on the next page lest I should extend this nonsense to the bottom of that also. . . ."

This was playful. It was partly a joke on himself, and it was a kind of nonsense. It was also a serious credo of sorts: the best way to deal with emotional pain was to suppress it, to minimize its toxic potency by immersing oneself in work and books, by concentrating on the small pleasures obtained from daily obligations and realities, by sustaining long-term friendships, by stimulating intellectual and aesthetic activity, and by writing letters like this one. Some of this was disguise and evasion, a self-definition that suited his personality and needs. To some extent, it was self-conscious disguise, a purposeful alternative persona. But what was the persona to which it was an alternative? The less he thought about that, the better off he felt he would be.

The happiness of solitude was not the happiness he wanted. The energy of this letter, even in its evasions, was social, sexual, and patriarchal. He wanted to get married. He wanted children. And sometime in 1770, perhaps late in the year, he found a woman whom he wanted to marry and who wanted to marry him. He began to devote time, energy, and emotion to the courtship of Martha Wayles Skelton. He was twenty-seven; she was twenty-two. Martha's first marriage had left her with a young son, who would have been Jefferson's stepson if he had not died in June 1771, at a little less than four years of age, a death that Jefferson nowhere makes mention of, though he was already Martha's suitor. By local standards for a man of his class, he was a latecomer to the marital state. When they were married, in a traditional Anglican ceremony, Jefferson may have never had sexual relations with a woman, certainly not with a marriageable one, although the possibility had been on his mind probably even before his painful fiasco with Rebecca Burwell.

In 1766, at the age of eighteen, Martha Wayles Skelton had married twenty-two-year-old Bathurst Skelton, like Jefferson a former student of William Small at William and Mary and an heir of plantation wealth. Exactly a year later, she gave birth to a son. And less than a year after that, at the age of twenty, she was a widow. Perhaps Jefferson had met her in Williamsburg as early as 1768. By late 1770, he had fallen in love with this petite, attractive, well-read, and musically inclined widow who was now living with her father, John Wayles. Jefferson made a number of visits to Martha's father's home, his Tidewater plantation in Charles City County, called the Forest. A fifty-five-year-old, thrice-married widower, Wayles had at least eleven surviving children, six of them by a mulatto mistress named Elizabeth Hemings. In the convoluted kinship relationships of Virginia's upper class, John Wayles's third wife, Elizabeth Lomax Skelton, whom he married in 1760, had been the widow of Bathurst Skelton's older brother. A self-made lawyer, debt collector, entrepreneur, and slave trader, Wayles was a first-generation Virginian from Lancaster, England. Like Peter Jefferson, he had risen to the gentry class not by birth but by shrewdness and brains. His business touch had made him a member of the Tidewater elite. His plantation was a trophy, the result of, not the cause of, his wealth. Martha, his eldest legitimate child, whose mother, Martha Wayles Eppes, had died a week after she had been born, was the likely heir to a third of his fortune.

The courtship was successful. It seems likely that promises had been exchanged by early 1771. The two were from the start a compatible couple, both avid readers and musically inclined. Six months before the marriage, Jefferson ordered from London a mahogany piano, "the compass from Double G. to F. in alt. a plenty of spare strings; and the workmanship of the whole very handsome, and worthy the acceptance of a lady for whom I intend it." He was intending to have evenings in which he and his wife would be musical companions. The piano would be paid for, he promised his London agent, from the next tobacco crop. He also wanted his agent to help procure an architect for Monticello's expansion. A family with a piano needed more than one room.

That it was only one room did not discourage him from inviting guests. "Come then and bring our dear Tibby with you," he wrote exuberantly to Martha's brother-in-law, "the first in your affections, and second in mine. Offer prayers for me too at that shrine to which, though absent, I pay continual devotions. In every scheme of happiness she is placed in the fore-ground of the picture, as the principal figure. Take that away, and it is no picture for me." He was expecting much from the marriage. His brother-in-law encouraged him: "My sister Skelton . . . with the greatest fund of good nature has all that sprightliness and sensibility which promises to ensure you the greatest happiness mortals are capable of enjoying. May business and play music and the merriments of your family companions lighten your hearts, soften your pillows and procure you health long life and every human felicity!"

By February 1771, very shortly after Shadwell burned and a year before his marriage, Monticello was still one room. It "serves me for parlor for kitchen and hall . . . for bed chamber and study too . . . I too am in [the marrying] way," he wrote to a friend, though there was an obstacle to overcome, not from opposition from her "parents, nor perhaps want of feeling in the fair one, but from other causes as unpliable to my wishes as these." Monticello needed to be expanded, furnished, and made comfortable. Nevertheless, its limitations as a twenty-foot-square one-room home for the daughter of a rich man did not prevent their marrying on January 1, 1772.

Two weeks after the wedding celebration at the Forest, the couple set out for the home they were to share for the next ten years. They struggled by coach and then horseback through a heavy winter storm. Though the parents-to-be could not have known it yet, Martha was pregnant. Apparently, they were enthusiastic lovers. Jefferson wanted a wife who would bring him love, pleasure, children, and companionship. Martha seemed perfect. She was lovely. She was talented. She was compliant. She was a daughter of the world into which she had been born. She knew her place in the marital hierarchy in which the duty of a wife was serviceable compatibility, the keeper of the domestic keys, the ornament of hospitality, and the bearer of children. She was to be all these things.

Jefferson remained deeply in love and happily faithful during their ten years of marriage, their happiness limited only by her frequent illnesses, mostly related to her pregnancies. The marriage turned out to be exactly what Jefferson had hoped for. And John Wayles's death in 1773 theoretically doubled Jefferson's wealth. Clearly, though, he did not marry for money. And Martha's inheritance turned out to be a mixed blessing, partly because of Jefferson's own ineptitude with money and bad business judgment. He married, as was a given, a woman of his own class. That choice was inseparable from the class-based assumptions he shared with his Virginia contemporaries about status and patriarchy, about children, domesticity, slaves, land, and futurity. Like most married women of Martha's class, yearly pregnancy was almost inevitable, taken for granted in a society in which the ability of wives to endure pregnancies and produce heirs was highly valued. Birth control was primitive and undesired. Martha was to be constantly pregnant.

Not a word in writing between the couple has been preserved. It's reasonable to assume that they exchanged letters during their two-year courtship and later. At some unknown time, Jefferson and/or others destroyed whatever correspondence they'd had, from the time they first met to Martha's death in 1782. One letter of hers survives. It is not to her husband. It is not personally revealing. Almost everything about her that biographers provide is by surmise and indirection. Jefferson himself probably destroyed letters between them, although it is possible that, after Jefferson's death, his one surviving child and his grandson burned the letters. There's no record of a bonfire, supervised either by Jefferson or his descendants, like the flames that affirmed the privacy about his personal life that Charles Dickens ignited one afternoon late in his life on the lawn of his Gad's Hill home. If Jefferson was the arsonist, it's unlikely that his motive was suppression. For him, letters between a husband and wife were a sacred trove, exclusively theirs, not ever to be shared with anyone outside the family.

By the early 1770s, Jefferson had politics on his mind as much as his new home and his marriage. It was patriotism and politics, more than anything else, that made him a writer. His reading, though it made him super literate and knowledgeable about many things, had nothing to do with putting pen in hand, though of course it often contributed considerably to what he had to say in private and public. As a reader, his appetite was voracious, his taste classical—unlike John Quincy Adams, the literary son of his colleague, competitor, and friend, and unlike Lincoln, another president with literary genius, Jefferson never envisioned himself as a writer who desired to contribute to the literary canon. He read in every genre, but he did not conceive of himself as a writer of poetry, essays, plays, stories, or philosophical treatises. When he did write a book, it was not written to be published. It was written to convey information to a single person, a Frenchman of influence, to help advance a commercial and political alliance. The word *notes* in the title *Notes on the State of Virginia* was meant literally. It was not intended to be a polished or published literary work. To the extent that Jefferson was a writer, which was considerable, he was a writer for the political moment, for his intellectual engagements, and for his personal life.

In the 1770s Jefferson found a wife and built a home. Most of his six children were conceived in that decade. This was the much-desired fulfillment of his eagerness to become a patriarch. He had inherited land, slaves, income, elite status. Now he also had the domestic status that, if all went well, would give him happiness and heirs. He also began his life as a legislator, just one year before the start of the revolutionary decade that changed his life. By the end of that decade and the very beginning of the next, Jefferson had been for eight years a legislator in Virginia, briefly a member of the Continental Congress, the author of *A Summary View of the Rights of British America*, the Declaration of Independence, A Bill for Establishing Religious Freedom, and the writer of the first draft of *Notes on the State of Virginia*.

As a legislator, he was to be a productive success. Also, during four crucial years of the American Revolution, he was to be the governor of Virginia. Still, five years before the start of this momentous decade, though he had strongly opposed the Stamp Act, he was and always had been a loyal citizen of the British Empire. What happened to Jefferson that changed him from a loyal subject of King George III into a partisan of independence for Virginia and the American colonies?

Jefferson's Virginia world was both far from and close to the "sceptered isle." Literally, the distance was great. If the weather was reasonably good, the voyage took four to six weeks, if not longer, with no guarantee that you wouldn't come ashore hundreds of miles from the intended destination. Though the literal distance was great, the connection for people like Jefferson was close. London had a substantial American colony, much of it commercial, some of its members longtime residents of London. Some had brought their families. The daughter of one of them was to marry John Quincy Adams. Like many of his contemporaries, Jefferson relied heavily on his British business associate, Alexander McCaul of Glasgow. The connection with Great Britain was also legal and diplomatic, as well as cultural and educational, confirmed by the attendance of sons of the Virginia upper class at the Inns of Court and at English and Scottish universities, especially for medical studies. For Jefferson, the English connection closest to his heart was John Randolph, his cousin and companion on the violin. His brother, Peyton Randolph, one of Jefferson's political mentors, was the speaker of the House of Burgesses. John Randolph had studied law for four years at the Inns of Court. He enjoyed and admired London. He had returned to Virginia in 1749, when his young cousin was six years old, and soon rose to political prominence. Like his brother and all other Randolphs, in 1770 he had no thought of ever being anything less than a loyal subject of George III.

The Scotch merchant Alexander McCaul's view from Glasgow was unitary. His and Jefferson's correspondence kept Jefferson's tobacco flowing eastward and British goods flowing to Monticello. It was a business relationship. They had never met, but it was a bond that neither had any reason to sever. Jefferson needed to sell his tobacco; British law required that it be shipped first to Great Britain. McCaul then credited Jefferson's account for the tobacco and debited it for the items to be shipped to Monticello. The value of Jefferson's tobacco often was less than the cost of the merchandise. It was assumed that over time the account would be balanced. The credit British merchants provided to American planters also enabled luxurious flourishes, a style of life that the planter class thought its God-given right.

Jefferson's relationship with McCaul served them both well. From Glasgow, McCaul complimented Jefferson on his marriage. Jefferson asked McCaul to find a Scotch gardener for him, who would be an indentured apprentice. In 1770, McCaul asked Jefferson to be hospitable to a debt collector whom his firm was sending to Virginia to collect "outstanding debts. . . . We do not mean by this to give up our [American] trade, on the Contrary we mean still to carry it on and to have it more in our power to do it . . . by having less of our Money in the hands of negligent slothful planters." He did not consider Jefferson one of these. In fact, he had instructed his man "in all his General Court business solely to employ you." English was their shared language. Their national identities were distinctive but substantially overlapping. They had more in common with one another than with anyone who was neither British nor American.

In the summer of 1772, McCaul visited England for the first time. "I Spent two Months of this Spring and Summer in our Neighbor Kingdom," he wrote to Jefferson, "where I never was before and was much pleased and delighted. . . . It is Certainly the finest Country in the known World. You see their fields Cultivated with the utmost care, Covered with a rich Verdure, and abounding with everything to make Glad the heart of Man, the Towns and Villages crowded with Inhabitants, and Industry and its attendant Plenty to be seen everywhere I passed through." In London he "saw several of our old Virginia friends. . . . On the Change of London you would meet with many faces you had seen before." The stock and credit market had been going through a painful readjustment, many investors caught short when the Bank of England contracted credit and called in loans. "We however have escaped pretty well." But it would be some time "before public credit . . . is perfectly restored."

The Anglo-American connection was close, warm, and mutually profitable. Both countries, McCaul believed, had much to be pleased with in the pursuit of common interests. "It is happy for the Natives of Britain, they have such a resource as No. America . . . for there if they happen to be reduced, they may always have bread with Industry." English-speaking immigrants would help stock the labor-short, underpopulated colonies. Britain's excess population could sail westward, as did Jefferson's ancestors. The family's Albemarle home took its name from Jefferson's mother's London birthplace. The American colonists, McCaul observed, especially the Virginia planters, ought to "thank their stars they have so good a country to cultivate, though many of them are not sensible of the happiness they enjoy." Why did Americans not appreciate their good fortune? Why so many complaints? There is no extant response from Jefferson.

In 1773, Jefferson appealed to McCaul on a subject that had nothing to do with tobacco and money. It exemplified one of the strands in the bond between the British Isles and American colonists. It also dramatized the coexistence in Jefferson of a logical, legal, and rational element with a sentimental, idealizing element, the paradox of an Enlightenment man who also found irresistible the literature of sensibility. In 1760, James Macpherson, born in Inverness, Scotland, began publishing poems that he claimed he had translated from manuscripts written in Gaelic at some ancient time. Only he had access to these manuscripts. In 1762 he published his translation of an epic poem called *Fingal*, and then in 1765 *The Works of Ossian*, the putative author of the originals. Jefferson found *Ossian* irresistible, *Fingal* one of the great works of epic literature. Perhaps he also found in its depiction of dynastic struggles resonances of the tensions between the American colonies and Great Britain, suggesting that he had begun to think of American grievances in epic terms.

It is only the loosest of suggestions, and he had other reasons for being fascinated by *Ossian*. He thought it great poetry. He wanted to learn Gaelic to read it in the original. "I am not ashamed to own that I think this rude bard of the North the greatest Poet that has ever existed. Merely for the pleasure of reading his works I am become desirous of learning the language in which he sung and of possessing his songs in their original form." He got McCaul, through Macpherson's brother Charles, to convey his desire to have a copy of the originals. "I should be glad to accommodate any friend of yours," James Macpherson responded, "especially one of Mr. Jefferson's taste and character. But I cannot, having [re]fused them to so many. . . . The labor, besides, would be great. I know of none, that could copy them. . . . Make my humble respects to your American friend."

Ossian was a literary blockbuster, praised by many readers in Europe and America as a magnificent addition to world literature. It was translated into most European languages, translations of a translation based on a language that almost no one could read and the original of which no one other than Macpherson could consult. There were doubters. It seemed to them that the putative author was not "the greatest Poet that has ever existed" and that the translation was not a translation. When Samuel Johnson, usually a trustworthy arbiter of literary values, was asked, "Do you really believe that any man today could write such poetry?" he reputedly answered, "Yes. Many men. Many women. And many children." It was indeed inauthentic, a literary hoax. It was also bad poetry. Jefferson remained all his life a true believer. Napoléon also was an admirer until the evidence of fraud became convincing. What about Jefferson made him think the *Ossian* poems among the greatest poetry ever written? "These pieces have been, and will I think during my life continue to be to me, the source of daily and exalted pleasure. The tender, and the sublime emotions of the mind were never before so finely wrought up by human hand."

Jefferson's otherwise exemplary literary taste failed him. He had read the Homeric epics and Virgil's *Aeneid* in their original languages. To his credit, he wanted to read *Ossian* in Gaelic. That no manuscript was forthcoming to him or anyone else should have made him suspicious. There was also ample internal evidence to create doubt. Jefferson either did not see it or ignored it. There's no evidence that he re-reread *Ossian* in later years, though he took pleasure in the lines he had memorized and remained hopeful that the poem was authentic. It took almost a century for the scholarly consensus to determine that Macpherson, on the basis of a small number of fragmentary Gaelic sources, had vastly elaborated this pittance into an ersatz epic poem, most of which he himself created.

Ossian had a powerful effect on Jefferson. The poem appealed to desires and tensions within himself on a level of sufficient credibility that the semi-incredible and cliché-ridden evocation of the sublime became a treasured and spirit-moving reality. Macpherson was a minor poet who had the temperament and talent to create a text that appealed to the spirit of the times and to Jefferson's needs. It elevates sensibility and sensitivity. It values the Gaelic tradition over the British while also creating a modern epic in a language that makes English itself the vehicle of communication. It validates the English language and the English literary tradition, emphasizing the sensibility that prefaces the rise of Romanticism. Written in a room in London, it exemplifies both eighteenth-century English antiquarianism and the late-eighteenth-century English temperament. Jefferson's laudatory response was to a poem written in English. Fingal, the hero of this modern ersatz epic, hoax though it was, was a hero and a sensibility Jefferson could identify with. Like others, he was unable to distinguish its fake antiquarian language, simple rhymes and prosody, and incoherent evocation of the heroic life battling against its national enemies from the real thing. In the 1770s, Jefferson himself was at the start of an epic struggle, with life-or-death consequences. His passionate embrace of *Ossian* can be understood as both an escape from the present and an anticipation of what was to come.

One of Jefferson's friends in Virginia, James Ogilvie, embodied the ecclesiastical connection between Virginia and London. The underlying question was, why couldn't the American colonies have their own Anglican bishop? Early in the 1770s, Ogilvie was plunged into an epic battle of his own. It illustrates the personal and the public nature of the impending conflict in its ecclesiastical manifestation. Jefferson supported his friend's struggle to be ordained as an Anglican priest. It was not a matter of religion or religious belief; it was a matter of power and the relationship between the colonies and the mother country. Jefferson's involvement in Ogilvie's struggle seems a likely marker and motivator in his movement from loyal British subject to an advocate of independence.

Almost Jefferson's exact contemporary, Ogilvie, a Scotland-born son of a Presbyterian minister, had immigrated to Albemarle County in the early 1760s. Though not a close neighbor, he was close enough to Jefferson to soon become a friend. He earned his living as a tutor to gentry families. A former Presbyterian, he began to pursue ordination in the Anglican Church, which required intensive studies in a range of subjects, most of which he accomplished. Jefferson cheered him on, perhaps lent him books. The friendship transcended the gap between Jefferson's indifference to theology and distaste for any established church at all and Ogilvie's serious religiosity. Ogilvie's talents and interests made Anglican priesthood more attractive than tutoring the children of the wealthy. And he had fallen in love. He wanted to marry. He wanted a career. Having mastered the subjects required, with the exception of facility in classical Greek, he began the process by which an American aspirant became ordained. He needed the approval of the Bishop of London's representative in Williamsburg, James Horrocks. The test and interview did not go well. The obstacle was his deficiency in Greek. When he countered that another candidate with the same deficiency had been approved, he alienated his examiner.

Ogilvie asked the bishop's man for a second interview. He appealed to Jefferson for help. "We took proper measures," Jefferson wrote to his friend, "for prevailing on the commissary to withdraw his opposition." The "we" represented himself and some of his influential friends, including his highly placed Randolph cousin, the speaker of the House of Burgesses, whom he induced to write testimonials on Ogilvie's behalf. Eventually, the bishop's man agreed to write a letter of approval, with the provision that Ogilvie make up his deficiency in Greek. Ogilvie himself was to carry the letter to the Bishop of London for what he anticipated would be his ordination.

Jefferson provided a letter of credit for Ogilvie to obtain cash in London. "We shall do for you all that can be done in your absence," Jefferson wrote to him in February 1771. "But for god's sake" don't stay away "a moment longer than is of absolute necessity. Your settlement here would make your friends happy, and I think would be agreeable to yourself." He would always be a welcome guest at Monticello. "Whether my tenements be great or small homely or elegant they will always receive you with a hearty welcome." Ogilvie had in hand a list of items Jefferson had asked him to purchase for him in London. There was no point not taking advantage of the transit opportunity. And "if anything should obstruct your setting out immediately for Virginia," if you were to be delayed from returning, "I would beg the favor of you to send the things I asked of you to purchase by some careful captain coming to James river: such of them as were for my buildings, or for house-keeping I am in particular want of." In London, Ogilvie met with a shattering disappointment. The letter from James Horrocks damned with faint praise. Its general comments said nothing about a reparable deficiency in Greek, which an amiable and practical bishop with no ax to grind might have made a postordination requirement rather than a preordination standard. The Bishop of London apparently felt he had no choice but to conclude that his representative in Virginia did not find grounds on which to recommend Ogilvie. Why James Horrocks wrote as he did and why he allowed Ogilvie the illusion that if he undertook the expense and difficulty of a journey to London he would meet with approval and be ordained can only be guessed at. Apparently, he did not like Ogilvie not taking no for an answer. He seems to have enjoyed his make-or-break power over aspirants. It's also possible that he may have resented the efforts of Jefferson and his political allies to pressure him and may have taken pleasure in asserting his authority and power. The republicanism of which Jefferson was soon to become the leading embodiment was to have no place in it for any established church or authoritarian clergymen.

Meanwhile, in this case, it was a personal friend who was being tortured. "My life has been a continued scene of misfortune and disappointment," Ogilvie wrote to Jefferson. "I am naturally endowed with keen passions, and in the early part of my life they took a [bias] which has softened and rendered them most sensible of every accident that has befallen me." On appeal, the bishop reversed his decision, unwilling to let an otherwise well-prepared aspirant be denied Holy Orders because of a deficiency in one subject. Ogilvie took the oath of ordination. He "acknowledged the King of England as supreme governor of the church in all spiritual and temporal matters." He then set out to do some repair work with his English Presbyterian family, which eventually became reconciled to him. At first, though, it seemed to him that his Virginia friends loved him more. "I might to great advantage settle in England," he wrote to Jefferson, "yet my heart and thoughts are all eagerly bent upon Virginia." He wanted to return to the woman he loved. And to his friends, including Jefferson.

Ogilvie returned to Virginia in late 1771. He soon married the woman he loved, whom Jefferson referred to as "your Dulcinea," the peasant girl Don Quixote's disturbed mind transforms into a beautiful noblewoman. Jefferson probably correctly assumed that Ogilvie had read Cervantes. The rest of Ogilvie's Virginia years, though, were as heartbreaking as Don Quixote's anachronistic quest. He had sworn what he considered a sacred oath, that "the King of England [is] supreme governor of the church in all spiritual and temporal matters." He soon had a painful choice to make. Most of his parishioners in Hendricks County, Virginia, sided with the rebellion, the creation of a new regime that made any oath to King George incompatible with continued residence. Most voluntarily, some eagerly and others under pressure, tilted toward rebellion. Some hesitated, some refused at penalty of disapproval, ostracism, physical punishment, and confiscation of property. Some took it as an opportunity for enrichment, personal vengeance, and vigilante crimes.

In 1777, the new state required that every member of the community, especially those who seemed cautiously loyal to the previous regime, swear an oath of allegiance to what was now called the Commonwealth of Virginia. Ogilvie insisted that he had no politics, only a God. This was a political dispute; he was a clergyman. He would not take the new oath. In January 1778, the now dominant Patriot faction, in effect the new government of Virginia, led by Patrick Henry, evicted Ogilvie from his church, cut off his salary, assaulted him with insults, threatened his life, and pronounced an edict of perpetual banishment. Apparently, he was the only Anglican clergyman officially to be expelled, which suggests that he had been outspoken in his refusal to renounce his ordination oath. He left his wife and children behind. Never to see Virginia again, he made numerous attempts to bring his family to England. Each failed. He was never to see his wife again. And he was never again to see his American friends.

Jefferson had started the 1770s as a loyal subject of King George. So too had Ogilvie. As a clergyman, he had sworn an oath that Jefferson had not. In essence, though, every American colonist, especially lawyers and legislators, had sworn an oath of fealty to the king. Aware of the likely consequences of renunciation, Jefferson made his choice. Some made theirs gradually, some quickly, some under duress. There was no personal estrangement between Jefferson and Ogilvie, no harsh words or attempts at persuasion, as far as is known. Apparently, Jefferson was concerned enough about and loyal enough to his friend to offer in 1778 to pay one of his debts. What compelled Ogilvie one way and Jefferson another? Perhaps the religious nature of Ogilvie's oath made a difference. Perhaps Jefferson had more to gain by a successful rebellion than did his clergyman friend. Certainly Jefferson was a political creature at heart and Ogilvie was not. Perhaps it was simply that Ogilvie, married to the daughter of a pro-British colonist and whose father and brother were prominent clergymen in England, was more emotionally attached to king and country. There's no conclusive answer. As much as one examines the lives of individual colonists, their social, political, and economic situations, the difference between why one colonist sided with Great Britain and another opted for independence, despite oaths of allegiance, can be difficult to pin down. Contextual and rational matters often play a role. But it often seems a matter of the heart, the individual situation, the individual personality, and the individual's answer to the question: Under what circumstances shall an oath be renounced?

By 1771, Jefferson and his cousin John Randolph had developed a musical relationship. They played the violin together. The previous generation had joined the Randolph and Jefferson names. Randolph's father was Jefferson's mother's uncle, a wealthy planter and slave-holder, the Randolphs being among the earliest possessors of the native land and its imported labor. Like their Randolph predecessors, Thomas and John took their privileged lives for granted. The older cousin had studied at the Inns of Court in London. He had made a career for himself as a lawyer and legislator in Williamsburg. He also served the Crown as the king's official lawyer, Virginia's attorney general, a prominent member of the ruling class. Jefferson may have had opportunities to admire Randolph's violin in the early 1760s in the musical group that included Governor Fauquier and George Wythe. Randolph's enthusiasm for gardening produced the first American book on kitchen gardening. They saw each other regularly in Williamsburg. The cousins had much in common.

In 1771 they executed a legal agreement, partly serious, partly humorous. It was about Randolph's superior violin. Virginia did not have craftsmen who could make a violin of high quality. He had brought his back from London. Jefferson wanted it. In April, they drew up a document, signed by seven witnesses, including their Williamsburg associates George Wythe and Patrick Henry. It was a bit of good-humored seriousness. It stated that if Randolph should outlive his younger cousin, he would receive books from Jefferson's estate to the value of one hundred pounds sterling; if Jefferson should survive Randolph, "the Executors of the said John shall deliver to the said Thomas the violin which the said John brought with him into Virginia, but if the violin had been destroyed by accident Thomas could take its value in books from Randolph's estate."

Which of them originated this partly humorous assertion of Jefferson's hope to inherit his cousin's violin isn't known, but it was probably Jefferson. Randolph could simply have bequeathed it to his cousin in his will. This singular document had the effect of a codicil to a will whose point was the conveyance of a particular gift to the person who outlived the other. It was statistically likely that twenty-eight-year-old

Jefferson would outlive his older cousin. Randolph admired Jefferson's book collection. But he hardly needed more books and could always purchase any book that his cousin owned. Jefferson wanted the violin. Besides being a superior instrument, it also represented a bond between them, an instrument of connection, an embodiment of kinship and friendship. It attested to shared cultural values.

Between 1771 and 1775, the American world they lived in changed radically. Though the cousins positioned themselves in opposite corners, ideologically, politically, and physically, the personal bond was never broken. "Though we may politically differ in Sentiments," Randolph wrote to Jefferson, "yet I see no Reason why privately we may not cherish the same Esteem for each other which formerly I believe subsisted between us. Should any coolness happen between us, I'll take care not to be the first mover of it."

By late 1775, certainly by the summer of 1776, Jefferson had renounced his allegiance to George III. Whether directly or indirectly, he renounced his oath of loyalty to the Crown. In 1774, he had used his pen to make himself well known in the colonies and in London as a proponent of either reconciliation favorable to the colonies or independence. The risk was great. The potential rewards were equally great. Some Virginia planters hoped to liberate themselves from their dependence on British commercial credit. They hoped to be able to trade as free agents on the international market. The motivation on the whole, though, was resentment, a host of grievances whose most provocative public focus was taxation. They were wealthy white men of the British Empire, and Parliament had no right to treat them as second-class citizens. They felt insulted to the core. It was an insult to tax them without consent and to restrict settlement to the land east of the Alleghenies. It was essentially a matter of honor and self-definition, an assault on their status as freeborn British citizens, a displacement of the psyche from superior to subordinate, from master to slave. The members of Virginia's elite, at differing paces and with varying enthusiasm, some quickly, some slowly, some not at all, were reassessing the imperial relationship.

For Randolph, an oath to king and country was sacred. He wanted a reconciliation of differences. As literate as his cousin, in 1774 he urged arbitration and loyalty at book length, the maintenance of consanguinity and the common cultural history. By inference, just as Jefferson and he were cousins, so too were all the Anglo-Saxon males of the British Empire. Differences should be settled peacefully over time. However, Virginia was gradually becoming Jefferson's exclusive national identification. Although the process was gradual, the part of him that had believed he was a loyal son of the empire had sensed his loyalty gradually squeezed out of him. He still wanted reconciliation, but on his own terms, which he espoused in a long essay, *A Summary View of the Rights of British America*, published in 1774 without his permission as a pamphlet. Widely read, it made him well known in the colonies and infamous in Great Britain. Randolph's spoken and written words, in contrast, had made him unpopular in Virginia, a target of denunciation. He and his family were insulted, their persons and property attacked. His loyalty to the empire, though, was inseparable from his definition of himself as a Virginian. He could not separate them. You could not have one without the other.

In the summer of 1775, afraid for his and his family's safety, Randolph took refuge with Lord Dunmore, the now widely detested royal governor, on a British warship anchored in the James River. The alternative was seizure and imprisonment. Whether he stayed or fled, his property would be at risk. For Randolph there was no turning back. He was soon to become a permanent exile from the Virginia he had and always would love.

In late August 1775, from Monticello, Jefferson sent the price they had agreed on to Randolph's point of embarkation. Randolph was leaving much more behind than his cherished violin, particularly his brother Peyton and his son Edmund. With wife and daughters, he was about to sail eastward on a voyage from home to home, Virginia and England inseparable in his mind and feelings, a single country whose parts served a mutual interest far exceeding the potential benefits of any separation. He had no animus against his cousin. The sale of the violin was proof of that.

Jefferson expressed his affection at length in an eloquent letter. "My best wishes for your felicity attend you wherever you go," he wrote. It was not a personal matter; he still loved his cousin. "I am sorry the situation of our country should render it not eligible to you to remain longer in it." The fault was an "unnatural contest. There may be people to whose tempers and dispositions contention may be pleasing, and who may therefore wish a continuance of confusion. . . . My first wish is a restoration of our just rights; my second a return of the happy period when, consistently with duty, I may withdraw myself totally from the public stage and pass the rest of my days in domestic ease and tranquillity, banishing every desire of afterwards even hearing what passes in the world." In fact, "I would rather be in dependence on Great Britain, properly limited, than on any nation upon earth, or than on no nation. But I am one of those too who rather than submit to the right of legislating for us assumed by the British parliament, and which late experience has shown they will so cruelly exercise, would lend my hand to sink the whole island in the ocean . . . whether Britain shall continue the head of the greatest empire on earth, or shall return to her original station in the political scale of Europe depends perhaps on the resolutions of the succeeding winter. God send they may be wise and salutary for us all!"

Jefferson still hoped, he wrote, for a peaceful resolution, though blood had already been shed in Massachusetts, but only if the major issues could be settled favorably for the colonies. He preferred to be at home at Monticello with his wife, children, and slaves. It was a motif he was to repeat and insist on until he left the presidency in 1809, after almost thirty years of doing the opposite of what he claimed he preferred. All he wanted was "a restoration of our just rights." If they were not to be restored, he would lend his "hand to sink the whole island in the ocean," a resolution so extreme that it seems either a purposeful exaggeration or an expression of an intense anger beyond emotional control. The letter is a dramatic example of Jefferson in emotional turmoil, the rational man with an elegant and powerful pen, driven to say, as he habitually did, even with some excuse for rhetorical effect, that he would accept the deaths of millions of people rather than accept Parliament's right to have ultimate legal power over Virginia. If Britain should not become "wise and salutary," its conflict with America, he argued, would deprive it of its empire and make it a lesser power in Europe. The irony of that prediction is that, after the loss of the American colonies, Great Britain became even more dominant as a European and world power.

Still, Jefferson seems, even as late as August 1775, to have hoped that further conflict could be avoided. If only Great Britain would come to its senses. If only, by inference, his cousin would come to his. The contest is "unnatural," he grants. He regrets that his cousin is leaving. But what he writes is not an argument or a plea for him to remain. It is partly a justification for rebellion. It is also an emotionally intense diatribe, an anticipation of the passionately hostile tone of most of the Declaration of Independence. It raises the rhetorical stakes. It anticipates that rhetorical blood is likely to be turned into real blood. It assumes the premise of his oft-quoted later statement that "the tree of liberty must be refreshed from time to time with the blood of patriots and tyrants." In this and in the latter context, however, it was not his blood that was at issue.

His optimism that little blood would be shed was naive. A brief military campaign and one decisive battle, Jefferson believed, would settle the matter in favor of the colonies, including the union of Canada with the new American Confederation. It was not, he assured his cousin, that independence was his goal, let alone his highest priority.

"Believe me dear sir, there is not in the British empire a man who more cordially loves a union with Great Britain than I do." He would prefer to maintain that relationship. "But by the god that made me I will cease to exist before I yield to a connection on such terms as the British parliament propose and in this I think I speak the sentiments of America. We want neither inducement nor power to declare and assert a separation. It is will alone which is wanting and that is growing apace under the fostering hand of our king. One bloody campaign will probably decide everlastingly our future course; I am sorry to find a bloody campaign is decided on. If our winds and waters should not combine to rescue their shores from slavery, and General Howe's reinforcement should arrive in safety we have hopes he will be inspirited to come out of Boston and take another drubbing: and we must drub you soundly before the sceptered tyrant will know we are not mere brutes, to crouch under his hand and kiss the rod with which he deigns to scourge us."

These are hardly the words of a statesman seeking compromise and reconciliation. Whatever had made him an advocate of independence, that advocacy was now firmly in place. The question of what happened between 1771 and 1775 that resulted in his renouncing his oath to king and country, an oath taken in good faith in his admission to the bar and to the House of Burgesses, has no single and simple answer.

In his letter of late November 1775, Jefferson again explained himself to his cousin. But he also had news of a personal sort to report, "the melancholy intelligence of the death of our most worthy Speaker." John Randolph's brother Peyton had died. It would have been a heavy blow to the bereaved brother. With his usual stoic conciseness about such matters, Jefferson simply explained that "he was struck with an Apoplexy, and expired within five hours." Nothing more, though the speaker had been his mentor. Their kinsman in London would have found this flat conciseness far short of the language or substance that would have helped sustain him in his grief. What Jefferson had most on his mind and immediately segued to at length was further justification for rebellion and a boastful account of American success in its invasion of Canada, including the imminent fall of Quebec, which never occurred. "In a short time we have reason to hope the delegates of Canada will join us in Congress and complete the American Union as far as we wish to have it completed."

The conquest of Canada was to remain an American objective until the end of the War of 1812, an arrogant failure to recognize that the majority of Canadians had no desire to become part of the United States. It seemed a given to Jefferson that they would want to join the American experiment, an early manifestation of his belief in an American exceptionalism so extreme that it declined to recognize that Canadians (and, later, Cubans) might prefer their independence as distinct national cultures.

Clearly, for Jefferson, it was all George III's fault. "It is an immense misfortune to the whole empire," he generalized in *A Summary View of the Rights of British America*, "to have a king of such a disposition at such time. We are told and everything proves it true that he is the bitterest enemy we have . . . ignorance or wickedness somewhere controls him. In an earlier part of this contest our petitions told him that from our king there was but one appeal. The admonition was despised and that appeal forced on us. To undo his empire he has but one truth more to learn, that after colonies have drawn the sword there is but one step more they can take. That step is now pressed upon us by the measures adopted as if they were afraid we would not take it."

Ironically, George III and Jefferson had some qualities and interests in common. It was the context and circumstances that made the difference. For Jefferson, the war for independence had been forced on the colonies. George believed that his policies had been forced on him. Jefferson's view that the colonies had no other choice was an attitude characteristic of Jefferson throughout his public life. Someone else or some other country was always at fault. This simplification had its advantages. It allowed him to use his talents as a writer to create, between 1774 and 1776, two rhetorically powerful indictments of Great Britain. They were both works of literature and effective weapons of propaganda. The Declaration of Independence was to be, among other tools, a powerful weapon of warfare.

CHAPTER THREE

Our Great Grievances

1773–1776

On the morning of the last Sunday in May 1774, a batch of mail from Boston and Philadelphia arrived in Williamsburg. The House of Burgesses had been "unexpectedly dissolved" by the royal governor, Lord Dunmore, on May 26 for what he considered insubordination. The House had passed a resolution on May 24 designating a "Day of Fasting and Prayer," then a statement three days later, signed by a majority of the "members of the late house of Burgesses," that a newly formed correspondence committee recommended that every colony appoint delegates "to meet in general congress, at such place annually as shall be thought most convenient . . . to deliberate on those general measures which the united interests of America may from time to time require." No functioning Virginia legislature existed other than informal communications between former House members, some of them residents of Williamsburg and others dispersed to their home counties. "We were under conviction of the necessity of arousing our people from the lethargy into which they had fallen as to passing events," Jefferson wrote about forty years later in his *Autobiography*, "and thought that the appointment of a day of general fasting and prayer would be most likely to call up and alarm their attention."

On the next to the last day in May, Jefferson's cousin Peyton Randolph, in the role of moderator, convened a meeting of those he referred to as "the inhabitants of this city." It's unlikely that this description included ordinary working people. It was a meeting of the well-to-do, the elite. In Randolph's account of the meeting, written for distribution to the members of the discharged House of Burgesses, he summarized the general response to "the most interesting and important Subject of American Grievances." The news from Boston was alarming. Its citizens were in "a most piteous and melancholy Situation." In December 1773, a small number of vigilante Bostonians had destroyed a cargo of British tea in Boston harbor. The pricing of the tea was a ploy to undercut the smuggled Dutch tea that most Americans bought to avoid the import tax on British tea. Parliament and its constituency were outraged at this criminal activity. In retaliation, the Boston Port Act closed the port, halting most commercial activity. British warships patrolled the harbor. The act, to take effect on June 1, 1774, required repayment of the value of the tea as a condition for relief from the act's provisions, though how repayment was to be made was unclear. Whig opposition in London supported less confrontational ways to protect the Anglo-American relationship, fearing punitive actions would be counterproductive. Dominated by the king's Tory Party, Parliament insisted on reparations. Bostonians were outraged, angry, and afraid. Resistance increased.

In Williamsburg, twenty-five ex-legislators, including thirty-one-year-old Thomas Jefferson, made the strongest statement they could agree on. "The most effectual Assistance which can be given by their Sister Colonies," Peyton Randolph summarized, "will arise from a general Association against Exports and Imports, of every Kind, to or from *Great Britain*." It was a revival of a tactic that had been tried before, though the degree to which it had been successful was open to dispute. "Most Gentlemen present seemed to think," Randolph continued, "it absolutely necessary for us to enlarge our late Association, and that we ought to adopt the Scheme of Nonimportation to a very large Extent; but we were divided in our Opinions as to stopping our Exports." All the members of the "late House of Burgesses," they proposed, "should meet in Williamsburg on the first of August to express themselves on the situation. . . . We flatter ourselves it is unnecessary to multiply Words to induce your Compliance with this Invitation, upon an Occasion which is, confessedly, of the most lasting Importance to all America. Things seem to be hurrying to an alarming Crisis, and demand the speedy, united Councils of all those who have a Regard for the common Cause."

Jefferson signed. So did Peyton Randolph, Robert C. Nicholas, Edmund Pendleton, Richard Henry Lee, Mann Page, Charles Carter, James Mercer, Robert Wormeley Carter, George Washington, Francis Lightfoot Lee, Thomas Nelson, John Walker, James Wood, and Lewis Burwell, all of whom had played or were to play a role in Jefferson's life and future. All were men of wealth and standing. What determined the order of the signatures is unclear. Jefferson was not the first or even the second among equals. That was soon to change, mostly by the power of his mind and pen, his ability to use language and logic to express what many of his colleagues felt and thought, particularly those who were inching closer to the possibility, even the likelihood, that further measures would be forced on them, that their reaction to faraway events they could not control would change their lives.

The British also had grievances. The only taxation had been, from the start, on imports and exports. Customs agents collected the import tax at the ports of entry, particularly Boston, New York, Philadelphia, Baltimore, and Charleston. The export taxes were embedded in the mercantile system requiring American cargoes to submit to

British regulations. The import tax had never produced its anticipated revenue. Customs agents were easily bribed. Authorities and juries identified more with fellow colonists than with British regulations. Also, cargoes were often underreported by type and value or hidden from sight. Even more profitably, some American vessels avoided customs duties entirely. Smuggling was an age-old practice in Europe and America. Instead of docking at the established ports of entry, many ships unloaded at out-of-the-way places where there were no customs officials to deal with. Though even approximate figures are not available, it seems likely that many entered the colonies illegally. Outgoing ships were required to sail first to a British port, where a tax would be collected. Many attempted to sail directly to European ports. Others brought cargoes to proscribed destinations, like the West Indies.

Americans were superb smugglers. They had been refining the practice for over a hundred years. Hard as it tried, the British government found it almost impossible to curtail it, let alone end it. The cost of trying was immense. By the late 1760s and early 1770s, Great Britain devoted large amounts of money to establishing a partial naval blockade of the American coast for the purpose of limiting smuggling. Ships were seized, but many got through. Attempting to evade British enforcement, whether successful or not, made economic sense, and the seizure of ships usually prompted widespread American resentment rather than contrition. Many resented maritime regulations of any sort.

In return, Parliament and many non-American citizens of the empire resented the colonists' reluctance to accede to the authority of the central government. Why would they refuse to pay their fair share of the bills incurred by the cost of common defense? To the average British citizen, and to most British politicians, it seemed like greed and mendacity. The colonists' increasingly popular battle cry, "no taxation without representation," appeared to be a cover slogan for "no taxation at all," except of the most minimal sort, which would only occur, in the colonists' view, when those being taxed were in charge of setting the rates. This would result, Parliament and the king concluded, in little to no revenue from the American colonies.

The American colonies, the king and his ministers believed, were essential to their struggle to keep Great Britain an independent island kingdom. French economic and territorial aggression threatened its existence. London's attempts to force the colonies into helpful compatibility were motivated by need. The colonies were, in London's view, an essential element in its international competitiveness. Its competition with France was a matter of life and death. The focus on the degree of London's authority over the colonies arose as much, if not more, from England's struggle with France and the European balance of power as from imperial theory. From London, the view was simple: we need the colonies to be part of our effort to contain France. That's what the French and Indian War had been about. French Catholic Canada had been a threat to the American Protestant colonies and to the empire.

The dilemma was piercingly clear. Each British administration between 1765 and 1774 wanted obedience from the colonies, but none, until 1774, had been willing to use force to command it. Cabinets, ministers, and Parliaments made declarations and issued commands. From London, these looked reasonable and fair, more or less, even to some pro-American Englishmen. Whether they were prudent and wise was a different matter. Repeatedly, London flinched from the use of the only enforcement tool that had the best chance of working: military force. It would be politically controversial, vastly expensive, and bloody. It would deflect troops and ships away from other areas of conflict, especially European alliances and battlefields, to the advantage of Great Britain's most formidable worldwide enemy. Each British government had faced the same problem: either total capitulation to the American colonists or military force. And it was also a matter of mind-set. The American colonists seemed greedy, disloyal, and unlawful. Every British ministry believed it was in the right, legally and morally. There were pro-American dissenters, but the British press, public, and government had, on the whole, a stiff sense of rightness.

To the Virginia elite, the dissolution of the House added insult to injury. Jefferson's pen played some role, though exactly how much is unclear, in the three statements that he and his rump colleagues wrote for public distribution in the last week of May 1774. The first was a resolution designating the first of June as "A Day of Fasting and Prayer." It "devoutly" implored "divine Interposition for averting the heavy Calamity, which threatens Destruction to our civil Rights, and the Evils of civil War; to give us one Heart and one Mind firmly to oppose, by all just and proper Means, every Injury to American Rights, and that the Minds of his Majesty and his Parliament may be inspired from above with Wisdom, Moderation, and Justice, to remove from the loyal People of America all Cause of Danger from a continued Pursuit of Measures pregnant with their Ruin." There was disagreement about "just and proper means." There was, though, no need to define that yet, and there seems to have been a consensus that those means would be reactive, not proactive. The claim of loyalty required that.

The next resolution called for colony-wide communication and mutual support. Still, there were a lot of moving parts. "A tender regard for the interest of our fellow subjects, the merchants, and manufacturers of Great Britain, prevents us from going further at this time; most earnestly hoping, that the unconstitutional principle of taxing the colonies without their consent will not be persisted in, thereby to compel us against our will, to avoid all commercial intercourse with Britain." It was an attempt to influence British public opinion. However, the closing of the port of Boston made "going further" a serious consideration, and the slavery trope was irresistible. "With much grief we find that our dutiful applications to Great Britain for security of our just, antient, and constitutional rights, have been not only disregarded, but that a determined system is formed and pressed for reducing the inhabitants of British America to slavery, by subjecting them to the payment of taxes, imposed without the consent of the people or their representatives."

The corresponding committees, Jefferson and his colleagues believed, would make the "American" response to their grievances more unitary than before. The Virginia committee was instructed to write letters to its counterparts in every colony urging support of their Boston fellow colonists, proposing a colony-wide boycott of British products and recommending, if Virginia voters approved, that each send delegates to a "Congress" to meet in the near future at a convenient place, soon determined to be Philadelphia. In the meantime, the delegates to the dissolved House of Burgesses should return to their home counties to test the will of the Virginia electorate.

None of the three documents have the stylistic firmness and personal touch of the one sentence in Jefferson's autobiography that describes the motivation and context of the creation of the fast-day resolution: "With the help therefore of [a century-old source volume] whom we rummaged over for the revolutionary precedents and forms of the Puritans of that day . . . we cooked up a resolution, somewhat modernizing their phrases, for appointing the 1st day of June, on which the port bill was to commence, for a day of fasting, humiliation and prayer, to implore heaven to avert from us the evils of civil war, to inspire us with firmness in support of our rights, and to turn the hearts of the king and parliament to moderation and justice."

The two priceless phrases are "rummaged over" and "cooked up." The sentence is both dignified and colloquial. It is the private Jefferson writing about public events in a memoir that was not intended for publication, at least not in his lifetime. He allows "rummaged over" and "cooked up" to infiltrate the formal prose, to enliven the sentence, to give it a personal touch without the sentence being about Jefferson more than the event he wants to explain. That Jefferson took some part in writing the documents he and his colleagues had signed in May seems likely. Still, they are not in his characteristic style or tone. In his *Autobiography* he provides some context for the process but no certainty about attribution. They seem collective expressions, using language readily available to all the signatories. Jefferson, though, had already in a small way made a reputation for himself as a wordsmith, someone whose pen could be relied on to put words on paper quickly and effectively. Some of the eloquent passages apostrophizing the injustices being imposed on the colonists have a slight touch of Jefferson's exemplary flourishes, his combination of concision, eloquence, vigor, and logical force.

Jefferson returned to Albemarle in June 1774. He needed to make the case for his and his colleagues' resolutions and to stand for reelection. If reelected, he would return to Williamsburg on August 1. The House would then decide who would represent it in Philadelphia and what their instructions would be. Late in July, he wrote up in his own language the resolutions that had been approved at a meeting that had taken place at the Albemarle County courthouse. It is addressed to "the Freeholders of Albemarle County." The record doesn't show whether the resolutions were approved by voice vote, raised hands, or ballot, though probably not the latter. It doesn't show how many were in attendance. "Freeholders" were white male property owners. It seems unlikely that the sons of property owners, who were not technically landowners, could vote. Tenant farmers had no electoral presence. How many tenant farmers there were in Albemarle is unknown. The ballots cast were limited by tests of property, gender, and race. Voting preferences were openly expressed. It seems likely that Jefferson was reelected without opposition. The resolutions were not couched in exalted language, either of emotion or eloquence, but they made a claim in language that had already been shaped by Jefferson and his colleagues in their Williamsburg meetings. It was a clear anticipation of the level to which the language of natural rights was to be elevated in the next two years.

The colonists were entitled, Albemarle County's resolutions claimed, by custom, history, law, and natural rights, to make their own decisions about everything that concerned them internally. These were the "common rights of mankind." The original colonists were individual entrepreneurs, the Albemarle resolutions claimed, not representatives of the king or the Parliament. They were and should continue to be self-ruling, beholden to king and Parliament only by consent.

It is the opinion of this meeting, that we immediately cease to import all commodities from every part of the world which are subjected by the British parliament to the payment of duties in America. It is the opinion of this meeting that these measures should be pursued until a repeal be obtained of the act for blocking up the harbor of Boston, of the acts prohibiting or restraining internal manufactures in America, of the acts imposing on any commodities duties to be paid . . . and of the acts laying restrictions on the American trade. . . . Resolved . . . that this meeting do submit these their opinions to the convention of deputies from the several counties of this colony . . . and also to the general congress of deputies from the several American states . . . and that they will concur in these or any other measures which such convention or such congress shall adopt as most expedient for the American good. And we do appoint Thomas Jefferson and John Walker our deputies to act for this county at the said convention, and instruct them to conform themselves to these our resolutions and opinions.

Jefferson would have no difficulty conforming. The text was most likely written entirely by him. But he was far from completely satisfied with it. It was brief and perfunctory. It made its point, and it made known the will of the freeholders of Albemarle, in whose name the resolutions were stated. But to Jefferson's mind something more was needed, something much more.

In the last days of July 1774, at home at Monticello, preparing to join his legislative colleagues in Williamsburg, Jefferson began to write something astounding and consequential. It seems that the words and thoughts expressing his feelings about American grievances came irrepressibly to him. He was a man of intellect and feeling, and he was angry. He needed to put words on paper for his own relief and satisfaction. His words would also be exhortative. He hoped they would serve as guidelines, as talking points, to the delegates that the Williamsburg convention would be sending to Philadelphia. They also might add spine to their will. Whether he intended what he began writing as the extended essay of almost seven thousand words that it turned out to be is unknowable. It's probable that he had in mind that its impact would increase the likelihood that he would be elected one of the delegates to the Philadelphia Congress.

It is a strange and powerful essay. Strange because no one had asked him to write it; strange because of its historical inaccuracy and special pleading; strange because it totally refuses to even acknowledge the existence of a counterargument. It is powerful because of its no-holds-barred emotional intensity, its vivid combination of logical expansion and structural concision, and its inventiveness in combining feeling, argument, language, and ideology. It is the highest form of propaganda: propaganda as complex and interesting literature. Though it was eventually to be called *A Summary View of the Rights of British America*, it initially had no title. It was not intended for publication. When it was published in America and Great Britain, its anonymous authorship soon became known. It put Jefferson's name on the transatlantic map.

It also made clear to those who could read between the lines of its argument and eloquence that, if Jefferson had his way, unless the colonists could have reconciliation on their own terms, his energy, his elocution, and his anticipation were set in the direction of independence. The start of the voyage required only a precipitating act. For Jefferson, it was to happen at Lexington in April 1775. "My creed had been formed on unsheathing the sword at Lexington," he wrote many years later. By "creed" he implies that British responsibility for the first acts of violence had determined that he would commit himself to independence. In summer 1774, the skirmishes at Concord and Lexington were still almost a year off.

In July and August 1774, it was entirely a matter of words, the ventriloquist projecting sentences into the minds of a less articulate vehicle, an assembly. To take pen in hand, without encouragement, let alone assignment, without committee or institutional permission, suggests that Jefferson acted intuitively and impulsively. He could not be sure that his words would significantly affect his colleagues. He could not be certain that he would be chosen to go to Philadelphia. Clearly, though, he had the need to do this and had confidence that he could do it well. It's unlikely that, when he started writing, he had a clear view of the essay's length, substance, effectiveness, and usefulness. He needed to write this; he needed to have it put to the eyes of his fellow delegates, and he was entirely sincere.

What he created was the Jeffersonian version of the useful truths and fictional "facts" essential to the creation of the American story, the myth of the relationship between the colonists and the land they were attempting to possess. It was an example of what Robert Frost called the act of making the land their own. And the impending realization that "the deed of gift was [to be] many deeds of war." Years later, Jefferson referred to its origins with characteristic conciseness, as if the details of composition were irrelevant. "Before I left home to attend the Convention, I prepared what I thought might be given in instruction to the Delegates who should be appointed to attend the General Congress. . . . They were drawn in haste with a number of blanks, with some uncertainties and inaccuracies of historical facts, which I neglected at the moment, knowing they could be readily corrected at the meeting." The statement is an example of the characteristic gap between Jefferson's feelings and his manner of referring to them afterward, as if a denatured representation made them more factual, his words more commanding.

Jefferson wrote out two copies. Soon after setting out for Williamsburg, becoming sick, he turned back. The hint is that it was a stomach ailment. Apparently, he made no effort to postpone rather than cancel attendance, as if his illness would last for so many weeks that a timely journey would be impossible. His predilection for home and family may have influenced his decision. His second child, now four months old, had been born in April 1774. It's likely that she and her mother were weak, even sickly. The infant was to die five months later. His essay made the journey without him, copies sent to two members of the assembly—its moderator, Peyton Randolph, who laid it on the table, available to anyone who wanted to read it, and to Patrick Henry, whom Jefferson probably thought would identify with its argument. Whatever Randolph and Henry thought of it, the delegates concluded that it was not yet time for such a radical, angry, and confrontational statement.

Over fifty years later, John Quincy Adams, who had known Jefferson well, read it for the first time in the first posthumous edition of Jefferson's works. The tone and language of Jefferson's direct address to George III seemed to Adams unnecessarily insulting. And, point by point, Adams, who with his father was as much a proponent of the Revolution as Jefferson, eviscerated Jefferson's claims of historical fact. What Jefferson had created was passionate propaganda. The facts mattered less to him than to Adams, though what were fictions to Adams were facts to Jefferson.

Soon afterward, some of Jefferson's fellow Virginians who admired *A Summary View* took the initiative of publishing it in a small edition without its author's name. Two years later, it was published widely. Copies were available in London. Jefferson was known to be its author. *A Summary View of the Rights of British America* anticipated the version of the argument he was to make more concisely in 1776. The tone and substance of *A Summary View* implies that Jefferson was already almost there. "Tamer sentiments were preferred, and I believe, wisely preferred," he later wrote, "the leap I proposed being too long as yet for the mass of our citizens." On some of the major issues of his era, including rebellion and slavery, Jefferson preferred not to be a leader but a follower, in the hope that public opinion eventually would come his way.

At this point, it was Parliament that wielded the whip. It was the king, Jefferson argued, to whom an appeal should be addressed and through whom Parliament might be made to desist. And though Parliament's ears seemed closed, Jefferson and his colleagues could "hope that this their joint address, penned in the language of truth, and divested of those expressions of servility which would persuade his majesty that we are asking favors and not rights, shall obtain from his majesty a more respectful acceptance." The language would be plain; it would not be servile; it would assert rights. "Our grievances" would be "laid before his majesty with that freedom of language and sentiment which becomes a free people, claiming their rights as derived from the laws of nature, and not as the gift of their chief magistrate. Let those flatter, who fear: it is not an American art." The history and its intent were obvious. "A series of oppressions . . . too plainly prove a deliberate, systematical plan of reducing us to slavery . . . one free and independent legislature hereby takes upon itself to suspend the powers of another, free and independent as itself. . . . Shall these governments be dissolved, their property annihilated, and their people reduced to a state of nature, at the imperious breath of a body of men whom they never saw, in whom they never confided, and over whom they have no powers of punishment or removal, let their crimes against the American public be ever so great?"

From Jefferson's point of view, the question was rhetorical. "America was conquered," he claimed, "and her settlements made and firmly established, at the expense of individuals, and not of the British public. Their own blood was spilt in acquiring lands for their settlement, their own fortunes expended in making that settlement effectual. For themselves they fought, for themselves they conquered, and for themselves alone they have right to hold . . . the emigrants thought proper to adopt that system of laws under which they had hitherto lived, and to continue their union with her by submitting themselves to the same common sovereign, who was thereby made the central link connecting the several parts of the empire." It was by choice, not necessity or compulsion.

But "not long were they permitted, however far they thought themselves removed from the hand of oppression, to hold undisturbed the rights thus acquired at the hazard of their lives and loss of their fortunes. . . ." They were deprived of their ability to trade freely. It was their "natural right" to do so. Their right to make laws for themselves in their own assemblies was restricted and then denied. "The true ground on which we declare these acts void is that the British parliament has no right to exercise authority over us. . . . How is it acceptable that 160,000 electors in the island of Great Britain should give law to four millions in the states of America, every individual of whom is equal to every individual of them in virtue, in understanding, and in bodily strength? Were this to be admitted, instead of being a free people, as we have hitherto supposed, and mean to continue, ourselves, we should suddenly be found the slaves, not of one, but of 160,000 tyrants, distinguished too from all others by this singular circumstance that they are removed from the reach of fear, the only restraining motive which may hold the hand of a tyrant?"

Some of this was true; most, not. The best modern estimates of the population of the colonies, excluding slaves, is a little over two million residents, male and female, not four million: a total of 2,140,076 in 1770; 2,780,369 in 1780. It is true that more American than British males did qualify to vote as freeholders. After all, many colonists had emigrated in order to *become* freeholders, to have land of their own, which was unavailable to them in Great Britain. It's estimated that about 40 to 50 percent of male colonists owned sufficient land to be eligible to vote.

Jefferson's history of the settlement of the colonies was also flawed, partly true, often inaccurate. That it contained footnote citations exemplified the preciseness of Jefferson's cherry picking, not his objectivity. It was a self-serving narrative increasingly shared by many Americans. It was about who took possession of the land, under whose authority, and who consequently had the authority to govern in the present and with what limitations. The land had been "unstoried, artless, unenhanced," in Frost's phrase so dismissive of Native Americans. Actually, there *had* been a narrative, an historical record about the invaders. Whatever the amount of individual capital and labor they brought to the colonies, settlers from England proudly acted as English citizens, taking possession of new lands in the name of king and country, obtaining their first possessions or adding to what they already possessed—a territorial expansion of their self-identity as British nationals. They defined themselves as British citizens, "British American colonists," with the same status as Welshmen, Scotsmen, or Canadian men—hyphenated British citizens whose main distinctiveness was their accent.

What Jefferson and the colonists who shared his vision wanted was an alternate story, a believable and useful fiction. The replacement claimed that the American colonies had been founded by individuals as private actors rather than as British citizens, not as representatives of the British government or government-sponsored private companies.

Consequently, they were entitled to govern themselves independent of British constitutional and Parliamentary authority. Whatever about them was British was by free choice, Jefferson emphasized, entailing no obligation, legal or otherwise. For over a century and a half, Virginians, like their fellow colonists, had been expressing fealty in word and act to Crown and Parliament. They possessed their lands through royal charter and other entitlements attendant on emigration and settlement. The ownership of land required the approval of courts established by British law. Virginians had accepted the legitimacy of every royal governor. The actual story also had a legal and a constitutional narrative, inconsistent with the free-choice argument. It was to the king, not the Parliament, to which Americans owed fealty, and it was up to the king alone to redress American grievances.

Whigs, Tories, the Crown, and the government ministries considered themselves inseparable entities in a unitary empire, though Parliament had the right to treat each entity differently. No constituent of the empire since the late seventeenth century had claimed that one could swear loyalty to the Crown and reject the authority of Parliament. Accept the authority of the king and reject Parliament's authority? Inconceivable! The British Empire, London proclaimed, was not divisible into independent entities, each entitled to govern itself. Why would Jefferson and his colleagues believe that possible? How could any member of the elite of any unit of the empire think such an approach constitutional? And how could the British imperium, existing for mutual defense and prosperity and having Europe's best record for orderly protection of life, property, and justice, continue to exist if the constituent units of the empire had the legal power to reject the legal directives of Parliament and king? Why did Virginians think they had the right to make their own laws, to proclaim, in Jefferson's words, that the king "is no more than the chief officer of the people, appointed by the laws, and circumscribed with definite powers, to assist in working the great machine of government erected for their use, and consequently subject to their superintendence." When did Virginians begin to believe they had such rights, that the king, in effect, worked for them? Did Peter Jefferson believe that? When did Peyton Randolph get it into his head that this was so? When did Jefferson come to believe this? Certainly, by the summer of 1774, he had come to believe that government existed entirely by the consent of those governed rather than by any other rationalization. None of his predecessors in the theory of modern government, from Montesquieu to John Locke, had ever put it quite that way.

Emotional, psychological, ideological, and financial forces drove the substance and structure of Jefferson's argument. He felt that, as freeborn British citizens, American colonists were being exploited, lorded over, humiliated, and deprived of the wealth they had independently earned and were entitled to. Natural right could be appealed to. History could be massaged. Numbers could be manipulated. The same grievances, in the form of an indictment, were to be the body of the Declaration of Independence.

The original settlements, Jefferson argued, "had been arbitrarily divided into governing units for the benefit of the British governing elites," and the "colonies are controlled by the empire's mercantile system to the advantage of the British home market." He also claimed that "the regulation of trade is an abridgement of a natural right and a form of tyranny," that "liens and other debt instruments can be obtained by British creditors against the land owned by American debtors but Americans cannot do the same against British debtors." He protested that "our legislatures are suspended so that we cannot make laws for ourselves, making us the slaves of Parliament." He objected that "because of the act of a small group of colonists, who have reacted to British oppression, the whole city of Boston is unjustifiably and cruelly punished, and those accused of crimes are deprived of the right to be judged by a jury of their peers in their home jurisdiction, to be deported to England for trial." Though an unrepentant slaveholder himself, he complained that "the king has vetoed our efforts to limit and then end the slave trade." He professed outrage that the king had gerrymandered our legislative representation through control of our Western borders; that "he has granted lands to himself, as if he had the right to dictate ownership for himself or his favorites" under the fictitious principle that all lands belong originally to the king. He argued that "he has sent troops to enforce his and Parliament's decrees" without the permission of colonial legislatures, though "his majesty has no right to land a single armed man on our shores; and those whom he sends here are liable to our laws for the suppression and punishment of Riots, Routs, and unlawful assemblies, or are hostile bodies invading us in defiance of law." These oppressions were intolerable and these acts were void, since "the British Parliament has no right to exercise authority over us."

The *Summary* ends with an eloquent, aggressive appeal to the sovereign:

> Let not the name of George the third be a blot in the page of history. . . . The great principles of right and wrong are legible to every reader. . . . The whole art of government consists in the art of being honest. Only aim to do your duty, and mankind will give you credit where you fail. No longer persevere in sacrificing the rights of one part of the empire to the inordinate desires of another: but deal out to all equal and impartial right. Let no act be passed by any one legislature which may infringe on the rights and liberties of another. This is the important post in which fortune has placed you, holding the balance of a great, if a well poised empire. This, sire, is the advice of your great American council, on the observance of which may perhaps depend your felicity and future fame, and the preservation of that harmony which alone can continue both to Great Britain and America the reciprocal advantages of their connection. It is neither our wish nor our interest to separate from her.

We are willing on our part to sacrifice everything which reason can ask to the restoration of that tranquility for which all must wish. On their part let them be ready to establish union on a generous plan. . . . Let them not think to exclude us from going to other markets, to dispose of those commodities which they cannot use. . . . Still less let it be proposed that our properties . . . shall be taxed or regulated by any power on earth but our own. The god who gave us life, gave us liberty at the same time. . . . This, Sire, is our last, our determined resolution: and that you will be pleased to interpose with that efficacy which your earnest endeavors may insure to procure redress of these our great grievances, to quiet the minds of your subjects . . . against any apprehensions of future encroachment, to establish fraternal love and harmony through the whole empire, and that that may continue to the latest ages of time, is the fervent prayer of all British America.

One of the most consequential deaths of Jefferson's life occurred in late May 1773. It left him a legacy that burdened him for decades. It did not leave him an orphan, as his mother's death had; it did not cause sustained aching misery, as the deaths of his wife and five of his six children were to do; and it came initially as a blessing of sorts. His wife undoubtedly mourned the death of her father, John Wayles, at the age of fifty-eight, not an early death for an eighteenth-century man once he had survived childhood. There was no special relationship between Jefferson and John Wayles. That Wayles was a successful businessman and prolific slave trader was a given of Jefferson's courtship of his daughter, not an impediment to Jefferson's mind or conscience. In principle, he thought slavery immoral. In practice, it was the world he lived in. As an heiress, Martha Wayles Jefferson came into a large but complicated fortune. She was one of three beneficiaries. What his wife inherited, Jefferson owned.

The other two legatees were his wife's brothers-in-law, Francis Eppes and Henry Skipwith. The former became one of Jefferson's closest lifelong friends. Wayles's 5,420 acres in Cumberland, Goochland, and Charles City counties could be sold. So too could the slaves, about a hundred of them. Some, though, were the children of John Wayles with his slave mistress Betty Hemings. Martha Jefferson did not intend to have her half siblings sold. They were to come to live with the Jeffersons. They were still to be slaves, but of a distinctive and privileged kind, never to work as field hands. Jefferson kept most or all of the other slaves. Owner of a large number of slaves, he was always reluctant to sell any of them, partly because he felt responsible as part of his "family," partly for humanitarian reasons, but also for utilitarian reasons, because his agricultural estates required slave labor. Slaves were to be disposed of only for cause.

John Wayles had been, among other things, an active and substantial buyer and seller of slaves, particularly from Africa. A shipload of about four hundred had recently been lost at sea. Litigation was under way to determine to what extent his estate was responsible for the loss. It would take time and money to free the estate from liability. The three heirs had different financial pressures and schedules. Despite his training as a lawyer, Jefferson and his colleagues made a number of flawed business and legal decisions in regard to the estate. In the end, Jefferson found himself responsible for a large sum that neither his own cash nor his fixed properties could readily repay. The result was a debt that weighed heavily on him for decades. His main benefit from the Wayles estate was to come many years later in the form of a young enslaved woman named Sally Hemings.

The mid-May 1773 death of his close friend of many years, Dabney Carr, married to one of his sisters, was deeply personal. He had him buried at Monticello, where Jefferson had started a family graveyard. He had a stonemason engrave on Carr's tombstone that he was being memorialized by "Thomas Jefferson, who of all men living, loved him most." That was a proprietary exaggeration, but it came from a grieving heart. Frequent deaths of familiars, whether protracted or sudden, were an eighteenth-century reality made slightly bearable by sentiment, stoicism, and religious faith. Jefferson had none of the latter. He was to make his home his sister's for the rest of her life. Dabney's son Peter turned out to be a very minor blessing. Jefferson and Carr had been colleagues in the House of Burgesses in 1773. Carr's much-praised debut speech had called for the creation of a committee of correspondence to unite the colonies in response to their shared grievances. The two friends had apparently talked their hearts and minds out on the road back to Albemarle to report to their constituents.

"Your" father's "character was of a high order," Jefferson wrote in a belated eulogy to one of Dabney's sons. "A spotless integrity, sound judgment handsome imagination, enriched by education and reading, quick and clear in his conceptions, of correct and ready elocution, impressing every hearer with the sincerity of the heart from which it flowed. His firmness was inflexible in whatever he thought was right: but when no moral principle stood in the way, never had man more of the milk of human kindness, of indulgence, of softness, of pleasantry in conversation and conduct. The number of his friends, and the warmth of their affection were proofs of his worth, and of their estimate of it." This was also a self-portrait, except for the "ready elocution." Otherwise, it was Jefferson's view of himself projected onto a friend who was valued for the qualities and values Jefferson believed they shared. It's unlikely to have been an entirely accurate depiction of Dabney Carr. An unintentional laudatory self-portrait, it left out a lot.

This pen portrait has no sharp edges. Jefferson had a predilection for smooth edges in his personal life and for sharp positions in public life only when core values and passions were engaged. They were deeply engaged in the spurt of writing he did between the summer of 1773 and the end of 1776, actually continuing until the end of the decade. His pen was almost entirely in public service, though of course there were personal letters and business letters. Still, the personal dimension of his life seems almost a shadowy background to the more vividly etched foreground, though Jefferson repeatedly stressed how much he valued his home life, his family, and his friends.

At Monticello, his domestic happiness was undercut by absence and loss. Martha's second pregnancy was less successful than her first. The first child lived, named after her mother; the second, also a daughter, whom they named Jane Randolph Jefferson after Thomas's mother, died in September 1775, less than a year and a half old. The next child, a boy, died so quickly after his birth in May 1777 that he had not yet been named. Jefferson has almost nothing to say that survives about these losses except that they occurred. Painful as they must have been, one survival out of three was not too far off the average for the time.

But what was pervasively frightening was Martha's fragility. Whatever the cause of her ill health, it was almost constantly evident, despite spurts of household management and wifely engagement. Never in his long life did Jefferson create a pen portrait of his wife, partly, it would seem, the result of his reticence about private matters, partly to control grief and pain. He was prone to compartmentalize this one relationship into the sacred, beyond and above and different from the written word. The result is that we have little to no concrete information about Martha Jefferson as a wife, mother, and lover, nothing that lends itself to memorable description or engaging detail. In Carr's case, idealized as the pen portrait is, it expresses Jefferson's capacity for friendship, especially for those with whom he shared values and experiences. The tombstone inscription associates male friendship with love, without the slightest inference that this love was sexual. *Love* is a word that Jefferson rarely uses, even when he is obviously in love, as he was with his wife and, years later in Paris, with Maria Cosway. But the emotion and the passion were evidently there.

Two other deaths that happened in the two years after the composition of *A Summary View* also touched his mind and heart in distinctive ways. They were of people who had been formative influences, his mother and his teacher William Small. He had almost nothing to say, as far as the written record reveals, about the unhappy news of the death of his mother in March 1776. He wrote in his pocket notebook that "my mother died at eight o'clock this morning, in the 57th year of age." And there is not a single word extant about what his mother thought of him. Did he also burn after her death any remaining letters between them? She had been a widow for nineteen years. Living in the house that had replaced Shadwell, she had been a near neighbor of her eldest son since he had moved into Monticello. There is no record that she attended his marriage service. They must have seen each other many times. He named his second, short-lived child after her. There is no reason to assume that, as her heir, he was not involved in her financial affairs, her health, her role as the mother of his siblings, and the grandmother of his only living child.

Still, the few words about his mother that survive other than his simple statement on the day of her death are in a letter to her brother William Randolph, written from Philadelphia to Bristol, England, in June 1776. "The death of my mother you have probably not heard of. This happened on the last day of March after an illness of not more than an hour. We suppose it to have been apoplectic." Nothing more. The inscription on her gravestone in the family cemetery, probably composed by her son, states her name, her dates, her place of birth, that she was the wife of Peter Jefferson and the mother of Thomas Jefferson, and that she died at Monticello. No words of praise or love, no hint of emotion, let alone the strong emotion recorded on Dabney Carr's gravestone. All this could mean very little, or very much, or nothing at all.

Jefferson's uncle William Randolph, a businessman in Bristol, was the secondary heir of one of his father's Virginia properties. "I heartily join with you in wishing you had chosen a residence among us," his nephew wrote to him. "I should have found myself happy in your neighborhood." Would they, if his uncle had been a near neighbor, have had the same view about the desirable relationship between the American colonies and Great Britain? What actually did this resident of Bristol think of the political views of his nephew, whose *Summary View* he may have read or would soon read in its London publication in 1776? Indeed, what were his London-born mother's views about Anglo-American tensions from 1765 to the time of her death, a month before her son was to depart for Philadelphia to take part in the most consequential act of his life and the origin of his future fame? Did Jane Randolph express any political views at all? Her brother John, another of Thomas's uncles, had fled to London, his sympathies and loyalties entirely with the mother country. Certainly, Jane Randolph must have been aware of her son's views. Did hers differ? In the Randolphs' and Jeffersons' physically, psychologically, and politically divided world, some kept silence, and some spoke up. Some spoke with their feet, and many residents of the British Isles who had American connections, including those within the Randolph-Jefferson world, had choices to embrace or to flee from.

Between 1764 and 1775, Jefferson corresponded with William Small, his mentor at William and Mary. Ten years older than his student, Small had returned to his native Scotland and then moved to England after a consequential but short American stay, eventually settling in Birmingham. Jefferson, over his lifetime, acknowledged his seminal influence. Why Small left Virginia is unclear: perhaps resentment at not being appointed president of the college; perhaps boredom and dissatisfaction with most of his colleagues, and especially with William and Mary's clannish, peremptory Board of Visitors. The ostensible rationale for his departure, to purchase scientific instruments, assisted by a letter of introduction by Benjamin

Franklin to the scientific community in Birmingham, assumed his return to William and Mary. A restless, provocative mind committed to Enlightenment values and learning, he was a godsend to Jefferson but not an easy fit in his Virginia environment. At any rate, he did not return; he earned a medical degree in Scotland, set up a practice in Birmingham, and established himself at the center of a society dedicated to scientific research. The record provides no hint of what his political views were. He left Williamsburg a short time before the explosive American response to the Stamp Act.

Only one letter from their correspondence survives, from Jefferson to Small, written in May 1775. It is a lovingly affectionate letter, though Jefferson could have had no idea that it would never be read by his friend. It had given him pleasure, Jefferson wrote, to have learned of Small's "welfare" from a recent traveler from England. He had frequently had Small warmly on his mind, having put aside for him seventy-two bottles of wine, half of which he was now sending off. Whatever his attempt at companionable pleasantries, Jefferson's mind was compulsively on politics. He probably could not be sure of Small's view on Anglo-American tensions. Small could not have known that gunfire had been exchanged and bodies shredded at Lexington and Concord just one month before. The news could not yet have reached Birmingham. Even if it had, Small would not have been able to hear it. Unknown to Jefferson, he had died in April, at the age of forty-one. The letter had been written to a dead man, who had spent only a few years of his life in Virginia. Jefferson himself did not yet have accurate information about the extent of the battles or the number of deaths. All he had was "the unhappy news of an action of considerable magnitude between the king's troops and our brethren of Boston. . . . That such an action has happened is undoubted, though perhaps the circumstances may not yet have reached us with truth. This accident has cut off our last hopes of reconciliation, and a phrenzy of revenge seems to have seized all ranks of people."

The tone, rhetoric, and demands of *A Summary View* had made it almost certain that by the summer of 1774 Jefferson had assumed and affirmed the handwriting on the wall embodied in the hand that drove his pen. By May 1775, there was no going back. The efforts to compromise on both sides were minority efforts. The British required Parliamentary supremacy; the Americans, self-rule by local assemblies. Whatever Small's views might have been, Jefferson assured him that the colonists were not at fault: they had made every reasonable attempt at reconciliation. For reasons Jefferson claimed not to fathom, the king, the only viable mediating agent, had declined to support a compromise. "When I saw Lord Chatham's bill," Jefferson wrote, "I entertained high hope that a reconciliation could have been brought about. The difference between his terms and those offered by our congress might have been accommodated if entered on by both parties with a disposition to accommodate." Jefferson had to have known that there was no disposition in Massachusetts or Virginia to accommodate. The colonies were already used to self-rule. The colonists already had de facto self-rule. There was no inclination, even among most conservatives, part of whose hearts still belonged to the mother country, to give it back. The British saw the American definition of compromise as British capitulation.

Jefferson made his case to Small, reciting his oft-recited litany of complaints against the mother country, focusing on the events in Boston leading up to April 1775. He hoped he was being tactfully brief but perhaps not brief enough, he realized, not to offend Small. He deleted in his draft a substantial paragraph of anti-British denunciation, the rhetoric of which may have seemed even to him excessive in a letter he intended to be personal and accommodating. Still, he was dedicated to half-truths: "But the dignity of parliament it seems can brook no opposition to its power." And to self-righteous denunciation: "Strange that a set of men who have made sale of their virtue to the minister should yet talk of retaining dignity!" Apparently, every

British minister was corrupt. Unable to resist what he was, understandably, obsessed with, Jefferson drew back. "But I am getting into politics though I sat down only to ask your acceptance of the wine, and express my constant wishes for your happiness. This however seems secured by your philosophy and peaceful vocation. I shall still hope that amidst public dissension private friendship may be preserved inviolate, and among the warmest you can ever possess" was his.

There was another passage that, as he wrote his draft, he decided to delete. They were words addressed to himself, a confessional statement that he would acknowledge only to himself. He began with a simple expression of self-correction and self-admonition. "But for god's sake where am I got to? Forever absorbed in the distresses of my country I cannot for three sentences keep clear of its political struggles." Where he had "got to" was not necessarily where he wanted to be. He could not know that the letter he mailed to England would never be read by the man it was intended for. But the sentences he had struck out were, he realized in the writing, a confessional moment of both anguish and commitment.

At home, in July 1774, he coauthored with John Walker, his colleague from Albemarle, an open letter of a few pedestrian sentences to the residents of his parish calling on them to implement the fast-day resolutions. They were to meet "to implore the divine interposition in behalf of an injured and oppressed people; and that the minds of his majesty, his ministers, and parliament, might be inspired with wisdom from above, to avert from us the dangers which threaten our civil rights, and all the evils of civil war." In response, the elderly Jefferson wrote, "the people met generally, with anxiety and alarm in their countenances, and the effect of the day through the whole colony was like a shock of electricity, arousing every man and placing him erect and solidly on his centre." It did come, apparently, as a shock to those who read the letter and the many more to whom it was read. There is no way to test the accuracy of Jefferson's later description of his fellow parishioners' response. The "shock of electricity" is a literary trope that came readily to the elderly and science-minded Jefferson. There is reason to assume that his neighbors were indeed shocked. Certain grievances were probably widely shared, though for many at a level that probably did not prey on their daily lives and thoughts. The phrase "the evils of civil war" set many atremble, whether or not prone to expressive grievance.

How to find the words that not only justified his grievances but made persuasive his view about the only way to resolve the impasse? And to do it in the collective voice of the Virginia delegates to the Philadelphia convention, with the hope that Congress might also take it up as its own? And how to warn, short of an outright declaration, that if Parliament did not provide a reconciliation favorable to the colonists, there would be revolutionary consequences? And who would be the best creator and expositor of those words? Probably the latter was not a question Jefferson asked himself.

CHAPTER FOUR

We Hold These Truths

1774–1776

The majority of Jefferson's colleagues in the newly elected House of Burgesses in Williamsburg did not feel comfortable enough with *A Summary View of the Rights of British America* to believe that it should be the basis, let alone the verbatim text, of their instructions to the delegates to the Congress scheduled to meet in Philadelphia in 1775. For many, it probably made all too clear what they were not yet ready to put into print and convey to the world. Jefferson's views were already part of the mind-set of many of his fellow Virginians and other colonists, especially in Massachusetts, but *A Summary View* seemed too aggressive, angry, demanding, and eloquent, at a length that advertised its singular authorship. His colleagues had no doubt that they had a writer of excellence among their numbers, but the majority wanted a brief, less confrontational consensus statement.

What was at issue, they declared in bland concision, were "unhappy disputes. . . . His Majesty's faithful Subjects . . . are in Danger of being deprived of their natural, ancient, constitutional, and chartered Rights. . . . It being our Opinion that the united Wisdom of North America should be collected in a General Congress of all the

Colonies, we have appointed Richard Henry Lee, George Washington, Patrick Henry, Richard Bland, Benjamin Harrison and Edmund Pendleton, Esquires, Deputies to represent this Colony in the said Congress, to be held . . . on the first Monday in September next." It was a stellar list of delegates. They were instructed to "express . . . our Faith and true Allegiance to his Majesty King George the Third, our lawful and rightful Sovereign; and that we are determined, with our Lives and Fortunes, to support him in the legal Exercise of all his just Rights and Prerogatives."

Jefferson was not present for the discussion and vote. His fiery words undoubtedly had been read by some members of the House. A few partisans, without Jefferson's permission, had *A Summary View* printed for wide distribution. Why did his Virginia colleagues not appoint him a delegate to the first Continental Congress? Did any of them think it had been presumptuous of him to attempt to put so many passionate and well-written words into their mouths? Not likely, given that Patrick Henry, whose radical rhetoric pleased some but frightened others, had been chosen a delegate. No one could have assumed that the illness that had prevented Jefferson's attending in August would necessarily keep him from attendance in Philadelphia. Perhaps a young man who was out of sight may have been out of mind. The assembly certainly had more than enough influential Virginians to choose from.

For Jefferson, there was work to be done in Williamsburg and pleasures and pains to be experienced at home. He spent his time between the summer of 1774 and the spring of 1775 at both places. The over one hundred slaves inherited from the Wayles estate had to be assimilated into field and domestic work. He had a two-year-old daughter and an infant daughter. He was also trying to make Monticello larger and more comfortable. Progress was slow. The embargo on English imports caused him tension and frustration. He returned to Williamsburg in the spring, where the legislature and the governor were at odds. The House of Burgesses now attempted to act as if it were an independent assembly.

Working with his colleague George Wythe, Jefferson initiated an inquiry into whether "his majesty" or the legislature had the right to make land grants. The Crown had been doing exactly that for over a century. Land, from the start, had been a gift from the king, outright or by other provisions, direct or indirect, from London or from royal governors, on the widely accepted belief that the king, as the embodiment of the English nation, had always, in theory and law, had ownership of the American colonies. Whoever, in a practical and local sense, possessed the land, had it in the long perspective as "a gift" from the Crown. That "gift," since the first settlements, had created the wealth that Jefferson's class enjoyed. Peter Jefferson, among other things a surveyor, would never have questioned that. Jefferson and his colleagues wanted to change that mind-set. A busy committeeman, he worked at revisions and resolutions. It was time to make clear that the land fully belonged to those who lived on it, as long as they were white men. They resolved that the royal governor could no longer make land grants in Virginia.

His colleagues had discovered that Jefferson, now in his fifth year as a legislator, was an indefatigable committeeman. His mind and pen worked quickly and well. And if Virginia were to become a province or a state (a word beginning to be used) in a "union" (another word that began to appear in documents coming from Philadelphia) or a "confederacy" of states that would be an independent country, there was much work to be done. Each state would need to write its own constitution and rewrite its laws to embody the new dispensation. The fear that Parliament and the king could make laws and rewrite charters to determine who owned what and how taxes were to be levied began to motivate otherwise conservative people to write radical words and anticipate radical actions. That might mean taking up arms, but it first or at least simultaneously meant taking up the pen to write new laws and fundamental documents. That would be the most pressing task. Jefferson had begun to show in 1774–1775 that he was extremely well suited for it.

The Congress in Philadelphia was laying the groundwork, tentatively and haltingly, for independence. Not every colony moved at the same speed. All left open the possibility of reconciliation, which strengthened the colony-wide resolve not to import products from Great Britain. The message to London was: "We are sufficiently united to resist governance by Parliament. We insist that our local assembles and they alone have the authority to legislate for the colonies." In Virginia, there was an accurate sense of what was likely to happen. In March 1775, the Williamsburg convention appointed a committee to create a resolution proposing "That a well-regulated militia, composed of Gentlemen and Yeomen, is the natural strength, and only security, of a free government." The committee should prepare a plan for the creation of a militia to put the colony "into a posture of defence." That it was a "free" government was news to London, depending on how one defined "free." Jefferson prepared the resolution. He was becoming the draftsman of first resort. At the same time, his colleagues elected him to replace Peyton Randolph, who was to return to Williamsburg to take up the speakership of the House, as a delegate to the next Congress. On June 11, 1775, Jefferson left for Philadelphia, America's largest city. He was about to become one of the most vocally silent, hardest working delegates to a quasi-legislative assembly for a government that did not yet exist.

By the time he arrived in Philadelphia on June 20, he and his colleagues knew that they had a war of sorts on their hands. It had not been declared by any authority in Great Britain or in the colonies, and what had happened had a different appearance and language on opposite sides of the Atlantic. Was it a rebellion? Was it an insurrection? Was it a civil war? Whatever one called it, blood had been shed in April at Lexington and Concord. That made all the difference.

Jefferson had no doubt that it was a war, best called a rebellion. Given what he believed were the irreconcilable views of the British and British Americans about American sovereignty, it was what he wanted. He was also optimistic. The realization was to be slow in coming that it was much easier to start than to end a war. On both sides of the Atlantic what had happened seemed partly inconceivable and partly inevitable, a long-delayed reckoning that would not take long to resolve. Both were to discover, over an expensive seven-year bloodletting, how wrong they were.

Two weeks after his arrival in Philadelphia, Jefferson was enthusiastic enough to write a paean even to New Englanders. The date was July 4, 1775. He was flush with the newly created collegiality, almost unity, of the Southern and Northern colonies. His fellow colonists in Massachusetts, he believed, were ready and fit for the fight. "The New Englanders are fitting out light vessels of war," he wrote to his brother-in-law, "by which it is hoped we shall not only clear the seas and bays here of everything below the size of a ship of war, but that they will visit the coasts of Europe and distress the British trade in every part of the world. The adventurous genius and intrepidity of those people is amazing. They are now intent on burning Boston as a hive which gives cover to regulars; and none are more bent on it than the very people who come out of it and whose whole prosperity lies there." This was admirable patriotism, self-sacrifice, and resolve. Jefferson was to have cause to envy it during his years as wartime governor of Virginia.

How to deal with cousins who did not want, in the view of London, to pay their fair share of family expenses had been, more or less, on the minds of various British ministries, especially since 1763. Now, in 1775, it was on their minds with the urgency of crisis. Wales, Scotland, and Ireland had been absorbed into Great Britain by force and political coercion. There was little to no sentiment in London to bring the American colonists in line in the same way. After all, the Americans spoke English, not Welsh; they were Protestants, not Catholics; they were not semi-barbarians like the Scotch Highlanders. They read Shakespeare in the language in which he wrote. When Jefferson and his colleagues appealed to Parliament or to the king, they did so in sophisticated, often forceful, and sometimes tactful English. No translation was required. Though there were differences of opinion among the Parliamentary factions about how best to relate to their American colonies, there was no inclination to use force. Much was against that, including practical matters like cost. And their American cousins were not alienated from their Britishness except on one issue: sovereignty. Everything else in the relationship seemed to London secondary and negotiable. British ministries had been for over a decade in search of some model of empire, some formula or compromise, that would satisfy the requirements of Parliament and be accepted by the colonists. They were, as a whole, not of one mind, but mostly not of a dictatorial mind about how to rule the American colonies. And when it came to the use of force, which Parliament and the British public viewed as a last resort, the initiative was at first slow and hesitant.

Two months before Jefferson's arrival in Philadelphia in June 1775, Lord Frederick North, the head of King George's government, had proposed a series of compromises. Parliament would not tax Americans if they would pay the salaries of British colonial officials and would contribute to the cost of defending the empire, the mechanism for fixing on the amount to be determined by Parliament on an annual basis. Essentially, the offer put on the table in what came to be called Lord North's Conciliatory Proposals was a compromise that recognized Parliamentary sovereignty but that granted the American colonies some local autonomy. By addressing the proposals to the individual colonies, the North government affirmed that it did not recognize that the colonies had created an entity that represented them collectively. For Jefferson and his colleagues, it was too little and too late. By the time the ship bringing the proposal had arrived, blood had been shed at Lexington and Concord. The battles, it soon became clear, had made reconciliation, short of capitulation by one side or the other, impossible. Lord North's proposals were dead on arrival.

Though other hands contributed to the writing of a "Declaration for Causes and Necessities of Taking Up Arms" and the "Resolutions of Congress on Lord North's Conciliatory Proposal," Jefferson played a major role in shaping and writing both. The 1774 Williamsburg edition of *A Summary View* had made its way to Philadelphia soon after publication. It was, in a sense, Jefferson's calling card. The first drafts of the Declaration and the Resolutions seem to have been his; the final drafts, the result of editing and revision by his colleagues, the standard way Congress proceeded. The Declaration was a partly pugnacious, partly defensive document, a shot across the bow from a crouching posture. It attempted to assure those who were not yet ready to declare for independence that there was not any necessity to go precipitously forward.

But it was not a conciliatory document. We assure "our Friends and Fellow-Subjects that we mean not to dissolve that Union which has so long and so happily subsisted between us, and which we sincerely wish to see restored. . . . We have not raised Armies with ambitious Designs of . . . establishing Independent States. We fight not for Glory or for Conquest. We exhibit to Mankind the remarkable Spectacle of a People attacked by unprovoked Enemies, without any imputation or even suspicion of Offence. . . . *In our own native Land, in defence of the Freedom that is our Birthright, and which we ever enjoyed till the late Violation of it—for the protection of our Property, acquired solely by the honest Industry of our fore-fathers and ourselves, against Violence actually offered, we have taken up Arms.*" Britain boasts of its "Privileges and Civilization, and yet proffer no milder Conditions than Servitude or Death." Such language and tone, Jefferson would had to have known, could not be taken in London as anything but insult. The American game was to be both victim and counterpuncher simultaneously.

The completed document definitively rejected Lord North's proposal. The language, tone, and arguments of the response had much in common with the declarations and statements of grievance that had been on paper and in public discussion since the Stamp Act in 1765. It is a point-by-point analysis of the inadequacy of the proposal, but it has an additional, well-stated, and particularly Jeffersonian appeal, though how much of it he wrote is unclear. It includes, for the first time in Jefferson's writings, an appeal to the judgment of the world. The time had come to make the case for independence to an international audience. There was no longer any point in making the case only to London. The world and history would judge whether there was sufficient justification for taking up arms.

> But when the world reflects, how inadequate to justice are these vaunted terms [in the Conciliatory Proposals]; when it attends to the rapid and bold succession of injuries, which, during a course of eleven years, have been aimed at these Colonies; when it reviews the pacific and respectful expostulations, which, during that whole time, were the sole arms we opposed to them; when it observes that our complaints were either not heard at all, or were answered with new and accumulated injury; when it recollects that the Minister himself on an early occasion declared, "that he would never treat with America, till he had brought her to his feet," and . . . when it considers the great armaments with which they have invaded us, and the circumstances of cruelty with which these have commenced and prosecuted hostilities; when these things, we say, are laid together, and attentively considered, can the world be deceived into an opinion that we are unreasonable, or can it hesitate to believe with us, that nothing but our own exertions may defeat the ministerial sentence of death or abject submission.

Jefferson in his draft did not end the final sentence with a question mark. Congress did not insert one. It was, in effect, a declarative statement.

From the colonists' point of view, they were asserting rights that were distinctively, almost exclusively, British. They were historically, culturally, linguistically, and politically citizens of Great Britain. The theoretical grounding of the Revolution was in British legal and political fundamentals. No other European country gave its citizens such rights or held its colonies so loosely. Great Britain was the least autocratic country in Europe, though far from the constitutional monarchy it was to become. It was inching forward with various reforms that were to bring it eventually to the same political principles and democratic values that Jefferson and his colleagues were envisioning. If the colonists had been Spanish Americans or French Americans, the foundation on which the American Revolution was created would not have been in place. Spain certainly would have repressed dissent with a brutal decisiveness. In fact, the British American colonists had the possibility of a successful revolution *because* they were British. They shared a commitment to the English tradition of common law, statute law, and government by a representative assembly. There was also a shared consanguinity, a blood relationship, a sense that family ties, from the generation of settlement to Jefferson's generation, that still made colonial Americans, especially the educated elite and their English relations, cousins by kinship and culture. It was understood that the American colonists were different from the residents of most other parts of the empire: they were white; they were Protestant; they were England's second-best trading partner (after the British West Indies); they spoke English; and their ancestors had come from the British Isles. They believed themselves entitled to the same rights as their peers across the Atlantic.

By midsummer 1775, Jefferson was back at Monticello, relieved of Philadelphia's oppressive heat. He was now briefly free to resume his domestic life. In the fall, he was in Williamsburg for the assembly session. Late in August, he wrote to his cousin John Randolph, who had had enough of the insults and threats to himself and his family in response to his outspoken pro-British views. He did not think of them as pro-British. He thought of them as allegiance to an oath he had sworn and believed that his fellow Virginians did not have sufficient reason in the eyes of the world and of God to take up arms. About to set sail for England, he and his cousin settled some small business matters in addition to the disposition of his violin. He could not take all his books with him. Jefferson wanted some of them. "My collection of classics and of books of parliamentary learning particularly is not so complete as I could wish. As you are going to the land of literature and of books you may be willing to dispose of some of yours here and replace them there in better editions." It was assumed that they might never see each other again. Whether called an insurrection or a rebellion, there was a civil war under way. In the case of Jefferson and John Randolph, the terms at which they were at war were as civil as the civility between them. "I shall be glad to hear from you as often as you may be disposed to think of things here," Jefferson wrote. "You may be at liberty I expect to communicate some things consistently with your honor and the duties you will owe to a protecting nation. Such a communication among individuals may be mutually beneficial to the contending parties. . . . My best wishes for your felicity attend you wherever you go."

Jefferson's letter was an expression of the self-delusions, the evasions, the emotions, the hardening of views, and the inconsistencies of a conflict between cousins. "I hope the returning wisdom of Great Britain" will soon "put an end to this unnatural contest. . . . My first wish is a restoration of our just rights; my second a return of the happy period when, consistently with duty, I may withdraw myself totally from the public stage and pass the rest of my days in domestic ease and tranquillity. . . ." This was to be one of the great rhetorical inconsistencies of Jefferson's lifelong posture. He loved the public arena as much as he loved privacy. In public life, his actions spoke louder than his private words, and in this case his private words were words he desired that his cousin transmit to the British ministry. Indeed, before there was an actual country to represent, Jefferson was writing as if he were his country's representative. That his claim for pastoral preference was a widely used cliché of the public leaders of Rome did not make his use of the trope hypocritical. For Jefferson, sincerity was inseparable from usefulness. It was useful for Jefferson to remind his cousin and to communicate to the North ministry, as if he spoke for all Americans, that he preferred peace to war. But that peace could be achieved only on his and his colleagues' terms.

He was certain that the ministry had been deceived. Their American representatives "have constantly represented the American opposition as that of a small faction, in which the body of the people took little part. This you can inform them of your own knowledge to be untrue. They have taken it into their heads too that we are cowards and shall surrender at discretion to an armed force. The past and future operations of the war must confirm or undeceive them on that head. I wish they were thoroughly and minutely acquainted with every circumstance relative to America as it exists in truth. I am persuaded this would go far towards disposing them to reconciliation. Even those in parliament who are called friends to America seem to know nothing of our real determinations."

The leaders in London had gotten the basic facts wrong. Unless they now got them right and changed course, he warned, the empire itself would sink into the sea rather than rule the waves. It was a comment that the secretary of state for the colonies must have found presumptuous, unrealistic, and offensive. Still, what Jefferson also wanted to convey was that a peaceful resolution was no longer possible through negotiation. When, months later, his letter reached the ministry, it would have recognized that the phrase "dependence on Great Britain, properly limited" was rhetorical sleight of hand. Sovereignty for America meant in effect no limitation on American independence at all.

By the time the minister for colonial affairs had Jefferson's letter in hand, it was too late for a nonmilitary accommodation. There was wide recognition that the colonies had become an American home-land, were developing an independent national identity, and deeply resented their subordination to British trade policies. If taxation without representation was unacceptable, no or hardly any taxes at all was even better. Jefferson gave no attention to the fact that the average British citizen was taxed more heavily than any Anglo-American. With his love of numbers and lists, he did a calculation of what a successful rebellion would cost. His expectations were to be proved totally false, the cost immensely more than anticipated. Despite occasional delusions to the contrary, there was no going back. Jefferson certainly knew that. Only the assertion, on both sides, of state power could stanch the wounds of Lexington and Concord and satisfy national pride. The colonies were in the process of creating state power. Great Britain already possessed it. National pride demanded national expression. Public opinion supported it, on both sides of the Atlantic. The ocean that both joined and separated the mother country from the colonies was about to become a battlefield. Those who had fought side by side in the French and Indian War were now to be on opposite sides of the cannons and bayonets on land and at sea.

By June 1776, a great deal had happened that added bold ink to Jefferson's pen. His *Summary View* had provided a kick-start to his statements, his declarations, and his drafts in June and July 1775 of the "Declaration for Causes and Necessities of Taking Up Arms" and his response to Lord North's Conciliatory Proposal. In July 1775, he had also annotated Benjamin Franklin's draft proposal for Articles of Confederation, a version of which Congress was to adopt in 1781. In the autumn and early winter of 1775, his hand was instrumental in numbers of congressional statements, his pen active in the Confederation's ongoing business, working through the problem of defining what powers the states would allow it to have. It had become the de facto governing body of what was still in the view of most English people and in the eyes of the world a British possession. Great Britain's enemies, particularly France and Spain, had pressing territorial and economic interests in what would come next. Would these colonies actually be able to establish and keep independence? Who actually owned—and by what right, legally or by force—the land that Jefferson and his colleagues stood on, that they seemed on the verge of claiming they possessed?

At Monticello in late 1775 and early 1776, Jefferson had elaborated in writing the argument that he had made in *A Summary View*: that from the first settlement, the land had belonged to its settlers, not to the Crown or Parliament. His evidence from historical sources convinced only those who were already convinced. Jefferson, though, needed this evidentiary plank to bounce on, to gain traction and momentum for the leap forward. No one paid much attention to this new version of his alternative history. The day after his arrival in Philadelphia in June 1776, the Williamsburg legislature adopted a Declaration of Rights. Jefferson's friend George Mason had drafted it. Before leaving for Philadelphia, Jefferson had written a draft of a constitution for Virginia, seemingly on his own initiative. It advocated an expansion of the suffrage, the appropriation of Western land to small farmers, a limited executive elected for a single year, and the gradual abolition of slavery. It was the most radical series of proposals Jefferson ever made. Most of it never saw the light of law. The response seems to have taught him that making law was a collective activity. New law, he was to conclude, followed rather than led public opinion.

"I arrived here [in Philadelphia] last Tuesday after being detained hence six weeks longer than I intended by illness," he wrote to his friend and colleague Thomas Nelson. "Should our [Virginia] Convention propose to establish now a form of government perhaps it might be agreeable to recall for a short time their delegates." Other colonies were doing that. "It is a work of the most interesting nature and such as every individual would wish to have his voice in. In truth it is the whole object of the present controversy; for should a bad government be instituted for us in future it had been as well to have accepted at first the bad one offered to us from beyond the water without the risk and expense of contest."

None of the three drafts for a constitution for the state of Virginia that Jefferson composed in the spring of 1776 deal with first principles. All contain proposals for the organization of the new government, i.e., "constitution-making," which was a large part of the debates in state legislatures in the summer of 1776: two legislative houses, an executive with limited powers to be elected annually by the House of Representatives, and a judiciary with a version of our modern Supreme Court, its members to be chosen by the Virginia House of Representatives. The constitution was to be the blueprint for the organization of the newly independent state, not a declaration of independence. It anticipates the Articles of Confederation and the national Constitution of 1787, organizing the government into three branches. It strictly limits the power of the executive and the judiciary. It gives the legislature supreme power. The executive (elected from the membership of the legislature) is subordinate to the legislature. So is the judiciary, which is appointed by a committee (Privy Council) of the legislature. It is an elitist document in that it keeps power mostly in the hands of the chosen few.

Throughout the summer of 1776, Jefferson was eager to return to

Williamsburg, to participate in constitution making. Large as Philadelphia was by colonial standards, it was a small city. European capitals dwarfed even the largest American city, and Europe had dozens of small cities larger than Philadelphia. No European could imagine that anything of worldwide importance could happen in any American city. For Jefferson, used to rural privacy, Philadelphia's frenetic commerce, noise, horses and carriages, human smells, and daily waste, even in its private places, were all too public.

To most delegates to the Confederation Congress, Philadelphia would have seemed gigantic. Some were city people; but most, like Jefferson, were not. And in June 1776, in the midst of a heat wave, it must have felt like the wrong place to be compared to their rural homes. Jefferson had a particular civic reason to prefer being in Williamsburg. And even for delegates from hot climates, their country residences had cooling comforts that stuffy boarding-house life could not provide. At Monticello, in a summer climate that specialized in heat, humidity, and insects in screenless rooms, there at least were cooling breezes, privacy, and quiet. At home, for exercise, Jefferson rode his horse every morning. In Philadelphia, he reached toward the rural outskirts, but his exercise opportunities were intermittent.

After staying for almost a month at a colleague's residence on Chestnut Street, he moved into two rooms in a house on Market Street, including a sitting room in which he could set up his writing desk. Jefferson knew what was expected of him as a delegate: hours of listening to debates and committee meetings. And he knew that his colleagues expected him to put his writerly skills, his discipline, and his efficiency at their disposal. Almost every day he sat with his colleagues at the nearby State House. Monticello seemed immensely far away. For much of the time he felt depressingly out of touch. No sooner had he arrived than he wanted to leave. He worried about his wife and his daughter. Martha had again stayed at home in the spring of 1776, probably for reasons of health. "I am here in the same uneasy anxious state in which I was the last fall without Mrs. Jefferson who could not come with me." When mail from home or news from others about home was slow in coming, Jefferson worried. Sometimes he imagined the worst. Even though he was one of the central figures at the highest level of the new government, he wanted out as quickly as possible.

On June 6, 1776, Virginia's Richard Henry Lee, a dramatically articulate speaker, acting on the instructions of Virginia's House of Burgesses, proposed that there be a resolution declaring complete independence. Congress soon appointed a committee of six: Lee, Benjamin Franklin, John Adams, Roger Sherman, Robert Livingston, and Jefferson, all leading voices in Congress for independence. They had, to varying degrees, declared themselves even before the battles at Concord and Lexington. Lee, though, was heavily engaged with work on the Articles of Confederation—and he had no special talent as a writer. Fiery, with an attitude, he exercised his ego in debate. The elderly Franklin, the most famous writer and personality appointed to the committee, had recently returned from years in London, where he mainly represented Pennsylvania. With an international reputation as a scientist, a diplomat, and a writer, he was smart, crafty, tactful, and soon to be assigned the French portfolio. John Adams, a constant, effective, and passionate participant in floor debates, a more powerful speaker than thoughtful listener, was overburdened with committee work, concentrating on war planning and international diplomacy. A lawyer by training and a talented writer, he was soon to become a successful but discordant diplomat. As a writer, he tended to be scholarly and thorough; as a speaker, passionately unrestrained. Later, he was to write the Massachusetts constitution, which became a nationwide model. Posterity was to discover his great gift for vivid narrative and description in the eventual publication of his private diaries and letters. The other two appointees, New York's Robert Livingston, the heir to wealthy Hudson River Valley estates, and Connecticut's

Roger Sherman, a talented lawyer, judge, and senior political leader, had demonstrated no special talents as writers.

All six, though, were of the same mind. So too was Congress. It wanted another summary document, this one a conclusive statement of what every delegate, more or less, had essentially already signed on to—a declaration announcing that the colonies were now free and independent states, exercising sovereignty in all matters. It was to be a document justifying to the world its reasons for this extraordinary assertion. It was to be a collective assertion, to be signed, it was hoped, by every delegate.

Jefferson's discipline, eloquence, logical mind, and previous accomplishments helped make him the committee's candidate for the assignment, especially because no one else on the committee particularly wanted it. It also helped that he was from Virginia, one of the two tails that wagged the dog. Every member of Congress understood that they would have their chance to weigh in at some stage of the revision process. At a much later date, John Adams wrote that he and Jefferson had a conversation about which of the two should write the draft. Each preferred that it be the other. Apparently, no dispute arose over who might be, as a writer, the better choice. Adams insisted that Jefferson was. The assumption would have been, among all concerned, that each met the applicable standard. Adams, at the time, felt he had more important work to do. Jefferson deferred to Adams. It's a conversation that may or may not have existed, or at least in the way that Adams later reported it. Jefferson, who in the 1820s became testy about doubts cast on his authorship, never disputed Adams's version.

The Declaration was to be a statement of principle and justification in the abstract. It was also to be an indictment in specifics of the historical circumstances that had made recourse to first principles necessary. The assumption was that the case, or the justification, had already been proved. It simply needed to be written up. His colleagues happily turned over to Jefferson the task of creating a first draft.

They might have decided differently if they had anticipated that its statement of first principles would become, with the preamble to the Constitution and the Gettysburg Address, one of the three most widely quoted statements by any American writer. Moreover, they could not have anticipated that, at a much later date, it would also become one of the most controversial in its claim that "all men are created equal." It was to be, for history, Jefferson's most remembered and celebrated accomplishment, though it was not entirely his own. Its arguments had been made before, by him and others, and he had helpful editors. It was to be a fulfillment of Alexander Pope's dictum: great writing is what has "oft been thought but ne'er so well expressed." Jefferson was to sear into the American mind, past and present, through the power of the language of the Declaration, the collective decision and political philosophy of the elite leaders of what was probably a narrow majority of the American population. It was to be philosophy, argument, and propaganda combined and raised to the highest level of political literature. Its purpose was to help make and change history.

In the seventeen days between June 7 and 24, Jefferson wrote his draft. He was pressured to get it done quickly. Still, given the shortness of the document and his usual rapid writing pace, it seems unlikely that he felt rushed. On what days he actually wrote, how much at each sitting, how many days he spent revising is known only to those who can no longer speak. What papers or books he had with him is partly known. He had a copy of Richard Henry Lee's brief Resolution of Independence, introduced to the Congress on June 7, seconded by Adams, and passed over the course of the month. In it, it was "Resolved That these United Colonies are, and of right ought to be, free and independent States, that they are absolved from all allegiance to the British Crown, and that all political connection between them and the State of Great Britain is, and ought to be, totally dissolved." Jefferson seems to have had no direct hand in its creation:

the language originates with and belongs to Lee and others. It was the consensus language of the convention. Jefferson also had in hand, in full or in an early draft, the proposal he had created for a constitution for Virginia, with its lengthy forensic indictment of George III. In its various drafts and in its final form, to which various hands contributed, it contained an amplified list of American grievances now directed exclusively against the king. Jefferson drew extensively on it.

He most likely had at hand some version of George Mason's Declaration of Rights, at a minimum an oral memory from discussions with Mason, though not the final text passed by the Virginia legislature on June 12, 1776. Its first three sections made use of concepts and language that are close to Jefferson's in the Declaration of Independence. That language has its historical grounding in documents Jefferson and Mason knew well, such as the 1689 English Bill of Rights. It contained language that Jefferson and Mason had in common before either of them put a word to paper. Mason wrote:

That all men are by nature equally free and independent and have certain inherent rights, of which, when they enter into a state of society, they cannot, by any compact, deprive or divest their posterity; namely, the enjoyment of life and liberty, with the means of acquiring and possessing property, and pursuing and obtaining happiness and safety. That all power is vested in, and consequently derived from, the people; that magistrates are their trustees and servants and at all times amenable to them. That government is, or ought to be, instituted for the common benefit, protection, and security of the people, nation, or community; of all the various modes and forms of government, that is best which is capable of producing the greatest degree of happiness and safety and is most effectually secured against the danger of maladministration. And that, when any government shall be found inadequate or contrary to these purposes, a majority of the community has an indubitable, inalienable, and indefeasible right to reform, alter, or abolish it, in such manner as shall be judged most conducive to the public weal.

Jefferson's charge in Philadelphia was to express in the communal voice the claim of natural rights, the force of a particular historical circumstance, and the eternal truths that he and most of his contemporaries believed to be the foundation of all reality, described as the "Laws of Nature and of Nature's God." His task was to create a consensus document based on the language and substance of what had been stated frequently before by some colonial legislatures and in debates between 1775 and 1776, making use of Lee's words, Mason's Declaration, and the ideas and language of his own *Summary View*. The Declaration of Independence was to be a synthesis and a culmination, a consensus document. He had not been assigned to be its author in the modern sense. It would be Congress's authoritative statement on the matter, not the voice of an individual. It was to be a document that all were to sign, as if the entire body had written it.

Jefferson substantially revised as he wrote. At the same time, the Virginia House was deliberating the creation of a constitution and an explicit statement about human rights, particularly about freedom of conscience. He urged one of his fellow delegates, still in Williamsburg, to bring news to him as quickly as possible of "the great questions of the session." In addition, "I suppose they will tell us what to say on the subject of independence. . . . When at home I took great pains to enquire into the sentiments of the people on that head. In the upper counties I think I may safely say nine out of ten are for it." It's unlikely that he thought that his contribution to the convention in Philadelphia would be more important than what he might have contributed in Williamsburg, but he could not be in both places simultaneously. He worked quickly. The committee did the same. Apparently, Franklin contributed a revision of the final paragraph. They soon had a draft ready. Two days before Jefferson's second request to be allowed to go home, the committee submitted it to Congress. Congress went through it paragraph by paragraph.

"When in the Course of human events, it becomes necessary," Jefferson began, "for one people to dissolve the political bands which have connected them with another . . ." This meant that separation had been forced on the colonies. They had not sought it. It implied that they had done everything they could to avoid it. Necessity had forced the colonies "to assume among the powers of the earth, the separate and equal station to which the Laws of Nature and of Nature's God entitle them. . . ." That the "Laws of Nature and of Nature's God" entitled the colonies to do this had a particular resonance for Jefferson and his contemporaries, but it was not a resonance that they could attach to a substantive and specific body of law or theology. The extent to which "natural rights" were granted to exist, what they were, where they came from, and how they were to be implemented was a matter of dispute. By use of these terms, Jefferson's argument touched on theology without attaching itself to any particular sect; he steered clear of associating these terms with any religious or philosophical tradition except the vague Deism shared by many of his colleagues, which allowed a reference to "Nature's God," a creator who has mandated the laws of nature by which it functions. The Declaration needed to be a secular document.

Most Europeans and Anglo-Americans would have been at a loss to define these terms without evading the crucial questions. Do these natural rights, these "Laws of Nature," exist? How do you know that? Where do they come from? Who gets to define them? Who gets to implement them? And how would different definitions, by various self-interested parties, be reconciled? King George and his ministers would have had a different set of correlative terms and values to bring to bear on the language and the issues. They would have been appropriated in defense of the claim that Great Britain, not the colonies, occupied the moral and legal high ground. To different people and governments, the definitions and their implementation would have arisen from particular religious or secular histories. Jefferson was not after a fair and balanced argument. Most important, Jefferson was creating propaganda as literature and literature as propaganda, a form of argument that declared truth rather than proved it.

Jefferson had recently read the most successful eighteenth-century example of the genre, Thomas Paine's *Common Sense*, published in January 1776. It had no direct influence on the language of the Declaration. Later, Jefferson was to write that "no writer has exceeded Paine in ease and familiarity of style; in perspicuity of expression, happiness of elucidation, and in simple and unassuming language." Paine wrote directly to the American ear and heart to strengthen its revolutionary morale at a time of national peril. Jefferson's immediate audience was his congressional colleagues. His wider audience existed mainly in Europe, the Anglo-American and European world that Jefferson refers to as "mankind." The Declaration exists because "a decent respect to the opinions of mankind requires that they [the colonies] should declare the causes which impel them to the separation." It is directed toward, among others, Louis XVI and his ministers, and to all other enemies of Great Britain who ought to conclude that the enemy of my enemy is my friend. Unlike *Common Sense*, which is propaganda to the moment, the Declaration was also written for the future, for posterity and the historical record. Paine's style would no more be suited for the Declaration than Jefferson's for *Common Sense*, although ideologically they are in sympathy and mutually supportive. Years later, comparing Paine to another writer he admired, it is as if he is also comparing Paine to himself: "They were alike in making bitter enemies of the priests and Pharisees of their day. Both were honest men; both advocates for human liberty."

The most influential sentence in the preamble states that it is a "self-evident" truth "that all men are created equal, that they are endowed by their Creator with certain unalienable Rights, that among these are Life, Liberty and the pursuit of Happiness." Mason's Declaration gives prominence to the right to possess property. It explicitly states that one of the primary "inherent rights" is that "of acquiring and possessing property." Jefferson's Declaration does not. Jefferson and his colleagues were wealthy landowners. They believed in the sanctity of private property. Property ownership made citizenship. Its omission in Jefferson's Declaration may have been in the interest of tact, since its preamble was intended to rise above class, wealth, and social status. Still, one of the charges against the king in the Declaration is that he is attempting to take "away our Charters, abolishing our most valuable Laws, and altering fundamentally the Forms of our Governments," an attempt to alter or even deprive Americans of their present and future ownership of property.

All three drafts of Jefferson's proposed constitution for Virginia provide that "all land heretofore granted or purchased or occupied shall be held in full and absolute dominion, of no superior whatever." And that no Western land "shall be appropriated until purchased of the Indian native proprietors; nor shall any purchases be made of them but on behalf of the public, by authority of acts of the General assembly to be passed for every purchase specially . . . the territories contained within the charters erecting the colonies of Maryland, Pennsylvania, North and South Carolina, are hereby ceded, released, and forever confirmed to the people of those colonies respectively, with all the rights of property, jurisdiction and government and all other rights whatsoever which might at any time heretofore have been claimed by this colony." The land no longer belonged to the Crown. And Jefferson ultimately had in mind "from sea to shining sea," including Canada and Cuba. The land and its wealth belonged to those who lived on it.

What Jefferson did not have in hand from his sources is the claim that "all men are created equal." The Anglo-American world agreed that all Englishmen were created equal in the possession of the same legal rights. London had no argument with that. But what the American colonists were claiming seemed to the British to be rights possessed by no other component of the kingdom: the right not to be taxed or regulated by Parliament. And Jefferson and his colleagues did not mean that "all men are created equal" in the modern sense. Very few Anglo-American or European contemporaries believed that. To eighteenth-century English minds, the phrase did not even readily include non-Englishmen. Most Englishmen would not have thought that any Frenchman, for example, was his equal, though this was not a matter of natural rights but of political status, religious culture, and national history. The phrase did not include women; it did not include slaves; and it did not include other races or colors. For most Anglo-Americans, it would not have included Catholics. Jefferson did not believe that all white Anglo-Americans were created equal in intelligence, wealth, and opportunity. He meant that all white Englishmen and Europeans were born with the right to life, liberty, and the pursuit of happiness. For many, these were rights exercised in the ideal, not in practice. It was, nevertheless, a radical claim, at least in its emphasis, with its tentative basis in certain schools of thought in seventeenth- and eighteenth-century political philosophy. Louis XVI certainly would have had a different view of what rights his subjects were born with.

As a work of literary art, the Declaration is structurally unbalanced. Most modern readers read only the opening paragraph. It is one of the best known and most quoted statements in American history and literature. It has become a founding text, interpreted in the modern era, from the presidency of Lincoln to the present, as the most important expression of fundamental American values and governance. Jefferson and his colleagues put more weight on the full body of the document. In the revision process, they tinkered with some of the wording of the preamble, but not very much or with substantive consequence. They tinkered considerably, though, with the wording in the list of accusations and grievances against George III, sharpening the language, adjusting some of the phrases, and omitting a full paragraph accusing the Crown of having inflicted the institution of slavery on the colonists. It was a tactful omission. It would have complicated the document, directing attention away from the main point, which had nothing to do with actual slavery. Also, though Jefferson and his colleagues said otherwise, the claim that the Crown was responsible for the existence of slavery in the colonies had no basis in fact. The colonists from the start had been complicit in the importation of slaves. Anglo-American colonists in the Northern and Southern colonies had worked the international slave trade. It provided the labor force that was the foundation of colonial wealth. Entrepreneurs on both sides of the Atlantic benefited from slave labor, including the Jefferson and Randolph families.

Modern editors have struggled to try to determine who made the various revisions to Jefferson's first draft and the Declaration's succeeding versions. There is no doubt, though, that Congress itself eliminated the accusation that the British Crown had forced slavery on the colonies. In Jefferson's unedited version, it had seemed to him desirable, by conviction or tactic, to hold the Crown responsible for the existence of slavery in America. The Americans themselves, apparently, were blameless victims. Congress decided to avoid the topic altogether. Jefferson resented its omission, as he did every other change made to the document.

The body of the Declaration, in its final form, consists of a list of offenses against the rights of the colonists that warrant separation and the establishment of an independent government. No contemporary American had to agree with the abstract claims of the opening paragraph in order to agree that separation was warranted. By June 1776, it was a given that many Americans wanted out of the British Empire in order to be in control of the self-interested realities of daily life: taxes, property, territorial growth, commercial regulation, and economic opportunity. Mistreatment could, it seemed, be relieved, and its continuation or intensification prevented, by the assertion of independence.

Anglo-American manhood had been insulted. Its rights denied. They were not second-class cousins; they were equals. Many colonists felt they had done their best to be cooperative and accommodating, but freeborn Englishmen were being deprived of their natural rights. The list of about thirty accusations that follow the preamble summarizes and synthesizes in legal and forensic structure the grievances that Jefferson and his contemporaries had been accumulating since the Stamp Act. Jefferson had listed most of them in his *Summary View of the Rights of British America.* The underlying objection was simple: Parliament and George III seemed intent on governing Great Britain's American colonies by command rather than by assent.

And Jefferson's list of accusations gains power from its concise inclusiveness. It gains rhetorical and argumentative effectiveness in its role as indictment and evidence combined by being exclusively directed against George III. The king now seemed the handiest personification of what Americans were rebelling against. George III was being transformed, rhetorically, psychologically, and politically, into a tyrant whose commands determined American law. He is made to represent all the crimes committed against American interests and rights. Every indictment in the first half of the list begins with the phrase "He has." It changes to "For" and then returns to "He has." "The history of the present King of Great Britain is a history of repeated injuries and usurpations" all directed toward establishing "an absolute Tyranny over these States. To prove this, let Facts be submitted to a candid world." The both overpersonalized and impersonal king has become the ritualistic target of the clash of differing Anglo-American and British interests.

It is a long list, powerfully presented by a master of the language of accusation and argument, a lawyerly wordsmith for the prosecution addressing a jury and seeking a conviction. The voice of the defense never appears in the Declaration. Ironically, Jefferson and George III had interests and traits in common. Both were polymaths. The recent unveiling of the treasure trove of George III's private papers reveals interests ranging from horticulture and astronomy to music and the gadgets of the dawning industrial age. Like Jefferson, he was a great list maker. Of course, by the nature of its purpose, the Declaration is a one-sided document.

By June 1776, there were two trials in progress, one by words, the other by fire. History would be the judge of who would win the trial by words. Jefferson had no doubt his side would. "That to secure these rights," the preamble stated, "Governments are instituted among Men, deriving their just powers from the consent of the governed,— That whenever any Form of Government becomes destructive of these ends, it is the Right of the People to alter or to abolish it, and to institute new Government, laying its foundation on such principles and organizing its powers in such form, as to them shall seem most likely to effect their Safety and Happiness." It was, overall, a very risky claim, even riskier to implement. All the delegates knew that. Still,

We must, therefore, acquiesce in the necessity, which denounces our Separation, and hold them, as we hold the rest of mankind, Enemies in War, in Peace Friends. We, therefore, the Representatives of the united States of America, in General Congress, Assembled, appealing to the Supreme Judge of the world for the rectitude of our intentions, do, in the Name, and by Authority of the good People of these Colonies, solemnly publish and declare, That these United Colonies are, and of Right ought to be Free and Independent States; that they are Absolved from all Allegiance to the British Crown, and that all political connection between them and the State of Great Britain, is and ought to be totally dissolved; and that as Free and Independent States, they have full Power to levy War, conclude Peace, contract Alliances, establish Commerce, and to do all other Acts and Things which Independent States may of right do. And for the support of this Declaration, with a firm reliance on the protection of divine Providence, we mutually pledge to each other our Lives, our Fortunes and our sacred Honor.

Like much good literature, especially in the classical style, the Declaration coheres in its structure, which is simple and conventional: a beginning (the abstract preface) followed by a statement of theme and purpose, a middle (the accusation and indictment), and an ending, which is a reprise and reemphasis of the declarative purpose. There is nothing original about this structure. That is part of its effectiveness. It serves its purpose perfectly. It is concise, eloquent, forensically powerful, and emotionally resonant. There is nothing original or groundbreaking about the language itself, or even the ideological concept that the language presents.

Still, it is a brilliant and powerful example of a state document as literature. It is literature that is also extraordinarily effective propaganda, the presentation in words of one side of a conflict, every element of which is in the service of a political movement and its underlying ideology. As much as it is desirable to recognize that pens other than Jefferson's made contributions to the final version, and to recognize that it is a consensus document influenced by other documents that Jefferson had absorbed, as well as by many debates, it is Jefferson's talent as a synthesizing mind and a brilliant writer that gives the document its power. Other people helped create it, and it was a product of a particular historical situation and moment. Like a typical author, Jefferson believed that his first draft was almost perfect. He resented the revisions he had to consent to. Still, in the end and in its final version, Jefferson was its author. It was to be his most memorable achievement as a writer.

As he was writing, rumor reached him that some of his Virginia colleagues doubted the commitment of one or more of their delegates to their instructions about independence. The rumor irked Jefferson into self-defensiveness, though he did not know exactly who was being criticized and by whom. Did it come from the governor, Patrick Henry? Or from some other hyperpartisans of independence who feared one or more of their delegation was less committed than they were? Sensitive even to a whisper of criticism, he found it a "painful situation to be 300 miles from one's country, and thereby open to secret assassination without a possibility of self-defense. I am willing to hope nothing of this kind has been done in my case, and yet I cannot be easy." "Secret assassination" was irrational hyperbole. At the same time, he was confident that the Declaration of Independence would speak for him, "if any doubt has arisen as to me. . . . This will give decisive proof that my own sentiment concurred with the vote they instructed us to give." He may indeed have had doubters, but his exaggerated rhetoric verged on paranoia, an expression of his lifelong vulnerability to even a hint of criticism.

On June 30, while still working on the draft and its revisions, Jefferson wrote to the head executive in Virginia, "I am sorry the situation of my domestic affairs renders it indispensably necessary that I should solicit the substitution of some other person here in my room. Delicacy . . . will not require me to enter minutely into the private causes which render this necessary: I trust they will be satisfied I would not have urged it again were it not necessary." Since he was now urging it again, it's likely that he had asked to be recalled before he had been appointed to the Declaration committee or before the committee had assigned him to write the first draft. As always, he was discreet about personal affairs. The "delicacy" that he referred to may have been a pregnancy or a miscarriage. He might have thought it possible that his wife was dying. He may also have thought his work in Philadelphia was almost done. It would also take time for letters to be exchanged between Philadelphia and Williamsburg, for a replacement to be appointed, and a new delegate to take his place. The actual event was inevitably at least a month or two off. By the end of the summer, Jefferson was on his way home.

CHAPTER FIVE

An Angel in the Whirlwind

1776–1781

L ondon social, political, and commercial society was semihys-
terical in May 1776. The weather was cool and gray, a typical
late-eighteenth-century London spring. In Kew Gardens, the rhodo-
dendrons were in full bloom. How to deal with the increasing crisis
in the relationship between the American colonies and the mother
country was much on the minds of the governing class. George III
was not a well-liked king. It was to take, years later, his genetics-based
madness to make him a sympathetic figure. But at least he spoke English. The first George spoke German only; the second, George III's
grandfather, spoke some English but mostly German. In 1714 Great
Britain had imported this foreign royalty because they were Protestants. That sent a message to the Catholic Stuart kings in exile.
George III's American cousins, equally Catholic-hating, had also welcomed the House of Hanover to the throne. A loyal husband, the father of heirs to the throne, George III was a man of settled habits and
an unostentatious life, unusual for a European king. He liked keeping
lists and records; he loved domesticity, his wife, his children, and his
gardens. Pastoral life appealed to him. And he had had the advantage
of ruling during the war that had made Great Britain the dominant

world power. His indictment in the Declaration of Independence seemed in London excessively personal. And it seemed to many Englishmen that they also were being indicted—unfairly.

In May 1776, what George III and his ministers most wanted was to keep the Protestant American tail from wagging the Protestant British dog. It was becoming increasingly difficult. Different factions had different ideas about how to keep the tail in place. Jefferson's *A Summary View of the Rights of British America* was available in London in 1774. Worse was soon to come. London had little idea of the spread and depth of American alienation. Jefferson's prosecutorial indictment in the Declaration of Independence, as if George III were a criminal before the bar, reached London by late summer. It was a shocker. To the British governing class, it seemed legally and morally unsound. It also seemed, in its personal attack on the king, an insult to the country. With power divided between Parliament, the Crown, and public opinion, Great Britain was evolving gradually into a constitutional monarchy dominated by a Parliament in which landed and commercial interests competed for power. The Crown, dependent on Parliament for the funds that supported its existence, was one of numbers of factors in the equation. Its power mostly resided in its authority to appoint the ministers who ran the country. It was called "His Majesty's" government. In fact, it essentially belonged to the landed and commercial elite; thus it had much in common with Jefferson's Virginia.

Americans in London in May 1776 had much to be concerned about. A substantial community of British Americans negotiated the interests of New England businesses and Southern planters. One of them, Joshua Johnson, a Maryland tobacco entrepreneur, was acting as his company's sales representative for the London tobacco market. His daughter, born that year, was to become the wife of the sixth American president and the daughter-in-law of the second. Another American in London was Arthur Lee, from one of Virginia's elite families. Like Benjamin Franklin, Lee represented the interests of a number of American colonies. By May 1776, he had committed himself, like the entire Lee family, to American independence. Trained as a doctor, then as a lawyer, Lee was ostensibly practicing law in London. By the mid-1760s, a member of the London Bill of Rights Society, he had begun spending much of his time writing pamphlets addressed to the British public in support of the colonies. Recently, his main activity was diplomacy, representing the Confederation Congress, shuttling between London, where he encouraged the possibility of a peaceful resolution, and Paris, where he lobbied for French support for the confederated states. A congressional committee encouraged him to elicit in both cities any information that might be helpful to the American cause. He was, in effect, America's first authorized spy.

On May 15, 1776, four extraordinary men dined together at the home of a London book dealer, Charles Dilly, who ran a press well known for publishing pro-American pamphlets. The bookshop was a gathering place for those who favored reform at home and in the colonies. The two least known of these men were dramatically articulate speakers, both in their midthirties, Lee and James Boswell. Boswell and Lee had become friends during the latter's residence in Edinburgh. The other two were famous in the English-speaking world. John Wilkes was a hero of radical London politics who had defied Parliament and the Crown. Samuel Johnson was the author of *London, Rasselas, The Lives of the Poets*, and *A Dictionary of the English Language*; he was the most revered literary guru of the late-eighteenth-century English-speaking world. Johnson would have known who Lee was. A supporter of the Tory government, Johnson had recently published *Taxation No Tyranny*, a defense of the Coercive Acts. He thought Lord North's Conciliatory Proposals more than the American insurrectionists deserved.

Sixty-five years old, a portrait in brown and pink, Johnson was a fleshy tall man with convulsive tics. His forceful voice dominated conversation. He had been tricked by Boswell, a mischief-making Scotsman who adored Johnson, into attending a dinner with John Wilkes, a man he despised. A journalist and politician in his midforties, Wilkes embodied radical populism, a mayor of London who led rather than controlled antiestablishment and anti-Catholic mobs, a member of Parliament, and an advocate of Parliamentary reform and American independence. Boswell was to become the author of the premier biography in the English language, his *Life of Samuel Johnson*. It uncannily captures almost exact representations of Johnson's conversations.

Johnson and Dilly were on friendly terms, despite political differences. Probably having in mind that it would make good copy for his biography, Boswell had orchestrated the entertainment, eager to hear and record what the Tory conservative and the London radical antigovernment politician would say to each other. Johnson had no forewarning that Wilkes would be among the guests. Boswell expected Lee, the American revolutionary, also to provoke Johnson's wit and bite. Lumbering into the room, Johnson was introduced to Wilkes and Lee. He withdrew into a window recess. When dinner was announced, he had already composed himself into sociability. Boswell records very little about the actual conversation. His emphasis is on the cleverness of his own achievement. Wilkes and Johnson apparently conversed amiably. Afterward, Johnson acknowledged that Wilkes could charm even those who deplored his populist politics. He congratulated himself on having behaved as a polite and sophisticated man of the world.

The insular Jefferson had never met either one, but he would have read Johnson. He would also have known much about Wilkes, who had been a presence in American revolutionary rhetoric since 1765. Wilkes's advocacy of American independence had made him a widely lauded comrade in words. Since the Stamp Act uproar, Americans had co-opted the London street slogan "Wilkes and Liberty." From Boston, the Sons of Liberty, with John Adams, Samuel Adams, and John Hancock as signatories, evoked Wilkes as the man "reserved by heaven to bless and perhaps save a tottering Empire." His anti-elitist advocacy of the extension of the suffrage and of Parliamentary reform emboldened sympathetic Americans. In Virginia, the Lee brothers, embodying the paradox of elite Virginia planters as revolutionaries, raised Wilkes's radical banner. In May 1776, though Jefferson was three thousand miles away, his opposition to British control of America was represented at that dinner in London by the presence of Wilkes and Lee. And he would have been aware of Johnson's view of the American colonists.

Johnson could sacrifice truth for wit; Jefferson could sacrifice truth for hope. Like Jefferson, Johnson knew how to exaggerate effectively. The British public did not argue with Johnson's statement that Americans "are a race of convicts." About fifty thousand had been sentenced to servitude in the colonies between 1700 and 1775, more than twenty thousand to Virginia. Rebellious Americans "ought to be thankful for anything we allow them short of hanging," he had written. Johnson of course knew that the Lees were not descended from convicts. Neither were the Jeffersons. Like any talented polemicist with a wicked wit and pen, he had a point to make. Every American had benefited from British investment and culture. The colonies had been "settled under English protection . . . constituted by an English charter; and have been defended by English arms." They were behaving as if they . . . had no regard for law or loyalty." And they were hypocrites, he pointed out: "How is it that we hear the loudest yelps for liberty among the drivers of negroes?" He did not have to have read *A Summary View of the Rights of British America* or the Declaration of Independence to mock a claim that "all men are created equal" from those who owned slaves.

And the slogan "No taxation without representation" was, in Johnson's view, self-serving: "To suppose, that Americans" should be exempted from paying for the common defense, "involves such an accumulation of absurdity, as nothing but the show," rather than the reality, "of patriotism could palliate." American colonists had made a choice. "A man . . . cannot have the advantages of multiplied residence. . . . He who goes voluntarily to America, cannot complain of losing what he leaves in Europe. . . . By crossing the Atlantic . . . by his own choice he has left a country, where he had a vote and little property, for another, where he has great property, but no vote." It was a reality from the beginning of settlement; it was an acknowledged given, a bargain made.

In creating the Declaration, Jefferson was writing as a propagandist; Johnson in *Taxation No Tyranny*, as a trenchant realist. Johnson had an equally self-serving but more factual presentation than Jefferson of the historical justification for British rule of the colonies. "We have now, for more than two centuries, ruled large tracts of the American continent, by a claim which, perhaps, is valid only upon this consideration, that no power can produce a better; by the right of discovery, and prior settlement. And by such titles almost all the dominions of the earth are holden, except that their original is beyond memory, and greater obscurity gives them greater veneration." To the British, it was as simple and historically obvious as that. Jefferson's attempt to rewrite the conditions of settlement were, the British believed, both fictional and irrelevant. What was at issue was power and possession. Discovery, conquest, and settlement determined possession. Length of ownership contributed to the right of ownership.

Actually, Jefferson and his colleagues in 1776, by inference and action, had no argument with Johnson's description of the origins of possession. But they differed in some important details of legality and ownership. Jefferson was adding and defending another category of possession: those who took possession by revolutionary proclamation and force, if necessary, of the land they already possessed by denying the legal chain of ownership that had put them in possession in the first place. Johnson deplored revolution of almost any sort, with the exception of the Glorious Revolution of 1688, reaffirming Protestant rule and Parliamentary supremacy. In 1776, Jefferson and his colleagues embraced revolution. It seemed the only way to take full legal possession of the land they believed they already had the right to have unconditional possession of.

The Declaration of Independence startled, even shocked, the British ruling class. It made claims about the sources of power and polity, especially about what arrangements of power best served a country's interests, that had never been made before. George III symbolically represented the British commitment to rule by those whom the British elite considered the best and the brightest, the well-educated owners of property, wealth, and lineage, which included Jefferson within the limits imposed by his American residence. And this elite, it seemed sensible to the British, was to a considerable degree determined by birth and inheritance—a self-perpetuating ruling class, though far from entirely so. There was room for the ascension of the self-made man, like Peter Jefferson. His son and his colleagues had only a partial argument with that. Like the British ruling class, they also did not believe that all men were created equal. However, for a variety of motives, separate from economic grievances though inseparable from them, they wanted a society in which there was more equality of opportunity for white males, as well as a greater representation of the voice of the voter, limited by ownership of property, gender, and race. Great Britain was not to see any enlargement of the suffrage until 1832. The United States, starting from a different starting line, was to move more quickly. In the end, or at least over the next few centuries, the American view prevailed.

During the first two years that Jefferson spent in Philadelphia he lived in dread that he would receive tragic news from Monticello. "The suspense under which I am is too terrible to be endured. If any thing has happened, for God's sake let me know it," he wrote to his brother-in-law Francis Eppes in November 1775. "I have set apart nearly one day in every week since I came here to write letters. Notwithstanding this I have never received the scrip of a pen from any mortal breathing." It was mostly the same in 1776. Probably the very literate Martha occasionally wrote to him regardless of illness, children, pregnancy, and domestic responsibilities. Still, there was good reason, in addition to missing her company, for Jefferson to be so worried. Close to mid-August 1776, his friend Edmund Pendleton confirmed "the indisposition of Mrs. Jefferson. May heaven restore her health and grant you a joyful meeting." Whatever letters there were between husband and wife did not survive Jefferson's compulsion for domestic privacy. He did get some news from fraternal travelers and colleagues, but at times he felt a thousand miles away from where he wanted to be. Duty, though, required that he stay in Philadelphia until replaced. A committee workhorse, he regularly reported news to Virginia colleagues about Congress and the war. He wrote numerous letters and memoranda on behalf of his delegation. Even while writing the Declaration, he sustained his other obligations. His mind and pen were engaged in what he sensed then and came to believe, unhesitatingly, was the greatest enterprise of his life.

In July 1776, the Confederation Congress was, after some revisions, pleased with Jefferson's and the committee's work. Some colleagues thought Congress had tampered too much with Jefferson's exposition and prose. They liked his pre-revision draft better. So did he. A little vain and overly self-confident, he objected to almost every one of the changes, a sensitive author who perforce accepted but objected to editing. In this case, he had no choice. And the final product had, so to speak, wings. "I am highly pleased with your declaration," his friend John Page wrote to him from Williamsburg. "God preserve the United States. We know the race is not to the swift nor the battle to the strong. Do you not think an angel rides in the whirlwind and directs this storm?" It was an irresistible temptation, inseparable from sincere conviction, to believe that God was on the side of their Revolution, whether in traditional Protestant terms, from Congregationalist New England to Anglican Virginia, or in the deistic terms that Jefferson had used in the Declaration: "the Laws of Nature" and "Nature's God."

Eager to return home, he had already begun singing his retirement song. "I hope you'll get cured of your wish to retire so early in life from the memory of man," his friend Edmund Pendleton wrote from Virginia, "and exercise Your talents for the nurture of our new Constitution, which will require all the attention of its friends to prune exuberances and cherish the plant." To some of his colleagues in Congress, who preferred that he stay with them in Philadelphia, it seemed desertion. There was grumbling about his giving priority to family concerns rather than patriotic duty. But his Virginia associates would be pleased to have him back in Williamsburg. His concern about his family was not his exclusive motivation. Jefferson also wanted to be in Williamsburg to participate in the creation of the state constitution. To his regret, the draft proposal that he had written in May 1776 and put in the hands of Wythe to bring to Williamsburg arrived too late to play a role in what was already under way. This first Virginia state constitution, passed by the General Assembly at the end of June 1776, was rushed through for political reasons, putting in place a document Jefferson thought weak and flabby.

As soon as his replacement arrived in Philadelphia in September 1776, Jefferson left for Virginia. It was, alas, already too late for the kind of constitution he had in mind and that his draft had provided. He wanted a constitution that would not be subject to ongoing manipulation by a legislative majority. His ideal constitution would have reformed a variety of laws that seemed to him not only feudal but antithetical to his hope for a prosperous Virginia in a more enlightened age: no more hoarding of property through entail; opportunity for land for all who wanted to farm; an extension of the suffrage that would create a more democratic balance between the Tidewater and the Piedmont; the end of the slave trade, and even the eventual end of slavery itself. Jefferson went from Monticello to Williamsburg in early October, in place on the opening day of what was now called the General Assembly. His intellectual sharpness and writerly skills were drafted immediately into the service of replacing or revising Virginia's code of laws. In Jefferson's mind, this was an opportunity to turn defeat into victory: a thorough revisal of Virginia's laws could contain provisions that would compensate for what the constitution lacked.

To his surprise, at the end of the first week of October, he received a letter from Congress that assigned a totally different role to him. The letter came by private messenger. He was informed that he had been appointed, pending his acceptance, to be one of a commission of three to embark for France to persuade the French government to provide recognition, money, and arms. His colleagues were to be Benjamin Franklin and Silas Deane, the latter a New England businessman turned politician and now diplomat. Congress assumed he would accept. It was his sacred duty as a patriot. His congressional colleague, Richard Henry Lee, urged acceptance: "In my judgement, the most eminent services that the greatest of her sons can do America will not more essentially serve her and honor themselves, than a successful negotiation with France." It was an offer that appealed to his long-standing desire to visit Europe. It was also a powerful appeal to his patriotism.

Jefferson kept the messenger waiting three days while he anguished about his response. Then he replied: "No cares for my own person, nor yet for my private affairs would have induced one moment's hesitation to accept the charge. But circumstances very peculiar in the situation of my family, such as neither permit me to leave nor to carry it, compel me to ask leave to decline a service so honorable and at the same time so important to the American cause. The necessity under which I labor, and the conflict I have undergone for three days, during which I could not determine to dismiss your messenger, will I hope plead my pardon with Congress." He may have been aware that Martha was pregnant with the child she was to give birth to at the end of May the next year. She was, though, well enough to stay with her husband in Williamsburg for much of the fall of 1776. But they had already lost one child. A late fall or early winter sea voyage for Martha seemed frighteningly risky. And to leave her at home without him through the pregnancy would have created an impossible distance between himself and his domestic responsibilities, especially if things went wrong again. "I wish my domestic situation had rendered it possible for me to have joined you," he wrote to Benjamin Franklin.

Jefferson was not readily pardoned for his declination. Richard Henry Lee expressed his disappointment: "I heard with much regret that you had declined both the voyage, and your seat in Congress. No man feels more deeply than I do, the love of, and the loss of, private enjoyments; but let attention to these be universal, and we are gone, beyond redemption. . . ." Clearly Jefferson felt the anguish of declining. He too, he implied to Franklin, would have benefited from immersion in the cultural treasures that Paris offered. But it was to be a blessing postponed, not renounced. He could not know then that he would have his own Paris years in the next decade. He was to have two more offers to become an American diplomat in France, the second of which he was to accept. Great Britain was now the enemy; France, the likely friend, the provider of financial and military help. Ruled by an authoritarian monarchy, it was also a police state whose economic, social, and political structures were feudal, most of its land and wealth owned by the aristocratic elite. That had nothing to do with the realities of the situation. To survive, the United States needed foreign assistance, money and arms. The enemy of my enemy is my friend. That Great Britain rather than France embodied some measure of the laws and political system that Jefferson desired for his own country was irrelevant. The paradox of an alliance between France and the United States against Great Britain seemed likely to be to the advantage of both. It turned out to be a great advantage to the United States. It was mostly a disaster for France.

As much as he regretted declining the offer, Jefferson needed to stay at home. Family obligations may have felt compelling enough to use them as his entire justification. He had been away from his wife for much of the past two years. He was rich in land and slaves, so his cash flow was minimally satisfactory. He had entirely given up his legal work. Monticello, as plantation and residence, might benefit from its master's attention, though he was not a knowledgeable or enthusiastic farmer. He loved possessing the land, not working or managing it himself. Moreover, the house itself was still small, its expansion a project more for the future than significantly under way. Whatever his multiple motives, though, he had returned also because of his desire to participate in rewriting Virginia's laws. "You are also wanting much in the revision of our laws and forming a new body," Pendleton had written to him in late July 1776, "a necessary work for which few of us have adequate abilities and attention." His colleagues in the General Assembly thought him a natural for the task. It appointed a committee of five, named the Committee of Revisal: George Wythe, George Mason, Edmund Pendleton, Thomas Ludwell Lee, and Thomas Jefferson.

The revision of Virginia's colonial laws was mainly Jefferson's work, with George Wythe and Edmund Pendleton making substantial contributions. Whether to start anew with blank sheets of paper and create an entirely new legal code or to take the existing code as the starting text needed to be determined. The committee decided that it would do some of both. Part was to be revision of centuries of common and statute law, but some new statutes would have to be created. The results needed to be acceptable to the majority of the General Assembly, which would be required to vote on each item or approve the code as a whole. The task required energy and vision. As Jefferson realized from the start, it would have to be a series of reforms and clarifications that embodied the vision of those who made it and those who approved it. It would be a statutory exposition that would remedy some of the defects of the Virginia constitution. Like all statutory and common law, it would embody the values and vision of its creators. It would be, to some extent, an ideological document, part by part, as individual statutes, or as a whole, the vision or lack of vision of the people who created it and of their society. Jefferson wanted what for him would be its most important parts to embody his vision, to reflect his mind, his values, and his pen. He was to spend much of the next three years at the task. It had its challenges and complications, and it inspired him to create one of his most enlightened and effective prose pieces. Its most radical provisions were inseparable from his vision and his voice. In some of its provisions, it was a step too far for his legislative colleagues.

As the 126 separate bills the committee created during three years of work came to the attention of the Assembly, some of the most controversial were tabled for future discussion, others rejected. It was a document in progress, parts of which the Assembly seriously deliberated, some of which it postponed for consideration in postwar years. The war was not yet being fought on Virginia's soil, but preparations for defense were central to the activities of the General Assembly, the Senate, and the governor. Moreover, no one knew for certain that there would actually be postwar years in which the United States would continue to exist.

Between 1776 and 1779, with the exception of the Battle of Saratoga in 1777, the war went badly for the new country. Virginia remained untouched, though nervously watching activities to the north. Jefferson and his colleagues kept persistently at the revision. They proposed some reworking of the language of the existing laws. They proposed some laws entirely new in conception and language. Each was designed to be presented to the Assembly as a separate bill, with the possibility that, after further consideration and revision, the totality might be voted on at a later date. The bills covered the basics of setting up a republican legal system, combining statute and common law, based on the English model: courts of justice, criminal offenses, capital punishment, trial by jury, habeas corpus, naturalizing foreigners, dividing counties, establishing a land office, and dealing with property belonging to loyalists. Most dealt with the creation of a governing structure: the powers of the governor and the legislature, emergency powers, tax and revenue provisions, a monetary system, private banknotes, ownership of property, estates and wills, and public health.

The second of the 126 bills addressed who would have the right to vote to elect the General Assembly, which would elect from its ranks the governor and Privy Council. Suffrage was to be limited to free white male householders worth a minimum of fifty pounds or possessing twenty-five acres and a house. It included an extensive list of other provisions and details, including a penalty for those qualified to vote who did not—an attempt, initiated by George Mason, to prevent elections being determined by a small turnout easily manipulated by special interests. That also was on Jefferson's mind, but in a broader way. In August 1776, he had expressed to Pendleton his belief that "the decisions of the people, in a body, will be more honest and more disinterested than those of wealthy men. . . . I was for extending the right of suffrage (or in other words the rights of a citizen) to all who had a permanent intention of living in the country." That had been the intent of his spring 1776 draft constitution for Virginia.

"Take what circumstances you please as evidence of this," he wrote Pendleton, "either the having resided a certain time, or having a family, or having property, any or all of them. Whoever intends to live in a country must wish that country well, and has a natural right of assisting in the preservation of it." That meant "equal representation" for all free white males. A short residence requirement would give the vote to immigrants. His premise was that anyone who chose to be a citizen should by that very choice be considered worthy of being a participant in its governance. It was a position Jefferson was never to deviate from. That truth could be polluted by demagoguery, voters suborned by ignorance or self-interest, and an electoral system manipulated to undermine "equal representation" had occurred to him as a possibility but an unlikely one. If the unlikely should occur, he believed it would be temporary. His ideal republic would be, over time, self-correcting.

The committee proposed two bills central to Jefferson's vision of America's future. Before 1774, there had been two ways of acquiring unsettled land: by royal dispensation, begun by King Charles in the seventeenth century, with fifty acres for each person imported as an indentured servant, and by land grants bestowed as reward or patronage by the royal governor. The committee's bills provided a broader, more republican procedure to advance one of the central beliefs of Jefferson's life: that small farmers are the backbone of American republicanism, that farming is inherently a more moral activity than any other, and that it would attract and breed civic-minded, patriotic citizens.

The first bill, meant to encourage freehold availability of Western land to new settlers rather than to speculators, was strenuously opposed. The bill allowed tracts of any size that had already been surveyed and approved to remain in the hands of their owners. That seemed fair to Jefferson, but the Assembly decided that, in the future, tracts no larger than four hundred acres would be permitted. Those who strongly opposed the bill in its entirety supported it in order for the bill to be moved forward for rejection as a whole. The bill regarding land purchase limitations went down without much of a fight. The amended version omitted the four-hundred-acre limitation. The final bill was noticeably slanted to the advantage of speculators and land syndicates. The rich continued to get richer. Another of Jefferson's bills, eliminating primogeniture and entail, which concentrated power and property in the hands of eldest sons, narrowly passed.

The committee introduced a bill for a "general scheme of education." It proposed a system of primary education for the creation of a literate public that the new nation, in Jefferson's view, required for a republican future. Illiteracy and ignorance were the seed-ground for tyranny and oppression. "It is believed that the most effectual means of preventing this would be, to illuminate, as far as practicable, the minds of the people at large, and more especially to give them knowledge of those facts, which history exhibiteth, that, possessed thereby of the experience of other ages and countries, they may be enabled to know ambition under all its shapes, and prompt to exert their natural powers to defeat its purposes."

New England had already taken the lead in free primary education. Jefferson's scheme, totally new to Virginia, called for the creation of a three-year statewide system of education for all "free [white] children." As in New England, *females* were to be included at the primary level. Children of the indigent would attend at public expense. Those families that could afford tuition would pay it. The small number of those whom "nature had endowed" with intellectual ability, excluding females, would later be selected for free attendance at William and Mary. All this would be done "as far as possible," a phrase that signaled to the Virginia elite that their preferences would determine financing. It was a loophole that could cover almost any contingency. It would determine who was to be educated above the level of the families into which they had been born. On the one hand, Jefferson viewed basic education for the masses as a safeguard against tyranny.

On the other, those born to supremacy would form the governing class, "a natural aristocracy of virtue and talent," a wise ruling elite. Even this was a step too far for the General Assembly. The Virginia taxpayer thought it an expensive and destabilizing innovation. The bill did not become law.

The committee proposed a bill to forbid importing slaves from Africa. For some it was entirely an economic issue; for others, entirely a moral one; for many, something of both. In Virginia, with an adequate labor force in place and a high birth rate, additional importation would reduce the value of slave property. Jefferson himself had more slaves than he needed, but he also had a strong moral position. Still, the bill to forbid importation was not a bill to free any current slaves. Jefferson may have thought or even may have expressed orally that he hoped the next step would be compensated emancipation, which would, over time, free future generations of slaves. He later stated that it was his intention to introduce such a bill. His committee colleague, George Wythe, was a late-eighteenth-century version of a semi-abolitionist; Pendleton, less so but still an opponent of the institution.

Even so, the committee did not go the next step. They were practical politicians. Compensated emancipation was a huge step too far. But it seemed to them possible, even likely, that the General Assembly would agree at least to ban future importations. If it did not, it would be clear that emancipation itself would have even less support. The Assembly emphatically rejected the nonimportation bill. Perhaps, over time, Jefferson hoped, his fellow Virginians would come to think as he did. The decisive rejection of the committee's nonimportation bill was a reality check from which Jefferson never recovered. Importation continued, though gradually every state except South Carolina banned it, and in 1808 the United States Constitution implemented total nonimportation.

———

Jefferson did not and had no need ever to retreat from bill number 82, A Bill for Establishing Religious Freedom. Not only was history on his side; so too were many of his fellow Virginians. It took, though, about a decade from when Jefferson first drafted his bill until a modified version was passed by the legislature as the "Virginia Statute for Establishing Freedom of Religion." It took time, debate, and verbal tinkering to satisfy the various constituencies about the degree to which the language of the bill should have a Christian bias. There was also, for much of that time, a debilitating war in progress. Jefferson's original draft, as best it can be reconstructed, was a powerful complement to the Declaration of Independence, extending the umbrella of natural rights to provide total protection for freedom of conscience, thought, statement, and practice on anything to do with religious belief. It required that the Anglican Church, in the process of being reborn as the Episcopal Church, be disestablished. The bill mandated that no taxpayer money ever be used to support any religious establishment. Virginia's increasingly large population of Protestant dissenters, after frequently petitioning the Assembly, had been relieved in 1776 of some establishment requirements. Jefferson's bill required much more than that. Former members of the Church of England would have to accept disestablishment. There would be no state-supported church. Beyond that, Jefferson wanted an explicit, broadly drafted affirmation of freedom of conscience in all matters relating to belief and its expression, regardless of religious sect, religious belief, or the absence of religious belief.

The bill in its 1777 draft and its later forms is one of Jefferson's most influential and frequently cited contributions to the literature of American ideas, principles, and practices. Its sentences, rhythms, and structure are not as elegant, concise, and engaging as those of the Declaration. It is more philosophical and historical than forensic. It is also more grounded in intellectual engagement and historical reality. Like the Declaration, it makes universalist claims, but they focus on a single topic, freedom of conscience. They have no immediate political agenda other than to establish in law a specific natural right, whose implementation in a just and free society determines what civic and political rights its citizens actually have.

Some of the ground had already been covered in George Mason's Declaration of Rights. The groundwork is also in Jefferson's 1776 Declaration and in the philosophical traditions that influenced his mind-set. For Jefferson, the highest level of freedom, on which all other freedoms depend, is freedom of thought and the right to express oneself freely, including the right not to express oneself at all. No force or institution other than freely determined individual choice had, in Jefferson's view, any sovereignty over belief or the expression of belief on any subject, including that most bitterly and destructively fought-over subject, religious belief. Though the emphasis is on religious freedom, its insistence that freedom of belief includes every form in which it may be expressed or refused expression makes it also an affirmation of free speech on any and all subjects, whether in speech or print. It points toward article one of the Bill of Rights in the 1787 Constitution of the United States.

Like its message, the language of the Bill for Protection of Religious Liberty and the authority for its claims are nonsectarian. Jefferson begins with a sweeping claim: "Well aware that the opinions and belief of men depend not on their own will, but follow involuntarily the evidence proposed to their minds; that Almighty God hath created the mind free, and manifested his supreme will that free it shall remain by making it altogether insusceptible of restraint." An effort by sectarian legislators to add the phrase that this was "the plan of Jesus Christ, the holy author of our religion" was successfully resisted. Sectarian theology of any sort, Jefferson believed, was inappropriate in a bill about universal religious freedom. George Mason had included in his Virginia Declaration of Rights a plea for "Christian forbearance, love and charity towards each other." Jefferson wanted his document to have no hint of biblical quotation, let alone specific reference to Christianity or any belief system. When the bill finally passed, it barely survived another attempt to insert the sectarian language Jefferson had rejected in his original draft.

His own beliefs were deistic, unitarian, and rationalist. Jesus to him was a powerful teacher of ethics, not a divinity or a worker of miracles. And Jefferson's bill protected the privacy of his own nonsectarian Deism. Later, some of his political opponents would damn him as an "infidel," by which they meant a non-Christian. That Jefferson knew that the United States was overwhelmingly populated by Christians was relevant only in regard to the promotion of tolerance among different sects. That was a subdivision of the argument for establishing universal tolerance by law. Jefferson's notes in preparation for the writing of the bill make that clear: the bill was intended to provide Jews, Catholics, Muslims, Hindus, and any other belief system freedom of conscience, worship, and speech.

In a series of clauses denouncing the attempts of religious institutions to limit the "natural right" to freedom of thought, Jefferson created a cascading series of phrases unified into a single sentence by semicolons. That long but well-modulated and rhythmically ascending sentence leads to the climactic resolution: "We the General Assembly of Virginia do enact" a bill that rejects any infringement on the natural right of freedom of conscience and religious expression. Because "to compel a man to furnish contributions of money for the propagation of opinions which he disbelieves *and abhors*, is sinful and tyrannical . . . that our civil rights have no dependence on our religious opinions, any more than our opinions in physics or geometry; that therefore the proscribing any citizen as unworthy the public confidence by laying upon him an incapacity of being called to offices of trust . . . unless he profess or renounce this or that religious opinion, is depriving him injuriously of those privileges and advantages to which, in common with his fellow citizens, he has a natural right; that it tends also to corrupt the principles of that *very* religion it is meant to encourage, by bribing, with a monopoly of worldly honors and emoluments, those who will externally profess and conform to it . . . *that the opinions of men are not the object of civil government, nor under its jurisdiction. . . . For truth is great and will prevail if left to herself; that she is the proper and sufficient antagonist to error, and has nothing to fear from the conflict unless by human interposition disarmed of her natural weapons, free argument and debate; errors ceasing to be dangerous when it is permitted freely to contradict them."*

This is one of Jefferson's most idealistic claims. It is precisely, concisely, and effectively phrased, an example of Jefferson the writer at his exclamatory best. As in the Declaration, the author avoids defining his fundamental terms. "Truth" is self-evident. For Jefferson, it is a fundamental assumption in the context of "natural rights." It is a given of hope, desire, and conviction. It cannot be defined or applied other than by assertion. Ironically, though an apostle of the primacy of reason, of the analytic mind, Jefferson claims rather than demonstrates or proves that there are universal "truths." But he needs them. And his language and assertions imply that, in the case of religious freedom, he knows what these truths are. He engages in no attempt to prove that they exist. His preference, as usual, is for sweeping assertion. A claim that freedom of conscience is necessary for the peaceful functioning of a society based on republican principles might in theory have been sufficient. Implementation, not theory, was at issue. But Jefferson believed in "natural rights," even though it was disputed what they exactly were and to whom they applied. Religious tolerance, for Jefferson and his contemporaries, had to have a basis in something less relativistic than social utility. "Self-evident" truths are required, and truth, in a free society, Jefferson believes, will always in the end triumph, a claim American history has not always confirmed.

————

Inevitably, the war came to Virginia. Norfolk was totally destroyed on January 1, 1776, by shelling from the British navy. The Virginia militia was preoccupied with looting the property of British loyalists. Fires incinerated the town's buildings. After that, the British sailed away. Thereafter, the war was fought at a distance, though it seemed likely that at some point Virginia would again become the target of a British invasion. It did not come until May 1779. Brutal battles were fought to the north. General Washington learned to fight an evasive and defensive war. Time and geography favored the Americans, and the long-hoped-for military alliance with France came in January 1778. It was a negotiation that, if he had not declined the appointment, Jefferson would have participated in. Brutal battles were also fought to the south, in Georgia and South Carolina. In June 1779, Jefferson was elected governor by his legislative colleagues. In a contested election, his friend John Page came in a close second. "It had given me much pain," Jefferson wrote to him, "that the zeal of our respective friends should ever have placed you and me in the situation of competitors. I was comforted however with the reflection that it was their competition, not ours, and that the difference of the numbers which decided between us, was too insignificant to give you a pain or me a pleasure. . . ."

Jefferson soon had reason to wish the numbers had been reversed. The Virginia constitution of 1776 mandated a weak executive and a strong legislature. The governor served a one-year term, limited to two reelections. And the job was semi-impossible. It was an office with heavy responsibilities, especially in wartime, and little power. Its governing structure discouraged decisiveness and speed.

From the start, Jefferson expressed his wish to be out of office as soon as possible. In June 1780, the reluctant governor allowed himself to be reelected, though with strong misgivings. He considered resigning, and he urged John Page to run in the next election. "Should you resign, you will give me great Uneasiness," Page responded, "and will greatly distress your Country." He was persuaded not to resign. By the end of the year, Page and others were pleading with him to accept a third term. "I know your Love of Study and Retirement must strongly solicit you to leave the Hurry, Bustle, and Nonsense your station daily exposes you to," Page wrote to him. "I know too the many mortifications you must meet with, but 18 Months will soon pass away." And he assured the dubious Jefferson that "all who know you know how eminently qualified you are to fill" the position. Actually, Jefferson was in a position for which he was not well suited. The demands of the office, with few support services, during what was simultaneously a revolution and a civil war, in circumstances in which Virginia had to be self-sustaining and also had to contribute to the national effort, put more strain on Jefferson's administrative competence than any office he was to hold in the future.

Daily executive decisions had to be approved by a Privy Council created by the legislature. Jefferson spent much of his time trying to supply arms and men to the patriot armies to the south and north. That required constant letters and memos about horses, wagons, tents, and food to almost every county leader and militia head; letters to the Continental military to explain why he could not supply as much as they had asked for or anything at all; letters about every conceivable supply problem; memos and records about who was being paid what and in what currency; letters about debt and inflation; letters, memos, and legislative conflicts about taxation, expenditures, and misuse of public money by traders, hoarders, and speculators; the need to raise money when there was barely any hard specie and paper currency quickly lost value; letters about whether or not Virginia should issue its own paper currency, which it did—the state motto on one issue was SIC SEMPER TYRANNIS ("Thus always to tyrants," the words of John Wilkes Booth in Ford's Theatre in April 1865); letters between Jefferson and his peers about the war itself, its dismal prospects, and their hopes for better; letters to persuade people to fill

positions; the exhortations and threats necessary to keep the war machine supplied; and letters to mollify and coordinate proud, prickly,
ambitious members of the military command who argued among
themselves as much as they fought the enemy. He had so "many letters of absolute necessity to write," he wrote to Richard Henry Lee,
"and an innate aversion to that kind of business." There was enough
administrative chaos, even in the keeping of records, to make Jefferson miserable.

Jefferson spent much of his time attempting to cajole and coerce
Virginians to support the war effort financially. The only material
resources were in the counties. Each was frequently called on to semi-
beggar itself in order to supply the Virginia militias, Washington's
Northern army, and the Southern armies. And if the Revolution
failed, how would Virginia be reimbursed for expenses requested by
Congress? If it succeeded, where would Congress get money, since it
had no power to raise revenue by taxation? Perhaps the national government would raise money by selling Western lands. But would the
states relinquish these territories? And, if so, would their sale provide enough revenue to repay the money spent on the war, most of
which had been borrowed from individuals and private banks, and
underwritten by promissory notes authorized by the state legislatures? Jefferson frequently had pen in hand, attempting to maintain
an accurate record of the state's financial transactions, attempting to
raise money through taxation, borrowing, printing money, and requisitioning war materials, like horses, from its own citizens, with the
promise to repay. How these debts were to be repaid was murky and
uncertain.

Jefferson's frequent communications with his boards of trade and
war indicate how much Virginia operated as a quasi-independent nation. The governor had the responsibilities of the chief executive of an
independent country managing its own domestic and foreign affairs.
At the same time, the state's policies needed to be coordinated with

the Confederation Congress. Congress could only make requests, not issue directives. Virginia had to respond to these requests, but it also needed to raise the money to pay for them.

This arrangement meant not only that Jefferson had to write more letters, but also that he had to make decisions usually reserved to a sovereign nation, including choices about trade, currency, and defense. Jefferson negotiated directly with the governor of Spanish Louisiana. The French envoy requested that French citizens and property be given special protection and privileges. In effect, Virginia was acting as a semiautonomous country. It had already been a partly self-governing colony. The conditions of the Revolution further encouraged the sense in Virginia that it was its own country and that its residents defined themselves first and foremost as Virginians, a mind-set that was to have long-term consequences. Jefferson, harried, overworked, anxious, and fearful, found himself with a range of responsibilities usually reserved to the leader of a sovereign state. He did it well enough, given the demands placed on him in a system set up to give the governor limited power and considering how foreign to his interests was creating and running a statewide military machine.

In 1776, Jefferson proposed that the state capital be moved to Richmond, farther inland and less vulnerable to attack from the sea. It also would give legislators to the west of the Tidewater, like Jefferson, easier access. It would make Monticello about sixty-five miles closer to the state capital, reducing travel time to about two days. The bill was defeated. In 1778 a similar bill was passed, the advantages of distance from the coast and a midstate location outvoting Williamsburg's historical and architectural attractions. The removal took place in March 1778. With about a few hundred people, Richmond was a cultural and commercial vacuum. It would need to be created almost from scratch. That necessity appealed to Jefferson, who had grand ideas for architectural marvels in the classical style. In the end, it too proved vulnerable to British attack, but it also allowed for quicker, safer flight westward into undeveloped countryside, where British invaders were less likely to pursue. Jefferson was soon to find that an advantage. But quicker access to and from Monticello allowed escape and respite.

In May 1777, two years before her husband became governor, Martha Jefferson gave birth to a son. He did not live long enough to have the distinction of being named. The Jeffersons spent time together in Williamsburg and at Monticello between legislative seasons. By November, Martha was pregnant again. A second daughter, Mary, was born on the first day of August 1778. The move to Richmond made marital time more convenient, or at least more possible. And at Monticello, even during the war years, he continued trying to have the house expanded and reconstructed. He made little headway. He had "free" labor, but he needed craftsmen and artisans. He tried to get them from Baltimore and Philadelphia. Even if he had had the cash to pay them, there were none available. Anyway, why would any craftsmen agree to travel to Monticello to stay for many months, especially in wartime, when there were other opportunities and so many contingencies, some of them dangerous? Slaves did what they were instructed to do, and Jefferson had a few special slaves with close connections to the family trained to do skilled work. Still, little of what required skilled work got done.

From London, a voice spoke to him without ever being heard, an undelivered letter from his Tory cousin John Randolph, written in late October 1779, congratulating him on his election as governor. If it had been received, it might have reinforced Jefferson's awareness of some of the larger moral issues that arose. "I must take the liberty to say," Randolph wrote, "that your constituents could not have chosen a man of greater abilities to conduct their affairs, than you possess; and permit me to add my hope, that futurity may speak as favorably, of your moderation." It was a hope not entirely fulfilled. Jefferson struggled with maintaining his sense of his own honor and humanity amid the brutalities of war. There were loyalists and deserters to deal with. What to do with prisoners of war? Should the standard be an eye for an eye? He knew that atrocities were committed on both sides. Many who surrendered were murdered. American prisoners were imprisoned on rotting, stinking, rat-infested hulks in New York harbor. Most died. However the British treated American prisoners, Jefferson announced, the Americans will so treat British prisoners. He struggled with the moral dilemma. General Washington, in November 1779, expressed to Governor Jefferson the "hope with your Excellency, that there will be no necessity for a competition in cruelty with the enemy." And under the new British command "the treatment of our prisoners has been more within the line of humanity, and in general very different from that which they experienced under his predecessors." Still, few Americans struggled to be humane, and those who did rarely succeeded. Jefferson was an impressive combination of humaneness and implacability.

The war came to Monticello in a revealing way. British soldiers captured at Saratoga were imprisoned in makeshift camps in Charlottesville. Officers were privileged by the eighteenth-century code that provided comforts and exchanges for equals in rank. At Monticello, the Jeffersons treated numbers of captured officers and their families as social equals, providing hospitality, even friendship—an expression of shared class values, the notion that the upper class has more in common with the enemy elite than with friendly inferiors. Still, the British needed to know that mistreating Virginians would result in British prisoners being treated the same way—but not officers, except in the rare instance in which an exchange proved difficult to make. "We know," Jefferson wrote to George Matthews, a Virginian officer captured at Brandywine and for whom he was trying to arrange an exchange, "that ardent spirit and hatred for tyranny which brought you into your present situation will enable you to bear up against it with that firmness which has distinguished you as a soldier, and to look forward with pleasure to the day when events shall take place against which the wounded spirits of your Enemies will find no comfort even from reflections on the most refined of the cruelties with which they have glutted themselves."

Matthews spent four years on a prison ship anchored in New York harbor. The situation created difficulties of conscience and morality on both sides. In this case, Jefferson had only words to offer Matthews. Resolute and optimistic, they implied that somehow the prisoner's fate depended on his devotion to the cause and his hatred of the British. Jefferson's words can hardly have been much of a comfort. He did his best to think as little as possible about the wartime "cruelties" with which his fellow Americans had also "glutted themselves." On both sides, the moderation that Randolph hoped for was in short supply.

Randolph would have approved of his cousin's hospitality to the captured British officers as an affirmation of shared values, a brotherhood of "friendship" and free speech. "If a Difference in opinion," Randolph wrote, "was a good Ground for an Intermission of Friendship, Mankind might justly be said, to live in a State of Warfare; since the Imperfection of human knowledge, has rendered Men's Minds as various as the Author of their Being, has shaped their Persons. The Man who condemns another, for thinking differently from himself, sets up his Judgment as the Standard of Conception; wounds the great Liberty we enjoy, of thinking for ourselves; and tyrannizes over the Mind, which Nature intended should be free and unconfined. That Tyrant, I cannot suppose You, to be."

The author of the Declaration of Independence and the Virginia Statute on Religious Freedom could not have disagreed. The cousins shared philosophical and political values, part of the British governing continuum. Name-calling aside, the conflict was about implementation of those values. Randolph and his family had had their property confiscated and their bodies insulted by their fellow Virginians because he thought differently than they. That had filled him, he wrote to Jefferson, with "the highest Resentment." But "as there is Nothing which I forget so soon as an Injury; and as animosity never rankles in my Bosom, I have cast the whole into oblivion. There let it lie buried; for Implacability belongs only to the unworthy."

It was Jefferson, Randolph believed, who was being implacable and immoderate. "Independence . . . is the fixed Purpose of your Determination. Annihilation is preferable to a Reunion with Great Britain." And as an exponent of their shared values, his cousin seemed inconsistent, even hypocritical. "To support this desirable End, you have entered into an alliance with France and Spain, to reduce the Power of this Country, and make Way for the Glory of America." American ambition for national sovereignty and wealth was driving the revolutionary effort, Randolph noted, even to the extent of an alliance with the enemies of the English-speaking Protestant world. "But be it remembered, that France is perfidious, Spain insignificant, and Great Britain formidable. . . . How far the French have been useful to you in America, you must be better qualified to determine than myself. Yet, I cannot avoid expressing my Wish, that you had never entered into any Engagements with them." The French "are a People . . . educated in an Aversion to the English, and hold our Constitution in the utmost Detestation. . . . Laws, they have none but such as are prescribed by the Will of their Prince. This is their only Legislature."

If he had received the letter and responded, Jefferson would have had little option other than to argue that the interests of nations sometimes give priority, especially in matters of survival, to power rather than consistency, to intemperance rather than moderation. For Jefferson and his colleagues, the alliance with absolutist Catholic France was a national necessity. Still, if it had only been a matter of necessity, it might, for Jefferson, have ended or at least diminished after the successful Revolution. Randolph touched on the paradox of what was to be Jefferson's unqualified pro-French policy. During the Revolution, it could be justified as a necessity for survival. But thereafter? For Jefferson, hatred of Great Britain and fear of its reasserting control over the United States made France a desirable long-term ally. Still, later, Jefferson and his pro-French party of the 1790s were not hesitant or even qualified in their French attachment. It had for Jefferson both a political and a personal advantage. The personal was his deep identification with French culture. The political was an anti-English strategy to thwart any attempt by Great Britain to reassert itself in North America. It was also an anti-Federalist strategy. Great Britain could be vilified as the tyrannical government that in fact the French continuum from Louis XVI to the Revolution to Napoléon more fully represented. Jefferson allowed himself to be pro-France despite its despotism in the same way that he allowed himself to be a slaveholder despite his condemnation of slavery as an institution. It was to his and his country's advantage.

Jefferson's enmity to an empire of which he had once been a loyal citizen had its most memorable reinforcement when, in early 1781, the British invaded Virginia. In May 1779, British troops briefly occupied and launched raids from Hampton Roads and Portsmouth. Another British coastal attack in December 1780 took Portsmouth and devastated nearby James River communities. The two years in which the threat of attack or of quick raids by small British units terrified the most populated area of Virginia created some of the most painfully enduring experiences of Jefferson's life. The pain had to do with the facts themselves: the inadequacy of resources, the failures of the legislature, the excessive demands on Jefferson's energy and time, his distaste for personal and professional conflict, his lack of military experience, and the accusation afterward that, as governor, he had been either incompetent or cowardly or both.

New York and Boston were occupied by the British. The Royal Navy controlled the coastline. Virginians anxiously peered eastward. A French fleet was on its way, but the wait seemed interminable, subject to wind and weather and to long delays due to accident and sickness. It was a constant concern that the British fleet, not the French, might appear on the horizon, at a destination that could not be determined until its masts suddenly materialized, small vertical sticks that grew larger and larger, its cannons pointing shoreward. Jefferson had good reason to worry about an attack from the sea, but there was no certainty. Information and resources were stretched thin. As battles raged outside Virginia, the Continental Army had a strategic advantage: the British could not hold the countryside, and the British supply depot was three thousand miles away. By 1778 the British had determined to squeeze Virginia into submission by an army moving northward from Georgia and an army and fleet moving southward from New York. At the end of 1778, Savannah fell to the British. They occupied Charleston in spring 1780. In order to protect Virginia, Jefferson needed to send southward as many men and as much military equipment as could be spared without undermining Virginia's readiness if it were attacked from the sea. Many Virginians did not give him their full cooperation. Why should they make sacrifices when their own homes and families were not yet under attack? Why should they allow their horses and crops to be requisitioned to fight an enemy whose armies were at a distance? And how could they accept in payment Virginia's printed scrip made almost valueless by inflation?

After occupying Charleston, a British army under Charles Cornwallis fought northward. Though weakened by losses and attrition, it was still a formidable force. No credible American force existed between the British and Virginia. As a legislator and then governor, starting in June 1780, Jefferson did everything in his limited power to reinforce the American army trying to halt the British advance and to shore up Virginia's own defenses. Virginia brigades were serving in the Continental armies in the North and South. Home defense was minimal, subject to calling up militias if and when needed. Jefferson and his colleagues resented the fact that Virginia gave more to the war effort outside Virginia than Congress gave to Virginia. Its own time of need seemed imminent.

A committee drew up a protest to Congress. "But when we came to look for our Northern allies, after we had thus exhausted our powers in their defence, when Carolina and Georgia became the theatre of the war, they were not to be found." It was an early expression of the Southern belief that the North had exploited and would continue to exploit the South. It was also an accusation of betrayal. The Northern states had broken, the remonstrance claimed, or least deviated from the Philadelphia agreement for mutual support and defense. It seemed an early indication that when push came to shove the North and the national government would not protect Southern institutions. Jefferson may have shared some of the anger of the committee, whose three members were later to oppose the Constitution. But he was probably among those who found the argument of the remonstrance strained, simplistic, counterproductive, and rhetorically exaggerated. The Assembly voted not to send it to Congress.

In Virginia, manpower was at a premium. Bounties were offered in notes and acreage for militia and Continental Army volunteers. Most Virginians preferred to keep their families, crops, and bodies intact. When their own county was attacked, they would, sensibly, fight or flee, as the circumstance required. But Jefferson's pleas for militia recruits never produced the numbers he asked for. And the money he got to establish communications between the coast and Richmond was insufficient to keep riders posted around the clock to report sightings. An invading army was likely to come by sea to a coastline that the undermanned and under-armed Virginians could not readily defend. But when and where? In addition, there were strong pockets of loyalists. Though loyalists and patriots in Virginia did not slaughter one another with the same vigor and barbarity as they did in the Carolinas, the Revolution in Virginia was also a civil war. That made it even harder to raise money and men. Resistance to the war was consequential. Some were indifferent as to which side won. Many preferred independence but had families and farms to look after. The legislature was bitterly divided into factions.

During his two years as governor, Jefferson had the challenge of making the Virginia war machine function. It was in constant need of parts and spare parts, of men and material. They were forthcoming only with difficulty, against obstacles of organization, availability, and corruption. The war ground down lives and property. Many who had supported independence when the British were mainly in the Northern states were increasingly reluctant to suffer, let alone die for it. Conditions both on and off the battlefield were onerous. How could Virginia be defended, Generals Friedrich von Steuben and Nathanael Greene asked, if the militia, which made up most of the fighting force, was unreliable? They asked, would Governor Jefferson and the legislature please provide reliable soldiers and the necessary materials to arm, clothe, and maintain them? There were widespread desertions. The everyday militia soldier found the battlefield a place to avoid. He had little training for it. His enlistment, forced or volunteered, was for three months or eight months, hardly enough time to do more than shoot and run. And he was likely to have a farm to tend and a family to feed, the cost of rebellion especially hard on those who lived hardscrabble lives, eking out a minimal livelihood. The foot soldiers of the county militias, especially when the war came to where they lived, had good reason to have second thoughts. Some militias refused to respond to the call to serve.

That Jefferson was able to assemble a sizable number of units for the Southern army, for the defense of Virginia in the West, and for General Steuben's attempt to attack Arnold's army at Portsmouth, speaks to his combination of effort and competence. In the face of immense obstacles, the Virginians held on. Time was on their side. So too were the French. In the end, Virginia was saved and the Revolution won by American stubbornness, British errors, French help, Dutch financing, and good luck. Jefferson's was a burdensome assignment, little suited to his temperament and talents. Despite this, he not only gave it ceaseless time and effort, but also he was having, on the whole, reasonable success in the face of almost intractable odds.

With malice aforethought, the British had appointed Benedict Arnold to lead the attack on Virginia. It came in two stages. It was not an attempt to conquer and occupy the state. It was a substantial marauding raid to disrupt if not eliminate the movement of supplies and soldiers from the North to the South, men and materials going through Virginia to the Continental forces attempting to stop Cornwallis's advance. It was also intended to create fear and chaos, to pillage, burn, and destroy, to locate loyalist allies, to paralyze Virginia's government, and to capture its leaders, especially the governor who had the added opprobrium of being the author of the Declaration of Independence. It still seemed to London that if they could defeat American armies, cut off the heads of its leaders, rouse up loyalist support, and crush patriot morale, the war could be won. A well-regarded and seasoned professional, Arnold had led the American invasion of Canada in 1776 and then plotted to turn West Point over to the British, who rewarded him with a military command. In late December 1780, Arnold's troops landed at Portsmouth. He terrorized the area but mainly remained in place. By early 1781, a decisive American victory at Cowpens in South Carolina and then a partial victory in March at Guilford Court House in North Carolina raised American spirits.

On March 20, 1781, a sizable British fleet with three thousand troops arrived at Portsmouth. It brought the formidable General William Phillips, who had been appointed to replace Arnold, who never had the full trust of the British. Just as Virginia had not defended Portsmouth against Arnold, it had no ability to defend it against the new commander. Communications from the coast to Richmond were unreliable. False reports and rumors kept Jefferson and his government confused and unable to act decisively. Jefferson delayed a few days, unsure if, when, and where the British fleet would arrive or had arrived. The fleet had the initiative. On April 18, Phillips's army, helped by a favorable wind and tide, sailed up the James River, catching the Americans by surprise, killing, looting, and burning on their way to Richmond. Jefferson ordered that state documents and armaments be hidden or removed and the city be evacuated. The British were about to occupy the state capital.

Jefferson rode northwestward to Monticello. His family was already there. It did not include his youngest child, Lucy Elizabeth. The five-month-old had died in Richmond on April 15, one month before the British arrived. Jefferson made note of the loss with characteristic terseness. "Our daughter Lucy Elizabeth died about 10. o'clock A.M. this day." Since "Mrs. Jefferson [is] in a situation in which I would not wish to leave her, I shall not attend [to public duties] today." The months of April and May 1781 were exhausting and miserable for him. He had had by now more than enough of the demands of being governor. On June 3, 1781, he resigned. His timing astounded his legislative colleagues. Why did he not wait until the legislature could meet and elect a replacement? Many had hoped that he would run for another term. Others were glad to see him go. Jefferson could have announced that he would continue to serve until a replacement was in place; or that he would accept election provided that as soon as the emergency had decreased or been eliminated he would resign with the understanding that the legislature would replace him immediately. Under the circumstances, his absenting himself from the governorship even by the legal and legitimate action of not putting himself forward for reelection—which could not have occurred immediately anyway, since the legislature was dispersed—left the state without a governor at this time of military crisis.

On June 12, his critics opened an inquiry into the conduct of the executive during the last twelve months. A faction, probably guided by Patrick Henry, introduced a motion of censure, citing his failure to call up the militia promptly enough to defend against the invasion. It did not focus on his questionable decision to abandon the governorship in the midst of an armed conflict and with the legislature dispersed, without a replacement in place. Later in the year, he was to be fully acquitted of the charge. It was acknowledged that he had done well under onerous conditions. He was also, between the lines, accused of cowardice for having left Richmond prematurely. It was not a sustainable charge, and he was not a military leader. He was not, in the traditional Virginian and frontier sense, even a fighting man, either with his fists or a gun. He was a capable peacetime governor, diligent, responsible, sensible, intellectually precise and thoughtful in all his administrative duties, but not a warlord. On the other hand, he could write tirelessly, endlessly, a talent that the situation required.

In early June 1781, fleeing from Richmond, Jefferson's colleagues had thought Charlottesville would be a safe haven. General Phillips, though, had already dispatched troops, led by Colonel Banastre Tarleton, to capture as many of Virginia's leaders as possible, especially the governor. Tarleton almost succeeded. From Monticello, Jefferson could see British troops in Charlottesville capturing slow-moving legislators. Warned that he was the next target, with minutes to spare he rode southwestward into the woods toward Poplar Forest, the ninety-mile-distant estate his wife had inherited from her father. His family was already there. For his enemies, it was another instance of Jefferson fleeing from the British. He was to remain a private citizen for the rest of the war.

In December 1781, he returned to Richmond to defend his

reputation as governor. The delegates, after hearing him, voted him a commendation of thanks. He appreciated the commendation but forever resented the charge. Fortunately, the June raid on Monticello had left minimal damage. Another of his plantations, Elk Hill, was ravaged. "I had had time to remove most of the effects out of the house," he wrote in 1788, but Cornwallis "destroyed all my growing crops of corn and tobacco, he burned all my barn . . . having first taken what corn he wanted, he used, as was to be expected, all my stocks of cattle, sheep, and hogs for the sustenance of his army, and carried off all the horses capable of service: of those too young for service he cut the throats, and he burnt all the fences on the plantation, so as to leave it an absolute waste. He carried off also about 30 slaves: had this been to give them freedom he would have done right, but it was to consign them to inevitable death from the small pox and putrid fever then raging in his camp."

Jefferson had had enough of being governor as long ago as before the start of his second one-year term. He had made others aware that he wanted out of the job as soon as possible. It's fair to say that the demands of the governorship, with few support services during a rebellion and a civil war, in circumstances in which Virginia had to rely on its own resources for self-defense and also had to contribute to the national effort, put more strain on Jefferson's competence than any office he was to hold in the future. His enemies had had a weak case when they charged him with dereliction of duty because he had not promptly enough called up the militia to defend Richmond. A less prudent, less deliberate man might have acted more swiftly. But he had had reason to hesitate. He wanted solid intelligence about the enemy and its movements. Still, caution and deliberativeness were not assets in this situation. And whose ships could those possibly have been, and whose forces could they have contained? They couldn't have been American; they were not likely to have been French. How could one not have concluded that it was a British fleet intending to invade

Virginia? Jefferson had a right to want more intelligence. Still, he was remiss in not acting on the probable and requisitioning the militia immediately. His hesitancy, though, is understandable. He had been painfully schooled in the reality of the impoverished Virginia war chest and the difficulty of mustering and keeping militia in the field. He did not want to waste the state's limited resources. He wanted some certainty about the nature and direction of the invading forces. He got it, but too late to save himself from criticism. He now had an additional reason to wish he had never been governor at all.

His bitterness at the charges made against him was not then or ever assuaged. From far inland, he learned in October 1781 of the decisive American victory at Yorktown, which, it was thought, would probably result in a peace treaty recognizing independence. It may be fair to say that the American victory in the Revolution was the result of British incompetence, bad luck, and bad judgment, French military assistance, loans from France and Holland, American endurance, and Washington's defensive strategy. Time was on the side of the patriots. So was the size of the colonies, the Western territories, and the Indian situation. The longer the patriots could hold out, sustaining loss of life and property, and as long as they could suppress the loyalists, the more likely the political and financial leaders of Great Britain would want to cut their losses. There were better ways to deal with their national debt than continuing to pour money into what London now believed was an unwinnable war. Better to make peace with its major trading partner. Great nations forgive and forget when it is in their interest to do so. Jefferson never forgave Great Britain, however. He was also never to forgive the attempt to censure him. In the heat of political warfare in the 1790s, responding to attacks on his character, he was to make public in his defense a diary kept in 1781 and other documents. If he had remained as governor through the Battle of Yorktown, he might have been given some share in the glory and the ending of the war. It would have put further back into the shadows what history has mostly forgotten: the attempt to censure him. That perhaps might have softened his resentment at the accusations.

Soon after he arrived at Poplar Forest in June 1781, no longer governor and immobilized by an injury after falling from his horse, he became immersed in another project of a vastly different kind, one that he was much better suited to undertake than wartime governor. The secretary to the French legation to the United States, François Barbé-Marbois, asked Jefferson in late 1780, as he asked all state governors, to help America's French allies learn more about his state by answering a series of questions. "I am at present busily employed . . . without his knowing it," Jefferson wrote, "and have to acknowledge to him the mysterious obligation for making me much better acquainted with my own country than I ever was before." He was taking "every occasion which presents itself of procuring answers." Still, he needed a sustained period at Monticello "where alone the materials exist which can enable any one to answer them." In March 1781, he had anticipated that he would be "in a condition when it shall certainly be one of my first undertakings to give you as full information as I shall be able to do on such of the subjects as are within the sphere of my acquaintance." By mid-June 1781, he was free from public responsibilities. He now had ample time to research and write. It was to be an off-again on-again writing project that went through various stages between 1781 and 1785. *Notes on the State of Virginia* was to be the first and only book Jefferson ever wrote, a unique, idiosyncratic, and autobiographical masterpiece of American literature.

CHAPTER SIX

Unmeasurable Loss

1781–1782

At Monticello, before his flight to Poplar Forest in June 1781 and before starting to write *Notes on the State of Virginia*, Jefferson made an impressive contribution to a new literary genre that hardly existed before and was to exercise the pens of American presidents for over the next hundred years: addresses and proclamations to American Indian peoples, especially heads of tribes. The subject was usually land, land, land. After all, Native Americans had been in possession of every bit of North American soil before any white settler had arrived on the continent. The conflict over ownership of land between the Appalachians and the Mississippi that had begun with the first settlements was made even more intense by the Revolution. One of the motivations for rebellion had been the British attempt to limit American settlement to the east of the Appalachians. It seemed best to London to keep the white and red inhabitants of North America geographically apart. Otherwise, there would be endless wars about possession, at great cost to Great Britain. Americans wanted the lands the Indians possessed, and the people themselves were in the process of taking them, regardless of whatever anybody else thought, said, or decreed.

Jefferson was briefly open to purchasing Western land for himself. Elite Virginians were keen on becoming richer through land acquisition, almost always for low or nominal payment, unkept promises of payment or coexistence, or simply by force. Politically influential landowners, like George Washington and George Mason, joined syndicates dedicated to buying huge tracts for development, rent, or sale. In 1776 or 1777, Jefferson recalled, he had "consented" to join some friends "in an application for [Western] lands." His partners dropped the scheme. In 1783, he was invited to invest in a company created by ex-governor Abner Nash of North Carolina, now a delegate to the Confederation Congress. The land, in western North Carolina, extended to the Mississippi and belonged to the Cherokee, among other tribes. "He has proposed to me," Jefferson wrote to his brother-in-law, a land syndicate "which I think is hopeful and great and which he desires may be entirely secret. I have never adventured in this way in my own country because being concerned in public business I was ever determined to keep my hands clear of every concern which might at any time produce an interference between private interests and public duties." Its property would be about two million acres. Each share would be "more than a hundred thousand acres. . . . He has admitted me a share, and I have got him to let yourself Mr. Skipwith and Mr. Lewis in for another share if you chuse it." Jefferson instructed Francis Eppes to raise money for his purchase. The transaction apparently never occurred. In 1784, he stated that he had withdrawn from the scheme.

The Revolution created a new reality for the Indian tribes, defined by blood and bodies. Which tribes would enter into alliance with the British, which ally with the Americans, and which stay neutral? Each alternative had life-and-death consequences. The Revolution, a battle for the independence of the thirteen colonies, was also a battle for possession of the land to the west and northwest. Virginians believed their royal charter extended infinitely westward, at least to the

Mississippi and beyond, perhaps as far as the Western ocean that very few Americans alive in 1775 were ever to see. Now, for Jefferson and his colleagues, it was essential to the success of their Revolution that every means of persuasion be used to prevent Indian tribes from siding with the British on what Americans had already begun to think of as their land. "Persuasion" meant words, threats, or, if necessary, genocide. Jefferson favored words, though that was not always what his mood and his fears recommended. Beginning in 1776, the western borders of Virginia, Pennsylvania, and New York and the territory between the established American settlements and the Mississippi, extending to Michigan, became a brutally contested battleground. The war to the west was as great a danger to Virginia and other states as the war on the Atlantic coast. The Indian tribes fighting on the British side needed to be pacified, turned, or annihilated.

From Philadelphia in August 1776, Jefferson expressed his resolve to John Page: "I am sorry to hear that the Indians have commenced war. . . . Nothing will reduce those wretches so soon as pushing the war into the heart of their country. But I would not stop there. I would never cease pursuing them while one of them remained on this side the Mississippi." He had the assurance of the self-righteous about a just war. "I hope the Cherokees will now be driven beyond the Mississippi. . . . This then is the season for driving them off. . . ." The United States was at war with those tribes that allied with the British. They had to be defeated.

But this was also an opportunity to drive them off their land, vacating it for possession and settlement by Americans, a convenient conjunction of self-defense, independence, and expansion. Its progress was complicated by disagreements about which states the Western lands belonged to. Those that had no historical claim required as a condition for the establishment of the new nation that all states benefit equally from the sale of land. First, though, those territories had to be secured and independence won.

In 1779, as governor, Jefferson had responsibility for Virginia's war to the west. His vehicle of advancement toward Ohio and then Detroit was George Rogers Clark, a surveyor, land entrepreneur, and Virginia militia officer whom Jefferson sent westward to fight against the British and their Indian allies. The intent was to establish American dominance from Ohio to Illinois. At the beginning of 1780, he gave Clark his orders: "The end proposed" for these Indian tribes "should be their extermination, or their removal beyond the lakes or Illinois river. The same world will scarcely do for them and us . . . and therefore the object of the war should be their total extinction, or their removal beyond the lakes or the Illinois river and peace."

Military necessity required removal or annihilation, he argued. "We have reason to believe," he wrote Clark,

> that a very extensive combination of British and Indian savages is preparing to invest our western frontier. To prevent the cruel murders and devastations which attend the latter species of war and at the same time to prevent its producing a powerful diversion of our force from the southern quarter . . . it becomes necessary that we aim the first stroke in the western country and throw the enemy under the embarrassments of a defensive war rather than labor under them ourselves. We have therefore determined that an expedition shall be undertaken under your command in a very early season of the approaching year into the hostile country beyond the Ohio, the principal object of which is to be the reduction of the British post at Detroit, and incidental to it the acquiring possession of Lake Erie. . . . If that Post be reduced we shall be quiet in future on our frontiers, and thereby immense Treasures of blood and Money be saved; we shall be at leisure to turn our whole force to the rescue of our eastern Country from subjugation, we shall divert through our own Country a branch of commerce which the European States have thought worthy of the most important struggles

and sacrifices, and in the event of peace . . . we shall form to the American union a barrier against the dangerous extension of the British Province of Canada and add to the Empire of liberty an extensive and fertile Country thereby converting dangerous Enemies into valuable friends.

This is Jefferson at his administrative best, with detailed instructions and a vision of how to accomplish a project, with a clear understanding of what the success of the venture would mean for the safety of Virginia and the American union. It is also a prime example of Jefferson's mastery of the eloquence of precision and restraint, his use of language to clarify and inspire at the same time as he analyzes and instructs. Explicit, aspirational, and dramatic, it also reveals the hypocrisies of Jefferson's and his contemporaries' definitions of the "Empire of liberty." In Jefferson's view, this Western campaign against the British and their Indian allies was not only to defend but to extend the American empire. To them, "liberty" did not apply to slaves and natives, even those who allied themselves with the American insurrectionists. In theory, the inhabitants of the Western territories would be small independent farmers, the backbone of American republicanism. In practice, this empire was to be created and managed by elites with large holdings of land accumulating the wealth that the land produces. It is Jefferson's late-eighteenth-century version of capitalism, which rewards "investment" (conquest) with possession and wealth. Small farmers and large investors, Jefferson implies, are compatible stakeholders. This "Empire" would provide liberty for all its white male American inhabitants.

Jefferson shared the widespread American genocidal anger against Indian tribes that sided with the British, but he also shared the view of William Christian, a brother-in-law of Patrick Henry, that some measure of justice and fairness was needed to leaven territorial greed. "The only great Inducements the Indians can have for treating are for us to do them Justice respecting their Land." After all, once independence had been successfully defended, the creation of an "Empire of liberty" required negotiations between the Indian warrior-hunting culture and the American agricultural culture, communal forest and grassland versus individually owned acres of farmland. At best, these "dangerous enemies" could be converted into "valuable friends." A means of communication between those who had no language (and few concepts) in common needed to be developed. As an amateur ethnologist, Jefferson tried to learn as much as he could about Indian languages, though he never learned to speak any of them. As a substitute for direct verbal communication, he and his contemporaries developed a particular genre that American political leaders and their representatives used in addressing Native Americans. A kind of "Indian-speak," its tone and words combined ostensible respect with condescension, persuasion with coercion, and unity with separation. It often used racial stereotypes to appeal to universalist concepts. It was often a language of hyperbole and dissimulation. At its worst, it was an unintentionally parodic use of English to express what Americans thought Indians could understand, a form of contemptuous stereotyping. It became a genre of its own, mostly confined to those assigned by the government and its people to persuade Indian chiefs and their tribes to be what most Americans wanted them to be: compliant or dead.

During the last days of his governorship, the legislature having reassembled in Charlottesville, Jefferson hosted a delegation of visiting Illinois Indians. John-Baptiste Ducoigne, their chief, was the mixed-race son of an Indian and a Frenchman. He and Jefferson already knew each other well enough for Ducoigne to have named his son Jefferson. Aggressively pro-American and anti-British, Ducoigne was to stay in Virginia long enough to join Lafayette's army as part of the American forces that trapped Cornwallis at Yorktown. Later, in Illinois, he experienced some of the results of his deracination at the hands of Indians who viewed him not only as a half-breed but as a traitor to his own people.

For Jefferson, in June 1781, with the British breathing down the necks of Virginians, with the war for independence in the balance, the opportunity to make a speech to Ducoigne and his other Indian guests was opportune. He took the time to write it out, his pen probably at work the previous night and even that morning. The speech was a contribution to the war effort, propaganda of persuasion to encourage an ally to continue steadfast. Stick with us, and you will be rewarded. And take my words to other tribes; tell them that they should fight with us against the British or at least remain neutral. His address to Ducoigne, unlike his addresses to Indian tribes during his presidency, assumes that Ducoigne has enough command of English for Jefferson to minimize Indian-speak, and Ducoigne was to translate Jefferson's words to his fellow Indians. The genre appears mostly in the syntax and word choice. The "Great White Father" and his Indian "children" are not yet part of the language of the genre, or at least Jefferson saw no reason for such phrases at this time, except for the reference to Louis XVI as "your old father, the King of France."

We, like you, are Americans, born in the same land, and having the same interests. . . . I have joined with you sincerely in smoking the pipe of peace; it is a good old custom handed down by your ancestors, and as such I respect and join in it with reverence. . . . You find us, brother, engaged in war with a powerful nation. Our forefathers were Englishmen, inhabitants of a little island beyond the great water, and, being distressed for land, they came and settled here. As long as we were young and weak, the English whom we had left behind, made us carry all our wealth to their country, to enrich them; and, not satisfied with this, they at length began to say we were their slaves, and should do whatever they ordered us. We were now grown up and felt ourselves strong; we knew we were free as they were, that we came here of our own accord . . . and were determined to be free as long as we should exist. For this reason they made war on us. . . . Your old father, the King of France, has joined us in the war, and done many good things for us. We are bound forever to love him, and wish you to love him, brother, because he is a good and true friend to us. . . . The English stand alone . . . hated by all mankind because they are proud and unjust. This quarrel, when it first began, was a family quarrel. . . . We, therefore, did not wish you to engage in it at all. We are strong enough of ourselves without wasting your blood in fighting our battles. The English, knowing this, have been always suing to the Indians to help them fight. We do not wish you to take up the hatchet. We love and esteem you. We wish you to multiply and be strong. The English, on the other hand, wish to set you and us to cutting one another's throats, that when we are dead they may take all our land. . . . If the English do you any injury you have a right to go to war with them, and revenge the injury, and we have none to restrain you. Any free nation has a right to punish those who have done them an injury. . . . But if they have not injured you, it is better for you to lie still and be quiet. This is the advice which has been always given by the great council of the Americans. We must give the same, because we are but one of thirteen nations, who have agreed to act and speak together. These nations keep a council of wise men always sitting together, and each of us separately follow their advice. They have the care of all the people and the lands between the Ohio and Mississippi, and will see that no wrong be committed on them. . . . The Americans alone have a right to maintain justice in all the lands on this side the Mississippi.

Jefferson promised that the Americans would take care of the natives.

You complain, brother, of the want of goods for the use of your people. We know that your wants are great, notwithstanding we have done everything in our power to supply them, and have often grieved for you. . . . I will tell you honestly, what indeed your own good sense will tell you, that a nation at war cannot buy so many goods as when in peace. We do not make so many things to send over the great waters to buy goods, as we made and shall make again in time of peace. . . . But peace is not far off. The English cannot hold out long, because all the world is against them. When that takes place, brother, there will not be an Englishman left on this side the great water. What will those foolish nations then do, who have made us their enemies . . . and laughed at you for not being as wicked as themselves? They are clothed for a day, and will be naked forever after; while you, who have submitted to short inconvenience, will be well supplied through the rest of your lives. Their friends will be gone and their enemies left behind; but your friends will be here, and will make you strong against all your enemies.

Jefferson concluded by addressing Ducoigne directly.

You ask us to send schoolmasters to educate your son and the sons of your people. We desire above all things, brother, to instruct you in whatever we know ourselves. We wish to learn you all our arts and to make you wise and wealthy. As soon as there is peace we shall be able to send you the best of school-masters; but while the war is raging, I am afraid it will not be practicable. It shall be done, however, before your son is of an age to receive instruction. This, brother, is what I had to say to you. Repeat it from me to all your people. . . .

It is an extraordinary speech, both sincere and duplicitous, especially in historical perspective. "I will not boast to you, brother, as the English do," Jefferson emphasizes, "nor promise more than we shall be able to fulfil." In 1780, a collaborative effort to persuade Indian tribes not to ally with the British, to remain neutral or, even better, to become allied with the patriots took precedence over all other considerations, including the American intention to create an "Empire of liberty" that required that American settlers take possession of all the land between the Appalachians and the Mississippi. The speech is burdened with hyperbole. It is wartime propaganda to assure the Indian tribes that it is in their best interest to keep the peace with those who pretend to have their best interest at heart.

Americans are "native" Americans, Jefferson claims, like the Indians, born on these lands, rather than invading strangers. Actually, a substantial percentage of Jefferson's contemporaries had been born in Europe, including his mother. Jefferson had to have known that his "Empire of liberty" would be based on the extinction of Indian culture. His lies are both astounding and understandable. He is laying the groundwork in his own mind and before the Virginia House of Delegates for the postwar future. Inherent in his presentation is the claim of the right to total possession, making some combination of eviction, sequestration, and annihilation a certainty. That the land between the Ohio Territory and the Mississippi was under the protection of the American government was a wish rather than a reality, but the intention implied control and sovereignty, i.e., ownership. "The Americans alone have a right to maintain justice in all the lands on this side the Mississippi," Jefferson asserts. Here he is edging into a policy of continental conquest. His so-called empire of liberty is an early version of Manifest Destiny. He views the Indian nations as valuable allies in the war and as malleable dependents, subject to American justice, defined as whatever Americans want.

When, in late July 1781, Jefferson and his family returned from Poplar Forest to Monticello, he had with him the manuscript which, with later additions and revisions, eventually was published as *Notes on the State of Virginia*. Apparently, he had written most of it in six weeks or so, though he had made memoranda and probably written some passages previously. The silence of Poplar Forest, his liberation from public office, and his need to stay still as he healed from his fall made his pen his best weapon. *Notes* was at first, among other things, a contribution to the war effort, though it blossomed into much more than that. Jefferson seems to have been the only one of his contemporaries who made the effort to provide more than cursory answers to the questions the secretary of the French legation, François Barbé-Marbois, had created. They had not come directly to him. In Philadelphia, Barbé-Marbois had addressed the questions to Joseph Jones, a member of the Virginia delegation to the Continental Congress. Jones forwarded the questions to Jefferson, whom he believed better equipped for the task. Jefferson's writing and research skills were well known to his colleagues. He also had the advantage of having his own research library. He probably had sent to him from Monticello relevant books and papers. And now he had time available. He assumed that he was creating a private document to be read by a select few, not a book for the public.

Notes on the State of Virginia has become a classic of a singular kind and genre. It is well known among historians and students of Jefferson, but hardly anyone else reads it, although the sections that deal with topics of modern interest attract some attention. *Notes* provides Jefferson's fullest comments on race and slavery. It has few parallels and no rivals. Its tone and exposition reflect Jefferson the naturalist and social scientist, the man interested in many things but not at all interested in writing a literary work for the general reader. It contains informative descriptions of and views about Jefferson's native state, which he loved with a nativist's passion. *Notes* was conceived and organized as a report rather than a narrative. Jefferson felt free to manipulate the topics into an order and emphasis that the questions did not require. Over time he added four appendices, one of which was the first appearance in print of An Act for Establishing Religious Freedom. Instead of chapters, *Notes* is organized into twenty-three queries, though Barbé-Marbois's list contained twenty-two. Each query has a descriptive title, from "Boundaries of Virginia," "Rivers," "Mountains" . . . to "Histories, Memorials, and State-Papers."

It is also a book about Jefferson, partly because Jefferson did not want it to be a book about himself. He did not want it to be a book at all. *Notes* is a rarity in conception and reception if judged by the usual standards of genre, cohesion, development, and unity. In June 1781, as he wrote, Jefferson did not think he was writing a book. That he called it *Notes* emphasizes his awareness that it was a disparate set of responses, at any length and depth he chose, to a series of questions, the answers to which would give the reader a substantial amount of information about Virginia. Most of it would be factual, though the facts were inevitably inseparable from interpretation and opinion. In Jefferson's hands, the questions became a subtext to an original creation. For modern readers, it is a book mainly for those already knowledgeable about Jefferson. Approached as a literary work, it is especially revealing of its author because of how much Jefferson tried to remove himself as a literary persona, to create an authorial absence. To this degree, it is autobiographical, but slantingly so. It is strikingly different from the work of classic American autobiographers, from Franklin to Grant to Henry Adams. It is a book by an author who is trying not to be autobiographical, not to be a presence himself, not to be personally revealing. In the end, he failed in that aim, but overall, that effort is the story. *Notes on the State of Virginia*, despite Jefferson's every effort to the contrary, turned out also to be *Notes on Thomas Jefferson*. It tells us a lot about its author. One of the things it tells us is that he is a strikingly fine writer.

Notes is also a political document, an attempt to communicate to the French decision makers and the Enlightenment elite of France that Virginia is a "country" to be appreciated and reckoned with. The questions were grist to the patriotic, intellectual, and scholarly mill of one of the major pro-French and anti-British leaders of the Revolution. Some of it is patriotic special pleading; some, a sales pitch to France and Europe: this is what we are, these are our resources, here is the material basis for our future relationship. It is a contribution to the revolutionary effort, the creation of a compendium of knowledge to serve the purpose of advancing the alliance, essential to the American war effort, between the United States and France. *Notes* is the contribution of a soldier who fights with his pen. His emphasis on descriptive botany, zoology, demography, geography, and ethnology is in the service of a patriotic mission. Jefferson could have answered Barbé-Marbois's questions at one-fifth the length or less. What drove his pen were, among other forces, his compulsion to be both specific and comprehensive; his love of facts, details, and lists; his pride in his state and its primacy; his objection to the claim made by the French naturalist Buffon that North America is an inferior place whose deficiencies result in less well-developed animal life and, by inference, human life, than in Europe; and his desire to do all he could to strengthen the alliance between France and the United States.

Also, as he wrote, Peter Jefferson, the surveyor, explorer, and mapmaker, the first settler of Albemarle County, the man from whom Jefferson inherited the land on which he built Monticello, had to have been on his mind. He was doing his version of what his father had done literally: he was putting Virginia on the map. The final edition of *Notes* contains as a frontispiece a reproduction of the well-known map of Virginia that his father and Joshua Fry had created in 1753. It is a map of an important part of Jefferson's life and patrimony. *Notes* both incorporates and extends his father's work. The inclusion of the map, reproduced at considerable cost, made *Notes* a collaboration between father and son. It is also an homage from son to father, a testimony to patrimony and continuity, an assertion of possession of the land, a literal extension of the actual map. It confirms and extends the map's assertion that this land is our land, in the broadest, most patriotic, and emotionally possessive sense.

For Jefferson, putting pen to paper was an act of implementation as well as abstraction. Jefferson begins *Notes* with a description of the "Boundaries of Virginia." In that sense, *Notes* contains Virginia. It is an embodiment of Virginia's reality as Jefferson saw it in 1781. It is an act of taking possession through language. Peter Jefferson's 1753 map was only of the "inhabited" part of Virginia, along with Maryland, Delaware, Pennsylvania, and portions of New Jersey, New York, and North Carolina. The Blue Ridge Mountains are its western border. Albemarle County is in almost the exact center of Virginia and the center of the map. Over thirty years old when included in *Notes*, the map could not have been intended by Jefferson to have direct relevance to the reality of Virginia in 1787 other than the topography. Its "inhabited parts" had been vastly extended. The only more recent map that Jefferson could have used had been published in Edinburgh in 1767. It also placed Albemarle County in the center of the state. Probably it had been based on the Jefferson-Fry map.

The response to Query II describes Virginia's rivers. Between the paragraph-length descriptions of the James and the York, Jefferson inserts the much-loved but insignificant river of his childhood, easily in sight from Monticello: "The *Rivanna*, a branch of the James River, is navigable for canoes and batteaux to its intersection with the South West mountains, which is about 22 miles; and may be easily opened to navigation through those mountains to its fork above Charlottesville," a much-hoped-for passageway that never opened. Jefferson loved rivers and mountains, and he loved literally to look westward from Monticello, and to a greater distance in his mind's eye. Looking westward in *Notes*, he extends his father's map and his remit to the Cumberland, the Wabash, which is "a very beautiful river," to the Monongahela and the Allegheny, all rivers he had never seen. And beyond is the Ohio, "the most beautiful river on earth. Its current gentle, waters clear, and bosom smooth." Young Samuel Clemens, who in 1857 journeyed on the Ohio to the Mississippi, had more realistic things to say about it.

Beyond the Ohio, from books and in Jefferson's mind's eye, was the Mississippi, which "will be one of the principal channels of future commerce for the country," and the Missouri, as well as New Orleans and Mexico. This was Peter Jefferson's map extended into a transcontinental map of the "Empire of liberty." In Jefferson's mind, it was not a map of territorial aggression but of American settlements and commerce. In Madrid, the custodians of the Spanish Empire, frequently at war with France, might have found this extensive view of their territories disconcerting. It implies imminent possession. In Jefferson's extended view, Virginia looks westward, limitlessly.

Two additional rivers were on his prose map, both of which he had seen, the Potomac and the Hudson. Jefferson was advancing the act of taking possession. Like numbers of his contemporaries, he believed the Potomac held the key to Virginia's future prosperity. There will be "a competition between the Hudson and Patowmac rivers for the residue of all the commerce of all the country westward of Lake Erie. . . ." He argued at length what he did not yet know was almost impossible: that the Potomac would become the major artery for the passage of goods from the Mississippi basin and the Southwest to the international market via Chesapeake Bay, with Alexandria expanding into a major port of embarkation to Europe. It would become the New York of Virginia. Unlike George Washington, he never bet money on this, but the future implied by his answer to Query II was a future that Virginians, including Jefferson, devoutly wished would become a reality. Physical barriers and then the Erie Canal took the wind out of that sail. However, in 1803 Jefferson had the chance and took it; through the agency of Lewis and Clark, he tried to transform his 1781 prose map of rivers into the poetry and prose of Western water and soil.

Much of *Notes* is a paean to Virginia's resources, history, and character, the latter with some reservations. In style, tone, and substance, it is quintessential Jefferson, both self-revealing and self-concealing. The prose is sometimes perfunctory, though always precise and accurate in word choice and syntax. He does not want himself to be in the text, to be a presence. Queries VI–X and XII, parts of XIII and XIV, XV, and XIX–XXII are essentially the facts about production, resources, climate, manufactures, commerce, revenue, and a list of his sources, the social scientist–scholar at work, a dry but useful primer to the French about all things Virginian that might be useful to bureaucrats and entrepreneurs. This is Jefferson the statistician, the man who loves facts, lists, and numbers. He takes pleasure in providing the data on which to base opinions, generalizations, and policy. It is also the Jefferson who envisions and promotes Virginia and the United States as a mighty agricultural-commercial power in the making. Its resources will make it a valuable ally and commercial partner.

Jefferson implies that he is being totally frank about Virginia's wealth and its potential growth. *Notes* is a sophisticated salesman's pitch, perfectly accurate but deceptive. "The value of our lands and slaves, taken conjunctly, doubles in about twenty years. This arises from the multiplication of our slaves, from the extension of culture, and increased demand for lands. The amount of what will be raised will of course rise in the same proportion" ("Public Revenue and Expences"). He says Virginia is rich and will be richer in the agricultural products that European markets need. It has an abundant and growing labor supply, and the value of the land, as the state population grows, doubles every twenty years. Nevertheless, Jefferson conceals numerous key facts: there is an oversupply of slave labor; the state's major crop, tobacco, had depleted the soil; much of the land is not suited for agriculture; and most of the wealth of the Virginia elite is compromised by heavy debt to British merchants and banks, so in the event of recession or depression, given the absence of specie and widespread indebtedness, the value of property will fall precipitously. Also, white Virginians, especially slaveholders, live in constant fear of slave rebellions, and the average white Virginian, the small farmer, the artisan, and the laborer, possesses only a tiny portion of the wealth. Jefferson knows much of this but deals with it by concealment, evasion, and acceptance.

His evasions are not systematic, however, and perhaps not always intentional. After all, the book is not intended to be a tell-all about Virginia. Also, Barbé-Marbois's questions provide a framework that Jefferson felt free to depart from. The departures and the length, tone, and emphasis of his answers to particular questions are his choices; they reveal what's on Jefferson's mind, what's important to him. In that sense, *Notes* is autobiographical. Three topics are of special concern to him, the Indian tribes, slavery, and race. They are also of interest to the French government, but not with the intellectual, ethnological, and moral intensity that they have for Jefferson. As an amateur ethnologist of Indian culture and customs—how they buried their dead and how they honored kinship, their sexual and reproductive values, the variety of their languages, the minimal amount of crime in their communities—Jefferson included in *Notes* all the facts he had about Indian tribes in the Eastern United States. He makes himself the memorialist and historian of peoples who mostly have no written history of their own. How did these people come to inhabit the land? Why so many distinctly different tribes and languages? Where did they come from? How long have they been here? He concludes that since "so many radical changes of language [have] taken place among the red men of America, [that] proves them of greater antiquity than those of Asia."

From early on, Jefferson had developed an interest in the differing cultures, languages, and values that the Indian tribes represented: hunters, warriors, skilled woodsmen, defenders of their land, the possessors of a linguistic and religious culture that valued honor, tribal loyalty, and personal bravery. At war, he saw them as merciless killers. At peace, they could be friends from whom one could learn. Most important, "their only controls are their manners, and that moral sense of right and wrong, which, like the sense of tasting and feeling, in every man makes a part of his nature." They are, in Jefferson's view, "aborigines" whose human nature is grounded in inherent moral feelings and natural rights. They have no legal code; they have tribal customs and a moral sense, and they prefer small and separate tribal governments to pan-tribal unity. It is questionable "whether no law, as among the savage Americans, or too much law, as among the civilized Europeans, submits man to the greatest evil." Jefferson would "pronounce it to be the last and that the sheep are happier of themselves, than under the care of the wolves. It will be said, that great societies cannot exist without government. The Savages, therefore break them into small ones." In the Revolution, or at least until the Revolution starts, the Americans are the sheep, the British the wolves; the colonies are attempting to separate themselves from the British Empire and govern themselves locally. Thus the Indian tribes already saw themselves as the sheep, no matter how many tomahawks they had, and the United States the wolf, despite Jefferson's protestations to the contrary.

Jefferson speculates about the origin of Native Americans on the assumption that they are of Asian origin. In regard to American plants, animals, and minerals, he is a categorizer, a creator of lengthy lists, an encyclopedic observer of the physical world he lives in, whose richness and variety he takes pleasure in recording. He is at ease with the plenitude of nature's gifts to the American landscape, but he is far from fully at ease with the historical dynamic of the competition between the Indian tribes and white settlement. Just as he had convinced himself that the historical record proved that American colonists were, from the first settlements, free and independent operatives, taking possession of their lands without any legal relationship to the British king or Parliament, Jefferson had another fiction to advance. It was in regard to American possession of land that had been possessed by "red Americans. . . . That the lands of this country were taken from them by conquest, is not so general a truth as is supposed. I find in our historians and records, repeated proofs of purchase . . . and many more would doubtless be found on further search. The upper country [of Virginia] we know has been acquired altogether by purchases. . . ." History does not support Jefferson's dismissal of the charge. Like most Americans, Jefferson believed that a hunting culture and an agricultural culture could not coexist, that the American "Empire of liberty" required intensive Western settlement. At best, the tribes needed to be peacefully dispossessed and pushed westward into confined spaces. The alternative was to annihilate them. In regard to Virginia, Jefferson needed to claim that, except for an occasional irregularity, the land that the settlers took possession of had been by "purchase."

The most often quoted passages in *Notes on the State of Virginia* deal with slavery and race. One of the revealing oddities of the book is that there is no section exclusively devoted to the topic, perhaps because none of the twenty-two topics on which Barbé-Marbois invited comments mentions slavery or race. He called for statistics about the number of Virginia's "inhabitants." Jefferson titled his response "Population" (Query VIII). For the topic "The administration of Justice and a description of the Laws," Jefferson titled his response "Laws" (Query XIV). When asked for comments on "The particular Customs and manners that may happen to be received in that State," Jefferson called his response simply "Manners" (Query XVIII). These three widely separated sections contain Jefferson's comments on slavery and race, a topic so important to him that he inserts it into sections in which the subject has no relevance, other than in regard to "Population." On the one hand, the subject is so challenging that he has no structural or thematic intention of highlighting it in a section of its own. On the other hand, the subject is so important that it has the subversive power to insist on asserting itself, though Jefferson's thoughts on it in *Notes* have no structural, descriptive, or argumentative cohesion. The first mention is both statistical and self-congratulatory: "the mild treatment our slaves experience." And the Virginia nonimportation act "will in some measure stop the increase of this great political and moral evil, while the minds of our citizens may be ripening for a complete emancipation of human nature." In "Laws" Jefferson sets out proposals for the revisions that he and his colleagues had worked on between 1776 and 1777, one of which is "to emancipate all slaves born after passing the acts," though he explains that "the bill reported . . . does not itself contain this provision." An amendment has been prepared that does. The Virginia legislature was never to pass the amendment, to Jefferson's disappointment and, gradually, to his resigned acceptance that the "ripening" of public opinion was not in the least imminent. Blacks will never forget their oppression; white prejudices are "deep-rooted."

Jefferson devotes most of the rest of the section to what was much on his mind: slavery and race. None of the topic headings call for this, certainly not the topic of "Laws." But Jefferson has overall reordered and reshaped the topics to reflect what interests him, what preoccupies him. Barbé-Marbois probably cared little about slavery and race in America, except in regard to Black labor as a material asset. Jefferson lived with slaves every day of his life, even intimately. He both thinks about this and represses some of his thoughts. It was for him a domestic reality and a national problem, one of whose epicenters was Virginia. Race is a distinct difference and qualifier. There are between Blacks and whites "physical and moral differences," he maintains. Blacks have distinctive physical, mental, and moral deficiencies. And Black "inferiority is not the effect merely of their condition of life."

There are reasons, he acknowledges, not to be conclusive. Much of the evidence is anecdotal and tentative. "I advance it therefore as a suspicion only, that the blacks are inferior to the whites . . . in the endowments of both body and mind." It is "a suspicion only," but it is a suspicion that, for Jefferson, exculpates slaveholders from renouncing the use of the whip, an instrument of control that Jefferson cannot live comfortably with but will live with anyway. The rationale is practical. When they are disobedient or criminal, how shall we punish them? Since, once free, they cannot remain among us, can we find a place to send them? Will property owners be compensated for their material losses? Who will pay for transport and resettlement? Because we cannot readily replace the loss of this valuable labor force, how will our crops be raised and our economy be sustained? Even with exemplary moral intentions and intellectual analysis, Jefferson, who deplores slavery, cannot liberate himself from the slavery trap: the practical complications and consequences of emancipation would shake the foundations of Southern life.

The paradox of slavery's complications, Jefferson says (Query XVIII, "Manners"), is the damage it does to slaveholders. The manners and mind-set of all Virginians, he implies, bear the burden of the effect that the master-slave relationship has on the temper of society. "There must doubtless be an unhappy influence on the manners of our people produced by the existence of slavery among us. The whole commerce between master and slave is a perpetual exercise of the most boisterous passion, the most unremitting despotism on the one part, and degrading submissions on the other. . . . Our children see this, and learn to imitate it. . . . This quality is the germ of all education in him. . . . The parent storms, the child looks on. . . . The man must be a prodigy who can retain his manners and morals undepraved by such circumstances." Virginians, Jefferson observes, tend to be arrogant, impulsive, and commanding; slavery makes the slave-owner abhor and reject "industry" (work).

With characteristic inconsistency, he then boasts that the steady increase of the slave population and consequently of slave-owners' wealth is due to "the mild treatment our slaves experience and their wholesome food," though there is a contradiction, Jefferson grants, between the values of the Revolution, that "all men are created equal," and the maintenance of slavery. How can those who hold slaves not devalue freedom as an ultimate value? "And can the liberties of a nation be thought secure when we have removed their only firm basis, that these liberties are of the gift of God?"—by which Jefferson meant that they are "natural rights." What would Barbé-Marbois, in 1781, a subject of Louis XVI, in a nation in which all gifts come from God's regent, not from "natural rights," have thought of this?

Jefferson digresses from his remit to provide practical information about Virginia when he bemoans the burden that slavery has inflicted on his country, almost as if his countrymen were victims rather than instigators. "Indeed I tremble for my country," hardly an assurance to his country's French ally, "when I reflect that God is just; that his justice cannot sleep forever. . . . The Almighty has no attribute" (surely Louis XVI did) "which can take side with us in such a contest. . . . I think," he optimistically concludes, "a change already perceptible, since the origin of the present revolution," an optimism that he could not sustain over time. He hoped his country was "preparing, under the auspices of heaven, for a total emancipation." Barbé-Marbois would come to see the irony in this, for America and for France. The French Revolution of 1789 almost put the aristocrat to the guillotine, but he lived to serve Napoléon, who likewise had no moral qualms about slavery and whom Jefferson detested for other reasons. Jefferson, who never describes the suffering and pain of individual slaves, hoped, until the hope became untenable, that "total emancipation" and colonization would be accomplished peacefully. The passages about slavery in Notes are more about Jefferson's anguish, evasion, hopes, and fears for his and his country's future because of the existence of slavery than they are about the reality of an enslaved person's life, let alone the moral and physical complexity for himself and those he owned, the slaves who were an economic and emotional part of every day of his life.

Notes has much to say about the attractions and advantages of the new country whose independence Jefferson is confident will occur. He worried about what would happen after independence, after all the words and declarations, when his vision of a republic in which the will of its citizens governed, in which legal rights and natural rights were guaranteed, had been achieved. History did not provide happy examples. His response to Query XIX ("Manufactures") triggered his almost ever-present anxiety. His first rule is stick to the land, to agriculture. He believed that those who till the soil become by that very act more moral and patriotic than those who don't. Those who congregate in cities create epicenters of greed, corruption, and illness. They are more dependent, subject to the whims and commands of the marketplace, and less likely to give priority to patriotism. "The mobs of great cities add just so much to the support of pure government, as sores do to the strength of the human body." Small towns and rural life promote domestic virtues. And in a country with many creeds the best way "to silence religious disputes, is to take no notice of them" (one of the four appendices added to *Notes* is his text for A Bill for Establishing Religious Freedom). Because America's future existence was likely to be threatened only by European sea power, no standing army would ever be necessary. Distance would prevent invasion. The best defense, in Jefferson's view, was no armed defense at all, not even American warships. Europe needed American agricultural products more than America needed European manufactures: embargo would be the best self-defense.

In Jefferson's view, the main threat was not the enemy without but the enemy within, the threat to "pure [republican] government by too much government and by corrupt government." "The spirit of the times may alter, will alter. Our rulers will become corrupt, our people careless. . . . From the conclusion of this war, we shall be going downhill. The people will forget themselves, but in the sole faculty of making money. . . . The shackles . . . will be made heavier and heavier, till our rights shall revive or expire in a convulsion." In *Notes*, Jefferson's optimism, often qualified, comes through a porous filter of fear for America's future. In its first version, the unresolved war barely inflects his mood. He believes the war will be won, but slavery casts a long shadow. The forces of irrationality and superstition also seem to Jefferson still strong. Once the republican fervor of the Revolution relaxes, what then? Jefferson hopes that republican idealism will prevail. It was a hope he would struggle to sustain.

In *Notes*, Jefferson provided Barbé-Marbois with more information than the secretary to the French legation could possibly have anticipated, but he also used the topics as the catapult by which to launch himself into the creation of a book that represents, directly and indirectly, his own concerns. It is a personal book, an expression of Jefferson's personality and also his gifts as a writer. It is structurally partly coherent, partly incoherent. Organizing a cohesive text, even in the revision process, was not his priority, though some rearranging of the topics, especially Jefferson's decision to start with geography and topography, expressed some interest, at least when he started writing, in a structural pattern, an awareness of what should come first and what topics needed to be added that did not appear on the list. Often enough, the prose represents Jefferson the statistician, the creator of lists, the social scientist, the rationalist, the intellectual. But there are two Queries, IV ("Mountains") and V ("Cascades"), in which his prose soars into creative self-expression. Within IV and V, Jefferson switches from geography and commerce to aesthetics and beauty, to what he has seen with his own eyes rather than through books and in dreams. His writing is lofty, vividly evoking the land and its natural wonders.

The facts are for Barbé-Marbois; the landscape descriptions are entirely self-expression, vivid description and powerful but controlled emotion. Perhaps the most riveting example is the description in Query IV of a site that was "worth a voyage across the Atlantic, the passage of the Patowmac through the Blue Ridge." It is a beautifully modulated combination of observation and emotion.

The Blue Ridge is perhaps one of the most stupendous scenes in nature. You stand on a very high point of land. On your right comes up the Shenandoah, having ranged along the foot of the mountain a hundred miles to seek a vent. On your left approaches the Potomac, in quest of a passage also. In the moment of their junction they rush together against the mountain, rend it asunder, and pass off to the sea. The first glance of this scene hurries our senses into the opinion, that this earth has been created in time, that the mountains had been formed first, that the rivers began to flow afterwards, that in this place particularly they have been damned up by the Blue Ridge of mountains, and have formed an ocean which filled the whole valley; that continuing to rise they have at length broken over at this spot, and have torn the mountain down from its summit to its base.... But the distant finishing which nature has given to the picture is of a very different character. It is a true contrast to the fore-ground. It is as placid and delightful, as that is wild and tremendous. For the mountain being cloven asunder, she presents to your eye, through the cleft, a small patch of smooth blue horizon, at an infinite distance in the plain country, inviting you, as it were, from the riot and tumult roaring around, to pass through the breech and participate of the calm below. Here the eye ultimately composes itself. . . . This scene is worth a voyage across the Atlantic . . . a war between rivers and mountains, which must have shaken the earth itself to its center.

In "Cascades" (Query V) he describes the *"Natural bridge,* the most sublime of Nature's works":

> It is on the ascent of a hill, which seems to have been cloven through its length by some great convulsion. You involuntarily fall on your hands and knees, creep to the parapet and peep over. Looking down from this height about a minute gave me a violent headache. This painful sensation is relieved by a short, but pleasing view of the Blue ridge along the fissure downwards . . . descending then into the valley below . . . the sensation becomes delightful in the extreme. It is impossible for the emotions, arising from the sublime, to be felt beyond what they are here: so beautiful an arch, so elevated, so light, and springing, as it were, up to heaven, the rapture of the spectator is really indescribable!

Jefferson finds correlatives in eighteenth-century lyrical prose for the emotions of his direct experience: his love of the beautiful materiality of nature and the sublime beauties of the American landscape. Each of these lyrical passages is an "effusion of the heart." In one of the appendices to *Notes,* Jefferson exclaims that he considers "social harmony as the first of human felicities, and the happiest moments those which are given the effusions of the heart."

With manuscript in hand, about one-third the size of the book he eventually published, Jefferson returned to Monticello in late July 1781. A private citizen, he resumed his domestic life with his usual commitment. He had a rendezvous with the legislature in Richmond, set for late December, to defend himself against the charge, created by political enemies, that he had been derelict in his duty to defend the state against British attack. He spent time preparing his defense. Before the legislative bar, now once again a member representing Albemarle, he spoke decisively and energetically. The Assembly unanimously voted him a commendation of thanks for his stewardship. That was satisfying but insufficient to erase the anger he felt at what were politically inspired charges. That he had been forced to defend himself was, he felt, an insult to his honor and competence. It exemplified how nasty politics could be, a reminder of the difficulty of serving two passions at the same time: private life and public service. Even unanimous vindication left a sour taste in his mouth. Always distressed by even the hint of criticism, he needed during his entire public career to reconcile his view of himself as above reproach and his realization that criticism was a given in political life.

In May 1782, he declined the opportunity to be reelected. Apparently intent on having his services, the Assembly appointed him to a committee to report on Virginia's ownership of Western land, part of the ongoing attempt by Virginia to strengthen its hand in the discussion among the states about boundaries, ownership, and profiteering on this valuable asset at the end of the war, assuming American victory.

After returning from Poplar Forest, he was unexpectedly presented in July 1781 with a second chance to go to France. His supporters in Congress had appointed him to join Benjamin Franklin, John Jay, and Henry Laurens to represent the United States in peace negotiations. Congress balanced two Northerners with two Southerners. Immediate departure would be required. For the second time, he declined. If it "were possible for me to determine again to enter into public business there is no appointment whatever which would have been so agreeable to me. But I have taken my final leave of everything of that nature, have retired to my farm, my family and books from which I think nothing will ever more separate me." This time he did not keep the messenger waiting three days. Franklin wrote to him from Paris that "I was in great Hopes when I saw your Name in the

Commission for treating of Peace, that I should have had the Happiness of seeing you here, and of enjoying again in this World, your pleasing Society and Conversation. But I begin now to fear that I shall be disappointed."

Jefferson felt that he was more needed and obligated at Monticello than in Richmond or Paris. It seemed inconceivable that Martha, who had never left Virginia, could leave home and cross the Atlantic. The only son born to them had lived only a few weeks. The daughter named after his mother had died in infancy. Five-month-old Lucy Elizabeth had died in mid-April 1781, only three months before the family's return to Monticello. Her loss must have been painfully felt by both of them. In the summer of 1781, his wife would have been grieving. Their two living daughters were eight and two years old. Now thirty-two years of age, Martha had been pregnant and delivered children in five of the nine years of their marriage, in addition to her pregnancy in her previous marriage. It was a typical pattern for wives of late-eighteenth-century Virginians. Birth control, except that which nature provided, was not practiced. Children were desirable, especially sons. Deaths were expected. Children and mothers were factors in a calculated life-and-death activity, a numbers game in which the survivors determined the future of families. It was a risky activity. And in many cases wives bore children every other year for twenty or more years. There is reason to think that Martha's body, slim and perhaps fragile from the start, had been by summer 1781 significantly weakened by her childbearing. There may have been other illnesses. Her reserves of strength had been depleted.

Whatever her burdens, Martha was a compliant wife, expressive of her class and time, partly an ornament, partly a companion, and the manager of her household when she was well. The marriage had also been from the start a love match. In regard to sexual intercourse, it would seem that only the natural protections of nature prevailed in the Jeffersons' relationship, an exemplification of the societies' norms.

And they were not yet finished with trying to have children. In July 1781, Jefferson had immediately decided, when offered a European assignment, that this was not a propitious time to leave his wife and children. It had been suggested that it would be for only about six months, a prediction that no sensible person could have believed. In September, Martha was pregnant again.

On May 8, 1782, she gave birth to a daughter, also named Lucy Elizabeth, a replacement for the Lucy Elizabeth who had died the previous April. There were ominous signs. She was not recovering. "Mrs. Jefferson has added another daughter to our family," Jefferson wrote to his young colleague James Madison. "She has been ever since and still continues very dangerously ill." At the end of June, Madison feared "that the report of each succeeding day would inform me [Martha] was no more."

Through the hot summer, suffering and declining, she was attended by doctors and family. Her husband spent much of his time by her bedside in a state of "dreadful suspense." Late in the summer, she had enough strength to copy some lines from a book the couple shared and loved, Sterne's *Tristram Shandy*: "Time wastes too fast: every letter I trace tells me with what rapidity life follows my pen. The days and hours of it are flying over our heads like clouds of windy day never to return—more. Everything presses on—" Apparently, she couldn't continue. Her husband completed the quotation: "and every time I kiss thy hand to bid adieu, every absence which follows it, are preludes to that eternal separation which we are shortly to make!" They both knew what was happening.

On the morning of September 6, 1782, thirty-nine-year-old Thomas Jefferson became a widower. That cold word contained a new reality. Its template was painful anguish and unanticipated loneliness. A man who loved domestic satisfactions found himself without the main pillar of their existence. Shadowy now to us, how vivid and substantive she must have been to him. He still had Monticello, which he could continue to give life to, and two daughters, but the companion of his bed, the mistress of the house who had given her life to him and for him, the mother of his children, was dead. It was a loss without redemption. There's no evidence that he consoled himself with Christian aspirations, let alone beliefs, about reuniting with Martha in an afterlife that would allow him to see her or be with her again. He was not that kind of Christian. He turned to a pagan source that he knew as well as he knew the Bible, Homer's *Iliad*, for one of the inscriptions on her tomb, carved into the stone in Greek letters: "Nay if even in the house of Hades men forget their dead, yet will I even there be mindful of my dear comrade." Below the bare facts he wrote, in his own words: "Torn from him by death . . . This monument of his love is inscribed."

For weeks and weeks he was paralyzed by grief. He wailed, moaned, cried, and seemed to faint. He took to horseback and rode wildly, as if speed could make time move backward to when Martha was alive or propel him forward into a future in which he did not feel such pain. His observant ten-year-old daughter could not imagine that such a state of grief could exist. Jefferson's friend Edmund Randolph wrote to Madison, "Mrs. Jefferson has at last shaken off her tormenting pains by yielding to them, and has left our friend inconsolable. . . . I scarcely supposed, that his grief would be so violent, as to justify the circulating report, of his swooning away, whenever he sees his children." There were rumors about his sanity. There were two young daughters whose welfare was his responsibility. His own siblings, one of whom lived at Monticello with her children, and his wife's half siblings all had to have been frightened. The Monticello slaves would have been concerned about their master's stability and their own futures. If nine-year-old Sally Hemings had been in the house or close by, as seems likely, she would have remembered for the rest of her life the emotions of the day on which her half sister had died and the weeks thereafter.

By October he was able to express himself coherently to another of his wife's half sisters, Elizabeth Wayles Eppes. His mind was on his daughters. It seemed to him that they had not been affected by their mother's death. "The girls being unable to assure you themselves of their welfare the duty devolves on me. . . . They are in perfect health and as happy as if they had no part in the unmeasurable loss we have sustained." They did, of course, have a part, especially her mother's ten-year-old namesake. Young Martha and Mary were looked after by servants and family. Aunt Elizabeth and Aunt Martha, the latter the widow of Dabney Carr, had kept them as emotionally protected as possible during the months preceding their mother's death.

The eldest daughter never forgot how frightened she had been at her father's expressive grief. It was helpful to Jefferson not to see this. If they were happy, it made his own misery, which he was now articulate about, more sustainable: "This miserable kind of existence is really too burthensome to be borne, and were it not for the infidelity of deserting the sacred charge left me, I could not wish its continuance a moment. For what could it be wished? All my plans of comfort and happiness reversed by a single event . . . and myself thrown on the world at a time of life when I should be withdrawn and nothing answering in prospect before me but a gloom unbrightened with one cheerful expectation. The care and instruction of our children indeed affords some temporary abstractions from wretchedness and nourishes a soothing reflection that if there be beyond the grave any concern for the things of this world there is one angel at least who views these attentions with pleasure and wishes continuance of them while she must pity the miseries to which they confine me."

The angel in heaven was hypothetical, a literary metaphor for his moral obligation. His daughters needed him. He had that responsibility on moral grounds. It was also a debt, an obligation, owed to his deceased wife. There is no evidence that he felt in any way responsible for her death. Still, he may have kept to himself his awareness of the burden he had helped create by so many pregnancies so quickly. The bearing of as many children as possible was the expectation of Virginians of Jefferson's class. A wife who was not a mother bore a special stigma. Amid his misery, once the hysterical stage had passed, Jefferson showed his resilience. He was increasingly aware that he had reasons to live, that vivid mourning would gradually become shadowy, and that he had private and public obligations. In November 1782, just three months after Martha's death, he began committing himself to a new stage in his career as a public servant.

There was another long-term consequence of Martha's death. She had asked him to promise that he would never marry again. He pledged that he would not. The pledge was not to celibacy but remarriage. It required that he would not have any more legitimate children. It would have been assumed that a young widower like Jefferson, wealthy, handsome, and accomplished, would, in the future, have children by another wife, or even wives, as his father-in-law had. Perhaps the difference between legitimate and illegitimate children was not on Martha's mind. It was remarriage that mattered. With whatever focus and energy she had, her mind was on the future well-being of her three living daughters: the pledge mandated that they never would have a stepmother. She herself had had two stepmothers. After three marriages, her father had had a long relationship with a mulatto slave whose slave children became her half siblings. Martha had been in the direct line of inheritance of John Wayles; they were not. Her Virginia world had examples of children who had been ill-used by stepmothers. And such a stepmother might persuade her husband to favor her children from a previous marriage before his from his previous marriage. It was, from one perspective, an extension of a mother's protective love, but also meant that her daughters would never have a second mother. Despite her fears, a second might have nurtured and protected them. Her deathbed request was not an expression of confidence in her husband's judgment. It deprived him of the opportunity to have a second marital love, to exercise his own judgment about what was best for himself and his daughters.

Deathbed promises are coerced covenants, so they are sometimes subject to revocation or alteration. Jefferson's promise never to remarry may have seemed to him an emotionally satisfying expression of his commitment to his wife, a way of keeping her alive. He was to keep his word, perhaps as much because it suited him as because it had been made to a wife who became even more perfect in his memory than anyone could have been in life. If he had so chosen, he could have found a second bride among his social peers, a woman of property to help him support his life, especially Monticello's expansion, a companion for his bed and table who would have helped fulfill his need for companionship, a woman who might have provided maternal nurture and guidance for his motherless children. If that had happened, Sally Hemings would be, at most, a footnote in Jefferson's life and in American history.

That it did not happen may have had as much to do with his own inclinations as to his pledge. He became a disciplined flirt with numbers of woman and an immensely expressive verbal lover of one who had the salient characteristic of being married already. Jefferson seems likely to have been celibate for six years after Martha's death, and when he became sexually active again, it was with a woman he could not possibly marry. The fact that in 1788 he entered into a long-term sexual relationship with a young mulatto woman, a member of his household, who had been close to Martha's bedside when she died, speaks to the consequences of the promise he had made to his dying wife. It also speaks to Jefferson's human needs. It is neither to his credit nor discredit. Despite two centuries of doubt and denial, the preponderance of evidence, including DNA studies, scholarly analysis, and common sense, all say that it happened. To claim that it did not is to demand of Jefferson more than we have a right to demand of any human being. It is also to deprive ourselves of a meaningful gloss on human nature and on the world in which Jefferson lived.

CHAPTER SEVEN

Perpetual Gratitude

1783–1786

It had been a terrible few years for Jefferson. In retrospect, he might have considered them the worst of his life. He had lost his wife and a child. To his relief, however, he was no longer governor of Virginia. It had been a burdensome assignment, little suited to his temperament and talents. Despite this, he had not only given it ceaseless time and effort, but also he had, on the whole, had reasonable success in the face of intractable odds. His enemies in Virginia had had a weak case when they charged him with dereliction of duty. A less prudent, less deliberate man might have acted more swiftly, but he'd had reason to hesitate. Still, caution and rational deliberativeness were not assets in this situation. He had, over and over again, been painfully schooled in the reality of the impoverished Virginia war chest and the difficulty of mustering and keeping militia in the field. The experience left a lasting scar, mostly suppressed, later to be scratched at by political opponents. Revolution had been the determinative agent of his public life since 1773. It had also hung like a sword of Damocles over his personal life. It had made him only sporadically available to his family. It limited his efforts to create a handsome home for them all. Its exigencies probably had some effect on his wife's long-standing fragile health. She was not a war victim in the ordinary sense, but many people not on the battlefield paid a price for the Revolution. The fact that he had written *Notes on the State of Virginia* while the war was still being waged testified to his ability to compartmentalize, but he was never to allow himself to take particular pride in it.

Jefferson's commitment to revising Virginia's laws had motivated his return to the state in late 1776, as did his longing for his wife and home, especially his concern for Martha's health. He could have remained, as many of his colleagues hoped he would, as a delegate to the Confederation Congress, spending half the year at Monticello, the other half in Philadelphia or wherever the Congress retreated to on occasion. He chose to have the national Congress do its work without him. Some of his colleagues thought that a desertion of his duty, that the contribution his mind and pen could make to the effort to unite and govern the new country at the time of its birthing crisis should take precedence over local concerns, including revising Virginia's laws. It was usual for delegates to share their time between Philadelphia and their home states. Jefferson's decision to limit himself to Virginia eventually resulted in his difficult two terms as governor. When he resigned from the General Assembly, one of his warm supporters, twenty-four-year-old James Monroe, a war veteran and an aspiring politician, lectured him: "You should not decline the service of your country. The present is generally conceived to be an important era which of course makes your attendance particularly necessary."

He responded with a list of justifications, including his resentment of the criticism of his performance as governor. That seemed not good enough to supporters like Monroe and Madison whose encouragement implied political consanguinity. There now existed a network of "friends" of Jefferson who looked to him for guidance and who hoped he would return to public life. Virginia needed him, and Virginia, they believed, should dominate the Confederation government. This was not in 1781 a movement, let alone a political party, yet its tone, policies, and values were republican values that the Revolution and Jefferson's Virginia personified. He seemed to his friends and colleagues the perfect fit by age, education, experience, accomplishments, discipline, intellect, political gravitas, and talent as a thinker and writer to be the leader of what they represented. A household name among the ruling elite in Virginia, he had a national reputation. He knew almost everyone in Congress, and everyone knew or knew of him. In late 1782, his friends determined that for his and the country's interest he should be persuaded to return to public life. Deaths of wives and children were frequent enough for his withdrawal to seem self-indulgent, almost unpatriotic. In mid-November, less than three months after Martha's death, Congress gave him another chance to represent the United States in France.

He was, he confided to a friend, "a little emerging from that stupor of mind which had rendered me as dead to the world as she was whose loss occasioned it." A change of scene, he speculated, might do him good. Congress asked him to join John Jay, John Adams, and Benjamin Franklin in Paris, adding a Southern voice to the preliminary peace negotiations. He no longer had a sickly wife to justify a declination. His eldest daughter, Patsy, was now ten, a potential companion. The infant Elizabeth Lucy and her four-year-old sister, Mary, nicknamed Polly, could live with their aunt and uncle, Elizabeth and Francis Eppes, until he returned—probably, he thought, in a year or so. He seems not to have hesitated. Martha's ill health no longer restricted him. He had a good place to leave the younger children, with Elizabeth Eppes as a substitute mother. He was well aware that there were many instances of fathers in public service separating from their children, especially in wartime, his congressional colleague John Adams being a well-known example. Country came before family, as long as the family was safe and provided for.

Unexpectedly, in early February 1783, about to leave for France, he was frozen in place, literally. Patsy accompanied him to Philadelphia, where he stayed at the boarding house that had hosted him years before. The daughter of the house, Elizabeth Trist, was to become one of his lifelong friends. He had put Francis Eppes and his neighbor Nicholas Lewis in charge of his affairs with full power to run his estates, expecting that his farm income and government salary would give him ample cash flow. Due to his debts, his farm income alone was proving insufficient. In the transactions to settle the Wayles estate, he had accepted state-issued paper scrip, a decision that may have been a statement of faith in Virginia, poor judgment, or both. Inflation now made the paper money almost worthless. He owed large sums to English merchants. Unlike some others, he felt morally obligated to repay what he owed, though he objected to paying interest accrued during the war years.

In Philadelphia, he impatiently waited for his winter voyage to be under way in a vessel provided by the French government. The ship he originally thought he would be sailing on had left before he arrived. He wrote to John Jay in Paris that he would have a "little motherless daughter accompanying" him. When another French ship in open waters twelve miles outside Baltimore harbor arranged a private apartment for him and Patsy, all he had to do was get to it. The weather turned brutally cold. "The ice has since cut off all correspondence with" the ship "till yesterday, when I got a boat and attempted a passage. We got about half way with tolerable ease, but the influx of the tide then happening the ice closed on us on every side and became impenetrable to our little vessel, so that we could get neither backwards nor forwards." They were stuck. A sloop cutting through the ice rescued them.

The next day he was back in Baltimore, trying to decide among his options. The only sensible one, he concluded, was to wait for the weather to turn and sail on another ship. He returned to the comfort of his boarding house in Philadelphia to await word that the ice had cleared. "My situation is not an agreeable one, and the less so as I contrast it with the more pleasing one I left so unnecessarily." He soon learned that if he had sailed, he would have arrived in France with the reason for his having gone no longer valid. Almost three months before, in November 1782, a preliminary peace treaty had been signed. George III had accepted the inevitable. The United States, he told Parliament, would be declared "free and independent states . . . to take effect whenever terms of peace shall be finally settled with the court of France." Congress now had no reason to send him to France. He had reason to go home. He had not heard anything about his Virginia family for three months. He had been awaiting news, he wrote to Francis Eppes, "with fear and trembling, lest any accident should have happened."

By mid-May 1783, nine months after Martha's death, he and Patsy were back at Monticello. Jefferson had had a change of scenery, but not of the sort he had been anticipating. On his four plantations, two on each side of the Rivanna River, his overseer kept his field slaves at work; another overseer ran Poplar Forest. He had nothing to say with his pen about his absent wife or what he had done with her personal belongings. The house still would have had the aura of her presence. There were a number of brief references in letters to his grievous loss and his motherless children. He frequently expressed himself, sometimes eloquently, on his preference for a private life, for the pleasures of family and books, but his colleagues and friends kept emphasizing that he had a public duty. He responded that he had already served considerably. Whatever new duties he would undertake would have to be brief. That had been his mind-set when he accepted the appointment to the preliminary peace commission. His supporters in the Virginia legislature, his former congressional colleagues, and his political friends respected his ambivalence. They also knew, as he had recently shown, that he could be enlisted again in public service.

In spring 1783, he immersed himself in drafting a new constitution for Virginia. In Richmond, he had gotten the impression that there would soon be a convention to revise the 1776 constitution. What he thought a badly flawed document had been in place since then. Some of his miseries as governor had been, in his judgment, due to its flaws. The legislature was too strong, though often absent and irresponsible, and the executive too weak; there was no check on the legislature, no court of appeals, no provision for impeachment, and no flexibility for the executive to deal with crises. A better balance of power needed to be established. The inner workings of the legislature needed to be improved to allow it to function efficiently. A new constitution should, in his judgment, create a better balance of power among the legislature, the governor, the council, and the judiciary. It should include a statement guaranteeing religious freedom based on the unenacted statute he had created. It should affirm the right of habeas corpus, outlaw the slave trade, and provide for the gradual abolition of slavery. It should also, and most important, be recognized as a document that could not be altered by legislatively enacted statute law. Created directly by the will of the people, it should be able to be altered only by the will of the people.

Drawing on his previous efforts and a number of other documents, including a copy of the New York state constitution, Jefferson created a draft. The prose was efficient and lawyerly. In July, he sent a copy to James Madison, whose lengthy response, months later, showed that he was an equally good if not better constitution maker. If melded together, the combined result would have been a forerunner of what Madison and his colleagues created in 1789. Jefferson also sent copies to those members of the House of Delegates whom he knew favored revision. Heads were counted. Apparently, Patrick Henry, an influential delegate and soon to be elected to a second term as governor, opposed revisal. His opposition may partly have been based on the fact that it was Jefferson's initiative. Nothing came of it. Still, he had put in writing what he believed the fundamental provisions of a republican government should be.

No sooner had he finished his draft for a revised constitution than he allowed the General Assembly to elect him a member of its delegation to Congress. He committed himself to be away from Monticello for congressional sessions, starting in November 1783, which he assumed would continue to be in Philadelphia. He could have withdrawn his name. It was a given that if he allowed himself to be elected, he would be. Indeed, of the five-man delegation, only Jefferson had name and fame, though Arthur Lee, back from Europe, had some distinction. "The appointment with which you inform me I am honored," he wrote to an acquaintance, "will oblige me to stay pretty closely at home for some time to get my affairs into such a state as that they may be left." As usual, however he attempted to get his affairs in order, he did not get them sufficiently in order to deal with his debts. To do that, he would have had to sell land, which he was unwilling to do.

In September 1783, he revised and expanded *Notes on the State of Virginia*. He had given copies to a few friends in anticipation of corrections and additions. Others were asking to read it. He was not yet clear in his mind how that could be accomplished except by private publication, which he was considering, perhaps an edition of about two hundred that he himself would pay for. He still wanted to limit the book to private circulation.

Madison wrote to him from Philadelphia that the next session of Congress would meet in Princeton. The accommodations in Princeton, he predicted, would be "skimpy." Princeton was so unsatisfactory that Congress moved almost immediately to Annapolis, where Jefferson arrived in late November. Jefferson and Madison separately wrote up memos emphasizing the need for Southerners to be prepared to insist that the best site for a permanent capital city was on the Potomac. In Annapolis, in the next six months, Jefferson was to accomplish his last work as a legislator. Congress had serious, difficult issues to deal with. Jefferson had his guiding mind and pen in almost every one of them.

In a Confederation Congress that often seemed a floating crap game, Virginia and Jefferson were among the most reliable players. Virginia's delegation was fully represented when Congress convened in Annapolis. The delegations of various states were absent or underrepresented. Some appeared, then disappeared, then reappeared or not. Some states were late or remiss in paying delegates' expenses. The Virginians could afford to subsidize themselves, to be later reimbursed by the General Assembly. "Nine states appeared on the floor to-day," Jefferson wrote to a new friend, William Short, in early March, "but eight of them are represented by two members only, so that in every important question, as not only an unanimity of states, but an unanimity of members also will be requisite to carry propositions, we must expect to carry none, and that our time will be spent in proposing regulations, hearing one another a week on each, put them to the vote, and see them fall because one or two or more members are against them." Each state had one vote. The Articles required a supermajority to pass important legislation, nine of thirteen votes. And its powers were limited, an overreaction to the fear of the reestablishment of a strong executive and legislature, what the colonies had rebelled against. It could not levy taxes. It relied on voluntary funding from the states.

Jefferson's leadership role in Congress in 1783–1784 cannot be overemphasized. He played a major role in its sessions, mostly in committee work and drafting documents. He brought with him credentials and a reputation that had to be impressive to his colleagues. As one of the signers of the Declaration and its primary author, a distinction not widely commented on but increasingly well known, and as the former governor of Virginia, he added recognition of his high-level public service to the gravitas that came from his being an excellent listener, a deliberative legislator, and an energetic, capable, and eloquent writer. He was equally adept at legal logic and precision. Also, he was Virginia personified, the unofficial leader of his state's delegation. His state had more wealth, size, and clout than any other. It also laid claim to huge tracts of Western land, the cession of which it had with enlightened self-interest offered to the country, though the devil was still in the details. Virginia's aura radiated the power of influence. So too did Jefferson's work ethic. To the respect paid to his previous achievements he added his physical presence, unmistakably recognizable—a tall, sandy-red-haired man with a light complexion, lanky, informal, with sharply chiseled, almost handsome features. His quiet but unmissable presence in any room, ready with his pen and mind, expressed the aspirational aura of leadership.

"The winter here," Jefferson complained, "has been severe beyond all memory. Congress has been so thin that little could be done. We are constantly tantalized with the expectation of new members." He had lengthy exchanges with George Washington about a favorite project, the opening of the Potomac to west-east navigation. Hoping he could get Washington to associate his name or even his leadership with the project, he wrote to him, "All the world is becoming commercial." He was not referring to industry or manufacturing. His commitment was to agriculture, especially for the Western territories. Inland products needed river avenues to be brought to market on the East Coast and abroad. In return for agricultural products, commerce brought manufactured goods from Europe to America. "Was it practicable to keep our new empire separated from them," Jefferson argued, "we might indulge ourselves in speculating whether commerce contributes to the happiness of mankind. But we cannot separate ourselves from them. Our citizens have had too full a taste of the comforts furnished by the arts and manufactures to be debarred the use of them. . . . We must then in our own defence endeavor to share as large a portion as we can of this modern source of wealth and power." The "we" meant particularly Virginians. Washington also favored making the Potomac navigable to connect it to Western rivers. Jefferson in effect proposed a new career for the former commander in chief. Would he not consider becoming the chief executive, major fund raiser, and day-to-day manager/supervisor of a Virginia-dominated project to transform the Potomac into the main channel for the movement of goods from every area of the Western country to the Atlantic coast?

In this decades-long fantasy, Jefferson posited to Washington that the competition for the primary route between the Western territories and the East Coast was between Virginia and New York. Virginia's route would be across the Appalachians via the Potomac to the Monongahela, the Kanawha, and the Ohio. New York's access would be via the Great Lakes, then by portage to the Hudson down to New York City. Jefferson's Potomac proposal assumed that a port city in the Chesapeake area would be born from scratch or from an existing city. It would be the Southern equivalent of New York City but better, if only because it would be in Virginia and would embody its values and profits. He put on paper his dollar-and-cents projection of how the Chesapeake area would benefit financially. He did not have to make explicit that if Virginia grew richer, so would he and Washington. All Virginians would benefit from an additional tax base. Furthermore, if he and his fellow Southerners were clever and stubborn enough, Congress itself would have its permanent home on the Potomac.

Jefferson, though, could not avoid expressing his bleak mood about "the current . . . crippled state of Congress. . . . We have only 9 states present, 8 of whom are represented by two members each, and of course, on all great questions not only an unanimity of states but of members is necessary, an unanimity which never can be obtained on a matter of any importance. The consequence is that we are wasting our time and labor in vain efforts to do business. Nothing less than the presence of 13 states represented by an odd number of delegates will enable us to get forward a single capital point."

It was indeed a wonder that anything was accomplished. Actually, much was, though with difficulty and contention. Jefferson was a major contributor. In December 1783, he was on the committee appointed to report on the preliminary treaty of peace with Great Britain. It dealt with the controversial issue of "the restitution of all estates, rights and properties, which have been confiscated, belonging to real British subjects." The disposition of these properties would, for the time being, be determined by the individual states. Few Americans wanted to give back or pay for property they had seized. Jefferson's tactful prose, by deferral and postponement, kept the issue under control. In mid-December, Congress unanimously approved the provisions of the treaty.

Jefferson had the baton in his hand, but it was a challenge to his patience, and it took harmonizing skills to keep the players in their seats long enough to get business done. Rivalries within and between states became the central drama. Most Americans had begun to realize that the Articles of Confederation did not allow Congress to manage many of the matters that had to be dealt with. And to make matters even more difficult, the Articles required unanimity for amendment. The pressing question was: How strong a national government did the individual states think necessary for national prosperity and security?

Congress did make substantial progress on resolving the claims of Pennsylvania, Connecticut, and Virginia to vast tracts of Western land and the counterdemands of those states that had no claims at all. The existence of the union was at stake. Would states like Virginia cede their claims to the national government? If so, what would be the terms under which these territories would be divided and then new states be admitted to the United States? Could the money paid for the purchase of land in these territories be used to help pay the national debt? Jefferson took the pulse of all the state constituencies. The Virginia Assembly had already agreed, if fair terms could be worked out, to cede its claims. Greed and fear had to be detoxified in a compromise. The tacitly acknowledged leader of the session, with the backing of his state in hand, Jefferson was the moving force in working out a compromise. On March 1, 1784, Congress agreed to the terms of Virginia's cession. That brought Pennsylvania and Connecticut on board. The Western territories now belonged not to individual states but to the United States. The compromise language was not entirely to Jefferson's satisfaction. There were concessions, including a loophole favoring speculators. But the overall agreement embodied what Virginia had long accepted to and worked toward: the transference of ownership of Western claims in a way that all the states of the Confederation could accept.

In March, Jefferson wrote the Ordinance of 1784, a plan for the governance of the new territories. His colleagues made minor changes. No one disagreed with his assertion that these national territories *"shall forever remain* a part subject to the government of the United states in Congress assembled. . . . That they shall be subject to pay a part of the federal debts contracted or to be contracted. . . . That their respective governments shall be in republican forms, and shall admit no person to be a citizen who holds any hereditary title." But his final stipulation met with decisive objection: "That after the year 1800 of the Christian era, there shall be neither slavery nor involuntary servitude in any of the said states. . . ." North Carolina, seconded by South Carolina, made the motion to delete the provision, an anticipation of the slavery drama of the next seventy-five years. Only Jefferson and one Virginia colleague of all the Southern delegates voted for the antislavery provision. Every delegate, "including and north of Pennsylvania," voted for Jefferson's clause excluding slavery in the territories. "The lack of the vote of a single delegate determined the outcome." A New Jersey delegate was ill. "Sixteen delegates voted to retain the clause, whereas only seven voted to delete it; but the former represented only six states and the latter three. Thus, a minority of states and of delegates' votes determined the issue, for on the question as to whether the words moved to be struck out should stand, the required seven states could not be mustered, the question was lost, and the words were deleted."

This failure was a turning point in Jefferson's attitude toward abolishing slavery. Without eliminating the abolition clause, he could not get agreement on the settlement of the Western land claims necessary to the perpetuation of the union—and he had no doubt as to which was more important. It was a lesson in the politics of slavery and nation building that made a lasting impression. Like his fellow Virginians, he had no alternative labor force. He feared abolition without removal would threaten the lives and property of slave-owners, himself included. He was personally dependent on slaves for his economic and psychological well-being; they were necessary for the productivity of his farms, the maintenance of Monticello, and his everyday life, from dressing in the morning to dining at night. Personally, he never seems to have considered a life as a non-slave-owner. It was a practical and psychological impossibility. Even if he could cross one or more of those bridges, there would be very few white Americans crossing with him. He felt he had done his best, though, to prohibit slavery in the Northwest, but he failed.

Applause, toasts, embraces, and tears marked the celebratory public dinner in Annapolis on Monday, December 22, 1783, honoring the retirement of George Washington, the most revered leader of the Revolution. Hundreds of celebrants feasted and danced in the largest venue that Annapolis could offer. Washington honored every lady with his hand on the dance floor. The Confederation Congress hosted the celebratory occasion. The country believed that a singular man had made the Revolution successful. Others had contributed immensely—some, like Jefferson, exclusively with words and governance. But it was Washington's leadership in the field that had encouraged the British to make mistake after mistake in political and military judgment, though the most determinative ones originated in London. Washington's own military misjudgments weighed less heavily in the balance. His colleagues chose Jefferson to write a draft response to the address Washington was scheduled to deliver to a midday meeting of Congress.

Washington had already made two farewell addresses, one at Newburgh, the other at Princeton, both to his military colleagues. His message was succinct, aspirational, and prophylactic: "You now have a republic: see if you can keep it, and let resigning my commission, emphasizing that this is and should always be a republic of citizens, not soldiers, governed by elected officials to whom the military is subordinate, be an example to everyone." His resignation, he implied, should set the precedent. Revered by his countrymen, the man who could be king was setting the example that a republican government required. "Having now finished the work assigned me, I retire from the great theatre of Action; and bidding an Affectionate farewell to this August body under whose orders I have so long acted, I here offer my Commission, and take my leave of all the employments of public life."

Jefferson had in hand a copy of Washington's short address a day after the general's arrival. Congress appointed him and two colleagues to write its acceptance speech. Elbridge Gerry and James McHenry happily remitted the charge to Jefferson. "I send you the sketch," he wrote to his colleagues, "which I have been obliged to obliterate and blot after making what I intended for a fair copy. You will observe my plan was to make a short review in very general terms of those actions which redound to the General's particular credit. . . . Perhaps this answer is too short; perhaps it is too warm. A want of time must apologize for the one, and an exalted esteem for the other faults. Be so good as to handle it roughly and freely and make it what it should be." They had nothing to change or add.

Two days before Christmas, Washington entered the Senate chamber in the Maryland State Capitol. Every member of Congress had assembled. The clerk to the secretary of Congress announced his arrival, then escorted the general to his chair, saying, "Congress sir are prepared to receive your Communications."

"The spectators all wept," John McHenry wrote to his fiancée, "and there was hardly a member of Congress who did not drop tears. The General's hand which held the address shook as he read it. When he spoke of the officers who had composed his wartime family, and recommended those who had continued in it to the present moment to the favorable notice of Congress . . . his voice faltered and sunk, and the whole house felt his agitations. After the pause which was necessary for him to recover himself, he proceeded." After resigning, "he drew out from his bosom his commission and delivered it up to the president of Congress. He then returned to his station, when the president read the reply that had been prepared."

As soon as Washington took his seat, the secretary of Congress rose, with Jefferson's words in his hand, and read:

The U.S. in congress assembled receive with emotions too affecting for utterance this solemn Resignation of the authorities under which you have led their troops with Success through a perilous and a doubtful war. Called by your country to defend its invaded rights you accepted the sacred charge before it had formed alliances, and whilst it was without funds or a government to support you. You have conducted the great military contest with wisdom and fortitude invariably regarding the rights of the civil power through all disasters and changes. You have by the love and confidence of your fellow citizens enabled them to display their martial genius and transmit their fame to posterity. You have persevered till these United States, aided by a magnanimous king and nation have been enabled under a just providence to close the war in freedom safety and independence, on which happy event we sincerely join you in congratulations. Having defended the standard of liberty in this new world: having taught a lesson useful to those who inflict and to those who feel oppression, you *retire from the great theatre of action* with the blessings of your fellow citizens—but the glory of your virtues will not terminate with your military Command. It will continue to animate remotest ages. . . . We join you in *commending the interests of our dearest country to the protection of almighty god*, beseeching him to dispose the hearts and minds of its citizens to improve *the opportunity afforded them of becoming a happy and respectable nation* . . . that a life so beloved may be fostered with all his care; that your days may be happy as they have been illustrious, and that he will finally give you that reward which this world cannot give.

Jefferson had worried that his tribute might be thought too short. On the contrary, its brevity was a virtue. It was brief enough to be simple and direct. It was beautifully phrased, and at perfect length for the occasion. The phrase "the great theatre of action" was Washington's. Jefferson knew when there was a quote too good not to use. It was both complimentary and expressive to do so. It linked Washington's words and Jefferson's response as companion pieces. The syntactical surprise of the opening phrase of the first sentence catches the reader's breath and its final phrase, "through a perilous and a doubtful war," had to strike his audience as a heartfelt but disciplined reminder of what they had all been through, which they needed both to remember and forget. The past as prelude to the future was in the process of becoming the future of "a happy and respectable nation." To the degree that was to be possible, Washington's service and Jefferson's words had been and would continue to be, to an extent neither of them could predict, agents of a contested battle to create the shape and values of the new republic. After Jefferson's death, James Madison remarked that among Jefferson's "important literary compositions," his "answer of Congress to the resignation of the Commander in Chief . . . attracts attention by the shining traces of his pen."

Jefferson's praise was sincere. When Washington consulted him in April 1784 about his views of a new society proposed by the officers who had served under him, to be called the Society of the Cincinnati, its membership to be inherited from generation to generation, Jefferson responded that Washington himself exemplified the argument against inherited membership or titles. If the object of the society was to perpetuate friendships, it would likely fail. Worse, since this society was to give exclusive validation to military experience, it would undermine the proper subordination of the military to the civil necessary for republican government. Washington himself, Jefferson emphasized, had made that point by his decision to retire from government service. It was the shining example of the most powerful leader of a country affirming that no man is indispensable, that republican government requires rotation in office and rule by the people. "The moderation and virtue of a single character has probably prevented this revolution from being closed as most others have been by a subversion of that liberty it was intended to establish; that he is not immortal, and his successor or some one of his successors at the head of this institution may adopt a more mistaken road to glory."

This was a private letter, he assured Washington. "I consider the whole matter as between ourselves alone, having determined to take no active part in this or anything else which may . . . disturb that quiet and tranquillity of mind to which I consign the remaining portion of my life. I have been thrown back by events on a stage where I had never more thought to appear. It is but for a time however, and as a day laborer, free to withdraw or be withdrawn at will. While I remain

I shall pursue in silence the path of right." He was certain that he knew what right was.

At the end of April 1784, Jefferson wrote to William Short that "a disposition . . . seems to prevail to add to the present commission for negotiating foreign treaties of amity and commerce. . . . I am in truth indifferent. If they desire it I shall go." Congress did desire it. He was offered for the third time the opportunity to represent the United States in France. And his Virginia colleagues pressured him to accept. The South wanted to be represented by one of its own. Jefferson's college roommate, John Tyler Sr., regretted that Jefferson had not participated in the peace treaty negotiations. "Your Services might have been great indeed when the Preliminaries were entered into because Virginia would have had a friend who knew the circumstances of the people and how unjust it was to consent to the payment of the debts." The treaty even required prewar debts to be repaid with interest. Southerners resented that it did not compel Great Britain to return slaves who had fled to British protection. That the treaty had been negotiated by Northerners fueled Southern resentment of what felt like Northern dominance.

In Tyler's view, Jefferson could now best serve Virginia by remaining in Congress. It would be hard to replace him. Still, since Jefferson wished "to go abroad . . . mine would be to gratify you, if I had the power even to negative the Vote of Congress." Tyler would expect him to advance Southern commercial interests. And such treaties would also be de facto acknowledgments of American independence. "I shall pursue there the line I have pursued here," Jefferson told Madison, "convinced that it can never be the interest of any party to do what is unjust, or to ask what is unequal," a view of human nature that no amount of evidence to the contrary would ever change. In 1826,

William Short, who soon became one of Jefferson's close friends, remarked that Jefferson's "greatest illusions in politics have proceeded from a most amiable error on his part; having too favorable [an] opinion of the animal called Man."

Appointed a minister plenipotentiary, he was to be the third member of a commission headquartered in Paris, its purpose to negotiate treaties of commerce with every European nation with which it could be advantageous to trade. Jefferson immediately accepted the assignment, though its broad scope suggested that the commission would be active for numbers of years. At last he would be going to Europe, a fulfillment of his youthful fantasy, and to a country for whose culture and people he felt a special affinity and indebtedness. Now almost forty-one years old, he had been willing to go to France four months after Martha's death, hypothesizing that a change of scenery would help relieve his grief. Grief would be diluted by distance, time, and work. His recommended cure for any illness of the spirit was productive busyness. He had been taking his own medicine. The acceptance of a demanding assignment three thousand miles away from Monticello would certainly increase the dosage.

Once again, he gave power of attorney to Nicholas Lewis and Francis Eppes. They would have carte blanche to manage his estates. His long-term debts remained on semi-hold, with occasional payments and requests for extensions. Twelve-year-old Patsy would go with him. Polly and Lucy would be slotted into the same arrangement that he had had in place previously. Elizabeth and Francis Eppes would substitute for their dead mother and absent father. Leaving two daughters behind seemed to be no impediment. The appointment itself had no hint of a terminal date.

Jefferson had referred in his response to Washington's resignation to the "magnanimous king and nation" whose aid had helped make the United States an independent country. Neither Washington nor Jefferson cared that the "magnanimous king" was an autocrat serving his and his government's national interests: dominance of the European continent, revenge against Great Britain for France's defeat in the Seven Years' War, and competition with its island enemy in the international marketplace. This was irrelevant to the newly created republic's pursuit of its own interests. No American doubted that French assistance had made America's victory possible. To France, the enemy of its enemy was its friend, a strategic calculation. The centuries-long warfare between France and Great Britain had made the victory at Yorktown possible. But if the American colonies had been French possessions, Great Britain might have played the role in the American Revolution that France did. It was not personal; it was not ideological. It was about power, wealth, and national pride. Words of praise for the French came easily to Jefferson. He took to heart, even more than Washington, the general's words soon after the Battle of Yorktown: "The very important Share which our great Allies have taken in this Event, ought to endear them to every American, and their Assistance should be remembered with *perpetual Gratitude.*" Jefferson's definition of "perpetual gratitude" differed from Washington's. To Washington, France was a valued ally that had helped make the Revolution successful. It was a matter of national business, not of personal engagement, a matter of the head, not the heart. It had been determined by circumstances, not by cultural or personal preferences. Jefferson, though, multiplied gratitude into affection, if not love. He was to take "perpetual" almost literally, rather than as a loosely meant intensification of "gratitude."

In 1781, as the French fleet and American armies tightened the noose at Yorktown, Jefferson wrote to the three American peace negotiators in Paris that James Monroe, intending to travel to Europe, "will be able to give you a particular detail of American affairs and especially of the prospect we have through the aid of our father of France, of making captives of Ld. Cornwallis and his army." The phrase "our father of France" could not have been intended ironically.

It has a touch of the language with which Jefferson and his contemporaries addressed the Indian nations, as if Louis XVI were America's father rather than its ally. French financial support, most of it borrowed, and French military assistance, both of which helped make the Revolution successful, seemed to Louis XVI and his ministers a good investment. It was, though, not money invested in the United States but against Great Britain. To elevate Louis himself as if he were a Founding Father of the United States has its peculiar psychological resonances, perhaps particular to Jefferson. His "father of France" was an absolutist, anti-republican king, relatively unconstrained compared to George III. Jefferson's loss at a young age of his own father may have made the phrase comfortably available to him. And, as a rising patriarch himself, it may be that it came readily as a reference to the patriarchal power the new nation was indebted to for its life.

For both Jefferson and Washington, Britain was an ex-overlord to be wary of, a potential enemy that might try to reassert its power. Unlike Washington, however, Jefferson brought a leaven of hatred, even paranoia, to that fear, despite the preliminary peace terms being favorable to America. The Revolution helped to make Jefferson a Francophile. So too did his fear that Britain would attempt to do damage to its former colonies. Actually, there was no chance that any British ministry would attempt to reconquer what it had lost. Doubtless, Great Britain, not France, would be America's main rival in world trade, so powerful on the seas that it might severely limit the prosperity Jefferson expected to be one of the benefits of independence.

Jefferson had learned to read French. He had French friends, including Lafayette, a few of whom valued America for its republicanism. France had allure: culture, art, literature, theater; Paris was the center of the Enlightenment and its *Encyclopedie*, which Jefferson read and valued. The fact that France was Catholic and feudal seemed almost irrelevant. From Annapolis in the spring of 1784, all things French seemed attractive, and Paris seemed the appropriate center and point of departure from which the United States should extend its European outreach. America needed friends and trading partners. "In these circumstances," Jefferson wrote in mid-March, "we cannot be too careful to preserve the friendships we have acquired abroad, and the union we have established at home, to secure our credit by a punctual discharge of our obligations of every kind, and our reputation by the wisdom of our councils, since we know not how soon we may have a fresh occasion for friends, for credit and for reputation."

Two months later, in the darkness of four a.m. on July 5, 1784, sailing out of Boston harbor, the tide and breeze perfect, Jefferson was finally on his way to France. The ship was the newly built *Ceres*, named after the Roman goddess of agriculture, a propitious name for the passage of a man whose income depended on and whose ideology embraced the blessings the goddess bestowed. Jefferson had left Annapolis in late May for New York, searching for the first ship sailing to France, then Boston, with the hope that he could join Abigail Adams, who was scheduled to sail to London on the *Active*. He had in hand Congress's formal charge, which he had probably written, containing a list of European countries from which to solicit agreements of friendship and commerce. It was an ambitious list. Some of the countries would hardly know that the United States existed. In New York, where he had met with Robert Morris and other merchants to work up notes on the commerce of the Northern states, he had learned that the next packet sailing directly from New York to France was not to sail until July 15. He wanted something sooner. With letters of introduction, he made his way northward, stopping in New Haven to be the guest of Yale's president, Ezra Stiles.

He arrived in Boston so close to the departure of the *Active* that it was impractical to book passage. It seems likely that he had his first meeting, though brief, with Abigail Adams. What to do now? Return to New York and wait? He decided that his best course was to stay in New England, sail on the *Ceres* to Portsmouth, then cross the Channel to France. In the meantime, with the questionnaire he had worked up to help gather facts about the Northern states, he spent three weeks visiting cities in Massachusetts and New Hampshire, noting statistics about their agriculture, commerce, and population. When he returned to Boston on June 26, he knew that William Short, his Virginian acolyte whom he had agreed to accept as his unofficial secretary and to whom he had offered domestic hospitality in Paris, had sailed from Virginia. David Humphreys, an aide-de-camp to General Washington, had been appointed the commission's official secretary. They had all hoped to sail together, but Humphreys decided to wait in New York for the French packet.

As the *Ceres* made its swift way across the Atlantic, Jefferson did his usual thing: he recorded everything of interest to him, including "the position of the vessel at noon each day during the crossing . . . the number of miles covered . . . the direction of the wind . . . thermometer readings" and that the ship had "traveled 2,728 geographical miles from Boston," the longest trip he was ever to make. The only other crossing was his return five years later. On the one hand, he was a provincial Virginian who was never to travel westward beyond the Blue Ridge. On the other, his five years in Paris were to provide him with experiences that touched on the transformative without actually transforming him.

He arrived on French soil as a Francophile, though he could not make himself understood or understand conversational French, and he was to leave as much a Francophile as when he arrived. He was to work hard at advancing French-American commerce. In New York, the most astute and best-informed American merchant had told Jefferson that, in his judgment, Great Britain, not France, was the best long-term trading partner for the United States. Robert Morris, an exceptionally astute businessman, advised him that the United States should play off the two major European powers against each other. "If we are to chuse among the nations of Europe who shall be our carriers, many reasons give the English a preference." Jefferson had neither the heart nor mind to consider that view of America's best interest. His ideological and emotional preference transcended any assessments of national interest. It was an unshakable given, regardless of any evidence to the contrary, including his own frequent purchase of English manufactured goods.

When Jefferson and Patsy crossed from England to Le Havre at the end of July 1784, he discovered that he and the porters who helped them could not understand each other, as if his spoken French were a foreign language. He suspected that he was being cheated. "I understand the French so imperfectly as to be uncertain whether those to whom I speak and myself mean the same thing." He was to learn quickly, with the help of friends, a good deal about French society, especially the condition of the population as a whole. It was, he discovered, an acknowledged custom that the working class, especially domestic servants, would take what they could from wealthy gentlemen like himself.

In Paris, he was soon collaborating with Adams and Franklin, hard at work on the semi-impossible job of being in touch with more than a dozen European countries, hoping to make treaties with them. Most of the work of putting proposals onto paper fell to him. There were letters to write each day, memos to compose, and every morning letters to read and answer. Through his new French connections, he soon found a school for Patsy. After a brief stay at two hotels, he moved to a sizable house on the Right Bank, with gardens and a courtyard, which he rented and furnished at more than the cost of a year's salary. In November, William Short joined him. He was stretching his legs, seeing the sights of Paris, buying books for himself and Madison, to whom he'd sold the books that he'd had with him in Philadelphia. The books that he'd had in Annapolis he had sold to Monroe. His Paris years were to be costly, his government salary and much more spent to cover living expenses and his purchase of luxury items. For the future pleasures of his Monticello table, his deceased wife's half brother, nineteen-year-old James Hemings, who looked almost white, had been brought along. He was to be schooled in French cookery.

The first task of the commissioners was to implement a template of a model treaty. Jefferson had prepared a text, which, after some minor changes, Congress had approved. The challenge had been to find language affirming that the commissioners were negotiating on behalf of a united country rather than a confederation in which the parts were more than the whole. Europeans needed assurance that Congress spoke for the American nation. Many doubted that there was such a thing. In spring 1784, in Annapolis, Jefferson had composed drafts of treaties with Denmark, the Netherlands, and Prussia. The commissioners now took what he had composed and made appropriate changes.

A model treaty covering all conceivable situations, the template could be adjusted for any particular negotiation. It offered to establish relations on liberal principles that implied that the United States was a desirable trading partner; it promoted freedom of trade on mutually favorable terms; it required freedom of the seas; it established rules for the treaty's maintenance and protection; it set up trading mechanisms, including the exchange of consulships; it made provisions for how adjustments would occur if one or both signatories were at war with other nations or with each other; and it provided rules to guide every contingency Jefferson could think of that might arise in international trade, from piracy to port fees. It was a clear and concise legal document, its emphasis on the declaration of recognition and on mutual commitment to peace and trade under fair rules between equal parties. "There shall be a firm, inviolable and universal peace and sincere friendship between"—and though the text addressed Denmark and Norway, it was to be the binding template for every treaty. It also embodied Jefferson's desire to liberate official documents from archaic and technical language. Clarity and readability were his priority.

Jefferson and Adams composed the list of countries to approach. Franklin had the French portfolio. Negotiations proceeded slowly or not at all, partly because most European countries viewed the United States as unreliable, a weak government of contentious and conflicting parts. Jefferson, though he railed against British anti-American propaganda, recognized that the structure of the United States government was an international liability. Many agreed, especially Madison, who had pledged that he would serve via letters as Jefferson's eyes and ears in Congress. Jefferson would keep him informed about European affairs. It intensified an already flourishing correspondence that was to become central to their political partnership and their personal friendship.

Madison's letters kept Jefferson aware of American political developments. Jefferson, by virtue of his age and experience, was deferred to. By nature, Madison was deferential but independent of thought. Both were critical of Congress's weaknesses: the disadvantages of its rules for voting; its lack of checks and balances; its factiousness; its limited power to command support; and the structural misconception that made Congress the sole governing body, simultaneously both legislature and executive. Without a unified central government with the power to tax, the United States could not deal as an equal with the European powers. It was a widely shared view, though strong differences of opinion existed, even between Madison and Jefferson, about how much more power the central government should have. The letters between Madison and Jefferson in the five years that Jefferson was in Paris confirmed and advanced a friendship that was to be sacred to their lives and to their political partnership.

A relationship also had begun between Jefferson and twenty-six-year-old James Monroe, the war veteran from Virginia who had in

1780 started his own career in politics. Jefferson had become his mentor and facilitator. "Your kindness and attention to me in this and a
variety of other instances," Monroe wrote to him, "has really put me
under such obligations to you that I fear I shall hardly ever have it in
my power to repay them." Monroe had neither Madison's nor Jefferson's intellectual firepower. He was far from their equal in learning
and scholarship, but he had a ruggedly reliable intellect, a disciplined
work ethic, an ambition to be of service, and a commitment to the republican values that Madison and Jefferson believed in: that all power
comes from and resides in the people; that the new nation should
combine sovereign states, each in control of its domestic affairs, with
a national government in charge of international and multistate interactions; and that each state and the central government would be,
with certain safeguards, a modified vision of a democratic polity in
which educated, virtuous, and otherwise qualified leaders would be
elected to govern by freeholders. Also a strong Francophile, Monroe
eventually would ascend through local, national, and international
service to the presidency.

Jefferson and John Adams had been colleagues in the Second
Continental Congress. Jefferson had admired Adams's eloquent voice
and views in the debates about independence. Eight years older than
Jefferson, a self-made lawyer and political leader, Adams had been
ahead of Jefferson in calling for independence. By 1775–1776, they
were in full agreement. Jefferson's became the pen that synthesized
what Adams, Lee, Mason, and others had been voicing in debate.
When Abigail Adams joined her husband and eldest son in Paris,
Jefferson became a regular visitor at their home. Abigail Adams and
Jefferson had a cordial, affectionate friendship, teasing and gallant on
his part, charming and perceptive on hers. They did each other little
domestic courtesies. Later, in London, Abigail shopped for her Paris
friend; he did the reverse. Jefferson, Franklin, and Madison agreed
that Adams had a short fuse; that he was brilliant but impulsive; that

he was sometimes an intemperate diplomat, bluntly aggressive in his American patriotism. Franklin thought of Adams as a flawed genius who combined integrity and foolishness. The consummate diplomat, Franklin feared Adams's bluntness, especially in dealing with the French. Clearly not a Virginia gentleman, soft-spoken and discreet, Adams was the flinty New Englander who spoke his mind almost regardless of anything else. Jefferson valued him for his honesty, integrity, learning, directness, and energy. In Paris, they worked together amicably.

During 1784 and 1785, the commissioners proposed trade treaties with numbers of European countries, mostly without success. They had discussions with the French foreign minister about French-American trade, particularly tariffs and markets for tobacco and whale oil, mostly stymied by the difficulty of aligning in mutually profitable ways the heavily protectionist and highly taxed French structure with the American commitment to free trade, low taxes, and expanding markets. The French minister urged the speedy repayment of the loans that had helped make the Revolution successful. France's debts were immense, its tax structure corrupt.

There was also the challenge of dealing with the assault by North African state-sponsored pirates on American ships in the Mediterranean; the difficulties of dealing with the French and British governments about implementing the peace treaty, particularly differences about deference and self-interest between the French and American ministers; the disposition of American citizens stranded or imprisoned in Europe and in England during the Revolution, most of them impoverished; and, among other concerns, the adjudication with the French authorities about American vessels, whether acting legally or illegally, caught in the net of the French port authorities constantly seeking bribes and taxes through seizures and confiscations. Every matter, more or less, required a regular report to John Jay, Congress's secretary of foreign affairs. Jefferson wrote most of the reports.

In mid-1785, Franklin left for home. Appointed his successor as minister plenipotentiary, Jefferson spent most mornings writing official and personal letters. He took long afternoon walks in the Bois de Boulogne from a large, handsome, beautifully designed house he had moved to in the middle of October 1785, the Hôtel de Langeac at the corner of rue de Berri and Avenue des Champs-Élysées, almost at what was then the western boundary of Paris. It was, he felt, more suited to the dignity of an American ambassador. "I have at length procured a house," he wrote to Abigail Adams, "in a situation much more pleasing to me than my present. . . . It suits me in every circumstance but the price, being dearer than the one I am now in. It has a clever garden to it," which he was to have gardeners cultivate for flowers and vegetables, including American corn. It was to be his residence for the rest of his stay in Paris. In his mind, its grandeur was appropriate and useful. And he did a modest amount of entertainment, assisted by a staff of servants. As always, he felt entitled to live above his means.

And his French social and intellectual life was constantly expanding, especially his attendance at salons hosted by aristocratic French women and frequented by many prominent figures of the French Enlightenment and the intellectual establishment. They were all pro-American, embodying the paradox of French aristocrats who admired republican principles, led privileged upper-class lives, and had little to no influence on Louis XVI, his ministers, and French policies. When, in 1785, Lafayette returned from a visit to America, his home in Paris became one of Jefferson's second homes, where he and other Americans and French liberal aristocrats met for social pleasure and to work in the interest of French-American relations. Lafayette became Jefferson's closest French friend and colleague.

In addition to his official duties, Jefferson was also busy with his pen in ways that characterize his mind and skills as a writer, even if inadequately. In autumn 1784, soon after his arrival in Paris, he had available for the first time large numbers of English and European newspapers. The attacks in print on the viability of the United States as an independent nation infuriated him. British articles were widely reprinted throughout Europe. The British government subsidized articles depicting the American Confederation as dysfunctional, its people ungovernable, daily life controlled by mobs, and many citizens eager to reimpose British governance or immigrate to Great Britain. It was a powerful disinformation campaign. Great Britain had lost on the battlefield. It had not yet, though, given up on its propaganda war, especially in the popular press. Adams wrote a perceptive and informative letter to Congress about this pernicious anti-American propaganda. Jefferson had an idea of his own: a published rebuttal written in the first person by a pro-American English officer who has "lately returned from service and residence in the U.S. of America."

The officer was, of course, a fiction, the two-thousand-word essay Jefferson's invention. He hoped to publish it in two of the most widely read and respected European newspapers. It did appear in the *Gazette de Leyde*, through the efforts of a Dutch citizen, a friend of Adams who had been representing American interests in Holland. Jefferson, who read eighteenth-century essays with semifictional qualities, tried a genre that he had no experience with; it was also not a genre best suited to hit its target. That he chose to create a fictional character probably reflected his judgment that it would be unwise to publish a rebuttal with which he could be associated. It would not be compatible with the dignity of his office. The fictional disguise appealed to him as a viable alternative, and he was angry enough to give it a try. He did not give the narrator a name. He did not sign it with his own name. It was a genre that he was not to attempt again, a momentary and singular instance. The fictional narrator presented the American version of conditions in the United States, providing context and nuance, rebutting the British version point by point.

The intent was for the British nationality of the narrator to provide credibility that an American persona or Jefferson himself would
not have. A reader, the narrator argued, should gauge the reliance to
be placed on British newspapers by examining what account a Frenchman would "give of the affairs of France, if a Dutchman, what of the
United Netherlands; if an Irishman, what of Ireland. . . . If he finds
that those of his own country with which he happens to be acquainted
are wickedly misrepresented, let him consider how much more likely
to be so are those of a nation so hated as America. America was the
great pillar on which British glory was raised; America has been the
instrument for levelling that glory with the dust." Jefferson's narrator's
account is exculpatory propaganda. Neither depiction of the American scene was fully accurate. The United States indeed had serious
social, political, and economic tensions, especially about loyalists,
taxes, debt, currency, recession, and inflation. That American newspapers would corroborate Jefferson's views was a given. They were,
though, as biased as British newspapers.

In June 1785, Jefferson seized another opportunity to influence
European opinion, this time for a more select reading public. A young
well-connected French scholar, Jean-Nicolas Démeunier, the secretary to Louis XVI's brother, had been commissioned by the creators
of the newest attempt at a universal encyclopedia, the *Encyclopédie
Méthodique*, to write sections on the individual American states and a
separate article on the United States. The *Encyclopédie Méthodique*, a
huge undertaking, was a revised version of Denis Diderot's influential
earlier *Encyclopedie*. The first of the new encyclopedia's 210 volumes
had been published in 1782. Démeunier drew on the limited sources
available to him, particularly Guillaume Thomas François Raynal's
Philosophical and Political History of the Two Indies (1770).

Jefferson admired the ongoing *Encyclopédie Méthodique*. He despised Raynal's book, particularly its sloppy, ill-informed, but influential section on the American colonies and, in subsequent revisions,

the United States. Démeunier, who had reservations about Raynal, appealed to Jefferson for help. Would the American minister, the author of *Notes on the State of Virginia*, please read the manuscript section on the United States and offer whatever suggestions and corrections came to mind? Appalled by the inaccuracies and anti-American prejudices in Démeunier's manuscript, Jefferson put his pen to work. He wanted, in addition to correcting factual errors, to transform its anti-American slant into pro-American propaganda. Having himself no ax to grind, Démeunier was happy to have Jefferson's help, though he could not anticipate that the amount of help he would get might exceed his needs and his desires. The article on Virginia relied heavily on *Notes on the State of Virginia*.

From January to June 1786, Jefferson became the unacknowledged coauthor of the article on the United States. It was at greater length than the articles on any other country in the four volume *Économie politique et diplomatique* portion of the *Encyclopédie Méthodique*. Jefferson's secretary, William Short, with a keen critical mind of his own, succinctly summed up what had happened: Démeunier's article on the United States "was as erroneous and as false as might be expected from a man who had made the Abbé Raynal his model, and his own lively imagination his guide. Fortunately, he has candor, and after putting this article under Mr. Jefferson's inspection, he readily struck out and altered the most flagrant errors. It remains at present as different from what he had written it, as to matters of fact, as virtue from vice, and as to reflections it is changed from censure to eulogy. Still however this article is very imperfect."

The effort that Jefferson put into the revisions as copy editor, as overall editor, and as contributor was immense. His pen and energy expressed his patriotic outrage. At the same time, he was controlled and disciplined. He feared that if Démeunier's text were allowed to stand, the interests of the United States and his own efforts in France would be damaged. It would be a French intellectual version of British anti-American journalism. Whatever questions Démeunier asked, he answered in writing. As he read the manuscript, he commented in memoranda and letters, suggesting improvements and corrections. He created substantial new material, transforming Démeunier's hostile canards about the leaders of the Revolution, American social customs, and the conditions under which the Confederation Congress had created a new nation into complete approbation. Démeunier's original text was Eurocentric, anti-American, and inaccurate to an extent that drove Jefferson's pen into rebuttal, in the same way that, in *Notes on the State of Virginia*, he had rebutted the claims of the French naturalist Comte de Buffon about the inferiority of all life in the Northern Hemisphere.

On the whole, the prose of Jefferson's contributions to the *Encyclopédie Méthodique* is utilitarian. A few paragraphs, though, stand out as examples of his personal, patriotic, and moral preoccupations, and his eloquent command of written English. Like many French and European intellectuals, Démeunier particularly emphasized the prevalence and the cruelty of slavery in the United States. This was a sore point for Jefferson, and he responded with an evocative, measured, and eloquent statement on the subject. It is an emotional exclamation about an institution that he otherwise tried to stay as unemotional about as possible.

It also expresses his increasing awareness and acceptance of the pernicious consequences of his generation's indefinite postponement of emancipation: "What a stupendous, what an incomprehensible machine is Man! Who can endure toil, famine, stripes, imprisonment and death itself in vindication of his own liberty, and the next moment be deaf to all those motives whose power supported him through his trial, and inflict on his fellow men a bondage, one hour of which is fraught with more misery than ages of that which he rose in rebellion to oppose. But we must await with patience the workings of an overruling providence, and hope that it is preparing the deliverance of these, our suffering brethren. When the measure of their tears shall be full, when their groans shall have involved heaven itself in darkness, doubtless a god of justice will awaken to their distress, and by diffusing light and liberality among their oppressors, or at length by his exterminating thunder, manifest his attention to the things of this world, and that they are not left to the guidance of a blind fatality." The opening exclamation has a touch of Sophocles' *Antigone*: "Many are the wonders but nothing as wonderful as man," and the final sentence brings to mind Lincoln's affirmation in his Second Inaugural Address of the eventual assertion of cosmic justice. For Jefferson, in his lifetime, it seemed best to live as quietly as possible with an evil which seemed beyond his capacity to remove.

In Paris, in 1785, the subject came up in a different, more abstract, but still noteworthy way. At first Jefferson had intended *Notes on the State of Virginia* only for the eyes of the secretary to the French minister and a few others. Gradually, he expanded the audience. In Philadelphia, he looked into having a small private edition printed. When that seemed too expensive, he planned to have an edition printed in Paris or London, where the cost would be less. "I could not get my notes printed here," he wrote to Madison before leaving Philadelphia, "and therefore refer it till I shall cross the water where I will have a few copies struck off and send you one." "Struck off" meant privately printed. "If I do you shall assuredly have one," he wrote to the secretary of the Confederation Congress, who was an expert on Indian tribes. "I shall take the liberty of adding some of your notes. . . ."

In Paris, in late 1784, he had two hundred copies printed to distribute to those in his orbit he believed would be interested in the subject. The process of printing and private distribution at this stage was an exercise in authorial self-deceit. Publication was implicit in the venture almost from the start. If it had stayed in manuscript form, it might have remained a private document. But once Jefferson decided to print a private edition, public availability was inevitable. There were no copyright laws to prevent anyone from printing an edition for public sale. To his distress, he learned that a Frenchman who had obtained a copy had determined to translate *Notes*. Rather than trying to prevent the unpreventable, he offered to cooperate with a better-qualified translator. "Had I, at the time of writing them, had anything more in view than the satisfying a single individual," he wrote in early 1786, "they should have been more attended to both in form and matter. Poor as they are, they have been thought worthy of a surreptitious translation here, with the appearance of which very soon I have been threatened." He chose to accept the inevitable. In early 1787, he arranged with a London publisher for an authorized English-language edition.

Its reception was mixed, particularly in response to the paragraphs on slavery and race. David Ramsay, a distinguished South Carolinian, one of the first historians of the Revolution, who had also served in the Continental Congress, took issue with Jefferson's view of the intellectual and moral essence of negroes. "I admire your generous indignation at slavery," he wrote to him, "but think you have depressed the negroes too low. I believe all mankind to be originally the same and only diversified by accidental circumstances." For Ramsay, this apparent inferiority was the result of chance. He believed it likely that over time Blacks in the Northern states would become less black, the result of climate, not miscegenation, an early statement of a theory that was to become popular in the first half of the nineteenth century. "The state of society has an influence not less than climate." He had no doubt that what Jefferson claimed is racial essence was the result of cultural and educational deprivation. Indeed, "back country" white Americans "are as much savage as the Cherokees. I believe . . . that were it not for the commercial cities on the sea coast even the use of a plough would far to the westward be forgotten."

Jefferson responded to Ramsay: "I am honored with your letter . . . and obliged by your kind notice of what I had written on the subject of my own state. If I have any merit from it, it is in being fully sensible of its imperfections." The gradual whitening of the Hemings family, one of whose members was living in his household in Paris, was a reality that may or may not have come to mind. In fact, he had nothing to say in response to Ramsay's views about slavery and race. He thanked him for his general praise and then changed the subject.

Jefferson gave a copy of *Notes on the State of Virginia* to the Adamses, who had it in hand in June 1785 as they journeyed from Paris to Calais. Adams had been appointed the first minister of the United States to the Court of St. James's. They read it aloud to each other as their carriage jostled along the ragged roads of the French countryside. Sad to be leaving their Paris life and friends, they traveled through a drought-starved landscape. "I pity this people from all my soul," Adams wrote to Jefferson. "The Country is a heap of Ashes. Grass is scarcely to be seen. . . . The Flocks of Sheep and herds of Cattle, through the Country, stalk about the Fields like Droves of Walking Skeletons." The Virginia that Jefferson depicted in *Notes* made a verdant contrast to the barren French landscape. "I thank you kindly for your Book," Adams wrote. "It is our Meditation all the Day long. I cannot now say much about it, but I think it will do its Author and his Country great Honour. The Passages upon Slavery, are worth Diamonds. They will have more effect than Volumes written by mere Philosophers."

The Adamses, who deplored slavery, worried that it was the rock on which the union would founder. They deplored the Southern defense of slavery and resented that its continuance had been ensured over the objections of Northern antislavery voices in the Confederation Congress. Adams had reluctantly accepted the compromises that were necessary for the creation of a unified country. Both Adamses engaged with free Blacks and former slaves as civic equals. Their eldest son, who had recently sailed home to engage with his American aspirations, was eventually to favor immediate abolition. Race was not the issue. Slavery was. What the Adamses chose to see in *Notes on the State of Virginia* were its eloquent passages about the evil of slavery and the evocation of the cosmic justice that would someday put an end to it. Adams did not comment on Jefferson's theories about race.

Jefferson had asked Adams, as soon as he arrived in London, to hand-deliver a copy to Richard Price, a well-known pro-American British liberal, a dissenting minister, a mathematician, a moral philosopher, and a pamphleteer devoted to political and religious reform. Jefferson respected him. An abolitionist who recognized the obstacles to emancipation, Price eagerly read *Notes* "with singular pleasure," he wrote to Jefferson, "and a warm admiration of your sentiments and character. How happy would the United States be were all of them under the direction of such wisdom and liberality as yours?" Unlike Ramsay, Price chose not to respond to Jefferson's belief that negros were innately inferior to whites or to respond to Jefferson's comments on the impossibility of Blacks and Whites living harmoniously together. In his letter of thanks, Price limited himself to praise for Jefferson's antislavery moralism and his opposition to the slave trade. However, his own antislavery language in *Observations on the Importance of the American Revolution*, published in 1784, had been more pointed and severe than Jefferson's. Unlike Jefferson, he emphasized, as did Samuel Johnson, that it was absurd for those who enslaved negros to proclaim in their revolt from British rule that they valued liberty above all.

Price's optimism, though, was irrepressible, and misplaced, observing "with singular pleasure that the United States are entering into measures for discountenancing it, and for abolishing the odious slavery which it has introduced. . . . Till they have done this, it will not appear they deserve the liberty for which they have been contending. For it is self-evident, that if there are any men whom they have a right to hold in slavery, there may be others who have had a right to hold them in slavery." He prudentially concluded, sounding for a moment much like Jefferson, that he was "sensible . . . that this is a work which they cannot accomplish at once. The emancipation of the Negroes must, I suppose, be left in some measure to be the effect of time and of manners."

Price told his American friend, "nothing can excuse the United States if it is not done with as much speed, and at the same time with as much effect, as their particular circumstances and situation will allow. I rejoice that on this occasion I can recommend to them the example of my own country.—In Britain, a Negro becomes a freeman the moment he sets his foot on British ground." But if Southern attitudes about slavery persisted, he painfully remarked to Jefferson, "I shall have reason to fear that I have made myself ridiculous by speaking of the American Revolution in the manner I have done; it will appear that the people who have been struggling so earnestly to save themselves from slavery are very ready to enslave others." America's European friends would be mortified, he argued. To them, American slavery was scandalous. A resolute partisan of the American experiment, Price worried that it was or soon would turn sour. He also felt concerned that his strong language had offended those whom he hoped to persuade to do the right thing.

Still, Price and other British abolitionists felt betrayed. So too did many of France's friends of Black emancipation, including Lafayette, who frequently lectured Jefferson on the subject. Jefferson did his best to placate and assuage them. He responded to Price in a descriptive, explanatory, and conciliatory tone, as if he could find some middle ground on which to condemn slavery and do nothing about it. On the proslavery and antislavery temperature of the South and the North, he was frank. On his own views, less so, probably because he was aware that in *Notes* he had said both too little and too much about slavery and race.

Would his own book, Price asked Jefferson, find readers in America or would it be dismissed as an offensive rant? "Northward of the

Chesapeake," Jefferson answered, "you may find here and there an opponent to your doctrine as you may find here and there a robber and a murderer, but in no greater number. In that part of America, there being but few slaves, they can easily disencumber themselves of them, and emancipation is put into such a train that in a few years there will be no slaves." But "southward of the Chesapeake it will find but few readers concurring with it in sentiment on the subject of slavery." In Virginia, justice is "in conflict with avarice and oppression: a conflict wherein the sacred side is gaining daily recruits from the influx into office of young men grown and growing up. These have sucked in the principles of liberty as it were with their mother's milk, and it is to them I look with anxiety to turn the fate of this question. Be not therefore discouraged. What you have written will do a great deal of good." At his alma mater, William and Mary, the young men are "under the direction (most of them) of a Mr. Wythe one of the most virtuous of characters, and whose sentiments on the subject of slavery are unequivocal." You have no cause to regret what you have written, Jefferson assured him. "It can only have a good effect." The good effect, though, would be at some distant date. And between and beyond his words to Price, Jefferson's life as a planter and slave-owner is absent, as if there are two Jeffersons: the one who could partner with Richard Price and George Wythe in their abhorrence of slavery and the one whose slaves tilled his soil, made his money, and cooked his meals.

As if his days and writing energy were almost infinitely expandable, Jefferson took up another subject. It had nothing to do with his public life or private views about contentious public issues. He had discussed the subject of English prosody or metrics in April 1782 with a French visitor to Monticello, François-Jean de Beauvoir, Marquis de Chastellux, who was nine years older than Jefferson. The two had hit it off.

High in the French military command, Chastellux had served in the Revolutionary War as the liaison between Admiral Rochambeau and General Washington. He had contributed to the success of the Yorktown campaign. Apparently, his English was excellent. Chastellux's soon-to-be-published account of his visit to Monticello in his *Travels in North America in the Years 1780, 1781, and 1782* was to include a glowing idealization of Jefferson as a Renaissance man.

Among the many subjects they discussed was English poetry. They had an engaging disagreement: Jefferson believed that the metrical patterns of English poetry, the number of feet in a line and the arrangement of stressed and unstressed syllables, conformed to the metrics of classical poetry, based on long and short syllables, called quantitative meter. Chastellux believed that English poetry essentially was based on metrical lines in which the pattern of stressed and unstressed syllables conforms to where the stress falls naturally in each word as normally pronounced—a system called qualitative meter. Chastellux was correct; Jefferson, wrong. That Jefferson, as a native reader of English poetry, could have thought otherwise is astounding. Of course, from childhood on, he had been immersed in Greek and Latin poetry, and perhaps experiments by some eighteenth-century English poets with quantitative metrics influenced him. Perhaps he had given the subject little thought before his conversation with Chastellux. When he read English poetry, no doubt he read it as qualitative verse. He could only have put the stressed accents where the normal pronunciation of each word required. Otherwise, he could not have read it with any pleasure. His ear would have rebelled, just as it would have rebelled at hearing music played out of tune.

In Paris, in October 1786, he returned to the subject. "A daily habit of walking in the Bois de Boulogne," Jefferson wrote to Chastellux, "gave me an opportunity of turning this subject in my mind and I determined to present you my thoughts on it." He now entirely agreed with Chastellux. "I began with the design of converting you to my opinion that the arrangement of long and short syllables into regular feet constituted the harmony of English verse: I ended by discovering that you were right in denying that proposition. The next object was to find out the real circumstance which gives harmony to English poetry and laws to those who make it. I present you with the result." He had needed to put his thoughts and his argument into words on paper. He was not arguing against Chastellux. He was making more fully and at length the argument Chastellux had made against him. "Error is the stuff of which the web of life is woven," he wrote to his French friend, "and he who lives longest and wisest is only able to weave out the more of it."

To show how wrong he had been and how enlightened he was now, he wrote an approximately eight-thousand-word essay in the form of a letter, "Thoughts on English Prosody." Many of the words are not Jefferson's, for the argument and exposition required extensive quotations from a wide range of English poets, including Milton, Pope, Swift, Shenstone, Gray, Young, and even lines from Genesis and Psalms. To some extent, he may have had to rely on his memory. Did he have a copy of *Paradise Lost* with him in Paris? Perhaps. Some of the other poems were not likely to be at hand. It seems unlikely that he could have had in his memory extensive quotes from William Shenstone, a minor eighteenth-century poet. The essay-length letter was not for publication. Probably no one else in Jefferson's lifetime saw it other than Chastellux. The exposition has interest only because it was written by Jefferson. And its main interest is the light it throws on Jefferson's mind, energy, and compulsions, which expressed themselves, perhaps more than in any other way, in putting pen to paper. It was a way of life. It was his life. It was also a rare moment for him: he was self-correcting.

CHAPTER EIGHT

Getting into a Scrape

1786–1787

In mid-September 1786, forty-three-year-old Thomas Jefferson took a fall. He had attempted to jump over a fence near the promenade extending from the Seine westward from the Place de la Concorde. What motivated him he never commented on, though the presence of an attractive young woman is likely to have been relevant. How twenty-six-year-old Maria Cosway responded is unknown, as is the response of anyone else who might have seen the freckled, soft-spoken, well-dressed minister sprawled on the ground in pain. He had dislocated his right wrist. His crippled right hand never healed satisfactorily. It was a reminder of that fall for the rest of his life. "How the right hand became disabled would be a long story for the left to tell," he explained a month later. "It was by one of those follies from which good cannot come, but ill may."

An Italian-born painter and musician, Maria Cosway had come to Paris with her husband, Richard Cosway, a well-known English painter of miniature portraits. Introduced to the couple by his friend, the painter John Trumbull, Jefferson put his schedule at the Cosways' disposal. They toured Paris and nearby sites of interest. On some excursions, there were numbers of people, or just three or four, and perhaps just Jefferson and Maria, though most likely, whatever the size of the party, they had opportunities to walk as a twosome. There had been a strong mutual attraction from the start. It was an uncharacteristic holiday for Jefferson.

Maria Luisa Caterina Cecilia Hadfield had been born in Florence in 1760. Her father, an English Catholic, owned an inn catering to traveling British artists and aristocrats. Her talents and attractiveness were recognized in her childhood. Unlike her four surviving siblings, she was tutored and trained in art and music, in expectation of a genteel artistic career and a superior marriage. She had numbers of flirtations in Florence and in Rome, where she had gone to further her studies. In both cities, her talents had been recognized and appreciated. She studied with well-known artists, including visiting British painters, and socialized, often flirtatiously, with Italian artists and aristocratic visitors, but none of the men who adored her adored her enough or thought it enough to their advantage to propose marriage. In happy moods, she was social, engaging, and hardworking; her sketches and paintings, her love of music, including opera, and her performances as a musician and singer testified to her talents. In moments of disappointment and depression, she retreated to the Church. The life of a nun appealed to her, possibly as an escape from a controlling mother after her father's death in 1777.

In 1779, Mrs. Hadfield, with a small purse and few connections, took Maria and her siblings to London in search of a husband for her eldest daughter. Richard Cosway, eighteen years her senior, a successful portraitist for the London aristocracy, used to getting his way by flattery or manipulation, came courting. Maria's mother greeted him as an acceptable suitor for her daughter. Under pressure, Maria assented.

When Jefferson met Maria Cosway, he could have had no illusions about the future of their relationship. Petite and fashionably dressed, with engaging blue eyes, blonde curls, a light complexion, and lovely features, she was very attractive. She was also a married woman who spoke English with an Italian accent, equally at home in convents and in salons. Part of her yearned for the cloistered life in Italy, salvation through Jesus and the Church. As an artist, she was a niche person, the rare woman who thrived intermittently and had some fine successes as a painter. Her husband was neither good-looking nor rich, but he was successful enough to afford foppish clothes, a cash gift to Maria and her family, and a handsome London life, including a lavish home. Cosway had the reputation of being a bisexual serial adulterer, a short, ugly, witty, sophisticated man at home in the London world in which he earned his living. Maria accepted her obligations, even to playing second fiddle to her husband in their painting careers, though by 1781, the year of her marriage, her paintings were being exhibited at the Royal Academy. Married in an Anglican ceremony, she subordinated her pious Catholicism to material realities. Years later, Richard became a mystical Swedenborgian. By that time, the marriage was in name only, and Maria had returned to Italy to engage in her second career, an educator of young Catholic girls.

When they met in Paris in August 1786, Jefferson and Maria Cosway initiated a few months of romantic attachment that quickened Jefferson's sense of life and recharged his body, head, and heart. His initial response to John Trumbull's invitation that he meet the Cosways had been that he had no need of new acquaintances. When Trumbull tempted him to visit a new architectural sight in Paris, Trumbull arranged that the Cosways be there. Thereafter, they saw one another frequently. There are no letters extant between Jefferson and Maria Cosway before his fall on the promenade. Clearly, from the first, they adored one another. It was never easy for Jefferson to speak his feeling into words. With his first love, as a young man in Williamsburg, when the moment came to declare himself, he had been tongue-tied. He was always better at expressing himself with his pen than his tongue. His relationship with Maria Cosway is the one instance in which he provided for posterity a record of what he felt in response to romantic love and sexual arousal. The letters between Jefferson and his wife had been or were to be destroyed. He was never to permit any to exist between himself and Sally Hemings.

Jefferson was Maria's lover exclusively with his pen, except for an occasional touch of the hand or arm, the courteous gentleman always offering his help in the brief moments required by public decorum. Words dominated the relationship, and his letters to her are among the most personally expressive and revealing that have survived of any he wrote. He had been a widower for four years, apparently without any physical intimacy with a woman. Maria wrote to him in her Italian-inflected English. He wrote with his masterly pen. Both knew, from the start, that their relationship was not likely to lead to sexual embraces, and certainly not to a future together. Though partly disguised in her London public life as an Anglican, Maria was always a committed Catholic. Her husband's extramarital sexual life would not have pierced that. She may indeed have been indifferent to it, if not at first, then certainly during the years that led to their separation. Her beauty was widely noticed in London; so were her talents. But she found few friends in a city whose mists and rain she frequently bemoaned. To her husband, she seems to have been mainly an ornament, a useful adjunct to his life. She missed Italy. In London and elsewhere, she had admirers but apparently not lovers.

On the morning in early October on which the Cosways were to depart for London, three weeks after his accident, Jefferson wrote to Maria that he had "passed the night in so much pain that I have not closed my eyes. It is with infinite regret therefore that I must relinquish your charming company for that of the Surgeon whom I have sent for to examine into the cause of this change. . . . I am in hopes it is only the having rattled a little too freely over the pavement yesterday." That rattling had been experienced in Maria's company. "If you do not go to day I shall still have the pleasure of seeing you again. If you do, god bless you wherever you go . . . and let me hear of your safe arrival in England. Addio Addio. Let me know if you do not go to day."

Having received Jefferson's hand-delivered letter, Maria immediately responded that she was "very, very sorry indeed, and [forgive me?] for having been the Cause of your pains in the [Night]. . . . And why was I not more friendly to you and less to Myself by preventing your giving me the pleasure of your Company? . . . You repeatedly said it wou'd do you no harm. . . . We shall go I believe this Morning. Nothing seems redy, but Mr. Cosway seems More dispos'd then I have seen him all this time. I shall write to you from England . . . it is impossible to be wanting to a person who has been so excessively obliging . . . it will be with infinite pleasure I shall remember the charming days we have past together, and shall long for next spring. You will make me very happy, if you would send a line . . . that I may know how you are."

Feeling pain in his hand and his heart, Jefferson took a carriage to the Pavillon de St. Denis, about nine miles from the Hôtel de Langeac, to have one last touch of Maria's hand. There was the certainty that they would write to each other. There was the hope that they would meet again in Paris or in London. "Having performed the last sad office of handing you into your carriage at the Pavillon de St. Denis," Jefferson soon wrote to her, "and seen the wheels get actually into motion, I turned on my heel and walked, more dead than alive, to the opposite door, where my own was awaiting me." He had a companion with him, also a friend of the Cosways, with whom he rode in silence until they began "a mutual confession of distress. We began immediately to talk of Mr. and Mrs. Cosway, of their goodness, their talents, their amiability." They "spoke of nothing else . . . a mutual confession." For Jefferson, this was hardly a confession at all. He had his mind entirely on Maria Cosway, despite the use of the plural. That he was more "dead than alive" was for her ears and eyes only. Regardless of the condition of his wrist, it was a pain of the heart. "I was carried home," he wrote to her. "Seated by my fire side, solitary and sad, the following dialogue took place between my Head and my Heart." If he had felt half dead at their parting, he was much more than half alive when he took his pen in hand.

In much of Jefferson's experience, the affairs of the heart—wife, children, and friends—had been inseparable from pain and loss. His father was an early and determinative loss. His siblings were part of a network of loss. Dabney Carr was dead. Four of his six children were dead. His wife, Martha, had died, slowly, lingeringly, painfully, in his presence. The war for independence had taken comrades, known and unknown. From early on, Jefferson had embraced stoic acceptance. The challenge of life in a vale of woes was to protect oneself as much as possible from debilitating pain. It required an effort of the will. It required keeping oneself busy in work one believed in. It demanded a resolution that could be strengthened by constructive reading, by intellectual, moral, and social engagement. It had not been a cure-all. It had not been completely or always successful. His despair at the death of his wife had challenged his stoicism. But after no longer than a few months he had managed his pain, and his government had given him the opportunity for evasion and distraction. It had asked him to represent it and its values in France. Of course, he carried his scars with him, but his interaction with Maria Cosway provided renewal, a quickening of life, which had its first and fullest literary expression in October 1786.

The dialogue is written in the form of a letter of over 4,600 words, composed with his left hand, the early draft or drafts of which no longer exist. Jefferson kept a copy, made from the final draft; the original he sent to John Trumbull to deliver to Maria in London. "The left hand is learning to perform the functions of the right," he wrote to Trumbull. "This however it does awkwardly and slowly. . . . I take the liberty of putting the enclosed under your cover, and of begging you to deliver it personally." He arranged to keep his correspondence with Maria in private hands because "all letters directed to me are read in the post offices both of London and Paris." Jefferson's essay-length letter, in the form of a dialogue between the Heart and the Head, was astonishingly indiscreet. That "I turned on my heel and walked, more dead than alive, to the opposite door," so disoriented was he by his regret at their parting, is a unique statement in the Jefferson oeuvre of intense emotion in a personal relationship. He may have assumed that neither the original to Maria nor the copy he kept would be made public in his lifetime. It appeared in print two years after his death. Neither the original nor its copy nor earlier drafts are known to exist, though its print appearance in the *Virginia Advocate* suggests that the source was his copy. If so, it was uncharacteristic of him not to have destroyed it. He may have wanted it to be a part of his heritage, providing it was a posthumous publication. Though Maria was still alive, she was unlikely in her Italian world to learn of it or, if she did, be compromised in 1826 by a letter written to her in English forty years before. In this first letter to Maria, Jefferson went further than he had ever gone or ever would go again in creating a record of personal self-examination.

Like many eighteenth-century writers, Jefferson was attracted to the artifice of a dialogue between opposites as a literary artifice. Each is given a voice as a way of creating dramatic interaction in what is both a meditation and a dialogue. As a writer, Jefferson identifies, isolates, and projects his thoughts and feelings into opposite corners, like opponents about to fight it out. The philosophic and religious traditions that created and nurtured him were essentially dualistic. In their reductive forms, they divided the one into two, often in conflict, whether in the human body or the body politic: the body versus the soul, evil versus good, feeling versus thought, monarchy versus republicanism, country versus city, agriculture versus manufacturing, hard money versus paper money, the North versus the South, the United

States versus Great Britain, and so on. In the opposition between Heart and Head, Jefferson could talk to himself about himself. The intent is catharsis: there is a troubling, even painful conflict within him that needs to be resolved. It needs to find rest and resolution, either in victory to one of the disputants or a new synthesis.

Literature demands organization. The dialogue genre requires oppositional voices. It tames the otherwise unstructured intensity of feeling and thought. It creates the illusion of separability, the psychological representation of the binary opposites Jefferson set up in his intellectual life: One side is essentially good; the other, bad. Compromise or reconciliation between them may be undesirable. These, though, are ideological and linguistic conveniences. In matters of the heart and head, the opposition is a literary strategy rather than an objective reality. Jefferson knows that both exist simultaneously. They are a unitary force. When artificially separated, each has a claim on validity. In his public pose, Jefferson is a man of the head. He is in his private life also a man of the heart. Though he can separate them for literary exposition, he cannot separate them in reality. His battle between the two is an expression of the strategy he uses to keep life going, to keep pain from strangling effort and action, to keep feeling alive and strong while making reasonable, realistic, and practical choices about what to do in a particular situation. His attraction to Maria was a challenge to both heart and head.

To call the letter a dialogue is true in the sense of genre and form, but in its essence it is a monologue, a formalized version of a single individual talking to himself about his thoughts and feelings. It could easily be rewritten as a monologue, simply by dropping the explicit references to unreal or fictional entities, such as the Heart, which calls the Head "my good companion," and the Head, which calls the Heart "Thou" and uses other words of direct address. This is Jefferson talking to himself. The Head-Heart division is a formal device, an attempt to limit or slow down or evade the experience in which

Head and Heart do their thing together, inseparably. This is Jefferson as a skillful writer, doing what writers do, finding a way to create a literary analogue for experience. The Heart is given the assignment of expressing how wonderful were the days he spent with the Cosways. The Head is assigned the task of deflationary self-criticism. Of course, in actuality the two operate simultaneously. Both the enthusiasm and the reality check share the experience. And Jefferson, the man of rational enlightenment and of heartfelt sentiment, devotee of John Locke and Laurence Sterne, is not so far out of touch with himself that he would not have recognized who he was and what the reality required.

The dialogue is also a love letter from a lover who has not consummated his love. There is no reason to believe, from the record as we have it and from their letters, that Jefferson and Cosway ever made physical love. No doubt he fell in love in the ways in which that word is normally used. What he entertained in his mind and his dreams probably had physical explicitness, but the fact that Maria was married certainly made a determinative difference. In his youth, he had tried his hand at adultery. He had failed. It later caused him embarrassment and grief. Maria herself had a strongly Catholic and conservative commitment. Richard Cosway and others were frequently present during their Paris excursions. Windows of opportunity were short and limited. Anyway, where could an actual love relationship between them have gone in the life and world that Jefferson was committed to and looked forward to resuming in America? He could not and did not conceive of an actual future shared with Maria. That helped make the literary dialogue possible. It is both an exploration of Jefferson's feelings for her and a stoic elegy for the impossibility of the consummation or even the long-term continuation of the relationship. For all amatory purposes, even of the imagination, the relationship was already over when Jefferson wrote what is, except for the Declaration of Independence, his most sustained and accomplished work of literary prose. Unlike anything else he wrote, it is both imaginative literature and personal revelation.

The dialogue begins with the Head noticing that its opposite, the Heart, seems "to be in pretty good trim." The Heart, hearing the irony, responds, "I am indeed the most wretched of all earthly beings. Overwhelmed with grief, every fiber of my frame distended beyond its natural powers to bear, I would willingly meet whatever catastrophe should leave me no more to feel or to fear." The Head responds, in a "So, what's new?" tone, saying, "These are the eternal consequences of your warmth and precipitation. This is one of the scrapes into which you are ever leading us." Apparently, the Head objects to being dragged along into "scrapes" by the Heart. The Head must be present where the Heart goes and the reverse. From the start, then, as if in defiance of the dialogue form, the Heart and the Head recognize that they are not independent entities. They are indeed friends, though sometimes friendly enemies. The Heart responds, "Oh my friend! This is no moment to upbraid my foibles. I am rent into fragments by the force of my grief! If you have any balm, pour it into my wounds: if none, do not harrow them by new torments. Spare me in this awful moment! At any other I will attend with patience to your admonitions."

The Head takes it on itself now to provide redirection, to use reason and intellect to overcome pain through "repentance," which will allow "reformation." I kept telling you, the Head says, that this new "friendship" was dangerous "to our tranquillity" because the greater the attachment, the greater would be "the regret at parting." The goal of the Head is "tranquillity." And good works. "While I was occupied with these objects, you were dilating with your new acquaintances, and contriving how to prevent a separation from them. Every soul of you had an engagement for the day. Yet all these were to be sacrificed, that you might dine together. Lying messengers were to be dispatched into every quarter of the city with apologies for your breach of engagement. . . . I knew you were getting into a scrape, and I would have nothing to do with it." The Heart responds that he thanks his "dear friend" for reminding him that every moment he spent with Maria he remembers and cherishes. The world became more vivid, alive, and beautiful. "The wheels of time moved on with a rapidity of which those of our carriage gave but a faint idea, and yet in the evening, when one took a retrospect of the day, what a mass of happiness had we travelled over!"

When the Head, in response, acknowledges that the newly built architectural dome where Jefferson and the Cosways had met was "worth all we had yet seen in Paris," the Heart responds, "I thought so too. But I meant it of the lady and gentleman to whom we had been presented, and not of a parcel of sticks and chips put together in pens. . . . But you, forsooth, who are eternally getting us to sleep with your diagrams and crotchets, must go and examine this wonderful piece of architecture. . . . You then, Sir, and not I, have been the cause of the present distress."

This is comedy, a witty bit of self-mockery. Without the Head's obsession with architecture, mathematics, and science, the Heart would not have met the Cosways. Jefferson of course knew from the start that he was getting into a "scrape." The Heart recognizes the accuracy of the Head's criticism. The Heart knew that the end of the affair was inherent in its beginning, which the letter implicitly acknowledges. Jefferson had no intention or possibility of breaking up the Cosways' marriage. The possibility of adultery may have tempted him. But it would have been difficult to arrange, physically or morally. "Scrape" is a lightweight, dismissive word, but it carries considerable emotional and moral power. It also delivers a touch of self-irony, a low-impact word in a high-impact situation. It is a challenge to the power of the Head and an expression of the power of the Heart to feel misery and pain. It expresses Jefferson's struggle to distance himself from pain by deflating it: Maria is gone; she was never his, and there was never the opportunity to have her except as a temporary companion. There was never the remotest possibility of Maria Cosway becoming Jefferson's wife, stepmother to his daughters, and mistress of Monticello.

The Head's sharpest point is a dagger to the heart of the Heart. "Thou art the most incorrigible of all the beings that ever sinned!" the Head reprobates. "I reminded you of the follies of the first day, intending to deduce from thence some useful lessons for you, but instead of listening to these, you kindle at the recollection, you retrace the whole series with a fondness which shews you want nothing but the opportunity to act it over again." The Heart, though, will not give up on the continuation of the relationship. "But they told me they would come back again the next year." This was a first act, he argues, not a finale. The Head responds that the Heart should not expect that to advance its happiness. Give up that illusion. "May heaven abandon me if I do!" the Heart responds, a comically absurd bit of hand-wringing. The deistic and heaven-skeptic Jefferson resorts to hyperbole to express the pain of losing what he can never have. "Very well," the Head notes. "Suppose then they come back. They are to stay here two months, and when these are expired, what is to follow?" The Head indeed has another knife to stick into the Heart. "Perhaps you flatter yourself they may come to America?"

That Maria could ever be a member of the Monticello family was inconceivable. And the emphasis on "they" makes the point that Jefferson constantly resists and evades: Maria is a married Catholic. And it is always "they" who are inseparable from the Heart's hopes. So what is the Heart imagining? A platonic relationship in which Jefferson and Maria are "just friends"? That Richard Cosway approves or at least doesn't object? That they get to spend time alone together, perhaps in musical duets or long walks? Does Jefferson, at some level of evasion or deception, imagine a sexual relationship with her? The Heart's language throughout implies that there is an active body expressing itself, though that part of his desire for Maria's company is never explicitly addressed. And in response to the Head's insistence on asking the crucial question—"What in the world are you thinking?"—the Heart responds that it sees "nothing impossible in that supposition," that somehow Maria will magically appear in America. Jefferson's sentimental and fantasy-filled Heart gives itself to this moment of magical thinking. The mysteries of life have the power to give the Heart what it desires. "Thanks to a benevolent arrangement of things," the Heart tells the Head, "the greater part of life is sunshine."

For example, the Heart asks, what if the Cosways, by whom he means Maria, should need asylum? "With what sincere sympathy I would open every cell of my composition to receive the effusion of their woes! I would pour my tears into their wounds: and if a drop of balm could be found at the top of the Cordilleras, or at the remotest sources of the Missouri, I would go thither myself to seek and to bring it. Deeply practiced in the school of affliction, the human heart knows no joy which I have not lost, no sorrow of which I have not drank! Fortune can present no grief of unknown form to me! Who then can so softly bind up the wound of another as he who has felt the same wound himself? But Heaven forbid they should ever know a sorrow!" They should come to America. Where else "could they find such objects . . . for the exercise of their enchanting art? especially the lady, who paints landscape so inimitably. She wants only subjects worthy of immortality to render her pencil immortal. The Falling spring, the Cascade of Niagara, the Passage of the Potomac through the Blue mountains, the Natural bridge. It is worth a voyage across the Atlantic to see these objects; much more to paint, and make them, and thereby ourselves, known to all ages. And our own dear Monticello, where has nature spread so rich a mantle under the eye? mountains, forests, rocks, rivers. With what majesty do we there ride above the storms! How sublime," the Heart expands, paraphrasing and quoting from *Notes on the State of Virginia*, "to look down into the workhouse of nature, to see her clouds, hail, snow, rain, thunder, all fabricated at our feet! And the glorious Sun, when rising as if out of a distant water, just gilding the tops of the mountains, and giving life to all nature!"

The American landscape, Jefferson fantasizes, would allow Maria to realize her potential as an artist. Epitomized by the view from Monticello, the American sublime would be Maria's artistic inspiration. But, the Heart acknowledges, as it brings this fantasy riff to a close, this evocation is indeed a "distraction," a romantic indulgence about impossibilities and incompatibilities. "God only knows what is to happen," the Heart wails.

The Head now takes up the challenge of transforming this fantasy into a ballast of stability. "Well. Let us put this possibility to trial then on another point. When you consider the character which is given of our country by the lying newspapers of London . . . when you reflect that all Europe is made to believe we are a lawless banditti, in a state of absolute anarchy, cutting one another's throats, and plundering without distinction, how can you expect that any reasonable creature would venture among us?" The unitary Jefferson, the American minister to the Court of Versailles, now pokes sharply at his own Heart's effusions. The clever Head turns the tables on Jefferson's self-identification as an American. The dialogue moves from a dialogue about Jefferson and Cosway to a dialogue about Jefferson's greatest love: his two countries, Virginia and the United States. In effect, Jefferson now turns the dialogue between Head and Heart to political and diplomatic business.

The Heart and the Head can indeed agree about something. The unitary Jefferson is clear about this. These are European slanders. Actually, the United States is a place of "greater tranquillity" than Europe, the Heart asserts, "where the laws are milder, or better obeyed: where everyone is more attentive to his own business, or meddles less with that of others: where strangers are better received, more hospitably treated, and with a more sacred respect." The Head agrees: "True, you and I know this, but your friends do not know it," as if the knowledge of this would result in the Cosways (or at least Maria) coming to Monticello. That "your friends do not know it" is a throwaway line from the Head to the Heart. But the unitary Jefferson knows this also. It's not the European slanders against America that might make the Cosways reluctant to visit or settle in the United States. The Cosways are and always will be dedicated Europeans.

The Heart, missing the point, still resists. "But they are sensible people who think for themselves. They will ask of impartial foreigners who have been among us, whether they saw or heard on the spot any instances of anarchy. They will judge too that a people occupied as we are in opening rivers, digging navigable canals, making roads, building public schools, establishing academies, erecting busts and statues to our great men, protecting religious freedom, abolishing sanguinary punishments, reforming and improving our laws in general, they will judge I say for themselves whether these are not the occupations of a people at their ease, whether this is not better evidence of our true state than a London newspaper, hired to lie, and from which no truth can ever be extracted but by reversing everything it says." The Heart has turned into a patriotic propagandist, a spokesperson for the wonders of the new world of republican equality, progress, and prosperity. The list is almost Jefferson's own résumé. The Head, though, isn't convinced by the switch from Maria to Lady Liberty. "Leave the bustle and tumult of society to those who have not talents to occupy themselves without them," the Head emphasizes. Friendship is but another name for "an alliance with the follies and the misfortunes of others. Our own share of miseries is sufficient." In effect, protect yourself from inevitable disappointments.

The Head continues to make its case for prudence, caution, self-control, and rationality. Its premise is that of Stoic philosophy, from the Greeks to the eighteenth century, its primary antagonist the sentimentalism of Sterne, the late-eighteenth-century emphasis on the feelings, so attractive to Jefferson in certain moods and situations. The Head argues that the best antidote to the pain that life inevitably provides is stoic renunciation. Relationships, friendships, lovers, social engagements always will disappoint. Sustainable happiness comes from one's inner resources, from a life of intellectual and emotional self-sufficiency, from the life of the mind—reading, music, art, architecture, gardens, contemplation—free of the limitations and disappointments of dependence on other people. "Friendship is but another name for an alliance with the follies and the misfortunes of others . . . our own share of miseries is sufficient."

In oppositional response, Jefferson affirms the core values of his Heart and its relation to suffering, love, and friendship: "What more sublime delight than to mingle tears with one whom the hand of heaven hath smitten. . . . To watch over the bed of sickness, and to beguile its tedious and its painful moments!" The answer or response to loss and pain is not withdrawal from companionship and society. "This world abounds indeed with misery: to lighten its burthen we must divide it with one another. . . . For assuredly nobody will care for him who cares for nobody. . . . When Heaven has taken from us some object of our love, how sweet is it to have a bosom whereon to recline our heads, and into which we may pour the torrent of our tears! Grief, with such a comfort, is almost a luxury!" The widower Jefferson apparently is referring to his pain at the death of his wife and the death of four of his children. What would Maria have made of this? Would she have offered her bosom as a likely place for him to rest his head?

The days he and Maria had spent together, the Heart continues, shone with the "sunshine of life," its glow derived not from the landscape but from love and friendship. "On these indeed the sun shone brightly! How gay did the face of nature appear! Hills, valleys, chateaux, gardens, rivers, every object wore its liveliest hue! Whence did they borrow it? From the presence of our charming companion. They were pleasing, because she seemed pleased. Alone, the scene would have been dull and insipid: the participation of it with her gave it relish." The wisdom of the Stoic philosophers, the Heart argues, "is supreme folly: and they mistake for happiness the mere absence of pain. Had they ever felt the solid pleasure of one generous spasm of the heart, they would exchange for it all the frigid speculations of their lives."

The Heart has an additional lesson to teach. The Head, the Heart claims, having fixed on another convenient Jeffersonian binary, represents "science." But the Heart represents "morals," though they share "a divided empire." But the Heart, the Heart claims, is the better guide to moral conduct and happiness. Its directions should be followed. And to clinch the argument most tellingly, the American Revolution, Jefferson's Heart proclaims, was an implementation of the American heart. "If our country, when pressed with wrongs at the point of the bayonet, had been governed by its heads instead of its hearts, where should we have been now? hanging on a gallows as high as Haman's."

In the final sentences of the essay, Jefferson brings the Heart and Head into alignment. He allows for the utility and realism of the stoicism the Head represents. Pain and pleasure are alternative but coexisting realities; such is human nature, such is the human condition. The Heart rejects the Head's counterargument that giving priority to the Heart increases pain and misery. No, it was all worth it, the Heart says. "We have no rose without its thorn; no pleasure without alloy. It is the law of our existence; and we must acquiesce. It is the condition annexed to all our pleasures. . . . True, this condition is pressing cruelly on me at this moment. I feel more fit for death than life. But when I look back on the pleasures of which it is the consequence, I am conscious they were worth the price I am paying. Notwithstanding your endeavors too to damp my hopes, I comfort myself with expectations of their promised return. Hope is sweeter than despair, and they were too good to mean to deceive me."

Jefferson the optimist, the denier and evader of reality who can, with his chameleon capability, with the deepest sincerity, use whatever approach suits him most in the context, envisions a world of sunshine, a world that could not possibly be so cruel or unsatisfactory as permanently to deny him what he desires. Speaking as the Heart, he acknowledges that he is sufficiently in love to be a verbal lover but practical enough as the Head to know that neither he nor Maria are in a position even to try to make their relationship a physical let alone an enduring one. Still, the Heart proclaims, there is friendship. It will allow the Heart to prosper, to be the guiding moral beacon that gives the Head its due but the Heart its primacy. "In the summer, said the gentleman," they will return. "But in the spring, said the lady: and I should love her forever, were it only for that! Know then, my friend, that I have taken these good people into my bosom: that I have lodged them in the warmest cell I could find: that I love them, and will continue to love them through life: that if fortune should dispose them on one side the globe, and me on the other, my affections shall pervade its whole mass to reach them." Of course, "them" means Maria.

This essay-length dialogue between the Heart and the Head was to be the most intense expression of the relationship between Jefferson and Cosway. Jefferson could not and did not conceive of a future shared with her. That helped make the dialogue possible. It is both a celebration and exploration of Jefferson's feelings and an elegy for the impossibility of the continuation of the love relationship. For all amatory purposes, even of the imagination, their love relationship was in the process of becoming a loving friendship. Unlike anything else he ever wrote, it is both imaginative and personal. The Jefferson-Cosway relationship, after Maria returned to London in October 1786 and during the years afterward, including some brief time they spent together in Paris the next year, was to be mostly epistolary, and it dwindled over time. The relationship was, for Jefferson, at its most powerful, intense, and meaningful when he wrote about it in this extraordinary literary compromise between factual narrative and emotional fiction, between the intellect and the imagination. It was a high point in Jefferson's life as a writer.

As he was about to mail Trumbull the letter containing the dialogue, Jefferson received a letter of four pages postmarked from Antwerp. He eagerly opened it, assuming it was from Maria. Her name was at the bottom of the last page. But "I found that your name was to four lines only instead of four pages." The rest was by Trumbull about his own affairs. "I thank you for the four lines however because they prove you think of me," Jefferson responded. "Little indeed, but better a little than none. To shew how much I think of you I send you the enclosed letter of three sheets of paper," the large closely written sheets of the dialogue, "a history of the evening I parted with you."

His disappointment at getting only four lines from Maria, in comparison to his prolixity, prompted an attempt at humor. It is deflationary, mainly of Maria and of women. Its self-modesty both expresses and exemplifies self-praise. He is so confident that his dialogue's "only merit" is not its "length and dullness" that he can state that it is. And the joke implies that Jefferson is unaware that Maria might find it a touch insulting. "But how expect you should read a letter of three mortal sheets of paper? I will tell you. Divide it into six doses of half a sheet each, and every day, when the toilette begins, take a dose, that is to say, read half a sheet. By this means it will have the only merit its length and dullness can aspire to, that of assisting your coëffeuse [female hairdresser] to procure you six good naps of sleep. I will even allow you twelve days to get through it, holding you rigorously to one condition only, that is, that at whatever hour you receive this, you do not break the seal of the enclosed till the next toilette. Of this injunction I require a sacred execution. I rest it on your friendship, and that in your first letter you tell me honestly whether you have honestly performed it." He is jokingly suggesting that she read the dialogue while partly dressed and doing something distinctively feminine. There is a hint of Pope's extended parodic riff on Belinda's toilette in *The Rape of the Lock*, a poem Jefferson knew well and a female name he had made use of in his youthful correspondence with John Page.

It was a form of faux lovemaking by gesture and word. Even if her letters to him "are as long as the bible," he wrote, "they will appear short to me. Only let them be brim full of affection." His wrist, alas, mended slowly. But "my mind . . . mends not at all, but broods constantly over your departure." And he could treat his writing disability with humorous displacements, as if his hands were independent entities: "My right hand presents its devoirs [duties] to you, and sees with great indignation the left supplanting it in a correspondence so much valued. You will know the first moment it can resume its rights." When, late in October, she received his two letters, Maria had much to say about her tender feelings in a charming combination of her excellent Italian and poor English, though nothing that indicated that she had fully understood, let alone embraced, the implications of Jefferson's dialogue. Written in a literary genre she was unfamiliar with at a level of complexity for which she had not been educated, Maria still did feel its emotional power. Jefferson's letter overwhelmed her heart and her English.

Did she deserve the "kind things" that he wrote? she asked. Was it a love letter? A friendship letter? To what extent was the letter actually about her? "But what am I doing, that I write so much English when I can write in my own language, and become a little less involved," by which she meant involved in the syntax as well as the heart. She began in English. "How I wish I?] could answer the Dialogue! But I hon[estly think my hear?]t is invisable, and Mute, at this moment more than usual[l it is?] full or ready to burst with all the variety of Sentiments, which a very feeling one is Capable of; sensible of My loss a[t] separating from the friends I left at Paris, I have hardly time to indulge a shamisly tribute. . . . You seem to be Such a Master on this subject, that whatever I may say will appear trifelling, not well express'd, faintly represented but felt."

Her stumbling words and syntax spoke from the heart. "Your letter could employ me for some time, an hour to Consider every word, to every sentence I could write a volume, but I could wish that my selfishness was not reproching to Me, for with difficulty do I find a line but after having admired it, I recolect some part concerns Me. Why do you say so Many kind things? Why present so many opportunities for my feeling undeserving of them, why not leave me a free consolation in admiring a friend, without the temptation [. . .] to my Vanity?" She then turned, in Italian, exclusively to matters of the head, especially her dislike of London, plaintively bewailing its weather, tone, and spiritual climate in comparison to its Italian parallels. London depressed her, independent of any "melancholy" she felt on parting from her Paris friends.

Cosway's response to Jefferson's dialogue was not a love letter or a disquisition about love's complexities. She was, on the one hand, almost embarrassed by his effusiveness; on the other, she felt unworthy and at a loss about how to respond. Underlying her garbled English is her ambivalence about what feelings to express and how to express them. Purposely changing in the rest of the letter from English to fluent Italian, she turned away from expressions of the heart to the language of rational analysis and description: an account of her trip from Paris and her reaction to London, especially the spiritual and emotional void she felt in a city in which she was a cultural and psychological stranger. London was without the consoling Catholic markers of time and religiosity that Paris and, to an even greater extent, Florence and Rome pervasively contained. "Everything is tranquil, quiet and gloomy, there are no Bells ringing to announce to us some festival, service or celebration. . . . There are no Monasteries which contain men of God who at all hours pray for us and for all those who do not pray, all who are lost." She is a stranger in a strange land.

Did Jefferson, reading Maria's letter, with its Catholic religiosity, especially its evocation of the consoling voices of the priesthood, and her regret that there are no monasteries in England, give thought to how his own condemnation of the priesthood as a center of superstition and exploitation might have clashed with Maria's beliefs? In their golden September and October days, had there been any talk of serious things, of their divergent belief systems and worldviews, their differences in religion, culture, and values? Could it ever have been possible for Jefferson to imagine the piously Catholic Maria as the mistress of Monticello? The husband who, Maria writes, "sends you a thousand Compliments" and to whom she pretends Jefferson has equally directed his "attentions" ("I shall never forget your attentions to us") is a Protestant Londoner whom she has married outside of her faith for pecuniary reasons. The references and tone are of a woman who believes she has no alternatives, that her relationship with Jefferson in Paris was a transient escape, a transcultural episode with no possibility of a meaningful consummation. Since her marriage to Richard Cosway, she has never had an alternative except separation from him under circumstances that would allow her to return to Italy and the Church. The London weather burdens her spirits. Its Protestantism threatens her salvation. It is a sad letter, also evasive and resigned, not a love letter at all. Jefferson probably expected something more, and it marks for him his own awareness that, as much as the Heart has its powers, the Head, an overruling monitor in regard to illicit affairs, has already begun the transformation for both of them of something romantic and erotic into friendship alone.

During the last three months of 1786, Jefferson had Maria frequently in mind. "I am determined when you come next not to admit the idea that we are ever to part again." In response to her question regarding a good friend of theirs about to visit London, he wrote, "I wish she could put me into her pocket when she goes, or you, when she comes back.—Mercy, cramp! that twitch was too much. I am done, I am done." An erotic current flows through the courtly language and the playful pockets. At the same time, its comic exaggerations gently deflate; the intensity remains, but at a distance. While neither may have defined in their heads the nature of the communication, probably both felt in the heart and through their bodies the erotic charge, including Jefferson's "twitch." We know very little about Jefferson's erotic life. But this letter, among other indirect expressions, dramatizes the obvious fact that he had one. And if Maria was not to return to Paris soon, he was still "determined not to suppose I am never to see you again. I will believe you intend to go to America . . . that I shall meet you there, and visit with you all those grand scenes. I had rather be deceived, than live without hope. It is so sweet! It makes us ride so smoothly over the roughnesses of life."

In November 1786, he expressed once more his fear that she would never come to Paris again. His favorite trope is that his "poor heart has been duped by the fondness of its wishes. What a triumph for the head!" But, with Jefferson, that was and always would be the case: the head will triumph, though the heart will have its regular opportunity to express itself, almost as a condition that allows the head to win out. "I begin, my dear Madam, to write a little with the right hand, and you are by promise, as well as by inclination, entitled to its first homage. But I write with pain and must be short. This is good news for you; for were the hand able to follow the effusions of the heart, that would cease to write only when this shall cease to beat. My first letter warned you of this danger. I became sensible myself of my transgression and promised to offend no more. Your goodness seems to have induced you to forgive, and even to flatter me. That was a great error. When sins are dear to us we are but too prone to slide into them again. The act of repentance itself is often sweetened with the thought that it clears our account for a repetition of the same sin."

His letters of November 19 and 29 and December 24, 1786, are partly love letters, but they are undercut throughout by the realities of who they are and their situations. If he could write by the regular post, he explains, "I should trouble you too often: for I am never happier than when I commit myself into dialogue with you, though it be but in imagination. . . . When those charming moments were present which I passed with you, they were clouded with the prospect that I was soon to lose you: and now, when I pass the same moments in review, I recollect nothing but the agreeable passages, and they fill me with regret. Thus, present joys are damped by a consciousness that they are passing from us; and past ones are only the subjects of sorrow and regret." It is almost an adieu, a consoling and pleasurable evocation of gains and losses. It ends with a blessing: "God bless you! may your days be many and filled with sunshine! May your heart glow with warm affections, and all of them be gratified! write to me often. Write affectionately, and freely, as I do to you. Say many kind things, and say them without reserve. They will be food for my soul." But how can he expect Maria to write to him "without reserve"? And how can he expect her self-protective responses to turn into reciprocal effusions?

His letters could not have been understood by any contemporary as anything but love letters. For Jefferson and his culture, they are explicit enough. Maria's, though, had said no such things to him. And his courtly amorousness is not an approach to the relationship that he can sustain. As his Head knows, his "poor heart [has] been duped by the fondness of its wishes." But why, the Heart laments, had nature not "formed us like the birds of the air, able to fly where we please. . . . I was so unlucky when very young, as to read the history of Fortunatus. He had a cap of such virtues that when he put it on his head, and wished himself anywhere, he was there. I have been all my life sighing for this cap. Yet if I had it, I question if I should use it but once. I should wish myself with you, and not wish myself away again." He worked hard to negotiate between the priapic and the possible. "I do not know for what crime I must experience the punishment of Tantalus, every day I believe it near, but that day never comes."

Such explicit expressions of love can be presumed to have existed previously only with his wife. Jefferson was not alone among his contemporaries in finding Fortunatus's capabilities an apt embodiment of his hope to be restored to the presence of an absent loved one, to be, erotically, in her pocket or she in his. And Jefferson had more than the occasional inclination to indulge in magical thinking. The hope that Maria and her husband would come to America, as visitors or residents, was beyond absurd. In fact, because London was a lot closer, Jefferson did not need Fortunatus's magic cap. And what if Maria had responded, "Come and join me in London?" Would Jefferson have gone? Not likely. And in what role would Maria have welcomed him? He has an alternative. "Think of me much, and warmly. Place me in your breast with those who you love most: and comfort me with your letters." The untenable and compromised "affair" had been elevated to a conceit. Jefferson was happy to place it there. It had always been an expression of desire and resilience, of fantasy and idealism, of Jefferson's brilliance as a writer, of the conditions of his personality, and of the specificity of his values.

Through the winter and spring of 1787, Maria wrote to him with explicit realism. She had become for him something she was not, an object of a sort that she did not want to be and that might damage him as well. It was put partly in gender terms, partly as concern for his future, given the impossibility of a union between them. She felt unfairly and destructively targeted, no matter how good his intentions. His feelings were a burden to her and a danger to himself. She was herself not worthy of his unrealistic view of her, she wrote to him, the strength of his sentiments were not appropriate, and his depiction of himself in his letters as a forlorn romantic devastated by loss would undercut if not compromise his achievements and his intellect.

"Of all the torments, temptations, and weariness, the female has always been the principal and most powerful object," she wrote to him on February 15, 1787, "and this is to be the most feared by you at present, from my pen. Are you to be painted in future ages sitting solitary and sad, on the beautiful Monticello tormented by the shadow of a woman who will present you a deformed rod, twisted and broken, instead of the emblematical instrument belonging to the muses, held by genius, inspired by wit, from which all that is pleasing, beautiful and happy can be described to entertain, and satisfy a mind capable of investigating every minutia of a lively imagination and interesting descriptions?" No woman could live up to his romantic fantasy. And his fantasies, she feared, were self-damaging. She was wrong. Jefferson's dialogue between the Heart and the Head would become to posterity a Jeffersonian asset, testimony that he indeed had both a heart and a head, that he was not completely sphinx-like about his feelings, that at least in this relationship he had expressed himself with spontaneous emotion at the epitome of his gifts as a writer.

Cosway's February 1787 letter is one of complaint, pain, and disappointment in herself and her life. She cannot, she believes, live up either to her own or Jefferson's expectations. His letters became increasingly short, hers longer than before, a touch incoherent and self-pitying. He wanted and expected a muse, so she imagines. Even if there were no language barrier between them, she cannot, she thinks, be what she imagines he wants her to be, a muse to inspire and reward him. It is a riff of self-pitying pain, with little to no basis in or knowledge of Jefferson's personality. Older and wiser than Maria, tempered by the loss of wife and children, Jefferson apparently had already moved on. By mid-1787, what had been a brief romantic involvement had become a courtly correspondence between a very busy man and one of his many friends. Unable to work at her art, a victim of her gender, her marriage, her "melancholy," her detestation of London, and the restraints of patriarchy, Maria Cosway had a very different daily reality: "I attempt, I exercise and end by being witness of My own disappointment and incapacity of executing, the Poet, the Historian, or my own conceptions of imagination. Thus the Mornings are spent regretting they are not longer, to have More time to attempt again in Search of better success, or thinking they have been too long and have afforded me Many Moments of uneasiness, anxiety and a testimony of my not being able to do anything." Jefferson kept very busy.

Not long after receiving Maria's letter of New Year's Day 1787, Jefferson left Paris for four months. A tour of southern France and perhaps of northern Italy had been on his mind for some time. Much as he liked Paris, he did not like its weather, and the winter of 1786–1787 had been especially severe. He felt cold, he had a cold, his headaches came all too frequently, he got insufficient exercise, and the grinding day-to-day business of negotiating resolutions and agreements about the problems of individual Americans and about French-American trade wore on him. When Charles Gravier, Comte de Vergennes, the astute French minister of foreign affairs, whom Louis XVI heavily relied on, died in February 1787, Jefferson delayed his trip. Once he was on his way, he also prolonged his return, happy to stay away from his diplomatic duties and his private concerns for as long as seemed excusable. His fourteen-year-old daughter, Patsy, got only a few reassuring notes from her traveling father.

Soon after arriving in Paris, she had been enrolled as a boarding student in a prestigious Paris convent school, Pentemont Abbey. By mid-1787, she was going through an evolution of her own, including increasing attachment to the nuns and the Church. She had begun to consider conversion and the convent life. The decision to put Patsy in the convent school at all, no matter how highly regarded its superiors and teaching program, had its oddities and dangers. It disposed of Patsy for the weekdays and occasional weekends, giving Jefferson greater social freedom. A worshipful daughter, an avid and smart student, she made friends at the convent school, which became the center of her life. Jefferson had been assured that many non-French Protestant families sent their daughters there, that Protestant girls would be exempt from religious instruction, and that her education would focus exclusively on secular subjects. The assurances were partly unwarranted. Jefferson naïvely gave little weight to the influence that the Catholic atmosphere and the elite nuns might have on an impressionable young girl. That he could have put aside his hostility to Catholicism, particularly his detestation of clerical superstition, is less a testimony to his tolerance than to the absence of better alternatives and the influence of those whose advice he took. It was also convenient.

Jefferson had another daughter very much on his mind. He had left the infant Lucy Elizabeth and the child Mary, nicknamed Polly, with his in-laws, Elizabeth and Francis Eppes. When he learned of Lucy's death in October 1784, he had been shocked but resigned. He had hardly known the child. It became another addition to his many losses, almost a coda to the death of Lucy's mother two years before. It did, though, contribute to his determination that Polly join him and her sister in Paris. Arrangements were not easy to make. Polly did not want to leave her aunt and uncle. They had become parents to her, their family her own.

In spring 1787, she was partly forced and partly tricked into a voyage into the unknown. Attended by a fourteen-year-old Hemings half sister of her mother's, she arrived in London in early July. The Adamses took her into their home. Abigail coddled and mothered the unhappy child. When the time came to part, Polly did not want to leave. "She is a child of the quickest sensibility," Abigail wrote to Jefferson, "and the maturest understanding, that I have ever met with for her years. She had been 5 weeks at sea, and with men only, so that on the first day of her arrival, she was as rough as a little sailor, and then she had been decoyed from the ship, which made her very angry. . . . I was apprehensive I should meet with some trouble. But where there are such materials to work upon as I have found in her, there is no danger. She listened to my admonitions, and attended to my advice and in two days, was restored to the amiable lovely Child which her Aunt had formed her." The Adamses looked daily for news that Jefferson was on his way to claim his daughter. To their shock, he sent his non-English-speaking head housekeeper to bring Polly to Paris. "She told me this morning," Abigail wrote to Jefferson, "that as she had left all her Friends in Virginia to come over the ocean to see you, she did think you would have taken the pains to have come here for her, and not have sent a man whom she cannot understand."

Before leaving Paris at the end of February 1787 to tour southern France, Jefferson sent Maria Cosway, via Trumbull, a teasing message. "Tell Mrs. Cosway she is an inconstant. She was to have been in Paris long ago, but she has deceived us. The first evening that I find myself seated in a comfortable inn, warm, solitary, and pensive, I [will] invite her to sup, and will commit our conversation to writing. It will be a very scolding one on my part. In the meantime lay all my affections at her feet, desire her to write to me to comfort me on my journey."

His promise was not kept. He did not write to her, even when he was in the country of her native language. At the beginning of July 1787, almost a month after his return from his three-month journey to southern France and northern Italy, he responded to a complaining and scolding letter that was on hand when he returned. "You conclude, madam, from my long silence that I am gone to the other world. Nothing else would have prevented my writing to you so long. I have not thought of you the less. But I took a peep only into Elysium. I entered it at one door, and came out at another, having seen, as I past, only Turin, Milan, and Genoa. I calculated the hours it would have taken to carry me on to Rome. But they were exactly so many more than I had to spare. Was not this provoking? in thirty hours from Milan I could have been at the espousals of the doge and Adriatic. But I am born to lose everything I love. Why were you not with me? so many enchanting scenes which only wanted your pencil to consecrate them to fame."

Those scenes, Jefferson wrote, only lacked her paintbrush to translate his descriptions into visual splendors. "On one hand a mountain cloven through to let pass a gurgling stream; on the other a river, over which is thrown a magnificent bridge; the whole formed into a basin, its sides shagged with rocks, olive trees, vines, herds. . . . I insist on your painting it." These are the words of a correspondent who has no power to insist on anything in their relationship. "When are you coming here? If not at all, what did you ever come for? Only to make people miserable at losing you. Consider that you are but 4 days from Paris. . . . Come then, my dear madam, and we will breakfast every day . . . dine under the bowers of Marly, and forget that we are ever to part again." Why she was not with him was clear to both of them. And it was the same four days for him in the opposite direction. The statement is rhetoric, not sense, a flourish of the pen rather than the heart. Ah, if only she had been with him, what wonderful art she could have created. One of Jefferson's most imaginative fantasy letters, it is self-indulgent, almost sexually self-pleasuring. It is an invitation that neither can participate in except in words. They had already parted in the other possible ways. The language and sentiments are those of a lover. He "longs to receive another" letter, the next one to be "lengthy, warm, and flowing from the heart." An expression both of longing and renunciation, the letter is so rhetorically buoyant that it partakes of fantasy. It is an indication of loneliness and of longing but also of withdrawal.

On July 9, 1787, Maria responded. "Do you deserve a long letter, My dear friend? No, certainly not, and to avoid temptation, I take a small sheet of paper; conversing with you, would break on any resolution. I am determined to prevent it. How long you like to keep your friends in anxiety!—how many months was you without writing to me? and you felt no remorse?" Her limited English skills have the paradoxical effect of making her anger more expressive, as if the linguistic faults were the equivalent of emotional stuttering. She feels rejected, demeaned, as if she were but an appendage to his self-indulgent spouting about castles hanging from clouds and other scenic wonders. It is as if his sensitivity to the beauty of nature makes her an appendage to his travels. She had reason to feel "truly mortified." And to better express herself she switched, midway in her letter, to her native language.

"You spoiled me," she wrote to Jefferson, "in the beginning of our correspondence." But he had hardly done so thereafter. "I do not know that we shall come to Paris this year. I fear not. My husband begins to doubt it. . . . It seems a dream to have been there and I now wish it to be real, because of the impression it left upon me. At least console me by receiving news of a place which so much interests me. Tell me what comedies there are that are new and good, what operas, what works of art and . . . everything that can induce you to write me long letters." She seems to have had enough of his feelings. Paris was the major attraction, the life that she had led there, only a month or so of which had been shared with Jefferson. Their few meetings thereafter had none of the deeply felt magic, at least for Jefferson, as that of the golden late-summer days of the previous year. They were never to exchange letters of the heart again. And Maria, in Paris in the summer of 1787 and again in 1789, created a social schedule that had less opportunity for personal time between them. Two years later, when Jefferson returned to America, Maria became a receding memory revived by an occasional letter. She and her husband had a daughter in 1789. The couple separated in 1790. After the death of her daughter in 1796, she returned to Italy and became an educator of girls associated with the church she believed in. Before he left France in 1789, Jefferson found another, very different sort of woman to engage with. He was never to write any more love letters.

CHAPTER NINE

The Eloquence of Debt

1786–1788

Soon after his arrival in Paris in 1784, Jefferson had met Adrienne Catherine de Noailles, Comtesse de Tessé, through her nephew, Lafayette, who described Jefferson to his wife, Adrienne's sister, as "an admirable, cultivated and charming man, [who] overwhelmed me with kindnesses when he was Governor of Virginia." Two years older than Jefferson, married to the Comte de Tessé, she hosted a salon where Parisians distinguished in the arts, philosophy, and government regularly assembled for conversation and entertainment. It became Jefferson's premier social and intellectual home in Paris. Childless, Madame de Tessé became a semi-mother to Sophie-Ernestine de Tott, who was twenty-nine years old in 1787 and a member of the de Tessé household. A painter of talent whose aristocratic family history had a touch of the tragic, her love affair with the adopted blind son of Madame de Tessé was to create serious complications and conflicts for the principals and the families. Jefferson became almost as fond of Sophie-Ernestine de Tott as he did of Madame de Tessé. Immediately before leaving Paris in March 1787, he said his epistolary good-bye to Madame de Tessé: "I set out on my journey in the moment of writing this. It is a moment of powerful sensibility for your goodness and friendship, wherein I feel how precious they are to my heart."

One of his first letters from southern France was from Nismes (Nîmes), a city famous for its Roman monuments. It was to Madame de Tessé, also passionate about Roman antiquities. It overflows with vivid detail, witty turns of phrase, and personal excitement:

> Here I am, Madam, gazing whole hours at the Maison quarrée, like a lover at his mistress. . . . This is the second time I have been in love since I left Paris. The first was with a Diana . . . a delicious morsel of sculpture. . . . This, you will say, was in rule, to fall in love with a fine woman: but, with a house! It is out of all precedent! No, madam, it is not without a precedent in my own history. While at Paris, I was violently smitten with the hotel de Salm. . . . From Lyons to Nismes I have been nourished with the remains of Roman grandeur. They have always brought you to my mind, because I know your affection for whatever is Roman and noble. . . . At Orange too I thought of you. I was sure you had seen with rapture the sublime triumphal arch at the entrance into the city. . . . I thought of you again, and I was then in great good humor, at the Pont du Gard, a sublime antiquity, and well preserved. But most of all here, where Roman taste, genius, and magnificence excite ideas analogous to yours at every step, I could no longer oppose the inclination to avail myself of your permission to write to you. . . . Loving, as you do Madam, the precious remains of antiquity, loving architecture, gardening, a warm sun, and a clear sky. . . . I am immersed in antiquities from morning to night. For me the city of Rome is actually in all the splendor of its empire. . . .

From Marseilles, "a charming place . . . all life and . . . useful activity like London and Philadelphia," he wrote to Madame de Tott

a letter that was Jefferson at his most charming, a master of spontaneous prose and a witty, thoughtful observer of people and situations.
The trope of distant friends traveling with him, especially females,
appealed to him, an imaginative construct that created intimacy without actual presence, the feeling of closeness without physical touch,
as he had imagined himself traveling with Maria Cosway. "I presume
that you think," he wrote to Sophie de Tott, "as most people think,
that a person cannot be in two places at one time. Yet is there no error
more palpable than this. You know, for example, that you have been
in Paris and its neighborhood, constantly since I had the pleasure of
seeing you there: yet I declare you have been with me above half my
journey. I could repeat to you long conversations, word for word, and
on a variety of subjects. When I find you fatigued with conversation
and sighing for your pallet and pencil, I permit you to return to Paris
a while, and amuse myself with philosophizing on the objects which
occur. The plan of my journey, as well as of my life, being to take
things by the smooth handle, few occur which have not something
tolerable to offer me."

He took both Parisian friends by the "smooth handle" of his expressive prose. "I do not," he continued, "seek therefore for the good
things which [life] has not, but those which it has." He was a happy
traveler, with "all his effects contained in a single trunk," at night

all his cares circumscribed by the walls of his apartment, unknown
to all, unheeded, and undisturbed, writes, reads, thinks, sleeps,
just in the moments when nature and the movements of his body
and mind require. Charmed with the tranquillity of his little cell,
he finds how few are our real wants, how cheap a thing is happiness, how expensive a one pride. He views with pity the wretched
rich, whom the laws of the world have submitted to the cumbrous
trappings of rank. . . . Sometimes I amuse myself with physical
researches. . . . I should go on, Madam, detailing to you my dreams

and speculations; but that my present situation is most unfriendly to speculation. Four thousand three hundred and fifty market-women (I have counted them one by one) brawling, squabbling, and jabbering Patois, three hundred asses braying and bewailing to each other, and to the world, their cruel oppressions, four files of mule-carts passing in constant succession, with as many bells to every mule as can be hung about him, all this in the street under my window, and the weather too hot to shut it. Judge whether in such a situation it is easy to hang one's ideas together.

They indeed did hang together in the continuum of their *Tristram Shandy*–like wash of consciousness, into the digressions that are "the sunshine of life."

This is Jefferson as the master of personal and private prose, the interconnection between the flow of ideas, sensations, and language with a private voice, not the Jefferson of public documents and political persuasion. These two letters represent Jefferson's literary self-engagement at its best. He allows himself to talk about himself, to create playful and imaginative conversations, to create dialogues between made-up and colloquial voices. He amuses himself and his correspondents. His spirits are high. He seems genuinely and casually happy. His official obligations and his Paris routines are hundreds of miles away. With no sense that he is writing beyond the moment, he also knows that he is writing for the future, that his letters will be preserved in his own copies and by their recipients. The persona he creates is the person he sometimes is, though far from always, an easygoing philosopher of the ordinary and the daily, looking to get a "smooth handle" on life, the man who never wants to quarrel, who believes that "anger only serves to torment ourselves, to divert others," that public as well as private life is best conducted in a low voice, in a smooth tone of courtesy, minimizing confrontation. Whatever the circumstance, wherever he is, he believes he will find in his observation of daily life things to interest him; and in his reading and investigations he will find intellectual, scientific, and aesthetic immersions to stimulate mind and spirit.

Travel and travel writing itself, though, did not especially appeal to Jefferson. Unlike his visit to England in 1786, he did keep detailed notes during his four months in southern France and northern Italy. In April 1786, traveling with John Adams to English castles, gardens, and sites of historical interest, all within easy reach of London, Jefferson had made short observations, mostly about the garden features that he might adapt to his landscape at Monticello. Both Jefferson and Adams were lovers of Shakespeare's plays, but when they visited Stratford, Jefferson had nothing to say. In comparison, Adams, in his diary, is entertainingly descriptive, spontaneous, and personal about Shakespeare, English manners, customs, culture, and history. Adams was a diarist; Jefferson was not. Jefferson's English garden notes are confined to information of a dry sort, inflected toward the mathematical and the mechanical. Traveling together through some of England's most culturally fertile country, it is as if the two men were in different worlds. And Jefferson's disinterest in the English sites he visited with Adams, including Alexander Pope's Twickenham, contrasts with his fascination with the Hôtel de Salm in Paris and Roman ruins in southern France. Paradoxically, there's nothing French about Monticello, the house and the gardens, or classical, except the ersatz Corinthian pillars. It is eighteenth-century English through and through, the combination of an English version of a Palladian house with an informal or picturesque English garden. Monticello is Jefferson's vision of the earth writ small, of the connected community of kinship and friendship, a mostly self-contained, pastoral embodiment of the local. It is an idealization imposed on an intractable reality, an expression of his optimism about and his commitment to the "easy handle."

Pope would have been almost but not quite at home at Monticello. The unavailability of skilled craftsmen required compromises. Since much of the construction was paid for with borrowed money, including postponed payment to his workmen, the protracted building schedule eventually contributed to Monticello's deviations from strict Palladian principles. Also, the limited water supply and poor soil on a site chosen for its view rather than its practicality put it at a considerable disadvantage in comparison to Twickenham on the Thames. And Monticello combines the eighteenth-century English version of the Palladian villa with Jefferson's sometimes inspired, sometimes impractical architectural quirks. His Palladian fixation had its origins in Renaissance Italy and in antiquity, but Monticello was neither Italian nor French. Still, he preferred Paris to London, France to Great Britain, with only the slightest exceptions, mainly the superiority of English manufactured goods. In Paris, he swooned over the architectural brilliance and beauty of the Hôtel de Salm. In Nîmes, he sat "gazing whole hours at the Maison quarrée [Carrée]," the well-preserved ruins of an ancient Roman temple, "like a lover at his mistress."

Traveling in France in the spring of 1787, Jefferson focused mostly on what his eye observed, "a continued feast of new objects, and new ideas." There are occasional comments in his *Notes of a Tour into the Southern Parts of France* about culture and society, but what is mostly on display are facts about and descriptions of the landscape, its cultivation, and its workers. Jefferson was almost always sharply, persistently observant about the land and the people who earned their living from it. And he had a practical mission. Is there anything here of relevance to American farmers? Would the olive trees that are a staple of southern European life flourish in Virginia? "The olive tree . . . is assuredly the richest gift of heaven."

He had the eye of a lover of crops and agriculture, of man-made improvements, of a rural environment in which the things that grow, wild and cultivated, and the people who live on and make that landscape livable, are the cherished basics of a life worth living—not in villages or clusters but in separate homesteads. When the French live in villages, he disapproves. To be too close to one's neighbor in the country, let alone in city habitations, was to risk one's integrity and independence. "They are less happy and less virtuous in villages than they would be insulated with their families on the grounds they cultivate." Jefferson blames institutional Catholicism. "Are they thus collected by that dogma of their religion which makes them believe that, to keep the Creator in good humor with his own works, they must mumble a mass every day?" Jefferson brought to southern France the eye of an American separatist whose highest values are individualistic and anti-communitarian.

Jefferson is attentively observant about the details, so intent on the things themselves, their features and measurements, that ultimately the landscape becomes what Wallace Stevens called "description without place" in his poem of that title. Jefferson has an eye for things as they are, but he has a deeper eye for what things mean to him. His interaction with landscape becomes about essence, not particularity, about his own mind and the place his mind mostly lives in and always returns to. In the details, this world, any world, could not and would not exist for Jefferson without lists enumerated arithmetically and expanded descriptively, as if the fruits of the earth could not exist without his validating the specificity of every item in whatever garden he is in. An idealized Monticello is the ultimate template. In prose and in life, whether making notes, keeping records, writing the Declaration and *Notes on the State of Virginia*, the main point is personally existential and culturally defined: the state of Virginia and the vistas of the new republic as essential home, as earth's most valuable location, the place that gives him physical sustenance and moral meaning. Native soil is, for Jefferson, the material expression of American liberty and virtue. Wherever he is, everything else, by contrast, contributes to his vision of American virtue.

Notes of a Tour into the Southern Parts of France is mostly descriptive of landscape, with the emphasis on soil, weather, crops, productivity, laborers, prosperity, poverty, and the comfort or discomfort of where he puts up at night. Vineyards are of special interest. He explores rice production in northern Italy to see if he can be helpful to Carolina rice growers. Northern Italy, he notes, is poorer than southern France. He has nothing to say about urban architecture (with the exception of classical ruins), city life, social organization, or religion, and nothing about churches and cathedrals. The notes are chronological, with large gaps, partly due to travel conditions, and there are few generalizations that attempt an overview or comparisons that relate what he sees in France to American conditions. And there are no anecdotes about people; there is no narrative persona experiencing the life of the communities and the countryside he travels through. The landscape is particularized, its inhabitants generalized; people are not individuals. The *Notes* have no narrative beginning or end. They have only a time and place, a start and finish. There is no story. But the observations often are vivid and revealing about Jefferson himself.

From Lyon he wrote to William Short, "The people here were ill clothed, and looked ill, and I observed the women performing the heavy labors of husbandry; an unequivocal proof of extreme poverty." He is startled at the sight of women doing heavy labor. He disapproves. No white woman in America would be required or forced to do that. Poverty, he recognizes, often determines gender roles. Nevertheless, he also disapproves of French men doing what in Virginia would be considered women's work: "shoemakers, tailors, upholsterers, staymakers, mantua makers, cooks, door-keepers, housekeepers, housecleaners, bedmakers" and hairdressers. Likewise, he deplores French women doing men's work: "porters, carters, reapers, wood cutters, sailors, lock keepers, smiters on the anvil, cultivators of the earth." He concludes that it is no "wonder if such of [the women] as have a little beauty prefer easier courses to get their livelihood, as long as that beauty lasts. Ladies who employ men in the offices which should be reserved for their sex, are they not bawds in effect," by which he means sexually loose and immoral, not necessarily prostitutes in fact. It's not surprising, Jefferson concludes, that French women often prefer prostitution to the physically demanding jobs that in Virginia are reserved for men. A freethinker in matters of religious belief, his Enlightenment standards fail him in regard to gender roles.

In Champagne, Jefferson observed that "the soil is rich mulatto loam." As a color descriptive "mulatto" is for Jefferson a casual and uncomplicated use of the word. When he uses it as a color description, he seems to be without awareness of its other use, as if each use refers to a separate reality, an example of his ability to think, feel, and live without cross-referencing the givens of his racial assumptions. He segues from describing the soil as a "rich mulatto loam" to generalizing that "men, in a civilized country never expose their wives and children to labor above their force or sex, as long as their own labor can protect them from it." Apparently, Virginia, in this regard at least, is "a civilized country." He does not include Black men in the category "men." Slaves do not count. Do mulattoes count, male or female? Champagne, where he observes "women and children carrying heavy burthens, and laboring," apparently is not civilized. It does not occur to Jefferson to make it clear that he is referring only to white men. The conditions of Blackness and slavery create a different and separate category of human being. This is not a deliberative analysis but an un-self-conscious assumption, a given that is as much a part of his existence as the air he breathes. In Virginia, Black women and children do hard physical labor at the orders of their white masters. Their husbands and fathers are powerless to "protect them." When it comes to observations of this sort, Jefferson's mind is as white as his skin. The fact that the soil of Champagne is mulatto is simply a color description.

By contrast, in the prosperous provinces of Burgundy and Beaujolais, the women "do only light work in the fields, being principally occupied within doors." The people "were well clothed and appeared to be well fed. Here the hills become mountains, larger than those of Champagne." Burgundy resembles "our red mountainous country, but is rather more stony, all in corn and vine." He rambles "through their most celebrated vineyards, going into the houses of the laborers, cellars of the Vignerons, and mixing and conversing with them as much as I could." His spoken French continued to be modest. In Beaujolais, "nature has spread its richest gifts in profusion. . . . I have not visited at all the manufactures of this place: because a knowledge of them would be useless, and would extrude from the memory other things more worth retaining." He prefers that Virginia remain a non-manufacturing country, that agriculture continue to be the dominant driver of the economy of the United States.

"Architecture, painting, sculpture, antiquities, agriculture, the condition of the laboring poor fill all my moments. Hitherto I have derived as much satisfaction and even delight from my journey as I could propose to myself." But the weather had been terrible from the start. "Now and then a few gleamings of sunshine to cheer me by the way. Such is this life: and such too will be the next, if there be another, and we may judge of the future by the past." It was a witty way of describing and dispensing with bad weather and concerns about an afterlife. "I am now" in Aix-en-Provence, he wrote to William Short, "in the land of corn, wine, oil, and sunshine. What more can man ask of heaven? If I should happen to die at Paris I will beg of you to send me here, and have me exposed to the sun. I am sure it will bring me to life again."

It did not, though, bring his damaged right wrist to normalcy, as he had hoped the waters at medicinal spas might. "My hand recovering very slowly from the effects of its dislocation," he had written to the French foreign minister in February 1787, notifying the court that he would be absent temporarily. "I am advised by the Surgeons to try the waters of Aix in Provence." That his wrist had not improved at all worried him, he told Madison at the beginning of the year: "I have great anxieties lest I should never recover any considerable use of it." It was only somewhat better in the spring. If he resumed writing with his right hand, the posture for writing had to be an odd one, his wrist still damaged and his fingers still swollen. He claimed later that he was not able to write "for a long time," though between the October 1786 accident and August 1787 he wrote many letters and memos, perhaps with his left hand. Unfortunately, the curative waters at Aix did not seem to help. He was to conclude that in that regard it had been a "very useless voyage." Eleven months after the accident and soon after his return to Paris, he worried that his "dislocated wrist, badly set has . . . deprived me forever of almost every use of my right hand. Nor is the extent of the evil as yet known, the hand withering, the fingers remaining swelled and crooked, and losing rather than gaining in point of suppleness. . . . I am able however to write," apparently with his right hand, "though for a long time I was not so."

While traveling, he wrote few letters. Conditions were adverse, posting stations few, and apparently he gave priority to the writing of *Notes of a Tour into the Southern Parts of France*. In early May in Nice, hearing the singing of nightingales, his mind was partly on another kind of writer: "A poet is as much the creature of climate as an orange or palm tree. What a bird the nightingale would be in the climates of America! We must colonize him thither." He was devoting "every moment of every day almost, to the business of enquiry," as if this were the entire motive of his trip, justifying his long absence from Paris. The "almost" is significant. It was also a pleasure trip. And he still had hope in the beneficial effects of the curative waters. "The accident of a dislocated wrist had disabled me from writing," he had written to a French correspondent in November 1786, though he had written the entire Head and Heart letter to Maria Cosway with his left hand. He was "in constant hope of recovering its use. But finding that this hope walks before me like my shadow . . . I therefore employ my left hand in the office of scribe, which it performs indeed slowly, awkwardly and badly. . . . You enquire kindly the effect of the waters on my wrist," he wrote from Marseilles. "None at all. But time is doing slowly what they cannot do. It strengthens a little."

From Nice he wrote to Lafayette that he was constantly on the move, intent on taking advantage of what he expected he would never be in the presence of again, "to see what I have never seen before and shall never see again. In the great cities, I go to see what travelers think alone worthy of being seen; but I make a job of it, and generally gulp it all down in a day. On the other hand, I am never satiated with rambling through the fields and farms, examining the culture and cultivators, with a degree of curiosity which makes some take me to be a fool, and others to be much wiser than I am." The condition of the soil interested him wherever he was, the literal ground from which for Jefferson all human felicity arose. His eye constantly observed and commented on the condition of the laborers in relation to the quality of the soil. Apparently, it did not occur to him to compare the laboring poor of southern France with the slave laborers who worked his Monticello soil.

Two larger themes took form in his remarks to Lafayette. "The soil of Champagne and Burgundy I have found more universally good than I had expected, and as I could not help making a comparison with England, I found that comparison more unfavorable to the latter than is generally admitted. The soil, the climate, and the productions are superior to those of England, and the husbandry as good." What was not as good, he recognized, was the structural and legal arrangements that made French farmers less productive than English farmers. Much of the agricultural land of both European powers was owned by a small number of the wealthy elite. Lafayette was one of them. Most French farmers worked their land on short-term leases.

In England, long leases for twenty-one years, or three lives, to wit, that of the farmer, his wife, and son, renewed by the son as soon as he comes to the possession, for his own life, his wife's and eldest child's, and so on, render the farms there almost hereditary, make it worth the farmer's while to manure the lands highly, and give the landlord an opportunity of occasionally making his rent keep pace with the improved state of the lands. Here the leases are either during pleasure, or for three, six, or nine years, which does not give the farmer time to repay himself for the expensive operation of well manuring, and therefore, he manures ill, or not at all. I suppose, that could the practice of leasing for three lives be introduced in the whole kingdom, it would, within the term of your life, increase agricultural productions fifty per cent; or were any one proprietor to do it with his own lands, it would increase his rents fifty per cent, in the course of twenty-five years. But I am told the laws do not permit it. The laws then, in this particular, are unwise and unjust.

It had taken a bloody revolution and class turmoil for Americans like Jefferson to feel secure in the ownership of their land and wealth, to become certain that their freeholds were not still somehow owned or gifted to them with conditions by a distant king or alterable by the British Parliament. Great Britain had lost its American colonies. In England long-term leases and generational occupancy compensated to a degree for non-ownership, even though Jefferson did not approve. In France, however, the arrangement was considerably worse, bad for the farmer, for the community, and for the nation's productivity. It was "unwise and unjust." He implies that Lafayette and his fellow landowning aristocrats needed to reform French landowning and leasing legalities. Otherwise, he hints between the lines, there would be undesirable consequences. For Jefferson, justice, at least his version of it, especially in regard to the soil, would always eventually assert itself.

Many as were Jefferson's activities and pleasures in Paris, the activity he spent most time at in the aggregate was writing, mostly letters, though also memos and notes to himself and others and documents about trade issues. After all, he had been sent to France to negotiate trade agreements and to assist Americans attempting to do business there. That part of his mission was mostly unsuccessful. He did manage to persuade the French government, which collected trade-killing taxes through the power granted to a monopoly, to cooperate in American shipments of whale oil. An arrangement already in place controlled the amount and price of tobacco exports to France. Jefferson had no luck changing that. It didn't help that Gouverneur Morris, a talented and influential New York merchant and stateman who was playing a major role in creating a new constitution for the United States and who was to succeed Jefferson in Paris, had a financial interest in the existing arrangement. Though cordial with Jefferson, the wealthy and handsome Morris, who spent time with Jefferson during a visit to Paris in 1789, was an admirer and friend of Alexander Hamilton. Like most of the merchant class, he favored a strong central government. In the next decade, he was to become a Federalist of the sort that Jefferson hated. Ever the diplomatic gentleman, however, in Paris Jefferson kept on good but not warm terms with Morris.

As the American minister to France, Jefferson led a privileged life among the upper reaches of society, as he did in Virginia. As a stranger from away, he observed the obvious: the working people of France were physically and morally mistreated. And he was keen to emphasize how much better off were the "great mass of People" in the United States. It was certainly true that some Americans, particularly of Jefferson's class, were much better off, but not in the "great mass" nearly as much better off as Jefferson claimed. Compare the lives of the people of France, Jefferson wrote, with the lives of, presumably, people like himself in America. He emphasizes personal and marital happiness. In France, "intrigues of love occupy the younger, and those of ambition the more elderly part of the great." But "conjugal love" has "no existence among them," and "domestic happiness, of which that is the basis, is utterly unknown. In lieu of this are substituted pursuits which nourish and invigorate all our bad passions, and which offer only moments of ecstasy amidst days and months of restlessness and torment." It was characteristic of Jefferson to make such sweeping claims. He makes them in political documents, where justification and persuasion are his paramount aims. But when he generalizes to convey information and insight about French and American society he reveals more about himself than about his subjects.

French society, he claims, is "much, very much inferior . . . to the tranquil permanent felicity with which domestic society in America blesses most of its inhabitants, leaving them to follow steadily those pursuits which health and reason approve, and rendering truly delicious the intervals of these pursuits." Most of the inhabitants of America, he claims, are well-off and happy in their married lives, in their daily activities, in their work, and in their leisure time.

Jefferson had and was to have in his family and among his friends examples of unhappy marriages, domestic abuse, and alcoholism. Moreover, even if we exclude women, children, and slaves, Jefferson's eighteenth-century Virginia was often a nasty place for the working white population. There is enough statistical and anecdotal information to be certain that many white eighteenth-century Americans, especially in the South, and to a considerable extent in the major cities, lived subsistence existences with inadequate food in primitive conditions; many worked in semi-slave situations as indentured servants; heavy drinking and alcoholism were widespread; domestic abuse, theft, and violent crime were commonplace. Jefferson had enough experience as governor during the war to know that patriotism also was often a factor of immediate self-interest. Still, everything connected with Monticello and America is good, Jefferson implies, except bad weather and poor crops, his imaginative calculus omitting the Virginia that was poor, class ridden, and hierarchical; the Virginia that contained as many loafers, wastrels, alcoholics, gamblers, sexual adventurers, and abusive husbands, some of them tellingly close to Monticello, as anyplace else. There were certain truths Jefferson instinctively did his best to evade or deny.

From Paris, Jefferson wrote private and official letters to the Confederation Congress, particularly to its foreign secretary, John Jay, his immediate superior, and in much the same strain to James Madison, who, unlike Jay, shared many of Jefferson's views and values. In a letter written in late August 1785, he asked Jay's "permission" to write private letters, though that was more a rhetorical strategy than anything else. The fact of the letter precedes his receipt of permission, if permission ever explicitly came. It was a device to avoid transparency, even official accountability. It was a way of proposing an agenda, an effort to promote his own views and policies, though his role as minister to France did not warrant weighing in on matters that had nothing to do with France. But this was an insider's world, and Jefferson was an insider.

Those who till the soil, Jefferson wrote to Jay, are morally superior, by virtue of the experience of their occupation, to those who earn their living as artisans or sailors or in commerce. Those who work the soil (apparently including those who own the soil that others work) are "the most vigorous, the most independent, the most virtuous, and are tied to the country and wedded to its liberty by the most lasting bands." The latter phrase implies that ownership of agricultural property more closely ties the owner to the location and to the country as a whole than ownership of a private residence in a city, a flourishing business, or even human property.

Did Jefferson believe this superiority was based on the actual American rural agricultural world that he valorized? It seems that he never asks this question in this context. He is not entirely above and beyond the relevance of facts to generalizations, as he shows in *Notes on the State of Virginia*. But ideology, emotion, and self-interest often made facts irrelevant. His idealization of his slave-based version of the pastoral was ideological and emotional, more like religious faith than the science that he valued. Certainly, he had no evidence on which to believe that the farmers of Albemarle County were morally superior or more patriotic than the citizens of Boston or Philadelphia. Each had their self-evident share of the good, the bad, and the indifferent. Jefferson had ample opportunity, especially in his years as Virginia's governor, to observe examples of moral and immoral conduct, of the mixed nature of human nature, of patriotic and unpatriotic conduct among his neighbors and constituents. He often created belief structures independent of evidence or rational analysis.

Although he seemed blissfully unaware of this tendency, his view of the moral and patriotic superiority of those who till the soil was self-validating: he, his family, his friends, and his Virginia network and its extensions were tillers of the soil, though the class that Jefferson most identified with, plantation owners like himself, did so indirectly, through subordinates, particularly slaves. He seems unaware that the man to whom he is writing this letter, John Jay, the secretary of foreign affairs of the Confederation Congress, is the son of a wealthy family of New York City merchants. Jay was by profession a lawyer, a politician, and public servant. How did he feel on reading that he was morally inferior and less a lover of liberty than any person who tilled the soil? Or did Jefferson think of Jay as an exception? If so, were there other exceptions, such as Benjamin Franklin?

In addition to his view of the moral virtues that the agricultural life inculcated, Jefferson had a practical argument about why tilling the soil was a morally preferable occupation for Americans. Trade required competition with the major European powers for the shipping, sale, and purchase of raw materials and manufactured goods.

For Jefferson that meant that competitive tensions between American and European commercial interests might lead to physical conflict. And wars would endanger the independence of the United States. How best then, Jefferson asked, to avoid war? There were alternatives: one was to discourage conflict by having the means to defend oneself, which would be expensive; the other would be to strictly limit whom one trades with. Jefferson, as he wrote to Jay, conceded that Americans would want to and would trade, and that ultimately what the people want the people have a right to get. A navy would be necessary. And because a navy costs a great deal of money, the United States should first repay its debts and then do its best to avoid having to have a substantial navy. The best way to do that, if threatened by foreign adversaries, was to impose partial or full embargoes to limit or eliminate trade, as the colonies had done with the nonimportation agreements in 1769. That strategy would deprive adversaries of essential raw materials. The 1769 association became Jefferson's model for the embargoes he imposed during the second term of his presidency. The idea was in his head from early on. He had great faith in its efficacy, but like so many of his fixed ideas, it had little to no basis in evidence in the real world.

Despite assiduous efforts, Jefferson's successes with French trade restrictions were modest. Most European governments had higher priorities than improving trade with or lending money to the United States. Though he would never admit it, or only with begrudging indirection, including the frequent arrival of his luxury purchases from London, a rapidly industrializing Britain was America's best trading partner. Jefferson worked hard to help France become an alternative market. His Southern colleagues complained that they were still in bondage to British merchants. Jefferson felt the same way. Pre–Revolutionary War debts weighed heavily on the books and psyches of many American businessmen, especially Southerners and tobacco planters. Jefferson accepted moral responsibility for his own debts, though he argued that he should not have to pay the interest accrued during the war years. Other Americans hoped that repayment could be postponed indefinitely and perhaps, over time, forgiven or forgotten. British lenders and their government insisted that these were legally binding debts: treaty law and business morality required payment with accrued interest. To add salt to American resentments, Britain still offered the most profitable market for American products. Compared to trade with France, American-British trade was aboveboard, minimally bureaucratic, facilitated by easy credit arrangements, and legally protected. Why, Jefferson agonized, could France not lower tariffs, liberalize its trade policies, minimize corrupt practices, and create a credit apparatus for American merchants?

At the end of October 1787, a Charleston firm appealed to Jefferson for help. Like most American merchants, the firm accepted that there was no alternative to doing business with the British. It was a bitter pill to swallow. "Since the Peace, we have never had a single French House, that commanded Respect, or that has been entitled to it. At this moment, there is none at all. . . . Great Britain thus peculiarly situated, will no doubt leave no means unessayed to Continue, and confirm our Bondage, and it is certainly our Duty and Interest, to destroy it." Such was the view from South Carolina. "We are rejoiced in saying, that we think your Excellency has opened the Door for accomplishing so desirable an event." The door, though, was mostly shut. Having to do business with Great Britain, the Charleston correspondent bewailed, was like being enslaved. The comparison with slavery continued to come comfortably to many white Americans. The French door was only slightly open, no matter how hard Jefferson pried. With issues more demanding than trade, especially its huge national debt, much of it borrowed to help the United States, the French paid minimal attention to American hopes. Alas, "necessity has compelled us to accept" British credit, the Charleston merchant wrote to Jefferson, "and against our wishes, establish a preference in their favor. . . . To [in] any way, and in the smallest degree contribute to the effecting so happy a revolution, would be the height of our Pride and Ambition."

Jefferson spent a great deal of time helping Americans caught in the web of French restrictive policies and commercial exploitation. He tried to facilitate the sale of American rice in France. He had little success. He tried to establish French and Italian olive trees in American soil. Total failure. French wine was a niche market in the United States. Americans drank mostly beer and cider, cheap and easy to make from local products. Even when French women, in Jefferson's last two years in Paris, cried out for bread in the Paris streets, American wheat shipments had difficulty getting into France. Day in and day out, he wrote letters to officials on matters of trade, letters responding to pleas from merchants whose ships and cargoes had been confiscated, usually on trumped-up technicalities, letters to other American diplomats, and memo-reports to Congress on the situation in France and Europe. Letters arrived by the stack. With minimal secretarial help, a printing press he imported from England, and a primitive copying machine, he slogged away. Occasionally he had meetings with French officials. When required, he showed up at court. His spoken French had improved, but it was still poor. An uncomplaining workaholic, fit in mind and body despite the injured wrist, Jefferson kept at his writing desk. He answered every business letter he received, and he wrote personal letters in a style that was both characteristic of the age and personal to his own genius with language. If he had been a novelist, the number of words he wrote as a letter writer added to those for public documents would have made him more prolific than Smollett, Sterne, Scott, Dickens, Thackeray, Mark Twain, or Henry James. His only presidential competitor was to be John Quincy Adams.

When his seventeen-year-old nephew, Peter Carr, the son of his sister Martha and Dabney Carr, the much-loved friend of his youth, wrote to him in the summer of 1787 for advice about his studies, Jefferson responded at length with a letter that said more about the writer than we will ever know about the recipient. Jefferson could hardly ever resist a request for advice. Usually, he had a light touch as a didactic moralist. He was rarely brief but often concise, a paradox perhaps, though characteristic of his need to think aloud while writing and also to phrase effectively, sometimes elegantly, what he had to say. He had the gift of dramatizing his thoughts, as if while writing he was discovering what he had to say, spontaneously refining, elaborating, and discovering more to say and better ways to say it.

Peter Carr was a student at William and Mary, under the tutelage of Jefferson's mentor, friend, and fellow signer of the Declaration, George Wythe. Carr had two concerns: whether it would be advisable to continue his studies at a European university and what books he should read to qualify. The book list that Jefferson sent him hovers between a four-year liberal arts curriculum and a lifetime reading list. Carr was eager to travel abroad. Jefferson felt compelled to discourage him. With his usual attempt at fairness, he provided a seemingly balanced assessment of the pros and cons of young Americans visiting Europe. His advice was not personal. It was generic, as it often was, directed toward the next generation of the leaders who would ensure the stability and virtue of America's future. For travelers of every age, he wrote to Carr, European travel makes "men wiser, but less happy." If you are of "a sober age," it will make you more knowledgeable about the world. He especially had in mind useful knowledge. But it will also, he warned, provide temptations for immoral conduct and disconnection from America and its superior values.

Forty-four-year-old Jefferson was of "sober age." Still, the letter implies concern that his own Paris years might make him dissatisfied with his American home. The letter became a vehicle for starting to repress the nostalgia he anticipated he would feel for the attractions of the life he would one day no longer have: theaters, architecture, bookstores, and the daily pleasures of the greatest of European cities. His advice to Carr emphasized a prevalent theme among the American elite: Europe is dangerous to the character and virtue of young American men. "Be good, be learned, and be industrious," he wrote, "and you will not want the aid of travelling to render you precious to your country, dear to your friends, happy within yourself. I repeat my advice to take a great deal of exercise, and on foot. . . ." Keep walking, but on American soil.

Indeed, those who travel to Europe "are subject ever after to recollections mixed with regret, their affections are weakened by being extended over more objects, and they learn new habits which cannot be gratified when they return home. Young men who travel . . . do not acquire that wisdom for which a previous foundation is requisite by repeated and just observations at home." His age and years in Virginia, Jefferson implies, had given him that "previous foundation." But for young men, "the glare of pomp and pleasure is analogous to the motion of their blood, it absorbs all their affection and attention, they are torn from it as from the only good in this world, and return to their home as to a place of exile and condemnation. Their eyes are forever turned back to the object they have lost, and its recollection poisons the residue of their lives. . . . These observations are founded in experience. There is no place where your pursuit of knowledge will be so little obstructed by foreign objects as in your own country, nor any wherein the virtues of the heart will be less exposed to be weakened."

If this advice seems to modern Americans excessively prudent, some of the Founding Fathers were enough alienated from the European world to feel resentful, fearful, and vulnerable. There were numbers of variations on this common theme. Jefferson's Anglophobia had become self-definingly deep. However, the deepest level of vulnerability was not political but moral. Young American men were too liable to be corrupted by what was, from the American point of view, European immorality—that is, sexual pleasure. For example, Jefferson's secretary and colleague, William Short, had been having an affair with the daughter of a family he had gone to live with to improve his French. Jefferson disapproved. And vice was inescapably obvious in the streets of Paris, day and night. Jefferson was living in the city Americans judged to be the sensual center of European immorality. "These observations are founded in experience," he wrote to Carr. But whose experience is he referring to? He does not give any hint that Paris had corrupted him, and there is no evidence either way. He was, though, to return to the United States in a relationship that many of his contemporaries would have thought corrupt. He implied that he had gone to Europe when no longer young and prone to temptations. He had succumbed to an unavoidably chaste infatuation with Maria Cosway, to her beauty, her charm, her sexuality, but his flirtations all seemed to be more of the heart and mind than the body. All those who travel to Europe, he wrote to Peter, are in general "subject ever after to recollections mixed with regret."

Paris, indeed, had given him a socially, culturally, and aesthetically richer alternative to American life. The indefinite extension of that alternative was out of the question. He had assumed reappointment for another three-year term, which would keep him in Paris until 1791 or 1792. There was pressing business to attend to at home, including returning his daughters to their American culture and their future prospects. Even so, he assumed he would be returning as the beneficiary, not the victim, of his Paris years.

His lengthy didactic letter to Carr also contains Jefferson's most explicit statement of his belief in "natural law": the idea that human beings are endowed at birth with "a sense of right and wrong." It as well holds his most substantive statement that all claims of truth should be subject to the tests of reason and independent thought. "If there be" a God, he wrote, "he must be a God of reason." Miracles are so improbable as to be untenable. Probability is the standard. People should think for themselves, independent of authorities that claim to have the right to think for them. And Peter should know, Jefferson wrote, that each person, regardless of education or profession, has been innately endowed by "natural law" with a moral/ethical sense. He believed, no matter what evidence to the contrary, that people would, over time, make the right ethical choices, which also meant the right political decisions. For Jefferson, that was the basis for republican government and his version of democracy. "Natural law," combined with reason, provides the foundations for decision making in all human activities. "Your own reason is the only oracle given you by heaven, and you are answerable not for the rightness but uprightness of the decision. . . ." On the subject of religion, he wrote, if you conclude that "there is no god you will [still] find incitements to virtue in the comfort and pleasantness you feel in its exercise, and the love of others which it will procure you. If you find reason to believe there is a god, a consciousness that you are acting under his eye, and that he approves you, will be a vast additional incitement. If that there be a future state, the hope of a happy existence in that increases the appetite to deserve it; if that Jesus was also a god, you will be comforted by a belief of his aid and love. In fine, I repeat that you must lay aside all prejudice on both sides. . . . Read the bible then, as you would read Livy or Tacitus."

Jefferson makes no particular brief for Christianity or Deism or any belief system, for or against. He occasionally gives the impression that he is a Deist or a Christian or both, but only in the sense that these denominational terms are the lingua franca of his community. Their value is for ethical guidance. Even his Deism is "light." His highest standard in evaluating belief systems is reason and independent thought. He was already on public record advocating that other people's religion is their own business. It was a matter of concern only when used to coerce or control another person's right to make decisions about religion freely. For that to be possible, no church or state should be able to exercise any control over the free exercise of religious belief or nonbelief. Living in an increasingly pluralistic world, Jefferson encouraged its existence. Later, his political opponents were to call him an atheist, but for Jefferson, his beliefs were nobody's business but his own. The question, "Do you believe in God?" was not only inappropriate in the public sphere but dangerous. When he swore on the Bible to uphold the Constitution, he was merely affirming the role of the Bible as a widely revered cultural icon of ethical wisdom.

The day after writing his letter to Carr, Jefferson wrote another long letter, this one exclusively about education, European versus American. It was to Thomas Mann Randolph Sr. about his nineteen-year-old son, a student in Edinburgh who wanted to prolong his European stay. The young man had recently been in contact with Jefferson. Without a son of his own, he could never resist providing advice to young men he felt an interest in. "My proposition," he wrote to his cousin, "is that he shall pass his two first years of legal study in some one of the villages within an hour's walk of Paris." He will be "boarded with some good family wherein he may learn to speak the language, which is not to be learned in any other way. By this means he will avoid the loss of time and money which would be the consequence of a residence in the town, and he will be nigh enough to come to dine, to make acquaintances, see good company, and examine the useful details of the city." Because cost was an issue, Jefferson worked up a memo projecting the expense. The letter and memo took him hours to write.

Jefferson turned on its head his argument to Peter Carr. Young Randolph would learn French and study law in Europe, he argued, with greater benefit and at lower cost than in the United States. He is more likely to be studious, Jefferson maintained, if he is in Europe than if he is at home, where friends may tempt him from his studies.

It was the opposite of the rationale he had argued to Peter Carr the previous day. Jefferson apparently felt a personal interest in Randolph studying in or near Paris, which overrode the argument he had made to Carr. "I perceive by his letters that he has good genius, and everybody bears witness to his application, which is almost too great. It would be a pity therefore he should miss of giving them full improvement." Apparently, Randolph Jr. would not be vulnerable to the same European influences as would Carr. Perhaps he was anticipating that in the young man's nearby presence he would have a son of his own who would be protected by the proximity of his mentor.

Jefferson also had daughters whose futures he needed to consider. By summer 1787, he had decided that no matter how long he himself would be spending in France, he would soon take his daughters home to Virginia for American acculturation and appropriate marriages. The notion of either marrying a European was anathema. Perhaps, somewhere in the distances of Jefferson's mind, there gleamed the possibility that Thomas Mann Randolph Jr. and his eldest daughter might become sympathetic friends of the heart. Jefferson had long worried that the husbands Virginia would offer his daughters would mostly be "blockheads." He wanted his daughters educated within the framework of what was appropriate for genteel ladies of the Virginia elite. They would be teacher-mothers to his grandchildren. Martha would soon be of marriageable age. Beyond any further Randolph-Jefferson connection, Jefferson owed the young man's father affection and cooperation. He had no knowledge of Randolph Jr. other than what his and his father's letters revealed. "I must beg your pardon," he wrote to his cousin, "for thus intruding myself into a business belonging to yourself alone, and hope you will find its excuse in the motives from which it proceeds, friendship for yourself, for Mrs. Randolph, and your son, a wish to see you gratified and to be gratified myself in seeing him act the advantageous part which will naturally result from his talents, his merit, and the favorable ground from which he will start, a fear of seeing this endangered by a too early return to our own country . . . all these considerations have impelled me to take this liberty." His advice was not taken.

In late July 1787, soon after his return from southern France, Jefferson tried to face up to a personal crisis. Having proposed a repayment arrangement to his European creditors, he needed to raise money. The sale of crops plus his salary as a United States minister were insufficient to cover his ordinary bills and maintain his standard of living, so how could he get the additional cash to make the payments that, over time, would service and eliminate his debts? His assets were almost entirely in land and slaves. "The torment of mind I endure till the moment shall arrive when I shall not owe a shilling on earth is such really as to render life of little value." With pen in hand, he discussed with Nicholas Lewis three alternative ways to augment his income. We must lay "our shoulder seriously to the wheel of repayment. Honor requires it."

One alternative was to sell land. But "I cannot. . . . I have sold too much . . . already, and [my lands] are the only sure provision for my children." A second possibility was to rent out some or all of his estates, but that was not likely to bring in more money than the estates were already providing. Another option was to sell slaves, but he would not "willingly sell the slaves as long as there remains any prospect of paying my debts with their labor." However, "a number of slaves have been sold," he wrote to one of his creditors, "and I have lately received information . . . that the proceeds of that sale, with the profits of the estate to the end of 1781 would pay off the whole of the residuary debts. . . . I am desirous of arranging with you, such just and practicable conditions as will ascertain to you the terms at which you will receive my part of your debt, and give me the satisfaction of knowing that you are contented. . . . Substantial justice is my object, as decided by reason, and not by authority or compulsion. The first question which arises is as to the article of interest."

The losses he had suffered because of the invasion of Virginia, he argued, were all the fault of the British. Why should he not be compensated for his losses by having the interest dismissed? "Upon the whole then I propose that on your part you relinquish the claim to interest during the war, say from the commencement of hostilities April 19, 1775, to their cessation April 19, 1783, being exactly eight years: and that in proportion as I pay my third" of the Wayles estate liability, "I shall be acquitted as to the other two thirds," which by law and contract he was equally responsible for. "I agree to pay interest previous and subsequent to the war, and oblige myself to remit to you for that and the principal four hundred pounds sterling annually, till my third of the whole debt shall be fully paid; and I will begin these payments in August of the next year." The creditor declined Jefferson's proposal.

The best solution, Jefferson wrote to Francis Eppes in July 1787, was not to sell slaves but to rent them out for cash. "I feel all the weight of the objection that we cannot guard the negroes perfectly against ill usage. But in a question between hiring and selling them . . . the hiring will be temporary only, and will end in their happiness; whereas if we sell them, they will be subject to equal ill usage, without a prospect of change. It is for their good therefore ultimately, and it appears to promise a relief to me. . . . House negroes still to be hired separately. The old and infirm, who could not be hired, or whom it would be a pity to hire" should be given light assignments.

For Jefferson, a slaveholder's responsibility required the rationale that their happiness be one of his priorities. "In this I am governed solely by views to their happiness which will render it worth their while to use extraordinary cautions for some time to enable me to put them ultimately on an easier footing, which I will do the moment they have paid the debts due from the estate, two thirds of which have been contracted by purchasing them"—as if his purchase of them were their good fortune. In essence, his slaves would have to understand that any discomfort or extra burden this created was ultimately for their benefit also. Perhaps, he reconsidered, it would make more financial sense to rent out all his property, his slaves *and* his estate. "I look forward to it as my only salvation."

The subject was both demanding and obsessive. The practice of hiring out slaves was widespread. For Jefferson, all his slaves were part of his extended family, human beings to whom he had a responsibility, though limited by the law and by exigency. Exigency now dominated. Some of the slaves he had attained through marriage were half siblings to his deceased wife, blood relatives who served his family personally. Struggling with the need to raise cash, he had to have been aware that the mulatto servant who had accompanied Polly to France in July 1787 and resided in his Paris household was a blood relation of his children. So too was her brother James. Probably Jefferson's talent at compartmentalization was active. Clearly, he hoped to rent out only outdoor working slaves from his Cumberland and Goochland farms, though those with specialized skills would bring in the most income. The Hemings family slaves at Monticello had special protection.

Jefferson did not think of his slaves as machines. They were people, but they were also commodities. Their bodies and labor could be turned into income. He would not shrink, he wrote to Eppes, from stating clearly and fully what he was doing: "I put it in all its force, and I shall go through the operation, as a man does that of being cut for the stone, with a view to relief." His metaphor was dramatic. Renting them out was like surgery, as if it were his body that was being cut. "I have therefore written to Mr. Lewis to pray him to put my affairs on this footing immediately, in which I know your goodness will aid him. It is taking one great trouble in the lump, to be relieved from it in the detail." Another metaphor helped him: "When this arrangement shall be taken, I shall feel like a person on shore, escaped from shipwreck." His metaphors were about himself, not the slaves he was going to hire out. He would be safe on shore; others might be shipwrecked or drowned. "I am, like you," he wrote to Eppes, "on a bed of thorns till I am cleared of debt." By July 1788, he had again changed his mind about the best way to raise cash. Eppes had advised him to sell only land. "I therefore accede to your advice. . . ." Apparently, for the moment, land was less valuable than Black blood. He hoped, though, that it would be the last land he would ever have to sell. Land was life, sustenance, status, and independence.

Eloquent on the subject of his own and his country's debts, in his public life Jefferson was to advocate economy with a passion, as if freedom from debt was a condition of a virtuous national life. As a writer, one of his virtues is his economical use of words. His rhetoric is sometimes extravagant, but his overall aesthetic is one of understatement, of restraint in language and in structure. As a writer, he is economical—concise, pithy, the right word at the right moment, a classical but balanced syntax, the capability to combine colloquial rhythm with incisive rational analysis. As a man of the material world, he indulged in a self-destructive and contradictory economy, expertly graceful at deluding himself, except in rare moments of panic, spending beyond his means, usually by exaggerating what his means would be rather than what his means actually were. His extravagance seems to have been a matter of birth, class, personality, and optimism: the thought that everything will, over time, turn out right was his fallback certainty, including the relationship between his cash flow and his expenditures. All that was necessary for a happy life, Jefferson insisted, was a farm on which to raise crops, which would be independent of credit, creditors, paper money, and debts. The farmer's estate, he wrote, "supplies a good table, clothes itself and his family with their ordinary apparel, furnishes a small surplus to buy salt, sugar, coffee, and a little finery for his wife and daughter, enables him to receive and to visit his friends, and furnishes him pleasing and healthy occupation." This farm and farmer were Jeffersonian constructs. For many farmers, the soil was grudging and life was hard.

Made wretched by his own debts, Jefferson projected onto the national grid his own pattern for happiness. The Revolutionary War, Jefferson fantasized, had struck the right balance between income and expenditure. "Experience during the war proved this; as I think every man will remember that under all the privations it obliged him to submit to during that period he slept sounder, and awaked happier than he can do now. . . . I look back to the time of the war as a time of happiness and enjoyment, when amidst the privation of many things not essential to happiness, we could not run in debt because nobody would trust us; when we practiced of necessity the maxim of buying nothing but what we had money in our pockets to pay for; a maxim which of all others lays the broadest foundation for happiness." Looking back to the Revolutionary period as a Golden Age when everyone paid up front for whatever they bought distorted and denied the reality: rampant inflation, paper money, individual deprivation, widespread poverty, an army short of everything, including food and clothing, bills that the Congress could not and would not pay, and a monetary lifeline thrown to a sinking ship by French self-interest and Dutch capitalism. Austerity at the time was not a virtue; it was an imposition and a deprivation. Cash was scarce, state-issued paper money was next to worthless, an absence of credit brought the Revolution close to failure. The United States partly owed its independence to foreign loans and inflationary currency. Jefferson's claim that it was a time of happiness belies the misery of his experience as Virginia's wartime governor. It makes no allowance for the suffering of so many Americans: those crippled, those relieved of their misery by death, those whose property was destroyed or requisitioned, and those whose lives were thrown into other forms of turmoil and distress during what was simultaneously a rebellion and a civil war.

Some of Jefferson's most painful writing focuses on debt as a vice, partly because he was so monomaniacal about the subject, often writing as if the debt belonged to some anonymous, generalized mass of people, not at all to himself. It was a device of distancing and evasion, a trick of mind and language that enabled him to be financially irresponsible and at the same time the scourge of speculators, investors, bankers, and all those who pursued wealth and luxury: "I look forward to the abolition of all credit as the only other remedy which can take place." Jefferson conflated the personal and the national. Public indebtedness was to Jefferson a corrosive disease, a collective extravagance. He favored a legal mandate forbidding or at least controlling debt, as well as speculation in stocks and real estate. Debt was also a leadership failure, a government following a population characterized by "indolence, extravagance, and infidelity to its engagements." It was a sweeping indictment of his fellow Americans. The charge was also personal, and it provides context for his antagonism to the Federalist Party's effort in the 1790s to create national prosperity by expanding the money supply through credit. When he excoriated his materialistic countrymen, was he blocking out or acting on an awareness that he himself was an example of what he condemned? An inveterate optimist, like Dickens's Mr. Micawber, Jefferson usually, except in occasional moments of despair, expected that for himself something would turn up, that all would work out well in the end.

While Jefferson was dealing with his fractured wrist, his desperation about his debts, his heavy correspondence, and his daily obligations, other minds and pens were busy in Philadelphia conspiring to create a new constitution for the not-so-united United States. The effort was an ongoing end run around considerable resistance. As a delegate to the Confederation Congress from 1782 to 1784, Jefferson had experienced the resistance emanating from the various state legislatures, some more than others, aggressively guarding their privileges

and powers, particularly their taxing authority and their predilection to play fast and loose with the laws governing indebtedness and
property. Each state created its own internal and external tax laws. In
Virginia, a faction led by ex-governor Patrick Henry opposed giving
the Confederation Congress additional powers. Such a move required
unanimous approval, and Henry was aware that almost nothing of
consequence passes unanimously. When he left for France in July
1784, Jefferson had to have been relieved to escape the fractious opposition to ceding any additional authority to a national legislature
whose impotence suited the interests of many states. It was widely
feared that a strong national government would become at best indifferent to local interests, at worst tyrannical.

From his first attendance at the Continental Congress in 1775,
Jefferson favored a written constitution for the national government.
Franklin had submitted a proposal, which Jefferson supported, but
it was left in limbo. With constitution making much on his mind in
1775–1776, particularly a constitution for Virginia, he carefully annotated his copy of Franklin's draft. The difficulty of an agreement
on a national constitution surfaced from the start. Jefferson later
wrote that "the confederation of the States, while on the carpet before the old Congress, was strenuously opposed by the smaller states,
under apprehensions that they would be swallowed up by the larger
ones. We were long engaged in the discussion; it produced great heats,
much ill humor, and intemperate declarations from some members."
Attempting to defang the conflict, Franklin "at length brought the
debate to a close," observing that "'at the time of the Union of England
and Scotland, the Duke of Argyle was most violently opposed to that
measure, and among other things predicted that, as the whale had
swallowed Jonas, so Scotland would be swallowed by England. However, said the Doctor, when Lord Bute came into the government, he
soon brought into its administration so many of his countrymen that
it was found, in event that Jonas swallowed the whale.' This story

produced a general laugh, restored good humor, and the Article of difficulty was passed." Franklin was in Paris in 1777 when the Articles of Confederation became the first national Constitution. Jefferson was not in Congress but at Poplar Forest, working on *Notes on the State of Virginia*, when the states ratified it in 1781. His experience in the Confederation Congress in 1783–1784 made him keenly aware of its deficiencies.

Jefferson played no role in the deliberations in Philadelphia in the summer of 1787. "There is a general disposition through the states to adopt what the delegates shall propose," Madison wrote to Jefferson, "and we may be assured their propositions will be wise, as a more able assembly never sat in America." Washington, a strong supporter, sent Jefferson a copy of the proposed constitution. Destined by unanimous enthusiasm to be the first president in the new government, he may already have had in mind that he might offer Jefferson a position. Madison also sent him a copy. Both Jefferson and Madison wanted a stronger national government, responsible for foreign affairs, taxation, national defense, and interstate and international commerce. The new constitution would offer reassurance that the country could pay interest and principal on its Dutch and French loans by having a guaranteed tax base. "Happy for us," Jefferson commented, "that when we find our constitutions defective and insufficient to secure the happiness of our people, we can assemble with all the coolness of philosophers and set it to rights, while every other nation on earth must have recourse to arms to amend or to restore their constitutions."

Actually, ratification by two-thirds of the states was far from assured. Jefferson knew that opposition to numbers of the compromises was widespread, especially in Virginia and Massachusetts. It would be a close vote. Madison worried that, even if passed, the new constitution "will neither effectually answer its national object nor prevent the local mischiefs which everywhere excite disgusts against the state governments." Jefferson was more sanguine, at least in a letter to his Dutch representative, intended to assure Dutch bankers that the United States was taking a giant step toward economic stability. The letter hovers somewhere between sincerity and self-delusion. Jefferson boasted that Americans were creating a new constitution without internal strife and would soon have the power to tax themselves and sell Western land to pay their debts.

Ironically, the two most experienced constitution theorists and drafters, other than Franklin, were three thousand miles away from Philadelphia. How different the result of the deliberations might have been if Adams and Jefferson had been there with Madison, Hamilton, and George Mason. Jefferson and Adams were essentially in agreement about what needed to be done, and the new constitution mostly met their priority requirements: a balance of power between the executive and legislature; a federal judiciary to be established by Congress; the power of Congress to tax and regulate interstate and international commerce; foreign affairs to be the province of the executive, with the power to declare war exclusively reserved to Congress; and all matters of common law and its internal application to be reserved to the states. Adams favored a stronger executive than did Jefferson. He also favored more power in the hands of the federal government, though not much more, a difference varying from issue to issue and over time. Jefferson favored a minimal national judiciary. Madison, like Hamilton, with whom he was still on good terms, unsuccessfully argued for a radical proposal that Jefferson probably would have opposed: that Congress should have the power to veto state legislation. Otherwise, Madison feared, the tail would wag the dog; the national government would be too weak. "A Constitutional negative on the laws of the States seems equally necessary to secure individuals against encroachments on their rights." Later, Madison and Jefferson were to argue the opposite. One desirable asset, Jefferson thought, would be a Bill of Rights. The constitution that went to the states for ratification did not have one, mainly because Madison and others believed that the constitutions of the states protected the rights at issue.

By late 1787, as the debate about ratification intensified, Jefferson developed important doubts. "How do you like our new constitution?" he asked Adams in mid-November. "I confess there are things in it which stagger all my dispositions to subscribe to what such an assembly has proposed. The house of federal representatives will not be adequate to the management of affairs either foreign or federal." He did not anticipate the creation of a cabinet and of executive agencies. "Their president seems a bad edition of a Polish king. He may be reelected from 4 years to 4 years for life. Reason and experience prove to us that a chief magistrate, so continuable, is an officer for life." Yes, he agreed with one of his correspondents, it was nothing "less than a miracle" that any constitution that promoted national unity might be ratified, and he did not fully share Madison's pessimism about its adequacy. Jefferson, though, especially feared that the failure to limit the reelectability of the president would lead to tyranny, an American version of a Caesar or a George III. He favored a single four-year term. Many Americans worried that, without a strong chief executive who could serve for more than one term, the natural tendency of republics to settle disagreements by conflict would result in bloodshed and anarchy. Jefferson counterargued that there had been only one such armed rebellion in American history: the refusal in 1786 of farmers in western Massachusetts to pay what they felt to be unfair and ruinous taxes. Jefferson, the list maker, provided a statistical table to demonstrate to Madison that America was distinctive in how few rebellions it had experienced from as far back as the first settlement. Anyway, he wrote, "what signify a few lives lost in a century or two? The tree of liberty must be refreshed from time to time with the blood of patriots and tyrants. It is its natural manure."

If Jefferson had been alive in 1860, he might have granted that his database had been too small for his generalizations. His appeal to the desirability of the "tree of liberty" being refreshed "from time to time with the blood of patriots," not to speak of the difficulty of defining who was a patriot, made his argument, seemingly noble on first glance, actually superficial, imperceptive, ahistorical, and callous. What "signify," he asks, "a few lives lost in a century or two?" The American Revolution, which Jefferson naturally offered as his model of the right kind, had resulted in the deaths of at least fifty thousand human beings in battle and from disease, while the rebellion of 1860, in which firebrands persuaded many Southerners that it would at most shed only a little blood to nurture their version of the "tree of liberty," resulted in about seven hundred thousand dead. Such figures need not be exact to be depressing, and they do not include those casualties that were less than lethal but still horrible. What allowed Jefferson to be so epigrammatically cavalier about such losses? Did he think deaths in such large numbers could never happen in any future American rebellion? Did he put out of mind the horrors of the war that he himself had lived through, as if the "tree of liberty" between 1775 and 1781 had been so lightly watered with blood that he could, in 1787, dismiss the losses from his mind?

Jefferson often worked with large generalizations. In this case, he did not pause to consider whose blood would be shed, under what conditions, and in what quantity. In his mind, every drop of blood shed in the American Revolution had been worth shedding. Not everyone would have agreed. Moreover, without taking into account conflict between differing claims and communities about liberty itself, and without some precise definition of "liberty," Jefferson's comment seems almost outrageous. The French Revolution, whose initial violence had already begun by late 1787, almost within sight of Jefferson's Paris mansion, was to claim in its first three years the lives of about fifty thousand people and about 1.4 million between 1790 and 1802. Still, Jefferson meant it particularly about the American Revolution, which he idealized and romanticized, with little regard for those to whom it had brought suffering and death. In 1787, the word "liberty" was mostly in the service of an argument to provide strict term limits to the newly created office of the American presidency. If it had not been widely assumed that Washington would be the first president, the Constitutional Convention might have been guided more by fear of executive tyranny than of civil anarchy.

In any case, he was all right with the Constitution as a compromise document whose provisions could be changed, particularly limiting the presidency to a single term. He also believed it needed an explicit Bill of Rights, that it would not be enough to rely on the state constitutions. Gradually, Madison came to agree with him. The national debate over ratification eventually included the unanimous commitment that a Bill of Rights would be taken up in the first session of the new government's Congress. "You will perceive," Jefferson wrote, "that these objections are serious, and some of them not without foundation."

At the end of December 1787, Adams, who also had serious reservations, clarified his differences with Jefferson, which ultimately resided in their different views of human nature. Adams believed that Jefferson's relative optimism that the people could govern themselves and that they would instinctively elect educated, wise, and experienced leaders was unrealistic. He wrote to Jefferson, "You are afraid of the one," of a strong and continuously elected chief executive, "I of the few. We agree perfectly that the many should have a full fair and perfect representation.—you are apprehensive of monarchy; I, of aristocracy. I would therefore have given more power to the president and less to the senate. . . . You are apprehensive of foreign interference, intrigue, influence. So am I—but, as often as elections happen, the danger of foreign influence recurs. The less frequently they happen the less danger.—and if the same man may be chosen again, it is probable he will be, and the danger of foreign influence will be less. Foreigners, seeing little prospect will have less courage for enterprise [interference]. Elections, my dear sir, elections to offices which are great objects of ambition, I look at with terror. Experiments of this kind have been so often tried, and so universally found productive of horrors, that there is great reason to dread them."

A dominant populism, he feared, would create the danger of domestic and foreign corruption of American law and national security. Adams believed a strong executive would be the best guard against populist corruption. Jefferson believed the greatest danger to republican government was an overly strong executive. Actually, for Jefferson, the best government was the least government. "I own," he responded to Adams, "I am not a friend to a very energetic government. It is always oppressive. . . . After all, it is my principle that the will of the majority should always prevail. . . . I think our governments will remain virtuous for many centuries; as long as they are chiefly agricultural; and this will be as long as there shall be vacant lands in any part of America. When they get piled upon one another in large cities, as in Europe, they will become corrupt as in Europe. Above all things I hope the education of the common people will be attended to; convinced that on their good sense we may rely with the most security for the preservation of a due degree of liberty."

In 1787 and for the next four or five years, Jefferson and Adams were essentially on the same page. They were still there or on adjacent pages in later years, a matter of emphasis and nuance, and of anxieties about the use and misuse of power in a republican government, not of essential differences as to the government's overall structure. From the start, what Jefferson most feared was that the Constitution gave too much power to the executive. The specter of George III was always in his psyche.

Differences of personality and emphasis aside, Jefferson and Adams were mutually appreciative friends, each aware of the other's strengths and flaws. To Jefferson, Adams was a poor judge of human nature, too convinced of cupidity and sinfulness. To Adams,

Jefferson's rosy view of human nature misjudged the reality. Years later, Adams's son John Quincy was to best epitomize in his pen portrait of Jefferson the Adams family view of Jefferson as an example of well-meaning self-delusion. When, in early 1788, the Adamses sailed home from Europe, Jefferson hoped, he wrote affectionately, that "it will be only a change of service, from helping us here, to help us there. We have so few in our councils acquainted with foreign affairs, that your aid in that department, as well as others will be invaluable. . . . Be assured of the unchangeable esteem and respect with which I am Your friend and servant." In early 1789, from Massachusetts, Adams asserted, with an assurance that continued even in their years of estrangement, that "I am with an affection that can never die, your friend and servant." "Servant" was always an obligatory epistolary formality. "Unchangeable esteem" and "affection" were not.

CHAPTER TEN

His Masterly Pen

1787–1789

Jefferson's "masterly pen," in John Adams's assessment of his literary talent, was expressively at work in his Paris years, particularly in pen portraits of Adams, the Marquis de Lafayette, the Count of Vergennes, Louis XVI, and Marie Antoinette. Brief pen portraits were a highlight of eighteenth-century letter writing—short character descriptions that attempted through selective detail to capture the essence of a personality and career. Jefferson was "masterly" at it, though in that word Adams was referring particularly to the choice of Jefferson to create the first draft of the Declaration of Independence. Like many pen portraits, Jefferson's were not for publication, though the recipients often shared them within their own circles and among those whose views they hoped to influence. In Jefferson's case, the portraits, created spontaneously, without any anticipation that their subjects would ever read what he had written, have sharpness of wit and insight, vivid character evocations, and condensed narratives so brief that they concisely convey a personality.

For Jefferson, Adams was in a category of his own. Both were brilliant intellectuals, voracious readers, and obsessive writers. Only Madison played as large a role in Jefferson's literary and intellectual life. Madison disliked Adams; Jefferson did not. To Madison, Adams was boorish, loud, and argumentative, an unrefined New Englander without the courtliness that elite Virginians valued. To Jefferson, Adams was always

> my friend. . . . I afterwards saw proofs which convicted him of a degree of vanity, and of a blindness to it, of which no germ had appeared in Congress [in 1775–1776]. A 7-months' intimacy with him here [in Paris] and as many weeks in London have given me opportunities of studying him closely. He is vain, irritable and a bad calculator of the force and probable effect of the motives which govern men. But this is all the ill which can possibly be said of him. He is as disinterested as the being which made him: he is profound in his views: and accurate in his judgment except where knowledge of the world is necessary to form a judgment. He is so amiable, that I pronounce you will love him if ever you become acquainted with him. He would be, as he was, a great man in Congress.

Madison never came to love Adams. Jefferson, even in their years of alienation, never ceased loving him, though that love made its way gingerly and with reserve through difficulties of political disagreement and differences of personality. The record, including Adams's diaries and letters, corroborates the fairness and accuracy of Jefferson's pen portrait of the second president's strengths and flaws.

About Lafayette, a friend and collaborator during his Paris years, Jefferson's judgment was also balanced. "The Marquis de Lafayette is a most valuable auxiliary to me. His zeal is unbounded, and his weight with those in power great. His education having been merely military, commerce was an unknown field to him. But his good sense enabling him to comprehend perfectly whatever is explained to him, his agency has been very efficacious. He has a great deal of sound genius, is well remarked by the king and rising in popularity. He has nothing against him but the suspicion of republican principles. I think he will one day be of the ministry."

An honorary American and quasi-republican, Lafayette used the influence he had, more limited than Jefferson realized, to help Jefferson increase trade between France and the United States. Lafayette was praised for his valor and distrusted for his republicanism. He had enough influence to be helpful, but the aristocracy had its suspicions. They were confirmed between 1787 and 1791, when Lafayette led the effort to transform France into a constitutional monarchy. In the end, he made enemies among both right-wing conservatives and radical reformers. Jefferson collaborated with Lafayette and his circle of reformers. They leaned on him for advice and language in their attempts to help the nation avoid bankruptcy, anarchy, and bloodshed. In August 1789 Jefferson hosted a meeting of Lafayette and his colleagues at the Hôtel de Langeac, though the American minister was expected to absent himself from comment on or engagement with French internal matters. His pen portrait of Lafayette is incisive and perceptive. Its final sentence expresses the judgment of a friend who knows the best and the worst. "His foible is a canine appetite for popularity and fame. But he will get above this." "Canine appetite" has a special vividness and ambivalence in the dog-loving Parisian world. Jefferson himself detested dogs.

Jefferson often was kept waiting in the ornate anterooms of French power. He had numerous meetings with Louis XVI's foreign minister, the Count of Vergennes, until Vergennes's death in early 1787. Vergennes managed from the French side everything to do with Franco-American relations. Like the master he served, he detested the republican principles that Jefferson and his country embodied. Recognizing how minor a factor the United States was in French considerations and how little regard the ruling class had for republican principles, Jefferson needed to be both patient and assertive, a difficult combination. This was not a talent Adams could manage;

Jefferson did somewhat better, his manner better suited to maintaining some dignity for the United States in its posture as a client nation. The French doubted that its client state, governed by the weak Articles of Confederation, could survive, let alone pay its debts to France. "The count de Vergennes is ill," Jefferson wrote to Madison in 1787. "The possibility of his recovery renders it dangerous for us to express a doubt but he is in danger."

In a few lines, Jefferson captured the essence of Vergennes in the only aspect important to him: "He is a great Minister in European affairs but has very imperfect ideas of ours [and] no confidence in them. His devotion to the principles of pure despotism renders him unaffectionate to our governments but his fear of England makes him value us as a make weight. He is cool, reserved in political conversation, free and familiar on other subjects, and a very attentive, agreeable person to do business with. It is impossible to have a clearer, better organized head but age has chilled his heart. Nothing should be spared on our part to attach this country to us." The latter was the essence of Jefferson's mission. Vergennes was "a great and good minister . . . and an accident to him might endanger the peace of Europe." It's likely that this pen portrait was conveyed to Jay and to Washington. Madison was in constant touch with both, and the three were to be together in Philadelphia that summer.

Of even greater importance to Jefferson was Vergennes's master. From his first introduction to the Court of Versailles, where he submitted his credentials in May 1775, Jefferson acknowledged the obvious: France was ruled from the top by one man, whose character determined, in the whirlwind of conflicting influences, what policies would dominate at any one moment every aspect of the French state. However, he also knew that Louis XVI was not a unitary ruler, despite his absolute authority: the influence of his wife made her a de facto co-ruler, given her husband's pliable, irresolute, and often passive personality. Appropriately, Jefferson put his mind and pen to a character study of the king and queen. Although his view of the king did not substantially change through the years, it did, between 1787 and 1789, become more nuanced and textured. Unlike his other pen portraits, it is accretive, expressed in numerous letters over time. Jefferson's last summation of Louis XVI was written in 1821 in his autobiographical fragment.

From the perspective of his post-Napoleonic old age, Jefferson created his fullest portrait of Louis XVI and Marie Antoinette. From the start, he had thought kindly of the king, depicting him as a ruler whose vacillation made him as much a victim as a perpetrator of a system that could save itself and avoid civil war only by implementing the reforms that would turn it into a constitutional monarchy. As minister and diplomat, Jefferson needed to be careful to whom he expressed his views. In private letters, he could be scathing about a government that took from its citizens "an unjust proportion of their labor. . . . It is a government of wolves over sheep." The wolves were "to be seen as you would see the tower of London or Menagerie of Versailles with their Lions, tigers, hyaenas and other beasts of prey, standing in the same relation to their fellows. A slight acquaintance with them will suffice to shew you that, under the most imposing exterior, they are the weakest and worst part of mankind."

The king, Jefferson believed, was not the worst but the weakest, essentially a good man whose "concessions" in 1786 and 1787 came from his "very heart. . . . The king loves business," Jefferson wrote in 1787, "economy, order and justice. He wishes sincerely the good of his people. He is irascible, rude and very limited in his understanding, religious bordering only on bigotry. He has no mistress, loves his queen and is too much governed by her. She is capricious like her brother and governed by him, devoted to pleasure and expense, not remarkable for any other vices or virtues. Unhappily the king shews a propensity for the pleasures of the table. That for drink has increased lately or at least it is become more known."

In 1789, after two years of increasingly large crowds of hungry, angry, and violent people on the streets of Paris, Jefferson could still separate the king from the Court and the system. France should be "happy that he is an honest unambitious man, who desires neither money nor power for himself; and that his most operative minister, though he has appeared to trim a little, is still in the main a friend to public liberty." Jefferson was certain that *the king is a good man*, though how he could be so sure and by what standard he made this odd or at least irrelevant judgment is unclear. Jefferson continued to have no doubt that George III was a villain but Louis XVI was not. His eagerness to separate Louis from his context says more about Jefferson than about the king, as if the king were not complicit in the crimes against everything Jefferson otherwise stood for and believed in. Until 1774, Jefferson had believed that the Parliament, not George III, was entirely responsible for depriving the American colonists of their rights as freeborn citizens of British America and of their natural rights as human beings. But by 1776, he was exclusively a villain. To further exculpate Louis XVI, Jefferson depicts the queen as an exemplar of extravagance and absolutism. In his view, although the king ruled the country, the queen ruled the king.

For Jefferson, it was a supreme example of a deplorable reality that in France, so unlike in the United States, women of nobility were empowered to express themselves publicly about politics and government. Some indeed had significant influence, publicly and privately. "Our good ladies . . . have been too wise to wrinkle their foreheads with politics. They are contented to soothe and calm the minds of their husbands returning ruffled from political debate. They have the good sense to value domestic happiness above all other, and the art to cultivate it beyond all others. There is no part of the earth where so much of this is enjoyed as in America." He continued, writing to a beautiful, wealthy Philadelphia woman with whom he had recently become friendly, you think that Parisian women "are happier than American women. . . . You will change your opinion, my dear Madam, and come over to mine in the end. Recollect the women of this capital, some on foot, some on horses, and some in carriages hunting pleasure in the streets, in routs and assemblies, and forgetting that they have left it behind them in their nurseries; compare them with our own country-women occupied in the tender and tranquil amusements of domestic life, and confess that it is a comparison of Amazons and Angels."

Jefferson's squint focused exclusively on women of privilege, a narrow segment of the French population, a class-based exclusiveness typical of his propensity for extravagant generalizations. In November 1788, as he wrote this letter to Ann Willing Bingham, another kind of woman had been taking the public stage in France and in some of the provinces. These women wore ragged clothing. Their hands were worn. Their main interest was in food for themselves and their families. Their anger, Jefferson believed, could be placated by the redistribution of governing power that Lafayette and his circle were proposing. Jefferson's conviction that women's place was exclusively in the home, a support service to men of the world like himself and their families, allowed him to tip the balance of obliquity from the king to the queen, from the male to the female. Louis XVI had a good heart; clearly, Marie Antoinette did not.

And Jefferson's Francophilia and Anglophobia, as well as the situational differences between 1774–1775 and 1788–1789, allowed him to exculpate Louis XVI, to treat him as an individual independent of the system he headed, whereas George III was exclusively a representation of absolutist and oppressive monarchy. As late as the summer of 1789, Jefferson had "not a single doubt of the sincerity of the king," and believed "that there will not be another disagreeable act from him." Still, that same summer, he had a moment of lucidity about the king and the system he embodied. Though Louis XVI "is honest and wishes the good of his people," Jefferson wrote to John Jay, "the expediency of an hereditary aristocracy is too difficult a question for him.—On the contrary his prejudices, his habits and his connections decide him in his heart to support it." He would not be capable, Jefferson realized, of the kind of "*agreeable*" act that perhaps might allow France to evolve into a constitutional monarchy with republican features.

Jefferson returned to the subject in the autobiographical fragment he wrote in 1821. The king had "not a wish but for the good of the nation, and for that object no personal sacrifice would ever have cost him a moment's regret. But his mind was weakness itself, his constitution timid, his judgment null, and without sufficient firmness even to stand by the faith of his word. His Queen too, haughty and bearing no contradiction, had an absolute ascendency over him." She was in league with men "whose principles of government were those of the age of Louis XIV." No sooner had the king taken the good counsel of the liberal reformers than their advice "would be reversed in the evening by the influence of the Queen and court. But the hand of heaven weighed heavily indeed on the machinations of this junto . . . producing collateral incidents . . . powerfully co-exciting the nation to force a regeneration of its government, and overwhelming with accumulated difficulties this liberticide resistance. For, while laboring under the want of money for even ordinary purposes, in a government which required a million of livres a day, and driven to the last ditch by the universal call for liberty, there came on a winter of such severe cold, as was without example in the memory of man, or in the written records of history."

The cold winter of 1788–1789, Jefferson concluded, was apparently a collateral incident so sufficient in its damage to the food supply that the desirable balance of power between the king's competing constituencies failed to be achieved. "And here again was lost another precious occasion of sparing to France the crimes and cruelties thro' which she has since passed, and to Europe, and finally America the evils which flowed on also from this mortal source," apparently a reference to Napoléon and the War of 1812.

The king had now become a passive machine in the hands of the National Assembly. Had he been left to himself, Jefferson believed, "he would have willingly acquiesced in whatever they should devise as best for the nation. A wise constitution would have been formed, hereditary in his line, himself placed at its head, with powers so large as to enable him to do all the good of his station, and so limited as to restrain him from its abuse. This he would have faithfully administered, and more than this I do not believe he ever wished." Ironically, he would have been what George III was in fact. The queen was the villain. "I have ever believed that had there been no queen, there would have been no revolution," as if the systemic inequalities, feudal oppressiveness, and economic bankruptcy of France in 1789 had nothing to do with the bloodshed that was to follow. "I should have shut up the Queen in a Convent, putting harm out of her power, and placed the king in his station, investing him with limited powers, which I verily believe he would have honestly exercised, according to the measure of his understanding. In this way no void would have been created, courting the usurpation of a military adventurer, nor occasion given for those enormities which demoralized the nations of the world, and destroyed, and is yet to destroy millions and millions of its inhabitants." What happened was a total failure of "national morality."

In his depiction of Louis XVI, as to a lesser extent in his other pen portraits, Jefferson combines personal analysis with political context. The weakness of most of his pen portraits, exemplified in his description of Adams, is the absence of examples to illustrate his analysis. Too heavy a burden is placed on the reader's confidence in Jefferson's accuracy. Generalizations, rather than examples, dominate. Still, with the literary flair usual in his private letters, as if his reading from Cicero to Sterne is guiding his pen, Jefferson in these pen portraits delights and enlightens with his pithy, concise, and incisive language. At the same time, he falls short of full literary effectiveness, which requires examples and narrative, illustrations of what leads him to his insights. In general, Jefferson gives his correspondent what he is best at, but he leaves his modern reader wishing there were more, the evidence and narrative that would encourage greater assent or dissent.

His portraits, though, are not independent, self-conscious exemplifications of the genre; they aren't conceived separately from the letters they are embedded in. The depiction of Louis XVI in the autobiographical fragment is intended as a contribution to the historical record, as a statement by its author of what he observed and believed. Jefferson never thought of himself as a writer purposely creating a text intended to enlighten, entertain, and provide insights into and guidance about ways in which to think about people, human nature, and the world. Still, his literary talent and observational insight, inseparable from his interest in character and performance, personality and power, talent and achievement, give his pen portraits a vividness that literature at its best provides.

Hardly a year after his arrival, in May 1775, Jefferson considered writing a full-length essay on a subject larger than any that could be contained in a pen portrait—France itself. The possibility was embodied in an outline consisting of headings that exemplified every important aspect of the country as he had so far observed it. The headings are revealing indicators of what Jefferson found relevant topics for development, and like *Notes on the State of Virginia*, it had the potential for full-length treatment through revision and expansion. Government, of course, was central to Jefferson's interests. Under that heading, he defines France as a "Pure Despotism," with subheadings. It is badly governed, the outline states; corruption is widespread in public and private life; and commerce is impeded by heavy duties and taxes. The essay would also have dealt with Fine Arts and Society, comprising the subtopics Love, Friendship, Charity, Religion, Dogs, Theatres, Concerts, Balls, Meals, and Talkativeness. His observations about dogs and talkativeness would have had as much interest in regard to Jefferson's personality as about the French.

In the category of essays that might have been written, *Notes on the State of France*, to give it a title, would have had distinctive prominence. It might have been Jefferson's European version of *Notes on the State of Virginia*, perhaps at the same length, revised and expanded over time. The outline is all that exists, however. The fact that he sketched out sixty subdivisions for such an essay or book, covering governance, taxes, manufactures, agriculture, animals, labor, religion, charity, society, social manners, gardens, entertainments, music, poetry, architecture, and much more is a testimony to the liveliness of his mind, his gift for intellectual and cultural overview, and his conceptual energy. The unwritten text takes its honorable position in the list of works conceived but not written.

In the autumn of 1785, still making his way into the realities of France, Jefferson visited Versailles, fourteen miles from Paris. It was hunting season. Louis XVI and his court had taken up their seasonal occupancy of the ostentatious seat of the French monarchy that his great-great-great-grandfather Louis XIV had created to represent the glory of his reign and the unification of France under his absolutist rule. It was entirely a company town, a city that was not a city, a mirror with its own huge hall of mirrors to reflect the egos of the aristocratic rulers of the kingdom. It was an odd place for the republican minister from America in his simple dress and quiet dignity. He was, in his own way, as was Franklin before him, an object of curiosity, and of some respectful interest. On his tight budget, he could not and did not wish to compete with the richly dressed, etiquette-sensitive European ambassadors to the French Court. And other than as a curious anomaly, the Court was not interested in him. His presence was a formality.

The United States itself was of consequence mainly as an ally against Great Britain. Also, the French treasury hoped for quick repayment of the large sums of money it had borrowed and lent to the United States. In 1785, that prospect was minimal. Three years later, Adams and Jefferson were able to arrange to transfer some of America's French debt to Dutch banks. In 1785, the tremors about revenue, expenditures, and taxation were a serious concern for the French government. Jefferson did his best at Versailles and in Paris to maintain the expectation that the United States would repay its debt and remain a reliable ally. It was not an easy sell, and the Comte de Vergennes and his governing colleagues, especially the economists, were preoccupied by tensions in Europe, the king's expenses, the national debt, and the difficulty of raising money.

From his arrival in 1784, Jefferson had assumed a public stance of neutrality. In private, he was a scathing critic of French pomp and circumstance. In his first spring in Paris, he attended a Te Deum at Notre Dame Cathedral to celebrate the birth of Louis XVI's son, heir to the throne. The cathedral was packed, the streets so full that the Adamses' daughter wrote in her journal that "I may say with truth there were millions of people. Mr. Jefferson, who rode . . . with us, supposed there were as many people in the streets as there were in the State of Massachusetts, or any other of the States. Every house was full—every window and door, from the bottom to the top." The Court and clergy provided the power-asserting spectacle. For the populace, it was entertainment of the highest order. "You lost much by not attending," Jefferson wrote to William Short, who was away from Paris, immersed in his affair with a French woman. "It bids defiance to description. I will only observe to you in general that there were more judges, ecclesiastics and Grands seigneurs present, than Genl. Washington had of simple soldiers in his army, when he took the Hessians at Trenton, beat the British at Princeton, and hemmed up the British army at Brunswick a whole winter. Come home like a good boy and you will always be in the way of these wonders."

His request that Short return was, ironically, a request that he return to a city whose glamor offered erotic temptations, especially the availability of French women. Short may have been acting out a temptation that Jefferson sometimes felt. Soon the affable, handsome, well-bred Short, toward whom Jefferson was expressively paternal, would fall in love with the young wife of a much older well-known aristocrat and spend much of the next twenty years as her lover. Jefferson had to be aware that he too had the potential to live a variant of Short's relationships, a widower attractive to women in his high-level social life. In Paris, he was a desirable match, an object of erotic curiosity, eligible for the role of flirtatious friend, lover, or even husband.

Versailles was a spectacle; Paris, a city—one of misery and wealth, poverty and beauty, squalid quarters and upscale splendor, especially in buildings like Jefferson's Hôtel de Langeac. Paris reveled in public rituals dedicated to the Church, the royal family, the aristocracy, and the glory of the nation-state that Louis XIV had created. Its vulnerability was financial. Living on borrowed money, the regime was also living on borrowed time, its survival dependent on fiscal reform, which various ministers, like the eminent Jacques Necker, were being prevented from implementing. The obstacles were the vested interest of the aristocracy, the clergy, the royal family, and a history of overspending, overborrowing, and aristocratic privilege, including exemption from taxation. Minister of finance between 1777 and 1781, the talented and modernizing Necker had a second try at rationalizing the French economy during Jefferson's last two years in Paris, an effort that Jefferson observed intently, hoping Necker might be successful. In the summer of 1789, Jefferson provided John Jay with a pen portrait of Necker. If Necker should fail, Jefferson wrote, "probably a civil war" would follow.

It is a tremendous cloud indeed which hovers over this nation, and he at the helm has neither the courage nor the skill necessary to weather it. Eloquence in a high degree, knowledge on matters of account, and order, are distinguishing traits in his character. Ambition is his first passion, Virtue his second. He has not discovered that sublime truth that a bold, unequivocal virtue is the best handmaid, even to Ambition, and would carry him further in the end than the temporizing wavering policy he pursues. His judgment is not of the first order, scarcely even of the second, his resolution frail, and upon the whole it is rare to meet an instance of a person so much below the reputation he has obtained.

The words are Jefferson's, the view of Necker's character not from firsthand knowledge but from someone Jefferson knew. The source "is not indeed his friend, and allowance must therefore be made for the high coloring. But this being abated, the facts and ground work of the drawing are just." Apparently, Jefferson did not know that Necker had been instrumental in the French decision to provide the loans that helped make the American Revolution successful. "If the Tiers [Jefferson here seems to mean the three estates, the nobles, the clergy, and the commons] separate," Jefferson continued, "he goes at the same time: if they stay together and succeed in establishing a constitution to their mind, as soon as that is placed in safety, they will abandon him to the mercy of the court, unless he can recover the confidence which he has lost at present, and which indeed seems to be irrecoverable." Jefferson was right about the outcome but not about Necker's abilities or about the connection between virtue and political achievement. He continued to maintain, despite evidence to the contrary, that virtue and political achievement were inseparable. Jefferson believed himself to be an example of that synergy.

He had gotten it into his head that the French people "love us more I think than they do any other nation on earth." And that was very much the result of "the effect of the good dispositions with which the French officers," like Lafayette, returned from America. Jefferson's definition of the French people was narrow, however. He had only modest knowledge about them, and as a whole they had very little knowledge about or interest in the United States. He was to learn more about the French during his tour of southern France, his only venture outside Paris. But his inclination for generalizations about the French people remained, an expression of his desire that the French and the American people love one another, an ideological and a personal hope transformed into a claim of fact. His portrait of the king resulted from direct observation and also from what his sources, such as Lafayette, Condorcet, and other members of his Parisian aristocratic-intellectual circle, told him.

Visiting Versailles in October 1785, Jefferson set out one morning for a hike. He had wanted, he wrote to Madison, "to take a view of the place" from the surroundings hills, a wandering expedition into the countryside away from the Court.

> For this purpose I shaped my course towards the highest of the mountains in sight, to the top of which was about a league. As soon as I had got clear of the town I fell in with a poor woman walking at the same rate with myself and going the same course. Wishing to know the condition of the laboring poor I entered into conversation with her, which I began by enquiries for the path which would lead me into the mountain: and thence proceeded to enquiries into her vocation, condition and circumstance. She told me she was a day laborer . . . that she had two children to maintain, and to pay a rent . . . for her house . . . would consume the hire of 75 days, that often she could get no employment, and of course was without bread. As we had walked together near a mile and she had so far served me as a guide, I gave her, on parting 24 sous. She burst into tears of a gratitude which I could perceive was unfeigned, because she was unable to utter a word. She had probably never before received so great an aid.

This is a rare instance of Jefferson recording a conversation with a poor person, whether in France or America. "This little attendrissement [emotional episode], with the solitude of my walk led me into a train of reflections on that unequal division of property which occasions the numberless instances of wretchedness which I had observed in this country and is to be observed all over Europe." Characteristically, Jefferson moved quickly from a concrete example to an abstraction.

> The property of this country is absolutely concentered in a very few hands. I asked myself what could be the reason that so many should be permitted to beg who are willing to work, in a country where there is a very considerable proportion of uncultivated lands? These lands are kept idle mostly for the sake of game. It should seem then that it must be because of the enormous wealth of the proprietors which places them above attention to the increase of their revenues by permitting these lands to be labored. I am conscious that an equal division of property is impracticable. . . . Whenever there is in any country, uncultivated lands and unemployed poor, it is clear that the laws of property have been so far extended as to violate natural right. The earth is given as a common stock for man to labor and live on. If, for the encouragement of industry we allow it to be appropriated, we must take care that other employment be furnished to those excluded from the appropriation. If we do not the fundamental right to labor the earth returns to the unemployed. It is too soon yet in our country to say that every man who cannot find employment but who can find uncultivated land, shall be at liberty to cultivate it, paying a moderate rent. But it is not too soon to provide by every possible means that as few as possible shall be without a little portion of land.

In the late 1770s, Jefferson had proposed that the Virginia House of Delegates legislate the distribution of land not yet settled by whites to guarantee fifty acres to every homesteader. As he gazed westward to the Ohio Territory and beyond, he envisioned his panacea to poverty, a republic of farmers made independent in their livelihoods and in the exercise of their rights as citizens by ownership of property that would provide economic security and political independence. Western expansion was for him the key to population growth, prosperity, independence, and republican government. The legislation, to Jefferson's disappointment, was not enacted. The majority of the governing elite in Virginia had no intention of giving land away. Many, like Washington, had speculative investments in Western land, and even Jefferson did not envision an equal distribution of Western property. Fifty acres was his baseline distribution. Thereafter, wealth in property could be expanded by purchase or barter or any other accepted means. He did not oppose the accumulation of massive wealth in land. He himself had been the heir of large estates, and his proposal did not provide for redistribution of land already owned by legal title. For Jefferson, freeholding of land was sacred, untouchable. The land belonged to those European Americans who had settled it, he had argued in 1774 and 1776. Virginians like Jefferson valued their ownership above any proposal or thoughts about redistribution of wealth. Giving up even a small fraction of his own acres to the American equivalent of this French peasant woman would have been anathema to Jefferson.

In France, since every bit of land was already legally owned by a small number of people, "an equal division of property is impracticable," Jefferson wrote to Madison. "The consequences of this enormous inequality" produces "so much misery to the bulk of mankind, [that] legislators cannot invent too many devices for subdividing property, only taking care to let their subdivisions go hand in hand with the natural affections of the human mind." What the latter phrase means is unclear, an instance of Jefferson's propensity to propose improvements or solutions to inequities in vague phrases that are mellifluous but undefined. What indeed are "the natural affections of the human mind"? Do all human minds have them? Jefferson had two practical recommendations: the laws of inheritance in France, which he had helped democratize in Virginia, should be reformed. "Another means of silently lessening the inequality of property is to exempt all from taxation below a certain point, and to tax the higher portions of property in geometrical progression as they rise." For "whenever there is in any country, uncultivated lands and unemployed poor, it is clear that the laws of property have been so far extended as to violate natural right." For "the earth is given as a common stock for man to labor and live on." But if all available land is already appropriated "we must take care that other employment be furnished to those excluded from the appropriation."

Jefferson was, of course, aware that the Virginia elite had already appropriated most of the state's productive land. For those without land, some other type of employment must be found. Still, "it is too soon yet in our country to say that every man who cannot find employment but who can find uncultivated land, shall be at liberty to cultivate it, paying a moderate rent. But it is not too soon to provide by every possible means that as few as possible shall be without a little portion of land"—as long as there was uncultivated land. "The small landholders are the most precious part of a state."

It was the perfect solution and the perfect evasion. Uncultivated land should belong to those who cultivate it. Already cultivated land should remain in the possession of those who currently owned it. And without being explicit, Jefferson seems to anticipate that those Americans with money, initiative, energy, and competence would sooner or later obtain most of the land, including the Western venues, just as his own father had accumulated the large tracts that his son had inherited. There will be along the way many small landholders. But slowly and inexorably, wealth in the form of land and its equivalents, varying over time with individual fortunes, would resolve into the hands of the few, as it already had in his own lifetime and as it would do in the next centuries and to the present. Jefferson had no solution for wealth inequality. The fifty-acre proposal had been his most radical and innovative effort. It had not proved acceptable to land-hungry Americans, to the speculators in land for resale, and to the state governments dominated by landowners.

Madison responded to Jefferson in June 1786 that he had "no doubt that the misery of the lower classes will be found to abate wherever the Government assumes a freer aspect, and the laws favor a subdivision of property. Yet I suspect that the difference will not fully account for the comparative comfort of the mass of people in the United States. Our limited population has probably as large a share in producing this effect as the political advantages which distinguish us. A certain degree of misery seems inseparable from a high degree of populousness."

Both believed that the likely increase in the population of the United States, the Western territories notwithstanding, had the potential to create a society with the same features of land scarcity, surplus production, cutthroat commercial activity, income inequality, and government corruption as those of the European nations. How could the United States—whose dominant ethos, so it seemed to them, encouraged accumulating wealth, luxury, and security—avoid becoming like France and Great Britain? Yes, Madison wrote, "from a more equal partition of property must result a greater simplicity of manners, consequently a less consumption of manufactured superfluities, and a less proportion of idle proprietors and domestics. From a juster government must result less need of soldiers either for defence against dangers from without, or disturbances from within." But how in practice to pass laws that "favor a subdivision of property"? Why would current property holders consent? And would the result in fact be a more just government?

In Jefferson's and Madison's visionary logic, people who owned land would live a life of noble simplicity, a hallmark of which is the

rejection of foreign-produced luxuries. They won't want manufactured goods from Europe. They would happily do without what
Jefferson highly valued: European art, architecture, musical instruments, house decorations, books, wine, and cuisine. Neither Jefferson
nor Madison discussed whether the recipients of a more equal distribution of land would have servants or slaves—though why wouldn't
they? And wouldn't some of them want more land than the distribution had given them? Wouldn't they buy and sell land? Wouldn't
some be more enterprising, competitive, clever, opportunistic, ruthless, greedy, or criminal than others? Wouldn't the complexity and
variety of human nature and human beings, moral to immoral, saintly
to criminal, still determine the basic ambience in which republican
exemplars lived their individual lives? Madison, not always, and Jefferson, pervasively, assumed that human beings are what they wanted
them to be. Each placed heavy reliance on the belief that better government, as they spent their lives defining it, and the essential noble-
ness of human nature, would play the dominant role in determining
the well-being of their fellow citizens.

"But I forget that I am writing a letter not a dissertation," Madison
concluded, with a brief coda that in Virginia "the scarcity of money,
the low price of Tobacco and the high price of bread continue to be
the topics of complaint. The last evil is likely to be much increased
by a sudden vicisitude in the prospects of wheat." There had been
prayers for rain. "Shortly after we had a deluge of it . . . incessant rains,
and sometimes showers, or rather torrents that threatened to sweep
away everything." Crops failed, and the economy had plunged into
depression. Commerce and tax revenue had declined; discontent was
widespread.

Jefferson had a solution to the challenge of a more equitable distribution of land. "Within an hour after you left us," he wrote to John
Trumbull in September 1789, "I was taken with an illness which confined me to my chamber six days." It was one of his periodic disabling

headaches. Richard Gem, his highly regarded but uncredentialed doctor and a well-known radical republican, attended him. A talented British intellectual, Gem was also an economist, well known for his theoretical boldness. Gem shared an idea that appealed immensely to Jefferson. "The earth is given as a common stock for man to labor and live on," Jefferson had already written to Madison. Gem's similar idea now struck an intellectual and personal chord, adding a temporal limitation to Jefferson's idea of the spatial universality of the "common stock." "That one generation of men in civil society," Gem wrote in a memo which he read to his patient, "have no right to make acts to bind another, is a truth that cannot be contested. The earth and all things whatever can only be conceived to belong to the living; the dead and those who are unborn can have no rights of property." With a spurt of energy, Jefferson expanded the idea, sharing his detailed version with Lafayette and other French constitution makers.

Sick enough to be incapacitated for anything but a compelling idea, Jefferson had enough energy to rewrite it at length in a letter to Madison. The question "whether one generation of men has a right to bind another, seems never to have been started either on this or our side of the water. Yet it is a question of such consequences as not only to merit decision, but place also, among the fundamental principles of every government." Ironically, American voters had just ratified a new Constitution expressly binding future generations to its particulars, except through a difficult process of amendment. Jefferson had not in 1787 raised an objection. "The course of reflection in which we are immersed here on the elementary principles of society has presented this question to my mind; and that no such obligation can be so transmitted I think very capable of proof." It was the French attempt now to create their own constitution that had stimulated his hypothesis, which he hoped would influence the French constitution makers.

I set out on this ground, which I suppose to be *self-evident*, "that the earth belongs in usufruct to the living": that the dead have neither powers nor rights over it. The portion occupied by any individual ceases to be his when himself ceases to be, and reverts to the society. If the society has formed no rules for the appropriation of its lands in severality, it will be taken by the first occupants. These will generally be the wife and children of the decedent. If they have formed rules of appropriation, those rules may give it to the wife and children, or to some one of them, or to the legatee of the deceased. So they may give it to his creditor. But the child, the legatee, or creditor takes it, not by any *natural right*, but by a law of the society of which they are members, and to which they are subject. Then no man can, by natural right, oblige the lands he occupied, or the persons who succeed him in that occupation, to the payment of debts contracted by him. For if he could, he might, during his own life, eat up the usufruct of the lands for several generations to come, and then the lands would belong to the dead, and not to the living, which would be the reverse of our principle.

A restraint on inflicting debts on future generations would be the rule or law: "No generation can contract debts greater than may be paid during the course of its own existence." Jefferson has nothing to say about how that might be instituted or enforced in a society of the sort that had just been embodied in the 1787 Constitution of the United States. But he continued, "On similar ground it may be proved, that no society can make a perpetual constitution, or even a perpetual law. The earth belongs always to the living generation. They may manage it then, and what proceeds from it, as they please, during their usufruct. They are masters too of their own persons, and consequently may govern them as they please. But persons and property make the sum of the objects of government. The constitution and the laws of their predecessors extinguished then in their natural course with those who gave them being. . . . Every constitution then, and every law, naturally expires at the end of 19 years." That was Jefferson's calculation of the length of a generation.

> If it be enforced longer, it is an act of force, and not of right.—It may be said that the succeeding generation exercising in fact the power of repeal, this leaves them as free as if the constitution or law had been expressly limited to 19 years only. In the first place, this objection admits the right, in proposing an equivalent. But the power of repeal is not an equivalent. It might be indeed if every form of government were so perfectly contrived that the will of the majority could always be obtained fairly and without impediment. But this is true of no form. The people cannot assemble themselves. Their representation is unequal and vicious. Various checks are opposed to every legislative proposition. Factions get possession of the public councils. Bribery corrupts them. Personal interests lead them astray from the general interests of their constituents: and other impediments arise so as to prove to every practical man that a law of limited duration is much more manageable than one which needs a repeal. In effect, all laws and contracts should automatically terminate after nineteen years.

By inference, so should the ownership of all land, though Jefferson seems not to follow his own logic.

The undefined phrases "*self-evident*" and "*natural right*" once again came spontaneously to Jefferson's pen, as they had in 1776, the underpinning of his argument, his assumption that all must agree with his use of these concepts, and in this case the weight they are given to bear in a claim that for many would neither be self-evident nor a natural right. In effect, Jefferson argued that there was both no right of inheritance of property from generation to generation and that all contracts—from individual debt to public legislation or compacts such as constitutions—had a shelf life of no more than a single generation. Its central claim that "the earth belongs in usufruct to the living" resonates with existential obviousness. Nothing belongs to the dead. But that the earth belongs exclusively to the living, that the living have no obligations to future generations, that they are not stewards who pass on values, commitments, property, and contracts to future generations seems not to have intruded itself on Jefferson's considerations. Each generation had the right to write its own constitution and laws, regardless of the contracts created by the previous generation. Laws, constitutions, and contractual obligations needed to be revised, even canceled, every nineteen years so that the next generation should not be saddled with the mistakes of its predecessors or with what was right for the previous generation but no longer desirable. By this arrangement, it may have occurred to him, his own debts would become void at his death, though his argument makes no reference to his personal situation.

For Jefferson, the French situation in 1789 illustrates an important aspect of what he meant by the claim that the "earth belongs to the living." It is, as far as the French reality is concerned, a catchphrase for the redistribution of wealth by an equitable redistribution of land. The French would seize the moment, Jefferson hoped, to implement a new regime in regard to the obligations of succeeding generations to previous generations: that debts, laws, property rights, and constitutions would not be indefinitely binding, that each generation would have the right to refashion the world without the heavy hand of the past limiting its alternatives. That hope for his own country and for revolutionary France propelled the labor of writing out for Madison a variation of the version he had already created for Lafayette. He hoped to influence the French reformists in their effort to create a written constitution, which would, Jefferson expected, make France a republican brother to the new nation across the Atlantic. In its first version, which is not extant, Jefferson's document went through the agency of Gem to Lafayette and others.

Jefferson hoped that its main point would help the French sweep away the old and create an entirely new nation, established on principles of justice, with wealth equitably distributed, and with each new generation having no obligation to repay the debts of the old. Since the national debt of the ancient regime was unbearably heavy and since each generation, he argued, self-evidently had the *natural right* to have a fresh start, France would be starting anew, from square one, with no inherited limitations or restrictions and no obligation to honor the previous government's debts.

Jefferson's September 1789 letter reached Madison in February 1790, a letter Madison probably would just as soon not have received. He answered it calmly, point by point, efficiently, and with respectful refutation. As theory, it had its interest. As practical legislation, it could not be implemented. It was actually undesirable to attempt to do so. In their exchange, neither Jefferson nor Madison alluded to the implication that if one generation did not have the right to obligate or entail the next, one generation of slave-owners could not bind the next generation of slaves to "a contract in perpetuity."

Madison gently pointed out seriatim the flaws in Jefferson's argument. It was more than a bridge too far. It failed to take into account a host of matters central to stability, mutuality, fairness, justice, and continuity in finance and government. Though in principle it had abstract and philosophical interest, its implementation as legislation would create a formidable variety of illogicalities, injustices, and hostilities. For example, if one generation were to owe no contractual allegiance to the debts of the preceding, would it not follow that it had no right to the assets that generation had accrued and the improvements it had made? "The improvements made by the dead form a charge against the living who take the benefit of them," Madison wrote. "This charge can no otherwise be satisfied than by executing the will of the dead accompanying the improvements. Debts may be incurred for purposes which interest the unborn, as well as the living." For better or worse, "the spirit of philosophical legislation has never reached some parts of the Union," Madison generously summarized, "and is by no means the fashion here, either within or without Congress."

Jefferson's proposal, Madison knew, was at variance with the Constitution and inimical to the American commitment to the pursuit of wealth, the sanctity of contracts, and the role of government and the courts in establishing stability and predictability among competing interests and from one generation to the next. It also included by omission the affirmation that slavery was and would remain an American institution. The Constitution strengthened government, not limited it. "The evils suffered and feared from weakness in Government, and licentiousness in the people, have turned the attention more towards the means of strengthening the former than of narrowing its extent in the minds of the latter," Madison responded. "Besides this," he continued, sensitive to Jefferson's feelings, "it is so much easier to espy the little difficulties immediately incident to every great plan, than to comprehend its general and remote benefits, that our hemisphere must be still more enlightened before many of the sublime truths which are seen through the medium of Philosophy, become visible to the naked eye of the ordinary Politician." It was the ordinary politician who embodied the will and character of the people. In this case, Jefferson was far from ordinary enough. He was being the philosopher, not the politician.

The idea was also, implicitly, deeply embedded in and reflective of Jefferson's personal situation. It was an intellectual projection and a personal expression of his own financial and psychological dilemma, in one of the most extraordinary letters, in conception and literary power, Jefferson ever wrote, not so much eloquent as intellectually astounding and personally revealing. Jefferson would have liked himself and his heirs to be relieved of his debts. Between the lines of the expanded version sent to Madison, Jefferson was expressing indirectly his personal sense of having been victimized by the past. He had become heavily burdened by inherited debts. His wife had been a gift from John Wayles, but Jefferson's inheritance of land, slaves, and debts from Wayles had become a poison pill. What had at first seemed an enrichment was now an incubus. So too were his own expenditures on consumer products of all kinds, some of them for his European life, many to be shipped back to Virginia. In his Paris years, Jefferson added to rather than controlled his indebtedness. He did, though, have a plan to become solvent again. He would sell some of his land and rent out the rest, including Monticello and many of his slaves.

In theory, and for the republican nation that he hoped France would become, he proposed a rationale for renouncing the debts of the ancient regime. That also provided the rationale for the claim that his own debts should not burden his estate and his heirs. He could, so to speak, in his generational theory at least, spend extravagantly with borrowed money, without his heirs being responsible for his debts. As absurd as this might seem as a personal extension of usufruct, it has a touch of psychological plausibility, at least as a comfort zone for a man who spent beyond his means and eventually bankrupted himself and the next generation of his family. It is an example of Jefferson's genius for self-exculpation by evasion if not suppression of the obvious.

One evening in March 1788, in Jefferson's large and comfortable Paris home, probably in the library, two of Europe's most notorious proponents of republican government carried on their continuing discussion of the proposed constitution for the United States with the author of the Declaration of Independence. James Madison and his colleagues had created it in Philadelphia the previous year. It had not yet been ratified by enough state conventions to make it the law of the land. Debate throughout the country was contentious, heated, divisive.

The three men gathered in the Hôtel de Langeac strongly supported it, with reservations. One was a Frenchman, the Marquis de Lafayette. Another was a famous British-born writer and bridge designer, Tom Paine, who had spent the years of the American Revolution in the United States and fueled it with his stirring pamphlet *Common Sense*. He was now ferrying between London and Paris, contributing what he could to radical discourse in both places, riding the political waves into the tumultuous 1790s. He was beginning to feel at home in Paris, where his host for this evening, the American minister plenipotentiary, was culturally and physically as comfortable in a city as he was ever to be in his life. Paine and Jefferson also shared an interest and pleasure in inventions, gadgets, and technological improvements, such as Paine's design for a long-span iron bridge to replace the common wooden structures from the preindustrial age. Both were eager to learn about European, especially British, manufacturing and building processes that could be imported to the United States. "I have been to see the Cotton Mills, the Potteries, the Steel furnaces, Tin plate Manufacture, white lead Manufacture,—all those things might be easily carried on in America," Paine wrote to Jefferson.

When Paine got home that evening, "being alone and wanting amusement," he "sat down to explain to" himself his "ideas of natural and civil rights, and the distinction between them." Probably something in the discussion that evening had resulted in concern that he might have been misunderstood. The distinction was simple. Natural rights are the rights of speech, thought, and conscience. They are individual, inalienable, and permanent. Civil rights are those that communities agree on for mutual security and protection. They can be changed by the will of the people.

Paine apparently sent his brief memo on the subject to Jefferson and Lafayette. About this, Jefferson and Paine were then and always on the same page. So too were most of the American Founding Fathers, though not all of them had the intellectual and philosophical interest to focus at length on the subject, as did Paine, Jefferson, Adams, Madison, and Hamilton. The three men in Jefferson's mansion in Paris, reading and talking by candlelight, probably with glasses of Jefferson's wine in hand, made "a small ratifying convention of their own," as Jefferson's twentieth-century editor has remarked. In fact, the three men were literal outliers, three thousand miles away from the United States, with no direct influence on the state ratifying conventions. Having reservations about the absence of a Bill of Rights, worried that an elected president with no limits on reelection would become a president for life, Jefferson had reconciled himself to the constitution with the hope that it would be amended. He probably did not like the fact that its provisions made amendment difficult. Each generation, he believed, should have the right to legislate anew the basic contract.

Watching from his Paris grandstand seat in 1787 and for the next two years, Jefferson was optimistic that France would reform itself enough to avoid a bloody revolution. It was moving, he hoped, toward a version of what he had proposed in his argument to Madison, that "the earth belongs to the living," that each generation has the right to reject the past and start anew, to create a more just society honoring "natural rights" and to legislate just laws providing universal equality. Lafayette and his colleagues, inspired by the American Revolution, hoped for an improved version of the British structure without the corruptions that had alienated the American colonies. Advocating for the creation of a French version of a constitutional monarchy, Lafayette pressured the American minister for advice and help. Jefferson hardly resisted, though he knew that it was his "business . . . to be spectator only."

Anonymously, he contributed to the creation of the 1789 Declaration of the Rights of Man and of the Citizen. He also provided cover for Lafayette and other members of the National Assembly by secretly hosting them at the Hôtel de Langeac as they discussed their plans to keep the state from bankruptcy and to avert civil war. Concerned by his own indiscretion, the next morning Jefferson "waited on" the minister of foreign affairs "and explained to him . . . how it had happened that my house had been made the scene of conferences of such a character . . . I told him I knew too well the duties I owed to the king, to the nation, and to my own country to take any part in councils concerning their internal government, and that I should persevere with care in the character of a neutral and passive spectator." The foreign minister, it turned out, approved of Lafayette's efforts and Jefferson's role, irregular as it was. Jefferson's claim that he was and would be a neutral spectator was a diplomatic lie. The French foreign minister knew better.

As tension increased, Jefferson worried that without significant compromises about taxation, revenue, and representation, there might be a civil war. Still, he was on the whole optimistic. And his optimism did not prevent him from accurately describing in vivid prose the revolutionary scenes that he observed on the streets of Paris and in Versailles between 1787 and 1789. His gift for narrative was not one that normally dominated his mind and pen. He favored argument, abstraction, and analysis. But he had an obligation to describe to his American colleagues what was going on as he saw it, and the preciseness and vividness of his prose in these letters suggest that, though analysis was his usual epistolary mode, he took pleasure in the excitement of describing what he was seeing and feeling. Jefferson reported to Tom Paine, Richard Price, St. John de Crevecoeur, John Jay, John Adams, George Washington, and others on the "state of things," the ebb and flow of battle between constituencies as the General Assembly argued about whether and how to redistribute power and to create a financially stable state.

Jefferson was a frequent spectator in the Paris streets and at the General Assembly in Versailles. Attracted both to mathematical order and creative chaos, he found the tumult riveting. In August 1787, Jefferson wrote to Adams that huge crowds, "mobs of 10; 20; 30,000 people collected daily, surrounded the parliament house," within easy walking distance of Jefferson's residence, "huzzaed the members, even entered the doors and examined into their conduct, took the horses out of the carriages of those who did well, and drew them home. The government thought it prudent to prevent these, drew some regiments into the neighborhood, multiplied the guards, had the streets constantly patrolled by strong parties, suspended privileged places, forbad all clubs." To Jefferson the mob seemed useful leverage against a failing monarchy and an unreliable king, as if the mob had a rational commitment to peaceful protest. "I think that in the course of three months the royal authority has lost, and the rights of the nation gained, as much ground, by a revolution of public opinion only, as England gained in all her civil wars under the Stuarts," he wrote to Adams. Even in these circumstances, France was doing it better and quicker than England had. "I rather believe too they will retain the ground gained, because it is defended by the young and the middle aged, in opposition to the old only." It seemed to Jefferson that the crowds represented the coming generation and that the pressure of public opinion would elicit concessions from the aristocracy and the clergy. "A spirit of distrust in the government here and of confidence in their own force and rights is pervading all ranks."

But if agreement could not be reached on new taxes, the revenue shortfall would create a national bankruptcy so severe that violence would be inevitable. And many of France's wealthy entrepreneurs were speculating in stocks, Jefferson observed. "It will probably produce as total a depravation of morals as the system of Law did. All the money of France almost is now employed in this, none being free even for the purposes of commerce, which suffers immensely from this cause." Jefferson's contempt for financial speculation, for banks, and for paper money influenced his analysis of the French crisis. His response to speculation was reflexive, unchangeable, moralistic, and personal.

That France was now totally preoccupied with politics did not entirely please him. "The confusion here at present is really distressing," he noted in May 1788. "Society is spoilt by it. Instead of that gaiety and insouciance which has distinguished it heretofore, all is filled with political debates into which both sexes enter with equal eagerness." This was a different Paris than the city of theater, salons, and social sophistication that he had come to in 1784. And he was aware that he had reason to worry. "I sincerely wish that in this country they may be contented with a peaceable and passive opposition. At this moment we are not sure of this." In July 1788, he wrote to an American friend that "I imagine you have heard terrible stories of the internal confusions of this country." They were, though, mostly exaggerated rumors. "As yet the tumults have not cost a single life according to the most sober testimony I have been able to collect. Nine tenths of Paris believe that 200 were killed at Grenoble, where there was in truth but an officer wounded." There had been indeed one death. His optimism dipped and rose frequently. It was at its height in August 1788. "For some days I was really melancholy with the apprehensions that arms would be appealed to, and the opposition crushed in its first efforts. But things seem now to wear a better aspect." The liberal reformers seemed to be gaining ground against the Court and the clergy, but a poor crop had created a severe shortage of wheat, and bad weather further damaged crops.

"There is no remedy for the present evil," Jefferson wrote to his French-born American friend, St. John de Crevecoeur, "nor way to prevent future ones but to bring the people to such a state of ease as not to be ruined by the loss of a single crop. This hail may be considered as the coup de grace to an expiring victim." Though the country was at present "extremely agitated" by political stalemate, much of it, he observed, was suffering from hunger. An effort, indirectly initiated by Jefferson, to import wheat from America failed, with some temporary and unwarranted criticism directed at him. Still, he continued to believe that all would be saved by accommodations between the reformers, the aristocracy, and the clergy, that the vacillating king would become a force for compromise, and that the voices of the people would be given fuller representation. It seemed to him likely that a new government would be formed. Chaos and violence would be avoided. And there would be a redistribution of landed wealth. By the end of the summer of 1788, Jefferson was confident that "within two or three years" France would become a constitutional monarchy, on its way to joining its friend across the Atlantic in a brotherhood of republicanism with equal rights for all its citizens.

Of course, Jefferson had no crystal ball. In early 1789, he believed he had reason to expect a peaceful resolution. All it would take would be an agreement that the king would have no veto over legislation and the aristocracy would have limited but enough hereditary power to pacify it. Continuing to work on French-American relations, Jefferson's major accomplishment was the Treaty of Amity and Commerce, signed in early 1788, and an agreement for each country to exchange consulates. It was also a mutual defense treaty. That had divisive consequences in the next decade. Its provisions were well composed, though any competent American minister would have done as well. Their distinction is that they were done at a moment when one of the signatory nations was about to be radically transformed. By committing itself to mutual defense, the United States made itself vulnerable to being drawn into the next war between France and Great Britain. Still, in 1788 it seemed the necessary and sensible thing to do in the hope that France would replace Great Britain as America's major trading partner, a hope based more on anti-British anger and ideology than on realism. In addition, a commitment to mutual defense was part of the repayment of the financial, military, and moral debt owed to France, though different factions in the United States would calibrate differently the extent of the debt. For Jefferson, it needed to be honored and repaid at almost any cost.

In March 1789 "the public mind seems to be in a good train of preparation for the States General," Jefferson thought, "and I am in hopes that assembly will put this country into a course of prosperity and happiness which it never yet knew." He expected that something like what had happened in Philadelphia in 1787 would happen in Paris. In America, he wrote, things were going well, a promising new government in formation, Washington to be its president. His own state, he regretted, was "the most antifederal of the states. I am in hopes however that the addition of a good bill of rights, by removing the most material objections will reconcile the great mass of opposition." In fact, he now confessed, he was more concerned about the possibility of legislative than executive tyranny. The passage of a Bill of Rights as amendments might alleviate that. In France, the Revolution seemed "to be going on well." He expected the States General, with the cooperation of the king, to "establish some of the leading features of a good constitution. They have indeed a miserable old canvas to work on . . . covered with daubings which it will be difficult to efface. But some they will efface, and some soften, so as to make a tolerable thing of it, perhaps a good one." The French press had thrown off its shackles, and the air was crackling with political tensions, denunciations, and proposals. It seemed to Jefferson the start of a free press and other republican assets.

As Paris shivered through one of its coldest winters, Jefferson noticed ice skaters and heavy carriages cavorting on the Seine, as if everyone were having great fun. Just the thought of the brutal weather made him shiver. Eager to be an observer at the upcoming assembly, he hoped "to see this great meeting before my departure," he wrote to a French friend. Everything was going "on more auspiciously than the most sanguine could have expected." Paris, though, had become a desert, he wrote in March 1789, since "all the world here" was electioneering at Versailles. "All the world" was not. Many of the six hundred thousand Parisians and the twenty-eight million people of France were hungry. Street riots started in early May. It was, Jefferson noted, "a very considerable riot in which about 100 people have been probably killed . . . the most unprovoked and . . . the most unpitied catastrophe of that kind I ever knew." He had no sympathy for the rioters. They wanted nothing but to do mischief. The riot, he complained, "had no particular connection with the great national questions now in agitation."

He had just been at the opening session of the States General. "Viewing it as an Opera it was imposing; as a scene of business the king's speech was exactly what it should have been and very well delivered." To Jefferson, it was a riveting spectacle of political theater. A week later, he still denounced the rioters as mischief makers—indeed, criminals. "They were the most abandoned banditti of Paris. . . . Neither this nor any other of the riots have had a professed connection with the great national reformation going on. They are such as have happened every year since I have been here, and will continue to be produced by common incidents."

Except for this riot, the "revolution of this country has advanced thus far," he wrote to John Jay, "without encountering anything which deserves to be called a difficulty." Still, there were tremors. He expressed to Lafayette his concern for his friend's personal safety. And political theater might become political tragedy. "The three orders which compose the States General seem likely to stumble at the threshold on the great preliminary question How shall they vote, by orders or persons? If they get well over this question, there will be no difficulty . . . in the great points of constitutional reformation. If they do not get over this question (and this seems possible) it cannot be foreseen what issue this matter will take."

By mid-June the factions seemed stalemated on the question of taxation and revenue. For the first time, Jefferson thought a civil war likely. No one was sure whom the army would side with. "We shall know I think within a day or two whether the government will risk a bankruptcy and civil war rather than see all distinction of orders done away, which is what the commons will push for. . . . The Commons," representing the middle class, "have in their chamber almost all the talents of the nation; they are firm and bold, yet moderate. There is indeed among them a number of very hot-headed members; but those of most influence are cool, temperate, and sagacious. Every step of this house has been marked with caution and wisdom. The Noblesse on the contrary are absolutely out of their senses. They are so furious they can seldom debate at all. They have few men of moderate talents, and not one of great in the majority. Their proceedings have been very injudicious. The clergy are waiting to profit of every incident to secure themselves and have no other object in view. Among the commons there is an entire unanimity on the great question of voting by persons." Fascinated, worried, hopeful, Jefferson went almost every day to Versailles.

In late June 1789, Jefferson thought calamity was about to explode. His accounts were graphic. The ruling class was in turmoil. The king, who needed an increase in revenue to restock the empty royal treasury, had dismissed the Assembly of Notables, a subdivision of the States General assigned to resolve the need for increased taxation, whose members included Lafayette and other reformers. The States General had declared all current taxes illegal. The aristocracy and the commons were at each other's throats; the clergy looked to its own interests. At Marly, his estate near Versailles, the king and his associates considered whether to dissolve the National Assembly. Factions within the royal household disagreed, from mildly to vociferously, the queen among the latter group, "the king assailed by lies in all shapes," Jefferson wrote to Jay. "He was made to believe that the commons were going to absolve the army from their oath of fidelity to him and to raise their pay." A few days later, Jefferson stood at the entrance of the Church of St. Louis at Versailles as the factions assembled, the king himself still at Marly, refusing to make any decision. "This is the first time that the Churches have been made some good use of," Jefferson remarked to his friend Philip Mazzei.

The next day, from Paris, he wrote to Jay that

the Nobility were in triumph, the people in consternation. When the King passed . . . through the lane they formed from the Chateau to the Hotel des Etats (about half a mile) there was a dead silence. He was about an hour in the house, delivering his speech and declaration. . . . On his coming out, a feeble cry of "vive le roy" was raised by some children, but the people remained silent and sullen. When the Duc d'Orleans followed however their applauses were excessive. This must have been sensible to the king. He had ordered in the close of his speech that the members should follow him, and resume their deliberations the next day. The Noblesse followed him, and so did the clergy, except about 30 who, with the Tiers [the Third Estate and the commons] remained in the room and entered into deliberation. They protested against what the king had done, adhered to all their former proceedings, and resolved the inviolability of their own persons. An officer came twice to order them out of the room in the king's name, but they refused to obey. In the afternoon the people, uneasy, began to assemble in great numbers in the courts and vicinities of the palace. The Queen was alarmed and sent for Mr. Necker. He was conducted amidst the shouts and acclamations of the multitude who filled all the apartments of the palace. He was a few minutes only with the queen and about three quarters of an hour with the king. . . . The king . . . passed through the crowd to his carriage and into it without being in the least noticed. As Mr. Necker followed him universal acclamations were raised of "vive Monsieur Necker, [the savior of France." He] was conducted back to his house with the same demonstrations of affection and anxiety. About 200 deputies of the Tiers, catching the enthusiasm of the moment, went to his house and extorted from him a promise that he would not resign. These circumstances must wound the heart of the king, desirous as he is to possess the affections of his subjects. . . . I shall go to Versailles tomorrow, and be able to add the transactions of this day and tomorrow.

Late the next day, Jefferson continued his account.

On the 24th [of June 1789] nothing remarkable past [passed] except an attack by the mob of Versailles on the archbishop of Paris, who had been one of the instigators of the court to the proceedings of the seance royale. They threw mud and stones at his carriage, broke the windows of it, and he in a fright promised to join the tiers.— This day (the 25th) forty-eight of the Nobles have joined the Tiers. Among these is the Duke d'Orleans [the king's cousin]. The M. de la Fayette could not be of the number, being restrained by his instructions. He is writing to his constituents to change his instructions or to accept his resignation. There are with the Tiers now 164 members of the clergy, so that the common chamber consists of upwards of 800 members. The minority of the clergy however call themselves the chamber of the clergy and pretend to go on with business. I found the streets of Versailles much embarrassed with soldiers. There was a body of about 100 horse drawn up in front of the hotel of the states, and all the avenues and doors guarded by soldiers. Nobody was permitted to enter but the members, and this was by order of the king; for till now the doors of the Common room have been open, and at least 2000 spectators [including Jefferson] attending their debates constantly. They have named a deputation to wait on the king and desire a removal of the soldiery from their doors, and seem determined, if this is not complied with, to remove themselves elsewhere. Instead of being dismayed with what has passed they seem to rise in their demands, and some of them to consider the erasing every vestige of a difference of order as indispensable to the establishment and preservation of a good constitution. I apprehend there is more courage than calculation in this project. . . . Mr. Necker, seeing that all the trimming he has used towards the court and nobles has availed him nothing, would engage himself heartily and solely on the popular side, and view his own salvation in that alone. The confidence which the people place in him seems to merit some attention. However the mass of the Common chamber are absolutely indifferent to his remaining in office.

Soon matters seemed noticeably better. The two chambers, Jefferson wrote to Jay, had "entered into debate on the question whether they should obey the letter of the king," which was conciliatory to the commons. He continued:

There was a considerable opposition. When notes written by the count d'Artois [later to become King Charles X] to sundry members, and handed about among the rest, decided the matter, and they went in a body and took their seats with the Tiers, and thus rendered the union of the orders in one chamber complete. As soon as this was known to the people of Versailles, they assembled about the palace demanded the king and queen, who came and shewed themselves in a balcony. They rended the skies with cries of "Vive le roy" [and] "Vive la reine." They called for the Dauphin who was also produced, and was the subject of new acclamations. . . . Similar emotions of joy took place in Paris, and at this moment the triumph of the Tiers is considered as complete. Tomorrow they will recommence business, voting by persons on all questions: and whatever difficulties may be opposed in debate by the malcontents of the clergy and nobility, everything must be finally settled at the will of the Tiers. It remains to see whether they will leave to the nobility anything but their titulary appellations. I suppose they will not. Mr. Necker will probably remain in office. . . . A perfect cooperation with the Tiers will be his wisest game.—This great crisis being now over, I shall not have matter interesting enough to trouble you with as often as I have done lately.

He wrote to John Trumbull, still in London, that "all is settled . . . so that all danger of civil commotion here is at an end, and it is probable they will proceed to settle to themselves a good constitution, and meet no difficulty in doing it."

On July 4, 1789, the Hôtel de Langeac, in effect the American embassy, was the scene of a festive occasion and a celebratory party in honor of American independence. It was known to at least most of the guests that the host was the author of the Declaration of Independence. The congratulatory speech, composed by a few of his American friends, celebrated the "man who sustained so conspicuous a part in the immortal transactions of that day—whose dignity energy and elegance of thought and expression added a peculiar luster to that declaratory act which announced to the world the existence of an empire."

One of the many Americans present was Gouverneur Morris, the author of the preamble to the Constitution and the stylist of much of the text, who was to be Jefferson's successor in Paris. The Marquis de Lafayette with some members of his political circle and probably most of the diplomatic corps were there. Morris, who declined to sign the congratulatory address, and Jefferson were ideological opposites. A proto-Federalist from New York, Morris advocated the United States as a single unitary government with the states reduced to subordination or nonexistence. Taking Lafayette aside, Morris urged that the

French retain a significant role for the aristocracy in whatever new government was to be formed. Otherwise, he anticipated, there would indeed be civil war. Late in the month, Jefferson, with his usual courtliness, encouraged Maria Cosway to be hospitable to Morris in London. He is "a countryman and friend of mine of great consideration in his own country." He "deserves to be so everywhere." He and Jefferson were not friends in 1789, and less so thereafter.

Jefferson may have been in Paris when a mob attacked the Bastille on July 17. The States General was in session at Versailles. His own hotel had been attacked for the third time, apparently not as political theater but as ordinary burglary. He asked the Paris authorities to provide round-the-clock security. The thieves had stripped bare three of his apartments, though Jefferson did not say, in his report to Trumbull, what they took, except for the loss of "candlesticks," which he could not find replacements for, though he "searched every shop." He asked Trumbull to send him "4 pair plated from London. Mine were plated and came from there, and I am sure the pattern is common there. It was a fluted Corinthian column." Amidst the turmoil, he had multiple priorities, one of which was his eagerness to replace his candlesticks, another indicator that stressed how important to him were classical designs and elegant material possessions. The burglars were "common criminals," he wrote, rather than participants in the revolutionary activity of the thousands of working-class people who now dominated the Paris streets, as if it were easy to tell the difference or a meaningful distinction. In early August, he mistook a pause in street violence for a cessation, perhaps the start of a transition to a constitutional monarchy. "I never was more tranquil in my house than through the whole of it," an odd comment, given the recent burglary. "I went much too into the city, and saw there was no danger but for a very few characters. Property was sacred through the whole."

Jefferson, though, did fear personal assault, since he was being blamed for the delay of wheat shipments from America. He had iron bars and alarm bells installed in the windows of the Hôtel de Langeac, though he and Short, attracted to the energy and unpredictability, wandered by daylight in the streets of an increasingly anarchic Paris.

Jefferson still was hopeful, almost confident, that all would turn out well, and "should this revolution succeed, it is the beginning of the reformation of the governments of Europe," a prediction so wildly off the mark that it embodies Jefferson's mind simultaneously on two opposite tracks. Though "the body of the nobles are rankling at the heart . . . I see no reason to apprehend any great evil from it." All setbacks would be overcome: "The progress of things here will be subject to checks from time to time of course," he wrote to Paine. "Whether they will be great or small will depend on the army. But they will be only checks." It was a mantra he repeated and repeated. "The Declaration of the rights of man, which constitutes the 1st. chapter of this work," he wrote to Richard Price, "was brought in the day before yesterday. . . . You will observe that these are the outlines of a great work, and be assured that the body engaged in it are equal to a masterly execution of it. They may meet with some difficulties from within their body," particularly from the aristocracy, "and some from without. There may be small and temporary checks. But I think they will persevere to its accomplishment."

Vividly describing the events he observed, Jefferson's rose-tinted glasses and optimistic ideology transformed some violent activities into pacific language, as if a few beheadings were not only justified but necessary. "The people here attacked with stones a body of German cavalry and drove them off. On the 13th. they forced the prison of St. Lazare," he wrote to Price on July 17, "released the prisoners and got some arms." They supported a new constitution and voting rights.

They asked arms at the invalids [Les Invalides, a military hospital and armory] and being refused . . . forced the place and got here a large supply of arms. They then went to the Bastille and made the same demand. The Governor after hoisting a flag of truce and decoying a hundred or two within the outer drawbridge, hoisted the drawbridge and fired on them. The people without then forced the place, took and beheaded the Governor and Lt. Governor . . . arming themselves. . . . The Marquis de la Fayette was made commander in chief of the men raised. . . . these events carried imperfectly to Versailles. . . . The court and the king . . . believed that the Aristocrats of Paris were under pillage and carnage, that 150,000 men were in arms coming to Versailles to massacre the Royal family, the court, the ministers and all connected with them, their practices and principles. . . . The king determined . . . to comply with the desires of the states.

The queen disagreed.

The king went to them, told them so, asked their guidance, and their interposition to quiet Paris. . . . The king ordered away all the troops . . . and came this day to Paris in procession, having in his coach the most popular characters, the States General walking on foot in two ranks on each side of it, and the Marquis de Lafayette on horseback at their head. There were probably 60 or 80,000-armed bourgeois lining the streets thro' which he was to pass.

The king came to Paris, leaving the queen's faction in fear and consternation.

About 60,000 citizens of all forms and colors, armed with the muskets of the bastille and invalids as far as they would go, the rest with pistols, swords, pikes, pruning hooks, scythes . . . lined all the streets thro' which the procession passed, and, with the crowds of people in the streets, doors and windows, saluted them everywhere with cries of "vive la nation." but not a single "vive le roy" was heard. . . . Tranquillity is now restored to the capital: the shops are again opened; the people resuming their labors, and, if the want of bread does not disturb our peace, we may hope a continuance of it.

Throughout July and August 1789, Jefferson continued to put a positive spin on the attempt by the nobles, the king, the clergy, and the commons to transform an absolutist government into a constitutional monarchy, as if the powerful would voluntarily forgo power and as if the hungry, angry, anarchic mobs that had already cut off heads could be mollified by words and legalisms. The king had "opened his heart" to the people, "asked them what he could do to restore peace and happiness . . . and shewed himself ready to do everything for that purpose, promising particularly to send away the troops. . . . The heat of this city is as yet too great to give entire credit to this, and they continue to arm and organize the Bourgeoisie. But I think you may be assured . . . that no other act of violence will come from him." For a man who had excoriated George III, his confidence in Louis XVI seems weirdly inappropriate. That the French had no experience with trial by jury, habeas corpus, freedom of worship, or any of the protections that British Americans had possessed seemed to him relevant but not determinative. Still, it is clear that Jefferson never confronted or could acknowledge that in 1789 France was not in a position to reform itself into a society providing the security and liberties that the United States and Great Britain provided for its citizens.

Two days later, Jefferson continued his eyewitness account to Jay: "Troops to the number of about 25 or 30,000 had arrived and were posted in and between Paris and Versailles. . . . For this change, however sudden it may have been in the mind of the king, was, in that of his advisers, only the second chapter of a great plan, of which the bringing together the foreign troops had been the first." Jefferson assumed that the king was now under the control of his despotic advisers.

The news of this change began to be known in Paris about 1 or 2 oclock. In the afternoon a body of about 100 German cavalry were advanced and drawn up in the Place Louis XV [a short walk from the Hôtel de Langeac and soon to be renamed the Place de la Concorde] and about 300 Swiss posted at a little distance in their rear. This drew people to that spot, who naturally formed themselves in front of the troops, at first merely to look at them. But as their numbers increased their indignation arose: they retired a few steps, posted themselves on and behind large piles of loose stone collected in that Place for a bridge adjacent to it, and attacked the horse with stones. The horse charged, but the advantageous position of the people, and the showers of stones obliged them to retire, and even to quit the field altogether, leaving one of their number on the ground. The Swiss in their rear were observed never to stir. This was the signal for universal insurrection, and this body of cavalry, to avoid being massacred, retired towards Versailles. The people now armed themselves with such weapons as they could find in Armourer's shops and private houses, and with bludgeons, and were roaming all night through all parts of the city without any decided and practicable object. . . . The mob, now openly joined by the French guards, force the prisons of St. Lazare, release all the prisoners, and take a great store of corn, which they carry to the corn market. Here they get some arms, and the French guards begin to form and train them.

To Jefferson, all still seemed well or likely to be. "I went yesterday to Versailles to satisfy myself what had passed there; for nothing can be believed but what one sees, or has from an eye witness." Based on what he had seen, he believed his own account to be objective and reliable.

They believe there still that 3000 people have fallen victims to the tumults of Paris. Mr. Short and myself have been every day among them in order to be sure of what was passing. We cannot find with certainty that anybody has been killed but the three beforementioned, and those who fell in the assault or defence of the Bastille. How many of the garrison were killed no body pretends to have ever heard. Of the assailants accounts vary from 6 to 600. The most general belief is that there fell about 30. There have been many reports of instantaneous executions by the mob, on such of their body as they caught in acts of theft or robbery. Some of these may perhaps be true. . . . Bags of money offered . . . through fear or guilt, have been uniformly refused by the mobs.

The best in human nature had been asserting itself, Jefferson concluded, and peace and prayer had returned to Paris. "The churches are now occupied in singing 'de profundis' and 'requiems' for the repose of the souls of the brave and valiant citizens who have sealed with their blood the liberty of the nation."

Jefferson was tweaking the narrative to suit his preferences, his personality, and his ideology. It was sometimes difficult to do, even for him. Though the assault on property and life had only marginally begun, it was real and threatening. One week later, on August 12, 1789, he told a slightly different story to Jay. The narrative emphasis changed: Yes, there are summary executions in Paris "done on individuals, by individuals, . . . nobody is in condition to ask for what or by whom." In the country an "abundance of chateaux are certainly burnt and burning and not a few lives sacrificed." Jefferson had no difficulty writing two different narratives, partly an expression of his passionate desire for the Revolution to succeed and also because "the tree of liberty must be refreshed from time to time," as he had written in November 1787, "with the blood of patriots and tyrants." The phrase perhaps came too easily to a man who had never experienced the battlefield. Later in the month, he wrote to Maria Cosway that "my fortune has been singular, to see in the course of fourteen years two such revolutions as were never before seen. . . . The cutting off heads is become so much à la mode, that one is apt to feel of a morning whether their own is on their shoulders," he joked with a touch of callousness. His own was in no danger. He had apparently seen the head of one of the hated ministers "cut off, and his body drawn through the principal streets of the city. . . . Whether this work is yet over, depends on their catching more of the fugitives. If no new capture re-excites the spirit of vengeance, we may hope it will soon be at rest, and that order and safety will be reestablished except for a few of the most obnoxious characters."

To Jefferson, the Revolution seemed to be at an end. "I think there is nothing further to be apprehended," he informed Jay. "The harvest is so near that there is nothing to fear from the want of bread. The national assembly are wise, firm and moderate. They will establish the English constitution, purged of its numerous and capital defects." In early September, he was still optimistic, despite some significant discord. "Civil war is much talked of and expected: and this talk and expectation has a tendency to beget it. What are the events which may produce it? 1. the want of bread. . . . 2. a public bankruptcy. . . . 3. the absconding of the king from Versailles." Still, his optimism dominated. "Upon the whole I do not see it as yet probable that any actual commotion will take place. And if it does take place I have strong confidence that the patriotic party will hold together."

What had transpired, what he had been an eyewitness to, had been fascinating and encouraging. He had been eager to write about it, to create a narrative for Jay and others, to put his literary gifts and his pen to work, to track the progress of what seemed still a comparatively bloodless revolution. He expected it to end in the triumph of republican values. "I have multiplied my letters to you lately," he wrote to Jay, "because the scene has been truly interesting" He would not have missed these recent events, he admitted, for any alternative. He was about to depart, but he was glad he had been there. And he was expecting to return.

CHAPTER ELEVEN

The Stage of Public Life

1789–1794

As Jefferson sailed across the Atlantic in September and October 1789, he did not expect the voyage to mark his permanent departure from Europe. Regardless of expressions of homesickness, of missing his friends, of needing to get his affairs in order, of the importance of his two daughters growing up in an American environment, he expected the recently elected first president of the United States to reappoint him to the Court of Versailles. It was a special incentive to him that the Court he would return to would be different than the one currently in place. He hoped, almost expected, the new government to be a constitutional monarchy, with "a tolerably free constitution, and that without its having cost them a drop of blood." William Short had been left in what they both expected to be temporary charge of the embassy. Not that Jefferson left possessions or obligations behind, though he kept his Paris household in place. The hold of his cross-channel ship, sailing from Le Havre after a long delay, contained thirty-eight boxes and miscellaneous baggage, his portable printing press, and his personal and official papers. Sally Hemings, pregnant, and her brother James were members of the entourage.

Most of the caravan of luggage was intended for Monticello, an exemplification of his material self-indulgence, his collector's passion, his appreciation of fine objects, and his artistic sensibility—all this though he had every reason to believe he would be reappointed for another three-year term, at the end of which he would have shipped home more crates of fine furniture, art objects, wine, porcelain, silks, linens, and "colonies of plants and birds." The shipment also contained a beautifully crafted crane-neck carriage that he had had made in England, had had shipped to Paris, and was now transporting across the Atlantic. It would be for his daughters in Virginia. He intended to have another made for his own use when he returned to Paris.

Unable to locate a direct connection, his sea voyage required transit via England, which meant his possessions had to go through customs. In London, Trumbull petitioned the prime minister to instruct his officials to forgo inspection of Jefferson's possessions and payment of duties and have them moved directly to a warehouse, then to be loaded onto the Virginia-bound *Clermont*. "It is my Duty to return my warmest thanks for your goodness in this Business," Trumbull wrote to William Pitt, "and to repeat my assurances that it shall not be forgotten by me or my friends:—Mr. Jefferson will know by a letter which I write him this Evening to whom He is obliged for the politeness of his Reception." There is no indication that Jefferson wrote a note of thanks to the prime minister.

No matter how warmly he expressed in letters that his fervent wish was to retire to private life, his expectation (and apparent hope) was that he would be reappointed to another three-year term in Paris. After all, who could better serve the United States there than the man who had already been in place for five years, had learned so much, knew so many of the major players, and had finally mastered enough French to be comfortable in ordinary conversation? Jefferson's original appointment had assumed that his commission would expire in the spring of 1788. Congress could, he well knew, recall him at any time; he also could request to be recalled. In August 1787, he remarked that "my commission expires next spring, and if not renewed, I shall return then. If renewed, I shall stay somewhat longer: how much, will not depend on me altogether. So far as it does, I cannot fix the epoch of my return, though I always flatter myself it is not very distant. . . . My habits are formed to those of my own country. I am past the time of changing them and am therefore less happy anywhere else than there." His self-flattery was partly self-deception. When Congress indeed reappointed him, he did not decline. At first, he was happy enough in Paris not to take the initiative to determine a date of return for a six-month leave, though that had become his intent in 1788. Assuming that permission would be shortly forthcoming, he declined to renew his lease on the Hôtel de Langeac. Soon aware that he would be kept on hold until the new American government was in place, he renewed it for another year.

On the one hand, he yearned for his Albemarle world. "I consider myself here as a traveler only, and not a resident. My commission expires the next spring. . . . If renewed, I shall remain here some time longer. How much I cannot say; yet my wishes shorten the period." His wishes and actions were not synchronized. His fantasy of the simple life at home coexisted with his penchant for luxuries, including the crates of French and British furniture with which he would be returning. In early 1788, he wrote, "I had rather be shut up in a very modest cottage, with my books, my family and a few old friends, dining on simple bacon, and letting the world roll on as it liked, than to occupy the most splendid post which any human power can give." In the same letter, he casually affirmed that "I am not at this moment able to pay all my debts." His "modest cottage"? His "simple bacon"? There's a level at which this is self-indulgent nonsense, though beautifully written and with the deep sincerity of supreme self-deception. Was Monticello his vision of a simple cottage? By choice, he was living in a luxurious mansion in Paris, entertaining at table in high style, spending on wine and books. Still with large debts from the Wayles estate, he was contracting more debts, his $9,000 salary insufficient for his purchases and living expenses. Whatever his rhetorical commitment to a private life, the allure of the public arena always won out. Neither his garden, his residence, his hospitality, his indebtedness, his singular sexual relationship, nor his family complications would ever be simple.

His life soon became even more complicated. In November 1788, he had urged John Jay to allow him a visit home. He had "been led on by events to an absence of five years instead of five months," a phrase felicitous for its alliteration but not its accuracy. "In the meantime, matters of great moment to others as well as myself, and which can be arranged by nobody but myself, will await no longer," by which he meant his need to address his financial situation. "Another motive of still more powerful cogency on my mind is the necessity of carrying my family back to their friends and country. I must therefore ask of Congress a leave of short absence. Allowing three months on the sea, going and coming, and two months at my own house, which will suffice for my affairs, I need not be from Paris but between five and six months."

In December 1788, the start of a winter with "a Siberian degree of cold," he had communicated his plans to the relatives he had depended on since the death of his wife. He was concerned about his daughters' "future welfare." By that he meant their national identity. If they stayed in France, they would forever be Americans who had grown up in France, their language, culture, social life, perhaps even their religion, marriages, and children, at least as much French as American. He had been startled by the serious interest Martha had developed in a Catholic vocation. Apparently, he had never considered that enrolling his daughter (and then her sister) in an aristocratic convent school might attract a motherless, impressionable adolescent into its embrace. The likely consequences of a prolonged residence in France had been driven home to Jefferson. He would be returning with his daughters in the next sailing season. "Their future welfare requires that this should be no longer postponed." He intended to spend two of the six months of his American visit at Monticello, then return to Paris. But where would his daughters stay when he returned without them? Who would look after them? "As my time must be passed principally at Monticello during the two months I destine for Virginia, I shall hope you will come and encamp there with us a while. . . . Feasting we shall not expect," an allusion to his financial difficulties, "but this will not be our object. The society of our friends will sweeten all."

Sincere as was his evocation of the bliss of reunion with friends and family, this cannot be all that the invitation signified. Did his invitation to his sister-in-law and her husband that they join him at Monticello imply that he wanted and at least hoped they would stay when he left? And if he were to spend only two of his six months at Monticello, where did he plan to spend the other four? Probably in the political world of New York and Philadelphia, sharing with the new government his knowledge of French and European affairs. Or did he hope that his in-laws would take Polly, now often addressed as Maria, back to Eppington, which had already been a home to her, and to the companionship of her cousins? And perhaps that Martha would stay at Monticello, with the adult supervision of Jefferson's sister and the nurturing presence of his wife's half siblings? And what were his thoughts about sixteen-year-old Sally Hemings? Would she return to America with him? If she did, where would she live and in what role?

To further complicate matters, the disposition of Monticello and his other plantations was subject to his proposal that his estates be rented in order to pay his debts, though apparently he did not intend that the properties and slaves he would sell or rent would include Monticello. "Though I foresee that my two months in Virginia will be filled with business and disagreeable things," he wrote to Francis Eppes, "yet I look forward to it with desire for the pleasures also of passing some time with my antient friendships. . . . I suppose I must be at Monticello principally, and shall hope that your family . . . will contrive to encamp there with me, for a while at least. . . . I would wish that my return to Virginia should not stop any of the measures before recommended for selling my lands in Goochland and Cumberland" and "renting the rest of my estate."

While waiting, he took care of business, especially his efforts to accelerate trade with a country whose trade mind-set was still mercantile and protectionist. He wandered the tense Paris streets. He visited the proceedings at Versailles. He hosted and advised Lafayette and other political activists. He brought his daughters to live at the Hôtel de Langeac. He had a sexual relationship with Sally Hemings. By March 1789, he had begun to write letters of farewell to friends who had a special place in his heart. A voyage across the Atlantic was no small thing, and a return to Europe was never guaranteed. To Maria Cosway, the woman with whom he had had his most intense relationship since the death of his wife, he wrote touchingly about friendship, love, the difference between American and European values, and about the extraordinary changes taking place in Paris.

I leave here a scene of tumult and contest. All is politics in this capital. Even love has lost its part in conversation. This is not well, for love is always a consolatory thing. I am going to a country where it is felt in its sublimest degree. In great cities it is distracted by the variety of objects. Friendship perhaps suffers there also from the same cause but I am determined to except from this your friendship for me, and to believe it distracted by neither time, distance, nor object. When wafting on the bosom of the ocean I shall pray it to be as calm and smooth as yours to me. . . . Adieu, my very dear friend. Be our affections unchangeable, and if our little history is to last beyond the grave, be the longest chapter in it that which shall record their purity, warmth and duration.

It is a farewell that contains distance but not disengagement, a poetic conciseness, graceful and eloquent, merging friendship and love into a unity whose best resource is language. It expresses the feelings of a man whose intention was never to lose a friend, though he accepted that losses were the currency of life.

In late summer 1789, his mind and energy directed toward departure, he ceaselessly wrote letters, personal, practical, and professional, despite his "withered hand and swelled and crooked fingers. . . . I have forever lost the use of my hand, except that I can write." He needed to locate passage for himself, his daughters, and his two Hemings slaves. He confided to his closest American friend that he had to attend to his "private affairs" by which he meant his financial difficulties and the Americanization of his daughters. He confided nothing about his most singular private affair. Early in a pregnancy, Sally Hemings chose to return with him, to be a special kind of slave in Virginia rather than a free woman in France. He himself would stay only from April to October. It did not seem to concern him that he would be separated thereafter from Martha and Maria and the never-mentioned Sally for at least a year and, if reappointed, by another three. Between 1785 and 1787, he had frequently expressed his desire to have Maria with him in Paris. He had forced her departure from her home at Eppington. Now he seemed to have no difficulty anticipating that they would be separated again. And what would it be like for them to transit from cosmopolitan Paris to rural Virginia? That he was willing to "leave them," the phrase he used to Madison, might have come harshly to their hearts.

Did Jefferson ask himself these questions? He seems to have answered them by not asking them. As frequently, his gifts as a writer were inseparable from his use of language as self-persuasion and self-definition, as evasion and amelioration. He had his principles and his bottom line in place: he wanted his daughters to be Virginian Americans. They could not be that if they returned with him to Paris. He felt a duty, perhaps an inclination also, to return to France. Everything else was secondary. His daughters were going home, period. He was returning to Paris. In this case, as often, Jefferson's sense of his own integrity short-circuited self-analysis. He always assumed that he was doing the right thing. His literary gift, his ability to express himself so well, especially as a writer of letters, was the foundation of his self-mastery and his graceful willfulness.

The rapid twenty-six-day voyage across the Atlantic to Norfolk, Virginia, was uneventful, the *Clermont* swift and steady, the weather favorable. The arrival on November 23, 1789, however, was not. Heavy mists on the coastline limited visibility, and adverse winds kept beating the *Clermont* hard. Other ships were pushed out to sea; some were lost. An anxious Jefferson worried not only about lives but about his papers and account books. He had kept them with him in his cabin. The *Clermont* then replaced water with fire. An hour after the Jefferson entourage went ashore, the ship burst into flames. "In the middle steerage where was some spirits and oil, and the flame bursting through the cabin and out at its windows, consumed all the inside of that before it was extinguished. By a miracle our baggage which still remained in our staterooms, was untouched." Fortunately, their "trunks also had been put in our state rooms," Patsy wrote, "and the doors pulled to accidentally as our Captain acknowledged but seeing them open he thought it as well to shut them . . . the flames did not penetrate." Jefferson especially needed his account books to provide support for his request for reimbursement for his Paris expenses. He still assumed he would be returning to France. "I shall proceed first to my own house," he wrote to John Jay, "to arrange those matters which have called for my presence there, and, this done, go on to New York in order for my embarkation." And to talk with Jay and others "to take the sense of government on some subjects which required" face-to-face discussion. Among the others would be President Washington.

The dignitaries of Norfolk, a city still showing the scars of its wartime shelling, greeted Jefferson with an expression of their "fervent wishes . . . that you may be as happy in the important Station you are now called to by a grateful Country, as you have been successful in your negotiations." On landing, reading a newspaper, he had first learned what "the important station" was. Unknown to Jefferson, two weeks before he had sailed from Le Havre, the Senate had confirmed his nomination as secretary of state. In Norfolk, he now had good reason to believe, whatever his personal preferences, that he would not be returning to Paris in the spring and that, indifferent to his own mental twists and turns, the die had been cast for him by someone else. He responded in writing to the Norfolk people "that my country should be served is the first wish of my heart: I should be doubly happy indeed were I to render it a service." New York, Boston, Philadelphia, Charleston, London, and Paris knew of the appointment before he did. So did Virginia. Richmond happily anticipated having a native son in the highest counsels of the government. The House of Delegates appointed a committee to welcome him home. On December 11, at Eppington, he received President-Elect Washington's letter of appointment; the official document soon followed. The president required "to be made acquainted with your sentiments as soon as you shall find it convenient to communicate them to me."

From Eppington, where Maria must have been thrilled to be reunited with her aunt, uncle, and cousins, they went on to Monticello, presumably with Sally Hemings and her brother, arriving two days before Christmas. Later accounts proclaim that Jefferson was greeted rapturously by a cordon of dozens or hundreds of huzzahing slaves, some of whom cried with joy at their master's return, that Jefferson was lifted by Black hands out of his carriage as it ascended the twisting road, his slaves carrying their benevolent and now famous owner from the lower road to the house, with a laurel wreath with which to crown him and celebrate his return.

Whatever truth there is in these reports, we should take into account that the scene might have been a semi-scripted show of the sort slaves were well known to fake as essential to their own well-being, that some slaves might have known that Jefferson had intended to sell or hire out slaves to pay debts, and that some of the greeting may have expressed the pleasure felt by the Hemings family at their reunion with Sally and James. Jefferson, however, would have felt this welcome as sincere, the patriarch returning to his family, an instance of his lifelong ability to separate his own slaves and his responsibilities as a slave-owner from considerations about the institution itself.

He had addressed the topic in *Notes on the State of Virginia*, and the published version had extended his views to a wide audience in America, England, and France, where he had had discussions with Enlightenment luminaries and French admirers of the United States, particularly Lafayette, Nicolas de Condorcet, and Jacques Brissot, all three of whom felt that Jefferson stopped at a bridge far too short of where antislavery ought to go. They would not have known that at the Hôtel de Langeac Jefferson had had two mulatto servants who in America were legally his slaves. In France, they were not, and by their own simple declaration they would have been considered free, an opportunity which neither Sally nor James Hemings availed themselves of. They may not have known of this right, or they may have preferred a life of certainties with Jefferson to one of uncertainties in France. If this was their choice, it may have been by agreement with their master, including promises of special treatment and advantages. Aware that he was in violation of French law, Jefferson had quietly evaded the legalities. As always, when it came to his slaves, he did what was practical and in his own interest. As an intellectual, especially among friends and colleagues, he was rarely reluctant to make it known that he believed that slavery was, in theory, a moral iniquity, a stain on a civilized society. Still, his innate self-protective duplicity often came into play.

Lafayette, of course, knew that Jefferson owned many slaves. Who else among the members of Jefferson's salon and intellectual-political circle knew? When Jacques Brissot, a leading abolitionist and the founder in 1788 of the Society of the Friends of the Blacks, invited Jefferson to become a member, he declined. It would be incompatible, he said, with his official position. If Lafayette was ever disappointed in Jefferson, it was with Jefferson's refusal to act on his professed anti-slavery views, as well as his belief that Blacks were innately less intelligent than whites. Sometimes Jefferson leaned a little one way on this point; sometimes, the other. The idea that emancipated Blacks could become capable, competent, and self-supporting free laborers seemed to him problematic but possible.

In fall 1788, he had received a request from Edward Bancroft, an American doctor, scientist, and patriotic pamphleteer living in London, for information about an experiment by an antislavery planter in Virginia who had liberated his slaves and employed them as paid labor. Bancroft had told his London abolitionist circle that Jefferson had mentioned this incident when they were dinner guests of a mutual friend in 1785. Jefferson could not recall the occasion, but the subject was of interest to him. Bancroft had served as Franklin's assistant during the peace treaty negotiations in Paris in 1783. A double agent, he had been spying for the American colonies in London and Paris while also serving the British, though apparently of little consequential help to either side.

Jefferson responded early in 1789 that "as far as I can judge from the experiments which have been made, to give liberty to, or rather, to abandon persons whose habits have been formed in slavery is like abandoning children." To get them to work, they needed to be watched and even whipped. It was not the fault of the slaves, he said, for "a man's moral sense must be unusually strong, if slavery does not make him a thief. He who is permitted by law to have no property of his own, can with difficulty conceive that property is founded in anything but force. These slaves chose to steal from their neighbors rather than work . . . and in most instances were reduced to slavery again." Time, education, and proper modeling might, however, make slaves into morally responsible and productive free laborers.

Maybe, or maybe not, Jefferson thought. "I am decided on my final return to America to try this one. I shall endeavor to import as many Germans as I have grown slaves. I will settle them and my slaves, on farms of 50 acres each, intermingled, and place all on the footing of the metayers [tenant farmers] of Europe," which meant they were not to own the property they farmed. "Their children shall be brought up, as others are, in habits of property and foresight, and I have no doubt but that they will be good citizens [as] some of their fathers will be so: others I suppose will need government . . . to oblige them to labor as the laboring poor of Europe do, and to apply to their comfortable subsistence the produce of their labor, retaining such a moderate portion of it as may be a just equivalent for the use of the lands they labor [on]. . . ." Despite his intention to try the experiment, he never did, and his plan did not envision ownership, only tenancy. If the plan had been tried and been successful, Jefferson would still have been the legal possessor of the land.

Even if Jefferson felt discomfort when among his Paris associates about the conflict between his opinions and his ownership of slaves, his hypocrisy probably was disregarded. It may never have come up; it may have been tactfully avoided. For them, the reality of Jefferson as slaveholder apparently had much less presence than his moral opposition to the institution. None of his French friends owned slaves, a legal impossibility, which differentiated him from abolitionists like Brissot, Richard Price, Edward Bancroft, and the most distinguished intellectual whom Jefferson conversed with in Paris, the Marquis de Condorcet. Well known for his brilliance as a mathematician and social scientist, Condorcet may have influenced Jefferson's arithmetic in claiming that the length of a generation was nineteen years in his argument that each new generation should not be responsible for the debts of the previous one. Jefferson read Condorcet's denunciation of slavery in *Reflections on the Slavery of Negroes*, a powerfully eloquent screed, two copies of which Jefferson bought in 1788. He decided to translate it, a contribution to the effort to persuade the next generation of Americans to do what his generation could not.

In late 1788, he translated the opening passages. There's no evidence that he showed them to Condorcet or anyone else, and it probably was not his intention to have his name affixed as translator. He did not explain why he got no further. Perhaps he decided that the project was too risky. He kept the manuscript in his private possession. Two years later, Jefferson wrote to Condorcet about a free African American, a "worthy and respectable member of society," whose "very elegant solutions of Geometrical problems" he had seen. "I shall be delighted to see these instances of moral eminence so multiplied as to prove that the want of talents observed in them is merely the effect of their degraded condition, and not proceeding from any difference in the structure of the parts on which intellect depends."

Did Jefferson believe Condorcet's claim that nature had endowed Blacks "*with the same genius, the same judgment, the same virtues as the Whites?*" As he translated from French to English, were Jefferson's convictions as well as his pen committed to what the words explicitly claimed? The translation could have been exploration or conclusion, or both. Even if he agreed with Condorcet, the gap between principle and practice remained, between the continuation of his life as the benevolent slaveholder he thought himself to be and the moralistic philosopher for whom in the abstract slavery was a moral evil. The translation is another instance, though a slanting one, of Jefferson's commitment to writing, his reliance on the written word to engage with subjects of importance to him, and also of the oddly ironic situation in which he placed himself: his pen at the service of what his daily life did not embody, of what his intellect was capable of and what his moral principles supported but what his practical life and the world into which he had been born did not.

When Jefferson arrived at Monticello in December 1789, the welcome he received from his slaves must have seemed to him entirely compatible with the necessities of life and his sense of what he deserved. For him, slavery remained an essential reality of his time and place. Life as he had known it and as he expected it to be for some time did not admit of an alteration in its psychological and economic structure. The land that he returned to possessed him, and he possessed it. And his slaves, whatever his relationships with them, were inseparable from the land. Because it was inconceivable that he could work the land himself or pay people to do so, he believed it would be of little use to him without slaves, and the land and what he built on it were inseparable from the fundamental values he also deeply held—family, friends, education, knowledge, patrimony, and patriotism.

In December 1788, Jefferson had written to George Washington a subtly indirect job application. Much has been made of Jefferson's lack of interest in or ambivalence about pursuing a political career once his time in Paris was concluded. He assumed that he would be returning to Paris for at least 1789–1790, perhaps until 1792. It was a diplomatic position, though with an important political component. He had made it clear to the newly elected president that he would be at the chief executive's disposal in the service of his country, and he expected that to be in France. But his letter to Washington intimates his availability for other national service as well.

It is the kind of letter that does not make a case for anything specific but rules out nothing. It is a letter about public policy—to the man Jefferson knew would be the most powerful dispenser of positions.

Calculation has convinced me that circumstances may arise, and probably will arise, wherein all the resources of taxation will be necessary for the safety of the state. For . . . who can avoid seeing the source of war in the tyranny of those nations who deprive us of the natural right of trading with our neighbors? . . . The power of making war often prevents it, and in our case would give efficacy to our desire of peace. Whenever [the French] are in war with England, they must open the islands to us, and perhaps during that war they may see some price which might make them agree to keep them always open.

War might promote American economic prosperity.

In the mean time I have laid my shoulder to the opening the markets of this country to our produce, and rendering its transportation a nursery for our seamen. A maritime force is the only one by which we can act on Europe. . . . However before there is a necessity of deciding on this I hope to be able to consult our new government in person. . . . It is necessary for me to pay a short visit to my native country. . . . I shall hope therefore for the pleasure of personal conferences with your excellency on the subjects of this letter and others interesting to our country, of getting my own ideas set to rights by a communication of yours, and of taking again the tone of sentiment of my own country which we lose in some degree after a certain absence.

Washington would have found the policies advocated in Jefferson's letter consistent with his own, as if the two were of like mind about taxes, credit, neutrality, commerce, naval appropriations, and relations with France. Jefferson is, in effect, affirming that Washington's views are his own and that, if they are not, his "own ideas" will be "set to rights." If he became a member of Washington's administration, the president's policies would be his. It was already a stretch, perhaps for a purpose. Washington would have had no reason to doubt Jefferson's sincerity, though in the 1790s he was to discover to his disappointment that his secretary of state was not the team player he had claimed he would be and that his views were not always consistent with his earlier words. Probably in 1788, Washington already had in mind offering Jefferson the position of secretary of state. After all, Jefferson, a fellow Virginian of national reputation whom he had known since the 1760s, had executive and legislative experience. He had supported the control of Western expansion by the national government. He had deplored the limitations of the Articles of Confederation. He had collaborated with Washington on the effort to transform the Potomac into a navigable passage to the West. He could be counted on for assiduous hard work. As minister to France, he had become one of the Americans best informed about European affairs. Most important, the author of countless legal, political, and legislative documents could be relied on to wield his pen effectively in fulfilling the requirements of the office.

It was Jefferson's preference to stay on in Paris, if the Washington administration concurred. It suited him personally, professionally, and financially. Nevertheless, he may indeed have had in mind as early as 1788 that he might serve his country in an alternative and even more powerful position. This letter suggests that. It does not belie the sincerity of his disavowal of political ambition, his oft-repeated expression of how much he yearned to retire to Monticello, to his books, his family, and his garden.

In July 1789, two months before leaving France, he wrote to a friend that "to glide unnoticed thro' a silent execution of duty, is the only ambition which becomes me, and it is the sincere desire of my heart." The word "duty" neatly expresses the unresolved conflict between public and private. The conflicting aspirations coexist, incompatible in temporal and spatial simultaneity but not in mood and values—opposite sides, so to speak, of a singular personality. A master of direction and indirection, of a concealment that both reveals and obscures, Jefferson made known to Washington his value and his availability with a conciseness and tact that his correspondent, a man who also chose his words carefully, would appreciate. In this instance, though, the offer to be of service was unmistakable.

The day after the Constitutional Convention ended in September 1787, Washington had sent a copy of the constitution to Jefferson. It was certain that if the constitution were to be ratified, Washington would be elected president. It would have seemed sensible to make certain that his minister was prepared to present and extoll the constitution to the French and other European governments. His letter from Mount Vernon on New Year's Day 1788 was intended to assure Jefferson that they were on the same page about what America's relationship with France should be, the primacy of agriculture in the American economy, and the necessity for "energetic general government." They both still hoped that the Potomac would become the main avenue of commerce between the West and the East, and that the capital of the nation should be closer to Mount Vernon than to any Northern city.

Both believed that America should not get involved in European wars. For Washington that meant neutrality. It would be "extremely imprudent for us to take a part in their quarrels; and whenever a contest happens among them, if we wisely and properly improve the advantages which nature has given us, we may be benefitted by their folly—provided we conduct ourselves with circumspection, and under proper restrictions." For Jefferson it required that the United States continue to strengthen its alliance with France. Great Britain was not simply another actor in the great power struggle with which it was in the interest of the United States to relate to with dispassionate self-interest. It was a visceral enemy. The desideratum was to have the advantage of French support and protection without the disadvantage of having to go to war on its behalf. France had become an exotic and pleasurable second home to Jefferson, and he had reason to hope that over time it would evolve into a sister republic, the vanguard in Europe of the extension and ultimate triumph of the American Revolution. But Washington's statement that under an "energetic general government" the United States would create a nation that would attract respect and investment from European countries must have given Jefferson pause. For Jefferson, support and investment were desirable, but energetic government was not. Energetic government on a national scale was exactly what Jefferson did *not* want.

Two letters from Washington reached Jefferson as he traveled to Richmond in mid-December 1789. His "talents" were needed "for the service" of his country "and without being able to consult your inclination, or to derive any knowledge of your intentions from your letters either to myself or to any other of your friends, I was determined, as well by motives of private regard as a conviction of public propriety, to nominate you for the department of state, which, under its present organization, involves many of the most interesting objects of the executive authority." That Washington included an escape clause in his letter was a matter of propriety and courtesy, the gentlemanly rhetoric of one member of the Virginia elite to another. "But grateful as your acceptance of this commission would be to me, I am at the same time desirous to accommodate to your wishes, and I have therefore forborne to nominate your successor at the court of Versailles until I should be informed of your determination." John Jay, who would soon become the first chief justice and who had held the pre-Constitution version of the office of secretary of state, would handle its affairs in the interim.

Jefferson responded immediately. On the one hand, he wrote to Washington, he feared the criticism inevitably directed at the occupier of such a high office, "embracing as it does the principal mass of domestic administration, together with the foreign, I cannot be insensible of my inequality to it: and I should enter on it with gloomy forebodings from the criticisms and censures of a public just indeed in their intentions, but sometimes misinformed and misled, and always too respectable to be neglected. I cannot but foresee the possibility that this may end disagreeably for one, who, having no motive to public service but the public satisfaction, would certainly retire the moment that satisfaction should appear to languish." He would be a novice to the position, whereas reappointment as minister to France would continue him in a position he was already well qualified for.

"But it is not for an individual," he continued, "to chuse his post. You are to marshal us as may best be for the public good . . . be so good only as to signify to me by another line your ultimate wish, and I shall conform to it cordially. If it should be to remain at New York, my chief comfort will be to work under your eye, my only shelter the authority of your name, and the wisdom of measures to be dictated by you, and implicitly executed by me." In effect, he could not say no, though he needed an elaborate, circumspect, and self-protective letter to say in effect that he would accept the position unless Washington changed his mind, which it was clear he would not. Jefferson wrote to William Short in mid-December that "it was impossible to give a flat refusal to such a nomination," and he knew that the absence of a "flat refusal" meant acceptance. Anyway, what would Virginia and especially its elite have said if he had refused? Washington's word, under the circumstances, had to be his command. He emphasized that whatever criticism might come his way, he would bear it, under the protective shield of "the authority of your name, and the wisdom of measures to be dictated by you, and implicitly executed by me." He would be a good soldier.

At Monticello in mid-February 1790, Jefferson was greeted by a welcome from the prominent citizens of Albemarle to which he responded in writing with characteristic brevity and brilliance. It was both a heartfelt thanks for the warm welcome and the marking of another departure, for how long he could not tell and to what end he could not be sure. His farewell looked forward to another and lasting return, to his retirement in private life to his familiar world of family and friends and his Virginia community. He had expected to return to France. Now he was home, in the compromised sense that his home would for a time be someplace else, though in a city much closer than Paris. The new level of public service would place him at the highest level of national leadership short of the presidency. Of course, he could not and would not decline.

Once again he could accept public office while at the same time quite sincerely claiming that his ultimate happiness resided in a return to private life, a retirement that at the moment was in the indefinite future. What better time to emphasize his preference for private life than when he was committing himself to public life. Uncharacteristically, he chose to speak in personal terms about himself, partly because a welcome from his Albemarle friends had strong emotional and personal resonances. But his theme was the "we" of republicanism, with back references to the Declaration of 1776 and to the shared rigors and sacrifices of the war for independence. It is one of Jefferson's finest statements of his political creed, his prose at a level equal to the best he ever wrote:

> The testimony of esteem with which you are pleased to honour my return to my native county fills me with gratitude and pleasure. While it shews that my absence has not lost me your friendly recollection, it holds out the comfortable hope that when the hour of retirement shall come, I shall again find myself amidst those with whom I have long lived, with whom I wish to live, and whose affection is the source of my purest happiness. Their favor was the door thro' which I was ushered on the stage of public life; and while I have been led on thro' its varying scenes, I could not be unmindful of those who assigned me my first part. My feeble and obscure

exertions in their service, and in the holy cause of freedom, have had no other merit than that they were my best. We have all the same. We have been fellow-laborers and fellow-sufferers, and heaven has rewarded us with a happy issue from our struggles. It rests now with ourselves alone to enjoy in peace and concord the blessings of self-government, so long denied to mankind: to shew by example the sufficiency of human reason for the care of human affairs and that the will of the majority, the Natural law of every society, is the only sure guardian of the rights of man. Perhaps even this may sometimes err. But its errors are honest, solitary and short-lived.— Let us then, my dear friends, forever bow down to the general reason of the society. We are safe with that, even in its deviations, for it soon returns again to the right way. These are lessons we have learnt together. We have prospered in their practice, and the liberality with which you are pleased to approve my attachment to the general rights of mankind assures me we are still together in these its kindred sentiments. Wherever I may be stationed, by the will of my country, it will be my delight to see, in the general tide of happiness, that yours too flows on in just place and measure. That it may flow through all times, gathering strength as it goes, and spreading the happy influence of reason and liberty over the face of the earth, is my fervent prayer to heaven.

This was not a call to arms; it was not literature as propaganda. It was a personal testament, Jefferson's attempt to affirm to a small audience at a local occasion the unity of himself, the local community, and the national state, a unity created by his version of and his confidence in "the people." It is both an invocation of and an affirmation of "the holy cause of freedom." It deserves to be better known and more widely read. It connects Jefferson with Lincoln, no matter how different they were in regard to birth, words, and actions, especially about slavery and "energy" in government. To the extent that it is also a farewell, temporary as it was to be, to the Albemarle home to which he had just returned, it is suggestive of Lincoln's farewell to his Springfield audience when he departed for Washington in early 1861 to face the most challenging problem that Jefferson's generation had not resolved. It is Jefferson's post-Declaration declaration of republican values, of "reason" and "liberty," of what he expected of himself and his fellow Americans in the republic now under a new Constitution, which he expected to affirm and to implement as a premier adviser to the president in what was to be soon defined as the president's Cabinet.

In a single paragraph of exemplary prose, Jefferson affirmed his faith that self-government, reason, and natural law would always be the guiding values and forces of the United States, and that ultimately the people would make the best choice or quickly self-correct. Natural law and the will of the majority were one and the same—an extraordinary claim, as if natural law and the will of the majority could never be at odds. He was to find that his faith exceeded what reality would provide. He would, though, continue to believe that the faith stated in this brief address was warranted: reason, natural law, respect for the independence and self-governance of others, and the commonsense instincts and views of the people as a whole would sustain and continue the republican values that the generation of 1776 had fought for.

To Washington's request that he come as quickly as possible to New York City, he asked for time. "Your desire that I should come on as quickly as possible is a sufficient reason for me to postpone every matter of business, however pressing, which admits postponement." But there were concerns and obligations at home that he still needed to attend to. His sale of some of his estates, probably with the slaves who worked them, relieved some of the financial pressure of his indebtedness. His creditors in Great Britain agreed to an extended repayment schedule guaranteed by long-term bonds. Monticello and some other properties were preserved, none of its slaves sold, though some were occasionally rented out. The debts that during his Paris years had been a gnawing anxiety seem to have become a secondary concern, real but not imminently threatening. He would be making or postponing annual payments for much of the rest of his life.

There was also a marriage to celebrate. Soon after Jefferson's Christmas 1789 return to Monticello, eighteen-year-old Martha Jefferson was courted by her father's second cousin, twenty-one-year-old Thomas Mann Randolph Jr., the heir to Tuckahoe, where Jefferson had lived for five years as a young boy. Just two months later, they married. Randolph had returned from Edinburgh in 1789 after five years of desultory education, educated but careerless. He now decided to try politics. Volatile and thin-skinned, he quarreled with his father. Soon Thomas Mann Randolph Sr. married a younger woman, disappointing his son's expectation of a substantial inheritance. Through Jefferson's mediation, his son-in-law purchased a small plantation close to Monticello. He and Martha set up housekeeping in stringent circumstances.

The marriage was likely to have been Martha's introduction to sexual experience. Nothing is known about what led to their marriage after an acquaintance of less than two months. Martha was not pregnant. Her first child, of the twelve she was to have, was born on January 23, 1791. Her father had given his blessing. He may have been distracted by other matters. He liked Randolph and thought well of him, though he did not know of his temper, vacillations, and irresolution about almost anything he set himself to. The couple represented themselves as being in love; Martha was of marriageable age, and Jefferson would have thought that another union of a Jefferson and a Randolph would be a fitting expression of the kinship of the two distinguished families. Apparently, he did not consider recommending that they set a later date for the marriage. Any such recommendation would have been taken by his daughter as a command. Randolph, whatever his desires, would have had to consent.

From New York, in April 1790, Jefferson wrote to his daughter, now pregnant: "I am anxious to hear from you, of your health, your occupations, where you are . . . ." Always the didactic father, he urged her not to neglect her music. "It will be a companion which will sweeten many hours of life to you. I assure you mine here is triste enough. Having had yourself and dear Poll to live with me so long, to exercise my affections and cheer me in the intervals of business, I feel heavily the separation from you." Polly may have been at Eppington, and would not have been receptive to an invitation or command to accompany her father to New York. "It is a circumstance of consolation," he assured Martha, "to know that you are happier; and to see a prospect of its continuance in the prudence and even temper both of Mr. Randolph and yourself." The Jeffersons were to learn that Randolph was not prudent, and did not have an "even temper." "Your new condition will call for abundance of little sacrifices. But they will be greatly overpaid by the measure of affection they will secure to you." As to married women, the conventional Jefferson emphasized that "the happiness of your life depends now on the continuing to please a single person. To this all other objects must be secondary; even your love to me, were it possible that that could ever be an obstacle. But this it can never be. Neither of you can ever have a more faithful friend than myself, nor one on whom you can count for more sacrifices. My own is become a secondary object to the happiness of you both."

At first the marriage seemed promising. Jefferson embraced Randolph, or at least the idea of him, as the son he never had. Randolph, though, became an erratic provider, sometimes intemperate, arrogant, jealous of the success of others, and often in unstable and irrational competition for his father-in-law's favor. It was to be a long and troubled marriage, for Martha a roller coaster with some highs, especially in her mothering, and many lows. Her husband took little active interest in his children. His career also had its highs and lows. He had the kind of successes as a farmer, politician, and then officer in the War of 1812 that are inseparable from the aura of failure, and he was always short of money. His moods ranged from optimistically loving to morbid loathing of self and others. He had a talent for undermining the successes he did have, and there were to be years of marital estrangement and bitter relations between Randolph and some of his children, especially Jefferson's namesake and favorite grandson.

Martha was to live much of her life at Monticello, her husband ill or far away or sulking nearby, and it is certain that in her hierarchy of love her father came first. Her husband became more a burden than a pleasure, emotionally volatile, financially unsuccessful, and undependable as husband and father. Stoic Martha may or may not have confided in her father. Jefferson would do his best to mediate discreetly. The fact that the couple parented twelve children says more about conventional conjugal rights in patriarchal Virginia than about Martha's desires. She was to become her father's housekeeper, companion, and hostess at Monticello, Randolph spending much of his life sulking, fighting, scheming, attempting to do better and failing. Jefferson did his best to help. He could never, though, improve the quality of the marriage to which he had so quickly given his blessing.

The next three years, from 1790 through 1793, as Washington's secretary of state, were to be Jefferson's most politically contentious and painful. The workload was heavy, the secretary being responsible for all aspects of foreign and domestic policy, except for the military, monetary, and legal. He did not like living in New York and then Philadelphia. The job was both underdefined and overconscripted. Like the entire government, it was a work in progress in its formative stage. In June 1789, James Madison, at work in the House of Representatives of the first Congress, had written to his friend in Paris that "we are in a wilderness without a single footstep to guide us. Our successors will have an easier task, and by degrees the way will become smooth short and certain." He was right about the former but not the latter assertion. Jefferson probably had during his three-year period as secretary of state more tension headaches than at any other time, one of which confined him for six weeks to inactivity in a darkened room in the small house on Maiden Lane that he rented soon after he arrived in New York City in late March 1790. Now "for the first time" he wrote to Paris "to put down my household, and wind up and [send home] my affairs. This was the first moment that I ceased entirely to hope I might" return to France.

It had taken three weeks to travel in winter weather from Monticello to the temporary capital. He had stopped in Philadelphia to visit the ailing Benjamin Franklin, who was to die the next month. James Hemings, Jefferson's Paris-trained slave chef, attended him. Hemings's sister had just given or was about to give birth to the first of Jefferson's children with her. There is no record of what he thought or felt about that, of what he said or did not say to her when he left Monticello. In New York, his plate was full. On the first day, he immediately reported to the president. He was late. The government had been in operation since March 1789. John Jay had been acting secretary of state until Jefferson's arrival. Henry Knox, from Massachusetts, the secretary of war, had been on the scene since September 1789; Edmund Randolph, the attorney general, had arrived a month before Jefferson; and Alexander Hamilton, a New Yorker, had assumed his office as secretary of the Treasury on September 11, 1789.

Hamilton had gotten immediately to work. He had been busy for over six months creating the Treasury Department, whose first priority was to establish a stream of revenue based on customs duties to repay foreign creditors the nation's war debts. He had additional debt-relief plans, especially finding reasonable formulae for buying back outstanding bonds issued to Americans during the war. For months he had been advocating to Congress the establishment of a national bank. He was also taking soundings about establishing a stable currency, banknotes to encourage reliable credit transactions and borrowing, as well as a national mint under the Treasury Department. Like Hamilton, Washington believed such devices and institutions were necessary for national credit, prosperity, and security. Jefferson was already late to the party.

Washington wanted comprehensive advice from his four appointees. He was deliberative and thoughtful; he would make decisions only after discussions with them. During the ratification struggle, a friend of Jefferson's visited Mount Vernon. "I never saw him so keen for anything in my life, as he is for the adoption of the new Form of Government. As the eyes of all America are turned towards this truly Great and Good Man, for the First President." Knox and Hamilton had been soldiers alongside Washington; that bond was strong. Randolph had served briefly in 1775 as the general's aide-de-camp. Jefferson, Randolph, and Washington were Virginians. All had seen battle except Jefferson. Hamilton, Knox, and Randolph, like Washington, desired a government energetic enough to create sufficient authority to unite the nation so that the totality would be more than the sum of its parts.

Jefferson argued for less. In his view, individual states should be more than the sum of the states together, except in regard to foreign affairs and revenue from import taxes. He opposed energetic national government. The Constitution had established the broad principles of organization and authority, but some of its articles and provisions were broad enough to admit of varying interpretations. It was not a blank slate, but, still, it had room enough between the lines for people to read into the text their own views and preferences about how it should be interpreted and implemented.

Jefferson was a textualist, a literalist. That suited his view of government long before the Constitution was created. He was soon engaged in arguments about how energetic the national government should be. For example, when Hamilton proposed the creation of a national bank for the deposit of federal revenue and for monetary transactions, Jefferson responded that the commerce clause could not and should not be interpreted to allow that. Actually, Jefferson disapproved of all banks. His antagonism had been generated from the economics of the Virginia world into which he had been born, from his own indebtedness, from his belief that banks encouraged speculation, and his fear that a national bank would favor commerce rather than agriculture. Moreover, he associated a national bank with the Bank of England, with deficit financing to pay for aggressive nationalism and colonialism, with mercantilism that limited free trade, with financing armies and navies, and with the British system that had led to the war for independence. If there had to be banks, he thought they should be chartered by individual states. A national bank would give excessive power to the federal government; it would use money to make money, which Jefferson thought immoral. Its resources would support a formidable military, which would provoke wars, and thus it would be one of the building blocks of oppressive government, even tyranny. In addition, it would be accompanied by other energetic government activities, which would undermine the freedoms for which the Revolution had been fought.

The passage of the bank bill particularly galled him. "Mr Madison and myself left nothing untried to obtain General Washington's negative to the law," he wrote years later, "but after a long struggle in his mind, Hamilton prevailed in the last hour and let in this torrent of swindling institutions which have spread ruin and wretchedness over the face of our country." The situation could only go from bad to worse. "What is the most disheartening it has still left such a hankering after those delusive establishments that no hope remains of their proscription in future."

To Jefferson, those who agreed with him were true Republicans. Those who did not, soon labeled Federalists, were anti-Republican. They wanted the United States to be essentially like Great Britain, with a hereditary king, whatever his title. Jefferson soon turned his claim into a certainty. Federalists like Hamilton were, he accused, closet monarchists who wanted hereditary leaders, aristocratic titles, a government controlled by the privileged, and patronage of the sort that had perennially corrupted the British government. It was a hefty charge to bring against Hamilton, a cultural and economic Anglophile who was deeply patriotic. Over time, Jefferson was to include in the accusation Knox and Randolph, and gradually to implicate Washington, who was in favor of sufficiently energetic government to make the United States a successful and independent nation-state. In Jefferson's view, his fellow Americans were less than patriotic if they were not Republicans and Francophiles. Between 1791 and 1793, he became a deeply engaged oppositional politician rather than a loyal member of Washington's team. It was to became an untenable situation.

Washington relied heavily on Jefferson for the details of foreign affairs, such as: possible war between Great Britain and Spain, consular vacancies and regulations, the overall diplomatic establishment, instructions to ambassadors, enforcement of the 1783 peace treaty and negotiations with Great Britain, the Barbary Coast state-authorized pirates, British impressment of sailors from American ships, tariff and trade relations with France, the ramifications of the 1788 American-French mutual-aid treaty and the extent to which it required the United States to help France against Great Britain, issues arising from possession of the Northwest Territories, negotiations with Indian tribes, tension with Spain about American access through the Mississippi to New Orleans and international trade, and attempts to elicit European support for freedom of the seas. All these issues and more, with multiple stages of discussion and negotiation, dominated Jefferson's portfolio during his three years as secretary of state. His pen was put to constant use drafting opinions to be submitted to Washington and corresponding with American ministers and foreign governments, particularly Great Britain, France, and Spain, the three sharks whose powerful jaws and appetites the weaker United States had to placate, avoid, bargain with, and play off against one another.

A consensus leader, Washington encouraged his advisers to express their views about every important matter, orally or in writing, in meetings or private discussions, as if they composed a deliberative body in which each member had an equal vote, a tie to be broken by the president. Consequently, each member had some purchase in their colleagues' territory. Knox and Randolph tended mostly to be in agreement with Hamilton. Hamilton and Jefferson usually disagreed: whether to raise revenue through internal taxes, whether and in what ways the federal government should redeem the debts of the states, the speed of the repayment of the debt to France, the degree to which the United States should support France against Great Britain or maintain neutrality, the creation of a national bank, whether to protect domestic manufacturing by tariffs, and where the national capital should be located, a question that eventually was reduced to Philadelphia versus an unsettled area bordering Maryland and Virginia, close to the village of Georgetown.

Jefferson and Madison had been lobbying for this Southern location for ten years, at least since 1784. It would keep the government physically close to Southern influence; it would help with the scheme to make the Potomac the gateway to the West; and it would cut down on travel time for Southerners, who expected to dominate the federal government. Two of the three Cabinet members were Virginians. Madison was the de facto speaker of the House of Representatives. He worked to get the votes for the Southern location. Various deals were proposed, arms were twisted, and rewards were offered to

Pennsylvanians and others. New Englanders and New Yorkers were not happy.

Simultaneously, members of the House were negotiating about whether the federal government should assume the states' war debts. Jefferson and Madison essentially controlled the outcome. Their aim was to ensure that the new capital would be a Southern city. Hamilton's highest priority was assumption of the state debts. It was one of the linchpins of his financial vision. Successful repayment would establish national credit, which would facilitate borrowing, tax collection, and commercial transactions. On June 20, 1790, at a dinner in lower Manhattan arranged by Jefferson, Hamilton agreed to Jefferson's terms, and Jefferson consented to Hamilton's priority. Both were praised and criticized by partisans on each side. The new capital was to be built in a semiwilderness by private funds raised by sale of local land. It would pay for itself, so to speak, an illusion that both Northerners and Southerners sustained. Two years later, in a lengthy letter to Washington, Jefferson distanced himself from the bargain, maintaining that he had been tricked by Hamilton, a self-serving fiction about both principals. "I was duped into [it] by the Secretary of the Treasury, and made a tool for forwarding his schemes, not then sufficiently understood by me; and of all the errors of my political life, this has occasioned me the deepest regret."

Most Southerners, of which many were Federalists, did not regret the deal. Washington himself strongly approved. He expected that he would one day be able to stand on his Mount Vernon porch and almost see in the distance the buildings of the new capital. Over time, history rejected Jefferson's views about debt, commerce, and the monetary system. On the issue of France, Washington sided neither with Francophiles like Jefferson nor Anglophiles like Hamilton. He opted for neutrality, and most Federalists, including Hamilton, essentially agreed with him. Jefferson did not.

Washington more often agreed with Hamilton than Jefferson,

especially on fiscal and monetary policies. Jefferson's claim that the president was unaware of Hamilton's "schemes" and supported them unwittingly is wrong. On the contrary, Washington approved of and supported them. The extent to which those disagreements expressed very different views of the functions of the federal government became the major drama of Washington's first term, of the relationship between Jefferson and Hamilton, and of the relationship between Jefferson and Washington.

In the dynamics of this drama, Jefferson began to develop the rhetoric of the life he was soon to embrace as a partisan politician. As he saw it, on one side were virtuous Republicans like himself: the powers of the federal government should be narrowly defined; borrowing and national debt must be kept to a minimum, exclusively for national defense; agriculture should be favored over manufacturing; the United States owed France a multilevel debt; and its Revolution in progress was the likely genesis of a new birth of Europe-wide republicanism. On the other side were Great Britain–loving proto-monarchists who embraced deficit financing, wars of aggression and colonization, energetic national government, and the use of debt, paper money, and patronage to create a corrupt system of government. He assumed that their major tool of congressional influence would be bribery, and he recycled the language of opposition to King George for use against those whom he now began to view as his internal political enemies.

Between 1790 and 1793, Hamilton earned his place at the top of Jefferson's list of ideological enemies. Jefferson communicated to Washington, without being explicit, that he believed Hamilton in his regular meetings with the British minster was betraying Cabinet and state secrets. To Jefferson, the differences of opinion between himself and Hamilton about monetary policy and about France and England distinguished honest patriots from corrupt monarchists, by which he meant traitors to the principles of the Revolution. Hamilton and his associates did not have, as did Jefferson, a preexisting political rhetoric to recycle. They did have at hand, though, an ongoing dynamic, a generator of attack rhetoric and labels: the French Revolution. While Jefferson was in Paris and for a year or so afterward, Lafayette and his moderate colleagues had attempted to transform France into a constitutional monarchy. They failed. Thereafter, factions competed for power, leading to the execution of Louis XVI in January 1793. Jefferson semireluctantly accepted that the king's blood had been shed to water the liberty tree and that the many deaths that preceded and followed did much the same, the necessary prelude to the rebirth of France as a republic. To Hamilton and his party, it was murder bred of anarchy, vengeance, cruelty, and the triumph of irrational mob rule over orderly government. To Hamilton and many Federalists, Jefferson and his associates were Jacobins in favor of mob rule by the uneducated, revolutionaries against the Revolution, proponents of class warfare, and endorsers of political and ideological murder who would, if they were in power, bring the guillotine to America.

The rhetoric became especially dramatic in 1793 when the new French minister, Edmund-Charles Genêt, attempting to enlist Americans and American facilities to help in France's conflict with Great Britain, interfered in American domestic affairs by outfitting French privateers in US ports in defiance of Washington's policy of neutrality. To protect his own flank, Jefferson eventually had to side with Washington, Hamilton, and Knox. The administration asked that Genêt be recalled. Meanwhile pro-French Americans in support of Genêt and France were forming Jacobin Clubs, the very name of which provoked Federalist fear and anger. Pro-British Americans denounced them. Washington denounced them. Jefferson did not, though he granted that Genêt's breach of diplomatic propriety needed to be appropriately rebuked. Though they were still without formal structures, there were now two political parties in the United States. Jefferson believed his was the true heir of the principles of the Revolution.

Washington and Jefferson were not personal friends. They shared few interests. The president had been a surveyor, a speculator in Western land, a farmer, a businessman, a military officer of mixed distinction, and a quiet member of the House of Burgesses and the Continental Congress. He had risen mostly on his own initiatives from the minor gentry, with the help of a favorable marriage, to become in 1775 the choice of Congress to lead the Continental Army. His military record had been limited and mixed. He would have much to learn as events developed. He had no special gift for writing or legislating; his interest in ideas was modest. Neither was he devoted to art, literature, and intellectual pursuits, but he was a commanding presence. His silences spoke louder than words. "His passions were naturally strong," Jefferson was to write, "but his reason, generally, stronger." He possessed the essence of what his contemporaries called "character," a leader whose judgment, capability, and presence inspired his troops and made him an icon thereafter, the inevitable first president of the new nation. Loyalty, competence, and courage were his highest values. He had good reason to believe that Jefferson was competent. How loyal he was and how much he could be a team player remained to be seen. That he was a patriot could never be doubted.

The two Virginians had been allies in the Revolution, both committed to independence and the sacrifices that required. The governor of Virginia and the commander of the Continental Army had corresponded on matters of mutual urgency. Before the Revolution, they had served together in the House of Burgesses. As fellow Virginians, they were bound into consanguinity by class, slaveholding, and patriotic commitment. They were allies in hoping to make the Potomac navigable, the key to a Virginia-based water route to the West. Jefferson had written on behalf of Congress its formal response to Washington's resignation speech, and the two had corresponded on matters of mutual interest while Jefferson was in France. By 1787, their political paths had begun to diverge. Washington envisioned a stronger role for the federal government than did Jefferson. Jefferson favored a weak executive, preferably limited to one term; Washington, a stronger executive. Washington still wanted him in his administration. Soon after Jefferson arrived in New York, suffering from what seemed an interminable headache, he accepted an invitation to accompany the president on a fishing trip off Sandy Hook, New Jersey. It might help rid him of the headache. Washington probably thought it a friendly gesture toward his newly arrived secretary of state.

They were at the start of an adventure in government. Between 1791 and 1793, Jefferson was to write extensive memoranda, summarizing events, Cabinet meetings, and conversations. He later collected them in three bound volumes. The only formal unifying device is the date that heads each note. He did not have a notebook or a pen in hand during these conversations and meetings. The president would not have known that Jefferson was afterward creating his version of what had been said. He wrote each note or group of notes on whatever piece of paper was at hand, literally within reach. "I made memorandums on loose scraps of paper, taken out of my pockets in the moment and laid by to be copied at leisure, which, however, they hardly ever were." He included some press clippings. Some of the lengthy notes had to have been created some hours after the event, probably on the same day but at a time that would permit a few hours of concentration. The writer's motivation is not entirely clear: perhaps an expression of his habit of keeping records, certainly as an aid to memory, probably as evidence of what had been said that might have some relevance for the historical record. The most substantial contain Jefferson's records of his private conversations with the president. A man who never threw away anything he had written, he did not envision these notes as building blocks in a totality. Indeed, there was no notion of a totality at all.

In March 1792, Washington began convening regular Cabinet meetings for discussion and resolution. In his memoranda, Jefferson summarized the flow of debate, occasionally with critical comments, some personal, some speculative. He was usually the odd man out on the issues that meant most to him. About Indian affairs, after internal debate, they were all eventually in agreement. If they could not persuade the tribes to be with them, they would be against them. Most settlers favored genocide. Washington and Jefferson favored accommodation, fairness, compensation, and eventual assimilation of the tribes into the American polity. There was also the absolute necessity, in Jefferson's view, for the United States to affirm and enforce its special and primary relationship with France as France evolved, he hoped, from an absolute monarchy to a republic. But startling events beyond his anticipation and control needed to be accommodated and absorbed into his Francophilia and his optimism. His fellow Cabinet members and the president could not do that as readily. They warmly debated what American policy toward France should be. The execution of Louis XVI, then of his wife, had weight. Washington was appalled. "I remember," Jefferson wrote in March 1792, that "when I received the news of the King's flight and capture," and told Washington, "I never saw him so dejected by an event in my life."

The excesses of the Reign of Terror were more than off-putting. Jefferson did his best with his fellow Cabinet members and the president to emphasize the financial debt and the moral debt of honor the United States owed to France, to assert that the 1778 treaty of alliance was still valid, and to point out the advantages to the United States of the ideological affinity between the two countries as France moved toward becoming a republic. The Directory, the latest regime in France, was not, though, a plausible republic. Jefferson supported it anyway as another step toward the establishment of a real French republic. In late 1792, Washington instructed Jefferson to encourage Gouverneur Morris in Paris to "effect a stricter connection with

France." The president wanted more counterweight against the pressures coming from England and Spain. Jefferson's response was personal and ideological: "I was much pleased with the tone. . . . It was the very doctrine which had been my polar star. . . ."

In spring 1793, the Girondist (moderate) government of France sent thirty-year-old Edmund-Charles Genêt to represent it in America. When Genêt landed in Charleston, he began to recruit American ships to serve as privateers in the French war against the British, the start of months of pro-French activities on American soil, including raising soldiers to attack British Florida. Jefferson wrote detailed memoranda of the Cabinet meetings in which the president and his colleagues gradually decided that this was impermissible. It put the country in danger of being drawn into war. It was an insult to the president, to the neutrality policy, and to Congress that even Jefferson could not tolerate. He ultimately agreed with Washington, Hamilton, Knox, and Randolph about what had to be done. In his heart, unlike his colleagues, he agreed with the ideology and the priorities that Genêt represented, but Genêt's unauthorized implementation could not be tolerated. It was an assault on American sovereignty. When Genêt refused to moderate his conduct, Washington instructed Jefferson to request Genêt's recall. In his memoranda through the spring and summer of 1793, Jefferson's accounts of the Cabinet meetings capture the drama of the most dangerous crisis the Washington administration faced during his years as secretary of state. It caused Jefferson anxiety and anger. The country had become even more polarized than it had been.

Months before the Genêt affair, Jefferson had decided to resign. He was a good fit for the office he held but a bad fit for the administration in which he served, and he was on the losing side of its most consequential decisions. Washington believed he was adhering to the principles of the Revolution as he understood them. That the president's values and ideology were not republican would have struck him as an absurd accusation. His administration and its supporters were now being called Federalists. That didn't seem to him incompatible with republican values in the abstract or even, in many instances, in implementation. After all, what was not republican about creating a national bank or assuming the debts of the states? Couldn't a more centralized government be just as republican as a decentralized one?

Washington wanted Jefferson to stay. He was a well-experienced workhorse of distinction and intellect, a valuable voice in decision making at the highest level. The fact that anyone could even indirectly associate the president with monarchical tendencies seemed ludicrous to a man who wanted nothing more by early 1793 than to retire to Mount Vernon and never again play an active role in government. Still, as his arm was twisted and his patriotism appealed to, he decided he couldn't decline to run for a second term, despite the polarized environment in which he was being increasingly pilloried by an opposition so hostile that the political situation had developed into something the creators of the Constitution had never envisioned—political parties. Washington knew that Jefferson was playing some role, mostly behind the scenes, in the formation and expression of these differences. Even so, he valued Jefferson's contribution and wanted him to stay.

If there were any private discussions between Jefferson and Washington before February 1792, Jefferson either did not make a record of them or omitted them from the three volumes of notes that he was to create in 1818. The brief note of their February 28 meeting and the long memoranda of February 29, headed "Conversations with the President," set the subjects and the voices in place for the entirety, though Jefferson's voice dominates this first substantial dialogue. Late in the afternoon of the 28th, he raised with the president his view that the Post Office should be under the authority of the Department of

State rather than Treasury. "That in urging this measure," he told Washington, "I had certainly no personal interest, since if I was supposed to have an appetite for power, yet as my career would certainly be exactly as short as his own, the intervening time was too short to be an object."

Washington, irritated by political attacks, had told his Cabinet that he would not run for a second term. At sixty years of age, twelve years older than Jefferson, he had let it be known he did not care to continue to suffer the slings and arrows that were being directed at him. It was, they both knew, Jefferson's political friends who were shooting at him. The issue was not simply the Post Office. It was Jefferson's view that the secretary of the Treasury already had so much power that to give him more would add insult to injury. And the person most injured had been and would be Jefferson. He indeed had an ideological interest, more important to him than any personal interest.

The next day, having breakfasted together, Washington, "in an affectionate tone," told his fellow Virginian "that he felt much concerned at an expression which dropped from me yesterday, and marked my intention of retiring when he should." Since Jefferson rarely dropped any remark, it is likely that it was premeditated, and to some extent leverage against Hamilton, and Washington's support of Hamilton's policies. The mode is indirect narrative, a summary of Washington's words that intends to capture language and tone, as if we can hear Washington talking through Jefferson's mediation. "That he really felt himself growing old," the president continued, "his bodily health less firm, his memory, always bad, becoming worse, and perhaps the other faculties of his mind showing a decay to others of which he was insensible himself; that this apprehension particularly oppressed him; that he found, moreover, his activity lessened, business therefore more irksome, and tranquillity and retirement become an irresistible passion." It was an intimate and touching confession, perhaps partly meant to separate his condition from Jefferson's, for he hoped that his plans for retirement after one term would not cause Jefferson and others to resign, which would weaken the government and the confidence of the people. Ironically, years later, as Jefferson eagerly counted down the last days of his second term, he also felt that his energy had declined, his faculties weakened.

Jefferson responded: "No man had ever had less desire of entering into public offices than myself," a claim that might have seemed to Washington misplaced. It did not to Jefferson, who at length, in support of his claim to this distinction, reviewed his public career, his personal sacrifices, and his long-standing intention to resign as soon as possible and practical. Washington listened. Apparently without pause, Jefferson then spent the next hour in a full-throated attack on Hamilton's fiscal policies. The Treasury Department, Jefferson once again told the president, was a cancer at the heart of the government. "A system had there been contrived, for deluging the States with paper money instead of gold and silver, for withdrawing our citizens from the pursuits of commerce, manufactures, buildings, and other branches of useful industry, to occupy themselves and their capitals in a species of gambling, destructive of morality, and which had introduced itself into the government itself." Congressmen were being bribed through insider investments. And under the phrase *the general welfare,* the Constitution was being distorted to allow the creation of a corrupt financial system. The result would be, Jefferson implied, the end of republican government. It was not too late, he counseled Washington. The president could use his influence. "It is here stated," Jefferson wrote in his memoranda, "nearly as much at length as it really was; the expressions preserved where I could recollect them, and their substance always faithfully related." Jefferson had done most of the talking. But the conversation, its building blocks now set in place, was to go on for almost another year. Jefferson was not to wait until the end of Washington's first term to make public and dramatic his disagreement with the administration's policies.

Restless and worried, Washington called on Jefferson on April 6, 1792. An apportionment bill had passed in Congress on a straight North-versus-South vote. If he signed it, the president feared, it might appear that he was taking sides with the South. "He here expressed his fear," Jefferson noted, "that there would, ere long, be a separation of the Union; that the public mind seemed dissatisfied and tending to this." On May 23, Jefferson wrote to Washington another detailed indictment of Hamilton and his allies: they had created debts that the people would find intolerable; they had corrupted the legislature. He claimed, "That the ultimate object of all this is to prepare the way for a change, from the present republican form of government, to that of a monarchy, of which the English constitution is to be the model. That this was contemplated in the Convention, is no secret, because its partisans have made none of it. To effect it then was impracticable; but they are still eager after their object, and are predisposing everything for its ultimate attainment. So many of them have got into the legislature, that, aided by the corrupt squadron of paper dealers, who are at their devotion, they make a majority in both houses. The republican party, who wish to preserve the government in its present form, are fewer in number," though the next election, he thought, might chang that.

Still, sectional tensions were building. "Northern and Southern prejudices have come into conflict." The interests of the South were being "sacrificed" and those of the North "soothed . . . the owners of the debt are in the Southern and the holders of it in the Northern division." And Hamilton's policies, which penalized the South, were "a stepping stone to monarchy. . . . This is the event at which I tremble, and to prevent which I consider your continuance at the head of affairs as of the last importance. . . . Your being at the helm, will be more than an answer to every argument which can be used to alarm and lead the people in any quarter into violence or secession. North and South will hang together, if they have you to hang on."

Both were looking for an exit. But Washington, Jefferson emphasized, was the indispensable man. Jefferson continued:

I am perfectly aware of the oppression under which your present office lays your mind . . . and of the ardor with which you pant for retirement to domestic life. But there is sometimes an eminence of character on which society have such peculiar claims as to control the predilection of the individual for a particular walk of happiness, and restrain him to that alone arising from the present and future benedictions of mankind. This seems to be your condition, and the law imposed on you by providence in forming your character, and fashioning the events on which it was to operate: and it is to motives like these, and not to personal anxieties of mine or others who have no right to call on you for sacrifices, that I appeal from your former determination and urge a revisal of it, on the ground of change in the aspect of things . . . and I cannot but hope that you can resolve to add one or two more to the many years you have already sacrificed to the good of mankind.

As to himself, he assured Washington, he had no

selfish motive. . . . It is a thing of mere indifference to the public whether I retain or relinquish my purpose of closing my tour with the first periodical renovation of the government. I know my own measure too well to suppose that my services contribute anything to the public confidence, or the public utility. Multitudes can fill the office in which you have been pleased to place me, as much to their advantage and satisfaction. I, therefore, have no motive to consult but my own inclination, which is bent irresistibly on the tranquil enjoyment of my family, my farm, and my books. I should repose among them it is true, in far greater security, if I were to know that you remained at the watch, and I hope it will be so.

Jefferson's letter gave Washington additional heartache. That he could replace Jefferson from the "multitudes" of candidates equally qualified might have seemed to him an insult to the informed judgment he had exercised in having chosen Jefferson in the first place. There had arisen, the president observed, two political parties, in action if not in organization. Washington, of course, understood that Jefferson was now and would be even more so in retirement the acknowledged leader of the Republican faction. The division seemed to the president a potential deathblow to the new nation. Washington commented to Jefferson (in Jefferson's paraphrase), "That with respect to the existing causes of uneasiness, he thought there were suspicions against a particular party, which had been carried a great deal too far. There might be desires, but he did not believe there were designs to change the form of government into a monarchy. That there might be a few who wished it in the higher walks of life, particularly in the great cities. But that the main body of the people in the Eastern states were as steadily for republicanism as in the Southern."

To Washington, as he soon told Jefferson, what was at the core was "a difference of opinion" about policies, not fundamental values and aims, and "a difference of opinion must be tolerated . . . that in condemning the administration of the government, they condemned him." Washington's "they" was both literal and euphemistic. It was Jefferson who was doing the condemning, made more offensive and polarizing by his claim that the president was the unwitting dupe of those with whom, Jefferson implied, Washington in fact disagreed. "If these were measures pursued contrary to his sentiments," Washington sharply responded, "they must conceive him too careless to attend to them, or too stupid to understand them. That though, indeed, he had signed many acts which he did not approve in all their parts, yet he had never put his name to one which he did not think, on the whole, was eligible. That as to the bank, which had been an act of so much complaint, until there was some infallible criterion of reason, a difference of opinion must be tolerated." Jefferson repeated at length his views about debt, assumption, and the bank. Washington "said not a word on the corruption of the legislature, but took up the other point, defended the Assumption, and argued that it had not increased the debt, for that all of it was honest debt." He would, Washington concluded, "conquer his longing for retirement," since he was still needed. And, just as he would stay on, he hoped Jefferson would continue in office, at least for the remainder of the president's first term.

Washington left Philadelphia in July 1792 to summer at Mount Vernon. Jefferson went home to Monticello, to his daughters, to the catch-up duties of an absentee proprietor, to Sally Hemings, to his personal and public correspondence, and to his books. On his return to Philadelphia in October, he stopped first at Mount Vernon. "I had the following conversation with the President," he wrote later in the day.

> He opened it by expressing his regret at the resolution in which I appeared so fixed . . . of retiring from public affairs. He said that he should be extremely sorry that I should do it as long as he was in office, and that he could not see where he should find another character to fill my office. That as yet he was quite undecided whether to retire in March or not. His inclinations led him strongly to do it. . . . Still however if his aid was thought necessary to save the cause to which he had devoted his life principally he would make the sacrifice of a longer continuance. [He had been informed] that it was the universal desire he should continue, and the expectation that those who expressed a doubt of his continuance did it in the language of apprehension, and not of desire. But this, says he, is only from the North, it may be very different in the South. I thought this meant as an opening to me to say what was the sentiment in the South from which quarter I came. . . . That as to myself I had ever preferred the pursuits of private life to those of public, which had

nothing in them agreeable to me. . . . That I had constantly kept my
eye on my own home, and could no longer refrain from returning to
it [but] that he was the only man in the U.S. who possessed the confidence of the whole, that government was founded in opinion and
confidence, and that the longer he remained, the stronger would
become the habits of the people in submitting to the government
and in thinking it a thing to be maintained. That there was no other
person who would be thought anything more than the head of a
party. [Washington] then expressed his concern at the difference
which he found to subsist between the Sec. of the Treasury and
myself, of which he said he had not been aware. He knew indeed
that there was a marked difference in our political sentiments, but
he had never suspected it had gone so far in producing a personal
difference, and he wished he could be the Mediator to put an end
to it. . . . That as to the idea of transforming this government into a
monarchy he did not believe there were ten men in the U.S. whose
opinions were worth attention who entertained such a thought. I
told him there were many more than he imagined. . . .

Jefferson added "That the Secy. of the Treasury," who he said had
corrupted the legislature, "was one of these."

Washington was not convinced, and he had a different take on
government and human nature. He responded:

As to that interested spirit [in the legislature], it was what could not
be avoided in any government, unless we were to exclude particular
descriptions of men, such as the holders of the funds from all office.
I told him there was great difference between the little accidental
schemes of self-interest which would take place in every body of
men and influence their votes, and a regular system for forming
a corps of interested persons who should be steadily at the orders
of the Treasury. He touched on the merits of the funding system,

observed that there was a difference of opinion about it some thinking it very bad, others very good. That experience was the only criterion of right which he knew and this alone would decide which
opinion was right. That for himself he had seen our affairs desper-
ate and our credit lost, and that this was in a sudden and extraordinary degree raised to the highest pitch. I told him all that was
ever necessary to establish our credit, was an efficient government
and an honest one declaring it would sacredly pay our debts, laying taxes for this purpose and applying them to it. I avoided going
further into the subject. He finished by another exhortation to me
not to decide too positively on retirement, and here we were called
to breakfast.

In Philadelphia in the fall and winter of 1792–1793, there were meetings to attend and diplomatic business to take care of: Spain was
problematic, Great Britain continued to assert its North American
interests, Indian tribes needed pacification, the news from Paris was
not good, and Genêt's inappropriate activities caused domestic conflict. Jefferson twice told Washington that he had set a date for his
resignation. He would "be willing," he told the president, "to continue
somewhat longer, how long I could not say, perhaps till summer, perhaps autumn."

The president responded that

he had never mentioned to any mortal the design of retiring which
I had expressed to him, till yesterday having heard that I had given
up my house and that it was rented by another. [He] expressed his
satisfaction at my change of purpose [and] proceeded to express his
earnest wish that Hamilton and myself could coalesce in the measures of the government, and urged here the general reasons for it
which he had done to me on two former conversations. He said he

had proposed the same thing to Hamilton who expressed his readiness, and he thought our coalition would secure the general acquiescence of the public.—I told him my concurrence was of much less importance than he seemed to imagine: that I kept myself aloof from all cabal and correspondence on the subject of the government, and saw and spoke with as few as I could. That as to a coalition with Mr. Hamilton, if by that was meant that either was to sacrifice his general system to the other, it was impossible. . . . My wish was to see both houses of Congress cleansed of all persons interested in the bank or public stocks. . . . I subscribed to the principle that the will of the majority honestly expressed should give law. [There were] great discontents to the South . . . they were grounded on seeing that their judgments and interests were sacrificed to those of the Eastern states on every occasion, and their belief that it was the effect of a corrupt squadron of voters in Congress at the command of the Treasury. . . . On this subject he made no reply. . . . He expressed the extreme wretchedness of his existence while in office, and went lengthily into the late attacks on him.

In late May 1793, Washington discovered that Jefferson had hired Philip Freneau, a classmate and friend of Madison's, as a clerk in the State Department. Freneau was the editor of a virulent anti-administration newspaper, the *National Gazette*. Ostensibly employed as a translator, he knew no foreign language other than French. The president was not happy. In effect, Madison and Jefferson were using taxpayer money to subsidize the *National Gazette*'s opposition to the pro-Federalist *Gazette of the United States*, the main purpose being to attack Washington. When Jefferson arrived to discuss Genêt, the angry president was waiting with a copy of the *National Gazette* in hand. "I hired him exclusively as a translator," Jefferson explained. "But as to any other direction or indication of my wish how his press should be conducted, what sort of intelligence he should give, what essays encourage, I can protest in the presence of heaven, that I never did by myself, or any other, directly or indirectly, say a syllable, nor attempt any kind of influence." Of course, Jefferson knew that anti-Federalism was the very reason for the existence of the *National Gazette*.

Washington was furious. Jefferson noticed that "he had underscored the words our republic" in the issue of the *Gazette* in his hand.

He said that certainly ours was a republican government . . . that if anybody wanted to change its form into a monarchy he was sure it was only a few individuals, and that no man in the US. would set his face against it more than himself: but that this was not what he was afraid of: his fears were from another quarter, that there was more danger of anarchy being introduced. . . . He said he despised all their attacks on him personally, but that there never had been an act of the government, not meaning in the Executive line only, but in any line which that paper had not abused. . . . He was evidently sore and warm, and I took his intention to be that I should interpose in some way with Freneau, perhaps withdraw his appointment of translating clerk to my office, but I will not do it: his paper has saved our constitution which was galloping fast into monarchy, and has been checked by no one means so powerfully as by that paper . . . and the President, not sensible of the designs of the party, has not with his usual good sense . . . looked on the efforts and effects of this free press.

The president strongly disagreed with this judgment. Jefferson soon concluded that Washington "had not confidence enough in the virtue and good sense of mankind to confide in a government" run exclusively by the people. He submitted another resignation letter at the end of July. In early August, the president exploded at a Cabinet meeting. Jefferson afterward wrote out a paraphrase, adding his own comments and judgments. Secretary of War Knox,

> in a foolish incoherent sort of a speech introduced the Pasquinade lately printed, called the funeral of George W—n . . . where the President was placed on a Guillotine. The President was much inflamed, got into one of those passions when he cannot command himself. . . . Defied any man on earth to produce one single act of his since he had been in the government which was not done on the purest motives. . . . That he had rather be on his farm than to be made emperor of the world and yet that they were charging him with wanting to be a king. That that rascal Freneau sent him 3 of his papers every day [it was a biweekly], as if he thought he would become the distributor of his papers, that he could see in this nothing but an impudent design to insult him. He ended in this high tone. There was a pause.

A few days later the president called "on me at my house in the country." He had in hand Jefferson's latest resignation letter.

> He again expressed his repentance at not having resigned himself, and how much it was increased by seeing that he was to be deserted by those on whose aid he had counted: that he did not know where he should look to find characters to fill up the offices, that mere talents did not suffice for the department of state, but it required a person conversant in foreign affairs . . . that without this the best talents would be awkward and at a loss. [Hamilton had also] written to him, informing him that private as well as public reasons had brought him to the determination to retire, and that he should do it towards the close of the next session. He said he had often before intimated dispositions to resign, but never as decisively before . . . that our going out at times so different increased his difficulty, for

if he had both places to fill at one he might consult both the particular talents and geographical situation of our successors. He expressed great apprehensions at the fermentation which seemed to be working in the minds of the public . . . if I would only stay to the end of that it would relieve him considerably.

Jefferson, also filled with resentments, provided his explanatory self-justification, claiming that he knew nothing about the views of the Republican Party while at the same time, as if unaware of or indifferent to the inconsistency, assuring Washington that the Republican Party supported the current structure of the government. He existed, he believed, almost totally among enemies. He too was being maligned.

My excessive repugnance to public life, the particular uneasiness of my situation in this place where the laws of society oblige me to move always exactly in the circle which I know to bear me peculiar hatred, that is to say the wealthy Aristocrats, the Merchants connected closely with England, the new created paper fortunes that thus surrounded, my words were caught, multiplied, misconstrued, and even fabricated and spread abroad to my injury, that he saw also that there was such an opposition of views between myself and another part of the administration as to render it peculiarly unpleasing, and to destroy the necessary harmony. Without knowing the views of what is called the Republican party here, or having any communication with them, I could undertake to assure him from my intimacy with that party in the late Congress, that there was not a view in the Republican party as spread over the US. which went to the frame of the government.

Jefferson said this even though it was exactly the "frame of the government" that Washington's and Hamilton's implementation of the Constitution had created that Jefferson objected to.

The conciliatory and realistic president responded that

he believed the views of the Republican party were perfectly pure, but when men put a machine into motion it is impossible for them to stop it exactly where they would chuse or to say where it will stop. That the constitution we have is an excellent one if we can keep it where it is, that it was indeed supposed there was a party disposed to change it into a monarchical form, but that he could conscientiously declare there was not a man in the US. who would set his face more decidedly against it than himself.—Here I interrupted him by saying "no rational man in the US. suspects you of any other disposition, but there does not pass a week in which [the monarchical party proclaims that] we must knock [our government] down and set up something of more energy."—He said if that was the case he thought it a proof of their insanity, for that the republican spirit of the Union was so manifest and so solid that it was astonishing how anyone could expect to move them. He returned to the difficulty of naming my successor. . . . I told him that I had set my private affairs in motion . . . and that they had suffered immensely from my not going home; that I had now calculated them to my return in the fall, and to fail in going then would be the loss of another year, and prejudicial beyond measure.

Washington proposed that Jefferson might take temporary leave and then return.

I told him I did not think the public business would admit of it, that there was never a day now in which the absence of the Secretary of State would not be inconvenient to the public. And he concluded by desiring that I would take 2 or 3 days to consider whether I could not stay in till the end of another quarter, for that like a man going to the gallows he was willing to put it off as long as he could: but if

I persisted, he must then look about him and make up his mind to do the best he could: and so he took leave.

This ended Jefferson's "conversations with Washington." After two years and nine months as secretary of state, Jefferson left office on the last day of 1793. He had domestic and financial matters to attend to. "I have at length been able to fix that to the beginning of the new year," he wrote in late November. "I am then to be liberated from the hated occupations of politics, and to sink into the bosom of my family, my farm and my books. I have my house to build, my fields to farm, and to watch for the happiness of those who labor for mine." The president thought him disloyal and insufficiently patriotic. Licking his wounds, in January 1794, Jefferson went home to Monticello. He preferred the country to the city. He valued the company of his family and local friends. And most important, he would not and felt he could not give tacit support to an administration whose policies and whose view of America's future he opposed.

At Monticello, he extolled the advantages of a private life, expressing his disinclination ever to return to the public arena. His fellow Republicans would not accept that decision. Regardless of what he said and wrote, he would be conscripted as their leader, if conscription were necessary. It was not. To Washington, Jefferson's resignation seemed a desertion of duty, a premature retirement, the more galling because the reluctant president himself felt a patriotic obligation to stay on for another term. Moreover, he would have known that the attacks on his administration by Jefferson's surrogates through the rest of the 1790s had Jefferson's consent, though Jefferson himself would never publicly criticize the immensely popular president.

In January 1797, a portion of a letter written in April 1796 from Jefferson to his friend Philip Mazzei, now in Europe, became public in Paris in a French version. It was translated back from French into English in May 1797 and published in the United States. It contained a harsh judgment on Washington, whom Jefferson believed to have been a great leader who had fallen into error and iniquity. A quotation from it was to become a staple in anti-Jefferson allusions and diatribes in the election of 1800. Jefferson wrote,

> Against us are the Executive, the Judiciary, two out of three branches of the legislature, all of the officers of the government, all who want to be officers, all timid men who prefer the calm of despotism to the boisterous sea of liberty, British merchants and Americans trading on British capitals, speculators and holders in the banks and public funds a contrivance invented for the purposes of corruption and for assimilating us in all things, to the rotten as well as the sound parts of the British model. It would give you a fever were I to name to you the apostates who have gone over to these heresies, men who were Samsons in the field and Solomons in the council, but who have had their heads shorn by the harlot England.

The reference to "Samsons in the field" could not have been taken as referring to anyone other than Washington; "Solomons in the council," to anyone but Adams. Jefferson and his friends defended it as criticism of Washington's judgment, not an attack on his character. To many, that seemed a difference without a distinction. Jefferson had provided his political opponents with a weapon to use against him, and the breadth of the accusation embodied both rhetorical habit, a touch of paranoia, and an expression of irreconcilable differences rather than overlapping considerations.

Through the lens of Jefferson's Anglophobia, Washington had become at worst a villain, at best the dupe of villains, rather than a leader with whom he had policy disagreements. Apparently Jefferson expected the letter to be kept private. If so, it was one of numbers of mistakes in judgment about such matters. His friend Mazzei hardly ever resisted indiscretion. Consequential letters, either in full or in part, were then, as now, often made public by self-interested parties. Washington and Jefferson had little contact after 1793, except for an exchange of letters in which Jefferson overzealously defended himself against the accusation, which Washington had not given credence to, that he was the source of a leak of privileged Cabinet documents. After the publication of the selection from Jefferson's letter to Mazzei, the silence from Mount Vernon spoke loudly. Washington died on September 14, 1799, a little over a year before Jefferson very narrowly defeated Adams for the presidency.

When Jefferson visited Washington's widow at Mount Vernon in January 1801, "she assured a party of gentlemen . . . that next to the loss of her husband" Jefferson's visit was the "most painful occurrence of her life." If Washington had been alive in 1800, it is likely he would have voted for Adams, and if he had expressed publicly a preference for Adams, it's likely that Jefferson would not have become president. Jefferson later called his narrow electoral victory "the Revolution of 1800," as if it were as important and momentous as 1776. Regardless, in the long run, the policies of Washington and Hamilton on the role of government and the economy sketched out and sketched in America's future. Of course, they, like Jefferson, would in the America of the twenty-first century find themselves strangers in a strange land— but Jefferson considerably more so.

CHAPTER TWELVE

The Chains of the Constitution

1794–1801

It is "without comparison the most beautiful water I ever saw," Jefferson wrote from Lake George, New York, in late May 1791. The letter was to his eldest daughter, Martha. He was a long way from Virginia. It was to be partly a holiday trip for health and exercise. Jefferson had been secretary of state for a full year. Madison was the leader of his party in the House of Representatives. They both, so to speak, worked for the president, and both found themselves in a political landscape in which they were not comfortable, increasingly in opposition to the policies of the leader they were pledged to serve. Washington had left for Mount Vernon. "I think to avail myself also of the present interval of quiet," Jefferson wrote to the president in the middle of May, "to get rid of a headache which is very troublesome by giving more exercise to the body and less to the mind." To his daughter Mary he wrote, "I shall set out tomorrow for New York, where Mr. Madison is waiting for me, to go up the North [Hudson] river, and return down Connecticut river and through Long-island. My progress of the North river will be limited by the time I allot for my whole journey, which is a month." He also had political interests in mind. Unobtrusively, with

as little publicity as possible, he would search out allies who identified
with his anti-administration republicanism.

In early May, it had been cold in Philadelphia. "We have still pretty
constant fires here," he wrote to Mary. But "dogwood, Red bud, and
Azalea were in blossom." Wherever he was, he kept a calendar of the
dates at which different plants blossomed, partly the preoccupation
of Jefferson the farmer, partly his obsession with factual records,
keeping track of what interested him, especially climate, temperature,
landscape, and natural phenomena. The records he kept were also a
form of self-writing for the scientist, planter, historian, and autobi-
ographer. To the extent that he had a compass or another measuring
instrument in hand, the starting point was always himself and Monticello. Whatever lines and notations he wanted to make, he always had
his pen available; he was an obsessive writer. At Lake George, when
he ran out of paper, he wrote "on the bark of Paper birch, supposed
to be the same used by the ancients to write on before the art of making paper was invented, and which being called the Papyrus, gave the
name of paper to the new invented substitute."

No instance was too minor not to be a teaching moment. "I write
to you merely to tell you that I am well, and to repeat what I have
so often before repeated that I love you dearly, am always thinking
of you . . . and place much of the happiness of my life in seeing you
improved in knowledge, learned in all the domestic arts, useful to
your friends and good to all." She should not allow anything "to ruffle
[her] temper or interrupt that good humor which it is so easy and
so important to render habitual, and be assured that your progress
in these things are objects of constant prayer" with your affectionate
father. He had since late adolescence attempted to practice what he
preached, an exercise in socialization and repression.

The letter he wrote to Mary before leaving Philadelphia and a letter to Martha from Lake Champlain capture Jefferson the writer at
his casually intent and nonpolitical best, the writer about affection

and landscape, family and nature. To Mary he sketched out the route that he and Madison were to take. Always the didact with young people, he asked her to "take a map and trace this route." It was not a request but an imperative, both writer and recipient aware that his word was her command, patriarchy being the natural order of things. "I am glad you are to learn to ride, but hope your horse is very gentle, and that you will never be venturesome. A lady should never ride a horse which she might not safely ride without a bridle. I long to be with you all. . . . Adieu my dear."

The two politicians went sailing and fishing. Lake George, Jefferson wrote, is

> formed by a contour of mountains into a basin 35 miles long, and from 2 to 4 miles broad, finely interspersed with islands, its waters limpid as crystal and the mountain sides covered with rich groves of Thuya [hemlock], silver fir, white pine, Aspen and paper birch down to the water edge, here and there precipices of rock to chequer the scene and save it from monotony. An abundance of speckled trout, salmon trout, bass and other fish . . . have added to our other amusements the sport of taking them. Lake Champlain, though much larger, is a far less pleasant water. It is muddy, turbulent, and yields little game. After penetrating into it about 25 miles we have been obliged by a head wind and high sea to return, having spent a day and a half in sailing on it.

"We were more pleased," he wrote to his son-in-law, "with the botanical objects which continually presented themselves. Those either unknown or rare in Virginia . . . an Azalea . . . with very large clusters of flowers, more thickly set on the branches, of a deeper red and high pink-fragrance. It is the richest shrub I have seen." And "we have met with a small red squirrel, of the colour of our fox squirrel with a black stripe on each side, weighing about six ounces generally . . . twenty odd were killed at the house we lodged in . . . without going ten steps from the door." He took pleasure in killing three of them, "which were crossing the lake" where it was three miles wide, "one of them just as he was getting ashore." Against the high winds that were "blowing, he must have made it five or six miles." Jefferson did not comment on the squirrel's endurance and desire to live.

He took Virginia with him wherever he went, the reference point to which no other place compared well. With an atypical lack of statistical precision or even common sense, he complained that summer in northern New York State and New England was not only too hot but "as sultry hot through the whole as could be found in Carolina or Georgia. . . . I suspect indeed that the heats of Northern climates may be more powerful than those of Southern ones in proportion as they are shorter." He had a superficial and irrational explanation for this absurdity: "Perhaps vegetation requires this." In addition, "there is as much fever and ague too and other bilious complaints on Lake Champlain as on the swamps of Carolina."

The underlying point was that, as much as he recognized the attractions of New York and New England and the beauty of Lake George, his Southern parochialism, a form of regional patriotism, allowed him to disregard experience and fact. "On the whole I find nothing anywhere else in point of climate which Virginia need envy to any part of the world." In the North, "they are locked up in ice and snow for six months. Spring and autumn, which make a paradise of our country, are rigorous winter with them, and a tropical summer breaks on them all at once. When we consider how much climate contributes to the happiness of our condition, by the fine sensations it excites, and the productions it is the parent of, we have reason to value highly the accident of birth in . . . Virginia."

In this self-serving fantasy, Jefferson indulged an emotional state beyond rationality or fact. A product of the age of sentiment as well as the Enlightenment, like his favorite novelist, Laurence Sterne, whose

Tristram Shandy he probably had with him as he traveled, Jefferson ascribed to climate an influence on personality and well-being that his own experience as a Virginian would have contradicted, if he had allowed it to. Apparently hot, long, humid Virginia summers were a fiction; winter floods, fast falling snow, spring mud on soft and shallow soil, cloudbursts and heavy rains, months of drought—all the unhappy accidents of Virginia weather disappeared for Jefferson in this moment of affirming his allegiance to and his love for his home. New England was, in the sense of difference and contrast, a foreign country, one that he readily misrepresented.

Jefferson and Madison traveled 920 miles in thirty-three days, an extraordinary pace given the conditions of travel in late-eighteenth-century America. There were multiple motivations for the trip. It was an attempt to be refreshed by an excursion. It was also, for Jefferson, an effort to gather data about the Hessian fly disease that had been devastating wheat crops throughout the country. The trip also had an historical dimension: visits to Revolutionary War sites, particularly Saratoga, "which cost so much blood to both parties," and Ticonderoga. The two men also had an interest in visiting manufacturing activities, one of which, a nail factory, he was to attempt to replicate at Monticello, and the sugar maple industry, which he hoped would be tried in Virginia. Toward the end of the excursion, he visited an Indian community on the south shore of Long Island and recorded some of the native language. Throughout, he took notes, some brief, some extensive, about what was seen and experienced. He kept a table of distances between sites and ratings of the inns at which they stopped, the kind of notes made by someone who expected to return or to offer advice to other travelers, both of which were unlikely. It was as if the act of recording such data affirmed his own existence. It may have been partly habit, but it was also an existential assertion.

Jefferson was also in search of political and ideological allies, of a better sense than he already had of the political lay of the land. He had a good sense of the relative strength of his Federalist colleagues and his Republican friends in the South and in the middle states but not in New York and New England. This Northern trip only made full enough sense, in a world without technical tools for sampling public opinion, if he also had in mind taking political soundings, in getting some basis on which to judge the relative strength of the faction of which he and Madison were the leaders. These travelers were the secretary of state and a leading member of the House of Representatives. Their names appeared regularly in newspapers. Though not traveling in an official capacity, they were figures whose public presence attracted the attention of those who agreed with their political principles.

In New York City, they met with Republican sympathizers and allies, including Aaron Burr, an increasingly influential political operative, and in Vermont they met with the governor, Thomas Chittenden, and his circle. They made a point of not seeking publicity, but when circumstances were favorable, they quietly had, beneath and around other activities, unobtrusive but still palpable political conversations. Even more quietly, they spoke to and sounded out working people of every sort. The Revolution was less than ten years in the past, its scars and the changes it had wrought a prominent part of the American landscape. It seemed to the two travelers that, revered as the Federalist president was, even in the North there was the potential for reaffirmation and implementation of their own Republican principles. It was, they believed, just a matter of time.

Having relieved himself of his public commitments, Jefferson sought to relax his pen and enjoy his life at Monticello. He was partly successful, at least between 1794 and 1796. He no longer had drafts and documents to compose, Cabinet meetings to attend, and conversations with a president with whom he had fundamental disagreements. There were no more private memoranda attempting to persuade Washington to see things his way. Jefferson had hardly hesitated leaving Philadelphia. There were only a few people to whom he had an inclination to say good-bye. He was in a hurry to be at home, to resume his private life as a farmer, father, grandfather, and neighbor. The letters he wrote, fewer now that there were no professional demands, included some tag-end mopping up of matters left behind for the new secretary of state and others.

Still, many of his private letters dealt with public affairs, especially the letters he exchanged with Madison and James Monroe. Although Jefferson expected never again to serve in public office, his mind nevertheless was often on public matters. No matter how frequently he extolled the pleasures of private life, his Republican friends assumed that he was not to be taken at his word. Certainly key members of the Washington administration and Federalists in general expected that he would be a political presence again. In the meantime, he expressed his views only with trustworthy and like-minded colleagues.

Late in 1793 there had been unhappy news from France. Lafayette, out of favor with the new government and "for whom my heart has been constantly bleeding," had been imprisoned. "The influence of the United States has been put into action, as far as it could be either with decency or effect," Jefferson explained. "But I fear that distance and difference of principle give little hold to Genl. Washington on the jailors of La Fayette." In Paris, one of his friends had been "among the victims of the times. Sad times indeed! and much-lamented victim!" He blamed the times, not the perpetrators, and he lectured William Short, still in Paris and horrified at the executions, that the Jacobins were true patriots and that even if innocent people had been guillotined, their blood was a necessary sacrifice. It was an extraordinary rationalization, even for such a gifted rationalizer.

In the struggle which was necessary, many guilty persons fell without the forms of trial, and with them some innocent. These I deplore as much as anybody, and shall deplore some of them to the day of my death. But I deplore them as I should have done had they fallen in battle. It was necessary to use the arm of the people, a machine not quite so blind as balls and bombs, but blind to a certain degree. A few of their cordial friends met at their hands the fate of enemies. But time and truth will rescue and embalm their memories, while their posterity will be enjoying that very liberty for which they would never have hesitated to offer up their lives. The liberty of the whole earth was depending on the issue of the contest, and was ever such a prize won with so little innocent blood?

Indeed, some of the murdered were to be mourned as soldiers, Jefferson explained, as if they had enlisted for the privilege of being executed and had fallen in battle fighting for a noble cause. It was a reversal of the usual definition of martyrs, though limited, in Jefferson's exculpation, only to the innocent few who were actually "cordial friends" of the people. Their deaths were simply a mistake made in the heat of battle. They would be "embalmed" for future veneration. The others, apparently, deserved to be murdered by the mob, which was "the arm of the people," even if "blind to a certain degree," whose revolution, Jefferson was certain, would result in the "liberty of the whole earth. . . . My own affections have been deeply wounded by some of the martyrs to this cause, but rather than it should have failed, I would have seen half the earth desolated. Were there but an Adam and an Eve left in every country, and left free, it would be better than as it now is."

He claimed that his "sentiments are really those of 99 in a hundred of our citizens. . . . The universal feasts and rejoicings" of the Jacobin Clubs in America, "which have lately been had on account of the successes of the French shewed the genuine effusions of their hearts." The word "universal" was ideology, not fact, and saying that almost everyone in the United States agreed with him implied that anyone who disagreed, as many did, was either not a citizen or at best was in a minority of one in a hundred. Jefferson's eloquent ideological generalizations, impersonal and pseudo-statistical, had the ruthless bluntness of abstraction, the more comfortable the farther the sacrifices were from his own family and home.

There was also startling personal news. The fact that Maria Cosway had chosen the Church over her art and marriage shocked him, as if she had also rejected him. He wrote to one of Cosway's close friends, the beautiful Angelica Schuyler Church, the sister of Hamilton's wife, Elizabeth Schuyler Hamilton. Jefferson had had a friendship with Mrs. Church in Paris and continued an epistolary flirtation with her thereafter. "Madame Cosway in a convent! I knew that to much goodness of heart, she joined enthusiasm and religion," he began, "but I thought that very enthusiasm would have prevented her from shutting up her adoration of the god of the Universe within the walls of a cloister; that she would rather have sought the mountain-top." He meant his own peak, an allusion to and a repetition of the fantasy he had expressed in 1786 that she would join him at Monticello or at least visit him in Virginia. "I have one daughter married to a man of science, sense, virtue, and competence . . . in whom indeed I have nothing more to wish. They live with me. If the other shall be as fortunate in due process of time, I shall imagine myself as blessed as the most blessed of the patriarchs. Nothing could then withdraw my thoughts a moment from home, but the recollection of my friends abroad."

This was only partly and intermittently true. His recollections of his friends abroad never motivated him to travel to Europe again. What would be the purpose anyway, since the pre-Revolution Paris he had lived in had been forever radically changed? His description of his son-in-law had little basis in fact, as he might have suspected but was to learn definitively over the years. That his eldest daughter and her husband were living at Monticello made him a patriarch but also contributed to his financial responsibilities. Fortunately, his daughter Maria, whose futurity he prayed for, was to have better luck with a husband but not with longevity. His patriarchy, he wrote, equally resided in "the happiness of those who labor for me." That included his Hemings relatives. It also included the slaves who worked his fields and were the basis of every domestic and business activity at Monticello and his other plantations. He must have been aware, though without analysis or self-criticism, that his ability to make them happy was narrowly limited by the structure within which they all lived.

From January 1794 till March 1797, Jefferson was in voluntary exile from government. He had given up the law, which he had no desire to practice again. It was easy to turn down requests for legal advice. "A twenty years desuetude in matters of law, has produced a rust which will never be attempted to be rubbed off again," he wrote. "I rarely therefore permit myself to give opinions on the subject even in conversation." He no longer had a government salary. His income came from the sale of wheat and tobacco, his crops subject to the vagaries of weather and disease. Much of his daily satisfaction came from focusing on his crops, his soil, his gardens, his flowers, his botanical experiments, his sense of himself as a scientific and beneficent farmer who made enlightened use of his slave labor force and his resources. He got cash by hiring out some of his slaves. He satisfied two of his worried creditors by promissory transfers of ownership of some slaves in the event he defaulted. In one case, he mortgaged 150 of his slaves to a British creditor in order to obtain a loan with which to pay his debt to that same creditor, a sale that was not a sale as long as he could make the mortgage payments. None of this provided sufficient money to keep him from requesting postponements of repayments he had agreed to.

All Jefferson's creditors were in the British Isles, which dovetailed with the subject that his self-exile did not make any the less important to him: the "Monocrats & Papermen in Congress"; the influence of Hamilton on President Washington; British control of which countries the United States could trade with; the unfulfilled provisions of the 1783 peace treaty; the struggle between Anglophiles and Francophiles to determine American foreign policy, inseparable from domestic issues and conflicts; and the effort to find some leverage to use against Great Britain. An embargo, Jefferson thought and would always think, was potentially the most effective tool short of war. Actual war, he conceded, was an impractical alternative. It would cost too much; it probably could not be won. Consequently, national pride and military reality could not be reconciled. Monroe wrote to Jefferson that it seemed cowardice and degradation not to fight but that war would result in "the ruin of our commerce. . . . The prospect is most wretched and gloomy."

In spring 1794, Jefferson replied to Madison, his eyes and ears in Philadelphia, that "the rumor of a declaration of war has given an opportunity of seeing that the people here, though attentive to the loss of value of their produce, in such an event, yet find in it a gratification of some other passions, and particularly of their ancient hatred to Great Britain. Still I hope it will not come to that. . . . I have never seen a Philadelphia paper since I left it, till those you enclosed me; and I feel myself so thoroughly weaned from the interest I took in the proceedings there, while there, that I have never had a wish to see one, and believe that I never shall take another newspaper of any sort. I find my mind totally absorbed in my rural occupations." Though he probably thought that claim truthful as he wrote it, he soon subscribed to the anti-administration *Philadelphia Aurora*. He did his best to let "rural occupations" preoccupy him. Still, the national situation and his total estrangement from the Washington administration dominated his letters to Madison, and his relationship with the president further deteriorated in June 1796. The *Aurora* printed an anti-administration article to demonstrate that the president had all along been hostile to France.

In April 1793, prior to the publication of the administration's Proclamation of Neutrality, Washington had solicited the views of his Cabinet members in a series of nineteen questions. Jefferson had strongly argued against the proclamation. The president decided that the best interests of the country required neutrality. Honoring the alliance with France would risk war with Great Britain. Eager to damage Washington, in June 1796 the *Aurora* published the questions as evidence that the president had always been virulently anti-French. The intent of the attack was to rally anti-administration forces and discourage Washington from becoming a candidate for a third term. The identity of the man who had provided the *Aurora* with the spring 1793 Cabinet memos was of concern to all parties, especially Jefferson. He knew that the Federalists would assume it had been he who had broken Cabinet confidentiality. Jefferson may also have had in mind how the charge might affect the upcoming election. His supporters expected him to be a candidate for the presidency. The hope was that Washington would not make public his own preference unless provoked, but this might be provocation enough. Also, Jefferson felt, the charge compromised his honor. He immediately wrote what turned out to be his last substantive letter to Washington. It is a masterpiece of epistolary dexterity, eloquence, ambivalence, and evasion, an exculpatory letter to counter a charge that the president himself had not made.

In April 1791, Jefferson had assured the editor of the *Aurora*, Benjamin Franklin Bache, that despite his position as secretary of state he would continue to be a friend of the editor "from a wish to serve him, and from a desire of seeing a purely Republican vehicle of news established between the seat of government and all its parts." The *Aurora* had the approval and support of every opponent of the administration. Virulent personal attacks against the president, some viciously obscene, appeared regularly in its pages. Neither Madison nor Jefferson ever said or did anything to disavow their political alliance with its editor.

Jefferson, however, did not want Washington to believe that he had done something as dishonorable as to have betrayed the principle of Cabinet confidentiality. He was astounded, he wrote to Washington, or at least at a loss to explain how a confidential Cabinet document had gotten into the hands of the *Aurora*. He was not the guilty party, nor was Madison, the only person to whom he might have shown the list of questions. Jefferson's strained phrasing was noticeably self-exculpatory. "I cannot be satisfied as to my own part till I relieve my mind by declaring, and I attest everything sacred and honorable to the declaration, that it has got there neither through me nor the paper confided to me. This has never been from under my own lock and key, or out of my own hands. No mortal ever knew from me that these questions had been proposed. . . . I do not remember indeed that I communicated it even to [Madison]. . . . I may have read it to him . . . nor was a word ever copied or taken down from it, by anybody. . . . From myself then or my paper this publication has never been derived." Though Jefferson was in fact not the source of the leak, his interests were served by its publication as well as by his disclaimer. It was important that he make his innocence definitively clear to Washington. The language and length of the exculpation might have been read as a protest too much. That, though, did not make him the perpetrator.

Still, the letter evaded an important secondary issue, which Washington would have read between the lines. The publication of the Cabinet memo served one of Jefferson's political priorities. He did not want Washington to run for a third term. And whoever ran against Washington's preferred successor would be making the same arguments as the *Aurora* did. Consequently, it was not enough to deny his complicity. "I have formerly mentioned to you," he wrote to the president, "that, from a very early period of my life, I had laid it down as a rule of conduct never to write a word for the public papers. From this I have never departed in a single instance. . . ." An "intriguer . . . has thought it worth his while to try to sow tares between you and me, by representing me as still engaged in the bustle of politics, and in turbulence and intrigue against the government." That person had to have been the source. "I never believed for a moment," he continued, that this accusation "could make any impression on you, or that your knowledge of me would not overweigh the slander of an intriguer, dirtily employed in sifting the conversations of my table, where alone he could hear of me, and seeking to atone for his sins against you by sins against another who had never done him any other injury than that of declining his confidences. Political conversation I really dislike, and therefore avoid where I can. . . . But when urged by others, I have never conceived that having been in public life requires me to bely my sentiments, nor even to conceal them. When I am led by conversation to express them, I do it with the same independence here which I have practiced everywhere, and which is inseparable from my nature. Enough of this miserable tergiversator, who ought indeed either to have been of more truth or less trusted by his country."

After over a thousand words of disclaimer, Jefferson now changed the subject, as if he had been soiled by his own lengthy self-defense. Now "I put away this disgusting dish of old fragments, and talk to you," farmer to farmer, "of my peas and clover."

Washington's response gracefully refashioned Jefferson's awkward letter. Your "assurances," he wrote, had been unnecessary. The word "assurances" politely disengages the substance from the extent and language of Jefferson's denial. "The assurances you have given," Washington wrote, would have exculpated you entirely from any suspicions. "But the truth is, I harbored none. I am at no loss to conjecture from what source they flowed; through what channel they were conveyed; and for what purpose they, and similar publications, appear."

The original source had been, Washington believed, the thirty-three-year-old congressman William Branch Giles, soon to become a long-serving member of the Senate and then governor of Virginia. A close associate of Madison and an enthusiastic Jefferson supporter, Giles also hoped that Washington would not run for a third term. Washington would have assumed that the friend of my enemy could not be my friend. That, though, did not necessarily make Jefferson an active agent in the attacks on the president. Those who attacked the administration, Washington lamented, had been taking "every opportunity to weaken the confidence of the People—and by having the whole game in their hands they have scrupled not to publish things that do not, as well as those which do exist; and to mutilate the latter, so as to make them subserve the purposes which they have in view."

Both knew that Jefferson was the beneficiary of the leak. Since "you have mentioned the subject yourself," the president continued, "it would not be frank, candid, or friendly to conceal, that your conduct has been represented as derogating from that opinion I had conceived you entertained of me. That to your particular friends and connections, you have described, and they have announced me, as a person under a dangerous influence; and that, if I would listen more to some other opinions all would be well." Still, the president continued, his "answer invariably" had been "that I had never discovered anything in the conduct of Mr. Jefferson to raise suspicions, in my mind, of his insincerity; that if he would retrace my public conduct while he was in the Administration, abundant proofs would occur to him, that truth and right decisions, were the sole objects of my pursuit; that there were as many instances within his own knowledge of my having decided against, as in favor of the opinions of the person [Hamilton] evidently alluded to; and moreover, that I was no believer in the infallibility of the politics, or measures of any man living."

To Washington, Jefferson was no more infallible than Hamilton. And both were now party men. Jefferson had maintained that in the

Aurora affair he was, by implication, the injured party. Washington was on sounder ground. He explained himself:

> I was no party man myself, and the first wish of my heart was, if parties did exist, to reconcile them. To this I may add, and very truly, that, until within the last year or two, I had no conception that Parties would, or even could go, the length I have been witness to; nor did I believe until lately, that it was within the bounds of probability—hardly within that of possibility, that while I was using my utmost exertions to establish a national character of our own, independent, as far as our obligations, and justice would permit, of every nation of the earth; and wished, by steering a steady course, to preserve this Country from the horrors of a desolating war, that I should be accused of being the enemy of one Nation, and subject to the influence of another . . . and that too in such exaggerated, and indecent terms as could scarcely be applied to a Nero; a notorious defaulter; or even to a common pickpocket. But enough of this; I have already gone farther in the expression of my feelings than I intended.

Washington turned to his version of "peas and clover," farmer to farmer. Except for a brief note, which accompanied documents Jefferson requested, this was the end of their relationship.

Between early 1794 and March 1801, Jefferson wrote comparatively little. He wrote fewer letters than was his usual pattern and nothing at all for the public that could be identified as having been written by him. He attended to the business that required letters, notes, and accounts of a nonpublic nature even when they were about public affairs, including his correspondence with Washington and his exchanges with Madison and Monroe. The latter two kept him informed about

Philadelphia and Richmond politics. They had much to say privately about the divisive national traumas: the Jay Treaty in 1795–1796; the election of 1796, which made Jefferson vice-president; the Adams administration and the quasi-war with France; the XYZ affair; the Alien and Sedition Acts; the successful effort to avoid war with France; and the election of 1800 and its complications. In his First Inaugural Address, in March 1801, Jefferson the writer became once again, in a way he had not been since 1776, the creator of an important written contribution to the national narrative.

The Jay Treaty (officially the Treaty of Amity, Commerce, and Navigation, Between His Britannic Majesty and the United States of America) was signed in London in November 1794 and was to be effective for ten years. It had been in the works when Jefferson had resigned as secretary of state. He thought it a betrayal of the national interest and the values of the Revolution, which he began to refer to as the "spirit of '76." It did make progress in implementing the 1783 treaty that had ended the war: The British began a phased withdrawal from their northwestern forts on American territory. The border between the United States and Canada was made subject to arbitration. Some travel and trade restrictions were lifted. And the British agreed to end their anti-American collaboration with Indian tribes and to allow limited trading between the United States and the British West Indies. Britain also agreed to arbitrate claims for indemnification for the hundreds of American ships that had been seized by the Royal Navy to interdict American commerce with France. It still declined to recognize the American claim to "freedom of the seas" and continued to define "contraband" in a way that limited American trade with France. In return, the United States affirmed its obligation to repay American prewar debts to British citizens and to indemnify those pro-British Americans whose property had been confiscated during the war. The American claim to the return of or payment for the loss of slaves who had fled to British protection remained unresolved, to the disappointment, even anger, of many Southerners, including Jefferson. They wanted their property back or compensation.

It was not a treaty that most Americans cheered. Its ratification became a divisive partisan issue, but it served Washington's purpose: the avoidance of a new war between the United States and Great Britain. To Jefferson, it exemplified the pro-British, pro-monarchy policies of the Federalists, a pact with the devil in which the devil had gotten the best of it. "I am not satisfied we should not be better without treaties with any nation," he commented. "But I am satisfied we should be better without such as this. The public dissatisfaction too and dissension it is likely to produce, are serious evils. . . . I hope also that the recent insults of the English will at length awaken in our Executive that sense of public honor and spirit which they have not lost sight of in their proceedings with other nations, and will establish the eternal truth that acquiescence under insult is not the way to escape war." That the United States was incapable of successfully fighting a war against Great Britain provided no qualification to Jefferson's rhetoric. "I have never known the public pulse beat so full and in such universal unison on any Subject since the declaration of Independence." The Senate ratified without a vote to spare. Soon, to Jefferson's enthusiasm, "the House of Representatives . . . manifested its disapprobation. . . . We are yet to learn whether they will exercise their constitutional right of refusing the means which depend on them for carrying it into execution. . . ."

Madison and his Republican colleagues attempted to subvert the treaty by denying funds for its implementation. Otherwise, Madison argued, the people would have law made for them without the approval of the people's House. Jefferson agreed. The country is "looking to you," he exhorted Madison, "as their last hope to save them from the effects of the avarice and corruption of the first agent [Hamilton], the revolutionary machinations of others, and the incomprehensible acquiescence of the only honest man who has assented to it," by which he meant the president. A stretch of the Constitution, the argument did not prevail. The treaty became law in early 1796. One of Jefferson's Republican colleagues from South Carolina, Edward Rutledge, reminded him that "had you remained at your post," and not resigned, "you might have prevented" Jay being sent to London to negotiate a treaty. . . . But I am lamenting when it is too late, and will therefore quit the Subject for a private one." The possibility of Jefferson's future service to his colleagues and what was now a political party or at least a faction in opposition was implicit in the rebuke.

Between the lines of his July 9, 1796, letter to Jefferson, Washington acknowledged, without direct reference to the Jay Treaty, what Jefferson had never said publicly: that Jefferson was in tacit alliance with those who accused the president "of being the enemy of one Nation, and subject to the influence of another." He knew that his successful effort to steer "a steady course, to preserve this Country from the horrors of a desolating war" had made him the object of personal attacks that Jefferson did not disassociate himself from. To maintain his own honor, Jefferson granted Washington his, at the cost of depicting the president as the unwitting victim of politicians and policies that he was not smart enough to know were pernicious.

By early 1796, Jefferson's supporters assumed he would run for president if Washington declined. In March, Congress was still debating the Jay Treaty. Jefferson praised a speech by a young member of the House from western Pennsylvania, Albert Gallatin, that excoriated the Federalist support of the Jay Treaty. It was, Gallatin claimed, an exemplification of a thirst for unlimited powers for the federal government and a rejection of the defined-powers clause of the Constitution. "I wish," Jefferson commented, that the president's "honesty and his political errors may not furnish a second occasion to exclaim 'curse on his virtues, they've undone his country.'" That same month, from Philadelphia, a doctor, political activist, and signer of the Declaration, Benjamin Rush, tactfully urged Jefferson to become the leader of the country. "You drew up the Act of Independence of the United States. The wishes and prayers of thousands are, that you may live to realize that Act, by giving us the principles, and habits of an independent people." In September, Washington announced that he would not seek a third term.

Between the start of 1793 and early 1797, Jefferson stayed mostly at Monticello, putting his affairs in order as best he could, sustaining and improving his farmland, expanding the building itself with Palladian and neoclassical features, and attending to the day-in day-out enjoyments of domestic life from which, he frequently claimed, all social harmony emanated. Apparently he had Sally Hemings in his arms sometimes. Harriet Hemings [Jefferson] was born in 1795 and died in 1797. A son was born in 1798, and a daughter, also named Harriet, was conceived a short time before his election to the presidency, a naming that paralleled Thomas and Martha Jefferson naming a daughter Lucy after a dead previous Lucy. Secrecy and repression in regard to private matters were hallmarks of Jefferson's personality. How much the immediate and extended family at Monticello knew about the Sally Hemings–Jefferson relationship and what they knew is unknown. Common sense and experience suggest that some people knew and others suspected.

The Monticello house itself needed to be made more habitable and comfortable. Maintenance was costly. During 1795–1796, there was modest progress. In 1796, Jefferson had the second floor and roof taken down and then rebuilt. During the next twelve years, there would be little chance to do much more. Its otherwise hospitable owner lamented his inability to provide accommodations for visitors, hoping that additions and renovations would be finished soon, the roof fully covered, the new portico in place, and bedrooms refurbished, so that he could be a cosseting host once again, especially to his daughter Maria, who was to marry John Wayles Eppes in 1797. Jefferson was to have better luck with this second son-in-law, whose mother was also Sally Hemings's half sister and whose home at Eppington had been Maria's home during her father's first two years in Paris. A member of Congress during Jefferson's presidency, Eppes, after Maria's death, became the father of children to his grandmother's mixed-race granddaughter, also a Hemings and a slave, thus repeating the pattern of previous generations of the Wayles family.

"In truth if anything could ever induce me to sleep another night out of my own house," Jefferson wrote in August 1795 to Mann Page, "it would have been your friendly invitation." To bring in much-needed cash he started, with slave labor, to manufacture nails. His neglected farms needed regeneration. "I am become . . . a real farmer," he wrote to Maria Cosway in September, the month Harriet Hemings was born, "measuring fields, following my ploughs, helping the haymakers, and never knowing a day which has not done something for futurity. How much better this than to be shut up in the four walls of an office. . . . From such a life, good lord deliver me."

It was a self-indulgent fictional riff. In his public life, Jefferson had never been shut up in an office for much time, and he had always exercised on foot and horseback. At Monticello, his daily work, mostly outdoors, also had its moments at his desk, keeping accounts and writing letters. In one, to John Page's father, he eloquently combined personal sentiment and philosophical Stoicism, with two striking metaphors. He was happy to take "up a pen for an old friend . . . I feel the warmth of earlier years rekindle in my heart. While writing to you I am (in imagination) at Rosewell, 25 years old, in all the vigor of love and liberty. It is unpleasant that we should have been made, like our watches, to wear out by degrees, lose our teeth, and become unfit for our functions. A musical glass would have been a better type, sound, strong, and vibrating in all its harmony till some accident shivers it to atoms."

For Jefferson, 1795 seemed mostly a year of blessings. Perhaps he considered the birth of a daughter by Sally Hemings one of them.

Maybe not. Certainly the "blessings" were moments of self-satisfaction in which the land, the landscape, the weather, and his mind and body worked together in a routine that both tired and energized him. With pen in hand, he was at least as good at describing it as living it. He was the independent owner of the time and space he occupied, the happy master, like his idealized yeoman farmer, of the land he owned. On some days, he was blissfully happy in his enactment of his life as the exemplification of republican virtue. As a farmer, he was learning "to practice innocence towards all, hurt to none, help to as many as I am able," he wrote to Maria Cosway, as if, having already lived for fifty-two years, he had not practiced these virtues before. "But I am rambling again, my dear friend," he concluded, "and must recall myself to order." To him, "order" seems to have meant attention to serious practical and political matters, such as agricultural practice and theory, the Jay Treaty, and a potential existential crisis for the republic.

In fact, he was seldom without thoughts and theories about what he believed to be the connection between agriculture and republicanism. Agriculture, he believed, was the key to the financial and moral prosperity of the country, but he was slow and loathe to recognize that commerce had an increasingly substantial part to play in an economy in which capital, shipping, insurance, trade, and credit systems were indispensable. That part of the economy was mainly situated in the North. That was not Jefferson's "country," and his vision as well as his analyses of what was best for the country had their origin in parochial experiences and loyalties. Agriculture needed commerce, he thought, but as a handmaiden, not an equal.

In 1788, he had written from Paris that "in general it is impossible that manufactures should succeed in America from the high price of labor. This is occasioned by the great demand of labor for agriculture. A manufacturer going from Europe will turn to labor of other kinds if he find more to be got by it, and he finds some employments so profitable that he can soon lay up money enough to buy fifty acres of land, to the culture of which he is irresistibly tempted by the independence in which that places him, and the desire of having a wife and family around him." This was projection, not necessarily fact or persuasive argument. Furthermore, in Jefferson's language, "manufacture" sometimes included the process of growing and marketing staples, such as tobacco and wheat, partly overlapping but still different from the factories and artisanal workplaces that Hamilton thought of as manufactures. For Jefferson, the land was the pastoral canvas on which America's prosperity was being painted.

Jefferson predicted in 1798 that "if any manufacture" can succeed in the South "it will be that of cotton." He was prescient. Cotton was not yet king, and its success would not make Virginians prosperous, except those who left Virginia for rich cotton land to the south and southwest. His view that settlers from the East Coast and from Europe would prefer farmland to an urban residence was based on his premise that farming would be more profitable to laborers than factory or artisanal work or any work that required the networks available in cities. It was also, in Jefferson's view, morally superior work. It promoted personal independence. The landowning farmer could not be pressured by economic powers to be anything other than a good citizen, promoting the best interests of his community and the nation. "Our citizens are divided into two political sects," he wrote to an influential French political philosopher, Constantin François de Chassebœuf, Comte de Volney, "one which fears the people most, the other the government. You will readily judge in which of these the people themselves are. For my part I have no fear of a people, well-informed, easy in their circumstances, dispersed over their farms, and occupied on them. I say over their farms, because these constitute the body of our citizens. The inhabitants of towns are but zero in the scale."

Jefferson granted that manufacturing had its importance, but it was secondary to agriculture. He had traveled in the Northeast, but his were Southern eyes. He did not understand New York or Boston or even Philadelphia and Baltimore, and thus he misunderstood the power of commerce, urbanization, product manufacturing, national and international trade, and the carrying trade. Would he like America to have its own Paris? Not really. He was hardwired to assert that city life is essentially corrupt; rural life, essentially moral. He had enjoyed, even blossomed, in Paris; but it was a place to visit, not to be re-created in the United States. Any urban concentration in America would, he believed, erode the republican values he associated with the independent farmer. That was the view, near and far, from Monticello. His slaves were airbrushed out. So too were the great numbers of people who lived in one- or two-room wooden houses, humid, hot, and bug-ridden in the summer, cold and drafty in the winter, as well as all the farmers who struggled to put food on the table, who never traveled unless looking for a place in which they could make a better living, where there was richer soil and better weather, where the land had not been bought by speculators or wasn't controlled by plantation heirs. Invisible to Jefferson were all those who wore homespun clothes because they couldn't afford manufactured fabrics. He seemed not to notice that rural life had at least its proportional share of crime, including rape, incest, sexual abuse of children, other forms of domestic abuse, drunkenness, drunken violence, sober violence, revenge violence, and murder.

These aspects of country living were not what Jefferson chose to focus on. He looked toward the southwest and west, enough territory for yeoman farmers for at least the next few generations. It would be inhabited by the white male American laborer, allegedly exemplary in his virtues and productivity. "Never was a finer canvas to work on than our countrymen," he wrote to Adams. "All of them engaged in agriculture or the pursuits of honest industry, independent in their circumstances, enlightened as to their rights, and firm in their habits of order and obedience to the laws." Adams would have had reservations about such claims. Jefferson had recently written to his friend Mann Page that he did not believe "that fourteen out of fifteen men are rogues: I believe a great abatement from that proportion may be made in favor of general honesty." Human nature was essentially good. It was "rogues" like Hamilton and others in the Federalist leadership who would "always contrive to nestle themselves into the places of power and profit." Adams had a different view: history, past and present, and human experience demonstrated that human nature, at every social and economic level, combined both darkness and light, and the dark side was formidable.

In 1796 Jefferson allowed himself to be nominated for the presidency by the Republican faction in every state legislature. His acquiescence seems contradictory. Early that year, when Adams sent his friend a book he thought of mutual interest, Jefferson replied that he might not read it. "It is on politics, a subject I never loved, and now hate." Adams assumed that Jefferson would also be a candidate for the presidency in the election. Jefferson's response expressed one of the paradoxes of his life: his commitment to two seemingly incompatible attractions. On the one hand, he claimed he hated politics. He wrote to Horatio Gates that

> my private business can never call me elsewhere, and certainly politics will not, which I have ever hated both in theory and practice. I thought myself conscientiously called from those studies which were my delight by the political crisis of my country. . . . In storms like those all hands must be aloft. But calm is now restored, and I leave the bark with joy to those who love the sea. I am but a landsman, forced from my element by accident, regaining it with transport, and wishing to recollect nothing of what I have seen, but my friendships. Some of these are indeed very dear to my heart.

Nevertheless, his pen and heart overruled his head. The values of the Revolution, he believed, were under assault. The United States was being transformed into a centralized state, a heavily taxed, well-armed, commercial power in the British mode. What Washington and Hamilton had wrought needed to be undone. His inclination, though, was to encourage someone else to lead the counterattack. His candidate was his political soul mate, forty-four-year-old James Madison. "There is not another person in the US. who being placed at the helm of our affairs, my mind would be so completely at rest for the fortune of our political bark." Madison would be in effect a surrogate for Jefferson. Jefferson could stay home at Monticello.

Whatever decision he himself made, he could also say with sincerity "that the subject [of Madison] had not been presented to my mind by any vanity of my own." No, it "was pure and unmixed with anything respecting myself personally. For as to myself the subject had been thoroughly weighed and decided on, and my retirement from office had been meant from all office high or low, without exception. . . . The little spice of ambition, which I had in my younger days, has long since evaporated." Exactly when and in regard to what office he left unstated. But now he knew himself and his "fellow citizens too well to have ever thought of it." Still, the idea has been "forced upon me by continual insinuations in the public papers, while I was in office" as secretary of state. "There had indeed been suggestions in the public papers that I was looking towards a succession to the president's chair. . . . I never in my life exchanged a word with any person on the subject till I found my name brought forward generally in competition with that of Mr. Adams." He claimed the suggestions came only from enemies, and indeed most Federalists, starting in 1791, believed that someday they would face Jefferson in a competition for the presidency.

Jefferson knew that in 1796 the Republican faction wanted him, not Madison. Though he would not openly attest to his candidacy, as state legislatures met to choose electors, he did not request that his name be withdrawn. When urged to allow his name to stand as a candidate, Jefferson responded that "I have not the arrogance to say I would refuse the honorable office you mention to me." Unlike most Republicans, especially Madison, Jefferson had praise for the titular leader of the opposition, Vice-President Adams. A moderate Federalist, his colleague from 1776 and in their Paris days, Adams was also an Anglophobe, though a more realistic one than Jefferson. Adams also had reservations about some of Hamilton's fiscal policies. Unlike Jefferson, though, he favored a strong navy that could compete with Great Britain on the seas. With characteristic indirect coercion, Jefferson wrote to Adams, "I am glad to see that whatever grounds of apprehension may have appeared of a wish to govern us otherwise than on principles of reason and honesty, we are getting the better of them [the British]." He did not really believe that. "I am sure, from the honesty of your heart, you join me in detestation of the corruption of the English government, and that no man on earth is more incapable than yourself of seeing that copied among us, willingly." That was a hope, not a conviction. "I have been among those who have feared the design to introduce it here, and it has been a strong reason with me for wishing there was an ocean of fire between that island and us.—But away politics."

Adams and Jefferson knew early in 1796 that they were competing for the presidency. As was the custom, the campaign was fought by surrogates. The divisive issues were the Jay Treaty and Hamilton's fiscal policies. The campaign was a muted rehearsal of the campaign of 1800, when both sides descended from policy arguments to slanders and lies. Like Adams, Jefferson took no responsibility for his supporters' words. In matters of partisan politics, he absolved himself, and assumed that what people said in his name reflected entirely on those who had provoked them. His personal honor, he maintained, was sacrosanct and unimpeachable. "I know my own principles to be pure," he wrote in 1798, "and therefore am not ashamed of them. On the contrary I wish them known, and therefore willingly express them to everyone. They are the same I have acted on from the year 75 to this day, and are the same, I am sure, with those of the great body of the American people." Self-examination was limited to private silence. He prided himself on never responding to criticism. Response, he was convinced, would only trigger more attacks.

Any criticism pained him. "It has been so impossible to contradict all their lies," he was to write in the heat of the campaign of 1800, "that I have determined to contradict none; for while I should be engaged with one, they would publish twenty new ones. Thirty years of public life have enabled most of those who read newspapers to judge of me for themselves." There were massive lies on both sides. By late fall and early winter 1796, ballots were being counted, the electors chosen over a three-month period, mostly by state legislatures. Jefferson told his son-in-law that "it is not the less true however that I do sincerely wish to be the second on that vote rather than the first. The considerations which induce this preference are solid, whether viewed with relation to interest, happiness, or reputation. Ambition is long since dead in my mind."

In early December 1796, Madison wrote Jefferson that it is still "not possible yet to calculate with any degree of certainty whether you are to be left by the Electors to enjoy the repose to which you are so much attached, or are to be summoned to the arduous trust which depends on their allotment." Jefferson warily responded, "I know well that no man will ever bring out of that office the reputation which carries him into it. The honey moon would be as short in that case as in any other, and its moments of ecstasy would be ransomed by years of torment and hatred." If he must serve, he would rather be vice-president, he claimed. The Constitution, whose creators had not anticipated political parties, required that the candidate who got the second-most votes become vice-president, even if the president and vice-president had different allegiances. "It is both my duty and inclination therefore to relieve the embarrassment should it happen," he told Madison, "and in that case I pray you and authorize you fully to solicit on my behalf that Mr. Adams may be preferred." He instructed Madison to use his own judgment about telling Adams and others what he claimed he preferred. Adams "has always been my senior . . . and [if] the expression of the public [is] equal, this circumstance ought to give him the preference. When so many motives will be operating to induce some of the members to change their vote, the addition of my wish may have some effect to preponderate the scale." His preference, if that was indeed his wish, would have needed to have been expressed months earlier.

He also had a strategic concern. Foreign affairs "never wore so gloomy an aspect since the year 83," he continued. "Let those come to the helm who think they can steer clear of the difficulties. I have no confidence in myself for the undertaking." It was to his advantage to let Adams be responsible for a likely war either with France or Great Britain or both over their confiscation of American ships. "The second office of this government is honorable and easy. The first is but a splendid misery."

Madison declined to show Adams the letter. Though Jefferson emphatically granted that few would believe him, he did, at this point, insist that he sincerely wished "to be the second on that vote rather than the first." In the end, Adams got 71 electoral votes, Jefferson 69. Jefferson had allowed himself to be elected vice-president. "You must prepare yourself," Madison wrote to him, "to be summoned to the place Mr. Adams now fills." It was expected "that as you had made up your mind to obey the call of your country, you will let it decide on the particular place where your services are to be rendered . . . that as you submitted to the election knowing the contingency involved in it, you are bound to abide by the event . . . it seems essential that you should not refuse the station which is likely to be your lot." Another

Federalist, Thomas Pinckney, had received 59 votes. If three of Pinckney's or three of Adams's votes had gone to Jefferson, he would have been elected president in 1796.

Oddly and awkwardly, Jefferson was to be Adams's vice-president. He hoped that Adams would reign as a moderate, independent of the Hamilton circle and its policies, leaning neither toward Great Britain nor France. That he himself would be sitting in Philadelphia as the relatively powerless president of the Senate for about half of the next four years was not a happy prospect. "I become more and more disgusted with the jealousies, the hatred, and the rancorous and malignant passions of this scene, and lament my having ever again been drawn into public view," he soon wrote. "I have seen enough of political honors to know that they are but splendid torments. . . . The real difficulty is that being once delivered into the hands of others, whose feelings are friendly to the individual and warm to the public cause, how to withdraw from them without leaving a dissatisfaction in their mind and an impression of pusillanimity with the public." He could have been thinking of his situation in the Washington Cabinet. He could not allow himself now to withdraw from the vice-presidency. And it was not a prospect without a plan, or at least a hopeful likelihood. "There can be no doubt," a supporter wrote to him in the summer of 1797, that when Adams "relinquishes the high office which he now fills, that you will be his successor." In the next four years, the Republican press, the Republican constituency, Madison, and Jefferson himself were to do everything in their power to elect a Republican Congress and a Republican president in 1800. And no one doubted who the candidate would be.

In the next four years, the pendulum swung from one extreme to the other. Between March 1797, when Adams took office, and the election of 1800, events more than individuals controlled the electoral dynamics that were to make Jefferson president. The Federalists, though, did much to defeat themselves. And Jefferson's Republicans, in Congress and in the press, did everything they could to advance a change of regime. It was a rocky four years.

Three situations dominated: an undeclared war with France, the XYZ affair, and the passage of a series of laws known as the Alien and Sedition Acts. In their life-and-death jockeying for power and provisions, France and Great Britain seized American commercial vessels regardless of location or cargoes. For a time, France seemed the greater perpetrator. Outraged American public opinion, led by Federalists, especially its pro-Hamilton anti-French leadership, called for a declaration of war. Public opinion and Federalist detestation of the French Revolution beat the war drums. National honor and commerce needed to be asserted and defended. Adams hesitated, and a quasi-war, consisting mostly of embargoes, privateering, and piracy resulted. Adams twice sent peace missions to France. The first was stymied by French demands for bribes (called the XYZ affair) to initiate negotiations. American national honor was insulted. War fever swept the country. The Republican pro-French leadership feared the worst. Fortunately for Jefferson and Madison, Adams's determination to do everything possible to avoid war, earning him more Federalist enemies than Republican friends, worsened the domestic crisis. He sent another peace mission to join the one member of the first delegation who had stayed on in France, Elbridge Gerry of Massachusetts, a Federalist-turned-Republican. Adams's next mission was successful. France no more wanted war than Republicans and moderate Federalists like Adams.

Still, in 1798 and 1799, when war with France seemed likely, the Federalist-controlled Congress passed a series of laws called the Alien and Sedition Acts aimed against French nationals in the United States. The acts also lengthened the time it would take for immigrants to become naturalized citizens, an attempt to limit suffrage.

Worse, the acts allowed the executive to indict anti-Federalist editors who criticized the government. This grab bag of repressive laws of the sort that governments often enact in the name of national security were set to expire, unless renewed, in 1800. Adams signed them on the grounds that free speech had to be limited during a national crisis. They were also an exercise in political power by a Federalist leadership worried about the increasing Republican strength. In addition, the vitriolic Republican newspaper attacks on the Adams administration touched the raw nerves of a constituency that valued decorum and order. "Politics and party hatreds destroy the happiness of every being here," an unhappy Jefferson wrote to his daughter Martha. "They seem, like salamanders, to consider fire as their element."

The Federalist mind-set privileged stability, decorum, respect for authority, and government by those qualified by education, experience, and talent. To many Federalists, the country seemed on the verge of anarchy, the mob and the guillotine impending. On a Monday in May 1798, Jefferson wrote to Madison that a group of young men, strong anti-French partisans, wearing "the black (or English) cockade," had met with President Adams, apparently urging the president to take action against France. "The next day numbers of the people appeared with the tri-colored (or French) cockade: yesterday, being the fast day, the black cockade again appeared. On which the tricolor also shewed itself. A fray ensued, the light horse were called in, and the city was so filled with confusion from about 6 to 10 oclock last night that it was dangerous going out. . . . Environed here in scenes of constant torment, malice and obloquy," he had moments in which he felt that "no effort to render service can avail anything." It was "a dreary scene, where envy, hatred, malice, revenge, and all the worst passions of men are marshalled to make one another as miserable as possible."

The Alien and Sedition Acts were, to Jefferson, an assault on the "spirit of '76," which now became his catchphrase for the values by which he defined the Revolution: widening the franchise, liberty of speech, fiscal economy, hard money, a priority on agriculture, limited government, aggressive Western expansion, and a foreign policy that identified with France. To these goals he now added an interpretation of the Constitution that narrowly defined the powers of the national government, as if the "spirit of '76" now absorbed the Constitution of 1789. That spirit needed to be restored. The phrase suggested a return to an idealized past. It had, though, both a radical and a conservative glow. It was restorative, but it also promised significant change, its linchpin an increase in the self-esteem and patriotic commitment of many previously disenfranchised white male voters.

It was Jefferson's view of what the Revolution had existed to accomplish. It represented a nostalgic, simplified, and semifictional version of a Revolution that was an elite leadership-driven event, its popular support mostly a response to British restrictions, including London-imposed taxation, the prohibition of settlements west of the Appalachians, and the Quebec Act of 1774, which closed British ports to American trade in retaliation for the Boston Tea Party, gave the vote to Catholics, and mandated the quartering of British soldiers in colonial homes. About 40 percent of colonial Americans had wished to remain British Americans. About 40 percent had favored full independence. Many sat on the fence as long as they could, and the most salient problem the Continental Congress and the Revolutionary army faced was the resistance in Congress and in the colonies to raise money to pay for the rebellion, which also had class and economic implications, a revolution within a revolution, partly a civil war.

With his wide brush of criticism and contempt, Jefferson seems to have believed or at least was comfortable with implying that the Federalists rejected the principles of the Declaration of Independence. Any policies that Jefferson opposed were ipso facto not republican, not true to the spirit of '76, as if the issues of 1799—a national bank, national debt, relations with Britain and France, how to maintain peace during a war between the major powers of Europe, neutrality as a national policy, the cost of a standing army and navy, government support of infrastructure, appropriate levels of taxation, the Constitution as the governing document—could all be addressed simply by evoking the "spirit of '76."

In fall 1798, Jefferson and Madison devised a plan: anti–Alien and Sedition Acts resolutions to be submitted to the legislatures of Kentucky and Virginia. They would serve multiple purposes. They would be simultaneously legislative, legal, philosophical, and political documents, Jefferson's to be directed to the Kentucky legislature, Madison's to Virginia's, their explicit purpose to persuade these and other state legislatures to exercise their right to declare "null and void" the Alien and Sedition Acts because their enactment exceeded the power granted by the Constitution to the national government. The "spirit of '76" would be their political sound bite in preparation for the election of 1800. Their authorship anonymous but hardly a secret, these resolutions would, Jefferson hoped, become the template for similar resolutions to be passed by other state legislatures, asserting that each state had it in its power, inherent in the Constitution as a compact among sovereign states, to nullify any congressional legislation it believed unconstitutional. "Let the honest advocate of confidence read the Alien and Sedition acts," Jefferson wrote on a rhetorical high note, "and say if the constitution has not been wise in fixing limits to the government it created, and whether we should be wise in destroying those limits?" The present government had created an executive tyranny. "In questions of power then, let no more be heard of confidence in man, but bind him down from mischief by the chains of the constitution."

Jefferson's Kentucky Resolution is an explicit statement of the Republican Party's and Jefferson's view of constitutional philosophy and law. Its purpose was to affirm that the Constitution mandated restrictions on the national government, that the "necessary and proper clause" was to be understood to be bound tightly by the "chains of the Constitution." A well-argued, sometimes passionate brief against the Alien and Sedition Acts, it was also a political document, both propagandistic and philosophical, a contribution to the impending 1800 campaign for the presidency and the House and Senate, an argument about constitutional interpretation, and a campaign document. It drew on Jefferson's legislative experience and his expertise as a draftsman. The Jefferson who knew and had practiced the language of law also made his contribution. It is not an especially eloquent or dramatic document, though it has elements of both. In some of its phrasing and tone, the resolution has a distant resemblance to *A Summary View* and the Declaration of Independence, though tailored for a different context and different purposes. It also draws on Jefferson's literary skills to make a case against injustice and executive tyranny. In 1775 and 1776, it had been Parliament and George III who had been the perpetrators. Now it was the Adams administration and its collaborators. For Jefferson's America to be restored, they needed to be replaced.

The "chains of the Constitution," Jefferson argued, "bound the federal government to precisely, exactly, and no more than its enumerated powers." Legislation concerning crime, education, the suffrage, elections, property, slavery and other forms of human bondage, private life, and the common law were reserved to the states. The national government should be invisible except in foreign affairs, interstate commerce, national defense, and a postal service. In 1776, Jefferson had co-opted the language of master and slave to dramatize his view of the tyrannical relationship that British rulers had imposed on the American colonies. Restrictions on the liberties and natural rights of Virginians had impelled his revolutionary mentality. He had wanted to protect what he felt rightfully his by birthright. In 1798, he believed that Federalist monocrats and aristocrats were transforming the Constitution into an instrument of centralization, a threat equal to the tyranny of Parliament and king that the colonists had rebelled against. An interpretation of the Constitution that gave the national government powers other than those specifically enumerated had no lawful legitimacy. Limiting federal power and protecting the rights of the states would keep the people free.

In early 1799, Jefferson's mood lightened, and his energy and enthusiasm increased. On February 19, he wrote three long letters about what seemed to him a happy improvement in American-French relations. The French had been forthcoming with overtures and some acts that signaled that they too, like Adams, did not desire war. Jefferson welcomed the division between the pro-peace and anti-peace Federalists. He encouraged the creation of a new pro-Republican newspaper. He sniffed the wind and saw in the distance, particularly in Pennsylvania, New York, New Jersey, and New Hampshire, the popular tide rejecting war with France, rebelling against higher taxation, and opposing the creation of a large standing army and expensive navy. He envisioned the possibility of Republican majorities in the House and perhaps the Senate. In his behind-the-scenes way, with a surge of partisan energy, acting mostly through surrogates, Jefferson campaigned, encouraging friends and allies to write letters and newspaper articles to make the possibility of a Republican wave higher and stronger.

The heartfelt and engaging letter that he wrote on February 21, 1799, to Tadeusz Kościusko, the leader of the Polish struggle to establish a free republic, reveals Jefferson's political and emotional calculus at its most admirable. He had been corresponding irregularly with Kościusko for some years. The Polish patriot had made himself an American hero during the Revolutionary War. With Jefferson's financial assistance, Kościusko returned to Europe in 1798. He had made Jefferson executor of his American property, which Jefferson was attempting to liquidate for him. Jefferson concluded,

On politics, I must write sparingly, lest it should fall into the hands of persons who do not love either you or me. The wonderful irritation

produced in the minds of our citizens by the X.Y.Z. story has in a
great measure subsided. They begin to suspect and to see it coolly
and in its true light. . . . France is sincere in her wishes for reconciliation; and a recent proposition from that country . . . puts the matter out of doubt. What course the government will pursue I know
not. But if we are left in peace I have no doubt that the wonderful
turn in the public opinion now manifestly taking place and rapidly
increasing, will, in the course of this summer, become so universal,
and so weighty that friendship abroad and freedom at home, will be
firmly established by the influence and constitutional powers of the
people at large. If we are forced into a war, we must give up political
differences of opinion and unite as one man to defend our country.
But whether at the close of such a war, we should be as free as we
are now, god knows. In fine, if war takes place, republicanism has
everything to fear; if peace, be assured that your forebodings and my
alarms will prove vain, and that the spirit of our citizens now rising
as rapidly, as it was then running crazy, and rising with a strength
and majesty which shews the loveliness of freedom, will make this
government in practice, what it is in principle, a model for the protection of man in a state of freedom and order. May heaven have in
store for your country a restoration of these blessings, and you be
destined as the instrument it will use for that purpose. But if this
be forbidden by fate, I hope we shall be able to preserve here an asylum where your love of liberty and disinterested patriotism will be
forever protected and honored and where you will find in the hearts
of the American people a good portion of that esteem and affection
which glows in the bosom of the friend who writes this, and who
with sincere prayers for your health happiness and success and cordial salutations, bids you, for this time, adieu.

In June 1799, he responded at length to a letter from William
Green Munford, a young disciple. Munford's letter has not survived,

but Jefferson's response is frequently quoted. "I am among those who think well of the human character generally," he wrote, affirming his idealism and optimism with a claim so abstract and assertive that the lessons of history and of personal experience seem irrelevant. "I consider man as formed for society and endowed by nature with those dispositions which fit him for society. I believe also . . . that his mind is perfectible to a degree of which we cannot as yet form any conception." Fascinated by scientific inquiry and its possibilities, having in mind pioneer scientists like Benjamin Franklin and Joseph Priestley, Jefferson located the reach toward perfection in the acquisition of knowledge in the sciences, especially geometry, anatomy, chemistry, and medicine. "It is impossible for a man who takes a survey of what is already known, not to see what an immensity in every branch of science yet remains to be discovered, and that too of articles to which our faculties seem adequate."

He was hardly alone in exalting the potential for advances in science, though the nineteenth century was to begin to be fearful that, in the poet Tennyson's phrase, "Knowledge comes, but wisdom lingers." Jefferson continued, "I join you therefore, in branding as cowardly the idea that the human mind is incapable of further advances. This is precisely the doctrine which the present despots of the earth are inculcating, and their friends here re-echoing; and applying especially to religion and politics; 'that it is not probable that anything better will be discovered than what was known to our fathers.' . . . But thank heaven the American mind is already too much opened, to listen to these impostures; and while the art of printing is left to us science can never be retrograde; what is once acquired of real knowledge can never be lost."

For Jefferson, the difference between science on the one hand and religion and politics on the other was a difference without a distinction of consequence. The "present despots of the earth" included his political opponents, unless he had in mind actual despots, rulers like

Napoléon, Frederick, or Catherine the Great, though even European absolute rulers had for centuries selectively sponsored scientific research. Great Britain was experiencing a remarkable expansion of knowledge during George III's realm. Jefferson's mind and pen turned to the immediate political context, the Alien and Sedition Acts and the imminent election. "To preserve the freedom of the human mind then and freedom of the press, every spirit should be ready to devote itself to martyrdom; for as long as we may think as we will, and speak as we think, the condition of man will proceed in improvement." It is Federalism, he implies, the "reign of witches," his phrase for the Washington and Adams administrations, which has suppressed scientific inquiry. Such repression was, in Jefferson's view, inseparable from oppression and censorship in religion and politics. The Federalists, Jefferson claimed, rejected rational and scientific progress; they believed "that it is not probable that anything better will be discovered than what was known to our fathers."

That assertion arose from Jefferson's simplification of Federalist discourse. In spring 1798, Adams had responded to a "patriotic address" from the "Young Men of Philadelphia." The "Young Men" proclaimed their commitment "to preserve the honor and independence of their Country." France had received America's "propositions of peace with determined hostility and contempt, have wounded our national Independence by insulting its Representatives and calumniated the honor and virtue of its Citizens by insinuating that we were a divided insubordinate nation."

Adams responded, "I should, with the tenderest affection recommend to your serious and constant consideration that science and morals are the great pillars on which this country has been raised to its present population, opulence, and prosperity, and that these alone can advance, support, and preserve it. Without wishing to damp the ardor of curiosity, or influence the freedom of inquiry, I will hazard a prediction, that, after the most industrious and impartial researches, the longest liver of you all will find no principles, institutions, or systems of education more fit, in general, to be transmitted to your posterity, than those you have received from your ancestors." He and Jefferson were in fact themselves "ancestors." What was at issue between Jefferson and Adams was not a difference about science, freedom of inquiry, and morals. They differed about what government structure would best advance these values.

Both Jefferson and Adams were students of history and human nature. Adams's glasses were more darkly tinted than Jefferson's. Progress was hardly guaranteed, and he had a different sense of the desirable balance between freedom and restraint in public life. That Federalists like Adams would lift "parricide hands against freedom and science" was Jeffersonian campaign rhetoric at its most hysterical. In signing the Alien and Sedition Acts, Adams believed he was protecting the country from foreign enemies and internal sedition, as other American presidents have done during wartime, just as Jefferson argued in 1807–1809 that the restrictions his Embargo Act imposed on personal and commercial freedom were justified by semi-wartime conditions. Both Adams's Alien and Sedition Acts and Jefferson's embargo policies were counterproductive, the offspring of their political and ideological contexts; both skirted constitutional correctness; and both were quickly rejected by national sentiment. Jefferson's letter to William Munford expresses much about the sciences, freedom of thought, and Enlightenment values that most Federalists would have considered givens. In moments of calm rationality, Jefferson would have agreed with Adams that in morals and education the wisdom of the past required attention and respect. Even if Jefferson had wanted to begin the world anew, in many aspects of human existence, he could not. Even if Adams had wanted to stop the world from changing, he could not. Neither, though, embraced change or stasis entirely. Jefferson's letter of June 1799 was a political document as well as a statement of principles. It is one of many self-rehearsals of what he never tired of repeating.

Jefferson omitted from the final draft of this extraordinary letter the sentence that those "who like myself are going off the stage have deserved well of mankind for the struggles they have made." But he was not going "off the stage." He was the leader of a political movement. He was about to run for president. And Jefferson, Madison, and their colleagues were better politicians in 1796–1800 than Adams and his factionalized Federalist associates. Jefferson and Madison did not want war with France, but they preferred to keep the risk high rather than cooperate with Adams in any peace effort that would take Adams off the hot seat. They both had preferred that Adams win the presidency in 1796 precisely because he, not they, would have to deal with the dangerous and double-edged French problem. Despite Jefferson's gracious public words about Adams during the run-up to the election, he had had no intention of making good on them. They were a cover for what he conceived of as the best political tactic available: supportive words and uncooperative withdrawal. That left Adams holding the presidency and the bag. Out of the latter, hornets would fly and sting. Contemptuous of party and faction, hostile to the use of political wiles and himself proudly unskilled in wielding them, Adams would have to face the French crisis without any help from Jefferson and with implacable enemies of France dominating his Cabinet.

Jefferson skillfully played a double language game. On the one hand, he offered public verbal support. His language was graceful, respectful, even affectionate, but substantially misleading. On the other, he and Madison, now with one, now with the other taking the lead, implemented their political strategy. Madison played the public role, Jefferson the puppet master working privately offstage. Quickly finding strategic clarity, Jefferson soon had his rhetorical and emotional formula for success. One of its expressions was the Kentucky Resolution. The gradual public disapproval of the Alien and Sedition Acts, especially as the likelihood of war with France receded, worked to Jefferson's advantage. So did assiduous electioneering by Aaron Burr, Jefferson's Republican ally in New York, a state whose votes were crucial.

As the election of 1800 approached, Jefferson was far from a sure winner. He would, though, be the beneficiary of the hatred the implacable anti-French Federalists had for Adams, whose peace overtures they took as betrayal and treason, and who attacked Adams and his French policy, weakening his electoral viability. Peace with France came slightly too late to help the president. And Jefferson had the advantage of a block of Southern votes augmented by the three-fifths rule of the Constitution, the portion of the slave population that counted toward the Electoral College vote, which Southern slave-owners had insisted on as the price of union. By mid-December 1800, the election result was in: Jefferson had 73 electoral votes, Adams 65. There was no tally of the popular vote. Adams may have had a majority. Jefferson had barely been elected the third president of the United States, or so it seemed.

CHAPTER THIRTEEN

The Fugitive Occurrence

1801–1805

From the window of the newly built president's mansion, still smelling of plaster and paint, that the Adamses had occupied briefly, Thomas Jefferson looked out in March 1801 at the rudimentary village that was now the capital city. Its limitations did not disturb him. He hated cities anyway, and this was hardly a city, miniscule compared to Philadelphia, New York, and Boston. He had attained an office that he had said to himself and others that he did not want. An exemplar of contradiction and inconsistency, he had accepted since the late 1760s one government assignment after another, his mix of motives calibrated with slight differences at different times. He had frequently expressed his desire to be always at Monticello. Washington was a three- to four-day one-hundred-mile-plus journey away from his eldest daughter, from grandchildren, and from Sally Hemings, who had borne him three children, a fourth to be born that May. He would never reveal whether she was one of his reasons to prefer Monticello to any other place in the world or even whether, in March 1801, she was on his mind at all, whether he ever thought of her when he was away from home. In just a few years, he would refuse to respond, understandably, to the widely publicized and widely denied accusation that she played any role in his life.

At almost fifty-eight, Jefferson had enough perspective and self-awareness to know that age had brought changes. His sandy-red hair had flecked into mouselike grayness. His aquiline face had lost some of its angular sharpness. His freckled skin tended to peel. A tall man at six foot two, still slim at about 190 pounds, he slouched when sitting, usually raising one shoulder higher than the other, appearing both relaxed and uncomfortable at the same time. He needed to awkwardly lift his feet when walking. He still sat on his horse well and rode capably. He continued having weeks-long incapacitating headaches, and he had begun to have a sense of aging, the language of retirement, even of discharge from life, coming readily to stoic expressions of the inevitable "as we see that the candle of life is burning out." The first occupant of the presidency had died at the age of sixty-seven, exhausted, disgusted with political life. Adams, though he had desired reelection, preferred Quincy and his farm to any other place in the world. Jefferson never tired of stating that he hated politics with a passion. Annual payments on debts took almost all his income from the farms he had rented out. Monticello barely sustained itself, and he kept spending on improvements to a house barely capable of hosting guests comfortably. Every expense of his presidency had to be paid out of his salary. He was to leave office as much in debt as when he entered.

Jefferson was not to be a happy occupant of the executive mansion during his eight-year tenure. He had been triumphant in his conflicts with his presidential predecessors, both Federalists. His simplistic, angry, and condemnatory anti-Federalist rhetoric dominated his political discourse during the 1790s. Federalists were enemies of the people, Federalism equal to monarchy. He did not exclude any Federalist, including Washington, though he conveniently believed or at least maintained that Washington had been tricked and deluded by clever connivers like Hamilton. It was a necessary or at least convenient explanation, given Washington's national popularity. All Federalists, though, were enemies of his vision of republicanism, of the "spirit of '76," though he never tired of repeating that it was a difference in ideology, not a personal disagreement between individuals. He did his best to assert that personal relations and politics, like church and state, should not contaminate each other, asserting in his Inaugural Address on March 4, 1801, that "every difference of opinion is not a difference of principle. We have called by different names brethren of the same principle. We are all Republicans: we are all Federalists." He was not honest in that claim; it was certainly not true. His sincerity was tactical, an effort at provisional unification. He needed to bring factions together, given the bitter campaign and its controversial conclusion.

It had appeared for a short time in late 1800 that Jefferson had been elected president, a narrow victory made possible by a Constitution that favored the slave states. A complication arose: Aaron Burr, the Republican candidate for vice-president, had gotten the same number of votes. The Constitution stated that the candidate with the most electoral votes would be president; the candidate with the second most, vice-president. The Republican plan to have one of their electors leave blank his vote for Burr had misfired. Everyone knew that the intention had been for Jefferson to become president.

The tie turned into a crisis. It was widely acknowledged that Burr had made Jefferson's election possible. His exertions in New York City had swung the state's electoral slate to Jefferson by a narrow margin. The vice-presidency was his reward. It was expected that he would now cooperate in finding a mechanism to set things right. What that would be, no one exactly knew. If not, the Constitution required that the crisis be resolved by the House of Representatives. Each state would have a single vote. To Jefferson's surprise and disappointment, Burr said nothing, a passive-aggressive assertion of his desire for the presidency. Perhaps the Federalists in Congress, Burr apparently hoped, would prefer him to Jefferson. Jefferson was elected on the thirty-sixth ballot. Burr had gambled and lost. He was to become one of the three or four enduring hatreds of Jefferson's life. Over time, Jefferson did his best to revenge himself.

Jefferson's policy priorities had been clear from the start: to reverse Hamilton's financial program; to eliminate government debt, the national bank, and internal federal taxation; to keep the military as small and inexpensive as possible; to use American agricultural productivity and diplomacy as weapons against the European powers; to expand trading opportunities beyond the mercantile restrictions imposed by Great Britain; to protect and expand America's Southern and Western borders; to encourage Western settlement and the creation of new states to promote national unity, growth, and prosperity; to obtain by purchase lands claimed by Indian tribes; and to sustain as much as possible the "chains of the Constitution," the narrow interpretation that left states in charge of their internal affairs and the national government mostly invisible in the daily lives of Americans. He favored a functionally effective and influential executive but one that respected the explicit distinction made by the Constitution between the powers reserved to the states and those granted to the national government.

Jefferson had come to maturity in an empire dominated by a king. For many, the 1787 constitutional model for the presidency had a royalist mold. From the start, Federalists and Republicans assumed that the president would be the leader of the government. But how powerful? The president, created by a people who had been George III's loyal subjects, had the potential to become as powerful an executive as George III had been a king. Throughout the 1790s, Jefferson feared that the Federalists would transform the presidency into a form of monarchy. Would there be, Jefferson worried, a balance of power in which the executive and Congress would act as checks on each other, as the Constitution intended, or would the president be almost a monarch? Between 1787 and 1789, a substantial part of the electorate opposed ratifying the Constitution. The notion of a powerful executive without term limits seemed anathema. It was not what they had fought for. The presidency might become a version of royalty, reconceived and reclothed in the garments of Federal silk or even Republican homespun. In contrast, a narrow majority had come to believe that the country needed a strong executive, a figure around whom the nation could unite in a world in which it seemed possible that Great Britain would take it back by force, or that France and Spain would, if not swallow it whole, nibble and bite at its perimeters. The country needed an American and republican version of kingship, a master of foreign policy and national security who would keep the country safe from occupation or dismemberment. The actual "chains of the Constitution" could be loosened, even broken, by exertions of executive power.

Each half of the divided electorate in 1800 believed that the opposition was the devil in disguise. The Federalists' theological language had its base in the Calvinist tradition. The Republicans drew on the anti-Church, anti-institutional terminology of the Enlightenment. Jefferson was as gifted and inventive at the language of exaggeration and distortion as were his Federalist opponents, whom he cast as exemplifications of anti-republican evil: the monocrats, the speculators, the centralizers, the Anglophiles, and the warmongers. It was for both sides politics as a kind of theological either-or. Jefferson's rhetoric had as much emotional demagoguery in it as that of any Calvinist Congregationalist.

In reality, what the electorate was divided on was not always self-evident, though the rhetoric was. And neither side was unitary. In the 1796 and 1800 elections, the Federalists probably represented more people, if slaves are excluded; the Republicans, more states. Both elections were about anger and fear. They were also substantially about patronage. Jefferson's initial mission was to unite the country. He hoped that many Federalists would over time share his main policy aims. He recognized that not all Federalists were alike. In both parties there were those whose ambition and financial advantage dominated their political views and allegiances. They could be swayed. Eventually, moderate Federalists might became Republicans, including those who favored a stronger national government than did Jefferson. To Jefferson, a two-party system was anathema. His party was on the side of the angels, of the spirit of '76. He needed to persuade moderate Federalists to become Republicans: at the same time, he needed to reward Republicans, who had made his victory possible, and he needed to isolate and diminish the presence and power of the obdurate ultra-Federalists.

Jefferson's first task as president was to write an inaugural address. He may have used a quill pen, as he did when writing the Declaration of Independence, or a pen with a metallic nib, which he started using sometime at the start of the new century. His address went through at least three drafts, though the extant first is not substantively or rhetorically different from the final draft, with one exception.

For the swearing-in ceremony on March 4, 1801, he walked the short distance from his boarding house to the Capitol, without, unlike his two predecessors, a ceremonial sword, and plainly dressed, as befitted this most unmilitary of men. A single cannon was fired as he left his boarding house. Accompanied by a company of local riflemen, with swords drawn, the small parade was augmented by some of his fellow citizens, members of Congress, the marshal of the district of Maryland, and the deputy marshals. When Jefferson arrived at the Capitol, the officers opened ranks and saluted. Another discharge of the artillery was sounded. "Senators sat on one side" of the Senate chamber "and the other was given over by the members of the House to the women who were in attendance." About a thousand people had squeezed in. No member of Jefferson's family was present, and neither former president was there. One was dead, the other on his way home. Jefferson received a standing ovation. Vice-President Burr "rose to relinquish" to Jefferson "the chair of the presiding officer of the Senate." Jefferson read his address in almost a whisper. Apparently, hardly anyone could make out his words.

For the short essay that history records as his First Inaugural Address, Jefferson put on his pacific rhetorical robe. His mission was to bring Republicans and Federalists together. He felt, he later wrote, that he had to "face all the terrible passions of federalism in the first moments of its defeat and mortification, and to grapple with it until completely subdued." But his task was to do that not by reconciliation or confrontation but by pacification through generalized verbal assurances. "We are all Republicans: we are all Federalists," he proclaimed as his explicit theme.

Most Federalists would have thought that claim sophistical. Federalist officeholders, though, hoped that it at least meant that the new administration would not deny them some of the spoils of office. Some Federalist congressmen had believed, when they gave Jefferson his victory in the House, that that had been promised or at least vaguely assured. What Jefferson really meant was that we are all Federalists in that we are committed to national unity, but the nation should now unite under the principles of republicanism as he defined them. There was little nuance in his definition. You were either entirely and purely a republican or entirely a monarchist. The "monarchists" had to go, gradually if not sooner. And, since there should be only Jeffersonian Republicans, why should there be two political parties, a view he was gradually to soften when the reality became unavoidable.

Jefferson the writer had his fiery and legalistic side. His First

Inaugural Address, though, has the precise rhetoric demanded of a conciliatory document. It was his most sophistically compelling attempt at the language and structure of pacification. Brilliantly effective, it actually appealed to and received the praise of as many if not more Federalists than Republicans. An effective palliative, it promised that the mass of Federalists would not pay a price, other than verbal, for their defeat; that Republicans, especially if patient, would have most of the rewards of victory; and that almost everyone's best interests would be served by an adherence by affirmation, inattention, or indifference to the restoration of the spirit of '76. The "chains of the constitution" and Jefferson's policies would keep states' rights entirely secure. The internal economy would be left to do its own thing. However, as Jefferson implied, there was no going back to an entirely pre-Hamiltonian economy. He made no claim to eliminate, nor even did he refer to, the Bank of the United States, as if the antibank passion of the 1790s deferred to the realities of 1801. It was advantageous for the time being to allow the bank to continue to exist.

Soon Jefferson was to acknowledge that much of the Hamiltonian financial structure was irreversible, even if the national bank could be eliminated. In a private letter in early 1802, he wrote,

> When this government was first established, it was possible to have set it a going on true principles. But the contracted, English, half-lettered ideas of Hamilton destroyed that hope in the bud. We can pay off his debt in 15 years: but we can never get rid of his financial system. It mortifies me to be strengthening principles which I deem radically vicious. But this vice is entailed on us by a first error.... In other parts of our government I hope we shall be able by degrees to introduce sound principles and make them habitual. What is practicable must often control what is pure theory; and the habits of the governed determine in a great degree what is practicable. Hence the same original principles, modified in practice according to the

different habits of different nations, present governments of very different aspects.

It was his begrudging way of accepting a version of the Hamiltonian reality as a permanent feature of American life.

Many Americans held some views that were Republican, some that were Federalist, and most, regardless of affiliation, were dominated by a combination of ideology and self-interest. Not every Republican was committed to a minimalist navy, a small army, the dominance of agriculture, loyalty to France, and as limited a central government as Jefferson advocated. Not every Federalist objected to hard money and the elimination of the national debt; some regretted the Alien and Sedition Acts. Jefferson knew that the widespread antipathy to the acts had turned what might have been a narrow defeat into a victory. To the extent that his popular appeal had force, it coalesced around his antitax position and gained momentum from the conjunction of views about the extension of the franchise. A growing number of Americans found the rhetoric and reality of that attractive. Western Republicans wanted as much access to land as cheaply as possible. They wanted ongoing access to the port of New Orleans. Most Americans wanted minimal taxation, preferably none at all. At the same time, some Republicans wanted what seemed incompatible with minimalist government: a navy to protect shipping, an army to protect Western settlers, national security against Spain and Great Britain on the borders, and a monetary and credit system that supported without dominating the flourishing economy Jefferson had inherited.

Jefferson's speech was designed to make all this seem not only possible but the likely result of his policies. The address required generalized aspirational claims and a linguistic dexterity that navigated creatively between sincerity and the irreconcilable. He needed to assure fellow Republicans that their victory would be rewarded with the spoils of office, but also to assure Federalists that they would not be excluded from government and its rewards. He also needed to find a way to create at least the operative illusion of unification that would allow him to govern effectively. It was a challenging task. He began with the classic assertion of personal inadequacy, as if he were an epic poet proclaiming that, though his talents were not up to the task to which he had been called, he would invoke the assistance of his sources of inspiration, in this case the counsel of the citizens who had elected him, especially the wise legislators who were to be his partners in government. He lamented that the

task is above my talents . . . when I contemplate these transcendent objects, and see the honour, the happiness, and the hopes of this beloved country committed to the issue and the auspices of this day, I shrink from the contemplation and humble myself before the magnitude of the undertaking. Utterly indeed should I despair, did not the presence of many, whom I here see, remind me, that, in the other high authorities provided by our constitution, I shall find resources of wisdom, of virtue, and of zeal, on which to rely under all difficulties. To you, then, gentlemen, who are charged with the sovereign functions of legislation, and to those associated with you, I look with encouragement for that guidance and support which may enable us to steer with safety the vessel in which we are all embarked, amidst the conflicting elements of a troubled world.

It was an effective display of humility and a tactical display of deference to the Congress and the voters who had just elected him.

He also found it effective to use one of his favorite metaphors: the ship of state sailing on troubled waters, a staple of political discourse that eventually had its most effective expression in Whitman's poem "O Captain! My Captain!" a rare instance of brilliance redeeming cliché. The 1800 campaign had been a nasty combination of ambition, detestation, and ideology. Eager for the nation to move forward,

Jefferson alluded to the campaign only in evasive generalities. That he expected to find founts of wise guidance in Congress was a rhetorical palliative. He did not have a high opinion of its members: the newly elected Republican majority in the House had little in common with Jefferson's well-educated sophistication of mind and pen. Still, he needed to work with them. Most Republicans revered the leader who had brought them to power, and his low-key, hospitable cleverness at encouraging their agreement and compliance with his policies was to be one of the successes of his presidency.

He now elevated into his Cabinet two of the most capable Republican legislators, his co-conspirator James Madison as secretary of state and Albert Gallatin, the Republican congressman most astute in financial matters, a Geneva-born Pennsylvanian with a French accent, as secretary of the Treasury. A financial genius, Gallatin was a match for Hamilton in mind and vision, but a compatible match. Over time, his vision of the economy had much in common with Hamilton's, though to start with, like Jefferson, he was committed to eliminating the national debt as quickly as possible. It could be done, but only on the assumption that the nation did not need much of an army or navy, that the cost of war could be avoided regardless of provocation, that the Mississippi and the port of New Orleans could be kept open and West Florida obtained by peaceful means, and that at least until some distant date the infrastructure of the country could be left mostly as it was, except for limited improvements made by individual states and private enterprise. It seemed to Jefferson that, until debt and internal taxes were entirely eliminated, it was none of the concern of the national government that it took four days to travel on miserable roads from Washington to Monticello.

Jefferson made one significant revision from an earlier to the final draft. He had written that "I do not believe there is one native citizen of the US. who wishes to dissolve this union: I am confident there are few native citizens who wish to change its republican features."

The revised version proclaimed that "if there be any among us who would wish to dissolve this union, or to change its republican form, let them stand undisturbed as monuments of the safety with which error of opinion may be tolerated, where reason is left free to combat it." The emphasis, the tone, and the assertion had changed. It was a revision prompted by caution and pacification: in a country inhabited by a substantial number of first-generation immigrants, including his secretary of the Treasury, "native citizens" was not a well-chosen phrase. It implied that "native citizens" had a stronger attachment to the country than did immigrants, not a desirable emphasis for Jefferson's pro-immigrant party. What first came to Jefferson's pen had a touch of the nativism of the class into which he had been born, the elitism of long-established ruling-class Virginians, who had prospered in the shadowland of a labor force that at the start had been created partly by the indentured labor of impoverished white immigrants. It was possible to have nativist impulses, especially among the long-established elite, and also be pro-immigration.

The revision also took the original in another direction, from a general statement that most Americans, including those who had voted against him, favored a republican government to a broader assertion of the power of free speech to defeat false speech, errors "of opinion. . . . I know indeed," he continued, "that some honest men fear that a republican government cannot be strong. . . . But would the honest patriot, in the full tide of successful experiment, abandon a government which has so far kept us free and firm, on the theoretic and visionary fear, that this government, the world's best hope, may, by possibility, want energy to preserve itself? I trust not. I believe this, on the contrary, the strongest government on earth. I believe it the only one, where every man, at the call of the law, would fly to the standard of the law, and would meet invasions of the public order as his own personal concern." These men would be native and non-native citizens. Either kind of citizen would be exclusively white.

To Jefferson, "citizen" meant self-government, and self-government required the ownership of private property or some equivalent by white males, national unity under Republican principles, and peace at home and abroad. "Sometimes it is said that man cannot be trusted with the government of himself. Can he then be trusted with the government of others? Or have we found angels, in the form of kings, to govern him? Let history answer this question. Let us then, with courage and confidence, pursue our own federal and republican principles; our attachment to union and representative government."

For Jefferson, the viability of representative government required an almost infinite expanse of real estate for agricultural settlement by morally grounded, patriotic landowners from coast to coast. He was soon to send Meriwether Lewis and William Clark toward the Pacific, partly a scientific expedition, mainly a gesture of anticipatory possession. Ownership of land was essential to the existence of liberty, so there seemed almost no western terminus to American expansion. America's isolation would enable it to expand and prosper without the expense of wars. Its spiritual needs would be "enlightened by a benign religion," as if Christianity as an ethical code would always manifest itself in tolerance and love, an anticipation of Jefferson's own edited version of the Bible. America would, in Robert Frost's words, find "salvation in surrender" to its already manifest continental destiny.

Jefferson articulated for his fellow citizens his own edited version of America:

> Kindly separated by nature and a wide ocean from the exterminating havoc of one quarter of the globe; too high minded to endure the degradations of the others, possessing a chosen country, with room enough for our descendants to the thousandth and thousandth generation, entertaining a due sense of our equal right to the use of our own faculties, to the acquisitions of our own industry, to honor and confidence from our fellow citizens, resulting not from birth,

but from our actions and their sense of them, enlightened by a benign religion, professed indeed and practiced in various forms, yet all of them inculcating honesty, truth, temperance, gratitude and the love of man, acknowledging and adoring an overruling providence, which by all its dispensations proves that it delights in the happiness of man here, and his greater happiness hereafter; with all these blessings, what more is necessary to make us a happy and a prosperous people?

The rhetorical question answers itself. It assumed more than sober realism would normally permit, and it made no allowance for the traditional need in religion and literature to "justify the ways of God to man" in a world, including the United States in 1801, in which there were poverty, pain, bondage, slavery, genocide, illness, hostility, unmerited suffering, and natural disasters.

There was, though, in Jefferson's view, only one thing more that was needed: "a wise and frugal government, which shall restrain men from injuring one another, shall leave them otherwise free to regulate their own pursuits of industry and improvement, and shall not take from the mouth of labor the bread it has earned. This is the sum of good government; and this is necessary to close the circle of our felicities." The policies that would close "the circle of our felicities" needed to be reemphasized: "the preservation of the general government in its whole constitutional vigor, as the sheet anchor of our peace at home, and safety abroad"; equal justice to all men regardless of birth, political views, or religious beliefs; international trade but no "entangling alliances"; all domestic matters under the control of the states; free and fair elections; a militia as the first line of national defense; "the supremacy of the civil over the military authority"; strict economy and the elimination of debt; and the primacy of agriculture, with "commerce as its handmaid." To these he added the precepts of the Bill of Rights that the first Congress had added as amendments:

freedom of religion; freedom of the press; and freedom of person, under the protection of the Habeas Corpus:—These principles form the bright constellation, which has gone before us and guided our steps through an age of Revolution and Reformation. The wisdom of our sages, and blood of our heroes have been devoted to their attainment:—they should be the creed of our political faith; the text of civic instruction, the touchstone by which to try the services of those we trust; and should we wander from them in moments of error or of alarm, let us hasten to retrace our steps, and to regain the road which alone leads to peace, liberty and safety.

This was Jefferson at his most idealistic and aspirational, an elevation of partial truth into ultimate verities, a brilliant play with words and concepts that wove an American tapestry into a seamless and united whole, without a gap between ideal and implementation, a tapestry so rhetorically affirmative that the aspirational could seem the actual. One could not see through it or behind it, and for Jefferson in 1801 there was nothing to see through or behind. This America was an exemplification of the best of all possible worlds. His text creates the possibility of perfection. Imperfection is not even alluded to. It is Jefferson's vision of the American reality and the even more perfect American future.

The 1801 Inaugural Address is an optimistic, aspirational document. It has no place for those whose land it first was, and no place for the labor force that made the land productive and produced much of the nation's wealth. It evades human flaws and cultural divisiveness. It is one of Jefferson's supreme acts of creative mythmaking, of writing the story of the America that he believed in and the American future he envisioned. It reasserts Jefferson's republican ideals within the structure reserved for Jefferson's special people in their exceptional country. It demands small and prudent government; it projects Jefferson's Virginia writ large across a continent. It expresses his sincere belief that his countrymen have the ability to disagree without being disagreeable and that no matter the differences of opinion about priorities and values, his vision of government eventually would be embraced by everyone.

Jefferson had begun his address with a statement in the classical mode about his own inadequacy. He prefaced his conclusion with a personal note. It was also a confession of inadequacy but framed in the language of self-assertion, the voice of experience predicting that his presidency, like most, would sometimes be a bed of thorns and that the work of even an honest laborer in the vineyards of the Lord would sometimes produce sour wine—criticism rather than praise. All he could claim, he asserted, then and in the future, was that he had done his best, always with the best in mind: "With experience enough in subordinate offices to have seen the difficulties of this the greatest of all, I have learnt to expect that it will rarely fall to the lot of imperfect man to retire from this station with the reputation, and the favor, which bring him into it." He reached toward his climax. "I repair then, fellow citizens, to the post you have assigned me." Oddly, and clearly without any regard to the subtext, Jefferson then evoked President Washington as the highest example of public service. "Without pretensions to that high confidence you reposed in our first and greatest revolutionary character, whose pre-eminent services had entitled him to the first place in his country's love, and destined for him the fairest page in the volume of faithful history, I ask so much confidence only as may give firmness and effect to the legal administration of your affairs."

Jefferson had paid his respects to Martha Washington at Mount Vernon two months before his inauguration. She was icily polite to a man she despised. Soon after the publication of his Inaugural Address, she dismissed his praise of her husband as "sarcastic" remarks, his election the "greatest misfortune our nation has ever experienced." She was likely to have been an accurate embodiment of her deceased husband's opinion. At the same time, Jefferson had no difficulty, so it seems, in declining to acknowledge that her contempt was an expressive version of what her husband had felt about his former colleague. The new president had a gift for remaining politely poised and quietly amiable, no matter the situation and its undercurrents. When Martha Washington died, in May 1802, Jefferson, in a letter to an aristocratic Englishman, praised her "benevolent and virtuous" life. "This loss is the more felt too as it renews the memory of a preceding one, of a worthy of that degree which providence, in its wise dispensations, sees fit rarely to bestow on us, whose services in the cause of man had justly endeared him to the world, and whose name will be among the latest monuments of the age wherein he lived, which time will extinguish."

It was both slick and sincere, a willing suspension of the reality of their relationship and his view of Washington's policies. His graceful letter had the language and tone of conviction that transcends its element of hypocrisy. "I feel a pride in the justice which your lordship's sentiments render to the character of my illustrious countryman Washington. The moderation of his desires and the strength of his judgment enabled him to calculate correctly that the road to that glory which never dies is to use power for the support of the laws and liberties of our country, not for their destruction, and his will accordingly survive the wreck of everything now living."

Jefferson's evocation of Washington in his Inaugural Address had not the slightest touch of duplicity, the useful myth having replaced the reality. "I shall often go wrong," he concluded, "through defect of judgment. When right, I shall often be thought wrong by those whose positions will not command a view of the whole ground." That he himself, unlike Washington, would always "command a view of the whole ground" is implied.

I ask your indulgence for my own errors, which will never be intentional; and your support against the errors of others, who may condemn what they would not if seen in all its parts. The approbation implied by your suffrage, is a great consolation to me for the past; and my future solicitude will be, to retain the good opinion of those who have bestowed it in advance, to conciliate that of others by doing them all the good in my power, and to be instrumental to the happiness and freedom of all. . . . I advance with obedience to the work, ready to retire from it whenever you become sensible how much better choices it is in your power to make. And may that infinite power, which rules the destinies of the universe, lead our councils to what is best, and give them a favorable issue for your peace and prosperity.

It was a brilliant composition for the context and the country. The next day, in a personal letter, he resorted again to the image of the ship of state whose "tough sides . . . have been thoroughly tried. Her strength has stood the waves into which she was steered with a view to sink her. We shall put her on her republican tack, and she will now shew by the beauty of her motion the skill of her builders. Figure apart, our fellow citizens have been led hoodwinked from their principles by a most extraordinary combination of circumstances. But the band is removed, and they now see for themselves." Washington had been "hoodwinked." So had all Federalists. Hamilton had been the main hoodwinker. Now, in Jefferson's view, the ship of state was back on its true republican course. His fellow citizens had been blinded, but now they could see.

Between Jefferson's First Inaugural Address and his Second, the American world changed radically. One of its transformations was more substantial than Jefferson and his colleagues had anticipated would happen in their lifetimes. His Second Inaugural Address summarized the achievements of his first term. It evoked an equally strong view of American exceptionalism and its continental destiny, but its occasion quietly resonates with Jefferson's sense of what had not been accomplished and of problems to come. It is more of a report than an aspirational agenda. Its tone is comparatively flat; its eloquence, low-key. Its lower register mirrors what Jefferson had privately acknowledged: the American presidency indeed could be a bed of thorns. The tone corroborates what he wrote in private letters: he had no enthusiasm for these next four years. Actually, he had already decided that under no circumstance would he run for a third term. If he could have anticipated the difficulties of the next four years, he might have had second thoughts about running even for a second. As writing, the Second Inaugural differs noticeably from what he is most remembered for: the fiery eloquence of *A Summary View*, the sweeping beauty of the preamble to the Declaration, and the aspirational affirmation in his First Inaugural of America's impending national greatness.

Between 1801 and 1805, many of Jefferson's goals had been reached. He had been almost unanimously reelected, his majority in 1804 in contrast to his squeaker in 1800. The land mass of the United States had been approximately doubled: the Pacific was almost in sight, its shores envisioned eventually to be in American hands; the Mississippi and New Orleans had become American possessions; and the Native Americans were being increasingly neutralized, dispossessed, and massacred. Also, the national debt had been substantially reduced, revenue far exceeding expenses, and the economy was flourishing. The Alien and Sedition Acts no longer existed, and, as Jefferson happily wrote at the beginning of 1802, "the majority of the present legislature are in unison with the agricultural part of our citizens," his fondest wish.

Most important, the off-again mostly on-again battle between England and France for international supremacy allowed America to dominate commercial traffic on transatlantic routes, in what was called the carrying trade. In Jefferson's view, American ships had the right to transport goods not acknowledged to be war materials to any port in the world. It was a claim that the reality of warfare did not readily support. It was a tricky, dangerous, but profitable exploitation of wartime circumstances. It was to America's advantage for Great Britain and France to continue to be at war, leaving most of the world's carrying trade to American ships. Such trade produced most of the federal government's revenue. The British resented it. So did the French. Both had interests to protect in regard to what Jefferson insisted was the "freedom of the seas." The absolutely last thing Jefferson wanted was war with either of the great European powers, but he also wanted the tax revenue derived from the carrying trade so that he could eliminate internal taxes. He needed to maintain peace while advancing policies that might result in war.

Then there were the sectional tensions. Jefferson did not want to antagonize Northern commercial or Southern agricultural Republicans, both important constituencies, neither of whom respected, let alone trusted, the other. In early 1801, James Monroe, one of Jefferson's most trusted confidants, wrote to the president-elect that "the eastern people have no thoughts of breaking the union," though some had threatened that, "and giving up the hold they have on the valuable productions of the south. They only mean to bully us, thereby preserve their ascendancy, and improve their profits." Despite a Southern president and Southern-dominated Congress, many Southerners, especially of the elite class, believed they were too much under the thumb of Northerners. And they feared worse, especially Northern pressure to reduce or even eliminate slavery. Jefferson hoped to maintain a satisfactory economic balance between North and South. The South would grow crops, particularly tobacco, wheat, and cotton. The North would carry these crops to markets around the world. Manufactured imports would be taxed, providing revenue for the federal government. If Britain and France would stay at war and keep within tolerable limits their all-too-frequent confiscation of American ships, the United States could keep military expenditures to a minimum.

Jefferson had good reason to have France and Spain on his mind in 1803. If the United States could not be guaranteed free passage on the Mississippi with access to international waters through New Orleans, his Western constituency might look to Spain for help. Jefferson needed French cooperation. It had become a challenge to continue to approve of almost all things French, especially its Revolution. At its start, he was optimistic that it would make France a sister republic. He had feared the possibility of war with France in the late 1790s, and now he needed the cooperation of an anti-Republican French tyrant to reduce or even eliminate the Spanish threat on America's Southern and Southwestern borders.

In the middle of July 1803, Jefferson reminisced by letter with a French friend about how happy and optimistic his days in Paris had been. "Bliss was it in that dawn to be alive," as Wordsworth was to write in *The Prelude*. France under Louis XVI had not been entirely comfortable for Jefferson, but he had made the best of it, and there was much that was engaging and fine. He had welcomed the start of the Revolution. "In those days how sanguine we were!" When the Revolution turned bloody, he made allowances. His allowances, though, had limits. "How soon were the virtuous hopes and confidence of every good man blasted! how many excellent friends have we lost in your efforts towards self-government . . . but let us draw a veil over the dead, and hope the best for the living."

In 1763, France had ceded Louisiana to Spain. The territory extended from West Florida to unspecified boundaries in Texas and northward to the Great Plains. In 1801 Napoléon forced Spain to cede Louisiana back to France. In response, in late 1801, Jefferson appointed Robert Livingston, his colleague on the committee to write the Declaration of Independence, to be ambassador to France, with two main charges: to negotiate American purchase of the city of New

Orleans and attain French affirmation of free transit on the Mississippi. Jefferson had reason to fear that without access to New Orleans to move their agricultural produce to international waters, Western settlers might not remain committed citizens of the United States. The administration had four main foreign-policy objectives: to secure rights in or possession of New Orleans and free transit on the Mississippi; to obtain Florida, particularly West Florida; to push away European predator nations, exclusively Spain, France, and Great Britain, as far as possible from American borders; and to prevent the United States becoming an active participant in the conflict between France and Great Britain.

Napoléon did not welcome the American overture. The United States was a small fly in his huge jar of ointment. It was on his list of possible future conquests. Eager to advance his ambition for international dominance, he decided to reestablish France as the major colonial power in the Caribbean and in North America. First he needed to reestablish French control of Haiti, formerly a major contributor to French wealth, now a bloody battleground between French colonists, free mulattoes, and former slaves. Great Britain was an engaged predator. The United States surreptitiously traded with all Haitian elements. In 1798, the Adams administration established diplomatic contact with the Haitian government formed by liberated slaves. Jefferson shut that down, hoping to please France and appalled by the possibility of a nation of free Blacks close to American shores. Napoléon reestablished slavery in Haiti. Jefferson had no problem at all with that. In early 1803, he sent James Monroe to Paris to bolster Robert Livingston's mission. "For on the event of this mission depends," Jefferson believed, "the future destinies of this republic." The United States would have to go to war on this matter if there were no peaceful solution, perhaps even make an alliance with Great Britain, both a bargaining chip in negotiations and an alliance to be feared.

America was not prepared for conflict. It would require borrowing huge sums, which would scuttle if not eliminate Jefferson's domestic priorities. For reasons of his own, Napoléon, who despised the United States, became Jefferson's supreme benefactor. When the fleet and army he had sent to reconquer Haiti was demolished, mainly by yellow fever, he decided that it would not be worth the huge expense necessary to reestablish France as a major colonial power in North America. Instead, he would devote his resources to making himself absolute ruler of the European continent. For that he needed money. It was a cost-benefit calculation. Before Monroe arrived in Paris in April 1803, Napoléon had done an about-face. The United States, he told a flabbergasted Livingston, could buy all of the Louisiana Territory as it had been defined in 1763, excluding West Florida. Fearing that he might change his mind, Livingston, joined now by Monroe, after negotiating the best price they could, agreed to a purchase which they had no authority to make. The news reached the District of Columbia in July 1803. For a short time, Jefferson was almost as popular as Washington had been, although he himself had had nothing directly to do with the purchase. It was a great accidental triumph, indeed "a fugitive occurrence," in Jefferson's nice phrase.

The unanticipated purchase was Jefferson's major foreign-policy achievement. It came at a price that had difficulties far beyond the monetary. Three aspects of it had tense national consequences. It exacerbated North/South tensions. The Northeastern states, particularly Federalists in New England, believed that the new states to be formed from the territory would diminish their electoral influence. The heart, the population, and the wealth of the nation would move south and westward. And how could republican principles be affirmed and implemented in the huge land mass that the United States would now become? It was a concern that Madison had overcome in 1787 in his argument that size and diversity actually would benefit republican values and government. But the puzzlement about how that could be the case without a centralized national government was largely undiscussed, especially by those, like Jefferson and Madison, who opposed centralization, which they believed would be to the detriment of states' rights. The question of whether slavery would be legal in the Louisiana Territory and the new states, and, if so, under what stipulations, had a major potential for sectional tension. And how was it possible for the United States to take possession of a foreign territory and a foreign population when the Constitution made no provision for that occurence?

All three issues had considerable purchase on Jefferson's actions. First, as a believer in the "chains of the Constitution," he needed to find a way to overcome the constitutional difficulty. He had little concern for those who feared that the purchase would diminish their own national clout, especially because the Northeast was not his main constituency. The purchase helped implement his vision of an "Empire of liberty," an American agricultural empire to the west for future generations of Americans. He had no desire to create Southern opposition to the purchase, so he decided that slavery would be legal in most of the territory. It would be subject to some geographical limitations, as well as the prohibition on importing slaves, banned by law starting in 1808. National unity and the balance among North, South, and West needed to be handled thoughtfully. However, there was never any doubt that the Republican majority would defeat Northern opposition to the purchase, and although the slavery issue produced some hotly argued divisions within Congress, the Republican majority handled them easily. For Jefferson, the constitutional issue had the most bite. The purchase impinged on his commitment to republican values and to the "chains of the Constitution." Both were crucial to why he had become president. The Constitution made no provision for the United States to add territory by purchase, cession, or conquest. How could a Republican president transform a foreign population into American citizens and make their land American territory simply by buying them and it?

At first Jefferson insisted that an amendment was required, though over the next few months, he allowed himself to be convinced that it could be dispensed with. It was argued that Napoléon might change his mind, which was unlikely but possible. Time was of the essence. It was a convenient rationale. The president could make the initial decisions and appointments on executive authority, as if this were a national emergency. Popular enthusiasm in the South and West made Congressional approval and funding a certainty. Congress could legitimize the purchase through legislation rather than initiate the time-consuming amendment process before accession or even afterward. The executive could appoint administrators and establish a process that over time would make non-English-speaking foreigners Americans. With a few exceptions, all Republicans and some Federalists approved. The "chains of the Constitution" needed to be broken in what Jefferson believed to be the national interest. It was, he convinced himself, an exception forced on him by circumstances. National interest required it. Practicality came before principle. He wanted that territory. So did most Americans. "The Constitution has made no provision for our holding foreign territory," he wrote in August 1803, "still less for incorporating foreign nations into our union. The executive in seizing the fugitive occurrence which so much advanced the good of their country, have done an act beyond the Constitution. . . . It is the case of a guardian, investing the money of his ward in purchasing an important adjacent territory; and saying to him when of age, I did this for your good; I pretend to no right." In effect, Jefferson rationalized, it was the necessary thing, not the right thing.

Jefferson also wanted West Florida, which he argued, unsuccessfully, was included in the purchase. Furthermore, he joined many Southern colleagues in hoping, even expecting, that Cuba would become an American possession, perhaps even Mexico. Many

Americans assumed that Canada would become, sooner or later, part of the United States, especially if the United States and Great Britain went to war, which sometimes seemed to Jefferson to verge on certainty. Over time, these territories and countries would become, Jefferson believed likely, republics of liberty, either as part of the United States or as independent soul mates. He anticipated, almost expected, that one day even the European nations would embrace republican principles. If in the case of the Louisiana Territory there needed to be an end run around the Constitution, it was in a good cause. It was desirable for the executive to take an extra constitutional initiative, with the certainty of later legislative approval, rather than to forgo a golden opportunity that was in the national interest.

Of course, the purchase would cost money and extend the time to repay the national debt. Jefferson assumed that the money generated by land sales eventually would compensate for the cost and that, though the initial cost would be substantial, over time the benefits would be immense. However, he well knew that it would exacerbate the Indian and slavery problems, requiring a more costly army and increasing North-South tensions. In addition, though at the time this effect was unforeseen, it would puff up American pride in its worldwide destiny and contribute to the costly and unnecessary War of 1812.

Jefferson's attitude about the Louisiana Purchase paralleled his handling of his own money, the self-justifying optimism that, in the end, all such matters would work out well, or well enough. Jefferson's personal debt was not working out well, and in the long run the national debt, despite his efforts, became the Hamiltonian way of national life. Jefferson himself found some mental relief by projecting personal debt into a generalized reality for most Virginia farmers. "The unprofitable condition of Virginia estates in general, leaves it now next to impossible for the holder of one to avoid ruin. And this condition will continue until some change takes place in the mode of working them." The fault was in the structure, not in the person. "In the meantime nothing can save us and our children from beggary but a determination to get a year before hand, and restrain ourselves rigorously this year to the clear profits of the last. If a debt is once contracted by a farmer, it is never paid but by a sale." Lack of financial discipline was partly to blame, but the fault, he maintained, was not in himself but in the seemingly unalterable givens he had inherited, including the labor force he had to depend on. The Louisiana Purchase turned out to be a sustainable bargain but also a purchase whose price would include a civil war.

Slavery was a national problem, a state problem, a financial problem, and a personal problem: unproductive slaves, runaway slaves, renting slaves, purchasing slaves, rebellious slaves. At Monticello, each was an individual case. Though he abhorred slavery in principle, Jefferson still defined slaves as property, his irreplaceable labor force. He also concluded that it was a labor force that doomed his farms to be unprofitable, as if he himself played no role in his indebtedness. And the slave labor force was potentially violent. In 1797, he had expressed himself strongly about the probability of slave insurrection. "If something is not done, and soon done," he wrote to St. George Tucker, "we shall be the murderers of our own children . . . only a single spark is wanting to make that day tomorrow. If we had begun sooner, we might probably have been allowed a lengthier operation to clear ourselves, but every day's delay lessens the time we may take for emancipation." Virginia, he feared, was a powder keg certain to explode. The example of Haiti made slave-owners tremble. Moreover, he surmised, almost no other state would likely come to Virginia's assistance if there were a slave rebellion. When there was a bloody insurrection at Richmond in 1800, Jefferson approved Governor Monroe's harsh suppression and punishments. As president, he dealt with the Haitian slave rebellion as a pawn in the diplomatic power struggle with France and Britain. The fear that Black government there would be an inspiration for

American slaves worried him. He felt relief when Napoléon reestablished slavery in Haiti.

The colonization of American slaves (by shipping them back to Africa) seemed to him the best way to remove the threat to the lives of the next generation of American slave-owners, but in practice Jefferson saw no way to do this. And how could Monticello operate without slaves? Where would a substitute labor force come from? It was, in his resigned acceptance, a conundrum to be resolved by future generations. In the meantime, he had other pressing matters to think about. And he could emphasize the satisfaction that he expressed in his annual address to Congress in December 1806 that the constitutional protection of the importation of slaves would soon expire. "I congratulate you, fellow citizens, on the approach of the period," he wrote, "at which you may interpose your authority constitutionally, to withdraw the citizens of the US. from all further participation in those violations of human rights, which have been so long continued on the unoffending inhabitants of Africa, and which the morality, the reputation, and the best interests of our country have long been eager to proscribe." Actually, the American slave population was growing rapidly without importations. Still, in 1806 Jefferson at least had something in regard to slavery to feel good about.

In his first term, as the Constitution required, Jefferson sent four annual messages to Congress. Each set out a summary of the "state of the union," all of them concise and effective but not memorable. As was to be the future pattern for presidents, they were part report and part preview. It was clear between the lines that he was carrying out his mandate as best he could. Some of the challenges were intractable. Some needed more time to be resolved. He had tried, he emphasized, to keep all factions and provocations domestically manageable and internationally peaceful. Putting in long and tiring hours, he felt that his physical and mental strength had diminished. He was especially peeved at the aspects of the job he did not like. One was patronage. It seemed a Sisyphean task. "Yet, like the office of hangman, it must be executed by someone." Another was working with Congress. His preference was to exert influence privately. Almost every day, he hosted dinners for small groups from both parties, probably his single largest expenditure. And he wrote letter after letter. Madison and Gallatin helped keep the Republican legislative troops in line and moving. Jefferson's word was almost law. Nevertheless, he did not enjoy being president.

In January 1803, he played with the possibility that one term would be enough. In autumn 1804, he fantasized about not running for a second. The "winter campaign," as he put it, was soon to begin. "I dread it on account of the fatigues of the table in such a round of company, which I consider as the most serious trials I undergo." He had never been a happy warrior. "I wish much to turn it over to younger hands and to be myself but a guest at the table, and free to leave it as others are; but whether this would be tolerated is uncertain," another way of saying that it was impossible for him not to be a candidate again. He had to console himself with the thought that he would become a private citizen "in 1809 at the latest."

Not enough has been made of Jefferson's Second Inaugural Address. The first has its merits: its mission to unite the nation under his program and his attempt to alleviate, counter, absorb, and discharge the dynamically destructive tensions between Federalists and Republicans that had dominated the 1790s. Its core mission was to provide the illusion of calm after a storm, and the pledge that there would be no more storms; that the enemy would reconcile itself to the superiority, indeed the purity, the truth, and the inevitable ascendency of the Jeffersonian view of government and morality. It has its moments of conviction and eloquence, but it also has the thrust of self-exculpation, of triumphalism disguised as modesty. It calls for reconciliation on terms entirely set by the victor, headlined by the sophistical tagline "We are all Republicans: we are all Federalists." Many frightened Federalists would have seen them as reasonable terms and policies, especially the implication that Federalists would not be excluded from patronage positions. The dispersal of patronage in general, and which Federalists to fire and which keep in place, became one of Jefferson's most onerous presidential burdens.

During his first term, Jefferson found the sweet spot, combining his Republican policies with what moderate Federalists could accept, if not embrace. There were to be thorny patches, the most imminent being Jefferson's successful attempt to revoke the Judiciary Act of 1801, passed immediately before he took office. It had established federal district courts, with Federalist judges, with the certainty that a federal judiciary staffed by Washington's and Adams's appointments would be hostile to Jefferson's agenda. How to get rid of them? Impeachment perhaps. Or term limits. Why shouldn't Congress have the right to replace judges appointed by a previous administration? The elimination of the district courts eliminated a cadre of newly created Federalist judges. The constitutionally mandated Supreme Court, though, could not be eliminated except by constitutional amendment. To Jefferson, it was a viperous nest of anti-Republican judges led by the quietly charismatic John Marshall. Almost its every ruling was a thorn in Jefferson's side. He got some minor satisfaction in forcing them, having eliminated the district courts, to ride the judicial circuit again, a time-consuming inconvenience that every member of the Court hated.

Jefferson's Second Inaugural Address, in March 1805, is his most subtle, self-deceptive, self-congratulatory, and idealistically affirmative synthesis of the issues and emotions that had been his, more or less, from the start of his public career. It was written in the expectation that it would be his last term. He would follow Washington's example and not run for a third, though he had reason to believe that he could be reelected easily. He had made up his mind even before the 1804 election, though he kept his own counsel. "I determine to withdraw at the end of my second term. The danger is that the indulgence and attachments of the people will keep a man in the chair after he becomes a dotard, that reelection through life shall become habitual, and election for life." He had devoted his first term to guiding his country back to what he believed the true path of republicanism, and to keep it on a state-by-state rather than a national highway. In his view, he had done much of the first goal. The second, he was gradually to realize, was an impossibility. After his second inauguration, he had little to say beyond what he had already said. He sometimes did and sometimes did not face reality. The country's problems could be either alleviated or exacerbated by political, social, economic, and military realities beyond his or any president's control. Jefferson's idealistic vision of a fully united country at peace in a mostly pastoral decentralized world of Republican brothers had been a narcotic-like delusion.

In March 1805, he felt he had victories to celebrate. He wrote to a European friend that "the two parties which prevailed with so much violence when you were here are almost wholly melted into one." He had, to great self-satisfaction, "received 162 votes against 14. . . . Pride keeps [Federalists] hostile, they brood over their angry passions and give them vent in the newspapers which they maintain. They still make as much noise as if they were the whole nation." They were not, but neither were the Republicans, and they were dividing into factions. There were radical Republicans, moderate Republicans, and conservative Republicans; sectionalist Republicans and nationalist Republicans; agrarian Republicans and commercial Republicans; Republicans who favored war to protect the carrying trade; those who wanted more energetic government and those who preferred the least possible; and Republicans in New England who did not have the same priorities as Republicans in the South. There was, though, almost unanimous agreement on one subject: internal taxes were anathema. During Jefferson's second term, the Republican Party began to become multiple parties under the same name.

Still, in early 1805, an optimistic Jefferson asserted unified Republican integrity and achievement embodied in himself and his policies. "On taking this station on a former occasion," he wrote to Congress referring to March 1801, "I declared the principles on which I believed it my duty to administer the affairs of our commonwealth. My conscience tells me that I have, on every occasion, acted up to that declaration, according to its obvious import, and to the understanding of every candid mind." His formula for how he had conducted foreign policy exemplified republican values: "We are firmly convinced, and we act on that conviction, that with nations, as with individuals, our interests soundly calculated, will ever be found inseparable from our moral duties; and history bears witness to the fact, that a just nation is taken on its word." He sincerely believed this to be the case.

Jefferson was proud that he had kept his promises: "It may be the pleasure and pride of an American to ask, what farmer, what mechanic, what laborer, ever sees a tax-gatherer of the United States?" Import duties alone "enable us to support the current expenses of the government." The surplus revenue would soon effect the "final redemption" of the national debt "and that redemption once effected, the revenue thereby liberated may, by a just repartition among the states, and a corresponding amendment of the constitution, be applied, in time of peace, to rivers, canals, roads, arts, manufactures, education, and other great objects within each state." He insisted that the use of federal money for infrastructure projects required a constitutional amendment.

As long as the import duty continued and with the passage of such an amendment, the surplus revenue—channeled through the states, of course—could fund national infrastructure for transportation and education. Even if the nation were forced to go to war, "it could meet . . . all the expenses of the year, without encroaching on the rights of future generations, by burdening them with the debts of the past. War will then be but a suspension of useful works, and a return to a state of peace, a return to the progress of improvement." It was a rosy and overgeneralized optimism that events and policies would soon deny and that the next president would find impossible to sustain. The acquisition of Louisiana, Jefferson assured Congress, had not and would not endanger the union. "The larger our association, the less will it be shaken by local passions; and in any view, is it not better that the opposite bank of the Mississippi should be settled by our own brethren and children, than by strangers of another family? With which shall we be most likely to live in harmony and friendly intercourse?"

Also to the good, the lapsed Alien and Sedition Acts no longer denied the press a free voice.

> During this course of administration, and in order to disturb it, the artillery of the press has been levelled against us, charged with whatsoever its licentiousness could devise or dare. These abuses of an institution so important to freedom and science, are deeply to be regretted . . . they might, indeed, have been corrected by the wholesome punishments reserved and provided by the laws of the several states against falsehood and defamation; but public duties more urgent press on the time of public servants, and the offenders have therefore been left to find their punishment in the public indignation.

Jefferson believed that his government deserved unanimous approval. His administration, he told Congress, "conducting itself in the true spirit of its constitution, with zeal and purity, and doing no act which it would be unwilling the whole world should witness," had the strength to overcome "falsehood and defamation . . . truth and reason have maintained their ground against false opinions in league with false facts, the press, confined to truth, needs no other legal restraint." But "if there be still improprieties which this rule would not restrain, its supplement must be sought in the censorship of public opinion." If ineffective, then the "laws of the several states would enforce fidelity to truth and fact. . . . I offer to our country sincere congratulations." He was also congratulating himself. There should be no "doubt that truth, reason, and their own interests, will at length prevail" even among the small Federalist remnant. They will be gathered "into the fold of their country, and will complete their entire union of opinion, which gives to a nation the blessing of harmony, and the benefit of all its strength."

It was a utopian vision, defined in Jeffersonian terms. It placed absolute faith in people being innately moral, especially those who tilled the soil, which the vast majority did, and that an "entire union of opinion" was desirable. His almost unanimous reelection was evidence to Jefferson that that was so. He granted that he was not infallible. He might make mistakes. But "I am sensible of no passion which could seduce me knowingly from the path of justice; but the weakness of human nature, and the limits of my own understanding, will produce errors of judgment sometimes injurious to your interests. I shall need, therefore, all the indulgence I have heretofore experienced—the want of it will certainly not lessen with increasing years." It was both an acknowledgment and an affirmation that imperfection, including his own, was not a barrier to the perfection of the state, or at least to the pursuit of that perfection. He defined his own nature and that of most Americans as virtuous, peaceful, truth loving, and benevolent.

He believed that human nature, at least in its American version, had no need of the supernatural and of traditional religions. Its standard needed only to be ethical. His Second Inaugural Address makes not the slightest bow in the direction of Christian belief. It is in part the manifesto of a Deist, especially in its evocative peroration. "I shall need, too," he concluded, "the favor of that being in whose hands we are, who led our forefathers, as Israel of old, from their native land, and planted them in a country flowing with all the necessaries and comforts of life; who has covered our infancy with his providence, and our riper years with his wisdom and power; and to whose goodness I ask you to join with me in supplications, that he will so enlighten the minds of your servants, guide their councils, and prosper their measures, that whatsoever they do, shall result in your good, and shall secure to you the peace, friendship, and approbation of all nations." In other words, Providence favors Americans. America is a land of milk and honey because Providence guides it and has a special commitment to its virtue and prosperity. In fact, in Jefferson's mind and heart, Providence was a Jeffersonian Republican.

CHAPTER FOURTEEN

The Ladies of Williamsburg

1805–1809

Jefferson had had a long engagement with what was known as "Indian affairs." During the Revolutionary War, his message to the tribes of the Eastern seaboard and the Ohio Valley had been that you are either with us or against us in our fight against the British. It is in our mutual self-interest, he argued, to be allies in war and in peace. When, in June 1781, as governor of Virginia, he had met with John-Baptiste Ducoigne, the pro-American chief of the Kaskaskia nation, he eloquently addressed in a written text the inevitable postwar issue: How were the Indian tribes and white American settlers to share the same land? Jefferson's answer was couched in what he and his contemporaries believed to be the enlightened liberal view of the proper relationship between white Americans and Native Americans: we urge you to be more like us. All will be well, or at least for the best, if you become tillers of the soil and at peace with one another. The first message was well-intentioned, though self-serving; the second was well-intentioned but hypocritical: white people were killing one another as frequently as were Indian tribes and, as in the Revolutionary War, on a much larger scale.

In Jefferson's view, American Indians were not inherently inferior to white Americans. They were, though, behind in their cultural development. They were roamers, not settlers. They killed game and one another rather than grew crops. Like many of his contemporaries, Jefferson believed there was a natural pattern of cultural development from the primitive gathering to hunting and fishing to the highest stage of all, agriculture, much as infants became children and children became adults. To him, American Indians were immature; his white contemporaries were adults.

Jefferson was sincere: he respected Indian culture and tribal identity, and he was fascinated by Indian languages, devoting time and energy to studying them. In 1781 he had addressed Jean-Baptiste Ducoigne and his people as "brothers." The language and tone of his paternalism was in a minor key, but by 1805 Indians were less brothers than "children." In his address to Ducoigne, he had further developed his personalized version of the language that white Americans used to communicate with Indian leaders, a dialect recognizably English but in the form of Indian-speak, English inflected into what Americans thought non-English-speaking Indians or those with a slight knowledge of English would understand. It was a language developed to communicate from superior to inferior, from the father in Washington to his Indian children. Astoundingly, even in this Indian-inflected English, Jefferson sometimes manages to be eloquent, affecting, and empathetic.

His address to Ducoigne was to a chief who had accepted the necessity of adapting to white-style agrarian life. By the time of Jefferson's Second Inaugural Address, Americans had been pushing across the continent for almost a century, regardless of European nations or Indian tribes claiming right of possession. The territorial realities had changed. The push had become a shove. "The aboriginal inhabitants of these countries," he told Congress in March 1805, "I have regarded with the commiseration their history inspires." They are "endowed with the faculties and the rights of men, breathing an ardent love of liberty and independence, and occupying a country which left them no desire but to be undisturbed." But "the stream of overflowing population from other regions directed itself on these shores; without power to divert, or habits to contend against, they have been overwhelmed by the current, or driven before it." They could no longer be hunters, he said. "Humanity enjoins us to teach them agriculture and the domestic arts; to encourage them to that industry which alone can enable them to maintain their place in existence, and to prepare them in time for that state of society, which to bodily comforts adds the improvement of the mind and morals."

But there were "powerful obstacles." Those, though, came from internal tribal dissensions, "a sanctimonious reverence for the customs of their ancestor," and the belief that "reason is a false guide . . . the action and counteraction of good sense and bigotry; they, too, have their anti-philosophers, who find an interest in keeping things in their present state . . . ." Noncompliant Indians, like anti-Jeffersonian Federalists, needed to be encouraged to accept Enlightenment Republicans as overlords. For it was the national destiny that white Americans occupy the entire continent, including Canada and Florida, probably Cuba, and perhaps Mexico, a continent-wide expansion of freeholders under the aegis of Jeffersonian republicanism. To perpetuate the spirit of '76, Republican government required westward expansion, real estate for American citizens to transform into rural harmony and agricultural prosperity.

Between 1801 and 1806, Jefferson wrote at least five addresses to different Indian tribes. He also hosted tribal leaders in Washington. Indian affairs occupied prominent paragraphs in his messages to Congress. In his State of the Union Address in December 1801, he had emphasized the success of his Indian policy. All was going well. All would be well. "Among our Indian neighbors . . . a spirit of peace and friendship [is] generally prevailing and I am happy to inform you that the continued efforts to introduce among them the implements and the practice of husbandry, and of the household arts, have not been without success; that they are becoming more and more sensible of the superiority of this dependence for clothing and subsistence over the precarious resources of hunting and fishing." If they became farmers, they would need much less land. It was always almost entirely about real estate—to purchase, to trade for, to create treaties establishing legal ownership, to persuade Indians that conciliation with overwhelming force was better than confrontation, to try to prevent the white settlers who wanted their land and the Indians who desired to keep it from killing each other singly or en masse.

In January 1802, in Washington, Jefferson offered the olive branch of amity—though, as always, in the framework of assimilation or else—to the chiefs of the Miami Indians from Ohio, led by Little Turtle, whom Jefferson had met before.

On our part, we shall endeavor in all things to be just and generous towards you, and to aid you in meeting those difficulties which a change of circumstances is bringing on. We shall with great pleasure see your people become disposed to cultivate the earth to raise herds of the useful animals, and to spin and weave, for their food and clothing. These resources are certain: they will never disappoint you. While those of hunting may fail, and expose your women and children to the miseries of hunger and cold. We will with pleasure furnish you with implements for the most necessary arts, and with persons who may instruct you how to make and use them. I consider it as fortunate that you have made your visit at this time when our wise men from the sixteen states are collected together in council, who being equally disposed to befriend you can strengthen our hands in the good we all wish to render you.

Jefferson believed in the argument he made, duplicitous as it seems when read within the overall history of what the "wise men" of Congress decreed and what the facts on the ground actually were. In other contexts, Jefferson might have referred to congressmen as "wise men" with tongue in cheek. In reality, the communications between whites and natives and the treaties of amity signed between them always required that the Indians permanently trade their land for temporary peace.

Little Turtle accepted that reality. Most of his Miami colleagues did not. Little Turtle, whom Jefferson thought "the most intelligent man of his Race," made the case for his world. He already knew what Indian-speak meant. Apparently, his spoken words were taken down in shorthand and then transcribed for the record.

Father, it has again fell to my lot to make known to you the wish of your children. . . . My Father, and Brothers, by the Treaty it was mentioned that certain reservations should be made for the white people in our Country that the white people should not settle over the line described by the Treaty, that no individual of the white people should be allowed to purchase any land of the Indians, nor any Indians to sell to individuals of the White people, but that when your children were willing to sell any of their lands it should be sold to the United States, which we think a very happy circumstance, because the United States will not allow their Red Brothers to be cheated. Father some parts of the Treaty has not been so well understood as could be wished. . . . Father, we think some of the white people are settling over the line and we are fearful some of our young men may interrupt the harmony which prevails between the red and white people. . . . Father, by the Treaty of Greenville your children were promised a certain quantity of goods and money should be paid them annually, and this they expected would have been done.

As always, the promises were broken or were kept partially or badly, as Jefferson well knew.

Little Turtle's directness had its own power. He needed the help of the American government to keep his warriors from fighting to keep their land, and their own people being slaughtered in reprisal. Jefferson had to promise what he knew he couldn't deliver, but he believed he had to advocate a coercive process that was, in his judgment, preferable to genocidal extinction. It was also a policy that no American politician could oppose and that most Americans believed necessary for national prosperity—because it was their God-given right as a superior race. This policy had been determined from the first settlements, as European Americans advanced from the Virginia coast to the Blue Ridge Mountains and beyond. It required an unlimited western horizon to sustain the republic as an "Empire of liberty." Without Indian sequestration or elimination, Jefferson feared that the white American conquest would be stained by more blood, mostly red. Better, he had concluded, to persuade the tribes to take up farming on land set aside for them by the wisdom of the leaders of white America.

> Made by the same great spirit, and living in the same land with our brothers the red men, we consider ourselves as of the same family; we wish to live with them as one people, and to cherish their interests as our own. The evils which of necessity encompass the life of man are sufficiently numerous. Why should we add to them by voluntarily distressing and destroying one another? Peace, brothers, is better than war. In a long and bloody war, we lose many friends, and gain nothing. Let us then live in peace and friendship together, doing to each other all the good we can. The wise and good on both sides desire this, and we must take care that the foolish and wicked among us shall not prevent it.

Jefferson had reassured his Indian "brothers," who had reminded him of what he had said to them "when you visited me the last winter, that the lands you then held would remain yours, and shall never go from you but when you should be disposed to sell. This I now repeat, and will ever abide by. . . . This was done in the late case of which you complain. . . . All was reported to be free and fair. The lands were your property. The right to sell is one of the rights of property. To forbid you the exercise of that right would be a wrong to your nation." However, he continued, as he always did, telling them that selling would likely be to their advantage. In fact, as he told Congress in his special message on Indian policy in 1803, "in preparing them ultimately to participate in the benefits of our government, I trust and believe we are acting for their greatest good."

Writing in February 1803 to Benjamin Hawkins, the government's agent to the Creeks in Georgia, a tribe under great pressure to forfeit their lands, Jefferson used a revealing metaphor.

> The wisdom of the animal which amputates and abandons to the hunter the parts for which he is pursued, should be theirs, with this difference that the former sacrifices what is useful. The latter what is not. In truth the ultimate point of rest and happiness for them is to let our settlements and theirs meet and blend together, to intermix and become one people, incorporating themselves with us as citizens of the US. . . . Surely it will be better for them to be identified with us, and preserved in the occupation of their lands, than be exposed to the many casualties which may endanger them while a separate people.

In fact, he argued, and perhaps convinced himself, self-dismemberment for survival was the better part of wisdom.

It was crucial, he wrote in 1807 to his secretary of war, to go to great lengths to prevent the Indians from thinking "that these preparations are meant to intimidate them into a sale of their lands, an idea which would be most pernicious and would poison all our professions of friendship to them. The immediate acquisition of the land is of less consequence to us than their friendship and thorough confidence in our justice." It was an obvious shell game. "We had better let the purchase lie till they are in better temper," though the eventual "sale" of the land was a political, economic, intellectual, philosophical, and even, in Jefferson's eyes, a humanitarian necessity. "I feel it consistent with pure morality to lead them towards it, to familiarize them to the idea that it is for their interest," even though, like a wolf caught in a trap (to clarify Jefferson's intended metaphor), the Indian nations would have to self-amputate to escape certain death.

The trap was American expansionism, the "Empire of liberty," and to that end there was rarely anything that was not acceptable, in Jefferson's view, if it suited his purposes. Debt could be used as a weapon to pressure the Indian tribes—a revealing choice for a man himself deeply in debt. He again used the metaphor of self-amputation. "We shall push our trading houses, and be glad to see the good and influential individuals among them run in debt, because we observe that when these debts get beyond what the individuals can pay, they become willing to lop them off by a cession of lands. . . . As to their fear, we presume that our strength and their weakness is now so visible that they must see we have only to shut our hand to crush them, and that all our liberalities to them proceed from motives of pure humanity only."

At his second inaugural, Jefferson, as he had done since his first appearance on the political stage, looked westward with the Indian problem in the front view. It was always a double mirror, westward toward the lands that had already been cleared of Native Americans for white settlement, then farther westward toward those that still needed to be made available and safe for agrarian occupancy and national security. Assimilation was official government policy, but it had little impact on reality, partly because white settlers wanted instant ownership of all Western land, and partly because most natives, with some exceptions, did not want to assimilate. Still, Jefferson kept try-ing. Nevertheless, with or without Indian acquiescence, the "Empire of liberty" required its Western borders to be cleared for expansion and national security. As president, Jefferson's policy of

> "obtaining lands" resulted in the acquisition of about 200,000 square miles of Indian territory in nine states of the modern United States. . . . For the most part they were chosen primarily to clear Indians from the banks of the great rivers, the Ohio and the Missis-sippi, and to compress the eastern tribes into an interior region west of the Appalachians and east of the Mississippi, where they would be easier to dominate. It was essentially a military strategy: secure the supply lines and encircle the enemy . . . connecting American forts, frontier settlements, and centers of commerce. Jefferson had seen to the national security and the future expansion of the grow-ing white population into the remaining Indian territory east of the Mississippi, a task which Jackson would nearly complete a few years after Jefferson's death.

His and Andrew Jackson's heirs would, over the century, fulfilling Jefferson's expectation, do the same from the Mississippi to Califor-nia. By the end of 1805, his secretary Meriwether Lewis, a Virginian, and William Clark, leading the "corps of discovery," had the Pacific Ocean in sight.

Between 1805 and 1808, Jefferson made regular use of the lan-guage of Indian persuasion. The arguments and strategies were the same to the Creeks, Cherokees, Shawnees, and a half dozen other Indian nations. They had become "my children." He would be their protector. They would never be forced to sell. At the same time, strat-egies and tactics were put in place, and realities on the ground were tolerated, often with mild and unimplemented rebuke, that made In-dian resistance unavailing. He assured Congress in his annual address

in late 1806 that "we continue to receive proofs of the growing attachment of our Indian neighbors, and of their disposition to place
all their interests under the patronage of the United States. These
dispositions are inspired by their confidence in our justice, and . . . as
long as we discharge these high and honorable functions with the integrity and good faith which alone can entitle us to their continuance,
we may expect to reap the just reward in their peace and friendship."
He also reported on the success of the Lewis and Clark expedition,
his vanguard of far western territorial expansion.

Addressing the "People of the Mandan Nation," his mastery of
Indian-speak rose to unusual heights of eloquence and casuistry. Fact
and reason were beside the point, as had essentially been the case in
the Declaration and his First Inaugural Address. It is one of Jefferson's best and most multilayered uses of this special language:

> My children . . . I take you by the hand of friendship hearty welcome
> to the seat of the government of the United States. The journey
> which you have taken to visit your fathers on this side of our island
> is a long one. . . . I thank the great spirit that he has protected you
> through the journey and brought you safely to the residence of your
> friends, and I hope he will have you constantly in his safe keeping,
> and restore you in good health to your nations and families. My
> friends and children, we are descended from the old nations which
> live beyond the great water, but we and our forefathers have been
> so long here that we seem like you to have grown out of this land.
> We consider ourselves no longer of the old nations beyond the great
> water, but as united in one family with our red brethren here.
>
> The Europeans are gone, never to return.
>
> Remember the words I now speak to you, my children. . . . We are
> now your fathers; and you shall not lose by the change. . . . I felt the

desire of becoming acquainted with all my red children beyond the Mississippi, and of uniting them with us . . . in the bonds of peace and friendship. I wished to learn what we could do to benefit them by furnishing them the necessaries they want in exchange for their furs and peltries. I therefore sent our beloved man, captain Lewis, one of my own family, to go up the Missouri river to get acquainted with all the Indian nations in its neighborhood, to take them by the hand, deliver my talks to them, and to inform us in what way we could be useful to them. Your nation received him kindly, you have taken him by the hand and been friendly to him. My children, I thank you for the services you rendered him, and for your attention to his words. He will now tell us where we should establish trading houses to be convenient to you all, and what we must send to them.

My friends and children, I have now an important advice to give you. I have already told you that you and all the red men are my children, and I wish you to live in peace and friendship with one another as brethren of the same family ought to do. How much better is it for neighbors to help than to hurt one another; how much happier must it make them. If you will cease to make war on one another, if you will live in friendship with all mankind, you can employ all your time in providing food and clothing for yourselves and your families. . . . Remember then my advice, my children, carry it home to your people, and tell them that from the day that they have become all of the same family, from the day that we became father to them all, we wish, as a true father should do, that we may all live together as one household, and that before they strike one another, they should go to their father and let him endeavor to make up the quarrel. My children, you are come from the other side of our great island, from where the sun sets, to see your new friends at the sun rising. You have now arrived where the waters are constantly rising and falling every day, but you are still distant from the sea. I very much desire that you should not stop here, but go and see your brethren as far as the edge of the great water. . . . By the time you come back the snows will be melted on the mountains, the ice in the rivers broken up, and you will be wishing to set out on your return home. My children, I have long desired to see you; I have now opened my heart to you, let my words sink into your hearts and never be forgotten. If ever lying people or bad spirits should raise up clouds between us, call to mind what I have said, and what you have seen yourselves . . . let us come together as friends and explain to each other what is misrepresented or misunderstood, the clouds will fly away like morning fog, and the sun of friendship appear and shine forever bright and clear between us.

Jefferson may not have been purposely duplicitous. He may have convinced himself, at least in the process of writing so eloquently, that his message was sincere and morally sound. "With our Indian neighbors the public peace has been steadily maintained," he reported to Congress in his last annual message. "Some instances of individual wrong have, as at other times, taken place," he admitted, "but in nowise implicating the will of the nation." The Mississippi "now belongs to us," he told the Cherokees. "It must not be a river of blood." Tell other Indian tribes "that their father here receives them all into his bosom as his children. . . . They will find in me an affectionate father." Given the domestic realities, including his vision of an agricultural "Empire of liberty," he skillfully defined himself as acting in the best interest of the victims, transforming them into beneficiaries, justifying as moral what otherwise might have been seen, even by some whites, as manipulative and exploitative. "With the whole of these people, in every quarter, I shall continue to inculcate peace and friendship with all their neighbors and perseverance in those occupations and pursuits which will best promote their own well-being." It was necessary, though, he emphasized to the Senate in 1808, "to obliterate from the Indian mind an impression deeply made in it, that we are constantly forming designs on their lands. . . . I have thought it best, where urged by no peculiar necessity to the pressure of their own convenience only, to come forward with offers of sale to the United States." Most Cherokees, Choctaws, and Creeks would have seen things differently.

Jefferson kept up the attempt at persuasion. Language was his medium. He wrote out all his addresses. The message was always the same. The key phrases sometimes repeated themselves. And the assertive tone sometimes had, in its register and rhetoric, a plaintiveness, a touch of sadness, even a touch of desperation, as if he well knew that the Western drama would play out with a tragic and inevitable finality. He played the hand he had been dealt, and he dealt the cards himself. It was his inclination, by personality and personal history, to make the best of what he believed he could not change, at least not without an effort and a loss he was not willing to sustain.

In the case of the Indian tribes, it was assimilate or die. It may not have been fair, he recognized, but there was no other way, even for "noble savages." In the case of slavery, there were no "noble savages," and Jefferson, ignorant of Africa, doubted the potential for Blacks to move up the ladder of civilization. There was manumission for those slave-owners who could afford it, and in theory there was colonization, forced removal to a distant land they had never personally known for a race and a population Jefferson believed could never live in peace with their former white masters. In practice, of course, the Black labor force needed to stay for an indefinite time. American Indians, though, had hardly ever been a labor force for white settlers, certainly not a major one. They needed to be and could be disposed of, and assimilation seemed to Jefferson the most humane way.

Over and over again, he used Indian-speak to try to get them to hear and obey. Did he at some time acknowledge, at least to himself, that voluntary dispossession was incompatible with Indian tradition, history, religion, and culture? Did he not, at least in passing moments, recognize the tension if not opposition between the spirit of '76 and a policy that required that the Indian nations be forcibly deprived of territory, self-rule, and communal self-identity? Assimilate or die was the harsh subtext of Jefferson's language of persuasion, of his claim of patriarchal concern for the welfare of "my children." His language sometimes concealed, sometimes revealed; sometimes it did both simultaneously. It seems likely that Jefferson, in his expression of the will of the American people and his own vision of expansion, knew what he was doing, what the tragic finale of the slowly unwinding end of this drama would be. Even if so, he was apparently incapable of envisioning an alternative. Some version of Indian removal was necessary for the creation of his "Empire of liberty." And he was very good at accepting by repression or accommodation realities that he had neither the power nor the will to change. In 1818 he wrote to Albert Gallatin that there was only one passage in President Monroe's "message which I disapprove, and which I trust will not be approved by our legislators. It is that which proposes to subject the Indians to our laws without their consent. A little patience and a little money, are so rapidly producing their voluntary removal across the Mississippi, that I hope this immorality will not be permitted to stain our history." Gallatin knew better.

For much of his life Jefferson had believed that the right to vote should be limited to owners of agricultural property rather than given as a right to all adults. He believed that freeholders, by virtue of ownership, the tie that binds them to the local soil, would have a more principled, independent, and disinterested attachment to the welfare of their community, state, and country than those who rented land or worked for a salary or made products, as did most urbanites. Those who earned their living in commerce, on land or sea, had an equally tenuous hold on republican virtue and citizenship. Landowners would best embody and express republican principles. "From 40 years of intimate conversation with the agricultural inhabitants of my country," he wrote to a French friend in early 1802, "I can pronounce them as different from those of the cities, as the inhabitants of any two nations known. The sentiments of the former can in no degree be inferred from those of the latter."

Jefferson had spent a substantial part of his career as a legislator eliminating laws that favored inherited estates and land speculation, land being transferred from one generation to another under restrictive covenants created by a granting entity, such as a royal charter, generational inheritance, or legislative act. Eventually, to Jefferson's distress, that made it possible for land to become a commodity to be bought, sold, or rented in a capitalistic system in which the rights of ownership were totally invested in an individual or consortium that could dispose of it in any way desired. Jefferson never envisioned agricultural property as the basis of an agricultural industry in which land would be bought and sold for profit, a salable commodity in an economy in which the primary reason for the ownership of anything was its marketplace value. Jefferson wanted Virginia to embody his vision of independent freeholders who owned farms of modest size. He believed that those who worked the land would be inclined to love their communities, to have strong local attachments; they would be fair and peace loving, would value personal and political independence, would be more free than nonlandowners to exercise their own judgment as citizens, and would be republican in their political and moral embrace of the principles of the Revolution. Land would always be, Jefferson believed, the soil in which virtue and citizenship would grow from generation to generation. Out of that soil would come republican leaders.

His first mission as president had been to reduce to a minimum, without counterproductive turmoil and hostility, the Federalist hold on government offices, particularly in the judiciary. "I found the country entirely in the enemy's hands. It was necessary to dislodge some of them." By 1804, he had done that. Congress was in the hands of Republicans, with a huge majority in the House, a small majority in the Senate. But enemies, who did not share his republican vision and the value he attached to agriculture and freeholds, still held the judicial reins, though less tightly than previously. In 1805, he conspired and collaborated with the House of Representatives to impeach Supreme Court Justice Samuel Chase, an outspoken Federalist who epitomized for Jefferson the use of the judicial bench for partisan purposes. Anyway, why should a previous administration have the right to saddle the next with its judicial appointments any more than a previous generation should require the present generation to pay debts that it had incurred? Chase was impeached, but the Senate, in a close vote, failed to convict. Jefferson would have to wait for retirements or deaths to appoint Republican judges, and he soon discovered that his appointees did not always meet his expectations. Most distressingly, he had to endure a chief justice with a considerably different view than his of what should be the powers of the Court and the federal government.

Jefferson believed in government by majority, but his democracy had a small *d*. He governed in a country in which only a small fraction of the population had the right to vote, though it was a larger fraction than had been the case previously and much larger than anyplace else in the world. And though he favored a further expansion of white male suffrage, he also placed his faith in the belief that the electorate would always be overwhelmingly white, male, and Republican, that it would be self-correcting, and that it would elect the best qualified to be its leaders. "It will be for ever seen that of bodies of men, even elected by the people," he wrote in 1803, "there will always be a greater proportion aristocratic than among their constituents." These would be the "natural aristocrats," natural by talent, virtue, education, and experience, men like himself, Madison, and Gallatin. Jefferson was too sincere in his delusions to have doubts, let alone concede, that his own leadership had any self-serving element of class, ideology, or sectional interest.

He proclaimed the superiority of common men as voters, not leaders. It was the foundation of his belief in widespread representation for white males. If the mass of such people were ever a violent mob, then "a little blood" sometimes was necessary to water the liberty tree. If their elected representatives made unwise or self-serving decisions, then over time that would be corrected: a republic contained the self-correcting mechanism of the practical common sense of the people. It was rhetoric that justified a government controlled by the Southern proprietors of wealth in alliance with independent farmers and the slave-profiting merchant class of the North. It favored Western expansion, agriculture, and trade. They were its engines of growth and prosperity.

Jefferson's pen was almost always at work during his presidency. The right wrist that he had damaged decades before had never properly healed. Over time, his right hand did become useful again, with some aches and slight deformation. Other than exercise on horseback and dinner table hosting of congressmen, he spent a good part of most days writing, with his newly purchased steel-nib pens, notes and memoranda, drafts of legislation, proclamations, addresses to Congress and to Indian chiefs, and many letters. He wrote instructions to his Cabinet members. He prepared notes for meetings. He managed business correspondence about Monticello and his farms. Correspondence with friends often dealt with political issues and the state of the country, sometimes at considerable length. In a minimalist government, with few employees, almost everything of any consequence at all came to his desk. A meticulously clean man by the standards of his time, his fingers were frequently ink stained.

As a man who would rather write than talk, and with only one secretary, he was often, as a matter of exigency, habit, and self-definition, at his writing desk. That pose and that activity defined a major part of his life. In the latter part of his second term, he felt it even more than ever a tiresome chore, partly because some major domestic problems seemed irresolvable, partly because of the ever imminent likelihood that the United States might be at war with Britain or France or both, and because there seemed no satisfactory formula for maintaining prosperity, peace, and national honor. It was not a situation that inspired Jefferson's pen.

From 1803 to 1805, Jefferson and his party basked in the glow of the Louisiana Purchase. His agenda still included Florida, Texas, Mexico, Cuba, and Canada. He expected that through diplomacy the "Empire of liberty" would eventually obtain them. And he wanted "freedom of the seas." That meant an end to Britain and France restricting American trade, especially in the Caribbean. "Freedom of the seas" also meant that American ships would be free from restraint or interference anyplace and that the status of the United States as a neutral nation would be respected, its cargoes and crews immune from seizure. "Freedom of the seas," for Jefferson, had the aura of a natural right. Neither France nor Britain agreed. Each believed it had the right to confiscate materials that helped its enemy's war efforts. Britain ruled the seas. France controlled the continent. Each passed decrees retaliating against the other. Britain had reason to believe its survival was at risk. Both European powers decreed real and phantom blockades. They boarded American ships, searching for contraband, always loosely defined by each in its own interest. They confiscated American vessels at will, to different degrees at different times and with varying justifications.

Despite all this, the advantages the Napoleonic Wars provided the United States were substantial: the economy prospered, and import taxes provided the revenue to pay for the federal government and pay down much of the national debt. For Jefferson, the challenge was to keep the United States at peace. Only peace would perpetuate the profits and revenues from the carrying trade. Better to accept confiscations and insults than retaliate militarily. The threat of going to war was a legitimate tactic; going to war, a likely disaster. Jefferson and the country needed to zig and zag. It was not a pretty sight, and not everyone agreed with Jefferson's approach, though to different degrees and at different times between 1805 and 1809.

In his third annual message, Jefferson congratulated Congress and himself on having avoided the latest incitements to war with Britain or France. Providence and geography, he explained, were on the side of the United States.

> We have seen with sincere concern the flames of war lighted up again in EUROPE, and nations with which we have the most friendly and useful relations engaged in mutual destruction. . . . In the course of this conflict, let it be our endeavor, as it is our interest and desire, to cultivate the friendship of the belligerent nations by every act of justice and of incessant kindness; to receive their armed vessels with hospitality from the distresses of the sea; . . . to restrain our citizens from embarking individually in a war in which their country takes no part; to punish severely those persons, citizen or alien, who shall usurp the cover of our flag for vessels not entitled to it; . . . to exact from every nation the observance, toward our vessels and citizens, of those principles and practices which all civilized people acknowledge; to merit the character of a just nation, and maintain that of an independent one, preferring every consequence to insult and habitual wrong. . . . Separated by a wide ocean from the nations of Europe, and from the political interests which entangle them together, with productions and wants which render our commerce and friendship useful to them, . . . it cannot be the interest of any to assail us, nor ours to disturb them. We should be most unwise, indeed, were we to cast away the singular blessings of the position in which nature has placed us, the opportunity she has endowed us with of pursuing, at a distance from foreign contentions,

the paths of industry, peace, and happiness; of cultivating general friendship, and of bringing collisions of interest to the umpirage of reason rather than of force.

Jefferson's prose in his third annual message had some of its usual power and precision, but it also had the hollowness of a futile policy. Without the power to defend itself, the United States provided neither Britain nor France reason to respect America's definition of "freedom of the seas" although neither wished to be at war with the United States. Jefferson wanted to avoid war at almost all costs, though not every American agreed. Some Republican members of Congress let him and the public know that they were contemptuous of his zigs and zags.

Napoléon dismissed the United States as insignificant. London had more complicated considerations. British society was less autocratic than the French. There were competing ideological, political, and commercial interests, each with somewhat different attitudes toward their American cousins, and though the United States was its most important trading partner, Britain had a worldwide network. It could do without American trade if necessary. Jefferson assumed it could not. In his mind, Britain was dependent on trade with the United States. It was his model and his mantra, starting with the nonimportation policies of the American colonies in 1774. In his Anglophobic delusion, he believed that Britain was so dependent on American agricultural products that, if deprived of them, it would eventually cry uncle. In fact, Britain had higher priorities and more critical concerns. It was absolutely essential to its survival that it defeat Napoléon's aggressions. The homeland was at stake. Consequently, Britain believed it necessary for national survival that the Royal Navy maintain control of the seas. No change in ministry altered that conviction.

Controlling the entire Atlantic, British warships regularly boarded

American commercial ships to retrieve British-born sailors. Great Britain defined citizenship by birth as irrevocable. The United States did not. Serving in the Royal Navy was onerous. American ships provided better working conditions, pay, and safety. And the United States considered British-born immigrants and citizens to be under the protection of the American flag. To the British, these were deserters, and it appears likely that the number of these deserters roughly equaled the number of sailors impressed from American ships. British impressment was deeply and bitterly resented by all Americans. A diplomatic resolution, though, was not impossible. Britain intimated that if the United States would cooperate in detaining and returning proven British-born deserters in American ports, the impressments at sea might be halted. American pride and Jefferson's Anglophobia rejected that behind-the-scenes overture. Impressments and confiscations continued throughout Jefferson's presidency.

The American economy flourished as long as Britain and France were at war. American privateers and trading ships threaded the Atlantic and initiated a Pacific presence. In December 1805, Jefferson warned that aggressive British tactics that amounted to piracy threatened American prosperity and peace. This was about ships, not sailors.

> Our coasts have been infested and our harbors watched by private armed vessels, some of them without commissions, some with illegal commissions, others with those legal form. But committing piratical acts beyond the authority of their commissions they have captured in the very entrance of our harbors, as well as on the high seas, not only the vessels of our friends coming to trade with us, but our own also. . . . The same system of hovering on our coasts and harbors under color of seeking enemies has been also carried on by public armed ships to the great annoyance and oppression of our commerce. New principles, too, have been interpolated into the law

of nations, founded neither in justice nor the usage or acknowledgment of nations.

Jefferson proposed defensive measures "to place our seaport town(s)
out of danger of insult" and to modernize the militia system so "we
may draw from it when necessary an efficient corps fit for real and active service. . . . Considerable provision," he reminded Congress, "has
been made . . . for the construction of ships of war of 74 gun."

Jefferson's call to arms was more sound that fury. Congress was
reluctant to allocate money for an effective defense. Navy yard inef-
ficiencies and corruption had slowed construction. Jefferson, in fact,
did not push hard, and the notion of an offensive force was anathema to him. Many Americans, though, fantasized about and some
argued for war. Canada, ripe fruit for the picking, would then become
American territory. Still, whatever his verbal zigs and zags against
France, Britain, and Spain, Jefferson did not want to go to war. He
believed that refusing to trade with Britain or France or, if necessary,
a total embargo on international shipping would bring the major European powers to their knees. He sent James Monroe to London in
1806–1807. Monroe got nowhere. The British were preoccupied with
Napoléon. They also objected to American port cities giving sanctuary to British-born sailors, and they had reason to believe American
neutrality was to the advantage of France. It seemed to the British
that the Jefferson administration had at a minimum an unconscious
bias in favor of its ally in the war for independence. Jefferson's appeal
to "international law" or the "law of nations," as had all such previous American appeals, went nowhere. It was, in fact, an appeal to
something that mostly did not exist. Jefferson had done a great deal
of reading about what the law of nations should be. His library was
filled with the standard authorities. He gave, though, only minimal
recognition to the reality, especially when American interests were at
stake. He argued, with moral passion, that "freedom of the seas" was

a national right, that nation-states had or ought to have a moral conscience, and that human rights transcended national self-interest. The
fact that "international law" was mostly the aspirational optimism of
idealists mostly escaped him. The reality was that each nation-state
defined it or dispensed with it in its own way for its own purposes.

When Jefferson left Monticello in October 1807, the travails of his
journey back to Washington added insult to injury. He left Monticello with regret. He hoped that he would soon be able to renounce
forever the four-day, 118-mile commute. He was having built from his
design an octagonal house about 90 miles southwest of Monticello on
a tobacco plantation called Poplar Forest, inherited from his father-
in-law. It was a project that engaged and delighted him, regardless
of cost and debts, probably without any sense of the irony that this
retirement home was being built by his slaves on property inherited
from an estate whose settlement had helped put him in debt. In May,
from Washington, he had written to Lafayette that "I am panting for
retirement, but am as yet nearly two years from that goal. The general
solicitations I have received to continue another term give me great
consolation, but considerations public as well as personal determine
me inflexibly on that measure."

The seventh year of his presidency had so far been particularly
difficult. Now, returning to Washington, his carriage fording the
Rapidan River, his horse unexpectedly lay down "waist deep" in the
water. Castor "nearly drowned," Jefferson wrote to his daughter, "before the servants, jumping into the water could lift his head out and
cut him loose from the carriage." The incident could have been seen
as an eerily private version of the watery dangers that American ships
encountered at sea. His horse Castor was saved from drowning. His
slaves did the heavy and dangerous work. "This was followed," he
wrote, "by the loss of my travelling money. . . . Two days after my

arrival here I was taken with the Influenza, but it was very slight, without either fever or pain and is now nearly passed off." His Washington miseries, though, were not to pass off quickly or ever. The last two years of his presidency were painful to him and to the country. Immediately ahead of him was the resolution of the *Chesapeake-Leopard* Affair, with war or peace hanging in the balance.

On June 22, 1807, the HMS *Leopard* had fired on the outgunned and unprepared USS *Chesapeake* off the coast of Norfolk, Virginia. A tragic comedy of errors by both captains resulted in three Americans dead and eighteen wounded. HMS *Leopard* had been blockading two French warships that had taken refuge in Chesapeake Bay. Its captain believed, correctly, that some members of the *Chesapeake* crew were British-born deserters. The American commodore, assuming that the encounter would be nonintrusive, was unprepared for an attack. The *Chesapeake*, after all, was an American warship, not a commercial vessel. To board it, let alone fire on it, was an act of war. The United States and Great Britain were not at war. When the British captain's search request was declined and an explicit warning disregarded, *HMS Leopard* fired a broadside into the *Chesapeake*, whose guns were unloaded and decks cluttered with unstowed supplies. The American commodore surrendered rather than see further casualties and his ship destroyed. Four sailors were removed, three of them British nationals and Royal Navy deserters; there were other British nationals on the *Chesapeake*. Both the British captain's and the American commodore's careers were damaged by the incident. The HMS *Leopard* had taken an unauthorized deadly initiative, an embarrassment to the admiralty in London, which did not want war with the United States. Eventually, there would be reparations.

Through the summer of 1807, the American public wanted revenge. War drums beat, and editorial trumpets demanded vindication. The possibility that public pressure would force him to ask Congress to declare war distressed Jefferson. Monroe, in London, was instructed in no uncertain terms to add reparations for the *Chesapeake* to his list of treaty demands and to make that inseparable from British agreement to stop impressments. The president was firm about that. For London, that was a nonstarter, even if a deal was struck on other matters. Without British renunciation of impressment, Jefferson would accept no treaty at all. At some level of self-awareness, he had to have known that Britain would not ever agree to desist from recovering Royal Navy deserters as long as Britain and France were at war. Without its huge fleet fully staffed, Whitehall and the Palace had reason to fear that Napoléon would soon be in London. But what was the level of restitution Jefferson could accept? Short of full satisfaction on impressment, would he urge Congress to declare war? If he did, how could his much-favored and low-cost light gunships be a match for powerful British warships? War would be immensely costly. "Reparation for the past, security for the future is demanded," he wrote in late July. It seemed likely to Jefferson that, since British pride would never accede and American pride was demanding action, a resolution would require war. In his mind, though, he still believed that commercial pressure on Britain would bring it to the negotiating table.

In April 1806, he had convinced Congress to pass a bill banning the importation of a list of British manufactured products otherwise unavailable in the United States. Its start was delayed in the hope that Britain would rethink its impressment policy. It effected no change in British policy, and the American public resented the deprivation. In July 1807, in response to the attack on the *Chesapeake*, Jefferson issued a proclamation, which he delayed delivering to Congress until November, hoping the British government would come to the table and giving American ships time to sail out of harm's way. American ships around the world, empty of cargo, began their voyages home. The proclamation also required that "all armed vessels bearing commissions under the Government of Great Britain now within the harbors or waters of the United States immediately and without any delay to depart from the same. . . ." Any Americans provisioning British ships, as had been regular practice, would be subject to criminal prosecution.

Calling for a special session of Congress to meet in October 1807, he recognized that Congress was "extremely disposed for peace, and as there is no doubt Gr. Br. will disavow the act of the Leopard, I am inclined to believe they will be more disposed to combat her practice of impressment by a non-importation law than by arms. I am at the same time not without all hope she may relinquish the pretension to impressment on our agreeing not to employ her seamen, which it is our interest to agree to." It was wishful thinking about both matters. But he also feared that "if we resort to non-importation, it will end in war and give her the choice of the moment of declaring it."

It seemed throughout the summer and fall of 1807 that war was likely. Jefferson hoped to avoid it by trade limitations, which he still believed to be an available and effective weapon. He could start by prohibiting some British imports. If necessary, this could be expanded into an embargo on all trade with Britain, or both Britain and France, or even a total embargo on exporting timber, cotton, tobacco, hemp, and wheat to Europe. From the start, it was not a popular policy. His Cabinet was not unanimously behind it. His secretary of the Treasury argued against it. Jefferson, though, was confident that he and Madison were right. Putting his pen to work, he himself drafted an embargo bill. A compliant Congress passed it. In January 1808, loopholes in the bill were closed. The legislation forbade any American ship to travel to any foreign port. In March 1808, directed by Jefferson, Congress added to the legislation a prohibition on the export of any goods at all from the United States to any other country.

In London, Monroe and William Pinkney signed a treaty that provided some concessions to American commerce but nothing about impressment. There was no progress on reparations for the *Chesapeake* slaughter, either. The British had rejected Jefferson's insistence that it be a part of the general treaty negotiation. Though the Monroe treaty breached Jefferson's instruction that no treaty on commercial matters would be acceptable if it did not deal with impressment, his London representatives reluctantly concluded that something was better than nothing.

The total trade blackout was a disaster. Both Great Britain and France found alternate sources of agricultural products. Government revenue, most of which had come from the carrying trade, plunged. European traders and ships quickly exploited the opportunity. From the European standpoint, it seemed self-inflicted American folly, and unsustainable. At home, Jefferson supporters defended the embargo. It was better than military conflict. Others accepted the call to sacrifice. Southern farmers and Northern business interests suffered. New England deplored the stranglehold on its economic lifeblood. So did other parts of the country. Smuggling flourished; the American smuggling industry had always been among the best in the world. Hunger and money were powerful motivating forces, and policing every point of exit and entry was a geographical nightmare. Angry and stubborn, Jefferson expanded and empowered law enforcement by executive fiat, an oppressive act by America's best-known libertarian. However, even rigorous enforcement efforts could not prevent illegal trade.

It was a sectionally divisive policy. Some New Englanders revived thoughts of secession. The entire country suffered. So did Jefferson. It initiated one of the worst two years of his life. Motivated by ideology rather than practicality, there was also a personal dimension: apparently, the privileged farmer from the agricultural South felt compelled to believe that Europe would starve without American farm products. It was a narrow and inaccurate perspective. By the turn into the nineteenth century, it was a misreading of international reality. Alas, Jefferson attributed the failure of his policy not to inherent flaws but to lack of self-sacrificing patriotism, a betrayal of the spirit of '76. He did not have much sympathy for those on whom his policy inflicted economic misery.

In early 1808, Jefferson was disappointed at his granddaughter's "bad account of the patriotism of the ladies of Williamsburg who are not disposed to submit to the small privations to which the embargo will subject them. I hope this will not be general." Naïvely out of touch, as if in a time warp, he invoked the good old days of national sacrifice, oblivious to or contemptuous of the craving of Americans for manufactured goods from Europe, which later generations would assume to be a given of daily life. "I can assure you from experience," he asserted, "that we never lived so comfortably as while we were reduced to this system formerly; because we soon learnt to supply all our real wants at home." He evoked what he thought of as the spirit of '76, though in 1776 and certainly thereafter definitions differed about exactly what that spirit was or should be. As Jefferson's embargo became a continuing fact of life, it became increasingly clear to the people as a whole, whatever their political views, that this was not a sustainable sacrifice. Jefferson kept trying, but in March 1809, a few days before the end of his presidency, he reluctantly allowed the embargo to be repealed, freeing his chosen successor of this political incubus. During its two years, Jefferson had no inspiring words to put to paper to help his constituents. His pen was active in other public ways but was not effective or eloquent. As each day went by, he was more and more looking forward to his moment of release.

In the three years leading up to the miseries of the embargo policy, Jefferson had another major controversy to deal with, one that his emotional involvement exacerbated and that he felt compelled to write long letters, memos, and policy directives about. The source of the mess was Aaron Burr, a man he detested, though Jefferson contributed substantially to making the Burr affair much worse than it had to be. From early on, Jefferson had been repressively masterful at concealing from public display his feelings about those he disliked. Two emotions that he did his best to repress were anger and hatred. They were incompatible with his ideal model of himself, his moral self-definition. Philosophically and intellectually, he gave high value to stoic self-control, and he had long developed a commitment to knowing when and how a Virginia gentleman should express his feelings, especially undesirable ones. Valuing social comity as the essential foundation of a harmonious community, he assumed that quiet amiability in the face of disagreement or personal attack best served himself and society. It was better for all concerned, he believed, never to allow oneself to be seen as a victim, as aggrieved or angry, let alone resentful.

Sometimes, though, his dislike rose to hatred. In many cases, those who rose to that level of vileness in Jefferson's opinion were political enemies, especially Alexander Hamilton and Aaron Burr. It's probably accurate to say that Jefferson hated only three other men, Benedict Arnold, John Marshall, and Patrick Henry, though about Henry he had some positive things to say. Arnold had betrayed the Revolution and led an invasion of Virginia. The Federalist John Marshall was, like Hamilton, an enemy of the spirit of '76 and republicanism. When President Adams sent John Marshall to negotiate with France, Jefferson intemperately and incorrectly claimed that the XYZ dish was "cooked up by Marshall, where the swindlers are made to appear as the French government." Shortly before leaving office, Adams nominated Marshall to be chief justice of the Supreme Court. Jefferson's hostility to Marshall as an exponent and embodiment of Federalism was so great that it amounted to hatred, which, as with Burr, allowed him to elevate malicious rumor into fact. One of his fondest hopes was to have Marshall impeached.

With Burr, he had a suspect character to deal with; with Marshall, he did not. Marshall, who believed the Court had the authority to determine constitutional law, represented to Jefferson the exploitation of judicial power to thwart his attempt to revivify American republicanism and to limit the powers of the federal government. Marshall twice had the duty to administer to Jefferson the oath of office. By an accident of jurisdiction, he also became the presiding judge at the Jefferson administration's trial of Aaron Burr for treason.

Patrick Henry was a political and a Revolutionary War ally, but he also was the man who had been, Jefferson believed, the power behind the attempt of members of the Virginia House of Delegates to censure him, charging that he had failed to competently defend Virginia against the British invasion. It was an attack on his reputation that Jefferson bitterly resented. In 1799, a month before Henry's death, he wrote that Henry should be known more for his "intriguing and cajoling talents" than "for his eloquence."

In responding to Henry's first biographer, Jefferson began, as he often did, by making a character assessment with a seemingly balanced overview: "We had a very familiar intercourse for upwards of 20 years, and ran our course nearly together. During this our political principles being the same, we acted in perfect concert until the year 1781. . . . He was certainly the man who gave the first impulse to the ball of revolution." But his character was "of mixed aspect. I think he was the best humored man in society I almost ever knew, and the greatest orator that ever lived. He had a consummate knowledge of the human heart, which directing the efforts of his eloquence enabled him to attain a degree of popularity with the people at large never perhaps equaled. His judgment in other matters was inaccurate in matters of law it was not worth a copper: he was avaricious and rotten hearted. His two great passions were the love of money and of fame: but when these came into competition the former predominated." Jefferson's knife is slowly applied, with an eloquent twist. It then strikes deep into the heart. The balanced assessment becomes a death thrust.

There were many colleagues in public life whom Jefferson had differences with, particularly Adams and Washington. He had strong feelings about both, but not hatred. For Jefferson, they were full personalities, associates with whom he had political but not personal differences. They were men of character. In his heart, he respected both and had affection for Adams. The relationship with Washington was a formal one, befitting a man whose personality did not lend itself to informality. His friendship with Adams was, on and off and on again, an intimate one. He could never feel comfortable with Adams's confrontational personality. Cultural differences kept them from a close embrace, the difference between Virginia and Massachusetts always a factor. Their shared love of and deep immersion in the classics provided an enduring bond. So also did their status as fellow warriors in the events of 1776. Adams's moderate Federalism, though, seemed to Jefferson insufficiently republican; Jefferson's idealism seemed too unrealistically rosy to Adams. Their friendship, though it barely survived Jefferson's defeat of Adams in the nasty election of 1800 and was in hiatus for over a decade, was to be resumed after Jefferson's retirement from the presidency, at first tentatively, then with a frequent exchange of expressive letters in which both were at their best as writers, intellectuals, and human beings. They were to be among Jefferson's best writing in his later years, the last sustained flowering of his gift as a writer of letters, a genre in which both he and Adams were masterful.

While preoccupied with Burr, Jefferson also had another difficult man to deal with, John Randolph. A Republican ultra-anti-nationalist from two elite Virginia families, six times elected to Congress between 1799 and 1813, Randolph was speaker of the House and chairman of the Ways and Means Committee during Jefferson's presidency. An extreme advocate of states' rights, controversially flamboyant in speech and style, Randolph was a version of Tristram Shandy without the sentimentality, an immensely talented eccentric but also arrogant, biting, and egomaniacal. He had, by 1805, made himself almost anathema to a large majority of his fellow Republicans. To add insult to injury, his frequent verbal evisceration of his colleagues combined satirical rhetoric, sometimes verging on madness, with irrepressible Ciceronian eloquence. When he took to the House floor, he often held it for two or more hours. Seated, he expressed himself loudly regardless of the rules. His rhetorical talents and verbal energy dominated debate. Sacrificing leadership for performance, he amused, riveted, and horrified many of his colleagues, an irrepressible congressional circus performer, usually accompanied in the House by his two massive dogs, who made themselves comfortable in all ways. Members of both parties found his indecorous behavior insulting.

Between 1801 and 1803, Jefferson thought he could work with Randolph, but he was gradually disabused of that notion. Randolph excoriated Jefferson's and Madison's modest nationalistic and egalitarian policies. Both men, in Randolph's view, were traitors to the true principles of republicanism, and he particularly despised Madison.

Randolph had a point, but it was pushed to excess. Moderate Republicans and moderate Federalists had more in common with one another than with their colleagues to the left or the right. At times they created a viable center for governing. Firmly on the side of elite rule and hostile to any extension of federal power at all, Randolph's extreme states' rights republicanism differed from Jefferson's as much as Adams's Federalism differed from that of ultra-Federalists like Hamilton. Energetically self-destructive, Randolph led a small subgroup of like-minded colleagues, mostly Southerners. They became in essence a third party. If Jefferson could be pushed out of the presidency in 1804, Randolph imagined himself secretary of state to the man he hoped would be Jefferson's successor, James Monroe. And Randolph hoped to be Monroe's successor. It was the self-delusion of a man who felt himself superior to everyone else. Superior he was in many ways, but not that much and not in constructive ways. After 1805, his verbal cannonades were frequently aimed at Jefferson.

With Arron Burr, character and experience drove Jefferson's hostility. Burr devoted himself in mind and heart to the party and principles of Burr. He wore his ambition on his sleeve. Successful in legal practice, he was widely granted to be a master organizer and a brilliant trial lawyer. Known as Colonel for his commendable Revolutionary War service, he was an effective force in New York State politics, especially in New York City. An experienced politician, he had served in the state assembly and as attorney general. In October 1795, thirty-nine-year-old US senator Aaron Burr made a one-day visit to Monticello. In the late 1790s, Jefferson wanted Burr on his side. New York was a necessary piece in the electoral puzzle that might make him president and elect a Republican Congress.

In June 1797, he continued his conversations with Burr: "Though the newspapers give so minutely what is passing in Congress that nothing of detail can be wanting for your information," Jefferson wrote, "it will give me an opportunity of recalling myself to your memory, and of evidencing my esteem for you." The politeness was an affirmation of mutual self-interest. Writing at length, with his usual graciousness of phrase, Jefferson detailed his views about the state of the nation. "I had always hoped that the popularity of the late president [Washington] being once withdrawn from active effect, the natural feelings of the people towards liberty would restore the equilibrium between the Executive and Legislative. . . . I consider the future character of our republic as in the air; indeed its future fortunes will be in the air if war is made on us by France. . . . However, what with the English influence in the lower and . . . the upper parts of your state, I presume little is to be hoped."

The Eastern states, especially New York, would be crucial to rejuvenating the spirit of '76.

If a prospect could be once opened upon us of the penetration of truth into the Eastern states, if the people there, who are unquestionably Republican, could discover that they have been duped into the support of measures calculated to sap the very foundations of republicanism, we might still hope for salvation, and that it would come, as of old, from the East. But will that region ever awake to the true state of things? Can the middle, Southern and Western states hold on till they awake? These are painful and doubtful questions: and if, in assuring me of your health, you can give me a comfortable solution of them, it will relieve a mind devoted to the preservation of our republican government in the true form and spirit in which it was established.

His concern for Burr's health had more to do with the body politic than with Burr's physical well-being. He feared, Jefferson emphasized, "that what with currents and countercurrents, we shall in the end be driven back to the land from which we launched 20 years ago." Though never a fisherman, he made his point more vivid with an effective metaphor uniting angler with Anglophobia. "Indeed, my dear Sir, we have been but as a sturdy fish on the hook of a dexterous angler, who letting us flounce till we have spent our force, brings us up at last. . . ." War with France seemed imminent. "Thus we see two nations, who love one another affectionately brought by the ill temper of their Executive administrations to the very brink of dipping their hands in the blood of each other."

In early 1799, Burr advocated for Jefferson's and Madison's Virginia and Kentucky Resolutions. They were, though, a nonstarter in the Federalist-dominated New York legislature. "I have not thought it discreet to urge a determination in either house," he wrote to Jefferson. "It would be divisive and undermine the passage of desirable legislation. . . . Considerable changes will probably take place in this

State within two Years—Some Symptoms are already obvious even to you at a distance."

The subject of Haiti came up in regard to a possible war with France. What relationship should be established with the newly independent French colony ruled by a Black government? "The Southern states," Jefferson wrote to Burr, oppose President Adams's "bill authorizing the President to admit Toussaint's subjects to a free commerce with them, and free ingress and intercourse with their black brethren in these states. . . . However if they [the Federalists] are guarded against the cannibals of the terrible republic," he continued with heavy irony, "they ought not to object to being eaten by a more civilized enemy [the British]." That Burr favored abolition was not a part of their epistolary conversation.

The 1800 election kept them on the same page. In late December, when it seemed that all might work out well, Burr wrote that "my whole time and attention shall be unceasingly employed to render your administration grateful and honorable to our country and to yourself." He intimated that he would withdraw from the electoral tie in Jefferson's favor if Jefferson would agree to appoint him to some high position. He probably had in mind secretary of state or of the Treasury. A wary Jefferson preferred to have Burr become vice-president, an office without authority or clout.

Notoriously, then and thereafter, Burr dug a political grave for himself, particularly when in July 1804 he killed Alexander Hamilton, his arch Federalist enemy. A duel between gentlemen of that stature was not supposed to result in the death of either. Both had a talent for dramatic self-destruction. Obsessed with each other as alter egos, each saw the other as his evil opposite. They were inescapably drawn to the dueling ground. Burr's failure to withdraw in Jefferson's favor in 1801 and Hamilton's death by his pistol killed Burr's political future. In killing Hamilton, he killed himself. By allowing Burr to kill him,

Hamilton killed Burr's opportunities for public service. Burr became a man without a political party.

Federalists cheered on his disaffiliation from Jefferson and the Republicans, but they also bitterly blamed him for Hamilton's death. With one shot, Burr had eliminated two of Jefferson's rivals, the Hamilton of the 1790s, whom the Federalists might have turned to again in 1804, and himself. Jefferson would have been even better served if they had killed each other. Burr immediately became a wanted man in New York and New Jersey. His Republican rival in New York State, George Clinton, became Jefferson's second vice-president. Still, Burr had admirers, and some potential supporters. Resourceful and energetic, a charismatic personality, he made plans for an eventual triumph of some sort. In 1805, and then with energy in 1806, he turned westward. It was the only direction open to him.

In mid-April 1806, Jefferson wrote, "About a month ago, in which he mentioned that a little before my coming into office I had written to him [Burr] a letter intimating that I had destined him for a high employ, had he not been placed by the people in a different one; that he had signified his willingness to resign as V. President to give aid to the administration in any other place; that he had never asked an office however; he asked aid of nobody, but could walk on his own legs, and take care of himself: that I had always used him with politeness, but nothing more: That he had aided in bringing on the present order of things, that he had supported the administration, and that he could do me much harm: he wished however to be on different ground: he was now disengaged from all particular business, willing to engage in something, should be in town some days, if I should have anything to propose to him."

Jefferson had nothing to offer him. He kept his temper in response to what was an explicit threat and replied with a carefully phrased insult.

I observed to him that I had always been sensible that he possessed talents which might be employed greatly to the advantage of the public, and that as to myself I had a confidence that if he were employed he would use his talents for the public good: but that he must be sensible the public had withdrawn their confidence from him, and that in a government like ours it was necessary to embrace in its administration as great a mass of public confidence as possible, by employing those who had a character with the public, of their own, and not merely a secondary one through the Executive.

Was Jefferson, Burr responded, relying on newspaper accounts for his views? No, Jefferson said. "There was not a single voice" in favor of his renomination or for any other position. "As to any harm he could do me," Jefferson wrote in a private memo,

I knew no cause why he should desire it, but at the same time I feared no injury which any man could do me: that I never had done a single act, or been concerned in any transaction, which I feared to have fully laid open, or which could do me any hurt if truly stated: that I had never done a single thing with a view to my personal interest, or that of any friend, or with any other view than that of the greatest public good: that therefore no threat or fear on that head would [ever] be a motive of action with me.

Burr, Jefferson went on in his long private note, "has continued in town to this time; dined with me this day and called on me to take leave 2 or 3 days ago. I did not commit these things to writing at the time but I do it now." Then, at length, he summarized the electioneering that had led to his election by the House of Representatives. His defensive point was that his election had been untainted by electioneering; that he had made no promises; that he had authorized no one to bargain on his behalf and he was certain no one had done so.

The detailed length of the note, written for himself and the historical record, was Jefferson's edited version of history. There's no evidence that he and Burr ever met again.

Burr, though, would not go away, even when he went away, westward to Kentucky and Ohio, then toward New Orleans, in the interest of some achievement, the exact specificity of which no historian has been able to demonstrate. Jefferson heard rumors and then accounts of Burr enlisting men, equipment, and financial support for an expedition of some sort, either directed against the Spanish, if war should break out between Spain and the United States, as seemed imminent, with the conquest of Mexico in mind; or the same if war should not break out; or the above and also or alternatively the capture of New Orleans as his base for encouraging the secession of as many of the Western and Southwestern states as were dissatisfied with what they felt to be Jefferson's failure to protect their interests. Such secession would have created a separate nation under Burr's leadership. A Burr-led military expedition against Spain would have been a crime. An attack on Spanish territory would have been a violation of the Neutrality Act. Secession would have been treason. Initially, in September 1806, Jefferson took rumors and informants with a grain of salt. Urged to act, he hesitated. He waited for reliable news; he had only unsubstantiated rumors. As had been the case in Virginia in 1781, he wanted reliable information before acting.

In late November 1806, he announced that he had learned "that sundry persons, citizens of the United States . . . are conspiring and confederating together to begin and set on foot, provide, and prepare the means for a military expedition or enterprise against the dominions of Spain." All arms of the government should exert themselves to search out and bring "to condign punishment all persons engaged or concerned in such enterprise, in seizing and detaining, subject to the disposition of the law, all vessels, arms, military stores, or other means provided or providing for the same, and, in general, in preventing the carrying on such expedition or enterprise by all lawful means within their power."

In December 1806, he informed Congress that "a great number of private individuals were combining together, arming and organizing themselves contrary to law, to carry on military expeditions against the territories of Spain . . . ." He did not know how many or exactly where. General James Wilkinson, the head of America's Western military force, Jefferson reported, had successfully held back the Spanish on the Louisiana-Texas border. But New Orleans was in danger. Though Jefferson did not mention Burr, it was widely understood that it was Burr he was referring to. He was ordering, he continued, the governor of New Orleans to raise militia troops. "I inform you with great pleasure of the promptitude with which the inhabitants of those territories have tendered their services in defence of their country." As he was soon to tell Congress, he was already convinced that Burr was conspiring against the United States.

Jefferson received a letter from General Wilkinson, enclosing a deciphered version of a letter that Wilkinson claimed Burr had written to him. The letter, if authentic, showed that Burr was organizing treasonous activity. In his letter, Wilkinson accused Burr of raising a force of disaffected Westerners whose purpose was to separate the Western states from the United States. The ex-vice-president had, Wilkinson reported, attempted to persuade him, unsuccessfully, to become a co-conspirator. Jefferson gave Wilkinson's deciphered letter immediate credence. He eagerly waited for more information and evidence. It did not come, except as rumor.

In late January 1807, he wrote to Congress. "I received intimations that designs were in agitation in the western country, unlawful and unfriendly to the peace of the Union; and that the prime mover in these was Aaron Burr, heretofore distinguished by the favor of his country. The grounds of these intimations being inconclusive," a phrase characteristic of all that was to follow, "the objects uncertain, and the fidelity of that country known to be firm, the only measure taken was to urge the informants to use their best endeavors to get further insight into the designs and proceedings of the suspected persons." Exclusively on the basis of Wilkinson's claims and the deciphered letter, Jefferson accused Burr of engaging in treasonous activities. "The general, with the honor of a soldier and fidelity of a good citizen," he told Congress, "immediately dispatched a trusty officer to me with information of what had passed." As if he were prosecutor, judge, and jury, Jefferson announced his verdict to the country. Burr had been and was committing treason.

Driven by anger and hatred, disregarding common sense and law, Jefferson wanted Burr to be held to account for what he was certain were treasonous actions. In Jefferson's eyes, Burr had committed passive treason against the Republican Party in 1800. That itself was, for Jefferson, unpatriotic. He seemed certainly guilty now of an even greater crime. Consequently, Jefferson stated at length to Congress that Burr had committed treason; that he had raised an army with the intention of capturing New Orleans and invading Mexico; that he intended to separate the Western states from the United States; that he wanted to create the Empire of Burr. Burr was guilty of all of the above, though as yet Jefferson had no hard evidence, let alone a grand jury indictment. Due process required evidence, as defined by the Constitution.

It was soon revealed that Wilkinson, as Jefferson would never admit, had lied in his own letter and doctored the deciphered letter to disguise his own role in whatever it was that Burr intended to do. Eager to punish Burr for crimes Jefferson was certain he had committed, he had to have known that Wilkinson was untrustworthy, vain, boastful, and mercenary; that he had risen to military leadership on thin grounds and performed poorly. It had even been rumored that he was in the pay of Spain. It was well known that Wilkinson's priority was his bank account and that he profited from his military command much beyond his government salary. From Wilkinson's point of view, the scenario could not have been more ironic. Jefferson was praising Wilkinson's patriotism, and the less compromised former vice-president with none of the accusations proved was being denounced as a traitor who deserved the ultimate punishment.

Jefferson's address to Congress denouncing Burr as a traitor was a political, not a legal, document, an address to the court of public opinion. But a court of law would have to determine the truth, to the extent it was knowable. The Constitution itself was explicit about what constituted treason: "Treason against the United States, shall consist only in levying War against them, or in adhering to their Enemies, giving them Aid and Comfort. No Person shall be convicted of Treason unless on the Testimony of two Witnesses to the same overt Act, or on Confession in open Court." Jefferson from the start had no doubt that Burr was guilty of treason, but the challenge was to prove it. The charge against Burr was that, in a specific place and at a specific time, he had raised and armed a small army in preparation for acts of treason.

The trial, in the summer and early fall of 1807 in Richmond, Virginia, was a national sensation, replete with drama, bombast, a colorful cast of famous lawyers, especially for the defense, including Burr himself. Wilkinson found himself forced into the role of star witness for the prosecution. From Washington, Jefferson directed and manipulated every aspect of the case in the control of the prosecution and government. Wilkinson was a disastrously bad witness. The defense demonstrated that the deciphered letter that had implicated Burr had almost certainly not been written by Burr and had been doctored to exculpate Wilkinson. It was demonstrated that the defendant had not been at the site of the alleged treasonous acts at the time charged. Also, the prosecution could not produce the required two witnesses. And there was an instrumental irony that made Jefferson even more bitterly angry: Chief Justice John Marshall's Supreme Court position required that he serve, because of the location of the trial, as circuit court judge.

The definition of treason was at issue. Was intent sufficient? Was a material act required? Marshall had to distinguish between treason as defined by the Constitution and a form of treason, operative in British common law but dubious in its American applicability, called constructive treason, which meant that anyone distantly or even innocently connected to the alleged crime had committed treason. A superior lawyer and resourceful judge, neither a friend of Burr's nor of Jefferson's, Marshall ruled for the literal words of the Constitution. There was no "overt act." Burr's thoughts and intentions were another matter. Ironically, Burr's trial contributed to setting legal precedent for a definition of treason protecting the rights of the accused by requiring the highest standard of evidence for conviction. That the situation was legally complicated escaped Jefferson. He refused to acknowledge that Marshall's rulings, especially about the constitutional definition of treason, were sound. And when the Richmond, Virginia, jury in effect dismissed all the serious charges against Burr, Jefferson was shocked, furious, and more eager than ever to have Marshall impeached. Burr's acquittal and Marshall's continuance in office was for Jefferson one of the great disappointments of his presidency. Nevertheless, he never for a moment thought that he had acted emotionally, self-interestedly, or unwisely. He was the patriot, true to the principles of 1776. Marshall was not.

His willingness to embrace, despite obvious warning signs, Wilkinson's account of Burr's activities and the accuracy of Wilkinson's information testified to Jefferson's hatred of Burr. A man of intellect, analytic skills, and legal training who was also a constitutional textualist, Jefferson nevertheless had taken a position privately and publicly that in the end disappointed, embarrassed, and pained him. He had no doubt that Burr was guilty of treason. He may indeed have been, almost. But Marshall, a better lawyer with a better legal mind than Jefferson's, emphasized that the Constitution provided a strict definition of treason. It was an act, not an intention. And it needed to be proved in a court of law. With no evidence but Wilkinson's contradictory, partly fabricated, and obviously self-interested claims, Jefferson had stated unequivocally to Congress and the nation that Burr had committed treason. Detesting Burr and vengeful, Jefferson had eagerly and compulsively suspended his critical faculties. It was one of the sorriest performances of his career.

What Jefferson missed most during his presidency was the personal touch and presence of his daughters and grandchildren. He did have two extended visits from his eldest daughter, Martha, his cherished Patsy. While visiting in winter 1806, she gave birth to her eighth child, the first born in the White House. His daughter Polly's death in 1804 was a devastating blow. Characteristically, as with all such blows, he had a way of carrying on, a combination of resilience and compartmentalization, leavened with an optimism of an almost airy sort that had a bit in it of Voltaire's Pangloss, that this was the best of all possible worlds and all would somehow work out well or well enough.

He continued to practice what he preached. Work, especially of the serviceable kind, and social engagement, in Washington and at Monticello, kept dark spirits away and gave life whatever happiness it could have. To two of his grandchildren, Anne Cary Randolph and Ellen Wayles Randolph, he wrote delightfully playful brief letters, among his most charming, tailored to a child's attention span. They express an aspect of his personality he kept mostly private: his combination of light didacticism, lighter than it had been with his daughters, and inventive playfulness, the child's version of the many playful, imaginative, and expressive letters he had written, especially in the 1780s, to his women friends.

From Washington in May 1803, he wrote lovingly to his eldest granddaughter, now twelve years old. He enclosed with it a present of verses and a gift of an ABC for Anne's sister, a report on the weather, questions about the fruit trees at home, and a message for her "papa" in a diction and syntax that shows Jefferson's talent at creating a level of language best suited to tightening the bond between grandfather and grandchild. "It is very long, my dear Anne, since I have received a letter from you. When was it? In the meantime verses," which he clipped from newspapers, "have been accumulating till I find it necessary to get them off my hands without further waiting. With them I send an A.B.C. for Miss Cornelia, and she must pay you a kiss for it on my account." Cornelia was four. He continued:

The little recipe about charcoal is worth your Mama's notice. We had peas here on Tuesday the 17th and every day since. We had then also full-grown cucumbers: but I suppose they had been forced. What sort of weather had you from the 4th to the 10th. Here we had frost, ice and snow, and great damage in the gardens and orchards. How stands the fruit with you in the neighborhood and at Monticello? and particularly the peaches, as they are what will be in season when I come home. The figs also, have they been hurt? You must mount Midas and ride over to Monticello to inform yourself, or collect the information from good authority and let me have it by next post. . . . Present my tenderest affections to your Mama, and accept my kisses for yourself and the little ones.

As with all his correspondents, Jefferson kept a logbook of his exchanges with his granddaughters, a routine that he turned into a didactic joke in a letter in 1805 to then eight-year-old Ellen. He began with an account of how many letters she had written to him in a fifteen-week period. They had agreed that they would exchange letters every three weeks. Alas, there was a "balance due" to him.

So stands the account for this year, my dear Ellen, between you and me. Unless it be soon paid off, I shall send the sheriff after you. I enclose you an abundant supply of poetry, among which you will find Goody Blake, which I think you wanted. I will thank you if you will put on your boots and spurs and ride to Monticello and inform me how my thorns live. This part of the country is beautifying with them so fast that every ride I take makes me anxious for those at Monticello. Your Papa in his last letter informs me the mumps have got into the family. Let me know who have it and how all do. Kiss your dear Mama for me and shake hands with all the little ones.

When Anne was in arrears with her letters, he playfully took ownership of his own remissness, relieving both of them of responsibility for the lapse.

I do not know whether it is owing to your laziness or mine that our letters have been so long intermitted. I assure you it is not to my want of love to you, and to all of those about you, whose welfare I am always so anxious to learn. But it is useless to discuss old bankrupt scores. We will therefore burn our old accounts, and begin a new one. . . . Deliver my endearments to all the family, and above all to your mama: and accept kisses and salutations for yourself.

In 1807, waiting eagerly for a letter from then ten-year-old Ellen, he extended his expression of hope that one was on the way into a statement about his preference for optimism, for hoping for the best. "Hope is so much pleasanter than despair, that I always prefer looking into futurity through her glass." What he had done with a heavy didactic hand in preaching to his two daughters in their childhoods he did with a much lighter hand with his granddaughters.

I send you some poetical gleanings. Our newspapers have been rather barren in that ware for some time past. Whether the muses have been taking a nap, or our news writers have been prevented from making their weekly visits to mount Parnassus, by their occupations with Burr and the Chesapeake I cannot decide. But we will leave these idle ladies to their dreams in the Castalian valley, and descend to the more useful region and occupations of the good housewife, one of whom is worth more than the whole family of the muses. How go on the Bantams? I rely on you for their care, as I do on Anne for the Algerine fowls.

Like their mother, Anne and Ellen were being educated into the lives of appropriately well-read, musical, and capable managers of domestic and plantation affairs, of marriage and child-rearing, the daughters of the Virginia elite. It was a cultural predicate inseparable from Jefferson's idealization of family life and his epistolary expressions of love to his granddaughters. Later that year, he sent Ellen a clipping of an "old song. . . . I have nothing better to send you . . . but indeed I could send you nothing better. It was much in vogue when I was of your age, and has lost nothing of its pathos by time. It shews the wonderful sources of comfort which open themselves to every condition of man." He found some of that comfort, as he soldiered through the crises of his second term, getting letters from and writing to his granddaughters. It was one of the most charming and endearing uses of his pen. The man who wrote the Declaration of Independence could also write lovingly in the voice of an adoring grandfather adored by his grandchildren.

CHAPTER FIFTEEN

Sowing the Wind

1809–1826

No longer president, happy to be rid of an office that no longer interested him and from which he had gotten less and less satisfaction, Jefferson still had important uses to which to put his pen. He was glad to leave the presidency in the collegial hands of James Madison. He worried that his faculties were losing their sharpness. During his last six months, he reserved most significant decisions for the next president, confident that he was passing the baton to an ideological brother. In regard to politics and governance, there were hardly any extant Tories or monocrats to excoriate except some New England revenants who opposed the War of 1812. Jefferson led his party in denouncing them: "Your character of the Federalists is not exaggerated," he wrote to his son-in-law. "Bitterer enemies to their country do not exist in France, England or Spain. Those in Congress . . . would be delighted that Great Britain could conquer and reduce us again under her government." Timothy Pickering, a now powerless longtime antagonist, "would rather France should do it than that we should remain under a republican administration."

Actually, the mostly one-party rule that Jefferson preferred had become the reality, though he was aware that not all Republicans agreed with one another. Within seeming solidarity there were fissures and factions, ideological differences disguised as moderate distinctions, and regional priorities that set different parts of the country against one another about Western expansion, international trade, internal improvements, taxation, and slavery. On the one hand, the Jeffersonians won most of the elections. On the other, the actualities of the country, with fluctuations, were increasingly Hamiltonian. Few Americans believed that those who tilled the land were inherently more virtuous and patriotic than those in commerce, trade, building, and finance, though Jefferson believed it until his dying day. Still, in his last years as president, he had begun to recognize that most of Hamilton's and Washington's economic and nationalistic policies, with Chief Justice Marshall's help, were irreversible. Financing the debts incurred during the War of 1812 made that reality a certainty. And by 1817 it was becoming apparent that the other side of the political triumph of republicanism was the economic triumph of Federalism.

Jefferson would have agreed with his friend and secretary from their Paris days, William Short, that Federalists-turned-Republicans, like John Quincy Adams, "now say that they do not change sides, but that the Government has become ultra-federalist in their measures." Most Republicans, even Jefferson, began to favor using federal funds for national infrastructure, provided that either an end run could be done around the "chains of the Constitution" or the Constitution could be amended. During the War of 1812, Jefferson had a Federalist epiphany. For the first time, he enthusiastically supported the manufacturing section of the economy. The United States should further advance its independence from Britain by becoming self-sufficient in manufacturing as well as agriculture. Whether Jefferson gave thought to it or not, this meant, as many of his colleagues intended, that eventually the United States would become equal to and perhaps replace Great Britain as the leading mercantile and manufacturing economy of the world.

On the day of the inauguration of his successor in March 1809,

Jefferson responded with eloquence and verbal graciousness to an "affectionate address" of "patriotic sentiments" from the citizens of Washington. He had been their neighbor and leading citizen for eight years. He predicted a great future for the city. "I see the true character of the National Metropolis." It was to be the symbolic and physical representation of a great nation, for the time being "the only monument of human rights, and the sole depository of the sacred fire of freedom and self-government." It would inspire the nation's citizens "to maintain harmony and union among ourselves, and to preserve from all danger this hallowed ark of human hope and happiness. . . . That differences of opinion should arise among men, on politics, on religion, and on every other topic of human enquiry, and that these should be freely expressed in a country where all our faculties are free, is to be expected." But be warned: "these valuable privileges are much perverted when permitted to disturb the harmony of social intercourse, and to lessen the tolerance of opinion. To the honour of society here, it has been characterized by a just and generous liberality, and an indulgence of those affections which, without regard to political creeds, constitute the happiness of life."

That Jefferson himself had been less than libertarian, indeed sometimes intolerant of factions and opposition, he left unsaid. His message was one of optimism and gratitude. "That the improvement of this city must proceed with sure and steady steps, follows from its many obvious advantages, and from the enterprising spirit of its inhabitants, which promises to render it the fairest seat of wealth and science," where he hoped there would be created a national university. "It is very gratifying to me that the general course of my administration is approved by my fellow citizens, and particularly that the motives of my retirement are satisfactory." He ended on a personal note. "I part with the powers entrusted to me by my country, as with a burthen of heavy bearing: but it is with sincere regret that I part with the society in which I have lived here. It has been the source of much happiness to me during my residence at the seat of government, and I owe it much for its kind dispositions. I shall ever feel a high interest in the prosperity of the city, and an affectionate attachment to its inhabitants." Over fifty years later, another citizen was to write an even more moving farewell, with similar phrasing, in his case to the citizens of Springfield, Illinois, as he began his journey not away from but toward the nation's capital.

As he left Washington, Jefferson had to have had in mind the certainty that he would never return. He wanted no part of anyplace but home. As he made his way toward Monticello in mid-March 1809, it is unlikely that he could have imagined that he would ever leave Virginia again. He never did, though he was to live, in his own words, an "unmercifully long" seventeen years more, the last years in illness, disappointment, and debt. Again at Monticello, this time permanently, the sixty-five-year-old ex–public servant was decidedly finished with "the distressing burden of power." The phrase was sincere, despite how often he had pursued power and how often accepted the power that had pursued him.

In early April, he wrote an address to the people of Albemarle County, a touching, eloquent, and unusually personal expression of relief and happiness at his return to his "native country." This single passage from his pen captures and encapsulates Jefferson's heart, mind, and values. It is the most beautifully written expression of some of his defining characteristics: the tension he felt between public service and the private life, between the head and the heart; his belief in the sustaining and redeeming power of social harmony; his belief in his own moral self-worth and rectitude as a servant of the people and a patriot; and his fundamental attachment to home, land, and family as the touchstones of the happy life.

Returning to the scenes of my birth and early life, to the society of those with whom I was raised, and who have been ever dear to

me, I receive, fellow citizens and neighbors, with inexpressible pleasure, the cordial welcome you are so good as to give me. Long absent
on duties which the history of a wonderful era made incumbent on
those called to them, the pomp, the turmoil, the bustle and splendor
of office, have drawn but deeper sighs for the tranquil and irresponsible occupations of private life, for the enjoyment of an affectionate
intercourse with you, my neighbors and friends, and the endearments of family love, which nature has given us all, as the sweetener
of every hour. For these I gladly lay down the distressing burthen of
power, and seek, with my fellow citizens, repose and safety under
the watchful cares, the labors, and perplexities of younger and abler
minds. The anxieties you express to administer to my happiness,
do, of themselves, confer that happiness: and the measure will be
complete, if my endeavors to fulfill my duties in the several public
stations to which I have been called, have obtained for me the approbation of my country. The part which I have acted on the theatre of
public life, has been before them; and to their sentence I submit it:
but the testimony of my native country, of the individuals who have
known me in private life, to my conduct in its various duties and
relations, is the more grateful, as proceeding from eye witnesses and
observers. . . . Of you then, my neighbors, I may ask, in the face of
the world, whose ox have I taken, or whom have defrauded? Whom
have I oppressed, or of whose hand have I received a bribe to blind
mine eyes therewith? On your verdict I rest with conscious security.
Your wishes for my happiness are received with just sensibility, and
I offer sincere prayers for your own welfare and prosperity.

Between 1809 and 1821, Jefferson had much to say in private letters
about his favorite political and philosophical topics. He also had much
to say, some of it gracefully and lovingly written, to those he loved. He
had business to attend to in writing about his debts and the difficulty

of raising cash, of economic depression, of the devaluation of Virginia land, including his farms, and the likelihood that he would have nothing of value to leave to his heirs. What he valued most, though, was his reputation, not only relating to his personal life but in the historical record. Late in life, Jefferson became a novelist of history. He put his pen to use on several projects, some of them in response to current events, about which many valued his opinion. One of the others was the creation of his own version of the New Testament, though it was an editing, not a writing job. Another was an introductory essay for and explanation of the collection of his notes written during the Washington administration. It became known to later generations as the *Anas*. He wrote an autobiographical fragment. There were also the letters written in a substantial correspondence between himself and John Adams. And the most revisionist of all, his long letter, which he concluded with a non-apology apology about how "unmercifully long" this letter had become, to Martin Van Buren in June 1824. He did his best to encourage history to see him and what he had done the way he wanted himself and it to be seen. Among other things, that's what pen and paper were for. They were to write and rewrite history for future generations.

Jefferson always kept public silence about his religious beliefs. He had attempted in Virginia to legislate a code of religious freedom, finally passed into law in 1786. Adherents of the established church often took that to be an attack on religious belief itself. Its call for religious tolerance, freedom of conscience, and separation of state from church associated its author in the minds of many Christians with hostility to Christianity, an attack on the relevance to the legal life of American citizens of the theological claims of the established church or any other Protestant sect. The battle over the bill inevitably had a political dimension, which became nationalized in the 1790s. Federalists assumed that Francophiles were atheists. Accusations of irreligion, of anti-Christianity, of atheism became staples of Federalist attacks on Republicans. Sensitive to criticism, Jefferson responded just as he had to the accusation that he had a Black mistress. He said nothing. Religion was entirely a private matter. The public had no right to know anything about his personal beliefs or his personal life.

Religion, though, was a subject he thought about, read intensely in, and wrote about in private letters. He was, from early on, clear in his own mind about what he believed and what he did not. In the late 1790s, he had had discussions about Christianity with Benjamin Rush, a prominent physician, Republican, and pamphleteer on political subjects. In 1803 he recalled to Rush "some of the delightful conversations with you . . . the Christian religion was sometimes our topic: and I then promised you that, one day or other, I would give you my views of it. They are the result of a life of enquiry and reflection, and very different from that anti-Christian system, imputed to me by those who know nothing of my opinions. To the corruptions of Christianity, I am indeed opposed; but not to the genuine precepts of Jesus himself. I am a Christian, in the only sense in which he wished any one to be; sincerely attached to his doctrines, in preference to all others; ascribing to himself every human excellence, and believing he never claimed any other." To many of his contemporaries that would have meant that Jefferson was not a Christian at all.

Jefferson did not believe in miracles, past or present; the order, patterns, and laws of nature, as he observed and interpreted them, applied to all aspects of life, including the natural rights of people. He felt that the organization of Christian belief into churches had created instruments of psychological and physical oppression to be resisted, reformed, or eliminated. The primary merit of Christianity resided in its ethical code, superior to that of every other religion, expressed in the words of Jesus. Jefferson believed Jesus to be the wisest teacher of morals in human history. His Jesus was entirely a human being. He believed that if there were a transcendent extra-human creator, that it was not available in any imminent and personal way, but that a first cause could be extrapolated from the logic that said that something could not be made from nothing, that existence could not have been self-generated. Like his friend Joseph Priestley and other Deists, Jefferson believed the universe had been started by a first cause, call it whatever you will, that did not interfere with the ongoing laws of nature. He was in agreement with the Unitarians, who rejected the Christian tripartite division of that first cause as hocus-pocus and mystification, though he sometimes consoled himself and others with the possibility that there might be some form of existence for human beings beyond the life of the body. That, however, was the province of theology, which Jefferson preferred to have as little to do with as possible.

It was human conduct that preoccupied him, the standards of ethical behavior for individual and communal life. Though he had never published a word about religious belief, he began in the early years of his presidency, perhaps with his words to Rush in mind, an idiosyncratic project about the relationship between Christianity and ethics. Much of the New Testament seemed to him to detract from its significant essence: the words of Jesus. The essence of the Gospels needed to be liberated from miracle and transcendence, theology and metaphysics. The New Testament needed an Enlightenment revision. It was an undertaking rooted in Jefferson's lifetime of reading, especially of classical authors, to his take on the history of Christianity and its institutions, to the latitudinarian Anglican world into which he had been born, and to his observation that traditional Christian belief had produced more human misery than happiness. It had been often an enemy of personal liberty and freedom of conscience. Its alleged institutional ethics were often inconsistent with its material actions. Jefferson did not think it presumptuous to create his own version of the Gospels. He assumed he was scholar enough to distinguish between Jesus's actual words and those falsely attributed to him. He wanted to rescue Jesus from those who had misused him.

It was a satisfying moral and intellectual diversion. And, in its own idiosyncratic way, it was also political, a private way of rejecting the perversions of Christianity he associated with the Federalists and all those he believed were enemies of human freedom. He was not interested in revising the Old Testament. Its ethics seemed to him irredeemable. If he could abstract "what is really [Jesus's] from the rubbish in which it is buried, easily distinguished by its luster from the dross of his biographers, and as separable from that as the diamond from the dung hill, we have the outlines of a system of the most sublime morality which has ever fallen from the lips of man: outlines which it is lamentable he did not live to fill up."

Jefferson did have second thoughts about the history of the Jewish people when he read a pamphlet about Jewish history and Judaism. He praised its literary style and corresponded with its Jewish author. Still, the Old Testament seemed to him ethically deprived; the New Testament, a corrupted text that needed to be purified. He began to think about and work toward a New Testament that would present exclusively the Jesus he admired. Whom he would present it to seems not to have been a consideration. He intended it to be a private document. "I have ever thought religion a concern purely between our god and our consciences, for which we were accountable to him, and not to the priests. I never told my own religion, nor scrutinized that of another. I never attempted to make a convert, nor wished to change another's creed. I have ever judged of the religion of others by their lives."

As he traveled to Washington in 1804, prompted by a pamphlet from Joseph Priestley comparing Jesus to Socrates, he arranged in his mind "a Syllabus, or Outline, of such an Estimate of the comparative merits of Christianity, as I wished to see executed, by some one of more leisure and information for the task than myself." In Washington he attempted "too hastily," he wrote years later, to put it on paper. "It was the work of 2 or 3 nights . . . after getting through the evening task of reading the letters and papers of the day." This was to be a private discussion, he emphasized to Rush. His views, if they became public, would be used against him and his republican principles. If he had the time, he would "proceed to a view of the life, character, and doctrines of Jesus." No copies of what he wrote in 1804 survive. In 1815, he emphatically denied that he ever intended to publish a book on the subject. "I should as soon think of writing for the reformation of Bedlam, as of the world of religious sects. Of these there must be at least ten thousand, every individual of every one of which believes all are wrong but his own. To undertake to bring them all right, would be like undertaking, single handed, to fell the forests of America."

"To bring them all right" meant that most if not all were wrong. "The genuine system of Jesus, and the artificial structures they have erected to make him the instrument of wealth, power, and preeminence to themselves are as distinct things in my view as light and darkness. . . . I place him among the greatest of the reformers of morals, and scourges of priest-craft, that have ever existed." The historical Jesus was for Jefferson a political radical who combined moral wisdom with revolutionary action, such as his expulsion of the money changers from the temple. That was the Jesus Jefferson could identify with, though by 1804 he had recognized that despite all his efforts the Hamiltonian money changers could never entirely be expelled from the temple of the American republic. They could only, at best, be restrained and controlled. And he would have found it abhorrent, as he did when others made political use of religion, to have his views used for political purposes of whatever kind. The subject, though, continued to preoccupy him. When in late 1815 he read a synopsis of the Gospels created by his longtime colleague in Congress from revolutionary days, Charles Thomson, he wrote to Thomson that "I too have made a wee little book, from the same materials, which I call the Philosophy of Jesus."

He called it *The Life and Morals of Jesus of Nazareth*. "In extracting the pure principles," he had stripped off "the artificial vestments," he wrote to John Adams, "in which they have been muffled by priests, who have travestied them into various forms, as instruments of riches and power to them." It was a razor-and-paste job, its multiple texts arranged in columnar neatness, a polyglot use of a Latin and Greek version of the Bible, the Geneva Bible, and the King James Version to weave extracts that Jefferson believed to be Jesus's words. "It is a paradigm of his doctrines, made by cutting the texts out of the book, and arranging them on the pages of a blank book, in a certain order of time or subject. A more beautiful or precious morsel of ethics I have never seen. It is a document in proof that I am a real Christian, that is to say, a disciple of the doctrines of Jesus." Those "who call me infidel, and themselves Christians and preachers of the gospel," who draw their "dogmas from what its Author never said nor saw," will deplore my purified New Testament. But Jesus, "the greatest of the reformers of morals, and scourges of priest-craft, that have ever existed," would, he believed, have approved of his demystified version of the New Testament, stripped of the supernatural, a testament that embodied Jesus's moral and ethical wisdom unobstructed and unimpeded by the language of those who had transformed him for their own purposes into what he had never been. Between 1816 and 1820, Jefferson showed his New Testament to a few friends. It was then stored away in his archive at Monticello, not to be published until the early twentieth century.

Jefferson had another sacred but also malleable document, the Constitution. It too, he believed, was being corrupted, in this case by false readings and self-serving interpretations, threatening the existence of the Republican nation that the "spirit of '76" had created. He had two basic constitutional principles: that the "enumerated powers" listed all the powers of the federal government and that they could be added to only by amendments. But, as he had written in 1789 to Madison, he believed that each new generation should have the right to modify or reject the laws of previous generations. He proposed that there should be a regular mechanism other than amendments for each generation to rewrite the Constitution to be a more effective instrument for its times, even to create a new one, if the popular will desired that. The present Constitution restricted the federal government to its enumerated powers. In practice, though, phrases like "to lay taxes to provide for the general welfare" and "promote the general welfare" were being used to "establish corporate bodies," to expand national infrastructure, and to make the federal government a visible presence in daily life. Such additions to the power of the government should be done by amendment, not by legislation or executive dictate. He did not mention his own unconstitutional use of executive power in purchasing the Louisiana Territory, an argument for the broader interpretation. Actually, his preference was that the president act unconstitutionally in response to emergencies and be subject to later approval or disapproval rather than that the Constitution itself be interpreted to give the president powers beyond those enumerated.

But the Constitution, Jefferson argued, was not a static, stable, and sacred document. Each generation could and should do with it as it chose, to suit its needs and changing times. Some mechanism should be found to make it easier to do that than the current Constitution allowed. "Some men look at constitutions with sanctimonious reverence, and deem them, like the ark of the covenant, too sacred to be touched," he wrote in July 1816. "They ascribe to the men of the preceding age a wisdom more than human, and suppose what they did to be beyond amendment. I knew that age well: I belonged to it, and labored with it. It deserved well of its country. It was very like the present, but without the experience of the present: and 40 years of experience in government is worth a century of book-reading: and this they would say themselves, were they to rise from the dead."

If his Revolutionary-era contemporaries were alive, they would,

Jefferson believed, agree with him. They had accomplished much. They were the founders of the nation. But they were not perfect. And if they had lived into the present they would, he was certain, be among the first to support changes to the Constitution—that to its authors it was not a document written in stone but the start of an experiment in republican government to be regularly amended or rewritten to meet the challenges of the future.

I am certainly not an advocate for frequent and untried changes in laws and constitutions. I think moderate imperfections had better be borne with; because when once known, we accommodate ourselves to them, and find practical means of correcting their ill effects. But I know also that laws and institutions must go hand in hand with the progress of the human mind. As that becomes more developed, more enlightened, as new discoveries are made, new truths disclosed, and manners and opinions change with the change of circumstances, institutions must advance also, and keep pace with the times. We might as well require a man to wear still the coat which fitted him when a boy . . . let us provide in our constitution for its revision at stated periods . . . so that it may be handed on, with periodical repairs, from generation to generation to the end of time, if anything human can so long endure. . . . This corporeal globe, and everything upon it, belongs to its present corporeal inhabitants, during their generation. They alone have a right to direct what is the concern of themselves alone, and to declare the law of that direction: and this declaration can only be made by their majority. . . . But how collect their voice? this is the real difficulty.

The voice of the people, Jefferson believed, was not expressed by any court, especially the unelected Supreme Court, whose life terms Jefferson thought an affront to democracy, an embodiment of Federalist anti-republican policy. It was as if Hamilton were still alive. The chief justice had persuaded the Court to claim that it alone had the power to interpret the Constitution; that it was the final legal arbiter on what its words meant and how they should be implemented. Jefferson disagreed.

> The constitution, on this hypothesis, is a mere thing of wax in the hands of the judiciary which they may twist and shape in to any form they please. It should be remembered as an axiom of eternal truth in politics that whatever power in any government is independent, is absolute also; in theory only, at first, while the spirit of the people is up. But in practice as fast as that relaxes. Independence can be trusted nowhere but with the people in mass. They are inherently independent of all but moral law. . . . Each of the three departments [of government] has equally the right to decide for itself what is its duty under the constitution, without any regard to what the others may have decided for themselves under a similar question.

In effect, the Supreme Court, one of the three, had usurped for itself ultimate authority in all matters concerning the Constitution. This, Jefferson insisted, the writers of the Constitution had not intended. It should not be a feature of republican government. It was, in effect, judicial tyranny. And it had resulted in the perpetuation and intensification of a consolidating nationalism that the people had rejected when they had elected and reelected him president.

He put in writing in 1816 a concise outline of his fundamental principles of desirable government. They had had their first expression in his 1776 draft of a constitution for Virginia. Time, history, circumstance, and experience had clarified in his own mind what he believed the structure of republican government should be.

> The mother-principle [is] that governments are republican only in proportion as they embody the will of their people, and execute it.

Hence, our first [state] constitutions had really no leading principle in them. But experience and reflection have but more and more confirmed me in the particular importance of the equal representation then proposed. . . . We should thus marshal our government into 1. the General federal republic, for all concerns foreign and federal; 2. that of the State for what relates to our own citizens exclusively. 3. the County republics for the duties and concerns of the county, and 4. the Ward-republics, for the small, and yet numerous and interesting concerns of the neighborhood: and in government, as well as in every other business of life, it is by division and subdivision of duties alone, that all matters, great and small, can be managed to perfection. . . . The sum of these amendments is 1. general suffrage. 2. equal representation in the legislature. 3. an Executive chosen by the people. 4. judges elective or removable. 5. justices jurors, and sheriffs elective. 6. Ward-divisions. and 7. periodical amendment of the Constitution. I have thrown out these, as loose heads of amendment, for consideration and correction: and their object is to secure self-government by the republicanism of our constitution, as well as by the spirit of the people; and it is to nourish and perpetuate that spirit. I am not among those who fear the people. They and not the rich, are our dependence for continued freedom.

Between 1812 and 1815, Jefferson, like other Republicans, was challenged by circumstances that both supported and tested the principles that had been the bedrock of his policies and electoral victories. The War of 1812 was the war that had been threatening almost since the end of the Revolutionary War. Whether it would be with Great Britain or France, or both, varied as depredations changed in frequency and extent. Jefferson wanted war with neither, but he also wanted concessions neither was willing to grant. In 1799 Adams got the country off the hook with France, a war neither country wanted.

Jefferson threatened countermeasures against the British. Both parties recognized that they were not likely to be implemented. To the British, this was mostly the noise made by a powerless, undeveloped nation. America's complaints and demands seemed unrealistic. Britain's very existence was threatened by the Napoleonic Wars. And it did not concede that the United States had an inherent right to all or most of the territory of North America.

In the last month of his presidency, Jefferson reminded his successor that "we should have such an empire for liberty as she has never surveyed since the creation: and I am persuaded no constitution was ever before so well calculated as ours for extensive empire and self-government . . . no limit can then be drawn for our future acquisitions." The only cautionary limitation on how and when was "the principle which ought to limit our views. Nothing should ever be accepted which would require a navy to defend it." A navy was expensive to build and maintain. This empire should and would be obtained with as little expenditure as possible.

Jefferson believed that Canada was rightfully America's for the taking, an extension of the "Empire of liberty." Great Britain was determined not to give up Canada. There was, though, no appetite in Britain, preoccupied with its struggle with Napoléon, for war with the United States. To the extent that the British had an American policy, it was to keep the United States from siding with France. From the American point of view, all would be well if only Britain would respect its commercial neutrality and its version of the law of nations, a bookish canon of claims about the rights governing international relations that hardly affected anything that nations actually did, especially in wartime. The British assumed there would be words, not acts, of resistance from the United States. There was some sentiment to put America in its place, to flick the fly away. And there were some in Britain who had never reconciled themselves to American independence.

Still, the notion of a second British-American war seemed mutually counterproductive, except to those Americans lusting for Canada and eager to twist the tail of the British lion. Jefferson counseled patience and even respect for America's British heritage. In 1810, he emphasized to a Republican newspaper editor that "our laws, language, religion, politics, and manners are so deeply laid in English foundations, that we shall never cease to consider their history as a part of ours, and to study ours in that as its origin." But what directed Jefferson's counsel was the cost of a military conflict. It would undermine if not void some of the bedrock policies of his republicanism. It would require increasing the national debt, which he had been working to decrease. It might require a centralized bank to facilitate borrowing to pay for the war. It would accelerate the tendency toward national consolidation.

In June 1812, the United States declared war against Great Britain. New British restrictions on trade intensified American pro-war fervor. And Canada and Florida beckoned. Madison had held pro-war momentum in check. The United States was unprepared. But the pro-war faction of American public opinion had its way. Actually, by the time the United States declared war, the British restrictions had been rescinded, though neither Madison nor Congress knew that. Thousands were to be killed or crippled as victims of slow transatlantic communication. Jefferson, of course, supported the war, and once it had begun there was no turning back. His attitude toward the principals in the Napoleonic Wars was "a pox on both your houses." Britain exemplified the nation-state powered by indebtedness, taxation, commercial dominance, military might, disregard for the law of nations, and an aristocratic anti-republican government. Jefferson did, though, make the distinction between Shakespeare and George III. But once the United States was at war, the distinction was irrelevant. And France, under Napoléon, had betrayed its own Revolution. Ever the optimist, Jefferson believed that one day redemption would come. France would again become the republic that Napoléon's tyranny had aborted.

In 1813–1814, like many Americans, Jefferson suffered financial misery when what most chest-pumping Americans thought would be a short war turned out to be a long, suffering muddle, mostly of incompetence and defeat. Jefferson wrote to William Short in February 1814 that he believed that "by the combined effects of blockade embargo and drought, I have suffered more than any other individual," a forgivable inaccuracy. "The two former would but have left me where I was, but the last threw me back by forcing me to buy a year's subsistence for my whole family."

There was, though, good news. "I sincerely rejoice that the career of Bonaparte is at length arrested, and that Europe is likely to be restored to its antient divisions and governments: for bad as they were, they were better than the military despotisms of Bonaparte. . . . The only thing to be lamented is that the tyrant of the ocean is not also dismounted. Peace I suppose we shall have; but on the condition of navigating under her licenses; and although I believe we have greatly overtraded ourselves," he would prefer continuous war "to a peace on that condition. It will very possibly end in the total suppression of our navigation and commerce, and leave us to be a world by ourselves." And he had a savior in mind. "My whole confidence as to the salvation of commerce is in Alexander, that he will not yield to the subjugation of the ocean." He would be more than pleased if the Russian tyrant, Czar Alexander I, who had a reputation as a liberal in royalist circles, would limit or end Great Britain's control of the seas.

Alexander's liberalism proved to be a chimera. He soon exchanged liberal rhetoric for ultranationalistic and expansionist goals along with fanatical Russian Orthodox beliefs. When in December 1814 the Treaty of Ghent ended the war, Britain did not renounce impressment. The prewar status quo was resumed. But with its security no longer threatened, Britain had no need to impress sailors. The United States, though, was once again deeply in debt. A new national bank was needed. The war had empowered the federal government.

The centralization that Jefferson feared had been facilitated. In its economy, its fiscal structure, its reliance on debt, its manufacturing capability, its federally supported infrastructure projects, its expansionism, and its use of national power, the United States was becoming increasingly like the country it had declared its independence from. Jefferson was unhappily well aware of this.

On a spring day in May 1818, a congressman from New Hampshire caught sight of Jefferson "through the window among the trees, a tall, spare man, walking towards the house, throwing his legs about unmindful of his steps, like a man in a reverie." To reach Monticello, the visitor had "travelled through a poor country, and over bad roads." There "are many log huts, and a very few good houses. . . . The chimneys are at each end, and outside. . . . Every step I take makes me love New Hampshire better." To the eyes of a New Englander, Virginia seemed a primitive country—bad roads, few towns, almost no cities, a wealthy elite, some beautiful houses built by slaves, an unstable labor force, and log huts for the ordinary people. Jefferson at Monticello, as his visitor recognized, had created a singular and personal paradise. It also had its imperfections. They were built into the structure of its economy, into the complexity of Jefferson's family life, into his character as an intellectual, a designer, and a builder, and into the mood of the most prominent still-living remnant of a Revolution increasingly going in a direction he had attempted to prevent. In Jefferson's eyes, looking backward as an historian or forward to the future, the country as a whole had gone astray. Whatever at that moment of observation in May 1818 Jefferson was musing about, what was predominantly on his mind in his conversation with this visitor and through much of the last decade of his life was American history and his place in it. Both had become problematic, especially the former.

As Jefferson advanced into retirement, still on his feet and on horseback, still reading and thinking though convinced that his mind and memory were fading, he began to seem to his younger contemporaries, and to the post-Revolution generation, a repository of history. There were questions raised, some with partisan intensity, many whose intent was to fill in gaps in the record or to get the record right. Who could testify exactly to what had been said in the debates leading up to the Revolution? Who had been responsible for this decision or that, especially in sessions which had been pledged to secrecy? Had Jefferson been the sole author of the Declaration or was it created by a committee? Whose notes and memory were to be trusted? As each year went by, fewer of the original participants were alive.

Still, Jefferson felt the impulse to keep his pen and mouth shut about such matters. As piles of letters stacked up on his desk, he resented what seemed to him an epistolary plague. Sometimes this supreme letter writer wanted never to write another one again, except those required by family and farming. Many felt they had the right to ask him his opinion. And that he had an obligation to reply. He did in many cases feel compelled to reply, even if briefly, as he had done all his life. Often, when the request was for him to help fill in the record, he replied at length. He had always kept ledgers and records. He had written memoranda and taken notes. Facts mattered immensely. Although his preference was to write nothing more about public matters, he had an interest to protect. Inevitably, the notes, memoranda, and letters he was to write that added to or corrected the record were inflected by his desire to assert the integrity of his own role in the Revolution and its aftermath.

There were some overriding epistolary imperatives. One was a request from Gideon Granger, his postmaster general, to help counter partisan disinformation. Jefferson responded in March 1814,

Nothing is so painful to me, as appeals to my memory on the subject of past transactions from 1775 to 1809. My life was an unremitting course of public transactions, so numerous, so multifarious, and so diversified by places and persons, that, like the figures of a magic lantern, their succession was with a rapidity which scarcely gave time for fixed impressions. Add to this the decay of memory consequent on advancing years, and it will not be deemed wonderful that I should be a stranger as it were even to my own transactions. Of some indeed I retain recollections of the particular, as well as general circumstances; of others a strong impression of the general fact, with an oblivion of particulars; but of a great mass, not a trace either general or particular remains in my mind.

He was being sincere, but also self-protective. He wanted the record to be accurate. An accurate record, he believed, would always be in his favor. But to publish his notes, or a memoir, or even explanatory letters would seem exculpatory, self-defensive. It would make him once again a public figure to be scorched in the "furnace of politics."

In 1816, obliged by correspondence "to be anchored to a writing table," Jefferson was urged by his friend and protégé William Short to write a memoir. "I thought that the tracing your own memoirs might be a soothing labor and a most valuable legacy to your country. . . . If your own experience has induced you to change or modify any of your political opinions . . . you might leave this as a legacy to your successors." Short had a particular topic in mind. "For instance if you think it a dangerous policy to admit foreigners into our political rights, if you think it would increase the love and pride of country to make birth the sole and exclusive door of entry into this sanctuary, if you think that this Republic may be, as Rome was, lost by this kind of bastard amalgamation, your voice and solemn warning would, I think be listened to."

Jefferson had not changed his mind about immigration. It was key to the growth of the country. He encouraged immigration from

Europe. It would bring agricultural experience and skills. Immigrants would extend America's "Empire of liberty." They would create the small settlements and endless fields of wheat of what he envisioned would eventually be a continental country. It was also the case that such immigrants tended to vote for Republicans. He responded,

> To your encouragements to take up the political pen, I must turn a deaf ear. My repugnance to that is insuperable, as the thing itself is unnecessary. The present generation will be as able, as that which preceded them to do for themselves what is necessary for their own happiness; and that which shall succeed them will do what they shall leave undone. Constitutions and laws should change with the changes of times and circumstances. Those made now may as little suit our descendants, as we should be suited by those of our Gothic ancestors. The concerns of each generation are their own care.

Jefferson was being radical in principle and conservative in practice. Each generation should have a blank slate to write on or freedom to revise extensively what existed. In practice, leaving radical change to future generations maintained a status quo from which he benefited. He would not lead where public opinion would not follow, whatever his own views. He felt he had done enough. His strength was now in his refusal not to allow his pen ever again to be used for a political purpose. Again he was urged. Again he declined. He may have taken pleasure in self-protectively exaggerating his cerebral decline. It was partly true and mostly useful. Within the parameters of age-related memory loss, he was still very capable. "You say I must go to writing history. While in public life, I had not time: and now that I am retired, I am past the time. To write history requires a whole life of observation, of enquiry, of labor and correction." But his excuse had at its heart his useful exaggeration of not being quite as physically and mentally energetic as he used to be. The materials of history "are not to be found among the ruins of a decayed memory," he wrote. "If anything has ever merited to me the respect of my fellow-citizens, themselves, I hope, would wish me not to lose it by exposing the decay of faculties of which it was the reward. I must then, dear sir, leave to yourself and your brethren of the rising generation to arraign at your tribunal the actions of your predecessors, and to pronounce the sentence they may have merited or incurred. If the sacrifices of that age have resulted in the good of this, then all is well, and we shall be rewarded by their approbation. . . ."

Jefferson indeed did not want published in his lifetime his corrections of misinformation about the Revolution and the people who created it—or his account of his service as governor of Virginia or as secretary of state or of his presidency. Over his lifetime, he had kept every letter he had received and a copy of every letter he had written. Though he could not control instances in which a recipient chose to release an extract or more, his personal archive was for posterity. In early 1818, he wrote an introductory essay as a preface to the notes he had composed while secretary of state and had them bound into three volumes. "After the lapse of 25 years, or more, from their dates," he explained, "I have given to the whole a calm revisal, when the passions of the time are passed away, and the reasons of the transactions act alone on the judgment. Some of the information I had recorded are now cut out from the rest, because I have seen that they were incorrect, or doubtful, or merely personal or private, with which we have nothing to do." It was his intention, he told a trusted visitor to whom he showed the volumes and his explanatory preface, that they be published after his death "but he wished that the knowledge of the existence of this paper should not be confined to members of his own family; and that he should shew it to Mr Madison . . . late President of the United States." But not to the public.

The passions had not entirely been left out. John Marshall had published a five-volume biography of George Washington during

Jefferson's presidency. Jefferson believed it inaccurate and politically biased. It infuriated him. A Federalist whose appointment Jefferson resented and whose decisions he detested, Marshall idolized Washington. He thought as little of Jefferson as Jefferson did of him. Jefferson's purpose was to correct the record. Marshall, Jefferson believed, had been an enemy of the true principles of the Revolution. He had cherry-picked and misused documents to the detriment of Jefferson, the Republicans, and the historical record. His "party feelings" have created a biography, Jefferson wrote in a preface to the notes he had gathered together, "as different from what Gen. Washington would have offered as was the candor of the two characters." Washington was a truth teller; Marshall, a liar. For Jefferson, the truth and spirit of the Revolution were at issue. His obstreperous prose soared: "The sufferings inflicted on endeavors to vindicate the rights of humanity are related with all the frigid insensibility with which a monk would have contemplated the victims of an Auto da fe! Let no man believe that Gen. Washington ever intended that his papers should be used for the suicide of the cause for which he had lived, and for which there never was a moment in which he would not have died."

The main "abuse" of Marshall's biography, though, was his "history of the period" of Washington's first presidency. "Were a reader of this period to form his idea of it from this history alone, he would suppose the republican party . . . who were in truth endeavoring" to be true to the Constitution "and prevent it from being monarchized . . . were a set of grumblers satisfied with no government" and "without fixed principles. . . ." He took Marshall's account to be a direct attack on him. Jefferson's three bound volumes of notes were his response. He believed that he himself had a firm unbiased knowledge of the facts, that his contemporaneous notes were objective historical documents.

Many of those he included in his bound volumes are indeed accurate copies of letters sent and received. Many of the descriptive accounts are inflected by Jefferson's opinions and analysis, without distinguishing between corroborated facts and his own views. Some of the entries are on consecutive days. Some are separated by days, weeks, even months. Why were the events of those days considered worth recording and others not? Also, the implied claim is that all the notes accurately represent what was said or happened. In other instances, Jefferson summarizes Cabinet discussions, often stating who favored which option or policy in response to a specific problem. If the three volumes had been published by a publisher in another era, its title could very well have been *Me and George: A Memoir from My Point of View* or *One Participant's View of the Administration of Washington and Hamilton*. Scattered throughout are brilliantly conceived and written passages, with the novelistic flair of having been written to the moment. They bring alive Jefferson's version of who did and said what and why. Through quotations, summaries, and narrative description, they create Jefferson's fascinating, partly reliable, partly unreliable, version of the events of 1792–1793. Jefferson wanted to shape the narrative for posterity.

The degree to which Jefferson edited these memoranda is unknowable. He had them bound "in marble paper," chronologically arranged. "In these three volumes will be found copies of the official opinions given in writing by me to General Washington while I was Secretary of State." There are other things as well, especially records of conversations with the president. The texts of the memoranda are preceded by "an explanation of the three volumes," an essay dated February 4, 1818. It is a substantial, sharply written, partisan account of the issues and people of 1792–1793 and thereafter, a prelude to what Jefferson believed to be the second American Revolution, a rededication of the United States to a republican future which culminated in his election to the presidency in 1800. After his death, his grandson, who published selections, gave them the odd title *Anas*, by which he meant table talk or miscellaneous writings. The title has stuck. The *Anas* were next published in an "incomplete and scattered arrangement" in 1854; the last book-length edition dates from 1903. Thereafter its entries have been published in the chronological place of their dating in the *Thomas Jefferson Papers*.

Unlike *Notes on the State of Virginia*, whose readership he gradually expanded, Jefferson seems not to have intended that the *Anas* be read in his lifetime by anyone but himself. Still, much about it implies an audience, particularly his creation of the introductory essay, his version of the historical context, in effect a brief for who were the bad guys, who were the good guys, what issues were at stake, and the truth about his role in his relationship with the president. The *Anas* is a book of sorts, a record of self-vindication, or at least a bound collection of materials, whether conceived of as a book or not, that has at its center a conflict the ultimate result of which was a victory for Jefferson and his principles.

At the beginning of January 1821, seventy-seven-year-old Thomas Jefferson, at his self-designed writing desk, set pen to paper to do something he had repeatedly said he would never do: write something about his personal history and career. "You express a wish and a hope that I may have been writing memoirs of myself," he had responded to William Short in May 1816. "While in public life, my whole time has been absorbed by the duties that laid me under; and now, when the world imagines I have nothing to do, I am in a state of as heavy drudgery as any office of my life ever subjected me to." He had too many letters he felt obliged to respond to. He had to manage his farms. He needed exercise, and his wrist was "beginning to stiffen so as to render writing painful and slow." Let the public documents he had written, the letters that were already in the public domain, and his private manuscripts be sufficient for future historians. A memoir was out of the question.

In January 1821, he changed his mind. He began writing a narrative to which his later editors gave the title *Autobiography, 1743–1790,* although *autobiography* was a word Jefferson never used. As with the *Anas,* his purpose was to set the record straight about his contribution to the major political and legislative events that he had participated in or witnessed. Few modern readers, with the canon of American autobiography from Benjamin Franklin to Henry Adams in mind, would think of it as a contribution to the genre, and its author did not intend it to be autobiography in the traditional sense. Jefferson was rarely desirous of self-exploration or self-revelation, except in private letters. In public, on public affairs, and on his role as a political leader, he was, as his last sustained piece of writing reveals, consistent to the end: discretion, concealment, management, self-editing, the use of language for discreet persuasion in the interest of political ends and the management of history.

The extant manuscript begins "January 6, 1821. At the age of 77, I begin to make some memoranda and state some recollections of dates and facts concerning myself, for my own more ready reference and for the information of my family." The narrative is chronological. It begins with Jefferson's brief account of his ancestry and marriage and continues with a selective account of his public career from his first legislative experience in Virginia until his departure from France in 1789. A substantial portion contains quotations from or entire public documents. His family, private life, education of the head and heart, the death of his wife and most of his children, his attempt to construct a persona and a life, his relationship with his mother, and any of the events and relationships, thoughts and feelings, that might give personal substance to an autobiographical narrative are absent. The final section, describing what Jefferson saw and did in revolutionary Paris in 1788–1789, contains the most vivid and interesting writing in the manuscript.

As a literary work, most of it is not gripping. And it adds only a few details to what's known about Jefferson's early life. It provides some additional context and evaluation of the Revolutionary period. It carefully avoids implicating Jefferson in anything that might be questionable. On the whole, it is his account of and revision of his public life, controlled by focused selectivity and the insertion of documents, particularly an annotated and marked up Declaration of Independence to support his assertion that his original was superior to the final version. He still felt resentful of the changes in the text that had been forced on him. In fact, he believed that the editorial changes forced on his final draft made the Declaration less powerful than it otherwise would have been. It also, inferentially, makes the point that he himself was the major author, not the other four members of the committee. He did not claim that the document was original in thought. He readily granted that it was intended to and could not help but capture the spirit of the times, the arguments and language that had expressed the American colonial experience since the Stamp Act.

Jefferson worked on the manuscript for about six months, revising and writing new material. There may have been some touching up afterward, particularly about his years in France and his description of the revolutionary ferment he observed. In addition to the Declaration and the Articles of Confederation, it contains Jefferson's lengthy version of the debate in Congress starting on June 7, 1776, in response to the Virginia delegates' instructions to move that the colonies be free and independent. It is presented as a contemporaneous document, notes taken at the actual time. Whether they were written as the debate was in progress or immediately afterward or later, and if so when, or revisited and revised perhaps more than once, is not clear. Jefferson's premier editor argues that the first draft was written before 1783, almost certainly between June and August 1776, and that it was revised over time, some of the revisions before 1783, some after, as late as between 1819 and 1825.

It seems certain that between January and June 1821, Jefferson tinkered with the debate notes he had written at earlier times. Writing and shaping history, he placed into his narrative a document claiming to be contemporary with the chronology of the manuscript's narrative. Some of it is likely to have been, but it also was being written, or at least made use of, in the present of the author's life. The awkward insertion of what pretends to be an accurate transcription of the 1776 debate expresses Jefferson's concern that a counter-Jeffersonian history of the Revolutionary era was being written by his political enemies. He needed to help correct the record. There was in progress, and there had been for some time, a battle over the possession of the Revolution and credit for the Declaration. It had recently intensified and was soon, between 1822 and 1825, to become dramatic. How much credit, one side asked, did Jefferson deserve as "author" of the Declaration of Independence? And the less the credit, the more credit to those whose historical affiliation was with the Federalists and the Washington administration. It was a struggle over who owned the narrative. For Jefferson, it was a personal and a political matter. He wanted his version to be available to posterity.

In 1822 two Federalist newspapers claimed that Jefferson deserved little credit for the authorship of the Declaration. Even granting, as Jefferson did, that it was a document expressing the consensus of this formative American age, he believed that the words themselves and the structure of the document were his. So did many others. But in 1823, at a Fourth of July celebration in New England, the keynote orator, Jefferson's and Adams's old enemy, Timothy Pickering, claimed that Jefferson had been given credit that he did not deserve. Pickering misquoted a letter from Adams implying that Adams agreed with him. He did not, though Adams was sensitive about how little credit he was being given for his role in the Confederation Congress of 1776. Jefferson affirmed Adams's leading role. "You have doubtless seen Timothy Pickering's 4th. of July observations on the Declaration of Independence," he wrote to James Madison in August 1823.

The committee, he continued, made only two or three alterations "and merely verbal. . . . Whether I had gathered my ideas from reading or reflection I do not know. I know only that I turned to neither book or pamphlet while writing it. I did not consider it as any part of my charge to invent new ideas altogether and to offer no sentiment which had ever been expressed before." He was not sensitive about the charge of lack of originality. The Declaration was "the genuine effusion of the soul of our country at that time." But he did care that it be acknowledged that he had written it.

In June 1824, he wrote one of the most passionate public letters of his life. Over 3,500 words long, it was retrospective and argumentative. It was an historical summary and rationale for his career and a review of a few of the major controversies of his life. The spark that motivated him to write with his crippled hand what he concluded was an "unmercifully long" letter was the receipt of a copy of what he described as Mr. Pickering's "elaborate Philippic against Mr. Adams, Gerry, Smith and myself." It had been sent to him by a rising senator from New York, Martin Van Buren.

I could not have believed that, for so many years, and to such a period of advanced age, [Pickering] could have nourished passions so vehement and viperous. It appears that, for 30 years past, he has been industriously collecting materials for vituperating the characters he had marked for his hatred; some of whom certainly, if enmities towards him had ever existed, had forgotten them all, or buried them in the grave with themselves. As to myself, there never had been anything personal between us, nothing but the general opposition of party sentiment; and our personal intercourse had been that of urbanity. . . . But it seems he has been all this time brooding over an enmity which I had never felt, and yet that with respect to myself, as well as others, he has been writing far and near, and in every direction, to get hold of original letters, where he could, copies where he could not, certificates and journals, catching at every gossiping story he could hear of in any quarter, supplying by suspicions what he could find nowhere else.

Pickering detested John Adams as much as he did Jefferson. They had been colleagues who had fallen out, the worst kind of enemies. Pickering may have had reasons for his hostility to Adams, Jefferson wrote to Van Buren, but it was excessive. "He arraigns me on two grounds, my actions, and my motives." But "the very actions however which he arraigns have been such as the great majority of my fellow-citizens have approved." Rather than end the letter with that statement Jefferson continued with a full reprise of his career, especially his activities as secretary of state and the election of 1800. Pickering had accused Jefferson of hypocrisy, ambition, pandering to the public, and the dishonorable use of a private letter. It was Pickering's negative portrayal of Jefferson's relationship with Washington that, of all the accusations leveled against him, Jefferson felt most needed to be countered. Hamilton and his ilk, Jefferson assured Van Buren, were the villains. They had suborned Washington. He was certain that Washington would have returned, if he had lived longer, to his true friends, to the spirit of '76 and basic republican principles.

For Jefferson, the historical record and his reputation were at stake. He did not request, as he almost always did with such letters, that this one be kept private.

My last parting with General Washington was at the inauguration of Mr. Adams in March 1797 and was warmly affectionate; and I never had any reason to believe any change on his part as there certainly was none on mine. But one session of congress intervened between that and his death the year following . . . as it happened to be not convenient to call on him, I never had another opportunity; and as to the cessation of correspondence observed during that short

interval no particular circumstance occurred for epistolary communication, and both of us were too much oppressed with letter-
writing to trouble, either the other, with a letter about nothing. The
truth is that the Federalists, pretending to be the exclusive friends
of General Washington, have ever done what they could to sink his
character, by hanging theirs on it, and by representing, as the enemy of Republicans, him who, of all men, is best entitled to the
appellation of the father of that republic which they were endeavoring to subvert, and the Republicans to maintain. They cannot deny,
because the elections proclaimed the truth, that the great body of
the nation approved the republican measures. General Washington
was himself sincerely a friend to the republican principles of our
constitution. . . . It is vain then for Mr. Pickering and his friends to
endeavor to falsify his character by representing him as an enemy to
Republicans and republican principles, and as exclusively the friend
of those who were so; and had he lived longer, he would have returned to his antient and unbiassed opinions, would have replaced
his confidence in those whom the people approved and supported,
and would have seen that they were only restoring and acting on the
principles of his own first administration.

There was more to say, "but my letter is already too unmercifully
long. . . . If of no other value, the present communication may amuse
you with anecdotes not known to everyone." The anecdotes were not
the point of the letter. Jefferson was rewriting history.

In 1816, Jefferson had complained about and abjured writing letters,
a constant refrain.

I am grown old, and worn down by the drudgery of the writing
table. Repose and tranquility are become necessaries of life for

me. . . . I have labored daily from sunrise . . . say from 7 to 8 hours a day, answering letters, few of which are of the least concern to myself; and that instead of their decreasing as I had long had the hope, I have been obliged for many months past to rise from table and write from dinner to dark: insomuch that no office I ever was in has been so laborious as my supposed state of retirement at Monticello. Unable to bear up longer against it, either in body or mind, I am obliged to declare myself in a state of insurgency, and to assume my right to live out the dregs of life at least, without being under the whip and spur from morning to night.

He did write fewer and more perfunctory letters between 1816 and his death in 1826, with notable exceptions like his long letter to Martin Van Buren, and he refused every writing project other than those few he felt compelled to undertake in the interest of history and his reputation. "Indeed my Physician interdicts me the writing table altogether," he wrote to one correspondent. "I am obliged therefore to abandon all correspondence," only partly true but an effective excuse. "Age, its ordinary infirmities, and extraordinary visitations of sickness have so broke me down that I am no longer able to maintain any correspondence by letters but such as my own affairs render indispensable."

Jefferson still had many good days, and a visitor in 1817 put the best spin on his aging body: "I found Mr. Jefferson tall in person, but stooping and lean with old age, thus exhibiting that fortunate mode of bodily decay, which strips the frame of its most cumbersome parts, leaving it still strength of muscle and activity of limb." By 1820 he kept his writing tasks for the mornings, as early as possible, always rising with the sun, after which he rode for exercise, whenever he was not ill, and attended to the daily business of his farms and his family. Reading and his grandchildren were his greatest pleasures. To John Adams, he explained that "three long and dangerous illnesses within the last 12 months must apologize for my long silence towards you." Ailments from boils to urinary tract infections and obstructions plagued him. His abhorrence of letter writing, though, and his illnesses did not affect his continuing to keep up his part of the ongoing letters that highlighted his revivified friendship with his former colleague and opponent in political life.

He had in 1816 still been optimistically rosy about the ledger of life being all on the side of happiness, especially if one maintained the right frame of mind. He wrote to Adams, "You ask if I would agree to live my 70 or rather 73 years over again? to which I say yea. I think with you that it is a good world on the whole, that it has been framed on a principle of benevolence, and more pleasure than pain dealt out to us." It still seemed to him the best of all possible worlds, except for the painfulness of "grief," which he could not account for. It did not fit into his cosmic accounting. He had lost a wife and five children. He had experienced alcoholism, wife beating, near-death violence, clinical depression, and touches of insanity in his immediate family. Increasingly tired, by late 1819 he accepted that it would be best if he no longer handled his plantation affairs. "Age, its ordinary infirmities, and frequent attacks of illness have rendered me unable to attend to my own affairs, which I have in consequence committed to the care of a grandson," his daughter Martha's eldest son. He refused to be drawn into any public dissension. "I am old and infirm, scarcely equal to the labor of common and necessary letters, and sickening for the downy bed of repose and quiet." He believed that he noticed signs of dementia. "When the body is sensibly decayed, we may well suspect that the mind is in some sympathies with it. When the coat is well-worn, we ought to expect that the lining also is becoming thread-bare. We are the last . . . in perceiving that wane of the understanding; and unfortunately the faculty of perceiving is still weakening with the progress of its own decay."

But neither Jefferson's mind nor crippled hand prevented him from writing vigorous letters about a national crisis that dovetailed with his own financial woes. It also drew on a deep reserve of anger about banks, the banking system, and specie versus paper currency. The depression of 1819 seemed to Jefferson reality's revenge on what Hamilton and the Federalists had wrought, a centralized banking system dependent on paper money that it printed. Both had always been anathema to Jefferson. The paper money issued by overextended state banks without sufficient specie reserve and the demand for re-payment from a highly stressed central bank plunged the national economy into chaos and bankruptcy. The price of land and every other form of real property, including slaves, fell off a cliff. Banks called in loans. Citizens wanted specie for their paper money. There was insufficient specie reserve. Banks failed. The absence of mone-tary regulation, the mixture of private ventures and public office, and an emerging high-stakes capitalism, one of whose major ingredients was greed, contributed to Jefferson's insistence that the baby needed to be thrown out with the bathwater. Paper money had become al-most worthless. Land in Virginia plunged in value. The market for wheat and cotton declined precipitously. Jefferson's crops brought in hardly the cost of planting and harvesting them.

Jefferson was both unhappy and angry, a Cassandra whose eco-nomic and financial policies he believed, if they had been implemented and continued, would have prevented the financial collapse. The basis of the economy, in Jefferson's view, should always be real property, especially land and hard currency. He had enough energy and focus in November 1819 to create a *Plan for Reducing the Circulating Medium*, the purpose of which was to restore the value of real property by leg-islating monetary policy to reduce available credit over a five-year pe-riod. It would create strict controls on banks and lending. Credit and paper money were the villains. He believed his plan would restore the economy. "In this way the value of property, keeping pace nearly with the sum of circulating medium, will descend gradually to its proper level at the rate of about 1/5 every year, the sacrifices of what shall be sold for payment of the first instalments of debts will be moderate, and time will be given for economy and industry to come in aid of those subsequent." The state needed to act quickly. "It is believed that harpies are already hoarding their money" in expectation of profiting from the depression. "We know that lands have been already sold under the hammer for less than a year's rent." In need of cash, he tried and failed to sell part of his Poplar Forest estate.

The year 1819 was dreadful for the country and for Jefferson. He had been in debt for decades, juggling outstanding notes, new borrowing, unprofitable crops, and now the decline in market value of everything he owned and produced. His financial difficulties, compounded by the cost of ongoing renovations at Monticello, constantly pressured him. Every attempt to help himself or of others to help him failed or had limited success, even a "fire sale" in 1815 of his books to the Library of Congress. He immediately began the expense of creating another personal library. Much of the nation was grateful for his services, but not financially. Ex-presidents were on their own. He had also designed a second home for himself, mostly built by skilled slaves, an upscale summertime retreat and a refuge from sightseers and visitors. It was on his Poplar Forest estate where, in the original plantation house, he had written the first draft of *Notes on the State of Virginia*.

"Four years of bad overseers, one of drought, and one of fly [predatory insects] have been making me drop behind hand by little and little year after year," he wrote in March 1818 to a friend, relative, and political colleague, Wilson Cary Nicholas. This will "submit me to painful anxieties until better management and a better season or two shall bring me relief." Nicholas's daughter Jane had married Jefferson's eldest grandson. They were family, in a kinship alliance that characterized the Virginia plantation elite. A former senator and recent ex-governor of Virginia, Nicholas was also president of the Richmond branch of the Second Bank of the United States, from which Jefferson had a large outstanding loan, approved by the bank's president. When he could not repay it, the bank extended the repayment schedule. Jefferson may not have known how speculatively invested Nicholas was in Western land. Before 1819, Nicholas's Virginia plantations had a high valuation. He was considered a rich man.

Jefferson himself was in deep financial trouble before the depression began. That he would ever find relief was delusory optimism. That he expressed this hope to Nicholas in 1818 was to add a painful irony to his situation. The next month, Nicholas made a request. "Will you do me the favor to endorse for me, two notes for ten thousand dollars each? The accommodation to cease at the end of twelve months at longest. I have already sold property to the amount of forty-five thousand dollars, I shall persevere until I have sold the whole of my estate," if necessary, "which by any estimate that can be made of it is worth $350,000." It was only a matter of a short time until he would have the cash to repay the loan. "I sincerely wish, that you should not comply with the request . . . if it should be either inconvenient or unpleasant to you. . . . I have taken the liberty to enclose two notes. . . ."

Jefferson expressed only one concern, his desire to bequeath his own estate as unencumbered as possible. "But this consideration yields to the desire of rendering you service. I willingly therefore return you the papers you enclosed, with my endorsements, as I shall those which may hereafter, be necessary for their continuance, reposing myself with entire confidence in your care and assurances for you well know that a Virginia farmer has no resource for meeting sudden and large calls for money." It seemed to make no difference to Jefferson that he had not the slightest chance of paying the debt if Nicholas defaulted. Nicholas's bank had favored Jefferson. Nicholas was family by marriage. He had been a longtime political supporter. On his way to Poplar Forest, Jefferson had slept numbers of times in a bedroom at Nicholas's home. Nicholas was assumed to be a rich man, and in April

1818 there may have been some truth to his valuation of his property. Nicholas believed that Jefferson would not lose by his endorsement, though even in spring 1818, he might have had some twinges of doubt, given how much money he needed to repay the notes due for land he had bought on credit. At the end of 1818, Jefferson provided further endorsements to the very kind of speculator he had been railing against.

In January 1819, the bank panic began. By mid-spring the roof had fallen in on Nicholas. A "mortified" Jefferson, himself deeply in debt, was now responsible for an additional $20,000. In June 1819, he received a letter from the American minister to the Court of St. James's, offering to act as his agent to purchase books. Richard Rush got a response he had not anticipated. It testified to Jefferson's anguish and the national crisis. "The enormous abuses of the banking system," he wrote, "are not only prostrating our commerce, but producing revolution in property." The abuses threatened to void one of his highest principles, land as the basic and best source of American values. "The banks themselves were doing business on capitals, three fourths of which were fictitious: and, to extend their profits they furnished fictitious capital to every man, who having nothing and disliking the labors of the plough" had dashed "into every species of mercantile gambling." That gambling "ended as gambling generally does. . . . This fictitious capital . . . is now to be lost, and to fall on some body; it must take on those who have property to meet it, and probably on the less cautious part, who, not aware of the impending catastrophe have suffered themselves to contract, or to be in debt, and must now sacrifice their property of a value many times the amount of their debt." He had to be aware that he was also referring to himself.

We have been truly sowing the wind, and are now reaping the whirlwind. If the present crisis should end in the annihilation of these penny less and ephemeral interlopers only, and reduce our commerce to the measure of our own wants and surplus productions, it will be a benefit in the end. But how to affect this, and give time to real capital, and the holders of real property to back out of their entanglements by degrees, requires more knowledge of political economy than we possess. I believe it might be done; but I despair of its being done. The eyes of our citizens are not yet sufficiently open to the true cause of our distresses. They ascribe them to everything but their true cause, the banking system; a system, which, if it could do good in any form, is yet so certain of leading to abuse, as to be utterly incompatible with the public safety and prosperity. At present all is confusion, uncertainty and panic.

If only he could be among those who could "back out."

Jefferson's rejection of banking, credit, and speculation had deep roots in his sense of well-being and privilege, the inheritance he had been born into, the property that gave him his sense of worth, the class he belonged to and its standards of honor and honesty, and the inseparability of ownership of land from his belief in home and family. For Jefferson, American virtue grew from its soil, not from Hamilton's banks and credit structures. He would have been less damaged by the panic and depression of 1819 if he had not all his life spent freely. There was no reserve. To produce an income that would support his establishment, his farms needed to be tightly and effectively managed. Jefferson hired people to do that. He was, understandably, interested in other things. And farm viability varied from year to year, dependent on weather, labor, pests, and sufficient credit to pay for essentials in the period between sowing and selling. Still, whether in his role as plantation owner or as public servant, as good a mathematician as he was, Jefferson did not have a head for balancing ledgers between expenditures and income. Books, art, architecture, gardens, and hospitality were, for him, necessities. It was not a matter of choice. It was who he was. In 1819, he could not pay any of his debts.

In regard to Nicholas, "I am indeed a sore sufferer myself by his failure, yet I cannot look to his situation but with the greatest commiseration." He was also commiserating with himself. Jefferson needed the indulgence of the creditors he could not pay. The most iconic American patriot still alive mostly got it. But it was one of the most painful experiences of his life. It had misery-making consequences for him and for the family he loved.

There was another dangerous and difficult property, both personal and impersonal, that he owned as an individual and was concerned about for his country—enslaved people. It's unclear what his relationship was with Sally Hemings in his aging years and in her still comparative youth. Apparently, she wore her light-skinned slavery lightly, a privileged member of the household with continuous access to Jefferson's private sanctum. We have no access to her thoughts or feelings. Clearly, he cared for his obligations, one of which was a promise he had made in France that she would have a degree of privilege in the Monticello world and that their children eventually would be set free or allowed to assume their own freedom. So too would she if she outlived him and her legal status mattered to her.

His position on slavery was clear to those who knew him. He was in favor of gradual emancipation and colonization, an "establishment on the coast of Africa, and the patronage of our nation until the emigrants shall be able to protect themselves." He had attempted as a Virginia legislator to advance gradual emancipation, without success; he had strongly favored ending the importation of slaves after 1808; and he favored the efforts of the Colonization Society to encourage free Blacks to emigrate. It seemed a certainty to Jefferson that any large number of free Blacks, especially of former slaves, and white Americans could not live together harmoniously.

As a public official, Jefferson had not been a leader on the issue of slavery. He deplored the institution; it was morally shameful; it was dangerous to the long-term health and prosperity of the country; but for the time being, it was a necessity, particularly for Southern farmers like himself. There was no substitute labor force available. It was the basis of economic viability. It was not in human nature, and it was not in Jefferson's nature, to encourage the emancipation of slaves without some process that enabled slave-owners to remain economically viable. No one had yet figured out how to implement a process that would not destroy the Southern economy, a major contributor to national prosperity. Even compensated emancipation would probably leave farmers like Jefferson, having lost their labor force, with unplowed fields. Moreover, in Jefferson's widely shared view, newly freed slaves would be useless workers, criminal marauders, and violently hostile to their former white masters. Beyond that, Jefferson, like most slave-owners, would have found it hard to imagine how, without slaves, his daily life would be maintained in the patterns that were psychologically and materially embedded in his consciousness and assumptions. In public and private life, whatever his own personal stake in the continuance of slavery, whatever his principles, Jefferson would not lead where public opinion would not follow. He had good reason to believe that American public opinion did not favor emancipation. Even for those who condemned slavery, the cost seemed daunting, even prohibitive. Like most Americans, he believed that such a mighty transformation of the society could occur only if widespread public opinion favored it. It did not.

In 1816, William Short urged Jefferson to lend his name to a legal prohibition on the domestic slave trade. Jefferson refused. It had, in his view, no chance of becoming law. And the use of his name would make him and his name a target in a public controversy. He had dedicated his postpresidential life to avoiding that. Even allowing his name to be used to support the Colonization Society was a step too far. "I shall be willing to do anything I can to give it effect and safety," he responded to a request that he make his views on colonization widely known, "but I am but a private individual, and could only use endeavors with private individuals." He claimed he "was ready and desirous to make any sacrifice which shall ensure" the "gradual but complete retirement" from Virginia of individually manumitted slaves and "establish them elsewhere in freedom and safety." But he was not offering to manumit any of his own. And emancipation? "I have not perceived the growth of this disposition in the rising generation, of which I once had sanguine hopes. No symptoms inform me that it will take place in my day. I leave it therefore to time, and not at all without hope, that the day will come, equally desirable and welcome to us as to them . . . to provide an estab-lishment on the coast of Africa for voluntary emigrations of people of colour," which "may be the corner stone of this future edifice." He was certain that it would happen eventually.

Decades before, in working to revise the laws of Virginia and in *Notes on the State of Virginia*, he had stated his view that Black slaves should and would eventually be free. In 1821, composing what came to be called his autobiography, he was of the same view. "The public mind would not yet bear the proposition" then "nor will it bear it even at this day. Yet the day is not distant when it must bear and adopt it, or worse will follow. Nothing is more certainly written in the book of fate than that these people are to be free. Nor is it less certain that the two races, equally free, cannot live in the same government." But if emancipation "is left to force itself on, human nature must shudder *at the prospect held up.*"

When, in 1819, Missouri's imminent entrance into the union as a free or slave state became a divisive national nightmare, Jefferson indeed shuddered. "The Missouri question is a breaker," he wrote to Adams, "on which we lose the Missouri country by revolt, and what more, god only knows. From the battle of Bunker's Hill to the treaty of Paris we never had so ominous a question." It was possible, he wrote the next year, that "a general emancipation and expatriation could be effected" by coloniza-tion or dispersal, "and, gradually, and with due sacrifices. . . . But, as it is, we have the wolf by the ear, and we can neither hold him, nor safely let him go. Justice is in one scale, and self-preservation in the other." He regretted that he was "now to die in the belief" that the sacrifices made "by the generation of '76 to acquire self-government and happiness to their country, is to be thrown away by the unwise and unworthy passions of their sons, and that my only consolation is to be that I live not to weep over it." He still hoped that a future generation would find the proper balance between morality and practicality. The Missouri issue and the simultaneous national depression weighed heavily on his spirits.

Until 1819, Jefferson maintained high optimism in America's future. The spirit of '76 would reassert itself. The country would fulfill the promise of its founders. "I have much confidence that we shall proceed successfully for ages to come," or so he had written in 1817 to the French diplomat whose questionnaire had prompted *Notes on the State of Virginia*, "and . . . that the larger the extent of country, the more firm its republican structure, if founded, not on conquest, but in principles of compact and equality." That "if" still seemed plausible to Jefferson. "My hope of its duration is built much on the enlargement of the resources of life going hand in hand with the enlargement of territory, and the belief [that] men are disposed to live honestly, if the means of doing so are open to them. With the consolation of this belief in the future result of our labors, I have that of other prophets who foretell distant events, that I shall not live to see it falsified. My theory has always been that if we are to dream, the flatteries of hope are as cheap, and pleasanter than the gloom of despair."

He kept dreaming. The extensive farmland of the Western "Empire of liberty" would make possible a nation of settlers who would live in the happy dialectic between agricultural prosperity and personal virtue. Of course there would be differences of opinion. Political parties had become an inevitability. "For parties must be wherever men are free," he wrote in 1818. Still it was ominous, he acknowledged, that Congress was stalemated, that the Republicans were divided, that there were still Tories, as if America now had Whigs and

Tories once again, though under different names, that there existed the threat of an overly strong executive, that the economy was fragile, and that slavery seemed an irresolvable reality. After the collapse of the economy and the Missouri Compromise, Jefferson kept flickers of his lifelong optimism—but only flickers.

In the last decade of his life, Jefferson picked up the educational cudgel he had tried so hard to wield during his days as a Virginia legislator. Eventually, and with great effort, he succeeded in getting state financial support for a university in Charlottesville. It was an exhausting struggle against intense opposition. The depression of 1819 made raising funds a Sisyphean task. Legislative opposition frustrated him. Supporters of William and Mary opposed the project. He also had to fight strenuously to keep the Virginia clergy from injecting religion into what he wanted to be a secular university. And the Virginia elite was mostly indifferent to higher education, especially for the non-elite.

Jefferson conceived of the new university as the apex of the educational meritocracy he had proposed in the 1780s, the fulfillment of his long-standing vision of a university to rival Yale and Harvard. It turned out not to be quite that. His vision of statewide free education with his university at the apex was constantly undermined by the difficulty of raising money and by the poor quality of many of its students. Still, it was a significant achievement, its future stature to be a credit to his name. It was the only public activity of his retirement. It demanded almost more energy than he had, more involvement in state politics than he wanted, and more writing sessions at his desk than his mind and body could sustain. But he won the hard-fought battle. The university became a major though partial fulfillment of his vision of universal education for Virginians.

Life at Monticello during the last six years of his life had its pleasures and pains. He had too many visitors eager to intrude. Incapable of not being a host, the guests cost him money and inconvenience. Family members died, including a favorite granddaughter, whose loss pained him deeply. Other grandchildren went off to their different destinies, one to New England. His eldest grandson, whose competence kept his farms productive and his financial affairs afloat, managed to keep the walls of Monticello from falling under the auctioneer's hammer. Keeping them from literally falling down was also difficult. Debts remained outstanding. He could neither mortgage nor sell property except at a fire sale. He encouraged the creation of a state lottery to allow Virginia's most famous son to die with debts repaid and Monticello saved for his family. It came to nothing. His own body, in its ninth decade, was failing him: feebleness, tiredness, repeated urinary tract infections, bouts of diarrhea. The thought of death became a hope. It was, he knew, an imminent inevitability. His long-held stoic expectations kept him, seemingly, quietly resigned.

In 1824, Daniel Webster visited Monticello. The eighty-one-year-old Jefferson, Webster noted, was "rather thin and spare. His head . . . is set rather forward upon his shoulders and his neck being long when he is in conversation, or walking, there is a considerable protrusion of his chin." He still had a full head of hair,

> which having been once red and now turning to white, is of an indistinct, light, sandy colour. His eyes are small, very light, and now neither striking nor brilliant. His chin is rather long and not sharp. His teeth are still good. His mouth well-formed. . . . His skin formerly light and freckled is now rough and bears the marks of age. . . . His limbs are uncommonly long and his wrists especially of extraordinary size. . . . He stoops a little, not so much from age, as from constitutional formation. When sitting he seems short & low, partly from not sitting erect & partly from the disproportionate length of his limbs.

He had the mistaken impression that Jefferson had an "extraordinary degree of health, vivacity, and spirit."

Actually, he was fragile and fading, though he still had a few brilliant moments with his pen.

During the first half of 1826, he was mostly in bed or feebly on his feet, attended by his fifty-two-year-old daughter, Martha, his only surviving child, and probably Sally Hemings. He still had use for his pen. He left instructions for his gravestone: "Here was buried Thomas Jefferson / Author of the Declaration of American Independence / of the Statute of Virginia for religious freedom / and Father of the University of Virginia." It included only the history Jefferson favored. It was later vandalized. On June 24, he had the energy to respond to an invitation from the citizens of Washington to attend the city's celebration "of the 50th anniversary of American independence." He regretted that "ill health forbids me the gratification of an acceptance." He had something to say as one of "the surviving signers of an instrument pregnant with our own, and the fate of the world." He did not need to mention that he was also its author. His mind was still, understandably, on 1776.

> It adds sensibly to the sufferings of sickness, to be deprived by it of a personal participation in the rejoicings of that day. . . . I should, indeed, with peculiar delight, have met and exchanged there congratulations personally with the small band, the remnant of that host of worthies, who joined with us on that day, in the bold and doubtful election we were to make for our country, between submission or the sword; and to have enjoyed with them the consolatory fact, that our fellow citizens, after half a century of experience and prosperity, continue to approve the choice we made. May it be to the world, what I believe it will be . . . the signal of arousing men to burst the chains, under which monkish ignorance and superstition had persuaded them to bind themselves, and to assume the blessings and security of self-government . . . the free right to the unbounded exercise of reason and freedom of opinion.

The letter was the last sustained effort to which he put his writing skills.

He was, on his deathbed, consoled by his preference for optimism about America's future. It was an optimism that the reality did not fully support. He was still worried about America's unsustainable debt, congressional and executive stalemate, judicial tyranny, military posturing, Indian genocide, the likely presidency of a proslavery racist without respect for the law, and the unsustainable acrimony between North and South about the expansion of slavery westward. But his eye was still on the American future of his happiest dreams, and the eventual triumph for all the world of his republican vision of a better future that he believed is the inherent right of every human being. For Jefferson, it was built into the nature of things by Nature or God, or even only by an innate sense in the nature of human nature and of right and wrong. "All eyes are opened, or opening," he predicted, "to the rights of man." It was a claim for which he had little evidence.

> The general spread of the light of science has already laid open to every view the palpable truth, that the mass of mankind has not been born with saddles on their backs, nor a favored few booted and spurred, ready to ride them legitimately, by the grace of god. These are grounds of hope for others. For ourselves, let the annual return of this day forever refresh our recollections of these rights, and an undiminished devotion to them.

This said everything he had to say. He died a little over a month later, the day of the fiftieth anniversary of his best known and most influential achievement as a writer.

ACKNOWLEDGMENTS

The acknowledgment that comes before any other expression of thanks is to the editors and publishers of *The Papers of Thomas Jefferson*, who over many decades and at least two generations have edited and published in books and online *The Papers of Thomas Jefferson, Main Series, 1760–1809*, and *The Papers of Thomas Jefferson, Retirement Series, 1809–1826*. Fuller reference to the editors and presses appears in the introduction to the notes section in this volume. The Library of Congress and the American taxpayer, in cooperation with *The Papers of Thomas Jefferson*, have done American history and its students a great service by creating Founders Online, which is far advanced in the project of making unedited versions of the letters and papers of all American presidents available online and at no cost to the reader. Without these editors and institutions this book could not have been written.

I gratefully acknowledge the assistance of the Georges Borchardt Literary Agency. Its agent-in-chief, Georges Borchardt, has, as always, provided wise counsel and business acumen in the creation and presentation of this project from proposal to book. My thanks to his coworkers Anne Borchardt and Cora Markowitz. This is the third book of mine to be published by HarperCollins. The thoughtful comments of its editor, Jonathan Jao, have once again made this book a better one than it otherwise would have been, and his editorial assistant, David Howe, has capably and effectively guided the book through the publication process. The designer of the elegantly dramatic book jacket, Milan Bozic, has my gratitude. It is distinctive and original. Kelly Doyle and the rest of the publicity and marketing staff at HarperCollins have my thanks as well. My gratitude to Peter Felsenthal and Jen Litchfield for the portrait photograph that appears on the dust jacket. It captures a rare instance of the subject smiling for the camera.

The main personal acknowledgment is to Rhoda Ackerson Weyr, to whom this book is dedicated. Friends and family have made their direct and indirect contributions, as is desirable and inevitable in a project of five or so years' duration. My thanks for encouragement and conversation and also simply for their presence in my life to Kate Boulay, Katy Emck, Leslie Epstein, Peter Felsenthal, Ed Geffner, Benjamin J. Kaplan, Chloe Kaplan, Julia R. Kaplan, Noah J. Kaplan, David Kleinbard, Mara Lemanis, Jen Lichfield, Kier Lynch, Peter Lynch, Carol Molesworth, Charles Molesworth, Suzanne Spinrad, Allan Teel, Talila Tobias, Garret Weyr, and Tara Weyr. Two distinguished Jeffersonians, Peter S. Onuf and Andrew Jackson O'Shaughnessy, kindly read and commented on an earlier version of this book. Their help and generosity are much appreciated.

A NOTE ON SOURCES

Jefferson biography has been written mostly by political historians. The biographical emphasis has been on Jefferson as a political figure and political thinker. There are many fine biographical and analytical books about different periods in his life, especially his authorship of the Declaration; there are fine studies of his intellectual development, his personality, his engagement with his peers, his family relationships, his life as a slave-owner, and his relationship with his mistress, Sally Hemings. Dumas Malone deserves credit for his pioneering six-volume biography. So too does Fawn Brodie for her pathbreaking *Thomas Jefferson: An Intimate History*, the prelude to later fine explorations of Jefferson in excellent books by Peter Onuf, Joseph Ellis, Annette Gordon-Reed, and a host of exemplary scholars whose names anchor the endnotes to this book. No Jefferson biographer can avoid an immense debt to Julian Boyd and his heirs, the editors of the main series and the retirement series of *The Papers of Thomas Jefferson*.

This biography is anchored in primary sources, particularly Jefferson's own words. It is also indebted to many secondary sources.

Some are broad biographies and/or historical and interpretive over-views of aspects of Jefferson's culture, context, career, mind, and life. Some are focused on a particular issue or period. It would be tedious to acknowledge repeatedly in my notes the books that have influenced my overall approach to Jefferson and his world. The selective bibliog-raphy that follows these notes will suffice to direct the reader toward this valuable secondary literature. In the instances in which the narra-tive draws on a focused subject, such as Jefferson as a lawyer or Jeffer-son and the French Revolution, I have cited these works in the notes as books that I have relied on for my narrative in some particular way.

The vast majority of the citations are to Jefferson's own words. All such quotations come from *The Papers of Thomas Jefferson, Main Se-ries, 1760–1809*, edited by Julian P. Boyd et al., vols. 1–42, currently to March 1804 (Princeton, NJ: Princeton University Press, 1950–); or from *The Papers of Thomas Jefferson, Retirement Series, 1809–1826*, edited by James P. McClure and Jefferson Looney et al., vols. 1–21, currently to April 1818 (Charlottesville, VA: Thomas Jefferson Foundation, 2015–). The Rotunda Press at the University of Virginia Press provides digital versions of both series. The National Archives Founders Online website created by the Library of Congress contains the *Thomas Jefferson Papers* without the annotation that the Rotunda and the printed versions provide. I have sometimes quoted from the footnotes in the main series, using Boyd as the citation attribution. The extraordinary contribution of these editors and sponsors has made this book feasible. No biographer of Jefferson can overpraise the editors of the *Thomas Jefferson Papers*.

With a rationale that will not please those editors, however, I have often modernized Jefferson's punctuation, abbreviations, spelling, and contractions (especially his use of "its" for "it's" and vice versa), as well as his practice of starting a sentence with a lowercase letter. In a book for a general readership, readability trumps originalism. I have also dispensed with the convention of "p." for page and "pp." for pages in citations when what is being indicated is already obvious. The name of every correspondent who has three or more instances in the citations appears as an abbreviation, as below. All of the citations from letters by and to Jefferson come from the *Thomas Jefferson Papers*, the main series or the retirement series, with the exception of those letters not yet published in the *Papers* but which are available in the Founders Online series. It seems to me an unnecessary formality to include in each citation anything more than the name of the correspondent and the date of the letter. Those interested in examining the citation in relation to the letter in which it appears can use a search engine to locate the letter in the *Thomas Jefferson Papers*, which requires paid access, or on Founders Online, made freely available by the Library of Congress. The same is the case for all of Jefferson's writings. I've given a fuller citation in the rare instances in which Jefferson's words come from a source other than these.

ABBREVIATIONS

AA: Abigail Adams

AB: Aaron Burr

AC: Angelica Church

AD: Alexander Donald

BF: Benjamin Franklin

Boyd: Julian P. Boyd, et al.

BR: Benjamin Rush

EP: Edmund Pendleton

EWR: Ellen Wayles Randolph (Coolidge)

FE: Francis Eppes

GG: George Gilmer

GRC: George Rogers Clark

GW: George Washington

JA: John Adams

JBD: John-Baptiste Ducoigne

JJ: John Jay

JO: James Ogilvie

JM: James Madison

JM1: James Monroe

JP: John Page

JR: John Randolph

JT: John Trumbull

MC: Maria Cosway

MP: Mann Page

MJ: Mary Jefferson (Eppes)

MJR: Martha Jefferson Randolph

MVB: Martin Van Buren

NL: Nicholas Lewis

PC: Peter Carr

RP: Richard Price

TJ: Thomas Jefferson

TJA: *Autobiography* (New York: Library of America, 1984).

TJP: Thomas Jefferson Papers

TJR: Thomas Jefferson Randolph

TMR: Thomas Mann Randolph Jr.

TP: Tom Paine

WCN: Wilson Cary Nicholas

WGM: William Green Munford

WS: William Short

WS1: William Small

WSS: William Stephens Smith

CHAPTER ONE: MY WATCH HAD LOST ITS SPEECH

1   a good poem: Robert Frost, *Collected Poems, Prose, and Plays* (Library of America, New York, 1995), 336. In Rodgers and Hammerstein's *Oklahoma*, the chorus sings a celebratory version of the theme of Frost's poem: "We know we belong to the land / And the land we belong to is grand." The United States government opened Oklahoma, the last of the territories labeled Indian Territory, to white settlement in 1907. The people of the musical *Oklahoma* are beneficiaries of the belief, from the colonial period on, that in regard to real estate owned by Indian tribes, white Christian expropriation has no moral implications. In his personal life, Jefferson was not an exponent or practitioner of expropriation. As a political leader, his synonym for expropriation was assimilation. In his personal life, he was owned by the land he inherited, "possessed" in Frost's sense. Regarding Indian land, see Daniel Immerwahr, *How to Hide an Empire: A History of the Greater United States* (New York: Farrar, Straus & Giroux, 2019).

3   Without land ownership: See T. H. Breen, *Tobacco Culture: The Mentality of the Great Tidewater Planters on the Eve of Revolution* (Princeton, NJ: Princeton University Press, 1985); Robert G. Kennedy, *Mr. Jefferson's Lost Cause: Land, Farmers, Slavery, and the Louisiana Purchase* (New York: Oxford University Press, 2003); Christopher Michael Curtis, *Jefferson's Freeholders and the Politics of Ownership in the Old Dominion* (New York: Cambridge University Press, 2012); and Simon Winchester, *Land: How the Hunger for Ownership Shaped the Modern World* (New York: Harper, 2021). There is an extensive literature on TJ and slavery, starting with TJ's own words in *Notes on the State of Virginia* (see chapter 10), in his discussions of slaves, slavery, manumission, colonization, and emancipation in his letters, and in prominent books in the Jefferson bibliography, especially overviews and biographies.

4   "on which I was born and live": TJA, 3–4.

5   the family home, Shadwell: See Susan Kern, *The Jeffersons at Shadwell* (New Haven, CT: Yale University Press, 2010).

6   "To state the differences between": TJ/William Wirt, 8/5/1815.

7   "had lost her speech": TJ/JP, 12/25/1762.

8   "This very day": TJ/JP, 12/25/1762.

8   "3d or 4th settler": TJA, 3.

8   "were somewhat greater": TJ/JP, 12/25/1762.

9   "When I went to bed": TJ/JP, 12/25/1762.

10   had fallen in love with: TJ/JP, 12/25/1762.

12   "the mountain": TJ/John Harvie, 1/14/1760.

12 "I was at Colo. Peter Randolph's": TJ/John Harvie, 1/14/1760.

12 "when I recollect": TJ/TJR, 11/24/1808.

13 earliest memory: H. S. Randall, *Life of Thomas Jefferson* (New York: Derby and Jackson, 1958), 11, 111. See "Tuckahoe" in The Jefferson Monticello, https://Monticello.org, in *Thomas Jefferson Encyclopedia.*

13 "Whatever misfortunes may attend": TJ/JP, 12/25/1762.

16 "will not accept of my service": TJ/JP, 7/15/1763.

17 "Perfect happiness I believe": TJ/JP, 7/15/1763.

18 "In the most melancholy fit": TJ/JP, 10/7/1763.

20 "I began a regular course": TJ/TJR, 12/7/1808.

23 "faithful and beloved Mentor": TJ/William Duval, 6/14/1806.

23 "my most affectionate friend": TJA, 4–5; TJ, *Notes for the biography of George Wythe,* 8/30/1820.

23 "Under temptations and difficulties": TJ/John Saunderson, 8/31/1820.

24 "I am certain that this mode": TJ/TJR, 11/24/1808.

24 to become a lawyer: See Frank L. Dewey, *Thomas Jefferson, Lawyer* (Charlottesville: University Press of Virginia, 1986), 65–70; Edward Dumbaul, *Thomas Jefferson and the Law* (Norman: University of Oklahoma Press, 1978); and "Jefferson, Thomas, and the Practice of Law," Encyclopedia Virginia, https://encyclopediavirginia.org.

CHAPTER TWO: BUILDING HOUSES

35 "as I am convinced": George Wythe/TJ, 3/9/1770.

36 "we find it can no longer": TJ and others, *Virginia Gazette,* 3/20/1773.

36 "his very affectionate speech": TJ, 5/8/1769. That the statement is "purely ceremonial in nature" (Boyd, *TJP* 1.26) is debatable. Those who engage in such ceremonies usually do so because the ceremony represents community values. Does TJ believe that "*the Interests of Great-Britain . . . shall ever be discussed on this ruling Principle, THAT HER INTERESTS, AND OURS, ARE INSEPARABLY THE SAME?*" Or has the 1765 Stamp Act controversy given him pause, reservation, or even opposition to the rule of London? There seems to be no evidence to that effect. Why was he selected to write this resolution? Weren't there more senior members of the House who might have been asked? Was it a routine task, easily assigned to a new member, something a senior person would be happy not to be assigned? The language of the 1766 and the 1768 resolutions of thanks to the governor differs considerably from the language of the 1769 resolution. See TJ/William Wirt, 8/5/1815; and Henry Read McIlwaine and John Pendleton Kennedy, *Journals of the House of Burgesses of Virginia: 1727/1734, 1736/1740* (Virginia State Library, 1905).

40 that it and other colonies could be provoked: There were additional issues in Virginia. The elite planters were finding it difficult to pay their debts to British merchants in a timely way or at all, partly because of the seasonal pattern

inherent in an agricultural economy. The gap between the delivery of products from Great Britain and the shipment of harvests to the European markets kept American balances usually in the red. British mercantile regulation required that foreign markets be accessed only through British ports. That made cash flow even more sluggish. Planters like Jefferson believed themselves to be rich. Extravagance was warranted, an expression of status and power. But credit, not tobacco, was king. And many planters spent beyond their means, avatars of extravagance. Sometimes they were victims of blight and bad weather. Bankruptcy lurked; it sometimes pounced. Even for the most competent, like Peter Jefferson, cash was in short supply. Debt was ever present. For some, it created high anxiety. The problem was the cyclic nature of eighteenth-century farming, but it was also the mercantile system, the coercive trading regulations that controlled commerce between Great Britain and its agricultural colonies. See Robert E. Sloan, *Principle and Interest: Thomas Jefferson and the Problem of Debt* (Charlottesville: University of Virginia Press, 1995); and Robert E. Wright, *One Nation Under Debt: Hamilton, Jefferson, and the History of What We Owe* (New York: McGraw Hill, 2008).

42 "If in the Course": Resolutions for an Answer to Governor Botetourt's Speech, 5/8/1769.

44 "Being deeply affected": TJ signatory, *Virginia Nonimportation Resolutions*, 5/17/1769.

47 "I passed through": TJ/JP, 5/25/1766.

47 "I was surprised": TJ/JP, 5/25/1766.

48 "after a long, but agreeable trip": TJ/Francis Willis, 7/23/1766.

48 his little mountain: See Jack McLaughlin, *Jefferson and Monticello: The Biography of a Builder* (New York: Holt, 1988); and Roger G. Kennedy, *Mr. Jefferson's Lost Cause: Land, Farmers, Slavery, and the Louisiana Purchase* (New York: Oxford University Press, 2003).

50 "a Mulatto slave called Sandy": TJ, 9/7/1769, Advertisement for a Runaway Slave, *Virginia Gazette*.

51 "by which I am burned": TJ/JP, 2/21/1770.

52 "I have often thought": TJ/Charles W. Peale, 8/20/1811.

53 "To your committee therefore": TJ/Archibald Cary and Benjamin Harrison, 12/9/1774.

54 "Indeed I should be much happier": TJ/JP, 2/21/1770.

54 "the happiest man": TJ/JP, 2/21/1770.

56 "the compass from Double G.": TJ/Thomas Adams, 6/1/1771.

56 "Come then and bring our dear Tibby": TJ/Robert Skipwith, 8/3/1771.

57 expecting much from the marriage: Bond for Marriage License, 23 December 1771. "Know all men by these presents that we Thomas Jefferson and Francis Eppes are held and firmly bound to our sovereign lord the king his heirs and successors in the sum of fifty pounds current money of Virginia, to the payment of which, well and truly to be made we bind ourselves jointly and severally, our joint and several heirs executors and administrators in witness whereof we have hereto

set our hands and seals this twenty third day of December in the year of our lord one thousand seven hundred and seventy one. The condition of the above obligation is such that if there be no lawful cause to obstruct a marriage intended to be had and solemnized between the above bound Thomas Jefferson and Martha Skelton of the county of Charles city, Widow [spinster], for which a license is desired, then this obligation is to be null and void; otherwise to remain in full force."

57 "My sister Skelton": Robert Skipwith/TJ, 9/20/1771.

57 "serves me for parlor": TJ/JO, 2/20/1771.

61 "We do not mean by this": Alexander McCaul/TJ, 8/26/1770.

61 "I Spent two Months": Alexander McCaul/TJ, 7/8/1772.

63 "I am not ashamed": TJ/Charles Macpherson, 2/25/1773.

63 "the greatest Poet": TJ/Charles Macpherson, 2/25/1773. See Thomas Curley, *Samuel Johnson, the Ossian Fraud, and the Celtic Revival in Great Britain and Ireland* (New York: Cambridge University Press, 2009).

63 "I should be glad to accommodate": James Macpherson/Charles Macpherson, 8/7/1773.

65 One of Jefferson's friends: See https://encyclopediavirginia.org/entries/ogilvie-james-1773-1820.

66 "We took proper measures": TJ/JO, 2/20/1771. See TJ/Thomas Adams, 7/1/1770; TJ/Peyton Randolph, 7/23/1770; TJ/Thomas Adams, 2/20/1771; JO/TJ, 4/26/1771; and JO/TJ, 7/19/1771.

67 "My life has been": JO/TJ, 4/26/1771.

68 "I might to great advantage": JO/TJ, 7/19/1771; and Agreement with JR, October [i.e., April?] 11, 1771.

71 "no Reason why": JR/TJ, 8/31/1775.

73 "my best wishes": TJ/JR, 8/25/1775.

74 "restoration of our just rights": TJ/JR, 8/25/1775.

75 "Believe me dear sir": TJ/JR, 11/29/1775.

75 "the melancholy intelligence": TJ/JR, 11/29/1775.

76 "It is an immense misfortune": TJ/JR, 11/29/1775. See Todd Cohen, "George III's Battle to Save an Empire," https://www.colonialwilliamsburg.org/trend-tradition-magazine/autumn-2018/george-iiis-battle-to-save-an-empire; and James P. Ambuske, "Mourning Thomas Jefferson's Estranged Father," Georgian Papers Programme. "The Georgian Papers Programme is an ambitious project to transform access to the extensive collection of Georgian papers held in the Royal Archives and Royal Library at Windsor Castle." See also Andrew Roberts, *The Last King of America: The Misunderstood Reign of George III* (New York: Viking, 2021).

CHAPTER THREE: OUR GREAT GRIEVANCES

79 "the inhabitants of this city": Peyton Randolph and Others to Members of the Late House of Burgesses, Williamsburg, 5/31/1774.

79   "The most effectual Assistance": Randolph and Others . . . , 5/31/1774.

81   Smuggling was an age-old practice: See Joshua M. Smith, *Borderland Smuggling: Patriots, Loyalists, and Illicit Trade in the Northeast, 1783–1820* (Gainesville: University Press of Florida, 2019).

83   "divine Interposition": Resolution of the House of Burgesses Designating a Day of Fasting and Prayer, 5/27/1774.

83   "A tender regard": Association of Members of the Late House of Burgesses, 5/27/1774; and Proceedings of a Meeting of Representatives in Williamsburg, 5/30/1774.

84   "With the help therefore": TJA, 8.

85   "the Freeholders of Albemarle County": At a meeting of the freeholders of the county of Albemarle, 7/26/1774.

86   "common rights of mankind": At a meeting of the freeholders of the county of Albemarle, 7/26/1774.

88   "My creed had been formed": TJ, "Memorandum on Instructions to Virginia Delegates to Congress in 1774," 1820 (?), "Historical and Bibliographical Notes on *A Summary View of the Rights of British America*," TJP 1.671.

88   "Before I left home": TJ, "Memorandum on Instructions . . . ," 671.

90   "Tamer Sentiments": TJ, "Memorandum on Instructions . . . ," 670.

90   "hope that this their joint address": TJ, Draft of Instructions to the Virginia Delegates in the Continental Congress [*A Summary View of the Rights of British America*], 7/1774.

91   "For themselves they fought": TJ, Draft of Instructions . . . [*A Summary View . . .*], 7/1774. The claim that the British colonies in America were "conquered" by individuals exclusively acting as private citizens rather than as British citizens and consequently entitled to govern themselves independent of British legal, constitutional, and Parliamentary authority is an ahistorical claim, an "alternative fact." It is belied by innumerable expressions and acts of fealty during the colonial period. Jefferson's father had accepted and affirmed the legitimacy of every royal governor. Also, it is hard to maintain one's rational perspective and still claim that in the eighteenth century the king was not "in Parliament" and the Parliament not in the king, that they were not unitary entities; that one could proclaim loyalty to the king and reject the authority of Parliament. Jefferson's predecessors had taken possession of the land in the name of the mother country, adding possessions to what they already possessed, a territorial expansion of their self-identity as British nationals.

91   "authority over us": TJ, Draft of Instructions . . . [*A Summary View . . .*], 7/1774.

93   "no more than the chief": TJ, Draft of Instructions . . . [*A Summary View . . .*], 7/1774.

96   "prayer of all": TJ, Draft of Instructions . . . [*A Summary View . . .*], 7/1774.

96   prolific slave trader: Boyd, TJP 1, 10/20/1772. "An advertisement in the *Va. Gaz* . . . for 8 Oct. 1772 (repeated 15 and 22 Oct.) reads as follows: 'Just arrived from *Africa*, the Ship *Prince of Wales*, *James Bivins* Commander, with

about four Hundred five healthy *Slaves*; the Sale of which will begin at *Bermuda Hundred* on *Thursday* the 8th of *October*, and continue until all are sold. *John Wayles. Richard Randolph.*'"

98 "loved him most": TJ/William Fleming, 5/19/1773.

98 "spotless integrity": TJ/Dabney Carr, 1/19/1816.

98 unintentional laudatory self-portrait: TJ/Dabney Carr, 1/19/1816.

100 "The death of my mother": TJ/William Randolph, 6/1776.

101 "I heartily join": TJ/William Randolph, 6/1776.

102 "the unhappy news": TJ/WS1, 5/7/1775.

103 "entertained high hope": TJ/WS1, 5/7/1775.

103 "the dignity of parliament": TJ/WS1, 5/7/1775.

104 "implore the divine": Resolution of the House of Burgesses Designating a Day of Fasting and Prayer, 5/24/1774.

104 "the people met": TJA, 9.

CHAPTER FOUR: WE HOLD THESE TRUTHS

106 "unhappy disputes. . . .": Virginia Resolutions on Lord North's Conciliatory Proposal, 6/10/1775.

107 "our Faith and true Allegiance": Instructions for the Deputies Appointed to Meet in General Congress on the Part of This Colony, 8/1–8/6/1774.

107 inherited from the Wayles estate: Boyd, 7/15/1773. "Notice of Sale of Wayles Properties . . . Two Thousand five Hundred and twenty Acres of land in *Cumberland*, commonly known by the Name of Saint James; one Thousand four Hundred and twenty Acres in the Counties of *Goochland* and *Cumberland*, on both Sides of *James* River, opposite to *Elk* Island; and one Thousand four Hundred and eighty Acres on *Herring* Creek, in *Charles City* County. The above Tracts of Land were of the Estate of the late *John Wayles*, deceased, devised to the Subscribers, and are now offered for Sale. Persons disposed to purchase may be informed of the Terms, on Application to any one of the Subscribers; and the Times of Payment will be made easy, on giving Bond and Security to Thomas Jefferson. Francis Eppes. Henry Skipwith."

109 "We are sufficiently united": Report of Committee to Prepare a Plan for a Militia, 3/25/1775.

110 "The New Englanders": TJ/FE, 7/4/1775.

112 "our Friends and Fellow-Subjects": Declaration for Causes and Necessities of Taking Up Arms, 6/26/–7/6/1775.

113 "But when the world reflects": TJ, Resolutions of Congress on Lord North's Conciliatory Proposal, 7/25/1775; the resolutions as adopted by Congress, 7/31/1775.

115 "My collection of classics": TJ/JR, 8/25/1775.

115 "returning wisdom": TJ/JR, 8/25/1775.

119 "I arrived here": TJ/Thomas Nelson, 5/6/1776.

120 "I am here": TJ/Thomas Nelson, 5/6/1776.

121 a dramatically articulate speaker: Resolution of Independence Moved by R. H. Lee for the Virginia Delegation, 6/7/1776.

121 a resolution declaring complete independence: There is a library of literature on the origins of the various proposals for independence, some of them in similar language, by the legislatures of the individual colonies, in pamphlet literature, and in the resolutions and voices in the Continental Congress, preceding and then including the Declaration of Independence, the most influential of which is Pauline Maier, *American Scripture: Making the Declaration of Independence* (New York: Random House, 1997).

124 "That all men": George Mason, The Virginia Declaration of Rights, America's Founding Documents, https://www.archives.gov/founding-docs/virginia-declaration-of-rights.

124 "acquiring and possessing property": Mason, Virginia Declaration of Rights.

125 "The great questions": TJ/Thomas Nelson, 5/16/1776.

126 "When in the Course of human events": See Julian R. Boyd and Gerard W. Gawalt, *The Declaration of Independence: The Evolution of the Text* (Washington, DC: Library of Congress, 1999).

126 a matter of dispute: See Mark Somos, *States of Nature: The Origins of Independence, 1761–1775* (New York: Oxford University Press, 2019).

127 "no writer has exceeded": TJ/FE, 1/19/1821.

128 "shall be appropriated": First Draft by Jefferson for the Virginia Constitution, before 6/13/1776.

134 "painful situation to be": TJ/William Fleming, 7/1/1776.

134 "I am sorry the situation of my domestic affairs": TJ/EP, 6/30/1776.

CHAPTER FIVE: AN ANGEL IN THE WHIRLWIND

137 Boswell and Lee had become friends: James Boswell, *Life of Samuel Johnson* (London, 1791), 2.177–84.

139 "reserved by heaven": *Committee of the Boston Sons of Liberty to John Wilkes*, 6/6/1768.

139 "race of convicts": James Boswell, *Life of Samuel Johnson* (London, 1791), 2.312.

139 "To suppose, that Americans": Samuel Johnson, *The Patriot* (London, 1774).

140 "We have now, for more than": Samuel Johnson, *Thoughts on the Late Transactions Respecting Falkland's Islands* (London, 1771).

142 "The suspense under which": TJ/FE, 11/7/1775.

142 "I have set apart": TJ/JP, 10/31/1775.

142 "the indisposition of Mrs. Jefferson": EP/TJ, 8/10/1776.

142 "I am highly pleased": JP/TJ, 7/20/1776.

143 "I hope you'll get cured": EP/TJ, 8/10/1776.

144 "In my judgment, the most eminent services": Richard Henry Lee/TJ, 9/27/1776.

144 "No cares for my own person": TJ/John Hancock, 10/11/1776.

145 "I wish my domestic situation": TJ/BF, 8/13/1777.

145 "heard with much regret": Richard Henry Lee/TJ, 11/3/1776.

146 "also wanting much": EP/TJ, 7/22/1776.

148 "decisions of the people": TJ/EP, 8/26/1776.

150 "to illuminate, as far as practicable": A Bill for the More General Diffusion of Knowledge, 6/18/1779.

153 "Well aware that the opinions": A Bill for Protection of Religious Liberty, 6/18/1779; Boyd 3.545. The bill was not made law until January 1786.

154 "We the General Assembly": A Bill for Protection of Religious Liberty, 6/18/1779.

156 "given me much pain": TJ/JP, 6/3/1779.

156 "Should you resign": JP/TJ, 9/22/1780.

157 "your Love of Study": JP/TJ, 12/9/1780.

158 "many letters of absolute necessity": TJ/Richard Henry Lee, 6/17/1779.

160 "I must take the liberty": JR/TJ, 10/25/1779.

161 "there will be no necessity": GW/TJ, 11/23/1779.

162 "Difference in opinion": JR/TJ, 10/25/1779.

163 "Nothing which I forget": JR/TJ, 10/25/1779.

163 "the fixed Purpose": JR/TJ, 10/25/1779.

166 "when we came to look": TJ to the speaker of the House of Delegates, 3/6/1781. Boyd: "The Remonstrance, containing exaggeration and inaccuracies, was not adopted, partially, no doubt, because the approach of Lafayette's army made some of its statements obsolete. TJ sent an urgent request to the Assembly for a revision of the militia laws when that body reconvened in May."

169 "daughter Lucy Elizabeth": TJ/David Jameson, 4/16/1781. "Mrs. Jefferson in a situation in which I would not wish to leave her." Boyd: "TJ's Account Book under date of 15 Apr: 'our daughter Lucy Elizabeth died about 10. o'clock A.M. this day.' Lucy Elizabeth was four and a half months of age."

171 "time to remove": TJ/William Gordon, 7/16/1788.

173 "at present busily employed": TJ/Charles Francois D'Anmours, 11/30/1780.

173 "in a condition": TJ/François Barbe-Marbois, 3/4/1781.

CHAPTER SIX: UNMEASURABLE LOSS

175 "in an application": TJ/FE, 2/15/1783.

175 "He has proposed to me": TJ/FE, 2/15/1783.

176 "I am sorry to hear": TJ/JP, 8/5/1776.

177 "The end proposed": TJ/GRC, 1/1/1780.

177 "We have reason to believe": TJ/GRC, 12/25/1780.

179 "only great Inducements": William Christian/TJ, 4/10/1781.

180 "We, like you, are Americans": TJ, Speech to JBD, c.1/6/1781.

182 "You complain, brother": TJ, Speech to JBD, c.1/6/1781.

187 "a very beautiful river": Thomas Jefferson, *Notes on the State of Virginia*, ed. William Paden (New York: Norton, 1954). The quotations from *Notes* are not referenced to the page in the Paden edition but can readily be located by the internal references to the sections in which the quotations appear. *Notes* is a seminal source for scholarly discussion of numbers of concerns of Jefferson and of Jefferson scholars, especially slavery and race.

200 If it "were possible for me": BF/TJ, 7/15/1782; TJ/Edmund Randolph, 9/16/1781.

200 "in great Hopes": BF/TJ, 7/15/1782.

202 "Mrs. Jefferson has added": TJ/JM, 5/20/1782.

202 "the report of each succeeding day": JM/TJ, 6/28/1782.

202 "and every time": Lines Copied from *Tristram Shandy* by Martha and Thomas Jefferson, *TJP* 6.196.

203 "even in the house of Hades": Epitaph for Martha Wayles Jefferson [after 9/6/1782], Homer, *Iliad*, book 22, lines 389–90, given here in the translation by Augustus Taber Murray (Cambridge, MA: Harvard University Press, 1924).

203 "Mrs. Jefferson has at last": Edmund Randolph/JM, 9/30/1782; Boyd, *TJP* 6.1782.

204 "The girls being unable": TJ/Elizabeth Wayles Eppes, 10/3/1782.

CHAPTER SEVEN: PERPETUAL GRATITUDE

209 "You should not decline": JM1/TJ, 5/11/1782.

210 "a little emerging": TJ/François-Jean de Chastellux, 11/26/1782.

211 "little motherless daughter": TJ/JJ, 1/3/1783.

211 "The ice has since": TJ/JM, 2/7/1783.

212 "free and independent states . . . to take effect": Boyd, 2/14/1783; and George III/Parliament, 12/1792.

212 "with fear and trembling": TJ/FE, 3/4/1783.

214 "The appointment with which": TJ/Isaac Zane, 6/17/1783.

215 "Nine states appeared": TJ/WS, 3/1/1784.

216 "The winter here": TJ/Isaac Zane, 3/17/1784.

216 "All the world is becoming commercial": TJ/GW, 3/5/1784.

217 "crippled state of Congress. . . .": TJ/GW, 3/5/1784.

218 "the restitution of all estates": Report on the Definitive Treaty of Peace and the Letter from the American Commissioners, 2/16/1783.

219 "subject to the government": See *TJP* 6.571–616 for the text and editorial notes.

220 a lesson in the politics of slavery and nation building: See Joseph Ellis, *The Cause: The American Revolution and Its Discontents, 1773–1783* (New York: Liveright, 2021).

221 "resigning my commission": GW, Farewell Address to the Army, 11/2/1783; and Washington's Address to Congress Resigning his Commission, 12/23/1783.

221 "Having now finished": Washington's Address to Congress Resigning his Commission, 12/23/1783.

221 "I send you the sketch which I have been obliged": TJ/Elbridge Gerry and James McHenry, 12/21/1783.

222 "The spectators all wept": Boyd, *TJP* 6.402–8.

222 "The U.S. in congress": TJ, Report of a Committee on the Response by the President of Congress, 12/22/1783.

224 "important literary compositions": Boyd, *TJP* 6.405.

224 "the shining traces of his pen": JM/Samuel Smith, 11/4/1826.

224 "The moderation and virtue": TJ/GW, 4/16/1784.

225 "seems to prevail": TJ/WS, 4/30/1784.

225 "Your Services might": John Tyler/TJ, 5/20/1784.

226 "greatest illusions": WS/John Hartwell Cocke, 8/12/1826, Library of Congress, WS Papers, 1778–1853.

226 "magnanimous king and nation": Report of a Committee on the Response by the President of Congress.

227 "The very important Share": GW/TJ, 11/30/1781.

227 "will be able to give you": TJ/BJ, JA, JJ, 10/5/1781.

229 "In these circumstances": TJ/Benjamin Harrison, 3/18/1784.

230 "the position of the vessel": TJ/David Humphreys, 7/4/1784.

231 "If we are to chuse": TJ, Abstracts of Gouverneur Morris' Letters on Commerce, 3/1784.

231 "I understand the French so imperfectly": TJ/William Temple Franklin, 8/18/1784.

232 "There shall be a firm": See *TJP* 7.261–71, Boyd: From Charles Thomson, with Instructions and Commissions, 16 May 1784, Enclosure I: Commission for Negotiating Treaties of Amity and Commerce, 16 May 1784, Enclosure II: Instructions for Negotiating Treaties of Amity and Commerce By The United States in Congress Assembled, 29 October 1783, Enclosure III: Instructions to the Commissioners for Negotiating Treaties of Amity and Commerce, 7 May 1784; and *TJP* 7.471–79, I. Summary Notes of Provisions in Treaties with France, the Netherlands, and Sweden, 6 February 1778, II. Classification of

Treaty Provisions, 1783, III. Notes for Consideration of the Commissioners, 7 May 1784, Draft of a Model Treaty, 1784.

234 "Your kindness and attention": JM1/TJ, 5/6/1782.

236 "I have at length procured": TJ/Abigail Adams, 9/4/1785.

237 "lately returned from": TJ, before 11/20/1784, TJ's Reply to the Representations of Affairs in America by British Newspapers.

238 "give of the affairs of France": TJ, before 11/20/1784, TJ's Reply.

239 "was as erroneous": WS/William Nelson, 1/25/1786; Boyd; *TJP* 10.3. See *TJP* 10.3–64, The Article on the United States in the *Encyclopédie Méthodique*; and Boyd, "The Article on the United States in the Encyclopédie Méthodique. I. Answers to DéMeunier's First Queries, 24 January 1786. II. Additional Queries, with Jefferson's Answers, [ca. January–February 1786]. III. From Jean Nicolas DéMeunier, [February? 1786]. IV. Jefferson's Observations on DéMeunier's Manuscript, 22 June 1786. V. To Jean Nicolas Démeunier, [26 June 1786]. VI. From Jean Nicolas DeMeunier, [26 June 1786]."

240 "What a stupendous": TJ/Jean Nicholas Démeunier, 6/26/1786.

241 "I could not get my notes printed": TJ/JM, 5/25/1784.

241 "you shall assuredly have one": TJ/Charles Thomason, 5/21/1784.

242 "at the time of writing": TJ/C.W.F. Dumas, 2/2/1786.

242 "I admire your generous indignation": David Ramsay/TJ, 5/3/1786.

243 "I pity this people": JA/TJ, 5/22/1785.

244 "with singular pleasure": RP/TJ, 3/21/1785; 7/2/1785.

245 "nothing can excuse": RP/TJ, 7/2/1785.

246 "Northward of the Chesapeake": TJ/RP, 8/7/1785.

247 "A daily habit": TJ/Chastellux, 10/1786.

248 essay in the form of a letter: TJ, "Thoughts on English Prosody," Library of America, 593–622.

CHAPTER EIGHT: GETTING INTO A SCRAPE

249 "How the right hand": TJ/WSS, 10/22/1786.

250 Maria Luisa Caterina Cecilia Hadfield: See Carol Burnell, *Divided Affections: The Extraordinary Life of Maria Cosway: Celebrity Artist and Thomas Jefferson's Impossible Love* (Lausanne, Switzerland: Column House, 1977); and Gerald Barnett, *Richard and Maria Cosway: A Biography* (Tiverton, Devon, UK: Lutterworth Press, 1995).

252 "passed the night": TJ/MC, 10/5/1786.

253 "very sorry indeed": MC/TJ, 10/5/1786.

253 "Having performed the last": TJ/MC, 10/12/1786, "Dialogue Between the Heart and the Head."

253 "I turned on my heel": All "Head and Heart" quotations are from TJ/MC, 10/12/1786.

254 "The left hand is learning": TJ/JT, 10/13/1786.

267 "I found that your name": TJ/MC, 10/13/1786.

268 "as long as the bible": TJ/MC, 10/12/1786.

268 "kind things": MC/TJ, 10/30/1786.

270 "sends you a thousand": MC/TJ, 10/30/1786.

271 "I wish she could": TJ/MC, 11/19/1786.

271 "determined not to suppose": TJ/MC, 12/24/1786.

271 "heart has been duped": TJ/MC, 11/29/1786.

271 "I begin, my dear Madam": TJ/MC, 11/19/1786.

272 "I should trouble you": TJ/MC, 11/29/1786.

274 "Of all the torments": MC/TJ, 2/15/1787.

275 "I attempt, I exercise": MC/TJ, 2/15/1787.

276 "She is a child": AA/TJ, 7/6/1787.

277 "Tell Mrs. Cosway": TJ/JT, 2/23/1787.

277 "You conclude, madam": TJ/MC, 7/1/1787.

278 "a mountain cloven": TJ/MC, 7/1/1787.

278 "Do you deserve": MC /TJ, 7/9/1787.

279 "You spoiled me": MC/TJ, 7/9/1787.

CHAPTER NINE: THE ELOQUENCE OF DEBT

280 "I set out on my journey": TJ/Madame de Tessé, 2/28/1787.

281 "gazing whole hours": TJ/Madame de Tessé, 3/20/1787.

281 "a charming place": TJ/WS, 4/7/1787.

282 "I presume that you think": TJ/WS, 4/7/1787.

282 "seek therefore for the good things": TJ/Madame de Tott, 4/5/1787.

283 "the sunshine of life": Laurence Sterne, *Tristram Shandy*, 1.22.

283 "anger only serves to torment": TJ/MJR, 4/7/1787.

285 "a continued feast": TJ/Chastellux, 4/4/1787.

285 "The olive tree": TJ, *Notes of a Tour into the Southern Parts of France, &c: Memorandums Taken on a Journey from Paris into the Southern Parts of France and Northern of Italy, in the Year 1787*, 6/10/1787–5/2/1788. See TJ/William Drayton, 7/30/1787.

287 "The people here": TJ/WS, 3/15/1787.

287 "shoemakers, tailors": *Notes of a Tour into the Southern Parts of France*, 6/10/1787–5/2/1788.

288 "the soil is rich mulatto loam": *Notes of a Tour into the Southern Parts of France*, 6/10/1787–5/2/1788.

289 "do only light work": *Notes of a Tour into the Southern Parts of France*, 6/10/1787–5/2/1788.

289 "Now and then a few gleamings": TJ/WS, 3/15/1787.

289 "My hand recovering": TJ/Vergennes, 2/11/1787.

289 "I have great anxieties": TJ/JM, 1/30/1787.

290 "very useless voyage": TJ/JA, 7/1/1787.

290 "dislocated wrist, badly set": TJ/Martha Jefferson Carr, 7/25/1787; and TJ/James Currie, 8/4/1787.

290 "A poet is as much the creature of climate": TJ/WS, 5/21/1787.

290 "every moment of every day": TJ/Chastellux, 4/4/1787.

290 "The accident of a dislocated wrist": TJ/GG, 8/12/1787.

290 "in constant hope": TJ/John Baptiste Le Roy, 11/13/1786.

291 "to see what I have never seen before": TJ/Lafayette, 4/11/1787.

291 "The soil of Champagne and Burgundy": TJ/Lafayette, 4/11/1787.

293 "great mass of People": TJ/Charles Bellini, 9/30/1785.

294 "very much inferior": TJ/Charles Bellini, 9/30/1785.

295 to write private letters: TJ/JJ, 8/14/1785; 8/30/1785.

298 "Since the Peace": Brailsford & Morris/TJ, 10/31/1787.

300 "wiser, but less happy": TJ/PC, 8/10/1787.

301 "Be good, be learned": TJ/PC, 8/10/1787.

302 "These observations are founded in experience": TJ/PC, 8/10/1787.

302 "a sense of right and wrong": TJ/PC, 8/10/1787.

304 "My proposition," TJ/Thomas Mann Randolph Sr., 8/11/1787.

305 "I must beg your pardon": TJ/Thomas Mann Randolph Sr., 8/11/1787.

306 "The torment of mind": TJ/NL, 7/29/1787.

306 "I have sold too much . . . already": TJ/NL, 7/29/1787; TJ/FE, 7/30/1787.

307 "I feel all the weight": TJ/NL, 7/29/1787.

307 "I am governed solely": TJ/NL, 7/29/1787.

308 "I look forward to it": TJ/AD, 7/28/1787.

308 "When this arrangement": TJ/FE, 7/30/1787.

309 "I therefore accede": TJ/NL, 7/11/1788.

309 "supplies a good table": TJ/James Currie, 8/4/1787.

310 "I look back to the time": TJ/Henry Skipwith, 7/28/1787.

312 "the confederation of the States": TJ, "Anecdotes of Benjamin Franklin," c. 12/4/1818; and TJA, 24–31.

313 "Happy for us": TJ/C.W.F. Dumas, 9/10/1787.

313 "will neither effectually answer": JM/TJ, 9/6/1787.

314 "negative on the laws of the States": JM/TJ, 10/24/1787.

315 "How do you like our new constitution?": TJ/JA, 11/13/1787.

315 "less than a miracle": Edward Carrington/TJ, 10/23/1787.

315 "what signify a few lives": TJ/WSS, 11/13/1787.

316 "from time to time with the blood of patriots": TJ/WSS, 11/13/1787.

317 "You will perceive": TJ/William Carmichael, 12/15/1787.

317 "You are afraid of the one": JA/TJ, 12/6/1787.

318 "I am not a friend": TJ/JM, 12/20/1787.

319 "it will be only a change": TJ/JA, 2/20/1788.

319 "with an affection that can never die": JA/TJ, 1/2/1789.

CHAPTER TEN: HIS MASTERLY PEN

320 Count of Vergennes: TJ/JM, 1/30/1787.

321 "I afterwards saw proofs": TJ/JM, 1/30/1787.

321 "a most valuable auxiliary": TJ/JM, 1/30/1787.

324 "an unjust proportion": TJ, Jefferson's Hints to Americans Travelling in Europe, 6/1788.

324 "The king loves business": TJ/JM, 6/20/1787.

325 "happy that he is an honest unambitious man": TJ/JJ, 5/9/1789.

325 *the king is a good man*: TJA, 80.

325 "Our good ladies": TJ/Ann Willing Bingham, 5/11/1788.

326 "not a single doubt": TJ/John Mason, 7/16/1789.

326 "honest and wishes the good": TJ/JJ, 6/17/1789; and TJA, 80–92.

328 "he would have willingly acquiesced": TJA, 92–93.

331 "I may say with truth": TJ/WS, 4/2/1785.

331 "You lost much": TJ/WS, 4/2/1785.

332 "probably a civil war": TJ/JJ, 6/17/1789.

334 "love us more": TJ/JM, 1/30/1787.

335 "This little attendrissement": TJ/JM, 10/28/1785.

335 "The property of this country": See Christopher Michael Curtis, *Jefferson's Freeholders and the Politics of Ownership in the Old Dominion* (New York: Cambridge University Press, 2012).

335 "It is too soon yet": TJ/JM, 6/19/1785.

336 "an equal division": TJ/JM, 10/28/1785.

337 "the earth is given": See "The Earth Belongs in Usufruct to the Living," 9/1–9/9/1789.

337 "The small landholders": TJ/JM, 6/19/1785.

338 "no doubt that the misery": JM/TJ, 6/19/1786.

338 "from a more equal partition": JM/TJ, 6/19/1786.

339 "But I forget that": JM/TJ, 6/19/1786.

339 "Within an hour": TJ/JT, 9/9/1789.

340 "That one generation": TJ/JM, 9/6/1789.

340 "whether one generation": TJ/JM, 9/6/1789.

341 "On similar ground": TJ/JM, 9/6/1789.

343 "the earth belongs": TJ/JM, 9/6/1789.

344 "a contract in perpetuity": JM/TJ, 2/4/1790.

345 "The evils suffered": JM/TJ, 2/4/1790.

347 "I have been to see": TP/TJ, 6/17/1789.

347 "being alone and wanting amusement": TP/TJ, n.d. 3/1788.

348 "a small ratifying convention": TP/TJ, n.d. 3/1788.

348 "to be spectator only": TJ/Madame de Brehan, 5/9/1788.

349 "and explained to him": TJA, 96.

349 "state of things": TJA, 95.

350 "mobs of 10; 20; 30,000 people": TJ/JA, 8/30/1787.

350 "I think that in the course": TJ/JA, 8/30/1787.

350 "A spirit of distrust": TJ/Ralph Izard, 8/1/1787.

351 "There is no remedy": TJ/St. John de Crevecoeur, 8/9/1788.

351 "within two or three years": TJ/JM1, 8/9/1788.

352 "the public mind seems": TJ/Fulwar Skipwith, 3/1/1789.

353 "to be going on well": TJ/William Carmichael, 3/4/1789.

354 "to see this great meeting": TJ/Eleonore François Elie, Comte de Moustier, 3/13/1789.

354 "a very considerable riot": TJ/William Carmichael, 5/8/1789.

354 "They were the most abandoned banditti": TJ/JJ, 5/9/1789.

354 "revolution of this country": TJ/JJ, 5/9/1789.

354 "The three orders": TJ/JA, 5/10/1789.

355 "We shall know": TJ/JM, 6/18/1789.

356 "the king assailed by lies": TJ/JJ, 6/24/1789.

356 "This is the first time": TJ/JJ, 6/24/1789. Boyd: "Mazzei related that he and TJ were together at the Church of St. Louis and that, as TJ stood on the threshold, he remarked: 'This is the first time that the Churches have been made some good use of.'" (Philip Mazzei, Mémoire 2.24, cited by Garlick, Philip Mazzei [Baltimore: The Johns Hopkins University Press, 1933], 126).

356 "the Nobility were in triumph": TJ/JJ, 6/24/1789.

357 "nothing remarkable past": TJ/JJ, 6/24/1789.

358 "entered into debate": TJ/JJ, 6/29/1789.

359 "all is settled . . .": TJ/JT, 6/29/1789.

359 "man who sustained": A Fourth of July Tribute to Jefferson, 7/4/1789.

360 "a countryman and friend": TJ/MC, 7/25/1789.

360 "searched every shop": TJ/JT, 8/5/1789.

361 "should this revolution succeed": TJ/RP, 7/12/1789.

361 "The progress of things": TJ/TP, 7/13/1789.

361 "The Declaration of the rights of man": TJ/RP, 7/12/1789.

361 "a body of German cavalry": TJ/RP, 7/17/1789.

363 "Troops to the number": TJ/JJ, 7/19/1789.

364 "I went yesterday to Versailles": TJ/JJ, 7/19/1789.

364 "the tumults of Paris": TJ/John Bondfield, 7/16/1789.

365 "done on individuals": TJ/JJ, 8/12/1789.

365 "the tree of liberty must be refreshed": TJ/WSS, 11/13/1787.

365 "my fortune has been singular": TJ/MC, 7/25/1789.

365 "his body drawn through": TJ/JJ, 7/23/1789.

365 "I think there is nothing further": TJ/Edward Bancroft, 8/5/1789.

366 "Upon the whole I do not see": TJ/JJ, 9/19/1789.

366 "I have multiplied my letters": TJ/JJ, 7/29/1789.

CHAPTER ELEVEN: THE STAGE OF PUBLIC LIFE

367 "a tolerably free constitution": TJ/JM1, 8/9/1788.

368 "colonies of plants": TJ/JT, 11/1/1788.

368 "It is my Duty to return": JT/William Pitt, 9/24/1789; and 10/9/1789.

369 "my commission expires": TJ/GG, 8/12/1787.

369 "I consider myself here": TJ/GG, 8/12/1789.

369 "I had rather be shut up": TJ/AD, 2/7/1788.

370 "been led on by events": TJ/JJ, 11/19/1788.

370 "a Siberian degree of cold": TJ/FE, 12/15/1788.

370 his daughters' "future welfare": TJ/Elizabeth Wayles Eppes, 12/15/1788.

371 "Though I foresee": TJ/FE, 12/15/1788.

372 "I leave here a scene of tumult": TJ/MC, 5/21/1789.

373 "withered hand and swelled and crooked fingers": TJ/GG, 12/16/1788.

374 "In the middle steerage": TJ/JT, 11/25/1789.

374 "I shall proceed first": TJ/JJ, 11/23/1789.

375 "that you may be as happy": Address of Welcome of the Officials of Norfolk, 11/25/1789.

375 "that my country should": TJ, Reply to the Address of Welcome from the Mayor, etc. of Norfolk, 11/25/1789.

375 "to be made acquainted": GW/TJ, 11/30/1789.

377 "as far as I can judge": TJ/Edward Bancroft, 1/26/1788.

379 "worthy and respectable member": TJ/Condorcet, 8/30/1791.

379 *"with the same genius"*: Jefferson's Notes from Condorcet on Slavery, n.d. 1788.

380 the service of his country: GW/TJ, 10/13/1789.

381 "Calculation has convinced me": TJ/GW, 11/4/1788; and 12/5/1788.

382 "to glide unnoticed": TJ/John Paradise, 7/5/1789.

383 "energetic general government": GW/TJ, 1/1/1788.

384 "embracing as it does": TJ/GW, 12/15/1789.

385 "But it is not for an individual": TJ/GW, 12/15/1789.

385 "it was impossible to give": TJ/WS, 12/14/1789.

386 "The testimony of esteem": TJ/WS, 12/14/1789.

388 "Your desire that I should": TJ/GW, 2/14/1790.

390 "I am anxious to hear from you": TJ/MJR, 4/4/1790.

392 "we are in a wilderness": JM/TJ, 6/30/1789.

393 "I never saw him so keen": AD/TJ, 11/12/1787.

394 "Mr Madison and myself": TJ/Elijah Griffiths, 5/15/1820.

397 "I was duped": TJ/GW, 9/9/1792.

400 "His passions were naturally strong": Thomas Jefferson's Explanations of the Three Volumes Bound in Marbled Paper (Anas), 2/4/1818.

401 "I made memorandums": Thomas Jefferson's Explanations of the Three Volumes Bound in Marbled Paper (Anas), 2/4/1818.

402 "when I received the news": Memoranda of Conversations with the President, 3/11–4/9/1792.

402 "a stricter connection": TJ, Notes of a Conversation with George Washington on French Affairs, 12/27/1792.

405 "That in urging this measure": TJ, Memoranda of Conversations with the President, 3/1/1792.

405 "in an affectionate tone": TJ, Memoranda of Conversations with the President, 3/1/1792.

405 "growing old": TJ/MP, 5/16/1796.

406 "No man had ever": TJ, Memoranda of Conversations with the President, 3/1/1792.

407 "He here expressed his fear": TJ, Anas, 74, 4/6/1792.

407 "That the ultimate object": TJ/GW, 5/23/1792.

408 "I am perfectly aware": TJ/GW, 5/23/1792.

409 "That with respect": TJ, Notes of a Conversation with George Washington, 7/10/1792.

409 "difference of opinion must be tolerated": TJ, Notes of a Conversation with George Washington, 7/10/1792.

410 "I had the following conversation": TJ, Notes of a Conversation with George Washington, 10/1/1792.

411 "As to that interested spirit": TJ, Notes of a Conversation with George Washington, 10/1/1792.

412 "to continue somewhat longer": TJ, Notes of a Conversation with George Washington, 2/7/1793.

413 "I hired him exclusively as a translator": TJ, Notes of a Conversation with George Washington, 5/23/1793.

414 "had not confidence enough": TJ, Notes of Cabinet Meeting on Edmond Charles Genet, 8/2/1793.

415 "a foolish incoherent sort of speech": TJ, Notes of a Conversation with George Washington, 8/6/1793.

416 "My excessive repugnance": TJ, Notes of a Conversation with George Washington, 8/6/1793.

417 "he believed the views": TJ, Notes of a Conversation with George Washington, 8/6/1793.

418 "I have at length": TJ/AC, 11/27/1793.

419 "Against us are the Executive": TJ/Philip Mazzei, 4/24/1796.

420 When Jefferson visited: See Kathryn Gehred, "Did Martha Washington Really Hate Thomas Jefferson?," WashingtonPapers.org, 5/18/2018; and Ron Chernow, *Washington: A Life* (New York: Penguin Press, 2010), 816.

CHAPTER TWELVE: THE CHAINS OF THE CONSTITUTION

421 "without comparison": TJ/MJR, 5/31/1791.

421 "I think to avail myself": TJ/GW, 5/15/1791.

421 "I shall set out tomorrow": TJ/MJ, 5/8/1791.

422 "We have still pretty constant fires": TJ/MJ, 5/8/1791.

422 "on the bark of Paper birch": TJ/MJ, 5/30/1791.

423 "take a map and trace": TJ/MJ, 5/8/1791.

423 "formed by a contour of mountains": TJ/MJ, 5/31/1791.

423 "We were more pleased": TJ/TMR, 6/5/1791.

424 "as sultry hot": TJ/MJR, 5/31/1791.

424 A product of the age of sentiment: See Andrew Burstein, *The Inner Jefferson: Portrait of a Grieving Optimist* (Charlottesville: University Press of Virginia, 1995).

425 "which cost so much blood": TJ/TMR, 6/5/1791.

427 "for whom my heart": TJ/AC, 11/27/1793.

428 "In the struggle which was necessary": TJ/WS, 1/3/1793.

428 "liberty of the whole earth": TJ/WS, 1/3/1793.

429 "Madame Cosway in a convent!": TJ/AC, 11/27/1793.

430 "the happiness of those": TJ/AC, 11/27/1793.

430 "A twenty years desuetude": TJ/Charles Rose, 4/17/1794.

431 "Monocrats & Papermen": TJ/JM, 4/3/1794.

431 "the ruin of our commerce": JM1/TJ, 3/16/1794.

431 "rumor of a declaration of war": TJ/JM, 4/3/1794.

432 "from a wish to serve him": TJ/Benjamin Franklin Bache, 4/22/1791.

433 "I cannot be satisfied": TJ/GW, 6/19/1796.

433 "I have formerly mentioned": TJ/GW, 6/19/1796.

434 "The assurances you have given": GW/TJ, 7/6/1796.

436 "was no party man": GW/TJ, 7/6/1796.

438 "I am not satisfied": TJ/Henry Tazewell, 9/13/1795.

438 "I have never known the public pulse": TJ/JM, 3/2/1796.

438 "looking to you": TJ/JM, 3/27/1796.

439 "had you remained": Edward Rutledge/TJ, 4/30/1796.

439 "being the enemy of one Nation": TJ/GW, 7/9/1796.

439 "honesty and his political errors": TJ/JM, 3/27/1796.

440 "You drew up the Act": BR/TJ, 3/1/1796.

441 "In truth if anything": TJ/MP, 8/30/1795.

441 "I am become . . . a real farmer": TJ/MC, 9/8/1795.

442 "to practice innocence": TJ/MC, 9/8/1795.

442 "in general it is impossible": TJ/Thomas Digges, 6/19/1788.

443 "if any manufacture": TJ/Thomas Digges, 6/19/1798.

443 "Our citizens are divided": TJ/Count de Volney, 12/9/1795.

444 "Never was a finer canvas": TJ/JA, 2/28/1796.

445 "that fourteen out of fifteen": TJ/MP, 8/30/1795.

445 "It is on politics": TJ/JA, 2/28/1796.

445 "my private business": TJ/Horatio Gates, 2/3/1794.

446 "There is not another person": TJ/JM, 4/27/1795.

447 "I have not the arrogance": TJ/William Cocke, 10/21/1796.

447 "I am glad to see": TJ/JA, 2/28/1796.

447 "I know my own principles": TJ/Samuel Smith, 8/22/1798.

448 "It has been so impossible": TJ/JM, 5/26/1800.

448 "it is not the less true": TJ/TMR, 11/28/1796.

448 "not possible yet to calculate": JM/TJ, 12/5/1796.

448 "I know well that no man": TJ/Edward Rutledge, 12/27/1796.

449 "It is both my duty": TJ/JM, 12/17/1796.

449 "to be the second": TJ/TMR, 11/28/1796.

449 "You must prepare yourself": JM/TJ, 12/19/1796.

450 "I become more and more disgusted": TJ/MJR, 6/8/1797.

450 "There can be no doubt": Elbridge Gerry/TJ, 7/6/1797.

452 "Politics and party hatreds": TJ/MJR, 5/17/1798.

452 "the black (or English) cockade": TJ/JM, 5/10/1798.

454 "Let the honest advocate": TJ, Kentucky Resolution, 10/1798.

454 "bind him down from mischief by the chains of the constitution": TJ, Kentucky Resolution, 10/1798.

455 bound tightly by the "chains of the Constitution": TJ, Kentucky Resolution, 10/1798.

455 The "chains of the Constitution," Jefferson argued: TJ, Kentucky Resolution, 10/1798.

456 "I must write sparingly": TJ/Tadeusz Kościusko, 2/21/1799.

458 "I am among those": TJ/WGM, 6/18/1799.

458 "present despots of the earth": TJ/WGM, 6/18/1799.

459 "with the tenderest affection": JA to Young Men of Philadelphia, 5/7/1798.

460 "parricide hands": TJ/WGM, 6/18/1799.

461 "who like myself are going": TJ/WGM, 6/18/1799.

CHAPTER THIRTEEN: THE FUGITIVE OCCURRENCE

464 "the candle of life": TJ/Elizabeth House Trist, 12/15/1786; and TJ/Francis Willis Jr., 4/18/1790.

465 "every difference of opinion": TJ, First Inaugural Address, 3/4/1801.

466 the "chains of the Constitution," the narrow interpretation: TJ, Kentucky Resolution, 10/1798.

467 The actual "chains of the Constitution": TJ, Kentucky Resolution, 10/1798.

469 "Senators sat on one side": Boyd, *TJP* 33.134.

469 "face all the terrible passions": TJ/WCN, 3/26/1805.

469 "We are all Republicans": TJ, First Inaugural Address, 3/4/1801.

470 The "chains of the Constitution" and Jefferson's policies: TJ, Kentucky Resolution, 10/1798.

470 "When this government was first established": TJ, First Inaugural Address, 3/4/1801.

472 "task is above my talents": TJ, First Inaugural Address, 3/4/1801.

473 "I do not believe": TJ, First Inaugural Address, 3/4/1801.

475 "Sometimes it is said": TJ, First Inaugural Address, 3/4/1801.

475 "Kindly separated by nature": TJ, First Inaugural Address, 3/4/1801.

476 "justify the ways of God to man": John Milton, *Paradise Lost*, book 1, line 26.

476 "a wise and frugal government": TJ, First Inaugural Address, 3/4/1801.

478 "With experience enough in subordinate": TJ, First Inaugural Address, 3/4/1801.

478 "greatest misfortune our nation": Boyd, *TJP*, 5/31/1802.

479 "This loss is the more felt": TJ/Thomas Law, 5/31/1802.

479 "I shall often go wrong": TJ, First Inaugural Address, 3/4/1801.

480 "have been thoroughly tried": TJ/John Dickinson, 3/6/1801.

481 "the majority of the present legislature": TJ/Pierre-Samuel du Pont de Nemours, 1/18/1802.

482 "the eastern people": JM1/TJ, 1/6/1801.

483 "In those days how sanguine": TJ/Pierre Jean Georges Cabanis, 7/13/1803.

484 "on the event of this mission": TJ/JM1, 1/13/1803.

485 "a fugitive occurrence": TJ/John Breckinridge, 8/12/1803.

486 as a believer in the "chains of the Constitution": TJ, Kentucky Resolution, 10/1798.

487 "The Constitution has made no provision": TJ/John Breckinridge, 8/12/1803.

488 an end run around the Constitution: See Jeremy D. Bailey, *Thomas Jefferson and Executive Power* (New York: Cambridge University Press, 2007).

488 "The unprofitable condition": TJ/MJ, 1/7/1798.

489 "If something is not done": TJ/St. George Tucker, 8/28/1797.

490 "I congratulate you, fellow citizens": TJ, Sixth Annual Message to Congress, 12/2/1806.

491 "the office of hangman": TJ/Larkin Smith Washington, 11/26/1804.

491 "the fatigues of the table": TJ/MJR, 10/7/1804.

493 "I determine to withdraw": TJ/John Taylor, 1/6/1805.

493 "the two parties which prevailed": TJ/Count de Volney, 2/8/1805.

494 "On taking this station": TJ, Second Inaugural Address, 3/4/1805.

494 "It may be the pleasure": TJ, Second Inaugural Address, 3/4/1805.

495 "During this course of administration": TJ, Second Inaugural Address, 3/4/1805.

496 "I am sensible of no passion": TJ, Second Inaugural Address, 3/4/1805.

CHAPTER FOURTEEN: THE LADIES OF WILLIAMSBURG

498 he had met with John Baptiste Ducoigne: See TJ/ JBD, 6/1/1781.

499 "The aboriginal inhabitants": TJ/JBD, 6/1/1781.

500 "our Indian neighbors": TJ, First Annual Message to Congress, 12/8/1801; and TJ, Annual Message to Congress, 1808.

501 "we shall endeavor in all things": TJ, First Annual Message to Congress, 12/8/1801; and TJ, Conference with Little Turtle, Jefferson's Reply, 1/7/1802.

502 "the most intelligent man": Samuel Mitchell/Catherine Mitchell, 1/13/1802.

502 "fell to my lot": Little Turtle to TJ, Conference with Little Turtle, Address of Little Turtle, 1/4/1802.

503 "Made by the same great spirit": TJ, Conference with Little Turtle, Jefferson's Reply, 1/7/1802.

503 "when you visited me the last winter": TJ to Handsome Lake, 11/3/1802.

504 "in preparing them ultimately": TJ to the Senate and the House of Representatives, confidential, 1/18/1803.

504 "The wisdom of the animal": TJ/Benjamin Hawkins, 2/18/1803.

504 "that these preparations are meant": TJ/Henry Dearborn, 9/2/1807.

505 "We shall push our trading houses": TJ/William Henry Harrison, 2/27/1803.

506 "For the most part they were chosen": Colin G. Calloway, *The Indian World*

of George Washington: The First President, the First Americans, and the Birth of the Nation (New York: Oxford University Press, 2018). See Anthony F. C. Wallace, *Jefferson and the Indians: The Tragic Fate of the First Americans* (Cambridge, MA: Harvard University Press, 1999). See Claudio Saunt, *Unworthy Republic: The Dispossession of Native Americans and the Road to Indian Territory* (New York: Norton, 2020).

507 "we continue to receive proofs": TJ, Annual Address to Congress, 12/2/1806.

507 "I take you by the hand of friendship": Thomas Jefferson to Chief Wolf and People of the Mandan Nation, 12/30/1806.

508 "My friends and children": Thomas Jefferson to Chief Wolf and People of the Mandan Nation, 12/30/1806.

509 "With our Indian neighbors": TJ, Annual Message to Congress, 11/8/1808.

509 "It must not be a river of blood": TJ to the Chiefs of the Cherokee Nation, 1/10/1806.

509 "to obliterate from the Indian mind": TJ, *Special Message to the Senate of the United States*, 1/15/1808.

511 "message which I disapprove": TJ/Albert Gallatin, 11/24/1818.

511 "From 40 years of intimate conversation": TJ/Pierre Samuel du Pont de Nemours, 1/18/1802.

512 in which land would be bought: See Christopher Michael Curtis, *Jefferson's Freeholders and the Politics of Ownership in the Old Dominion* (New York: Cambridge University Press, 2012).

512 "I found the country entirely": TJ/Pierre Samuel du Pont de Nemours, 1/18/1802.

513 "It will be for ever seen": TJ/Benjamin Hawkins, 2/18/1803.

516 "We have seen with sincere concern": TJ, Third Annual Address to Congress, 10/17/1803.

518 "Our coasts have been infested": TJ, Fifth Annual Message to Congress, 12/3/1805.

520 "I am panting for retirement": TJ/Lafayette, 5/26/1807.

520 "jumping into the water": TJ/MJR, 10/12/1807.

522 "Reparation for the past, security for the future": TJ/William Duane, 7/20/1807.

522 "all armed vessels bearing commissions": TJ, Proclamation re British Armed Vessels, 7/2/1807.

523 "extremely disposed for peace": TJ/TMR, 10/26/1807.

525 "bad account of the patriotism": TJ/EWR, 2/23/1808.

526 "cooked up by Marshall": TJ/EP, 1/29/1799.

527 "intriguing and cajoling talents": TJ/Tench Coxe, 5/21/1799.

527 "We had a very familiar intercourse": TJ/William Wirt, 8/4/1805.

530 "Though the newspapers give": TJ/AB, 6/17/1797.

531 "If a prospect could be": TJ/AB, 6/17/1797.

531 "I have not thought it discreet": AB/TJ, 2/3/1799.

531 "The Southern states": TJ/AB, 2/11/1799.

532 "my whole time and attention": AB/TJ, 12/23/1800.

533 "About a month ago": TJ, Notes on Aaron Burr, 4/15/1806.

534 "There was not a single voice": TJ, Notes on Aaron Burr, 4/15/1806.

535 "that sundry persons": TJ, Proclamation on Spanish Territory, 11/27/1806.

536 "I received intimations that designs": TJ, Special Message to Congress on the Burr Conspiracy, 1/22/1807.

541 "It is very long, my dear Anne": TJ/Anne Cary Randolph, 5/20/1803.

542 "So stands the account": TJ/EWR, 5/21/1805.

542 "I do not know whether": TJ/Anne Cary Randolph, 7/6/1805.

542 "Hope is so much pleasanter": TJ/EWR, 6/29/1807.

543 "I have nothing better to send": TJ/EWR, 10/19/1807.

CHAPTER FIFTEEN: SOWING THE WIND

544 "Your character of the Federalists": TJ/John Wayles Eppes, 3/24/1811.

545 "now say that they do not": WS/TJ, 10/5/1817.

545 done around the "chains of the Constitution": TJ, Kentucky Resolution, 10/1798.

546 "affectionate address": TJ, To the Citizens of Washington, D.C., 3/4/1809.

546 "That the improvement of this city": TJ, To the Citizens of Washington, D.C., 3/4/1809.

547 "unmercifully long": TJ/MVB, 6/29/1824.

547 "the distressing burden of power": TJ, Message to the Inhabitants of Albemarle County, 4/3/1809.

547 "Returning to the scenes": TJ, Message to the Inhabitants of Albemarle County, 4/3/1809.

550 "some of the delightful conversations": TJ/BR, 4/21/1803.

552 "I have ever thought religion": TJ/Samuel H. Smith, 8/6/1816.

552 As he traveled to Washington in 1804: TJ, *The Life and Morals of Jesus of Nazareth* (*The Jefferson Bible*).

552 "a Syllabus, or Outline": TJ/BR, 4/21/1803.

552 "It was the work of 2 or 3 nights": TJ/WS, 10/31/1819.

553 "proceed to a view of the life": TJ/BR, 4/21/1803.

553 "I should as soon think": TJ/Charles Clay, 1/29/1815.

553 "The genuine system of Jesus": TJ/Charles Clay, 1/29/1815.

553 "I too have made": TJ/Charles Thomson, 1/9/1816.

553 "In extracting the pure principles": TJ/JA, 10/12/1813.

554 "It is a paradigm of his doctrines": TJ/Charles Thomson, 1/9/1816.

555 his preference was that the president: See Jeremy D. Baily, *Thomas Jefferson and Executive Power* (New York: Cambridge University Press, 2007).

555 "Some men look at constitutions": TJ/Samuel Kercheval, 7/12/1816; and TJ/Henry Tompkinson, 7/12/1816.

557 "The constitution, on this hypothesis": TJ/Spencer Roane, 9/6/1819.

557 "governments are republican only in proportion": TJ/Samuel Kercheval, 7/12/1816.

559 "we should have such an empire": TJ/JM, 4/27/1809.

560 "our laws, language, religion, politics": TJ/William Duane, 8/12/1810.

561 "by the combined effects": TJ/WS, 1/28/1814.

561 "I sincerely rejoice": TJ/WS, 2/24/1814.

562 "through the window": See *Selma Hale's Visit to Monticello*. Selma Hale/David Hale, 5/5/1818, postscript 5/7/1818; Selma Hale/William Plumer, 5/8/1818; Selma Hale/Arthur Livermore, 5/16/1818; and *Selma Hale's Notes on His Visit to Monticello* [after 1818].

563 "Nothing is so painful to me": TJ/Gideon Granger, 3/9/1814.

564 "furnace of politics": TJ/Ann Willing Bingham, 5/11/1788.

564 "to be anchored to a writing table": WS/TJ, 7/18/1816.

565 "To your encouragements": TJ/WS, 8/10/1816.

565 "You say I must go to writing": TJ/Josephus B. Stuart, 5/10/1817.

566 "After the lapse of 25 years": Thomas Jefferson's Explanations of the Three Volumes Bound in Marbled Paper (*Anas*), 2/4/1818.

566 "but he wished that the knowledge": Joseph C. Cabell, Memorandum on the Introduction to the "Anas," 4/9/1818: "On 31st March 1818, I was drawn to Monticello by my duties as a Visitor of the Central College. Mr Jefferson then put into my hands for perusal a manuscript covering four and a half sheets of letter paper, entitled Explanations of the 3 volumes in marble paper. It was a commentary written by himself on Marshall's life of Washington. Mr Jefferson observed that it would be published at his death by Col: Randolph, and his Grandson T. J. Randolph, to whom he should leave his papers: but he wished that the knowledge of the existence of this paper should not be confined to members of his own family; and that he should shew it to Mr Madison of Orange, late President of the U. States."

567 "as different from what Gen. Washington": Thomas Jefferson's Explanations of the Three Volumes Bound in Marbled Paper (*Anas*), 2/4/1818.

568 "In these three volumes": Thomas Jefferson's Explanations of the Three Volumes Bound in Marbled Paper (*Anas*), 2/4/1818.

569 "You express a wish": TJ/WS, 5/5/1816.

570 "At the age of 77": TJA, 3.

572 "You have doubtless seen": TJ/JM, 8/30/1823.

573 "the genuine effusion of the soul": TJ/Dr. James Mease, 9/26/1825.

573 "elaborate Philippic against Mr. Adams": TJ/MVB, 6/29/1824.

573 "I could not have believed": TJ/MVB, 6/29/1824.

574 "the very actions however": TJ/MVB, 6/29/1824.

574 "My last parting with General Washington": TJ/MVB, 6/29/1824.

575 "I am grown old, and worn down": TJ/William A. Burwell, 2/6/1817.

576 "Indeed my Physician interdicts": TJ/William E. Richmond, 12/25/1819.

576 "I found Mr. Jefferson tall": Francis Hall, Account of a Visit to Monticello, 1/7–8/1817.

576 "three long and dangerous illnesses": TJ/JA, 11/7/1819.

577 "You ask if I would agree": TJ/JA, 4/8/1816.

577 "Age, its ordinary infirmities and frequent attacks": TJ/L'Aine Meinadier, 11/12/1819.

577 "I am old and infirm": TJ/John Brazier, 11/22/1819.

579 "Four years of bad overseers": TJ/WCN, 3/26/1818.

580 "Will you do me the favor": WCN/TJ, 4/19/1818.

580 "But this consideration yields": TJ/WCN, 5/1/1818.

581 "The enormous abuses": TJ/Richard Rush, 6/29/1819.

583 "I am indeed a sore sufferer": TJ/JM1, 8/17/1819.

583 "establishment on the coast of Africa": TJ/Thomas Humphreys, 2/8/1817.

584 "I shall be willing to do anything": TJ/John Lynch, 1/21/1811.

585 "I have not perceived the growth": TJ/Thomas Humphreys, 2/8/1817.

585 "The public mind would not yet": TJA, 44.

585 "must shudder *at the prospect held up*": TJ/JA, 12/10/1819.

585 It was possible, he wrote: TJ/John Holmes, 4/22/1820.

586 "I have much confidence": TJ/Barbé-Marbois, 6/14/2017.

588 "rather thin and spare": Extract from Daniel Webster's Account of a Visit to Monticello, Dec 14–19, dated 1825 but actually 1824, https://tjrs.monticello.org/letter/1855.

589 "Here was buried": Thomas Jefferson, Design for Tombstone and Inscription, before 7/4/1826.

589 "ill health forbids me": TJ/Roger C. Weightman, 6/24/1826.

590 "The general spread of the light": TJ/Roger C. Weightman, 6/24/1826.

BIBLIOGRAPHY

PRIMARY

Adams, Dickinson W., ed. *Jefferson's Extracts from the Gospels*. Princeton University Press, Princeton, NJ, 1983.

Betts, Edwin Morris, ed. *Thomas Jefferson's Farm Book, with Commentary and Relevant Extracts from Other Writings*. Princeton University Press, Princeton, NJ, 1953.

Betts, Edwin Morris, ed. *Thomas Jefferson's Garden Book, 1766–1824, with Relevant Extracts from His Other Writings*. American Philosophical Society, Philadelphia, 1944.

Betts, Edwin Morris, and James Adam Bear Jr., eds. *The Family Letters of Thomas Jefferson*. University of Missouri Press, Columbia, 1966.

Burstein, Andrew. *Letters from the Head and Heart: Writings of Thomas Jefferson*. Thomas Jefferson Foundation, Monticello, VA, 2002.

Capon, Lester J., ed. *The Adams-Jefferson Letters: The Complete Correspondence between Thomas Jefferson & Abigail & John Adams*. University of North Carolina Press, Chapel Hill, 1959.

Jefferson, Thomas. *The Jefferson Bible*. Smithsonian Books, Washington, DC, 2011.

———. *Jefferson's Memorandum Books*, 2 vols. Digital versions at National Archives, Founders Online, https://founders.archives.gov, and the fully annotated editions at the University of Virginia Press, Rotunda Collections.

———. *Notes on the State of Virginia*, ed. William Paden. Norton, New York, 1954.

———. *The Papers of Thomas Jefferson, Main Series, 1760–1809*, ed. Julian P. Boyd, et al., vols. 1–42, current to March 1804. Princeton University Press, Princeton, NJ, 1950–.

———. *The Papers of Thomas Jefferson, Retirement Series, 1809–1826*, ed. J. Jefferson Looney, et al., vols. 1–21, current to April 1818. Thomas Jefferson Foundation, Charlottesville, Virginia, 1950–2021.

———. *The Selected Writings of Thomas Jefferson*, ed. Wayne Franklin. Norton, New York, 2010.

———. *Writings*, ed. Merrill D. Peterson. Library of America, New York, 1984.

Smith, James Morton, ed. *The Republic of Letters: The Correspondence between Thomas Jefferson and James Madison, 1776–1826*, 3 vols. Norton, New York, 1995.

Wilson, Douglas L., ed. *Jefferson's Literary Commonplace Book*. Princeton University Press, Princeton, NJ, 1989.

SECONDARY

Ackerman, Bruce. *The Failure of the Founding Fathers: Jefferson, Marshall, and the Rise of Presidential Democracy*. Harvard University Press, Cambridge, MA, 2005.

Adair, Douglas. *Fame and the Founding Fathers*. Norton, New York, 1974.

Adams, Henry. *History of the United States of America during the Administrations of Thomas Jefferson, 1889–1890*. Library of America, New York, 1986.

———. *John Randolph*. Houghton Mifflin, Boston, 1898.

———. *The Life of Albert Gallatin*. Lippincott, Philadelphia, 1880.

Adams, William Howard. *The Paris Years of Thomas Jefferson*. Yale University Press, New Haven, CT, 1997.

Amar, Akhil Reed. *America's Constitution: A Biography*. Random House, New York, 2005.

———. *The Words that Made Us: America's Constitutional Conversation, 1760–1840*. Basic Books, New York, 2021.

Anderson, Fred. *Crucible of War: The Seven Years' War and the Fate of Empire in British North America, 1754–1766*. Vintage, New York, 2001.

Anderson, Fred, and Andrew Cayton. *The Dominion of War: Empire and Liberty in North America*. Penguin, New York, 2005.

Ansary, Cyrus A. *George Washington, Dealmaker-in-Chief: The Story of How the Father of Our Country Unleashed the Entrepreneurial Spirit in America*. Lambert Academic Publishing, OmniScriptum SRL, Chisinau, Moldova, 2019.

Appleby, Joyce. *Liberalism and Republicanism in the Historical Imagination*. Harvard University Press, Cambridge, MA, 1992.

Atkinson, Rick. *The British Are Coming*. Henry Holt, New York, 2019.

Bailyn, Bernard. *To Begin the World Anew: The Genius and Ambiguities of the American Founders*. Knopf, New York, 2003.

Banning, Lance. *The Jeffersonian Persuasion: Evolution of a Party Ideology*. Cornell University Press, Ithaca, NY, 1978.

Baptist, Edward E. *The Half Has Never Been Told: Slavery and the Making of American Capitalism*. Basic Books, New York, 2014.

Barnett, Gerald. *Richard and Maria Cosway: A Biography.* Lutterworth Press, Tiverton, Devon, England, 1995.

Beckert, Sven. *Empire of Cotton: A Global History.* Vintage, New York, 2014.

Beran, Michael. *Jefferson's Demons, Portrait of a Restless Mind.* Free Press, New York, 2003.

Berkin, Carol. *A Sovereign People: The Crisis of the 1790s and the Birth of American Nationalism.* Basic Books, New York, 2017.

Betts, Edwin M., and Hazlehurst Bolton Perkins. *Thomas Jefferson's Flower Garden at Monticello.* University of Virginia Press, Charlottesville, 1986.

Bilder, Mary Sarah. *Madison's Hand: Revising the Constitutional Convention.* Harvard University Press, Cambridge, MA, 2015.

Black, Jeremy. *George III: America's Last King.* Yale University Press, New Haven, CT, 2006.

Blackburn, Robin. *The American Crucible: Slavery, Emancipation and Human Rights.* Verso, London, 2013.

———. *The Overthrow of Colonial Slavery, 1776–1848.* Verso, London, 1988.

Boles, John B. *Jefferson: Architect of American Liberty.* Basic Books, New York, 2017.

Boles, John B., and Randall L. Hall, eds. *Seeing Jefferson Anew: In His Time and Ours.* University of Virginia Press, Charlottesville, 2010.

Boorstin, Daniel J. *The Lost World of Thomas Jefferson.* University of Chicago Press, 1948.

Bordewich, Fergus M. *The First Congress: How James Madison, George Washington, and a Group of Extraordinary Americans Invented the Government.* Simon & Schuster, New York, 2016.

Bouton, Terry. *Taming Democracy: The People, the Founders, and the Troubling End of the American Revolution.* Oxford University Press, New York, 2007.

Boyd, Julian P. *The Declaration of Independence, The Evolution of the Text.* Library of Congress Thomas Jefferson Memorial Foundation, Washington and Charlottesville, 1999.

Brands, H. W. *The Heartbreak of Aaron Burr.* Anchor, New York, 2012.

Breen, T. H. *American Insurgents, American Patriots: The Revolution of the People.* Hill & Wang, New York, 2010.

Brewer, John. *The Sinews of Power: War, Money and the English State, 1688–1783.* Knopf, New York, 1988.

Brodie, Fawn M. *Thomas Jefferson: An Intimate History.* Norton, New York, 1974.

Brookhiser, Richard. *James Madison.* Basic Books, New York, 2011.

———. *John Marshall: The Man Who Made the Supreme Court.* Basic Books, New York, 2018.

Browne, Stephen Howard. *Jefferson's Call for Nationhood.* Texas A&M Press, College Station, 2003.

Browning, Andrew H. *The Panic of 1819: The First Great Depression.* University of Missouri Press, Columbia, 2019.

Brumwell, Stephen. *Turncoat: Benedict Arnold and the Crisis of American Liberty.* Yale University Press, New Haven, CT, 2018.

Bullock, Helen Duprey. *My Head and My Heart: A Little History of Thomas Jefferson and Maria Cosway.* Putnam's, New York, 1945.

Bullock, Steven C. *Revolutionary Brotherhood: Freemasonry and the Transformation of the American Social Order, 1730–1840.* University of North Carolina Press, Chapel Hill, 1996.

Bunker, Nick. *An Empire at the Edge: How Britain Came to Fight America.* Knopf, New York, 2014.

Burk, Kathleen. *Old World, New World: Great Britain and America from the Beginning.* Atlantic Monthly Press, New York, 2008.

Burnell, Carol. *Divided Affections: The Extraordinary Life of Maria Cosway, Celebrity Artist and Thomas Jefferson's Impossible Love.* Column House, Lausanne, Switzerland, 1977.

Burstein, Andrew. *The Inner Jefferson: Portrait of a Grieving Optimist.* University Press of Virginia, Charlottesville, 1995.

———. *Jefferson's Secrets: Death and Desire at Monticello.* Basic Books, New York, 2005.

Burstein, Andrew, and Nancy Isenberg. *Madison and Jefferson.* Random House, New York, 2010.

Burton, Cynthia H. *Jefferson Vindicated: Fallacies, Omissions, and Contradictions in Hemings Genealogical Search.* Self-published, Keswick, VA, 2005.

Calloway, Colin G. *The Indian World of George Washington: The First President, the First Americans, and the Birth of the Nation.* Oxford University Press, New York, 2018.

Cheney, Lynne. *James Madison: A Life Reconsidered.* Viking Penguin, New York, 2015.

Chernow, Ron. *Alexander Hamilton.* Penguin Press, New York, 2004.

———. *Washington: A Life.* Penguin Press, New York, 2010.

Chervinsky, Lindsay A. *The Cabinet: George Washington and the Creation of an American Institution.* Harvard University Press, Cambridge, MA, 2020.

Cogliano, Francis D., ed. *A Companion to Thomas Jefferson.* Wiley-Blackwell, Chichester, UK, 2012.

———. *Emperor of Liberty: Thomas Jefferson's Foreign Policy.* Yale University Press, New Haven, CT, 2014.

———. *Thomas Jefferson: Reputation and Legacy.* University of Virginia Press, Charlottesville, 2006.

Colley, Linda. *Britons: Forging the Nation, 1707–1837.* Yale University Press, New Haven, CT, 1992.

Cornell, Saul. *The Other Founders: Anti-Federalism & the Dissenting Tradition in America, 1788–1828.* University of North Carolina Press, Chapel Hill, 1999.

Cost, Jay. *The Price of Greatness: Alexander Hamilton, James Madison, and the Creation of American Oligarchy.* Basic Books, New York, 2018.

Countryman, Edward. *The American Revolution*. Hill & Wang, New York, 2003.

Crawford, Alan Pell. *Twilight at Monticello: The Final Years of Thomas Jefferson*. Random House, New York, 2008.

Cunningham Jr., Noble E. *The Image of Thomas Jefferson in the Public Eye: Portraits for the People, 1800–1809*. University Press of Virginia, Charlottesville, 1981.

Curtis, Christopher Michael. *Jefferson's Freeholders and the Politics of Ownership in the Old Dominion*. Cambridge University Press, New York, 2012.

Davis, David Brion. *The Problem of Slavery in the Age of Revolution, 1770–1823*. Oxford University Press, New York, 1999.

Dawidoff, Robert. *The Education of John Randolph*. Norton, New York, 1979.

Delaplaine, Joseph. *Life of Peyton Randolph*. Philadelphia, c. 1817; repr. Scholar's Choice, Rochester, NY, 2015.

Dewey, Frank L. *Thomas Jefferson, Lawyer*. University of Virginia Press, Charlottesville, 1986.

Dunn, Susan. *Dominion of Memories: Jefferson, Madison, and the Decline of Virginia*. Basic Books, New York, 2007.

———. *Jefferson's Second Revolution: The Election Crisis of 1800 and the Triumph of Republicanism*. Houghton Mifflin, Boston, 2004.

Du Rivage, Justin. *Revolution against Empire: Taxes, Politics, and the Origins of American Independence*. Yale University Press, New Haven, CT, 2017.

Edling, Max M. *A Hercules in the Cradle: War, Money, and the American State, 1783–1867*. University of Chicago Press, 2014.

Elkins, Stanley, and Eric McKitrick. *The Age of Federalism: The Early American Republic, 1788–1800*. Oxford University Press, New York, 1993.

Ellis, Joseph J. *American Creation: Triumphs and Tragedies in the Founding of the Republic*. Knopf, New York, 2007.

———. *American Dialogue: The Founders and Us*. Knopf, New York, 2018.

———. *American Sphinx: The Character of Thomas Jefferson*. Knopf, New York, 1997.

———. *Founding Brothers: The Revolutionary Generation*. Knopf, New York, 2000.

———. *His Excellency: George Washington*. Knopf, New York, 2004.

———. *The Quartet: Orchestrating the Second American Revolution, 1783–1789*. Knopf, New York, 2015.

Ellis, Richard E. *The Jeffersonian Crisis: Courts and Politics in the Young Republic*. Oxford University Press, New York, 1971.

Fehrenbacher, Don E. *The Slaveholding Republic: An Account of the United States Government's Relations to Slavery*. Oxford University Press, New York, 2001.

Feldman, Noah. *The Three Lives of James Madison: Genius, Partisan, President*. Random House, New York, 2017.

Ferling, John. *Adams vs. Jefferson: The Tumultuous Election of 1800*. Oxford University Press, New York, 2004.

———. *Jefferson and Hamilton: The Rivalry That Forged a Nation*. Bloomsbury Press, New York, 2013.

———. *A Leap in the Dark: The Struggle to Create the American Republic.* Oxford University Press, New York, 2003.

Ferreiro, Larrie D. *Brothers at Arms: American Independence and the Men of France and Spain Who Saved It.* Knopf, New York, 2016.

Finkelman, Paul, ed. *Slave Rebels, Abolitionists, and Southern Courts: The Pamphlet Literature.* Garland, New York, 1988.

———. *Slavery and the Founders: Race and Liberty in the Age of Jefferson.* M.E. Sharpe, Armonk, NY, 2014.

Fleming, Thomas. *The Great Divide: The Conflict Between Washington and Jefferson That Defined a Nation.* Da Capo Press, New York, 2015.

Fliegelman, Jay. *Declaring Independence: Jefferson, Natural Language, and the Culture of Performance.* Stanford University Press, Stanford, CA, 1983.

Ford, Lacy K. *Deliver Us from Evil: The Slavery Question in the Old South.* Oxford University Press, New York, 2009.

Frazer, Gregg L. *The Religious Beliefs of America's Founders: Reason, Revelation, and Revolution.* University Press of Kansas, Lawrence, 2012.

Freehling, William W. *The Road to Disunion: Secessionists at Bay, 1776–1854.* Oxford University Press, New York, 1990.

Freeman, Joanne B. *Affairs of Honor: National Politics in the New Republic.* Yale University Press, New Haven, CT, 2001.

Freeman, Joanne B., and Johann N. Neem. *Jeffersonians in Power: The Rhetoric of Opposition Meets the Reality of Governing.* University of Virginia Press, Charlottesville, 2019.

Fried, Stephen. *Rush: Revolution, Madness, and Benjamin Rush, the Visionary Doctor Who Became a Founding Father.* Crown, New York, 2018.

Gabler, James M. *Passions: The Wines and Travels of Thomas Jefferson.* Bacchus Press, Baltimore, 1995.

Gaines Jr., William H. *Thomas Mann Randolph, Jefferson's Son-in Law.* Louisiana State University Press, Baton Rouge, 1966.

Gilje, Paul A., ed. *Wages of Independence: Capitalism in the Early American Republic.* Madison House, Lanham, MD, 2006.

Gordon-Reed, Annette. *The Hemingses of Monticello: An American Family.* Norton, New York, 2008.

———. *Thomas Jefferson and Sally Hemings: An American Controversy.* University of Virginia Press, Charlottesville, 1997.

Gordon-Reed, Annette, and Peter S. Onuf. *"Most Blessed Are the Patriarchs": Thomas Jefferson and the Empire of the Imagination.* Liveright, New York, 2016.

Gould, Eliga H. *Among the Powers of the Earth: The American Revolution and the Making of a New World Empire.* Harvard University Press, Cambridge, MA, 2014.

Green, Constance McLaughlin. *Washington: Village and Capital, 1800–1878.* Princeton University Press, Princeton, NJ, 1962.

Greene, Jack P. *The Constitutional Origins of the American Revolution.* Cambridge University Press, New York, 2011.

———. *Interpreting Early America: Historiographical Essays*. University Press of Virginia, Charlottesville, 1996.

———. *Political Life in Eighteenth-Century Virginia*. Colonial Williamsburg Foundation, Williamsburg, VA, 1986.

———. *Pursuits of Happiness: The Social Development of Early Modern British Colonies and the Formation of American Culture*. University of North Carolina Press, Chapel Hill, 1988.

———, ed. *Settlements to Society, 1607–1763: A Documentary History of Colonial America*. Norton, New York, 1966.

Gutzman, Kenneth R. C. *Thomas Jefferson—Revolutionary: A Radical's Struggle to Remake America*. St. Martin's Press, New York, 2017.

Guyatt, Nicholas. *Bind Us Apart: How Enlightenment Americans Invented Racial Segregation*. Basic Books, New York, 2016.

Hailman, John. *Thomas Jefferson on Wine*. University Press of Mississippi, Jackson, 2006.

Hammond, John Craig, and Matthew Masson, eds. *Contesting Slavery: The Politics of Bondage and Freedom in the New American Nation*. University Press of Virginia, Charlottesville, 2011.

Hatch, Peter J. *"A Rich Spot of Earth": Thomas Jefferson's Revolutionary Garden at Monticello*. Yale University Press, New Haven, CT, 2012.

Hayes, Kevin J. *George Washington: A Life in Books*. Oxford University Press, New York, 2017.

———. *The Mind of a Patriot: Patrick Henry and the World of Ideas*. University of Virginia Press, Charlottesville, 2008.

———. *The Road to Monticello: The Life and Mind of Thomas Jefferson*. Oxford University Press, New York, 2008.

Holochak, M. Andrew. *Framing a Legend: Exposing the Distorted History of Thomas Jefferson and Sally Hemings*. Prometheus Books, Amherst, NY, 2013.

Holton, Woody. *Forced Founders: Indians, Debtors, Slaves, and the Making of the American Revolution in Virginia*. University of North Carolina Press, Chapel Hill, 1999.

———. *Unruly Americans and the Origin of the Constitution*. Hill & Wang, New York, 2007.

Hoock, Holger. *Scars of Independence: America's Violent Birth*. Crown, New York, 2017.

Horn, James, Jan Ellen Lewis, and Peter Onuf. *The Revolution of 1800: Democracy, Race, and the New Republic*. University of Virginia Press, Charlottesville, 2002.

Hyland Jr., William G. *In Defense of Thomas Jefferson: The Sally Hemings Sex Scandal*. St. Martin's Press, New York, 2009.

———. *Martha Jefferson: An Intimate Life with Thomas Jefferson*. Rowman & Littlefield, Lanham, MD, 2015.

Immerwahr, Daniel. *How to Hide an Empire: A History of the Greater United States*. Farrar, Straus & Giroux, New York, 2019.

Isaac, Rhys. *Landon Carter's Uneasy Kingdom*. Oxford University Press, New York, 2004.

———. *The Transformation of Virginia, 1740–1790*. University of North Carolina Press, Chapel Hill, 1982.

Isenberg, Nancy. *Fallen Father: The Life of Aaron Burr*. Viking Penguin, New York, 2007.

Jensen, Merrill. *The Founding of a Nation: A History of the American Revolution, 1763–1776*. Hackett, Indianapolis, 1968.

Karp, Matthew. *This Vast Southern Empire: Slaveholders at the Helm of American Foreign Policy*. Harvard University Press, Cambridge, MA, 2006.

Katznelson, Ira, and Martin Shefter. *Shaped by War and Trade: International Influences on American Political Development*. Princeton University Press, Princeton, NJ, 2002.

Keane, Tom. *Tom Paine: A Political Life*. Little, Brown, New York, 1995.

Kennedy, Robert G. *Architecture, Men, Women, and Money in America, 1600–1860*. Random House, New York, 1985.

———. *Burr, Hamilton, and Jefferson: A Study in Character*. Oxford University Press, New York, 1999.

———. *Mr. Jefferson's Lost Cause: Land, Farmers, Slavery, and the Louisiana Purchase*. Oxford University Press, New York, 2003.

Kern, Susan. *The Jeffersons at Shadwell*. Yale University Press, New Haven, CT, 2010.

Kerrison, Catherine. *Jefferson's Daughters: Three Sisters, White and Black, in a Young America*. Ballantine Books, New York, 2018.

Ketcham, Ralph. *James Madison: A Biography*. University of Virginia Press, Charlottesville, 1990.

Kidd, Thomas S. *Patrick Henry: First Among Patriots*. Basic Books, New York, 2011.

———. *Thomas Jefferson: A Biography of Spirit and Flesh*. Yale University Press, New Haven, 2022.

Kierner, Cynthia A. *Martha Jefferson Randolph, Daughter of Monticello*. University of North Carolina Press, Chapel Hill, 2012.

Kimball, Marie. *Jefferson: The Scene of Europe, 1784–1789*. Coward-McCann, New York, 1950.

Klarman, Michael J. *The Framers' Coup: The Making of the United States Constitution*. Oxford University Press, New York, 2018.

Kranish, Jay. *Flight from Monticello*. Oxford University Press, New York, 2010.

Kukla, Jon. *Patrick Henry: Champion of Liberty*. Simon & Schuster, New York, 2017.

———. *A Wilderness So Immense: The Louisiana Purchase and the Destiny of America*. Knopf, New York, 2003.

Lapore, Jill. *These Truths: A History of the United States*. Norton, New York, 2018.

Larson, Edward J. *A Magnificent Catastrophe: The Tumultuous Election of 1800, America's First Presidential Campaign*. Free Press, New York, 2007.

Larson, John Lauritz. *Internal Improvement: National Public Works and the Promise of Popular Government in the Early United States.* University of North Carolina Press, Chapel Hill, 2002.

Ledgin, Norm. *Diagnosing Jefferson: Evidence of a Condition that Guided His Beliefs, Behavior, and Personal Associations.* Future Horizons, Arlington, TX, 1998.

Lengel, Edward G. *First Entrepreneur: How George Washington Built His—and the Nation's—Prosperity.* Da Capo Press, New York, 2016.

Lerner, Max. *Thomas Jefferson: America's Philosopher-King.* Transaction Publishers, Piscataway, NJ, 1996.

Levy, Jonathan. *The Ages of American Capitalism: A History of the United States.* Random House, New York, 2021.

Levy, Leonard W. *Jefferson and Civil Liberties: The Darker Side.* Harvard University Press, Cambridge, MA, 1963.

Lewis Jr., James E. *The Burr Conspiracy: Uncovering the Story of an Early American Crisis.* Princeton University Press, Princeton, NJ, 2017.

———. *The Louisiana Purchase: Jefferson's Noble Bargain?* Thomas Jefferson Foundation, Monticello, VA, 2003.

Lewis, Jan. *The Pursuit of Happiness: Family and Values in Jefferson's Virginia.* Cambridge University Press, New York, 1983.

Lockridge, Kenneth A. *On the Sources of Patriarchal Rage: The Commonplace Books of William Byrd and Thomas Jefferson and the Gendering of Power in the Eighteenth Century.* New York University Press, 1992.

Lockwood, Matthew. *To Begin the World Over Again: How the American Revolution Devastated the Globe.* Yale University Press, New Haven, CT, 2019.

MacLeod, Duncan J. *Slavery, Race and the American Revolution.* Cambridge University Press, New York, 1974.

Madison, James, Alexander Hamilton, and John Jay. *The Federalist Papers* (1788). Penguin, London, 1987.

Maier, Pauline. *American Scripture: Making the Declaration of Independence.* Random House, New York, 1997.

———. *Ratification: The People Debate the Constitution, 1787–1788.* Simon & Schuster, New York, 2010.

Malcolm, Joyce Lee. *The Tragedy of Benedict Arnold: An American Life.* Pegasus, New York, 2018.

Malone, Dumas. *Jefferson and His Time,* 6 vols.: 1. *Jefferson the Virginian* (1948); 2. *Jefferson and the Rights of Man* (1951); 3. *Jefferson and the Ordeal of Liberty* (1962); 4. *Jefferson the President: First Term, 1801–1805* (1970); 5. *Jefferson the President: Second Term, 1805–1809* (1974); 6. *The Sage of Monticello* (1981). University of Virginia Press, Charlottesville.

Mann, Bruce H. *Republic of Debtors: Bankruptcy in the Age of American Independence.* Harvard University Press, Cambridge, MA, 2009.

Manseau, Peter. *The Jefferson Bible: A Biography.* Princeton University Press, Princeton, NJ, 2020.

Mapp Jr., Alf J. *Thomas Jefferson: A Strange Case of Mistaken Identity*. Madison Books, Lanham, MD, 1987.

Mason, Matthew. *Slavery and Politics in the Early American Republic*. University of North Carolina Press, Chapel Hill, 2006.

Matson, Cathy, ed. *The Economy of Early America: Historical Perspective and New Directions*. Pennsylvania State University, University Park, 2006.

Matson, Cathy D., and Peter S. Onuf. *A Union of Interests: Political and Economic Thought in Revolutionary America*. University Press of Kansas, Lawrence, 1990.

Mayer, David N. *The Constitutional Thought of Thomas Jefferson*. University Press of Virginia, Charlottesville, 1994.

Mayer, Henry. *A Son of Thunder: Patrick Henry and the American Republic*. Grove Press, New York, 2007.

McColley, Robert. *Slavery and Jeffersonian Virginia*. University of Illinois Press, Urbana, 1973.

McCoy, Drew R. *The Elusive Republic: Political Economy in Jeffersonian America*. Norton, New York, 1982.

———. *The Last of the Fathers: James Madison and the Republican Legacy*. Cambridge University Press, New York, 1989.

McCraw, Thomas K. *The Founders and Finance: How Hamilton, Gallatin, and Other Immigrants Forged a New Economy*. Harvard University Press, Cambridge, MA, 2014.

McDonald, Forest. *Alexander Hamilton: A Biography*. Norton, New York, 1982.

———. *The American Presidency: An Intellectual History*. University Press of Kansas, Lawrence, 1994.

———. *The Presidency of George Washington*. University Press of Kansas, Lawrence, 1974.

———. *The Presidency of Thomas Jefferson*. University Press of Kansas, Lawrence, 1976.

McDonald, Robert M. S. *Confounding Father: Thomas Jefferson's Image in His Own Time*. University of Virginia Press, Charlottesville, 2016.

McDougall, Walter A. *The Tragedy of U.S. Foreign Policy: How America's Civil Religion Betrayed the National Interest*. Yale University Press, New Haven, CT, 2016.

McLaughlin, Jack. *Jefferson and Monticello: The Biography of a Builder*. Henry Holt, New York, 1998.

McLynn, Frank. *1759: The Year Britain Became Master of the World*. Grove Press, New York, 2006.

Meacham, John. *Thomas Jefferson: The Art of Power*. Random House, New York, 2013.

Mikaberidze, Alexander. *The Napoleonic Wars*. Oxford University Press, New York, 2020.

Miller, John Chester. *The Wolf by The Ears: Thomas Jefferson and Slavery*. Free Press, New York, 1977.

Moore, Roy, and Alma Moore. *Thomas Jefferson's Journey to the South of France*. Stewart, Tabori, & Chang, New York, 1999.

Morgan, Edmund S. *American Heroes: Profiles of Men and Women Who Shaped Early America*. Norton, New York, 2009.

———. *American Slavery, American Freedom*. Norton, New York, 1975.

———. *Inventing the People: The Rise of Popular Sovereignty in England and America*. Norton, New York, 1988.

Nagel, Paul C. *The Lees of Virginia: Seven Generations of an American Family*. Oxford University Press, New York, 1990.

Nash, Gary B. *Race and Revolution*. Madison House, Lanham, MD, 1990.

———. *The Unknown American Revolution*. Penguin, New York, 2005.

Nelson, Eric. *The Royalist Revolution: Monarchy and the American Founding*. Harvard University Press, Cambridge, MA, 2014.

Nelson Jr., John R. *Liberty and Property: Political Economy and Policymaking in the New Nation, 1789–1812*. Johns Hopkins University Press, Baltimore, 1987.

Newmyer, Kent. *The Supreme Court under Marshall and Taney*. Harlan Davidson, Arlington Heights, IL, 1968.

———. *The Treason Trial of Aaron Burr: Law, Politics, and the Character Wars of the New Nation*. Cambridge University Press, New York, 2012.

Norton, Mary Beth. *1774: The Long Year of Revolution*. Knopf, New York, 2020.

Oakes, James. *Slavery and Freedom: An Interpretation of the Old South*. Norton, New York, 1990.

O'Brien, Conor Cruise. *The Long Affair: Thomas Jefferson and the French Revolution*. University of Chicago Press, 1966.

Onuf, Peter S. *Jefferson's Empire: The Language of American Nationhood*. University Press of Virginia, Charlottesville, 2000.

———, ed. *Jeffersonian Legacies*. University Press of Virginia, Charlottesville, 1993.

———. *Jefferson and the Virginians: Democracy, Constitutions, and Empire*. Louisiana State University Press, Baton Rouge, 2018.

———. *The Mind of Thomas Jefferson*. University Press of Virginia, Charlottesville, 2007.

O'Shaughnessy, Andrew Jackson. *The Men Who Lost America: British Leadership, the American Revolution, and the Fate of Empire*. Yale University Press, New Haven, CT, 2013.

Parkinson, Robert G. *The Common Cause: Creating Race and Nation in the American Revolution*. University of North Carolina Press, Chapel Hill, 2016.

Patrick, Rembert W. *Florida Fiasco: Rampant Rebels on the Georgia-Florida Border, 1810–1815*. University of Georgia Press, Athens, 1954.

Paul, Joel Richard. *Without Precedent: Chief Justice John Marshall and His Times*. Riverhead, New York, 2018.

Peterson, Merrill D. *The Jefferson Image in the American Mind*. Oxford University Press, New York, 1960.

———. *Thomas Jefferson and the New Nation: A Biography*. Oxford University Press, New York, 1970.

———, ed. *Thomas Jefferson: A Reference Biography*. Scribner, New York, 1986.

———, ed. *Visitors to Monticello*. University of Virginia Press, Charlottesville, 1989.

Pole, J. R. *Equality, Status, and Power in Thomas Jefferson's Virginia*. Colonial Williamsburg Foundation, Williamsburg, VA, 1986.

Popkin, Jeremy D. *A New World Begins: The History of the French Revolution*. Basic Books, New York, 2019.

Potts, Louis W. *Arthur Lee: A Virtuous Revolutionary*. Louisiana State University Press, Baton Rouge, 1981.

Ragosta, John A., Peter S. Onuf, and Andrew J. O'Shaughnessy, eds. *The Founding of Thomas Jefferson's University*. University of Virginia Press, Charlottesville, 2019.

Rakove, Jack N. *Original Meanings: Politics and Ideas in the Making of the Constitution*. Knopf, New York, 1996.

———. *Revolutionaries: A New History of the Invention of America*. Houghton Mifflin, New York, 2010.

Randall, Willard Sterne. *Thomas Jefferson: A Life*. Henry Holt, New York, 1993.

Randolph, Sarah N. *The Domestic Life of Thomas Jefferson*. Thomas Jefferson Memorial Foundation, Monticello, VA, 1947.

Rasmussen, Dennis C. *Fear of a Sitting Sun: The Disillusionment of America's Founders*. Princeton University Press, Princeton, NJ, 2021.

Reardon, John J. *Edmund Randolph: A Biography*. Macmillan, New York, 1974.

———. *Peyton Randolph, 1721–1775: One Who Presided*. Carolina Academic Press, Durham, 1982.

Reid, John Phillip. *Constitutional History of the American Revolution*. University of Wisconsin Press, Madison, 1995.

Rise, Howard C. *Thomas Jefferson's Paris*. Princeton University Press, Princeton, NJ, 1976.

Ryerson, Richard Alan. *John Adams's Republic: The One, the Few, and the Many*. Johns Hopkins University Press, Baltimore, 2016.

Sanford, Charles B. *The Religious Life of Thomas Jefferson*. University Press of Virginia, Charlottesville, 1984.

Saunt, Claudio. *Unworthy Republic: The Dispossession of Native Americans and the Road to Indian Territory*. New York, Norton, 2020.

Scharff, Virginia. *The Women Jefferson Loved*. Harper, New York, 2010.

Schiff, Stacey. *The Great Improvisation: Franklin, France, and the Birth of America*. Henry Holt, New York, 2006.

Selby, John E. *The Revolution in Virginia, 1775–1783*. Colonial Williamsburg Foundation, Williamsburg, VA, 1988.

Shachtman, Tom. *How the French Saved America: Soldiers, Sailors, Diplomats, Louis XVI, and the Success of a Revolution*. St. Martin's Press, New York, 2017.

Shackelford, George Green. *Jefferson's Adoptive Son: The Life of William Short, 1759–1848*. University Press of Kentucky, Lexington, 1993.

Sharp, James Roger. *American Politics in the Early Republic: The New Nation in Crisis*. Yale University Press, New Haven, CT, 1993.

Sheldon, Garret Ward. *The Political Philosophy of Thomas Jefferson*. Johns Hopkins University Press, Baltimore, 1991.

Signer, Michael. *Becoming Madison: The Extraordinary Origins of the Least Likely Founding Father*. PublicAffairs, New York, 2015.

Simon, John F. *What Kind of Nation: Thomas Jefferson, John Marshall, and the Epic Struggle to Create a United States*. Simon & Schuster, New York, 2003.

Skowronek, Stephen. *The Politics Presidents Make: Leadership from John Adams to Bill Clinton*. Harvard University Press, Cambridge, MA, 1993.

Slack, Charles. *Adams, Jefferson, and the Misfits Who Saved Free Speech*. Atlantic Monthly Press, New York, 2015.

Slaughter, Thomas P. *Independence: The Tangled Roots of the American Revolution*. Hill & Wang, New York, 2015.

Sloan, Robert E. *Principle and Interest: Thomas Jefferson and the Problem of Debt*. University of Virginia Press, Charlottesville, 1995.

Smith, James Morton. *Freedom's Fetter: The Alien and Sedition Laws and American Civil Liberties*. Cornell University Press, Ithaca, NY, 1956.

Smith, Jean Edward. *John Marshall: Definer of a Nation*. Henry Holt, New York, 1996.

Smith, Joshua M. *Borderland Smuggling: Patriots, Loyalists, and Illicit Trade in the Northeast, 1783–1820*. Florida University Press, Gainesville, 2019.

Smith, Margaret Bayard. *The First Forty Years of Washington Society*. Scribner's, New York, 1906.

Spivak, Burton. *Jefferson's English Crisis: Commerce, Embargo, and the Republican Revolution*. University Press of Virginia, Charlottesville, 1979.

Stahr, Walter. *John Jay: Founding Father*. Hambledon Continuum, New York, 2006.

Stanton, Lucia. *Free Some Day: The African-American Families of Monticello*. Thomas Jefferson Foundation, Charlottesville, 2000.

Stearns, Peter N., and Jan Lewis, eds. *An Emotional History of the United States*. New York University Press, 1998.

Steward, Matthew. *Nature's God: The Heretical Origins of the American Republic*. Norton, New York, 2014.

Stewart, David O. *American Emperor: Aaron Burr's Challenge to Jefferson's America*. Simon & Schuster, New York, 2011.

———. *Madison's Gift: Five Partnerships That Built America*. Simon & Schuster, New York, 2015.

Stone, Cliff, and David McKean. *The Great Decision: Jefferson, Adams, Marshall, and the Battle for the Supreme Court*. PublicAffairs, New York, 2009.

Stuart, Reginald C. *The Half-way Pacifist: Thomas Jefferson's View of War*. University of Toronto Press, 1978.

Sweet, John Wood. *Bodies Politic: Negotiating Race in the American North, 1730–1830.* University of Pennsylvania Press, Philadelphia, 2003.

Taylor, Alan. *American Colonies: The Settling of North America.* Penguin, New York, 2001.

———. *American Republics: A Continental History of the United States, 1783–1850.* Norton, New York, 2021.

———. *American Revolutions: A Continental History, 1750–1804.* Norton, New York, 2016.

———. *The Internal Enemy: Slavery and War in Virginia, 1772–1832.* Norton, New York, 2013.

———. *Thomas Jefferson's Education.* Norton, New York, 2019.

Tucker, Robert W., and David C. Hendrickson. *Empire of Liberty: The Statecraft of Thomas Jefferson.* Oxford University Press, New York, 1990.

———. *The Fall of the First British Empire: Origins of the War of American Independence.* Johns Hopkins University Press, Baltimore, 1982.

Unger, Harlow Giles. *First Founding Father: Richard Henry Lee and the Call to Independence.* Da Capo Press. New York, 2017.

———. *Lion of Liberty, Patrick Henry and the Call to a New Nation.* Da Capo Press, New York, 2010.

Unger, Maurizio Valsania. *The Limits of Optimism: Thomas Jefferson's Dualistic Enlightenment.* University of Virginia Press, Charlottesville, 2012.

Van Cleve, George William. *A Slaveholder's Union: Slavery, Politics, and the Constitution in the Early American Republic.* University of Chicago Press, 2010.

Vidal, Gore. *Inventing A Nation: Washington, Adams, Jefferson.* Yale University Press, New Haven, CT, 2003.

Waldstreicher, David. *Slavery's Constitution: From Revolution to Ratification.* Hill & Wang, New York, 2009.

Wallace, Anthony F. C. *Jefferson and the Indians: The Tragic Fate of the First Americans.* Harvard University Press, Cambridge, MA, 1999.

Walters Jr., Raymond. *Albert Gallatin, Jeffersonian Financier and Diplomat.* Macmillan, New York, 1957.

Warner, Michael. *The Letters of the Republic: Publication and the Public Sphere in Eighteenth-Century America.* Harvard University Press, Cambridge, MA, 1990.

Wheelan, Joseph. *Jefferson's Vendetta: The Pursuit of Aaron Burr and the Judiciary.* Carroll & Graf, New York, 2004.

White, Leonard D. *The Jeffersonians: A Study in Administrative History.* Macmillan, New York, 1959.

Wiencek, Henry. *An Imperfect God: George Washington, His Slaves, and the Creation of America.* Farrar, Straus & Giroux, New York, 2003.

———. *Master of the Mountain: Thomas Jefferson and His Slaves.* Farrar, Straus & Giroux, New York, 2012.

Wilkins, Roger. *Jefferson's Pillow: The Founding Fathers and the Dilemma of Black Patriotism.* Beacon Press, Boston, 2001.

Wills, Garry. *Explaining America: The Federalist*. Doubleday, Garden City, NY, 1981.

——. *Inventing America: Jefferson's Declaration of Independence*. Doubleday, Garden City, NY, 1978.

——. *James Madison*. Henry Holt, New York, 2002.

——. *"Negro President": Jefferson and the Slave Power*. Houghton Mifflin, Boston, 2003.

Winchester, Simon. *Land: How the Hunger for Ownership Shaped the Modern World*. HarperCollins, New York, 2021.

Wood, Gordon S. *The Creation of the American Republic*. University of North Carolina Press, Chapel Hill, 1969.

——. *Empire of Liberty: A History of the Early Republic, 1789–1815*. Oxford University Press, New York, 2009.

——. *Friends Divided: John Adams and Thomas Jefferson*. Penguin, New York, 2017.

——. *The Radicalism of the American Revolution*. Knopf, New York, 1991.

——. *The Rising Glory of America, 1760–1820*. Northeastern University Press, Boston, 1990.

Wright, Robert E. *One Nation Under Debt: Hamilton, Jefferson, and the History of What We Owe*. McGraw Hill, New York, 2008.

Wulf, Andrea. *Founding Gardeners: The Revolutionary Generation, Nature, and the Shaping of the American Nation*. Knopf, New York, 2011.

Yarborough, Jean M. *Thomas Jefferson on the Character of a Free People*. University of Kansas Press, Lawrence, 1988.

Young Alfred F., and Gregory H. Nobles, *Whose Revolution Was It? Historians Interpret the Founding*. New York University Press, 2011.

Young, James Sterling. *The Washington Community, 1800–1828*. Columbia University Press, New York, 1966.

Ziesche, Philipp. *Cosmopolitan Patriots: Americans in Paris in the Age of Revolution*. University of Virginia Press, Charlottesville, 2010.

INDEX

Fred Kaplan is Distinguished Professor Emeritus of English at Queens College and the Graduate Center of the City University of New York. He is the author of *Lincoln: The Biography of a Writer*, which was named a Best Book of the Year by the *New York Times* and the *Washington Post*, among other publications. His biography of Thomas Carlyle was a finalist for the National Book Critics Circle Award and the Pulitzer Prize. He lives in Maine.